Introduction to Physical Education, Fitness, and Sport

Introduction to Physical Education, Fitness, and Sport

SEVENTH EDITION

Daryl Siedentop

The Ohio State University

 **Higher Education**

Boston   Burr Ridge, IL   Dubuque, IA   New York   San Francisco   St. Louis
Bangkok   Bogotá   Caracas   Kuala Lumpur   Lisbon   London   Madrid   Mexico City
Milan   Montreal   New Delhi   Santiago   Seoul   Singapore   Sydney   Taipei   Toronto

Higher Education

Published by McGraw-Hill, an imprint of The McGraw-Hill Companies, Inc., 1221 Avenue of the Americas, New York, NY 10020. Copyright © 2009, 2007, 2004. All rights reserved. No part of this publication may be reproduced or distributed in any form or by any means, or stored in a database or retrieval system, without the prior written consent of The McGraw-Hill Companies, Inc., including, but not limited to, in any network or other electronic storage or transmission, or broadcast for distance learning.

4 5 6 7 8 9 0 FGR/FGR 0

ISBN: 978-0-07337651-6
MHID: 0-07-337651-5

Vice President and Editor in Chief: *Michael Ryan*
Publisher: *William Glass*
Executive Editor: *Christopher Johnson*
Development editor: *Gary O'Brien*
Executive Marketing Manager: *Bill Minick*
Media Project Manager: *Thomas Brierly*
Production Editors: *Melissa Williams/Aaron Downey, Matrix Productions, Inc.*
Cover Designer: *Margarite Reynolds*
Senior Production Supervisor: *Richard DeVitto*
Composition: *10/12 New Caledonia by ICC Macmillan Inc.*
Printing: *45# New Era Matte Plus by Quebecor World Fairfield*

Cover images: © *Royalty-free/Corbis*

Credits: *The credits section for this book begins on page 401 and is considered an extension of the copyright page.*

Library of Congress Cataloging-in-Publication Data

Siedentop, Daryl.
    Introduction to physical education, fitness, and sport / Daryl Siedentop.—7th ed.
        p. cm.
    ISBN-13: 978-0-07-337651-6
    ISBN-10: 0-07-337651-5
 1. Physical education and training. 2. Physical fitness. 3. Sports. 4. Sports sciences.
I. Title.

GV341.S479 2008
613.7'1—dc22   2008041138

The Internet addresses listed in the text were accurate at the time of publication. The inclusion of a Web site does not indicate an endorsement by the authors or McGraw-Hill, and McGraw-Hill does not guarantee the accuracy of the information presented at these sites.

www.mhhe.com

Again, to B.J.—the best thing that ever happened to me.

Brief Contents

Contents

Preface

What a time to be in or to be preparing for one of the many physical-activity professions! The national concern about the high prevalence of overweight and obesity among children and youths and the health costs associated with illnesses related to obesity have brought the physical-education and fitness professions into the national spotlight as never before. Sport participation begins in childhood. The variety of sports available and the variety of levels of competition within them makes it possible for those who choose to do so to stay involved with sport throughout their lifetimes, thus creating the need for an increasing number of professionals who work to maintain the quality and quantity of those sport programs.

Most students who read this text share an important kind of knowledge about sport, fitness, and physical education—you have experienced them! Each reader will bring a viewpoint to the issues in this text. The seventh edition of *Introduction to Sport, Fitness, and Physical Education* will help you broaden your perspectives and test your opinions about the various issues raised in the text. This text is meant to emphasize quality services by physical-activity professionals—physical-education teachers, coaches, fitness trainers, athletic trainers, athletic administrators, and the like—both by emphasizing professionalism in developing and sustaining good programs and by activism to ensure that programs become more widely available to those who need them.

The various sections of the text provide you with up-to-date information about the status of the physical-activity professions, the kinds of programs offered to various groups, the educational path to service in the those professions, and the significant problems that are current in the professional practice of the various areas. You will be encouraged to think critically, to recognize and confront problems in various fields, to weigh various alternatives to solving problems, and to respect divergent points of view. No single answer is presented as the *only* answer. The text does present points of view but only to stimulate your thinking and the further development of your own perspective.

The quality and availability of sport, fitness, and physical education has the capacity to affect the nature of our common cultural life and the health of the nation. Cultures do evolve but they do not always necessarily "progress." If sport, fitness, and physical education are to become positive forces in this century, it will be because the new generation of professionals will provide positive solutions to the many problems that now exist in those fields.

The seventh edition of *Introduction to Physical Education, Fitness, and Sport* is divided into five parts. Part 1 provides the historical and philosophical foundation for understanding the current status of the various fields and how they developed. The main themes of the text are introduced: the desirability and possibility of ensuring a physically active lifestyle for all people and the infrastructure that will have to be developed to achieve that ambitious goal. Part 1 examines the important influences in the development of the various fields and the philosophical positions that shaped their evolution.

Parts 2–4 present detailed information about the fields of sport, fitness, and physical education, respectively. Each of these parts begins with a chapter describing the basic concepts in the field and its current stage of development. The next chapter in each part describes current programming efforts in the field and the qualifications expected of professionals who work within it. Each part concludes with a provocative look at the major issues and problems that confront the field.

Part 5 has a dual focus. First, Chapter 13 describes the national, state, and local policy and program initiatives that represent the infrastructure currently in place to support physical activity and healthy lifestyles. Chapter 14 outlines the major themes that need to be addressed if we hope to achieve the ambitious goals set forward in the national agenda. Chapters 15 and 16 describe the physical-science and social-science subdisciplines of Kinesiology, which provide research support to professionals working in the fields of sport, fitness, and physical education.

FEATURES OF THE SEVENTH EDITION

The seventh edition continues to update information about and expand coverage of the major developments in sport, fitness, and physical education. Special emphasis is given to issues, problems, and programmatic solutions that are of major importance in achieving national goals for healthy lifestyles and lifetime physical activity. Here are some examples of the topics discussed:

- New information related to the incidence of obesity and overweight
- New information on, and examples of, lifetime involvement in physical activity
- New and revised discussions of trends and issues in sport, fitness, and physical education
- Thoroughly revised physical-education chapters adding new discussions of skill themes and a variety of education models
- Changes in physical-education programs to meet public health goals
- New federal and state policy initiatives to develop and sustain infrastructures to support healthy lifestyles and physical activity
- New examples of programs at the national, state, and local levels to achieve those policy initiatives
- Updated information on preparation for careers in a number of sport, fitness, and physical-education professions
- Changing views on what constitutes fitness and how it is related to healthy lifestyles

As fields progress, the problems that arise change, sometimes subtly and sometimes quite markedly. The text deals with problems in ways that reflect the latest information from the various fields. I often state my view but not to the exclusion of other views and always in a way that encourages young professionals to develop their own views on the basis of sound evidence and information.

Finally, the *Introduction to Physical Education, Fitness, and Sport* Online Learning Center (www.mhhe.com/siedentop7e) includes a wide range of tools for instructors. Instructors will be able to download chapter-specific PowerPoint Presentations and an Instructor's Manual.

ACKNOWLEDGMENTS

My professional life and work have been influenced by a number of bright and caring people who took the time to share their insights and experiences with me and who respected me enough to offer their honest and sincere criticisms. My brother, Larry Siedentop, D.Phil., CBE, a Fellow of Keble College, Oxford University, is a world-class scholar in political theory; his commitment to quality scholarship has influenced me greatly. Ken Weller, past president of Central College, was my first mentor. Russ DeVette and Gord Brewer helped me understand and care about sport. Larry Locke, Charles Mand, Don Hellison, and George Graham have been close professional colleagues from whom I have learned in many different ways. The many years I worked on a day-to-day basis with Mary O'Sullivan, Deborah Tannehill, and Sandy Stroot were the best and happiest of my professional life.

I wish to thank the following individuals for their helpful reviews of the seventh edition:

Heather R. Adams-Blair, *Eastern Kentucky University*

Douglas R. Callahan, *Winona State University*

Sherri Hildebrand, *Black Hawk College*

John Hughes, *College of Southern Idaho*

John Paul Muczko, *Wesley College*

Scott Richmond, *University of Kansas*

The eighty doctoral students whom I have advised to completion have been a constant source of inspiration. That most of them have gone on to important professional careers of their own is a major source of pride in my professional career. My collaborative work with physical-education teachers in central Ohio has been a continuing source of information and inspiration—and a constant reality check for me. My thanks go particularly to Chris, Gary, Bobbie, Molly, Jane, Bob, and Carol.

I thank all the folks at McGraw-Hill who have helped with the successful transition of this text to their list after the Mayfield Publishing acquisition. My development editor, Gary O'Brien, the best I've ever worked with, navigated this edition from the revision process to completion with thoughtful caring and prodigious skill.

PART ONE

Understanding the Context for Lifespan Sport, Fitness, and Physical Education

Chapter 1 The Dilemma of Our Times: Lifespan Physical Activity and the Obesity Health Crisis

Chapter 2 The Heritage of Physical Education, Sport, and Fitness in the United States

Chapter 3 Changing Philosophies for Sport, Fitness, and Physical Education

When you become a professional in any area related to sport, fitness, or physical education, you must think critically about the issues related to your professional endeavors. Other people will expect you to have the knowledge and the ability to analyze issues differently from the way laypeople do. Put simply, you will be expected to know and to do things that nonprofessionals do not know and cannot do. To fulfill the expectations people have for you as a professional, you must know something of both the history of events and the philosophical positions that have characterized your profession. You will of course develop your own philosophy, but you should develop it critically, with respect for competing points of view. Your professional philosophy is not just your opinion; it is a coherent way of looking at your professional world, informed by an understanding of the events that have led to the current state of affairs.

The current state of affairs can best be characterized as a dilemma between the increased opportunity for lifespan physical activity and growing health concerns related to physical inactivity and obesity. The three chapters in Part 1 provide a beginning description of this dilemma and an overview of historical and philosophical developments in sport, fitness, and physical education that provide the background to understand Parts 2, 3, and 4.

1

The Dilemma of Our Times: Lifespan Physical Activity and the Obesity Health Crisis

The NCPPA mission is to unite the strengths of public, private, and industry efforts into collaborative partnerships that inspire and empower all Americans to lead more physically active lifestyles. The reality is that there is an unprecedented synergy building around the issue of physical activity as it pertains to lifestyle behavior patterns and accessible environments that promote physically active lifestyles.

National Coalition for Promoting Physical Activity (2002)

LEARNING OBJECTIVES

- To explain the current possibilities for lifespan physical activity
- To describe the problems of overweight and obesity and resulting health costs
- To describe the range of physical activity opportunities for different age groups
- To describe the new settings for sport, fitness, and physical education
- To discuss and analyze the characteristics of lifespan involvement
- To describe the concept of an infrastructure designed to support healthy lifestyles

We live in an era during which people in the developed world now understand that lifespan involvement in physical activity—through sport, fitness, and physical education—is both *possible* and *desirable*. People can become physical active very early in life and can continue to be physically active throughout their lives. We know more about the positive relationships among physical activity, health, and longevity. We understand that *lack of physical activity* creates a major health risk at all ages. Unfortunately, the possibility of lifespan physical activity has not yet been realized for many people.

We also live in an era when the major health crisis facing developed nations is the increasing prevalence of overweight and obesity among persons of

---

FOCUS ON   Body Mass Index   1.1

Body mass index (BMI) is a way to *estimate* the degree of underweight or overweight among children, youth, and adults. For children and youth, BMI is estimated by having measures of height and weight related to age, which allows for BMI percentiles to be calculated for each age group. Children and youth that have BMIs above the 85th percentile are considered to be overweight. Children and youth with BMIs above the 95th percentile are considered to be obese.

For adults, the formula for computing BMI is weight in pounds divided by height in inches squared and multiplied by 703. For adults, an optimal range for BMI is 18.5–25. A BMI lower than 18.5 is considered to be underweight, a BMI over 25 is considered to be overweight, and a BMI over 30 is considered to be obese.

BMI is used because of the availability of height and weight measures and is an *estimate* of actual levels of body fat. Its accuracy, especially among older youth and adults, can be distorted by factors such as fitness level, muscle mass, and bone structure.

---

all ages. Over the past quarter century, the prevalence of overweight and obesity among children and youth in the United States, as defined by body mass index (see Focus On Box 1.1 for definitions), has reached epidemic proportions, more than doubling in the 6- to 11-years age group and tripling in the 12- to 19-years age group (Koplan, Liverman, Kraak, & Wisham, 2006). About two-thirds of adults in the United States are overweight, and almost one-third are obese (Weight-Control Information Network, 2007). The Centers for Disease Control has determined that obesity is now the second leading cause of death in the United States, and the surgeon general estimates that the direct and indirect costs of obesity come close to $1.2 trillion annually (Senate Report 108-345, 2006).

Like many health and social issues in the United States, the overweight and obesity epidemics are not distributed equally across racial and socioeconomic groups. The incidences are higher for black children and youth than for white children and youth and still higher for those of Mexican origin (Anderson & Butcher, 2006). Children and teens from families living in poverty are more likely to overweight or obese (Meich et al., 2006), and children and youth with disabilities are at greater risk for becoming overweight than nondisabled peers.

This is the dilemma of our times: The opportunity for lifespan physical activity has never been so

available, yet our children, youth, and adult populations are more likely than ever to be overweight or obese (Focus On Box 1.2). As you will see throughout this text, our public health goals cannot be achieved by any one professional group working alone. Women and men involved in the physical-education, fitness, health, sport, and recreation professions must join forces in a coordinated effort to improve the quality of life for children, youth, and adults so as to improve the nation's health and reduce the nation's costs for combating diseases associated with overweight and obesity (Focus On Box 1.3). These professional persons are supported by the research done within the medical sciences and the kinesiology disciplines described in Part 5. Together, we must develop and sustain an **infrastructure for healthy lifestyles**, a concept that will be described later in this chapter and dealt with throughout the text.

This book is intended to introduce women and men who are interested in careers in various physical-activity fields—such as physical education, athletic training, coaching, fitness, recreation, and sport management—to the importance of physical activity at all ages for women, men, and people from all socioeconomic levels. This is an extraordinary era for people interested in sport, fitness, and physical education. There certainly has been no period in U.S. history to match it! If you enjoy physical

FOCUS ON — Precipitating Factors for Overweight/Obesity Epidemic   1.2

Overweight and obesity stem from the imbalance created when energy intake exceeds energy expenditure. This imbalance develops over time when caloric intake through eating/drinking patterns exceeds energy expenditure through physical activity.

Children and youth consume more energy-dense foods and are less physically active than they were 25 years ago. In food consumption, the primary factors are higher caloric intake, more dietary fat, higher caloric density of foods, and larger portions. These factors are related to less in-home cooking, greater reliance on take-out food, more fast-food meals, and overreliance on soft drinks, sport drinks, and fruit drinks that are high in calories and sugars.

Reductions in physical activity are the result of a number of factors related to what is typically referred to as the *built environment*. Factors such as commuting time, communities designed to foster driving rather than walking/cycling, and lack of public transport reduce physical activity. Children and youth spend increased amounts of time engaged in the *electronic culture* with playing video and computer games, watching TV, and connecting to the Internet. Lack of indoor activity space and programs limits physical activity during inclement weather. Urban communities are often unsafe for children and youth to be active in after-school hours.

SOURCE: Levi, Segal, & Juliano (2006); Anderson & Butcher (2006).

FOCUS ON — Health Impact of Overweight and Obesity   1.3

Research has shown that overweight and obesity are related to a significant number of health problems.

Type II Diabetes

- More than 80% of people with type II diabetes are overweight.
- More than 20 million adult Americans have diabetes.
- Another 54 million are "prediabetic."
- Diabetes is the sixth leading cause of death in the United States and accounts for 11% of all U.S. health costs.

Heart Disease and Stroke

- People who are overweight are more likely to suffer from high blood pressure, high levels of blood fat, and high LDL cholesterol—all risk factors for heart disease and stroke.
- Heart disease is the leading cause of death in the United States, and stroke is the third leading cause.

- One in four Americans has some form of cardiovascular disease.

Cancer

- Persons who are overweight have increased risk for several types of cancer.
- Approximately 20% of cancer in women and 15% of cancer in men is attributable to obesity.
- Cancer is the second leading cause of death in the United States.

Health Risks Earlier in Life

- Younger adults who are obese face greater health risks earlier in life. Women who are obese at age 30 are more likely to die at a younger age and significantly more likely to develop cancer.
- Some research suggests obesity in middle age may create higher risk for developing dementia later in life.

SOURCE: Levi et al. (2006).

activity, you are already well aware of trends that range from serious fitness work, both strength and flexibility and aerobic training, to half-hour walks in the park to meet the minimum expectation of 30 minutes per day of modest cardiovascular exercise. Fitness centers and sport facilities with fitness components have sprung up everywhere. The "athletic look" has replaced the "slim look" in fashion magazines. Activity clothing and athletic shoes have become standard dress, not only for workouts but also for dining, going to the movies, and casual outings. In addition to influencing fashion, the physical-activity movement is part of a larger health movement that seeks to influence diet, exercise, and other lifestyle habits. The emphasis on looking healthier and actually being healthier is often referred to as *lifestyle management* and is itself a part of the *wellness movement* that promotes a lifestyle focused on feeling and staying well through prevention rather than the remediation of illness.

Physical education in schools is one important setting for achieving the goals of a physically active, healthy lifestyle. Recognizing that, the U.S. Congress passed House Concurrent Resolution 97 in 1987, calling for high-quality, daily physical education. The facts are, however, that few students participate in daily physical education, and in many schools at various grade levels, the quality of physical education is often considerably less than "high." Recent evidence shows that since the inception of *No Child Left Behind Act* the time specified for physical education, especially at the elementary-school level, has been reduced to allow for more classroom time devoted to language arts, English, and mathematics (Jennings, 2006).

A major step forward in the effort to create a coordinated approach to reducing the overweight/obesity epidemic among children and youth was made in June 2004 when Congress passed Section 204 of the reauthorization of the National School Lunch Act. A portion of this legislation required that "each local education agency participating in a program authorized by the Richard B. Russell School Lunch Act or the Child Nutrition Act of 1966 shall establish a local school wellness policy" by the year

2006–2007. This important federal initiative also defined the minimum requirements that the local school wellness policy should address:

1. Includes goals for nutrition education, physical activity, and other school-based activities designed to promote student wellness.

2. Includes nutrition guidelines for all foods available on each school campus during the school day with the objectives of promoting student health and reducing childhood obesity.

3. Provides an assurance that guidelines for reimbursable school meals will not be less restrictive than regulations and guidance issued by the U.S. Department of Agriculture.

4. Establishes a plan for measuring implementation of the local school wellness policy.

5. Involves parents, students, and representatives of the school food authority, the school board, school administrators, and the public in developing the local school wellness policy.

As a result of this federal initiative, most states have passed legislation further defining the minimum requirements for school districts in the areas of school nutrition, nutrition education, and physical education/physical activity (see Focus On Box 11.2 for information on how some states have increased requirements for physical education/physical activity). The flurry of state legislation to further define the requirements of the federal legislation has already resulted in major improvements in school nutrition and, at least in some states, significant increases in requirements for physical education and physical activity.

In 1991 in its landmark publication *Healthy People 2000*, the U.S. Public Health Service created a new strategy to deal with the broad issues related to public health. A series of goals were established, and regular progress reports are made. In 2000 *Healthy People 2010* was published (U.S. Department of Health and Human Services, 2000). The report noted the progress made on goals in the initial 10 years and established revised goals for the next decade. (See Chapter 8 for details.) The first goal of

Healthy People 2010 (HP 2010) is to help individuals of all ages increase their life expectancy and improve their quality of life. The second goal is to eliminate health disparities among different segments of the population. These two goals focus on two main issues that will be addressed throughout this text: (1) Sport, fitness, and physical education need to contribute to healthier lifestyles, and (2) certain segments of the population need special, coordinated attention to achieve that goal. Physical activity and fitness is focus area 22 in *HP 2010*, and the stated goal is to "improve health, fitness, and quality of life through daily physical activity" (Spain & Franks, 2001).

Physical education in schools is obviously one important setting for achieving the goals of a physically active and healthy lifestyle. Recognizing that, the U.S. Congress passed House Concurrent Resolution 97 in 1987, calling for high-quality, daily physical education. The fact is, however, that few students participate in daily physical education and that in many places at various grade levels there is no quality physical education. (See Chapter 10 for details of state requirements for physical education.) It is clear that physical education is undergoing serious examination and that stronger programs need to be developed to both meet the challenges related to the public health issues and gain the confidence of the public.

LIFESPAN PHYSICAL ACTIVITY: A REVOLUTION NOT LIMITED BY AGE OR GENDER

Someday, historians will describe the current era as a watershed period characterized by the emergence of the possibility for lifespan physical activity—in sport, fitness, and physical education. Many have yet to achieve lifespan physical activity, but we now know that it is both possible and desirable. What has to be done now is to create the opportunity to achieve it.

When we consider the topics of sport, fitness, and physical education, what age and gender groups come to mind? If we observe our cultural traditions,

our thoughts may turn to children at play, youths involved in sport, and young adults perhaps continuing for a time in recreational sports, with involvement slowly diminishing as people grow older. Very young children are not typically included in such a scenario. We also may be less likely to imagine the involvement of girls than that of boys. In addition, although we may think of men as continuing some moderately active recreation as they age, we may not think of them as engaged in strenuous activity, and we will be less likely to think of older women as participating in even moderate physical activity. The traditional stereotype is that older people are largely inactive, except perhaps for a quiet walk in the afternoon.

Historically, sport, fitness, and physical education have been limited primarily to older children, youths, and young adults. Most people have believed that adults become much less active as they age. Furthermore, many people have viewed appropriate participation for girls and women as being less rigorous than male participation, and some have considered female participation to be out of bounds altogether. Leaders, who typically have been men, have been especially susceptible to those historically stereotypical views.

Many who have entered this current of dramatic change continue to think in terms of such stereotypes, but they are now being dismantled. Our old ideas are being replaced with a vision of lifespan involvement in sport, fitness, and physical education—not only for adolescents and young adults but also for very young children and for older people (at almost any level of intensity); not only for boys and men but also for girls and women (with equally intense activities). These changes in perception, and the changes in opportunity that accompany them, lie at the heart of the revolution that we are now experiencing—and these changes make this era unlike any before it. The possibility of lifespan involvement potentially touches every person. This revolution is not limited by age or gender.

Does this vision of lifespan involvement mean that every person must be a committed athlete from childhood through old age? Clearly not! Indeed, from a public health perspective, regular, moderate physical activity is more important than vigorous, athletic activity (Morrow & Gill, 1995). What the new vision does mean, however, is that people who want to be physically active, at any level of intensity, can now be so. It also means that people are increasingly likely to view involvement in some regular physical activity—sport, dance, fitness, or walking—as fundamental to living well, regardless of their age or gender.

The purpose of this chapter is to provide glimpses of the kinds of opportunities available in sport, fitness, and physical education, which together constitute the possibility of lifespan involvement. Each vignette presents a snapshot of involvement for particular people at particular points and places in their lives. None of the scenarios has been contrived. Each is based on *real* programs or people. Together, they paint a picture of lifespan involvement in sport, fitness, and physical education.

THE EARLY YEARS

Physical movement is the basic language of early childhood, from birth to age 6 or 7 years (Boucher, 1988). Young children learn about their world chiefly by moving about and physically exploring their immediate surroundings. In seeking to foster children's physical, social, and mental development, child-development experts have long recognized the fundamental importance of providing opportunities for physical movement and, later, for motor play. Traditionally, the movement experiences of young children have been only informally arranged and monitored, often with no specific purpose other than to keep children involved in some activity. Furthermore, those early movement experiences have been almost exclusively the responsibility of parents, most of whom have little or no knowledge of or training in motor development or early-childhood physical education.

Early-Childhood Physical-Activity Programs

Many families now have access to programs for young children that focus primarily on physical activity and the development of motor skills. Most of these programs are in the private sector; that is, they are franchises that are fee-for-service providers of physical-activity programs for young children. Because they are fee-for-service operations, they tend to be more frequently found in suburbs and in more affluent neighborhoods in cities. Some social service organizations provide early motor-skill programs for children in less affluent city neighborhoods, but these programs typically cannot afford the facilities and equipment that rival those in the private sector. If you search the Web sites described in Focus On Box 1.4 you can come to understand the differences in some of the programs that are franchised nationally.

A preschool movement curriculum for young children of all abilities, called *Smart Start* (Wessell & Zittel, 1995), was developed by physical-education professionals for use by parents, preschool teachers, Head Start, and private programs. Children in lower-income communities are much less likely to have access to any of these programs. They also tend to live in areas where play spaces for children are not common and it is not always safe for children to be outside playing. This theme of unequal access to opportunities for physical activity will recur throughout this text.

Sport opportunities are now being made available to children at an earlier age than in the past. It is no longer unusual to see 5-year-olds enrolled in a children's soccer or gymnastics program. Many infant swimming programs are available. Children's playgrounds are increasingly being designed with apparatus to accommodate activities that are developmentally appropriate for young children and that encourage children to explore and to use their entire movement repertoire.

Most evidence (Gober & Franks, 1988) indicates that children who have enriched motor experiences as infants tend to be more fit and more likely to

---

FOCUS ON   Early-Childhood Physical-Activity Program Web Sites   **1.4**

Baby Power Forever-Kids (www.babypower.com): Gymnastic and musical parent–child play programs for ages 6 months to 3 years

Pee Wee Workout (www.peeweeworkout.com): Health and fitness program for preschool and elementary-school children

Gymboree (www.gymboree.com): Children's play, fitness, music, and art programs

Fitwize 4 kids (www.Fitwize4kids.com): Innovative circuit-training program with specially designed resistance-training equipment

Kinderdance (www.kinderdance.com): Motor development, gymnastics, and fitness program for ages 2–8 years old

The Little Gym (www.thelittlegym.com): Movement skills, gymnastics, sports, and games for infants and toddlers

Jumpbunch (www.jumpbunch.com): Home-based physical-activity program to promote fun, fitness, and self-esteem

---

participate in sport throughout their lives. Sport psychologists even speculate that the drive to excel in sport may originate in infancy, when parents or child-care workers recognize and respond lovingly to infants' early motor efforts. There seems little doubt now that physical-activity habits originate in childhood and that the longer a child's bad habits are allowed to persist, the more difficult they are to change.

There is much debate about the *nature* of early-childhood motor-activity programs. Should they be mostly exploratory with adults providing only encouragement, support, and reinforcement? Should they aim to develop specific skills? At the moment, there is not enough evidence to decide the issue. Experts all agree, however, about the importance of providing rich, stimulating motor experiences for very young children.

Children's Sport

Sport opportunities for children have grown enormously in the recent past (see Chapter 5 for details). Both the number of children participating and the kinds of early sport opportunities available to these children have increased. Some sports, such as swimming and gymnastics, have age-group programs that are highly specialized, with children sometimes beginning to train year-round in their early elementary-school years.

Sport programs for children differ dramatically in how they are organized and supported. Some programs emphasize instruction and even competition for all children who want to participate, with practice and games one or two evenings a week. Other programs cater to families who want their children to have more intense training and competition, leading to a focus in that particular sport throughout their childhood and adolescence. Other programs include both of these opportunities by offering widespread participation and then the option for participating on the "select team" if the child is skilled enough and the parents are willing to support the increased demands that come with this level of participation.

Sport programs for children are sponsored by a variety of organizations. Community recreation programs often offer an array of sport experiences for children at modest fees. Many sport programs for children are sponsored by volunteer organizations such as local Lions and Kiwanis Clubs. Still others are organized and supported by interested parents who seek wholesome activity for their children (see Chapter 5 for further details). These organizations raise funds, make rules for participation, decide

Young children learn specialized skills early.

Elite-level women's gymnastic competitors are often young girls.

what activities to offer, and determine what levels of competition will exist within activities.

As Chapter 6 shows, there are many issues and problems in children's sport. I believe that well-designed, careful programs can provide a positive developmental experience.

Elementary-School Physical Education

It is clear that physical education for elementary-school children is very important. Yet only thirty-six states require elementary physical education, and only twenty-eight states require that those who teach physical-education classes at the elementary level have a physical-education license (NASPE, 2006). In many schools, students may get only one 30-minute physical-education class per week, far different than the national recommendation for daily physical education. In some schools, the physical-education period is hardly more than an organized recreation period; in fact, in some schools, recess is counted as physical education.

There are nonetheless extraordinary elementary-school physical-education programs—programs where students have physical education daily taught by a physical-education specialist. These programs typically emphasize the development of motor skills in the K–2 grades, using dance, games, and physical activities so that children learn to enjoy activity while also learning skills. A visitor to a first-grade class might find the children in a unit where they explore different ways to strike objects—using balloons, yarn balls, soft rubber balls, and balls that bounce more like tennis balls. They strike with different kinds of implements, some like stubby tennis rackets and others more like paddles. As the teacher directs their experiences, children eventually explore forehand stroking, backhand stroking, overhead stroking, and even something that begins to look like a tennis serve. There is enough equipment for all children to be active, and they clearly enjoy what they are learning.

Many schools now include adventure education units in their curriculum with gymnasium climbing walls that are brightly painted to represent mountain scenes. Children participate in cooperative games and group initiatives learning the value of working together and depending on one another to accomplish group goals.

Sport is part of the curriculum for the upper grades in elementary-school physical education. Children learn modified forms of volleyball, soccer, floor hockey, and flag football. There are gymnastics units in which students take the motor skills learned in the early grades and learn how to use them to develop floor exercise routines on mats. Folk and ethnic dancing are often introduced in the fourth and fifth grades.

YOUTH: THE TRANSITION YEARS

Students who are at the upper-middle-school grades and into high school tend either to become either more active or more sedentary than in elementary or early middle school. Although forty-two states require physical education at the high-school level, in most of those states the requirement is either one or two semesters. In many of those states, students who participate in school sport, band, ROTC, or school drill teams are exempt from physical education (NASPE, 2006). Still, for many of us, memories of our own youth are dominated by sport and fitness activities. In fact, those experiences may have been so influential that we decided to explore a professional career in teaching, coaching, athletic training, recreation, or sport management.

It is becoming increasingly common for high schools to develop fitness centers, often shared with the community during after-school, evening, and weekend hours. The facilities are used by students in physical-education classes and for drop-in activity by students interested in improving and maintaining their fitness levels. In addition, many high schools have well-developed strength-training facilities for school athletes. Additionally, it has become more common for cities, suburban communities, and rural towns to develop community fitness and recreation centers that are available to youth on a year-around basis. The point being made here is that there is now more opportunity than ever before for youths to have access to facilities for purposes of physical activity, either in the form of swimming laps, playing on intramural or recreation center teams, or just working out to maintain or improve your level of fitness.

The High-School Interschool Sport Program

In 2005–2006, for the seventeenth consecutive year, participation on high-school sports teams increased. Nearly 3 million girls and 4.2 million boys competed on school teams (NFHS, 2007).

Girls' softball has become increasingly popular.

Virtually every high school in the nation has some kind of sport program for its students. The programs differ according to the financial resources of the school district, the size of the school, and the state regulations under which the school operates. The programs are, however, more similar than different. The program described here is from a ninth-through twelfth-grade suburban high school with an enrollment of 1,650 students. The school competes in twelve varsity sports for girls and boys. Football, boys' basketball, girls' basketball, and girls' volleyball have ninth-grade, reserve, and varsity teams. The others have reserve and varsity teams. Eight hundred fifty of the students in the school compete at one time or another on one or more of these teams.

The school has a year-round weight-training facility and a full-time athletic trainer. Nearly every sport has a parents' or a booster club, which supplies extra funds for the program and acts as a communication link between coaches and parents. The school district cannot find enough qualified people to act as coaches from the ranks of certified teachers in the district, so they take advantage of a state regulation that allows them to hire noncertified people to coach if they cannot fill vacancies within the district.

Out-of-School Sport

Not all high school students participate in the interschool sport program, and some of those who do not participate have an active sport involvement outside

Some kinds of elite sports develop completely outside school programs.

the school. Two examples are Andrea and William. Andrea owns her own horse and has trained and competed for years in equestrian sports. She boards her horse at a nearby stable and goes there nearly every day after school to train and care for her horse. She hopes someday to compete in equestrian 3-day-event competitions. Thus, she trains both in *dressage* (precise replicating of figures and moves) and in jumping. Last summer and autumn, she competed in fifteen events, most of them against boys and girls her own age, but sometimes in more open competition against adults. Although her sport involvement is quite expensive, her training and competition are every bit as intense as those for less expensive sports such as basketball or volleyball. Nonetheless, many of her classmates do not know that she is such an accomplished athlete.

William has taken karate lessons for 6 years. He has slowly advanced in local karate competitions and is beginning to make a name for himself. He trains at a small karate studio, which occupies a storefront in one of the area shopping malls. He has grown very strong and can make very quick movements. His room at home is filled with trophies he has won in local competitions. Like Andrea's athletic accomplishments, however, his are not known by many of his classmates. He, too, has never played on a school team.

YOUNG ADULTHOOD

Young adults are women and men who have finished high school and have gone on to further education or have entered the workforce. They are in a time of separation from youth and of establishment of patterns of work and play that will last a lifetime. Young adults participate in sport, fitness, and physical education in so many ways that these ways can only be sampled here.

University Recreation and Fitness Programs

Private and public colleges and universities throughout the nation have developed sport, recreation, and

FOCUS ON   University Elective Fitness Classes   **1.5**

Making Fitness Fun and Attractive for University Students

- **20/Cycle/20:** 20 minutes of strength training, then 40 minutes of cycling, and then 20 minutes of core strength and flexibility work
- **Body Sculpt:** Focus on muscular strength and endurance with resistance tubing, free weights, and resistance balls
- **Boot Camp:** For students who want maximum exertion exercise focusing on running, jumping, squatting, and sprinting
- **Cardio Funk:** Mixed-level aerobics with funky dance steps
- **Cardio Kickbox:** Cardio-based class utilizing kickboxing choreography
- **Cardio Sculpt:** Equal balance of cardio and strength work
- **Express Abs:** A 25-minute express class of abdominal workouts
- **Get on the Ball:** A 1-hour class using resistance balls to add instability and greater challenge
- **H₂O Challenge:** Mixed-intensity water workouts with a cardio focus
- **Hatha Yoga:** Focus on mindful practice, breath work, tension release, and relaxation

- **Indoor Cycle:** 40–45 minutes of strength cycling followed by 15 minutes of strength and flexibility training
- **Mixed Aerobics:** A warm-up, then 40 minutes of mixed-impact aerobics
- **Personalized Training:** Individualized training aimed at developing your own pace and level of workout
- **Pilates:** Introduction to Pilates training, working toward improved posture, lung capacity, increased flexibility, and core strength
- **Power Yoga:** A 90-minute class teaching ujjayi breathing and bandha engagement for poses and floor work
- **Step Kickbox:** Step combos, kickboxing choreography and style, for strength and endurance training
- **Step/Sculpt:** 30-minute step combinations for cardiovascular work and 30 minutes of strength training
- **Sunrise S&S:** Early-morning strength and stretching using resistance tubing
- **Super Step:** 45 minutes of step combos for cardio work, finishing with 5 minutes of strength training and 5 minutes of flexibility work
- **Total Body:** Focus on muscular strength and endurance as well as cardio improvement

SOURCE: Ohio State University (2008).

fitness facilities for use by the general student body, faculty, and staff. They do this to attract students to their campuses and to keep them on campus during weekends and for those students who stay on campus during term breaks.

A new group of facilities at Ohio State University provide ample opportunity for students to work out, take fitness and sport classes, swim, participate on intramural teams, be members of sport clubs, and participate in adventure activities. The Sport, Fitness, and Health Program offers more than sixty elective sport and fitness courses each quarter and serves more than 13,000 students each year. The Recreation and Physical Activity Center opens early each morning and closes late each night. Nearly 300 fitness machines of various types are available throughout the building with ample provision for free-weight work also. More than 20 different types of fitness classes are available to students (see Focus On Box 1.5).

Students have the opportunity to participate by joining one or more of the seventy-nine sport clubs that are sponsored by the Intramural and Recreational Sport Department. Each club has a faculty advisor. Some clubs—such as the equestrian, women's rugby, and water-ski club teams—compete in regional and national championships. Others—such as the alpine-ski, cycling, and scuba clubs—take trips during quarter breaks.

The Outdoor Adventure Center includes a Climbing Center with two state-of-the-art climbing walls offering more than fifty routes for climbing. Classes are offered as well as workshops that prepare students for backcountry trips during weekends and quarter breaks.

The department offers a wide range of intramural competitions for men's, women's and coed teams and trains student officials and managers to ensure that intramural competitions run smoothly. During winter quarter, 386 basketball teams compete in nearly 900 games in men's, women's, and coed leagues. During the same winter season, competitions are also offered in ice hockey, indoor cricket, indoor soccer, volleyball, table tennis, and wrestling.

The entire group of programs is managed by a professional staff of more than 35 full-time persons with the assistance of more than 400 student assistants, many of whom are interns from academic departments such as recreation, sport and exercise education, exercise science, and sport management.

For many college students, easy access to good facilities and good programs contributes importantly to a successful college or university experience. It provides the opportunity to meet new friends, and it often has a very high "fun quotient." For example, every year Miami (Ohio) University holds an intramural "broomball" tournament. Broomball is an indoor hockey-type game played with a small rubber ball and an aluminum stick with a rubber head. More than 6,500 students compete on 475 teams in various league play. In a recent broomball season, all available slots for competition were filled within 30 minutes after registration began—30 teams had to be turned away! Fun competitions in attractive facilities can obviously attract the enthusiasm and loyalty of young adults.

COMMUNITY RECREATION

The same motivation that has influenced colleges and universities to provide recreation and fitness facilities for their students has also motivated communities to provide similar facilities for their citizens, young and old. Many of these facilities are built by and administered by community government, typically a parks and recreation department. These facilities are often financed by local taxes. Others are built by organizations such as the Young Men's Christian Association (YMCA), and still others are developed in the private sector as a business, but the vast majority of these are primarily fitness facilities. In most cases, these community facilities offer daily, monthly, or yearly memberships. These fees typically pay for the salaries of those who work within the facility. Corporations have also developed recreation and fitness facilities for employees (see Chapter 8). These facilities also hire a number of persons who have professional preparation in fitness, recreation, or recreation administration.

Community recreation facilities try to provide a variety of activities for all age groups, from infant/toddler programs to those for senior citizens.

Coed competition is popular among young adults.

Drop-in activities are typically covered by whatever fee is required by the facility. Special classes often require a small additional fee. The availability and quality of community recreation facilities is increasingly seen as an important way of attracting new residents to the community.

Communities also build and administer a variety of recreational sites such as parks, softball fields, and walking/biking trails. Rather than describe the full scope of programming for community recreation, this section focuses in more detail for the organization of one popular sport in one city, Columbus, Ohio.

Softball is one of the most popular participation sports in America. The number of "frequent" participants continues to rise each year with the current number more than 4.5 million (Sporting Goods Manufacturing Association, 2006). The typical "fast pitch" softball participant plays the sport on at least fifty-eight separate days. The Columbus Parks and Recreation Department organizes and administers 114 softball leagues competed on 126 city-owned softball fields, involving 878 local teams in organized league play and nearly 100 tournaments for 4,000 local and regional softball teams. Each year more than 13,000 games are played with an estimated 35,000 players. The center of softball activity is Berliner Park, a facility with thirty-one softball diamonds, two batting cages, two concession stands, and two play areas for children, all on 226 parkland acres. Leagues are formed for men's, women's, coed, and age-group players.

Informal Participation

Although the participation of young adults and adults in fitness and recreation activities is impressive, we should not forget the importance to fitness and well-being of informal physical activity. Walking for pleasure is the most frequent form of physical activity in America, with an estimated 176 million participating (NSRE, 2007). If pleasure walking is at a brisk pace and lasts for a minimum of 30 minutes, it becomes an important contributor to health fitness. Cycling, jogging, in-line skating, rollerblading, tennis, ice skating,

swimming, waterskiing, and golf are all outdoor activities that can provide healthful exercise. Most of these can be done alone or with small groups and do not typically require specialized facilities.

When you are out and about the area in which you live, what do you see in terms of activities? In my area, I see adults using the bike/walking path that runs along a nearby road. I see groups of cyclists headed out for a trek, all clad in the latest cycling gear. When the weather is decent, the local tennis courts and golf courses are busy. I see joggers, often in groups of two to four, talking among themselves as they jog down the street.

We also need to be aware of the physical activity that we are unlikely to see unless we are participating. Activities such as backpacking, mountain biking, and rock climbing are great physical activities pursued by large numbers of adults, as are rowing and kayaking and other water sports.

Young adulthood is an important transition period when lifestyle habits become developed. If young adults continue to be active and take advantage of opportunities to learn new ways of maintaining an adequate level of health-related fitness, they are much more likely to develop into healthy adults who maintain a healthy lifestyle.

THE OLDER ADULT

One of the myths that pervaded physical education and sport as late as the 1940s was that of the "athlete's heart." The myth was that vigorous exercise was inappropriate for young people because of the potential damage to the heart. We now know that lack of exercise is more likely to be detrimental.

Similar myths kept older adults from participating in many kinds of sport and fitness activities. Traditionally, only nonvigorous sports such as golf or bowling have been considered appropriate for older adults. If older adults cycled or jogged, they tended to do so in a leisurely fashion. Since the 1980s, the prejudices accompanying these traditional myths have been breaking down rapidly.

The Masters Athlete

In the late 1960s and early 1970s, a number of American and Canadian men and women who had competed in track and field were trying to find ways to continue participating in their sport. At first, they began to take part in age-group track-and-field meets and distance races in European countries where an age-group track-and-field movement had already begun. The first World Masters Games in 1985 attracted 8,000 athletes to Toronto, Canada. During these games, a steering committee was elected to plan an international governing body for masters track and field. The World Association of Veteran Athletes (WAVA) was founded two years later in 1987 at the second World Masters Athletics Championship in Sweden. WAVA later changed its name to World Masters Athletics and continues to be the sport's governing body.

By 2002, the fifth World Masters Games attracted 20,000 competitors to Melbourne, Australia. The organization now sponsors three regular events: outdoor track and field, cross-country, and indoor track and field. In the 2005 games in San Sebastian, Spain, a 78-year-old woman competed in nine events, and an 81-year-old man competed in seven. At the most recent championship, in Riccione, Italy, twenty-five new world records were set (www.world-masters-athletics.org). Fifty-year-old Marie Michel of Puerto Rico set new records in the 200 meter (25.65) and 400 meter (57.66) sprints. Ninety-year-old Frederico Fisher of Brazil set new records in the 100 meter (17.53) and 200 meter (38.57) sprints. Sixty-year old Phil Raschker of the United States set a new record in the 80-meter hurdles (13.35).

The masters track-and-field movement is not the only organized sport opportunity for older athletes. For example, the United States Masters Swimming (USMS) organization (www.usms.org) has 500 affiliated masters swim clubs for adults aged 18 or older in fifty-three regions throughout the United States, with a total membership of more than 42,000. These clubs offer structured workouts, often with a coach, and assistance in planning for training. The USMS publishes *Swimmer*

Exercise across the lifespan is an essential component of health.

magazine for its members. It also organizes ten National Long Distance Championships each year, ranging from a 3,000-yard race (25-yard pool) to a 6-mile race (open water). Several of these races are "postal" races where swimmers perform locally and mail their results to the national headquarters.

One can also find local, regional, and national age-group competitions in a number of sports. Local recreational leagues now often organize age-group competition for older adults. For example, the Columbus (Ohio) Parks and Recreation program offers "over-50" and "over-60" basketball leagues during the winter months.

Physical Activity Forever

People in the developed world now live longer than ever, so the number of elderly people is rising, as is the proportion of older people relative to other age groups. The 65–84 age group will increase to 12 percent of the total population in 2010 and to nearly 17 percent by 2025 (Cordes & Ibrahim, 2003). Estimates suggest that by 2030 more than a half-million Americans will be over the age of 100. It is increasingly clear that regular physical activity is important in helping elderly people maintain the quality and length of their lives. Whereas young people can increase physical function by 10 percent through regular exercise, older people can achieve an increase of 50 percent. A sedentary lifestyle, on the other hand, is estimated to account for 50 percent of the decline in strength, flexibility, and aerobic functioning among older people. The cost to the nation's public health bill for this loss of capacity is staggering.

The men and women who now constitute our "senior" generation grew up in an era that did not promote fitness in the same ways our current era does. Women particularly tended to be socialized away from vigorous activity and were exposed to the prejudice that it was not "feminine" to exercise or to compete vigorously. Also, the detrimental effect of tobacco smoking and of eating a poor diet were less well known.

Thus, the current senior generation is actually *learning* to be more active. Many contemporary seniors prefer *low-impact activities*, such as walking or water aerobics, which are designed to minimize the stressful impact of exercise on aging joints. Others, however, work out in much the same way that young adults do, using exercise machines or cycling. Many senior-citizen centers now offer fitness facilities to their clients. These fit seniors also provide excellent role models for their younger counterparts. The generations that follow them, who grew up in the current climate of knowledge about and support for sport and fitness as lifetime endeavors, are likely to alter further our perceptions of what is possible for the senior citizen.

THE NEW SETTINGS FOR SPORT, FITNESS, AND PHYSICAL EDUCATION

Traditionally, sport, fitness, and physical education have been restricted primarily to children, youths, and adults. Facilities, therefore, have most often been those associated with schools, communities, and family-oriented organizations, such as the YMCA. These agencies still provide such facilities and are expanding their programs. There is, however,

Exercise facilities are found in many private and public venues.

a host of facilities more widely available to more people than ever before. Many of these sport and fitness facilities are in the private sector, with users paying direct fees for the opportunity to use them.

Sport Clubs

Private-sector sport clubs are now regular features of any metropolitan area. Tennis may account for the largest number, but there are many types of clubs, with foci ranging from skating to trapshooting to racquetball. Typical is the Olympic Tennis Club where 2,500 tennis players of all ages play each week, primarily outdoors in the summer and indoors in the winter.

Sport clubs offer three primary services: instruction, organized competitions, and social play. At the Olympic Tennis Club, 350 adults take lessons each week. Lessons might range from a 30-minute private lesson for $32 per lesson to a 1½-hour group lesson costing $18 per lesson. Beginner lessons are typically given in groups of six, last for 1 hour, and cost $12 per lesson. Competitors are organized in several ways but primarily on the basis of skill level—that is, beginners, intermediates, and advanced. Leagues are formed so that players can participate regularly for an extended period of time.

Social play and practice require only that members sign up for court time. The cost of court time depends on the hour of the day and day of the week, with popular times more costly than off-peak times. Many members have regular court-time reservations and often play with the same person each week, thus emphasizing the social element often associated with adult involvement in sport.

Sport clubs often have attractive lounges, weight-training facilities, and child-care services available, as well as some kind of food service. The facilities are typically bright, clean, and attractive. The service at sport clubs is typically quick, courteous, and friendly. Amenities such as these keep customers returning.

Sport-Medicine Centers

People who participate in sport and fitness activities often need health-care treatment and rehabilitation—sometimes to remediate problems and sometimes to prevent problems from developing. Unheard of 20 years ago, specialized **sport-medicine** facilities and programs are now common in metropolitan areas.

A sport-medicine program serves a varied clientele. It might provide care for high-school athletic programs, serve adults who have sport-related injuries, implement sport/fitness education programs, or treat children in either remedial or preventive modes. The staff of sport-medicine organizations might include orthopedic surgeons, family-practice physicians, podiatrists, nutritionists, physical therapists, X-ray technicians, athletic trainers, and even sport psychologists.

Initially, sport-medicine programs were attached to hospitals or were operated out of a regular group medical practice as an additional service to clients. As their popularity has grown, however, they have tended to become separate facilities, specialized to serve clients of all ages.

Home Fitness

As our population ages and physical activity across the lifespan grows more important to sustaining a high quality of life, adults are finding ways to accommodate their activity interests within the home. This trend is no doubt due to several influencing factors: primarily, the convenience of having a fitness workout at home and the expense of belonging to a private or community fitness center.

Many homeowners have converted part of a basement or a spare bedroom into a "fitness room." Here they might have a stationary bike, a treadmill or elliptical trainer, and some weights for lifting. They might also install a TV so that they can watch news or sporting events as they do their workout. Many new homes are now constructed with a fitness center as part of the plan. The "home fitness" industry is booming, including both the construction of fitness rooms and the high-tech fitness machines that will be used in the fitness rooms (see, for example, www.homefitnessinc.com). None of this is inexpensive! New, so-called smart fitness machines monitor your pulse rate and automatically adjust speed and/or incline to maintain your target heart-rate zone (see, for example, www.landice.com).

We should expect that fitness technology will continue to develop and that the fitness industry will continue to develop and market new and better fitness machines with more and more features to help make fitness work more effective and fun.

Worksite Programs

Increasingly, employers are converting facilities into space for recreation and fitness programs. Newly constructed facilities often include fitness and recreation spaces. Corporations and businesses have found that an increasing portion of their costs is associated with paying for health-care insurance for their employees. Employees who are healthier simply cost less, not only in terms of medical expenses but also in days lost from work due to illness.

Most employers believe that fit employees, other things being equal, are better workers. They are absent less frequently and have more energy throughout the day. Thus, it is in the interest of the company to support worker involvement in fitness and recreation activities. Companies that cannot afford separate facilities of their own often financially support employees' joining local fitness and recreation centers.

The General Electric Company reported that employees participating in a worksite fitness program reduced health-care costs by 38 percent compared with nonparticipating employees (www.fitwellinc.com). The Coors wellness center estimates that the corporation saved $1.4 million in health-care claims from employees over a 6-year period.

Some corporations provide incentives, such as reductions in health-care premiums, for employees who exercise regularly and do not smoke. Other corporations provide disincentives. The Hershey Foods Corporation charges higher rates for health insurance if employees have high blood pressure, smoke, or are overweight. Clearly, worksite fitness is now big business. This opens a range of new professional opportunities for women and men who aspire to careers in the fitness and wellness professions.

Sport/Games Festivals

A type of sport festival recently added to our cultural landscape illustrates well the theme of lifespan physical activity. All across America, states have developed highly successful summer sport festivals for athletes of all ages. The first such event, New York's Empire State Games, attracted 5,000 participants in 1978 (*Albany Times Union,* 1992), and the idea spread quickly. Forty states now hold summer games, and fourteen states hold winter games (www.stategames.org). Nearly 500,000 athletes of all ages participate in these games. In Montana, a state with only 800,000 residents, the Big Sky State Games attract more than 10,000 competitors each year.

In 2007 the Kentucky Bluegrass State Games (www.bgsg.org) attracted more than 14,000 participants ranging in age from 3 years to 87 years. They competed in twenty-nine sports that included basketball, soccer, and softball but also croquet, chess, tee-ball, and kayaking. Many sports included categories for people with disabilities.

The Badger State Games in Wisconsin are now 23 years old. Over thirty-five communities host competitions for athletes of every age. There are summer games with competitions in thirty sports and winter games with competitions in twenty sports. All participants are welcomed with an ethic that "everyone plays regardless of age or ability" (www.badgerstategames.org).

Medal winners from the forty-eight state games nationwide qualify to compete in the State Games of America (www.stategames.org). The 2007 State Games of America competition was held in Colorado Springs, Colorado. Competitions were held in thirty sports, ranging from triathlon to bowling, gymnastics, archery, basketball, and volleyball.

THE EMERGING CHARACTERISTICS OF LIFESPAN PHYSICAL ACTIVITY

Lifespan physical activity is an emerging phenomenon. Although we cannot now predict how it will continue to evolve and mature, we can predict some characteristics of its future development, based on observations of its early stages.

1. *The importance of an early start.* Habits of participation in physical activity clearly begin in childhood. In addition, the skills developed in childhood can be used throughout life, whereas new skills become increasingly difficult to learn as people age. Also, many fitness problems may have a pediatric origin; that is, unfit children tend to become unfit adults. Although some programs aim at producing "superbabies," making exaggerated claims and perhaps doing more harm than good, most early programs do not.

2. *Breakdown of gender stereotypes.* We are approaching the time when girls and women will have full opportunities for lifespan physical activity in ways similar to those men enjoy. Being fit is

not gender specific: You do not have to be male to be an athlete. Sport, fitness, and physical education can no longer afford to organize or categorize activities or roles on the basis of gender rather than skill or interest. An important professional goal is to eliminate gender bias from how children and youths are socialized into physical activity and from the opportunities available to them throughout their lifespans.

3. *Breakdown of age stereotypes.* People are living longer than ever before. In the developed world, a large proportion of the population is in the postretirement age group. Health problems related to aging represent a major investment of national resources. Unfortunately, stereotypes have sometimes contributed to behavior that increased the likelihood of health problems. For instance, tradition once dictated that older adults should not engage in vigorous physical activity; based on such a stereotype, an older woman, for example, would be expected to avoid doing weight training. We now know that vigorous physical activity not only enhances older people's quality of life but also reduces their health-care costs—by decreasing the incidence and the severity of osteoporosis in postmenopausal women, for example. People who are currently in middle age are likely to change this stereotype as they advance to their postretirement years, but until then, we must encourage contemporary older people to be active, providing them with opportunities to do so.

4. *Shift in emphasis from youths to adults.* The median age of our population increases with each passing decade—America is becoming grayer! The median age is now over 30 years, will reach 35 by the year 2010, and will be above 40 by the year 2020. Sport, fitness, and physical education have traditionally been viewed primarily in terms of programs for children and youths. It is quite clear now that these fields are undergoing an important transformation, shifting their focus to primarily serving adults rather than children and youths (Ellis, 1988). This transformation will require new programs, new facilities, a newly trained group of professionals, and an entirely new outlook on program goals and the processes through which those goals can be achieved.

5. *Shift to the private sector.* Historically, opportunities for sport, fitness, and physical education have been most widely available in the public sector: in schools, community recreation, and public facilities such as parks. In the past several decades, we have witnessed the emergence of an enormous private-sector industry dealing with sport opportunities (the tennis club, the gymnastics center), fitness (the weight-training center, the aerobics center), and physical education (the multipurpose athletic club). The emergence of this new industry has brought bright new prospects for participation; it has also revealed certain problems such as the increasingly strong relationship between wealth and opportunity in sport, fitness, and physical education. Also, like most other industries, these are market oriented, catering to the interests and desires of the consumer and trying to influence those interests and desires through creative advertising.

6. *Increasingly strong scientific base.* Our scientific understanding of sport, fitness, and physical education has increased dramatically since the late 1960s (see Chapters 15–16). This knowledge has become widely available not only to physical-activity scientists and professionals but also to the general public. Many physically active people are highly knowledgeable about their activity, and they increasingly demand that professionals know the best and latest information. In addition, the high cost of medical services and health insurance provides a strong impetus for researchers to continue investigating the preventive benefits of lifespan physical activity.

7. *The new professionals.* Many of the professional roles described in this text have emerged only in this generation—sport management, cardiac rehabilitation, worksite fitness, and early-childhood physical education, to name a few. Each profession requires somewhat different preparation, and, increasingly, each requires a professional certification or license to practice. The new professions develop organizations and a specialized literature,

often spawning an even more specialized role such as the sport-marketing specialization within sport management.

8. *Greater amounts of more readily available information.* Check the sport and fitness sections of your local bookstore or video store. What will first impress you is the volume of books, magazines, and videos particularly the how-to books and videos such as how to stay fit, how to scuba dive, or how to help your child become more skilled in a sport. Cable television now has specialized sport channels—for example, a 24-hour golf channel that offers instruction as well as events. Not all the information represents the best of what sport and fitness sciences have taught us, but consumers are becoming more knowledgeable and selective.

9. *The use of technology.* Technology is transforming our lives in many ways, including both knowledge *about* sport, fitness, and physical education and how we *do* sport, fitness, and physical education. The World Wide Web is an extraordinary source of information, as the number of Web sites cited in this text will attest. High-tech exercise equipment allows for more specific workouts and more fun too! Nearly every sport has been influenced by technology breakthroughs in equipment—golf clubs, poles for vaulting, and shoes, to name just a few. The professional work of coaches, personal trainers, athletic trainers, sport managers, and physical-education teachers has been changed by information technology. We should expect that this trend toward technology will continue to change how we exercise, how we play, and how we learn.

THE MAJOR ISSUES THAT WE FACE AND WHAT WE NEED TO DO TO CONFRONT THEM

Most of this chapter is intended to introduce the wide variety of opportunities for people of all ages to participate in sport, fitness, and physical-education activities. Youngsters can start earlier, and older adults can continue to be active throughout their lifetime. We have more places, programs, and people to accommodate them. That's the good news!

The bad news is that America has an epidemic of overweight and obesity, starting in childhood and continuing throughout the lifespan. More bad news is that opportunities to be active and to learn and enjoy sport and recreation activities are not distributed evenly across the population. Race, place, and socioeconomic status (SES) severely affect the opportunity to be healthy and active. If you are poor, black, or Hispanic and live in an inner city, you have few places that cater to your activity needs and interest, the food you can afford to buy does not support a healthy diet, your local environment is unsafe for children and youths, and you have few support services. This phenomenon will be discussed in more detail in Chapter 9 as the *social gradient in health and fitness.*

Historically, educational and policy efforts to improve physical activity opportunities for persons of all ages have focused primarily on individuals. Although individual responsibility is important, there is increasing recognition that we must deal with the structural and environmental issues that are associated with poor health, obesity, and inactivity. Reductions in physical activity are caused by a number of factors related to what is now commonly referred to as the *built environment.* Communities are designed to foster driving rather than walking or biking. Physical activity among children and youth has decreased while time spent with video games, watching TV, or using the computer has increased. Forty years ago, more than half of all U.S. children walked or cycled to school while today only 10 percent do (ncdot.org). Parents cite five primary barriers to their children's participation in physical activity: transportation problems, lack of opportunities for physical activity in the immediate area, expense, parental lack of time, and concerns about neighborhood safety (*MMWR Weekly,* 2003).

In Chapter 13, the concept of a *physical-activity infrastructure* is fully explained. The infrastructure to support physical activity is weak throughout the nation and weakest in those places where it is most needed. Low SES rural and urban communities are much less likely to have adequate recreation, fitness, and physical-activity programs and facilities. It is unwise to think that the nation can confront and solve health problems that are due largely or partially to physical inactivity without developing a more supportive infrastructure.

After the three introductory chapters, this text is divided into sections that describe the sport, fitness, and physical-education professions, then a final section dealing with national, state, and local efforts to build and sustain a physical-activity and healthy lifestyles infrastructure, the crucial themes that define our future, and the kinesiological disciplines that support the professions. In one sense, it is important for you to understand the issues and opportunities available in the sport, fitness, and physical-education professions. In the fitness section alone, for example, there are multiple opportunities for different kinds of professional service. It is appropriate and necessary for you to understand these fields and the professional opportunities within them, but it will also be made clear to you that the problems that we face as a society cannot be solved by professionals working solely within their own profession. We must all learn to be *boundary crossers*. Sport, fitness, physical-education, health, and recreation professionals must work together to develop and sustain programs that address these health and activity issues that confront the nation. As you will see throughout this text, programs that bring professionals together—to work in a collaborative way to solve problems at the local and state level—do exist. As you learn about them, you will become increasingly aware of the cooperation needed to effectively address issues related to inactivity.

SUMMARY

1. Recognition of the possibility and desirability of lifespan involvement in sport, fitness, and physical education represents a fundamental change in our perception of human life.

2. Overweight and obesity rates among all age groups have increased markedly over the past 20 years, are associated with a number of serious medical problems, and represent an increasing share of the nation's medical costs.

3. The major societal problems related to inactivity, overweight, and obesity can be solved only when professionals from sport, fitness, physical education, health, and recreation work together at local and state levels.

4. The era of lifespan sport, fitness, and physical education represents a watershed period—one not limited by age or gender.

5. Physical activity in the early years represents a new and exciting field for the sport, fitness, and physical-education professions.

6. Sport, fitness, and physical education for children occur in both the public and the private sectors; each has its own problems and prospects.

7. Activity programs for youths are extensive, with opportunities both within and outside schools.

8. Young adults find many outlets for activity in community programs and in the growing private-sector activity and fitness industry.

9. Adults increasingly have activity programs available at their worksite, and the adult fitness and sport industry has become big business. The masters sport movement has shown that older people can stay active as competitive athletes throughout their lives.

10. The new settings for sport, fitness, and physical education include sport clubs, specialized sport/fitness centers, sport-medicine centers, home fitness areas, worksite programs, and sport/games festivals.

11. The emerging characteristics of lifespan involvement include recognition of the importance of an early start, the breakdown of gender and age stereotypes, the shift in emphasis from youths to adults, the shift from the public to the private sector, the increasingly strong scientific base, the creation of new professional

roles, the increased availability of information, and the use of technology.

12. Although the consumer of sport, fitness, and physical education typically does not recognize the specialized nature of each field, professional specialization is typical of career preparation. The resulting ambiguity forms the framework for this text.

DISCUSSION QUESTIONS

1. What physical-activity opportunities have you had growing up? Do you believe these opportunities are different for people from other backgrounds?

2. Describe three new facilities or programs that you have seen firsthand that are typical of the current boom in sport and fitness.

3. Describe five private-sector facilities for sport, fitness, and physical education in your region. What socioeconomic groups use these facilities most?

4. What specific experience have you had or what specific evidence can you present that shows that there is gender, race, or age discrimination or stereotyping in sport, fitness, and physical education?

5. Did the women in your family (mother, aunts, and others) have ample opportunity for physical activity when they were growing up (for example, sport teams and fitness classes)?

6. If you have children or when you do have children, do you expect that they will have physical-activity opportunities that are substantially different from the ones you had growing up? Why?

CHAPTER 2

The Heritage of Physical Education, Sport, and Fitness in the United States

Physical education must have an aim as broad as education itself and as noble and inspiring as human life. The great thought in physical education is not the education of the physical nature, but the relation of physical training to complete education, and then the effort to make the physical contribute its full share to the life of the individual, in environment, training, and culture.

Dr. Thomas Wood, 1893, speaking to the International Congress on Education at the Chicago World's Fair

LEARNING OBJECTIVES

- To discuss the influence of Greece and Rome

- To describe the cultural influences, including formal gymnastic systems and national sport forms, on the emergence of sport and physical education

- To discuss the birth of the physical-education profession and the institutionalization of sport

- To describe the emergence of the new physical education and the contributions of its early leaders

- To discuss the emergence of a national sport culture

- To describe the umbrella profession of physical education

- To describe the emergence of professional sport and changes in recreational sport

- To analyze the fitness crisis of the mid-1950s and the fitness renaissance of the mid-1980s–1990s

- To describe the academic discipline of kinesiology and the development of research disciplines

THE EMERGENCE OF A PROFESSION: 1885–1930

This chapter introduces the development of sport, fitness, and physical education in the United States. Chapter 3 reviews the major philosophical positions that influenced that development. America was settled primarily by European explorers and immigrants. Thus, early ideas about sport, fitness, and physical education were greatly influenced by the beliefs and perspectives that these newcomers to America brought with them. European culture and philosophy were much influenced by two great early civilizations—those of Greece and Rome. The major period of Greek influence occurred from about 500 BCE to 300 BCE, whereas the Roman Empire flourished primarily from 300 BCE to 476 CE.

Early Influences in Physical Education and Sport

The Greek Influence Greek culture had a major focus on physical development and sport. The two key elements of the education of Greek boys were "gymnastics" and "music." Gymnastics included a wide range of physical activities and sports. *Music* was the term used for all the other academic subjects. Only Greek male citizens were given the opportunity to be educated. Women were generally not educated and were permitted only modest involvement in physical activity and sport. All teachers were male. Education took place in temples; in the *gymnasium*, which was usually an outdoor facility for physical training and bathing; and in the *Palaestae*, which was a center for boxing and wrestling that also included changing rooms and bathing rooms. Physical prowess and beautiful physical form were much sought after and admired in early Greek culture, especially in the city-state of Athens.

Greek boys were encouraged to become athletes and to compete in the large number of "games" that made up the Greek sporting calendar. The Panhellenic Games consisted of the Olympic Games held at Olympia to honor the god Zeus; the Pythian Games held at Delphi, the sacred site of the god Apollo; the Isthmian Games held in Corinth to honor Poseidon, the sea god; and the Nemean Games held in Nemea to honor Zeus (Mechikoff & Estes, 2006). Contrary to popular belief, Greek athletes were not amateurs. Riches were bestowed upon winners in all these contests. Physical training and sport were also very much related to the need for all Greek men to fight in combat in the many small wars that erupted between Greek city-states and with other powers.

The two primary city-states of Greece were Athens and Sparta. The culture of Athens was home to Socrates, Plato, Aristotle, and Aristophanes and is credited with much of the development of drama, philosophy, and the spirit of democracy, although women, children, and slaves were considered inferior and were excluded from government. Sparta was the major military power whose goal was to rule all of Greece (Mechikoff & Estes, 2006). In Sparta all babies were examined by a council of elders and only the strongest and healthiest were allowed to live. Spartan boys left home at the age of 7 to be in the military where they were obligated to stay until age 50. Physical training and sports programs were taken very seriously in Sparta, all under the control of the military. Discipline, obedience, indifference to pain, and obsession with victory in competition were the primary values of the education system.

The Roman Influence The Roman Empire was built through wars whereby emerging civilizations were conquered and put under control of Roman leaders. Unlike the Greeks, who thought that other civilizations were barbaric and had nothing to offer Greek civilization, the Romans were quite willing to adopt practices of those they conquered if they appeared to be more useful than Roman practices. Whereas Greek city-states *created* philosophy, music, art, and drama, the Romans typically *adopted* cultural practices of those they conquered.

Military training was very important to Roman life. The education of boys was strongly slanted toward developing the obedience, discipline, and physical prowess to be a solider. Skills such as running, jumping, swimming, wrestling, horseman-ship, boxing, fencing, and archery were all taught both as appropriate healthy exercise and as military preparation.

Most sporting events in the Roman Empire were dedicated to the gods worshipped by the Romans, just as the Greeks dedicated their games to their own gods. Running events, wrestling, ball games, and equestrian events were common. Many sporting events grew into major entertainments that became both spectacular and bloody. Chariot races and glad-iatorial contests were often held in large facilities, the two most famous being the Circus Maximus and the Colosseum, both in Rome. Both women and men attended, and much betting took place prior to the contests.

Women were not as marginalized in the Roman Empire as they were in Greek city-states. Some sporting events were organized for young women. Participation in swimming, dancing, and light exer-cise was common, especially among the privileged classes. The fall of the Roman Empire in 476 CE ushered in a period of 1,000 years known as the Dark Ages, in which physical activity, sport, and fitness diminished in importance amid political and economic chaos.

The Birth of a Profession In 1885 William G. Anderson, who was to become the first secretary of what we now know as the American Alliance for Health, Physical Education, Recreation, and Dance (AAHPERD), was deeply concerned about his own lack of training and preparation to be a professional physical educator (Lee & Bennett, 1985a). Ander-son, who was then 25 years old, had graduated from medical school and was employed at Adelphi Acad-emy in Brooklyn as an instructor of physical training. His only real experience in his field, however, had been as a young participant at the German *Turn-verein* (a social, gymnastics, and sports club) in Quincy, Illinois.

In 1885 there were no institutions that prepared people to be what was then called a "gymnastics teacher." To become an instructor in physical training, apparently, a person needed only some knowledge of medicine and some experience in

gymnastics (a kind of gymnastics very different from what we now know as Olympic gymnastics). There were no professional organizations to bring together people who had common interests. There were few texts available to help people acquire understanding of the field. There were no professional journals. In fact, there was no profession.

Anderson, as his life's work makes clear, was a leader. He wanted to create a forum within which people interested in physical training, physical educa-tion, and the various gymnastic systems could discuss with, debate with, and learn from one another. To that end, Anderson invited a group of people inter-ested in these fields to meet at Adelphi Academy on November 27, 1885. Among those attending were local clergy, school principals, members of the news media, college presidents, and, of course, physical-training instructors (Lee & Bennett, 1985a). Sixty interested people gathered for that historic meeting.

On that day, the participants decided to form an organization, the Association for the Advancement of Physical Education. Dr. Edward Hitchcock, who had founded the first college department of physical education at Amherst College 24 years earlier and was still its head, was elected to be the first presi-dent. The director of the gymnasium at Harvard College, Dr. Dudley Sargent, was a vice president. The young Dr. Anderson earned the privilege of being the association's first secretary. Forty-nine of the sixty assembled participants took membership in the new organization. The distribution of their interests and affiliations is testimony to the breadth of interest in physical education at that time: Eleven were college teachers, thirteen were academy–seminary teachers (secondary level), three were practicing physicians, six were active in the early YMCA movement, and two were ministers.

That meeting marked the birth of a profession.

The Scene Before 1885

The second half of the nineteenth century marked the evolution of the United States from a predomi-nantly rural, colonial, and frontier nation to a more urban and industrialized nation. Sport, fitness, and physical education were certainly not unknown before 1885. In 1791 the first private swimming pool was built in Philadelphia. In 1820 the first college gymnasium was built at Harvard College. The first competitive football game was played in 1827. John Warren, a professor of anatomy and physiology at Harvard, published the first theoretical treatise on physical education in 1831; in the same year, Catherine Beecher published a book titled *A Course in Calisthenics for Young Ladies.*

Although there was virtually no physical education in schools before 1885, the idea of free, universal, public education was growing in the United States. In 1839 the first teacher-training school was founded in Lexington, Massachusetts. The idea that physical training (or physical education, as it was soon to be called) was to be a part of the school curriculum also took hold during that period. In 1866 the first state legislation requiring physical education in schools was passed in California.

The American Civil War was largely responsible for many of the subsequent developments, particularly in the field of sport. Many historians refer to that period as the transition time between local games and institutionalized sport (Spears & Swanson, 1978). The post–Civil War era saw an extraordinary development of organized sport. Baseball was first played as an intercollegiate game in 1859; the first intercollegiate football game was played a decade later. Tennis was introduced into the United States by Mary Outerbridge in 1874. The National Bowling Congress was formed in 1875, and badminton was first played in the United States in 1878. In 1879 the National Archery Association and the National Association of Amateur Athletics were formed.

Development during that pre-1885 period was not confined to schools and colleges. The YMCA movement had begun in England in 1844 and was devoted to character education and physical activity. In 1851 the first American YMCA was formed in Boston. The YMCA movement was so successful that it created the need in 1883 for the development of the International Training School of the YMCA in Massachusetts, later to become Springfield College. Springfield College has a long and noble history of contributions to the development of sport, fitness, and physical education. In Cincinnati, in 1848, German immigrants formed the first Turnverein, a forerunner of a movement that was to be widespread for the next half-century in cities where there was a significant population of German descent.

Those events portended what, in the first half of the twentieth century, would blossom into the profession of physical education—encompassing during that later period not only sport, fitness, and physical education but also recreation, the playground movement, dance, and outdoor education. Although there was no such overarching profession in the pre-1885 period, the roots of its eventual development are clear.

In 1825 Charles Beck became the first recognized teacher of physical education in the United States. He developed a program of German gymnastics at the Round Hill School in Northhampton, Massachusetts. Just 1 year later, another advocate of the German system, Charles Follen, started a gymnastics program at Harvard College. In 1837 Catherine Beecher founded the Western Female Institute, where her own Beecher system of calisthenics was an integral part of the curriculum. In the same year, the Mt. Holyoke Female Seminary offered a course in physical education to its students (Leonard & Affleck, 1947).

As Chapter 3 shows, a dominant philosophical movement of the first part of the nineteenth century was *muscular Christianity*, a philosophy that made exercise and fitness (if not yet sport) compatible with the Christian life. It was this philosophical movement that allowed a still-conservative nation to move gradually away from the Puritan prohibitions against play and exercise.

As religious prohibitions began to loosen, the idea that exercise and fitness were educationally important began to become accepted. (In contrast, recognition of the educational value of sport is much more a twentieth-century phenomenon.) That philosophical shift allowed physical education to become part of the school and college curriculum. In 1861 Edward Hitchcock became the director of the department of hygiene and physical culture at

An early twentieth-century physical-education class for college men.

Amherst College, marking the first such organizational arrangement in the United States. In 1879 Dudley Sargent was appointed assistant professor of physical training and director of the Hemenway Gymnasium at Harvard College. Hitchcock and Sargent were among the most important early leaders in physical education, and their emphasis on scientific approaches provided fundamental direction for the emerging field.

The attitudes and institutions developed before 1885 would later allow the full development of sport, fitness, and physical education (Lucas & Smith, 1978). The young nation was still conservative. Work was valued and there were still many formal and informal prohibitions against play. In schools, programs of manual labor were more common than were those of physical education. Sport was developing, even in colleges, but that was at the demand of students rather than of people in charge of the curriculum.

Those ideas, events, and people were, therefore, forerunners of the great expansion of sport, fitness, and physical education. They certainly did not constitute *physical education* in the sense that we

now know it. It is difficult to label each of these movements and the ideas that undergirded them; the terms *physical training*, *physical culture*, *gymnastics*, *sports*, and *play* were all used at one time or another. The term *physical education*, however, as an umbrella concept under which all the others might be understood, was not appropriate to those times.

> First, physical education, as we know it, largely had its origin in the United States. Second, although the name "physical education" appears in the literature before 1900, physical education is by and large a twentieth century phenomenon. (Bookwalter & Vander-Zwaag, 1969, p. 44)

Although the pious, hardworking Puritan is a common stereotype of early Americans, by the 1800s Americans certainly had sporting interests. For example, in 1862 (during the Civil War), more than 40,000 spectators watched a baseball game involving a New York regiment. In 1844 more than 35,000 spectators gathered at a racetrack in New York to watch a 10-mile footrace among professional runners. Horse racing, boxing, distance running, and rowing were popular spectator sports in the pre-1885 period (Lucas & Smith, 1978). People also participated in a variety of local sports and games, many of which later became standardized as national sports.

The Context for the Emergence of a Profession

The attempt to analyze the emergence of the sport, fitness, and physical-education professions from 1885 into the twentieth century has to be understood in the context of the general culture. To know why things happened as they did and why some directions rather than others were taken, we first have to understand the background of the culture within which sport, fitness, and physical education began to emerge toward the end of the nineteenth century and to grow into the umbrella profession of physical education in the first half of the twentieth century (see Focus On Box 2.1).

To understand that background, it is important to consider the major cultural developments that greatly influenced the emergence of the sport, fitness, and physical-education professions:

1. *Decline of religious opposition to sport and exercise.* The early development of physical education and leisure pursuits had been seriously hindered by religious sanctions. In the nineteenth century, however, religion and sport reached an accommodation in the philosophy of muscular Christianity, the idea that the body and physical pursuits were not antithetical to a good, Christian life.

2. *Immigration.* Between 1820 and 1880, 10 million immigrants came to America. From 1880 to 1890, 9 million more came! Immigrants brought with them new games and new attitudes, greatly enriching the sport and fitness culture of their new country. They settled mainly in cities and, with the rise of professional sport in large

FOCUS ON	CHRONOLOGY AT A GLANCE—The Emergence of a Profession		2.1
Western frontier expansion	1825	Charles Beck hired as first teacher of physical education in United States	
	1827	First competitive football game played	
	1827	First public swimming pool opened, in Boston	
	1834	First rules of baseball published	
Era of muscular Christianity	1837	Western Female Institute founded by Catherine Beecher	
	1848	First Turnverein formed, in Cincinnati	
	1851	First YMCA formed, in Boston	
	1861	Hitchcock appointed director of hygiene and physical culture at Amherst	
American Civil War	1861	Boston Normal Institute for Physical Education founded by Dio Lewis	
	1866	First state legislation requiring physical education passed, in California	
	1874	Tennis introduced in United States	
Expansion of Industrial Revolution	1879	Sargent appointed assistant professor of physical training at Harvard	
	1883	YMCA Training School started at Springfield, Massachusetts	
	1883	Swedish gymnastics introduced to United States by Nissen	
	1885	Adelphi Conference held; Association for Advancement of Physical Education formed	

(continued)

FOCUS ON	CHRONOLOGY AT A GLANCE—The Emergence of a Profession (*continued*)	2.1

Free, universal education	1885	Professional physical education program at Oberlin started by Delphine Hanna
	1887	Softball invented in Chicago
	1889	Boston Physical Training Conference held
	1890	Hartwell named supervisor of physical education for Boston
Urbanization	1891	Physical education recognized as curricular field by National Education Association
	1893	Department of physical education and hygiene formed in NEA
Substantial immigration	1895	First public golf course built
	1896	Olympic Games revived in Athens, Greece
	1896	Volleyball invented in Holyoke, Massachusetts
	1897	Society of College Gymnasium Directors formed
Expansion of public schooling	1901	First master's-degree program in physical education started at Teachers College
	1903	Gulick appointed director of physical education for New York schools
	1903	Delphine Hanna appointed first female full professor of physical education
	1905	National College Athletic Association formed
	1906	Playground Association of America formed
	1908	First high-school swimming pool built, in Detroit
	1909	National Association of Physical Education for College Women initiated
	1910	Four objectives of physical education identified by Hetherington
	1911	National Park Service formed
	1913	Intramural programs established by Michigan State and Ohio State
World War I	1916	First state supervisor of physical education named, in New York
Roaring Twenties	1924	Doctoral programs in physical education first offered by Teachers College and New York University
	1926	First dance major formed at University of Wisconsin
	1927	*The New Physical Education* published by Wood and Cassidy
Stock market crash	1930	*Research Quarterly* first published by Education Association
	1930	National Recreation Association formed

cities, found common loyalties with other immigrant groups and with groups already established in this country.

3. *Industrialization.* The American Civil War greatly intensified the move toward industrialization. Industrialization produced wealth—and some of that wealth helped to develop sport, fitness, and physical education. Industrialization created technologies for the development of facilities and equipment.

4. *Urbanization.* As immigrants poured into the country and industries developed in and around major cities, the population of America inevitably shifted from predominantly rural to predominantly urban. Whereas hunting, fishing, and other outdoor activities might sustain the leisure needs of a rural population, new activities had to be developed to meet the leisure needs of an urban population. Concentrated populations in cities and the wealth produced by industrialization were also necessary for the development of professional sport (Lucas & Smith, 1978).

5. *Transportation and communication.* The developing technologies in transportation and communication were especially important to the development and spread of sport. In 1830 only 23 miles of rail track existed in America; by 1880 there were 90,000 miles of track! The telegraph, invented in the 1840s, allowed instant communication of sport results. City newspapers became sufficiently sophisticated to have separate pages, or even sections, devoted to sport. In the twentieth century, the development of radio and television was to have an even larger influence on sport and fitness.

6. *Education.* So much of the development of sport, fitness, and physical education has occurred in schools that the development and extension of education was a fundamental influence. In 1862 the Morrill Land Grant Act created institutions of higher education, which provided greater access to university education; those same land-grant institutions would become leaders in the development of sport and physical education in the twentieth century. The American ideal of free, universal education began to become a reality in the middle to late nineteenth century. The courts decided that tax dollars could be used to support secondary education and paved the way for the model of the American comprehensive high school. Compulsory-attendance laws and emerging child-labor laws put more children into school and kept them there longer.

7. *Intellectual climate.* The nineteenth century is well known as one of the most active eras in history for the development of *ideas.* Charles Darwin challenged accepted theories of human life with his concept of evolution. Sigmund Freud challenged prevailing notions about human psychology and created the profession of psychiatry. Jean-Jacques Rousseau introduced new visions of the education of children. Karl Marx wrote *Das Kapital* and created the intellectual foundation for socialist and communist societies. Much of what we know now as modern science originated in the nineteenth century.

Those influences were crucial to the emergence of sport, fitness, and physical education toward the end of the nineteenth century. Together, those early influences created a context for fantastic development in how people played and watched sport, in how they viewed physical activity, and in what sport and fitness programs were available. We now turn to that development.

The Battle of the Systems

The period from 1885 to 1900 was marked by a competition among several approaches to what was then called gymnastics (which we now call physical education). That competition was for new converts to the systems and for places in school and college curricula. For that reason, at least for physical education, this period is most often referred to as "the battle of the systems" (Weston, 1962).

Almost all the early programs of physical education in America were gymnastic systems imported from Europe. Most of these gymnastic systems

An early twentieth-century rhythmic gymnastics class for college women.

Even in competition, activity costumes for women reflected nineteenth-century views of women.

were described as *formal* approaches to exercise, meaning that the movements were prescribed and were done in unison by a group of students.

To understand the various gymnastic systems and why they were so popular as early forms of physical education, you must be aware of two elements of the cultures within which they were practiced and debated. First, Europe at that time was a hotbed of nationalism. This fervor was accompanied by a strong military spirit. Loyalty to a particular system was not just allegiance to a particular approach to what was then called gymnastics; it was also a way to show pride in your country.

Second, a dominant psychological theory of that day, known as *faculty psychology*, held that the mind could be trained by precise, repetitive practice. Thus, gymnastic systems were thought to have cognitive benefits similar to those derived from practicing the conjugation of Latin verbs—each helped to "train the mind." A brief overview of the most prominent systems is provided in Focus On Box 2.2.

The Boston Conference in 1889   In 1889 Mary Hemenway financed a conference to promote Swedish gymnastics. The **Boston conference** was organized by Amy Morris Homans and was presided over by the U.S. commissioner of education, William Harris. The theme of the conference was an evaluation of the various physical exercise programs then in use, giving to the conference and to the era it represented the "battle of the systems" label.

A list of featured speakers at the conference now appears as a who's who of the fledgling profession of physical education: Hitchcock, Sargent, Hartwell, Anderson, and Posse. Also delivering papers at the conference were prominent American figures such as Henrich Metzner of the New York Turnverein and international figures such as Baron Pierre de Coubertin of France, who was soon to revive the Olympic Games (Lee & Bennett, 1985a).

That conference is considered by most historians to be pivotal in the development of American physical education. It brought together important persons in a context in which each was called to examine and evaluate current activities in physical education. Although each no doubt tried to promote

FOCUS ON   Gymnastic Systems   2.2

The German System

Main proponent: Friedrich Ludwig Jahn

Purpose: Build a strong, unified Germany by balancing academic and physical education

Activities: Jumping, running, throwing, climbing, vaulting, simple games of running and dodging

Apparatus: Horizontal bars, balance beams, vertical ropes, ladders, vaulting horses, parallel bars, running tracks, jumping pits

Brought to America by Jahn students Charles Beck, Charles Follen, and Francis Leiber

First American application: Round Hill School in Northampton, Massachusetts, and Harvard College

By 1890 with massive German immigration there were 300 Turnvereins (exercise, sport, and social clubs) with more than 40,000 members, mostly in the Midwest.

The Swedish System

Main proponent: Per Henrik Ling

Purpose: Regain vigor and national pride and renew spirit of Norse history with a scientific–therapeutic system of gymnastics

Activities: Swinging, climbing, vaulting, resistance exercises, passive therapeutic manipulation

Apparatus: Swinging ladders, rings, vaulting bars, stall bars

Brought to America by Hartwig Nissen, a Swedish diplomat who later built a gymnastics equipment manufacturing company doing business worldwide. Boston philanthropist Mary Hemenway gave funds to build Hemenway Gymnasium at Harvard College and invited Baron Nils Posse, a graduate of Ling's Royal Institute of Gymnastics, to introduce his system. Posse founded the Posse Normal School of Gymnastics, which provided a 2-year teacher-training program. Incorporated into the Boston school system in 1890 through Amy Morris Homans with Edward Hartwell as first director of physical training for the district.

The Beecher System

Main proponent: Catherine Beecher, director, Hartford Seminary for Girls and founder of Western Female Institute

Purpose: Develop a system of "appropriate" female activities

Activities: Archery, swimming, horseback riding, calisthenics done to music, calisthenics using light weights

Apparatus: lights weights, wands

Beecher created a system of 26 lessons in physiology and 2 in calisthenics with light exercise, all designed to correspond to the assumption prevalent at the time—that programs for men were too vigorous for women and required too much strength.

The Dio Lewis System

Main proponent: Dioclesian Lewis

Purpose: First effort to develop an American system based on grace of Beecher system and scientific nature of the Ling system

Activities: Exercise routines vigorous enough to raise heart rate but not as vigorous as prescribed in the German system; routines accompanied by music; social games and dance routines also

Apparatus: Beanbags, wands, dumbbells, clubs, hand rings

The Lewis system was adopted by progressive schools. In 1860 Lewis founded the Boston Normal Institute for Physical Education and in 1861 published the *Gymnastics Monthly and Journal of Physical Culture*, which can be considered the first American physical education journal (Weston, 1962)

The Hitchcock System

Main proponent: Edward Hitchcock, in 1861 appointed director of Hygiene and Physical Culture at Amherst College

Purpose: Physical development with measurement of bodily development baseline and progress over time.

Activities: Marching, unison calisthenics, exercises, some sports and games

Apparatus: Horizontal and rack bars, ladders, weights, rings, Indian clubs, ropes, vaulting horses

(continued)

FOCUS ON   Gymnastic Systems (*continued*)   2.2

Hitchcock created the first truly American program with an emphasis on its scientific base and consistent measurement. This provided a model that would be emulated in the twentieth century.

The Sargent System

Main proponent: Dudley A. Sargent, appointed to faculty of physical training and named director of the Hemenway Gymnasium at Harvard University in 1879.

Purpose: Amalgamated other systems into a scientifically defensible, comprehensive program of physical education

Activities: Calisthenics, German- and Swedish-style exercises, and specialized machine exercise

Apparatus: Bars, rings, vaulting horses, ropes, ladders, parallel bars, specialized exercise machines

Space: Gymnasium

---

her or his own system, it is also clear that the door had been opened to the larger question: To what purposes should physical education be devoted, and by what means might such purposes be achieved?

Sport was not a major topic at the conference. Sports and games were not fundamental to any of the systems and, at that time, had no place in physical education. If we look at what was happening with sport in the larger culture during the same period, however, we can easily see that the days during which physical education was defined as gymnastics were numbered.

The Emergence of Organized Sport

If the late nineteenth century is interesting for its early development of gymnastic-oriented physical-education programs, it is even more remarkable when viewed as a period of development in sport. During the post–Civil War period, sport grew up: It changed from loosely organized games having many local variations to standardized sports with widely recognized rules and national overseeing bodies. The standardization of sport could not have happened, of course, except in an increasingly industrialized, urbanized culture in which increasing wealth, transportation, and communication and an emerging middle class provided the framework for such developments.

When a sport becomes *standardized* (or *institutionalized*), rules governing its conduct become standard, bodies are formed to enforce those rules, standards of competition are set, the sport is promoted for both participants and spectators, championships are formed, records are kept, and traditions and rituals are developed and shared by people who participate and watch. What a remarkable period of history that was for sport! Sports that can be described as having "come of age" during the period were the following (Lucas & Smith, 1978):

archery	pedestrianism
baseball	polo
bicycling	roller skating
billiards	rowing
bowling	rugby
boxing	sailing
canoeing	shooting
cricket	skiing
croquet	soccer
cross-country running	swimming
curling	tennis
fencing	track and field
football	trapshooting
golf	trotting
gymnastics	volleyball
handball	water polo
ice hockey	wrestling
lacrosse	yachting

Baseball was probably our first truly national sport, having been spread widely by soldiers during the Civil War and having achieved professional success with its attendant organizational apparatus. Although many players were paid and teams competed for money in the very early days of baseball, and especially right after the Civil War, it was the Cincinnati Red Stockings of 1868 who provided the model that was to be emulated not only in baseball but in other sports as well. An entrepreneurial lawyer, Aaron Champion, hired an outstanding manager, Harry Wright, who then put together the best and most complete team of professionals that he could hire. The team was undefeated for more than a year, during which time they played before an estimated 200,000 spectators (Lucas & Smith, 1978).

Many of those developing sports, of course, had their roots in other countries. Some, like golf and tennis, were played in the United States as much as they were played in Europe. Other American sports, such as baseball and football, had origins in European games but had been modified substantially so as to become unique sports rather than variations of sports practiced elsewhere. Still other sports that came a bit later were derived from American sports that had origins in other countries. Softball, for example, which was invented in Chicago in 1887, was a variation of baseball, modified for use in smaller places and with less equipment. Basketball, on the other hand, which was invented by James Naismith in the YMCA school at Springfield, Massachusetts, in 1891, was strictly American and was created to meet the need for an indoor sport of skill and activity in the winter months. Likewise, volleyball, which was invented by William Morgan at the YMCA in Holyoke, Massachusetts, in 1896, is a particularly American sport that has since spread throughout the world.

Women were involved in this sport expansion from the beginning. For example, in the same winter that Naismith invented basketball, Senda Berenson adapted the game for her students at Smith College, a nearby institution. By 1899 a

Smith College women's basketball in 1904. Senda Berenson tosses up the ball.

committee had formalized a set of women's basketball rules, and the game was being played widely by women (Spears & Swanson, 1978). Volleyball, too, was played by women from the outset.

The revival of the Olympic Games in Athens in 1896 provided a fitting climax to a half-century in which sport had begun to assume the central role it would occupy in the cultures of developed countries for much of the twentieth century. The strongest impetus for reviving the games came from Baron Pierre de Coubertin, who greatly admired the moral and spiritual strength of ancient Greek culture as embodied in the early Olympic Games. Along with the revival of the games as a major sporting event, de Coubertin articulated the philosophy of "olympism," an educational program of peace and cultural understanding that sought to unite the modern world.

Sport on the College Campus

Perhaps the unique feature of the development of sport in America is the phenomenal way in which sport grew on college campuses and came to be an integral part of college and university life. In 1850 there was very little sport participation of any kind on American college campuses, and nowhere did intercollegiate sport exist. Yet, by the turn of the century, sport had assumed a critical social function on most campuses, and intercollegiate competition had begun to move to the central position it was to occupy in the general sporting scene in the twentieth century (Lucas & Smith, 1978).

A brief chronology of growth-period events:

1852   First collegiate competition—a crew race between Yale and Harvard

1859   First intercollegiate baseball game—Amherst versus Williams

1869   First intercollegiate football game—Rutgers versus Princeton

1873   First track-and-field competition as part of Saratoga regatta

1875   Intercollegiate Association of Amateur Athletes of America formed

1883   Intercollegiate Lawn Tennis Association formed

1890   First intercollegiate cross-country running meet—Cornell versus Penn

First women's tennis club at University of California

1891   Basketball invented at Springfield College

1892   University of California's women's basketball team formed

1895   First intercollegiate hockey competition at Johns Hopkins

1895   Intercollegiate Conference of Faculty Representatives formed (later became the Big Ten Conference)

1896   First intercollegiate swim meet (Columbia, Penn, Yale)

Intercollegiate football was a big spectator sport in the 1920s.

By the turn of the century, most universities had athletic associations that arranged schedules, purchased supplies, and generally began to offer the array of services now commonly found in athletic departments in universities. What is perhaps most remarkable about all of this rapid development is that it occurred largely through the efforts of students and, at the outset at least, despite the often serious opposition of administration and faculty. Still, as schedules grew more ambitious, travel became more costly, training tables began to become popular, and equipment became indispensable, it was clear that financial support was necessary. Although the student-organized athletic associations could handle those problems at the beginning, the problems soon became sufficiently complex that faculty and administrative intervention not only was necessary but also seemed to be the only way to solidify the venture and ensure its future success.

Thus, while early pioneers in physical education promoted gymnastic systems in school programs and began to develop college departments emphasizing scientific measurement and prescriptive exercise, the students were busy bringing organized sport into the life of the college and university, particularly for male students. The control over schedules and team membership was vested in the team captain, a student whose many roles included those now played by athletic directors and coaches. The truth is that the abuses in intercollegiate sport for males toward the end of the nineteenth century were so widespread that only faculty intervention and control could save the system. Intercollegiate sports for women, on the other hand, were controlled by faculty from the outset, accounting perhaps for both slower growth and fewer abuses in women's sports.

Faculty Control and the Beginning of a National Intercollegiate System

As we have noted, sport was not officially welcomed on campus with open arms. Many faculty and administrators were against it, especially in the early days. However, it became so popular among students and so integral to campus life that an accommodation had to be reached. In many cases, **intercollegiate sport** was replete with bad practices and serious abuses—some of which make current abuses look minor in comparison.

Lucas and Smith (1978) attribute the early abuses to two separate threads in the fabric of American society in the nineteenth century: the existence of the Puritan work ethic and the lack of a substantial "gentleman" class. The work ethic was straightforward. If there is a job to do (win the game), then you do everything you can to get the job done. The lack of a gentleman class meant that there were few restraining influences on that work ethic. Rather than "win within the rules," the practice often became "win at all costs." Although sport was well on its way toward standardization, with subsequent enforcement of rules and procedures that would provide a restraining influence, it had not yet matured to the point where the restraining influences provided by sport organizations (conferences, associations, and so on) were effective. In England, from which many of our sport practices derived, the desire to win was restrained by a sense of honor, fair play, and respect for rules that was taught to young British gentlemen in their schools. In England also, the work ethic among the sporting classes was entirely different from that in America.

The major abuses had to do with eligibility (there were no rules about it) and with how athletes were treated by their universities.

> One outstanding example was the captain of Yale's football team, James Hogan, who was twenty-seven years old at the turn of the century when he began his intercollegiate career. He occupied a suite of rooms at Yale's most luxurious dormitory and was given his meals at the University Club. His tuition was paid and he was given a $100 a year scholarship. He and two others were additionally given the privilege of selling game programs from which they received the entire profit. Furthermore, Hogan was an appointed agent for the American Tobacco Company and received a commission on every package of cigarettes sold in New Haven. If that wasn't enough for this "amateur" collegian, Hogan was given a ten-day vacation trip to Cuba during the school term after the football season was successfully completed. (Lucas & Smith, 1978, pp. 212–213)

Athletes often competed for different colleges or universities within the same season. Many intercollegiate athletes were paid, and many were for hire, often being enrolled as "special" students for a short time while they competed. Intercollegiate sport became so popular on campus, thus encouraging even greater abuses, that it threatened the real purpose of university education.

The beginning of faculty control was an important step in the continued development of intercollegiate sport. Because it was brought under the normal institutional control of faculty, sport was accepted as an appropriate and useful aspect of university life and as a contributor to the overall goals of a university education. The first faculty athletic committee was formed at Harvard in 1882. By 1888 the composition of this committee had changed to include representatives of alumni and students, and the committee's authority had been extended considerably. This pattern was gradually adopted by most universities.

The next important step in extending faculty control was the formation of associations of universities—what we now know as *athletic conferences*. In 1895 the Intercollegiate Conference of Faculty Representatives was formed, which immediately established eligibility requirements for entering students, for continued participation, and for transfer students. It also placed severe limitations on athletic aid and on how coaches were hired and retained. That conference, later to be known as the Western Conference or Big Ten, became the model through which other institutions, in other parts of the country, joined together to exert institutional control over intercollegiate athletics and, in so doing, ensured a continued role for sport in university life.

Intercollegiate sport for women was always under better control. On many campuses, women's athletic associations were formed; in 1917 Blanche Trilling of the University of Wisconsin organized a meeting through which the Athletic Conference of American College Women was formed (Spears & Swanson, 1978). However, the explosion in collegiate sport for women was to come more than a half-century later, with the advent of Title IX (see later in this chapter and Chapter 5).

The New Physical Education

In 1893 an International Congress on Education was held in conjunction with the Chicago World's Fair (Lee & Bennett, 1985a). Because the National Education Association (NEA) had 2 years earlier recognized physical education as a curricular field, a physical-education section of the congress was organized. That enabled physical educators from Europe and North America to meet for the first time as specialists in a fully recognized school subject. From that time on, the physical-education profession began to view education rather than medicine as its parent field. At that symbolically meaningful conference, a 28-year-old physical educator from Stanford University, Thomas Wood, presented to the audience a view for a *new physical education*:

> Physical education must have an aim as broad as education itself and as noble and inspiring as human life. The great thought in physical education is not the education of the physical nature, but the relation of physical training to complete education, and then the effort to make the physical contribute its full share to the life of the individual, in environment, training, and culture. (Lee & Bennett, 1985a, p. 22)

That conference symbolized the end of the era in which gymnastics dominated the physical-education curriculum, and it marked the beginning of the modern era of physical education. Wood's ideas about a physical education that had broad goals and contributed to a student's complete education were to become the dominant theme in physical education in the twentieth century—and they still dominate today. One of Wood's best students at Stanford was Clark Hetherington, who was to become a major force in the new American physical education, as was Luther Halsey Gulick, then director of the YMCA training school at Springfield. In 1927 Wood and Rosiland Cassidy, another great pioneer, published *The New Physical Education*, a landmark text.

The **new physical education** was to be embraced by many people but was articulated most clearly by four leaders—Wood, Cassidy, Hetherington, and Gulick. Wood went on to head the department of physical education at Teachers College, Columbia University, which became the great early training ground for leadership in physical education, marking the transition from medicine to education for advanced training in the field. Cassidy earned her doctorate at Columbia and became a major leader through her work at the University of California at Los Angeles (UCLA), later becoming a pioneer thinker in the field of human movement. Hetherington had a distinguished career at

An early-twentieth-century gymnastics class at a school for black girls.

several major universities, later becoming supervisor for physical education for the State of California. Gulick went from Springfield to become director of physical training for the New York City schools and was a major figure in the development of the playground movement.

The development of the new physical education was not the result of the influence of ideas alone. It is important to remember that the intellectual leaders in psychology, education, and physical education in the early part of the twentieth century were a small group of people who had frequent personal contact with one another. Wood went to Teachers College at Columbia University. The great psychologist Thorndike was also on the faculty there, as was John Dewey, America's greatest philosopher-educator. Hetherington was brought to Teachers College by Wood. Cassidy took her degree there also. Hetherington had studied under Hall, who was a close associate of both Thorndike

and Dewey. These people knew one another well and interacted both formally and informally—and this important intellectual circle lay the philosophical and programmatic foundation for the future of American physical education in the early years of the twentieth century.

The Spreading of the Physical-Education Umbrella

In the years between the turn of the century and World War I, the character of American physical education took shape. An umbrella profession—physical education—was created; it embraced a number of growing movements, including dance, YMCA/YWCA, playgrounds, recreation, outdoor education, sport, fitness, health education, and intramurals. It was during this period, as the umbrella profession formed, that much of the early organizational work in those separate yet related fields took place (see Focus On Box 2.3).

Dance, especially folk dance, became popular in school physical-education programs in the early years of the twentieth century. Together with the growing recognition of sport and games as curricular areas in physical education, dance helped push gymnastics out of the center of the curriculum. In 1916 the American Folk Dance Society formed.

The playground and camping movements grew out of a genuine social concern with the welfare of children, influenced strongly by the same philosophical and psychological theories that came together in the progressive-education movement. The Playground Association of America was founded in 1906 to guide that movement.

The Industrial Revolution of the nineteenth century had created a national concern about health, especially about the health of children. The emerging school health, health-education, and health-sciences professions were strongly backed by medical societies. In 1903 New Jersey passed legislation making a health examination compulsory for all schoolchildren.

Although this period was characterized primarily by the inclusion of sports and games in the school

---

FOCUS ON   Professional Organization Evolution Toward AAHPERD   **2.3**

- 1903—Association for the Advancement of Physical Education (AAPE) becomes the American Physical Education Association (APEA).
- 1937—APEA becomes the American Association for Health and Physical Education (AAHPE).
- 1938—The growing field of recreation is added to AAHPE, which becomes AAHPER.
- 1974—The emergence of district associations and the change from older divisions into national

associations (such as the National Association for Sport and Physical Education—NASPE) causes AAHPER to become an alliance of associations, named the American Alliance for Health, Physical Education, and Recreation

- 1979—The current name is created through the formal addition of dance: AAHPER becomes AAHPERD.

---

curriculum and by the development of a national sport culture, fitness was not neglected. In 1902 Dudley Sargent developed his widely used Universal Test for Strength, Speed, and Endurance. In 1910 James McCurdy set up standards for measuring blood pressure and heart rate. In 1915 William Bowen published his influential *Applied Anatomy and Kinesiology.*

Intramurals became important, particularly as a way of allowing guided sport competition in colleges and universities. In 1913 Michigan State and Ohio State appointed intramural directors, the first such positions recognized. By 1916 a survey indicated that 140 institutions had intramural programs (Weston, 1962). This development at the college level influenced the beginning of intramural programs in high schools a decade later; by 1930 such programs were national in scope.

The recreation movement began to form from a number of sources, including the YMCA/YWCA, the playground movement, camping, and parks. In the days when America was predominantly rural, there was little need for formal recreation organizations. As America became more urban, however, the need for formal recreation grew. The National Park Service was formed in 1911; by 1930 the National Recreation Association had formed from the Playground and Recreation Association.

During this period, America also was building a national sport culture. In 1911, 80,000 spectators watched the first Indianapolis 500 race. A championship boxing match between Jim Jeffries and Jack Johnson was a worldwide spectator event. In 1903 the first World Series was played. In 1905 the National Collegiate Athletic Association was founded. Ty Cobb in baseball and Jim Thorpe in football became national heroes of immense popularity.

In physical education, this period marked the transition from a gymnastics-oriented curriculum to one in which dance and sport began to share more equally. Physical education became associated with education rather than with medicine. Just after 1900, several universities—including Nebraska, Oberlin, California, and Missouri—offered professional preparation courses in physical education, expanding on the pioneer program begun in 1885 by Delphine Hanna at Oberlin College. In 1901 Teachers College offered the first master's degree in physical education. In 1905, at the University of Illinois, the first department of professional preparation in physical education was formed. By 1924 there was sufficient interest and need that both Teachers College and New York University began to offer doctoral programs in physical education.

Another important element in the maturation of the health, physical-education, and recreation professions was the creation of an academy of national leaders. In 1904 Luther Halsey Gulick created the Academy of Physical Education, whose membership was open only to those elected by fellows. That led in 1926 to the formation of the American Academy of Physical Education (AAPE), whose first elected members were Clark Hetherington, R. Tait McKenzie, Thomas Story, William Burdick, and Jay B. Nash. The purpose of AAPE was to create a forum of national leaders who could address major issues in annual meetings. The "Academy," as it came to be known, soon published the proceedings of its annual meetings as *The Academy Papers*.

The Golden Age: Post–World War I

The era between World War I and the beginning of the Great Depression in the early 1930s was a particularly interesting time in American history; it was an active period for the sport, fitness, and physical-education professions, too. America ended the war as an international power of the first order. The giant American industrial economy had moved into high gear. A middle class was emerging. People had money and wanted diversions. National interest in sports grew at all levels. The radio and the automobile had come within the means of many people— and each was important to the growth of sport, as the telegraph and the railroad had been in the mid-nineteenth century.

This was the era of Bobby Jones in golf, Babe Ruth and Lou Gehrig in baseball, Jack Dempsey in boxing, Man O'War the racehorse, Red Grange in football, Gertrude Ederle and Johnny Weissmuller in swimming, Bill Tilden and Helen Wills Moody in tennis, and Charlie Paddock and Mildred "Babe" Didrikson Zaharias in track and field. It was an era of heroes and heroines, of huge crowds (120,000 watched a high school football championship in Chicago), and of previously unparalleled media interest.

Except for media coverage of then hugely popular boxing matches, African American athletes were largely invisible in the majority-controlled media. These athletes were not allowed to participate in most professional and intercollegiate sports, but in sports such as baseball, Negro professional leagues developed and drew many fans, despite media neglect. Institutions of higher education for African American students, particularly in the South, developed intercollegiate sports programs of their own and organized into distinct leagues.

Education of or Education *Through* the Physical? As physical education made rapid gains in the post–World War I era, the major philosophical dispute among physical education professionals was "Should physical education be an education *of* the physical or an education *through* the physical?" The "of the physical" supporters, led by C. H. McCloy, argued that the main emphasis should be the development of the body and its systems for both health and skill. The "through the physical" supporters, led by Jesse Feiring Williams, argued that the mind and body were a unity and that physical education contributed to mental, emotional, and social development as well as physical development.

The new physical education, first advocated by Wood and later articulated most clearly by Hetherington, was the precursor to the *education through the physical* approach. These ideas were stated cogently in Hetherington's 1910 paper, "Fundamental Education":

> This paper aims to describe the function and place of general neuromuscular activities, primarily general play activities, in the educational process. We use the term *general play* to include play, games, athletics, dancing, the play side of gymnastics, and all play activities in which large muscles are used more or less vigorously. . . . To present the thesis four phases of the educational process will be considered: organic education, psychomotor education, character education, and intellectual education. (p. 630)

A women's tennis class, 1932.

Hetherington's four objectives for physical education (organic, psychomotor, character, and intellectual) were to be adopted with only slight variations in language and concept by virtually every important American physical-education spokesperson for 50 years (Siedentop, 1980).

The leadership of the new physical education began to pass in this era from the Wood–Cassidy–Hetherington–Gulick generation to the generation of physical educators trained by those pioneers, most notably to Jesse Feiring Williams and Jay B. Nash. Williams took his M.D. degree at Columbia in 1915 and joined the physical-education faculty at Teachers College in 1919, where he became an articulate and prolific writer. Jay B. Nash took his Ph.D. degree in physical education from New York University in 1929, where he already was a faculty member. Williams became the primary interpreter of Wood, whereas Nash became the main disciple of Hetherington. Both were dynamic and inspiring leaders, and it was through their teaching and writing that the modern curriculum in physical education was developed.

The notion of **education through the physical** became the modern interpretation of Wood's *new physical education*. This view was consistently challenged by C. H. McCloy, who argued that, of course, physical education could contribute to social and mental development but that its main emphasis and primary responsibility were to develop students physically and to make them more skilled. McCloy and those who supported the education of the physical perspective can be seen today as early advocates for what over time have become regular calls for a stronger emphasis on physical fitness and for the enormous importance now attached to regular physical activity as a contributor to health. In that sense, the battle still goes on within physical education.

The Beginnings of a Science of Physical Education

The early contributions of Hitchcock and Sargent had established the American gymnastic systems on a more scientific basis than that of their European counterparts. Emphasis on measurement and prescriptive exercises based on test data were unique features of those systems. Thus, as an American physical-education profession developed in the late nineteenth century, a scientific emphasis was ever present.

As sports, games, and dance began to move gymnastics out of the center of the curriculum and as the new physical-education philosophy gained strength, the scientific emphasis so notable early in the profession seemed to become less important. In fact, it was just temporarily overshadowed by the rhetoric and program changes that accompanied the new physical education.

The Sargent tests, McCurdy measurement innovations, and McCloy classification index provided continuing evidence of the scientific direction of the profession, firmly rooted in its medical ancestry. In 1921 Sargent developed his Sargent Jump Test, which is still used. The beginning of doctoral programs in 1924 provided a strong impetus for the research movement within the profession as doctoral candidates were trained in research methods and began to complete doctoral dissertations. In 1927 the Brace Motor Ability Test was developed, followed 2 years later by the Cozens' Tests for General Athletic Ability. In 1930 the APEA formally recognized this important emphasis within the profession by publishing the *Research Quarterly*.

This beginning of a research focus within the sport, fitness, and physical-education professions was vital for their increasing acceptance in university programs and as an important educational subject matter. It foreshadowed a period when the kinesiology scientific subdisciplines would emerge to stand on their own.

Access and Equity This era of expansion, in which our professions were born, needs also to be viewed realistically in the context of the inegalitarian nature of the times. Remember, most of the history reviewed in this chapter occurred *before* women were allowed to vote and *well before* blacks were granted their full constitutional rights. Women such as Delphine Hanna, Ethel Perrin, Jessie Bancroft, Amy Morris Homans, Elizabeth Burchenal, and Blanche Trilling were important and courageous pioneers, their advocacy of women in sport, fitness, and physical education made more difficult by the narrow and stereotyped views of femininity in those days. Their names appear less often in this history not because their roles were less important but because the power structures of almost all organizations were dominated by men.

Delphine Hanna, for example, is one of the remarkable figures in the history of American physical education. She graduated from Brockport State Normal School in New York in 1874, earned an M.D. degree at the University of Michigan and then a Bachelor of Arts degree from Cornell University. She taught in public schools, where she became concerned about the health and physical status of children. She completed a course at the Sargent Normal School of Physical Training in 1885 and then took a position at Oberlin College in Ohio where she developed the nation's first teacher-preparation program in physical education. Among her students at Oberlin were Luther Halsey Gulick, Thomas Wood, and Fred Leonard, all of whom went on to important positions of leadership and influence. In 1903 she became the first woman to be appointed a full professor of physical education.

Nor is there much mention in this history of black people. To be sure, black institutions, such as Hampton Institute and Howard University, pioneered sport and physical education for black students. To their credit, some notable institutions in the history of physical education and sport— such as Oberlin College, Springfield College, and the Sargent School for Women—admitted black students (Zeigler, 1962). In this period of emergence and growth, however, access and *equity* remained restricted to and dominated by white males.

That is where physical education stood as the era of affluence known as the Roaring Twenties ended and America plunged into the Great Depression of the 1930s.

FOCUS ON	CHRONOLOGY AT A GLANCE—Consolidation and Specialization	2.4

	1929	*Carnegie Report* published
	1930	*Journal of Health and Physical Education* first published
Great Depression	1935	NEA national study on teacher education in PE College Physical Education Association formed
	1937	AAHPE added as a department of NEA
	1938	La Porte curriculum guide first published
World War II	1943	*The Physical Educator* published
	1948	National conference on professional preparation
G.I. Bill	1950	National Intramural Association formed
	1951	National Athletic Trainers Association formed
Baby boomers	1953	Kraus–Hirschland fitness reports published in *JOHPER*
	1954	American College of Sports Medicine founded
Sputnik	1956	President's Council on Youth Fitness established
	1959	Operation Fitness started by AAHPER
	1960	President Kennedy's "soft American" article published
Civil rights	1961	President's Fitness Council's "blue book" published
	1963	*Quest* published
Environmental movement	1964	Henry's "academic discipline" article published
	1965	Dance added as a division of AAHPER
Women's rights	1972	Title IX passed AAHPERD's *Tones of Theory* published
	1975	Public Law 94-142 passed

CONSOLIDATION AND SPECIALIZATION: 1930–PRESENT

By 1930, at the end of the emergence era, sport, fitness, and physical education had begun to consolidate under the umbrella profession called "physical education."

The signs of approaching maturity for that umbrella profession were everywhere (see Focus On Box 2.4). In 1930 the APEA was on firm footing as *the* organization providing an umbrella under which physical educators, sport administrators, health educators, recreationists, and fitness experts found common ground and support. The APEA had just started two professional journals, the *Research Quarterly* and the *Journal of Health and Physical Education*. The organization also elected its first woman president, Mabel Lee of the University of Nebraska (Lee & Bennett, 1985b).

The battle between gymnastic systems and the new physical education had been clearly won by the adherents of "education through the physical," and physical education became firmly established within education rather than within medicine. Many states passed legislation requiring health and physical-education instruction in schools. Research on fitness and performance testing was being established within the profession. Sport was immensely popular within the culture, and there was a general perception that physical education was a vital aspect of the school curriculum.

The Cultural Context: 1930–1940

The years between 1930 and 1945 marked an important transitional period in American history. The Great Depression following the stock market collapse of 1929 shook the foundations of American society as well as the assumptions of free enterprise and rugged individualism on which the society had grown and prospered—businesses failed, savings were lost, banks closed, and unemployment rates reached intolerably high levels.

In the face of those economic and social threats, the nation elected Franklin D. Roosevelt as president in 1932 (and again in 1936, 1940, and 1944). President Roosevelt presided over a recovery era in which major changes were made in the social and economic systems within the nation. For example, the Social Security Act of 1935 created a national pension system as well as unemployment insurance and certain health benefits. The Wagner Act of 1935 encouraged the organization of labor, and unions grew in strength, securing wage and benefit improvements for workers. To pay for all these government programs, legislators developed new tax programs.

The Great Depression produced not only changes in the foundational structures of the government but also programs designed to provide immediate relief from the suffering brought about by the economic collapse. The Civilian Conservation Corps (the CCC), the Works Progress Administration (WPA), and the National Youth Administration (NYA) were three programs, among many, that had a direct effect on the sport, fitness, and physical-education professions.

World War I, the Russian Revolution of 1917, and the Great Depression produced worldwide problems that were to manifest themselves again in international conflict by the middle to late 1930s, as Germany and Italy went to war to expand their territories and influence. By 1940 it was clear that the war would involve more than continental Europe; by 1941, with the declaration of war against Japan by the United States after the Japanese bombing of Pearl Harbor, World War II had begun, and the era of the Great Depression had ended.

Other factors of major importance in understanding the continued evolution of the sport, fitness, and physical-education professions were the development of the automobile as a primary means of transportation, the widespread influence of the radio, and the beginnings of television. It also became clear that the airplane would soon further revolutionize the concept of travel and distance. Urbanization continued, and the emerging middle class grew.

Sport, Fitness, and Physical Education: The Depression Years

The decade of 1930–1940 saw major changes in sport and physical education. The economic collapse and the resulting widespread unemployment created substantial problems for the programs of sport and physical education that had developed so vigorously after World War I. These difficulties, however, led to new efforts and programs as the nation attempted to regain its economic and social balance. What follows are snapshots of the important developments of that decade.

Developments in Sport   The Carnegie Report in 1929 found widespread abuses in college sport, including use of professionals, eligibility violations, and compromises of academic rules (Spears & Swanson, 1978). With the negative publicity and general economic collapse, many sport programs in higher education were severely cut back.

Spectator sport fared poorly during the Depression because few could afford the price of admission. This precipitated a major shift to participatory sport, mostly at the local level. Youth sport, family sport, and informal kinds of participation increased substantially.

Softball exemplified this shift from spectating to participating. Invented in Chicago in 1877, softball required less space and less equipment than baseball. In the 1930s, softball became America's most popular recreational sport. By 1940, at the end of the Depression, there were more than 300,000 organized softball clubs, and the Amateur Softball Association had more than 3 million affiliated players (Gerber, 1974).

The shift to participation democratized sport participation during the Depression. Citizens at all socioeconomic levels began to participate in games and activities historically available only to a privileged class (Dulles, 1940).

Federal and Private-Sector Interventions

Ten federal agencies developed sport and recreation programs that had an immediate influence on participation as well as longer-term effects.

The National Youth Administration supplied part-time work for high school students, keeping them in school. Many of the projects students worked on were athletic and recreation facilities.

The CCC opened camps for men aged 18–25 whose families were on relief. These camps, in different parts of the country, provided work in parks and with recreational and sport facilities. The men lived in military-style barracks and engaged in well-organized intramural sports programs.

The WPA had the most visible and lasting influence of all federal Depression programs. The WPA constructed gymnasiums, swimming pools, auditoriums, ski facilities, and stadiums. Many of these facilities still host high school and university sport events.

The Boy Scouts, Girl Scouts, YMCA/YWCA, and Catholic Youth Organization all developed programs for youths, many of which were sport and recreation programs. This "youth sport movement," which began in the Depression, took a major symbolic step forward when Little League Baseball was launched in Williamsport, Pennsylvania, foreshadowing the enormous growth in youth sport in the following decades.

Organizational Consolidation   The umbrella profession of physical education weathered the Depression well. In 1930 the APEA had 5,700 members, but by 1940 when it had become AAHPE, membership had reached 10,000.

In 1931 the National Education Association organized a committee to evaluate teacher education in physical education, leading to a national code of standards in 1935, which exerted influence over teacher preparation in physical education for years to come.

In 1937 the newly named AAHPE (formerly APEA) became a department of the NEA, forming the organizational structure that would guide the profession for the next 30 years.

By 1938 a committee chaired by William Ralph La Porte had published *The Physical Education Curriculum*. The curriculum model proposed in this publication advocated a unit or block plan approach with activities lasting from 3 to 6 weeks. This quickly became the standard model for planning PE curricula.

Sport, Fitness, and Physical Education During the War Years

The war in Europe had begun in 1939, spreading over most of Europe by 1940. With the Japanese attack on Pearl Harbor, the United States was drawn into the conflict in 1941. More than 15 million people served in the American armed forces during World War II, including 216,000 women in newly created branches of the Army, Navy, and Coast Guard. The entire economic power of the United States turned toward the war effort and, in so doing, lifted itself out of the Depression.

The events associated with World War II had immediate and far-reaching effects on sport, fitness, and physical education. One of the most important was in the area of fitness, which had been the most important field in physical education during the nineteenth century, only to be gradually moved more to the periphery as the new physical education became popular in the early part of the twentieth century. Fitness was not a major issue in society during the Depression simply because basic needs such as food, shelter, and employment were dominant concerns. With the beginning of World War II, however, fitness became an issue immediately.

All the many women and men who were inducted into the armed forces underwent physical tests and then basic training. A large number failed the tests, and many had trouble with the physical aspects of basic training. At the War Fitness Conference in 1943, the assertion was made that school physical education had been a complete failure and that the emphasis on sports and games had to be replaced with fitness programs. Although that did not happen completely, it was clear that an emphasis on fitness would reemerge in not only school programs but also society as a whole. Research on fitness and fitness testing was greatly accelerated, and new fitness programs were put into place (Weston, 1962).

Spectator sport continued in the holding pattern it had entered during the Depression. Many great athletes were in the armed services, travel restrictions were severe, and discretionary leisure money was often diverted to the war effort. Participant sport, on the other hand, continued the growth that it had begun during the Depression. The War Department had invested substantial monies in sport equipment and personnel to provide activities for service personnel. Coaches and athletes often found themselves called to duty as trainers, coaches, and sport administrators. War-training camps developed large sport facilities and encouraged active participation both among camp personnel and between camps. The so-called recreational sports—such as badminton, archery, shuffleboard, volleyball, and table tennis—were promoted as *rest and recovery* activities for service personnel on leave.

School programs of physical education were forced to emphasize fitness objectives and activities more clearly but also fought to hold on to the more balanced approach that reflected the then-30-year-old development of the new physical education. Regardless of the objectives emphasized, physical education was once again considered to be an important part of the school curriculum; it had outlived the "frill problem" it had encountered when school budgets had been cut so drastically during the Depression.

There is little doubt that a major influence of World War II on sport, fitness, and physical education was the beginning of research specialization—a movement that would explode 20 years later as the kinesiology discipline movement. Before World War II, research activity in physical education was limited mostly to physical and motor testing. During World War II, the government funded a great deal of research that was to influence physical education (Weston, 1962). The obvious area was fitness where more had to be learned and testing and programming had to be improved. There were, however, other important areas. The beginnings of what we now call motor learning are clearly traceable to the war effort. Airplane gunners and aircraft lookouts needed to be trained. Those kinds of war skills were really motor skills and visual discrimination skills. The psychologists who studied them and produced both the knowledge and the programs for training were the first motor-learning specialists (see Chapter 15).

Adapted physical education also began as a major enterprise in World War II. Although rehabilitation had been a part of the American physical-education scene because of the influence of the Swedish gymnastic systems, the real impetus for the development of this specialization came during World War II as thousands of wounded soldiers needed both rehabilitation *and* activities in which they could experience satisfaction from leisure participation. Thus, the war years exerted great pressure for research in physical education and set the stage for the later period in which the specialized research fields would develop more fully into a discipline.

When the war ended in 1945, the nation settled back from the 15 years of turmoil and dislocation experienced in the Great Depression and the war. Service personnel came home with high hopes, new expectations, and the G.I. Bill, which could finance their college educations. Women, who had contributed significantly to the war effort both abroad and at home, had developed a new sense of what was possible for them and of what roles they could occupy in peacetime. The economy geared up to produce all of those things that had been put aside during the years of struggle. A boom time lay just ahead—and it was to be an important growth period for sport, fitness, and physical education.

Getting children to enjoy moderate to vigorous activity is a key goal for physical education.

Expansion and Growth in the Postwar Years

The decade following the end of World War II in 1945 changed the United States. Women and men who served in the armed forces came back to jobs and much greater opportunities in higher education. The economy was strong, and a nation that had postponed its desire for consumer goods spurred even further growth.

Developments in the General Culture

New housing was among the most wanted benefits of prosperity. Housing developments sprang up all over the country, especially around cities, giving rise to a new form of living, the "suburb."

College and university enrollments soared as women and men took advantage of a grateful government's programs, known collectively as the G.I. Bill, a major feature of which was support for higher-education tuition.

Many young couples who had postponed marriage and/or family because of the war began to start their families, producing what was perhaps the most significant aspect of that era—the "baby boom." The number of children born in the postwar decade was startling, representing a major shift in the demographics of the American population. The *baby*

boomers changed the social fabric of the nation as they moved through childhood and into adolescence, and they would dominate the cultural and economic life of the nation for the next 50 years.

The Expansion of Sport Although the solid foundation of participation developed during the Depression and throughout the war continued, the postwar years saw a marked shift back to spectator sport.

In 1946 the National Football League had ten teams. By 1977 the league had expanded to twenty-eight teams. In Major League Baseball, there were sixteen teams after the war, but this grew to twenty-five teams by 1977. The National Basketball Association was just starting as a financially shaky organization after World War II, but by 1977 it had become a financially sound league of twenty-two teams.

Golf changed from a country-club sport of the wealthy and began its long evolution into a mass market for participants and a major media sport. A large number of golf courses were built, both private and public.

The Olympic Games began again in 1948. The modern Olympic Games, begun in the late nineteenth century, had grown in importance, reaching its greatest modern status with the 1936 Berlin games, made famous in America by the stunning performances of the sprinter Jesse Owens. The wars in Europe and Asia caused cancellation of the next two games, but they resumed in London in 1948. These London games foreshadowed the enormous success the games were to have over the next half-century.

Intercollegiate sport also began its growth in numbers of sports and athletes and in the media coverage of collegiate sporting events. Teams began to play regionally and then nationally. Scholarships for athletes at larger universities became commonplace. More sports were added, and conference and national championships attracted widespread interest.

The baby-boom generation marked the emergence of sport for children and youth. Age-group competitions began to appear for not only baseball but also football, soccer, gymnastics, ice hockey, and tennis.

Toward the end of the postwar decade, it became obvious that the increasing attendance at sporting events, the widespread broadcasting of events on the radio, and the beginning of televised sport were ushering in an era when mass-media attention to sport of all kinds would become commonplace. Sport sections in newspapers increased in size. Sport magazines and books proliferated. Radio coverage increased, but it was soon clear that television would have the most profound effect on the growth of sport.

The Postwar Years in Physical Education

School programs of physical education, financially troubled during the Depression and World War II, participated in the economic comeback in the postwar decade. Physical-education programs generally followed the traditions of the *new physical education*. Activities taught in physical-education changed after the war as sports and games that became popular during World War II began to find their way into the curriculum, usually under the label of "lifetime sports." Among these were golf, bowling, and tennis.

The number of journals increased, and the level of scientific work in areas such as kinesiology, biomechanics, and exercise physiology expanded.

Immediately after World War II, physical education focused more on lifetime sports, and less

attention was paid to fitness either in school or in the general culture.

This all changed in the mid-1950s. In December 1954, Hans Kraus, a physician, and Ruth Hirschland published in the *Journal of Health, Physical Education and Recreation* an article titled "Minimum Muscular Fitness Tests in School Children." The article reported the results of a study comparing the performance of American and European children on tests of minimum muscular strength. The shocking results showed that 60 percent of the American children failed, compared with only 9 percent of the European children.

The results of the study led by Kraus were brought to the attention of President Eisenhower, who was an avid golfer and had been a leader of American forces in World War II. National newspapers and magazines picked up the story and made it into a national issue in which American youths were pictured as frail and soft. In 1956 a national conference on youth fitness was convened, which resulted in a presidential executive order to form the President's Council on Youth Fitness. In 1958 the nation celebrated its first "Presidential Fitness Week."

In 1960 newly elected President Kennedy published an article in *Sports Illustrated* titled "The Soft American." He also appointed legendary Oklahoma football coach Bud Wilkinson to head the President's Council on Youth Fitness. This flurry of activity and publicity around youth fitness resulted in strong pressures for school physical education programs to focus more on fitness.

The Mid-1950s and On: Forces That Shaped Our Current Culture

In the mid-1950s, events began to occur that would shape the social and cultural landscape in America for the remainder of the century. Those changes would be both tremendously exciting and very difficult. During the 1950s and 1960s, the baby boomers went through childhood and adolescence, changing our culture's language, clothing styles, and musical tastes—creating social turmoil between the generations that had not been seen before and has not been seen since.

In 1954 the Supreme Court upheld the decision in *Brown v. Board of Education* that eliminated the "separate but equal" ethic that had created segregated schools in America, a decision that ushered in the era referred to as the civil rights movement. In 1956 the civil rights movement gained momentum when Rosa Parks, a cleaning woman in Montgomery, Alabama, was arrested because she refused to give up her seat at the front of the bus when asked to do so by a white person. Her action led to a boycott of white-owned businesses in Montgomery. The boycott was led by a young black minister, Martin Luther King, Jr., and attracted national media attention.

In 1957 Russia launched the space satellite *Sputnik*. When Russia beat America into space, it startled both the education and scientific communities, who had assumed we were well ahead in such technological breakthroughs. The post-Sputnik era was known for concerns about American education, culminating 15 years later with the publication of *A Nation at Risk*, the report of the U.S. National Commission on Excellence in Education.

In 1962 Rachel Carson wrote *The Silent Spring*, warning Americans of the environmental dangers of pesticides and chemicals and setting off a major environmental movement. Certainly, the growth of wilderness sport and adventure education has direct ties to that movement. In 1965 an unknown named Ralph Nader wrote a book titled *Unsafe at Any Speed*, revealing the degree to which the auto industry neglected safety concerns in the production of cars. The book launched a consumer movement that eventually affected sport, fitness, and physical education through issues such as product liability, teacher or coach malpractice, and consumer participation in decisions about sport.

In 1972 Title IX of the Education Amendments passed the U.S. Congress, creating the framework within which girls and women might finally have equal access to sport, fitness, and physical-education opportunities. Title IX was one manifestation of what became known as the women's movement. In 1975 Congress passed Public Law 94-142, a far-reaching piece of legislation designed to ensure the rights of Americans with disabilities, particularly in education.

It was within this difficult and complex set of social events that sport, fitness, and physical education continued to develop into the current times. Much of what happened in those years in sport, fitness, and physical education forms the basis for the remainder of this text and, therefore, is reviewed only briefly here.

Sport in the Post-1950 Era The growth in sport in the postwar era was merely a prelude to the even more startling expansion in more recent times. America has become a great sporting nation! So much has happened within sport in recent years that it is difficult to catalog the main changes. Some trends do seem clear.

Title IX and the women's movement provided the framework for an explosion in women's sport, from youth sport all the way to the most elite levels of international sport. Not only do more women take part, but also the growth of women's sport has helped us partially to reconceptualize the role of women in society.

The environmental movement provided the framework for engaging in sport outdoors, especially in wilderness areas. Sports such as cross-country skiing and backpacking have grown enormously. The civil rights movement provided the framework for further collapse of racial barriers in sport. University teams were integrated. Black and Hispanic players became great professionals in the newly integrated competitions.

Road racing has become a national participant sport as well as a spectator sport. More than 30,000 people run the 26.2-mile New York City Marathon; millions more watch it on television. Youth sport expanded to include many sports other than football, baseball, and basketball; in fact, youth soccer may now be the largest program for boys and girls. Sport training started to become more specialized and to begin earlier in children's lives. Not too long

Commitment to environmental conservation and aerobic training come together in some outdoor recreational pursuits.

ago, most high-school athletes competed in a different sport each season, but now they tend to specialize, with year-round training and competition. Sport camps have developed for summer participation and have become highly specialized. The camps are seen by many parents and coaches as necessary adjuncts to year-round participation.

The money made by elite athletes has increased astronomically. Winner's purses for golf and tennis events are huge. Multimillion-dollar contracts are now commonplace. The sport-equipment business has expanded, along with the explosion in participation and spectating. Sport clothes have become fashionable, and athletes have major endorsement contracts with equipment and clothing companies.

The line separating the amateur from the professional has blurred considerably. Many sports

have moved to *open competition* in which there is no distinction (as in tennis, for example). Many amateurs (in track and field, for example) can make a good living while pursuing their sport on a full-time basis.

With the rapid growth and the economic overtones, sport has had more than its share of problems during the post-1950 era. Betting scandals, recruiting violations, point shaving, emotional trauma of young athletes, poor graduation rates for university athletes, and drug involvement have all created national concern. (Those issues and others are addressed in Chapter 6.)

The Fitness Renaissance and the Aerobics Era   Americans have been periodically concerned with physical fitness. Those concerns have typically been responded to but only briefly. Until recent times, there had been no abiding concern with fitness among the general population; then, however, fitness became very fashionable.

The media publicity in the late 1950s and early 1960s about the fitness of American children, along with a growing understanding of the relationships among various forms of fitness and health, laid the foundation for a continuing interest in fitness, both among professionals and, increasingly, among citizens. An additional powerful influence was that being fit became the "in" thing. The athletic look—slim, muscular, active—became the model to which many women and men aspired. Sport and fitness clothing became popular, not just for exercise purposes but also as standard casual wear. No longer were there taboos on going out for a jog or a bike ride. Indeed, such activity was applauded and supported.

When fitness became fashionable, the private sector became involved—it was clear that there was money to be made from catering to the fitness interests and needs of the society. Whereas several generations ago the thought of going to a gym for a workout was associated with dingy facilities and smelly locker rooms, to go to one of the fashionable spas or fitness centers today is a social event. The facilities are bright, colorful, and clean. The workout is social as well as physical.

In 1968 Dr. Kenneth Cooper published a small, paperback book that would wield enormous influence over the fitness movement for a generation and give us a new term that would become commonplace in our language system—the book was simply titled *Aerobics*. By 1973, just 5 years later, the book had gone through its twentieth printing and the term **aerobics** had come to represent an entirely new approach to cardiovascular fitness. Aerobic exercise became the preferred approach to fitness training. Aerobics classes became popular. Aerobics shoes were marketed. Aerobics videos sold well.

Dr. Cooper went on to establish the Cooper Aerobics Institute in Texas (www.cooperinst.org). This center played an important role in the modern fitness movement in several ways. First, it became one of the key fitness-research centers in the world. The institute also paved the way for increasingly useful forms of fitness assessment to be applied in schools and elsewhere.

As America moved toward the beginning of a new century, increasingly clear scientific evidence showed the importance of fitness throughout the lifetime. AAHPERD adopted as its major goal for students to *adopt and value a physically active lifestyle*. Everybody now understands that a modest amount of regular aerobic work, along with core strength and flexibility, are important for older citizens as well as for children and youths. Indeed, the burgeoning fitness industry is now driven by catering to older adults (Lauer, 2006). The dilemma of our times is we now have an increased interest in health/fitness while experiencing an obesity epidemic among children, youth, and adults! It is also clear that people in lower socioeconomic brackets are most seriously affected, and that of course also means people of color and ethnic minorities because race, ethnicity, and socioeconomic status in America are highly correlated.

Learning to cooperate to complete a task can be fun too.

School Physical Education Since the 1950s

The curriculum of physical education expanded greatly in the last half of the twentieth century. Lifetime sports (tennis, bowling, golf, and so on.) had joined the curriculum after World War II and during the 1950s were fully incorporated into existing philosophies and models. In later decades, the curriculum continued to expand, and a new curriculum philosophy challenged the primacy of the education-through-the-physical approach that had dominated since the early part of the century.

The curricular changes were interesting. They reflected a continuing trend for activities in school programs to be selected on the basis of what was popular in the larger culture. The academic reform movement that followed *Sputnik* in the early 1960s resulted in a countermovement in which competition was downplayed in favor of cooperation. Physical-education programs participated in this general trend by including activities such as new games and cooperative initiatives within its curricula.

The growth of scientific activity in what was coming to be called the "discipline of physical education" created a new emphasis on *knowing* as well as the more traditional emphasis on *doing*. In school programs, that trend was reflected in *foundations* courses. The courses typically used a lecture–laboratory approach and often focused on fitness and on the scientific aspects of sports, such as sports biomechanics.

Adventure education made its way into the curriculum. Not only did physical education go off campus to take part in the natural environment, but also school facilities were modified so that adventure skills such as climbing and rappelling could be learned. After-school, weekend, and vacation trips to adventure sites became common.

The largest conceptual change in the post-1950 era was **movement education**, the first serious philosophical challenge to the new physical education since the latter's inception early in the century. Movement education developed in England in the 1930s and was transported and developed even further as a curricular philosophy and program in America. The goals and values of movement education had great philosophical appeal to many professionals and were widely proclaimed in the 1960s and 1970s. Even AAHPERD began to define its subject matter as "the art and science of human movement." This approach has had a substantial influence on physical-education programs for young children but seems not to have been programmatically influential otherwise.

In the mid-1980s and early 1990s, several new approaches to physical education gained popularity in America and were exported to other countries. One was the *Social and Personal Responsibility* model (Hellison, 1984). Originally developed for application to work with troubled youth, this model was eventually mainstreamed in both elementary and secondary physical education. The major goal was to use an activity environment to help youngsters learn how to control themselves, be responsible for their own actions, and be supportive of others. A second approach was the *Sport Education* model (Siedentop, 1994; Siedentop, Hastie, & van der Mars, 2004), which offered a way of organizing students into small, mixed-ability teams who learned and competed in an activity season that was longer than typical physical-education units. This model, too, placed greater responsibility on students for their own behavior and for helping and

supporting their teammates. A third innovation was *Teaching Games for Understanding* (Almond, Bunker, & Thorpe, 1983), developed in Britain. The TGFU model started with helping students understand the tactical problems that one must solve to be successful in games and used this as a motivation for students to learn the skills necessary to play the games well. In the mid-1990s, TGFU spurred the development of what has been called the "tactical approach" to games teaching (Griffin, Mitchell, & Oslin, 1997). There is no doubt that the Sport Education, TGFU, and tactical models have led physical educators to a much stronger focus on tactical awareness in their teaching.

Title IX resulted in coeducational physical education beyond the elementary school, which in turn created new problems and opportunities for both curriculum planners and teachers as they tried to cope with an entirely new set of demands. The changes were also deeply felt in interscholastic sport programs where boys' teams and girls' teams now had to share their budgets and facilities more equitably.

The Academic-Discipline Movement

"I suggest that there is an increasing need for the organization and study of the academic discipline herein called physical education" (Henry, 1964, p. 32). Franklin Henry's now-famous statement appeared in a 1964 *JOHPER* article that was a milestone in the physical-education literature—the birth of the discipline movement. Henry outlined the relevant issues concerning the viability of physical education as an **academic discipline** and defined that discipline's parameters. The article also foreshadowed a major period of reconstruction for the umbrella profession under which the sport, fitness, and physical-education professionals had gathered early in the century and through which they had gained strength and legitimacy in the ensuing years.

Henry's call for an academic discipline of physical education can be seen as a logical outcome of the post-1950 reformist movement in education. Physical educators were forced to begin to redefine their field as an academic discipline rather than as an applied, professional enterprise. It was within that political–intellectual climate that programs for human-movement studies, kinesiological studies, human ergonomics, and exercise science developed.

The most well-developed scientific area at the outset of the academic-discipline movement was **exercise physiology**. Research in this field had a long and honorable history within the profession, and productive relationships with other scientific disciplines had been established. In 1954 the American College of Sports Medicine (www.acsm.org) was founded by physiologists, physical educators, and physicians. Joseph B. Wolffe, a cardiologist, was elected as ACSM's first president. In 1969 ACSM began to publish *Medicine and Science in Sports*, which quickly came to be one of the most respected research journals in the field. In 1974 ACSM began to certify practitioners, and now there are six certification fields. (See Chapter 8 for full information on certifications.)

The **subdiscipline** areas to develop were **biomechanics, kinesiology, motor control, motor-learning, sport psychology, sport sociology, sport history**, and **sport philosophy**. The North American Society for the Psychology of Sport and Physical Activity was founded in 1967 to provide a collegial group for the growing number of young professionals who saw themselves as either motor-learning or sport-psychology specialists and also to host the Second International Sport Psychology Congress after the Mexico City Olympics in 1968. Eventually, two journals were started to provide research outlets in those areas: the *Journal of Motor Behavior* (1968) and the *Journal of Sport Psychology* (1978).

The same pattern describes the development of sport history and sport philosophy in the early 1970s. The Philosophic Society for the Study of Sport was founded in 1972 at a regional meeting of the American Philosophical Association. In 1974 the first issue of the *Journal of the Philosophic Society for the Study of Sport* appeared. In 1973 the North American Society for Sport History was formed, an event soon followed by the appearance of the *Journal of Sport History*. Each of those scholarly associations was,

from the beginning, of interest to researchers from the older, parent disciplines—in these cases, philosophy and history.

The national umbrella association, AAHPERD, was quick to recognize the academic-discipline movement and to respond to it. In 1972 AAHPERD published its monograph *Tones of Theory* in which physical education was defined as the discipline of human movement and the emerging subdisciplines were accorded equal stature under the new, more academically oriented umbrella. AAHPERD also changed, in 1974, from an association to an alliance, a reorganization that gave greater visibility, self-determination, and autonomy to the seven member associations. The National Association for Sport and Physical Education (NASPE), one of the largest of the associations, formed academies that strongly reflected the academic-discipline movement—for example, the Kinesiology Academy. Much of that organizational restructuring represented an effort to maintain an umbrella and to minimize the splintering that inevitably occurred as the subdisciplines formed their own groups and developed their own loyalties and traditions.

AAHPERD remains the primary professional and academic organization seeking to hold together and serve a very diverse group of professional and academic interests. Focus On Box 2.5 shows the mission, purposes, and organizational structure of the alliance.

The discipline movement had an immediate and strong effect on the physical-education curriculum at the university and college levels. As graduate programs developed in the areas of specialization (sport sociology, biomechanics, and so on), so did new undergraduate courses that reflected the knowledge being developed in the subdisciplines. Because, at the beginning of the academic-discipline movement, most undergraduates were preparing to become teachers, many of the new courses found their way into teacher-education programs. Thus, it became common for teacher-education programs to include courses in motor learning, sport psychology, sport sociology, and other academic discipline-oriented subjects.

FOCUS ON The American Alliance for Health, Physical Education, Recreation, and Dance **2.5**

AAHPERD Mission Statement

AAHPERD's mission is to promote and support leadership, research, education, and best practices in the professions that support creative, healthy, and active lifestyles.

AAHPERD's national associations have the following purposes:

1. To develop and disseminate professional guidelines, standards, and ethics
2. To enhance professional practice by providing opportunities for professional growth and development
3. To advance the body of knowledge in the fields of study and in the professional practice of the fields by initiating, facilitating, and disseminating research
4. To facilitate and nurture communication and activities with other associations and other related professional groups
5. To serve as their own spokespersons
6 To promote public understanding and improve government relations in their fields of study
7 To engage in future planning . . .
8. To establish and fulfill other purposes which are consistent with the purposes of the Alliance

Alliance Associations

American Association for Physical Activity and Recreation

American Association for Health Education (AAHE)

National Dance Association (NDA)

National Association for Girls and Women in Sport (NAGWS)

National Association for Sport and Physical Education (NASPE)

Research Consortium

Alliance Districts

Central District—Iowa, Minnesota, Colorado, Kansas, Nebraska, North Dakota, South Dakota, Missouri, Wyoming

Eastern District—Connecticut, Delaware, Maine, Maryland, New Hampshire, New Jersey, New York, Pennsylvania, Vermont, Rhode Island, District of Columbia, Puerto Rico, Virgin Islands

Midwest District—Illinois, Michigan, Ohio, West Virginia, Wisconsin, Indiana

Northwest District—Alaska, Idaho, Montana, Oregon, Washington

Southern District—Georgia, Florida, Kentucky, Louisiana, North Carolina, South Carolina, Virginia, Texas, Arkansas, Tennessee, Oklahoma, Alabama, Mississippi

Southwest District—Hawaii, California, New Mexico, Arizona, Nevada, Utah, Guam

---

Inevitably, that produced a backlash from the leaders in physical education–teacher education. They argued that studying the discipline of physical education was perhaps important but did not replace the learning of sport skills and the acquisition of teaching skills. As teacher educators in physical education began to publish more research and to join together in their effort to make the teacher-education curriculum relevant to teaching physical education, they emerged as a specialized group themselves (concerned with *sport pedagogy*—see

Chapter 16), with a journal of their own, the *Journal of Teaching in Physical Education.*

In the early 1990s, sport-sciences faculty members launched an initiative to change the name of university programs from "physical education" to "kinesiology," thus reflecting the academic, rather than professional, focus of the programs (Newell, 1990b). The American Academy of Physical Education voted to call the discipline *kinesiology* and became the American Academy of Kinesiology and Physical Education (AAKPE). Many departments in colleges and universities voted to become departments of kinesiology, and others became departments of sport science or exercise science.

Part 5 of this text examines in detail each of the contemporary scientific and scholarly disciplines in the fields of sport, fitness, and physical education; charts the history of their development; discusses their current status; and addresses career options and relevant issues.

SUMMARY

1. The sport, fitness, and physical-education professions were born in the United States at the Adelphi Conference in 1885.

2. The pre–Civil War era was a time of transition from local games to institutionalized sport. The war itself helped to spread and standardize many sport forms.

3. Many sports were introduced in America in the period between 1850 and 1900. Several important sports, such as basketball and softball, were invented in America during the same period.

4. The decline of religious opposition to sport, fitness, and physical education and the philosophy of muscular Christianity greatly accelerated the growth of those fields.

5. Immigration, industrialization, urbanization, and advances in transportation and communication created the context within which sport and physical education rapidly developed in the late nineteenth century.

6. Formal gymnastic systems developed in Europe were adopted in America and competed with American systems for dominance in school and university programs. The Boston Conference of 1889 debated the various systems.

7. By the turn of the century, sport was becoming highly institutionalized at both the professional and the amateur levels through organizations, governing bodies, and sport conferences.

8. Abuses and problems in college and university sport led to the beginnings of faculty control and the formation of sport conferences.

9. The new physical education was heralded by Thomas Wood and marked the transition from a medical approach to an educational approach, ending the domination of physical education by formal gymnastic systems.

10. From the turn of the century to World War I, an umbrella profession of physical education was created. Under it gathered professionals from physical education, health, recreation, dance, playgrounds, camping, and sport.

11. In the early twentieth century, a national sport culture emerged with widespread participation and spectating and the beginnings of national traditions, as well as sport heroes and heroines.

12. The era between World War I and the Great Depression was the golden age of sport, fitness, and physical education. Schooling developed nationally with physical education as an accepted subject, and sport continued its domination of American popular culture.

13. "Education through the physical" became the dominant philosophy for the umbrella profession, but "education of the physical" continued to have a strong voice within the profession.

14. A science of physical education began to develop, tracing its roots from the work of Hitchcock and Sargent.

15. Access and equity for women and blacks were not features of this era, even though pioneering work was accomplished by women leaders and black students had access in some institutions.

16. By 1930 at the close of the emergence era, the sport, fitness, and physical-education professions were firmly consolidated under the umbrella of APEA, sport had reached new heights of cultural popularity, and many universities had begun to offer graduate-level programs in physical education.

17. The cultural context of the consolidation and specialization era was dominated by the Great Depression, World War II, the postwar recovery, and the post-1950 social ferment. The

Great Depression caused the first serious financial problems for sport, fitness, and physical education since the turn of the twentieth century, forcing both government and private sectors to seek new ways to fund programs. Participation rates increased, however.

18. The organizations supporting sport, fitness, and physical education were forced to consolidate further, with the APEA affiliating with NEA and changing its name to AAHPE.

19. World War II showed that fitness levels in the population were low, caused professional and other spectator sport to continue on hold, and further enhanced participation. Research specializations developed, greatly aided by the needs of the war effort.

20. Professional sport began to develop in the postwar years, becoming popular and taking on its modern forms. Recreational sports, such as golf, tennis, and bowling, also became popular. Youth sport, school sport, and intercollegiate sport also developed rapidly in the postwar years, assuming the central importance they now occupy in American culture.

21. In school physical education, lifetime sports became central to the curriculum. In the mid-1950s, the nation experienced a fitness crisis when American children were shown to perform less well than European children on so-called fitness tests.

22. The cultural context of the post-1950 years was dominated by consumerism, concern for ecology, the civil rights movement, and the Vietnam War, producing major changes in sport, fitness, and physical education, such as wilderness sports, Title IX, Public Law 94-142, and the racial integration of sports.

23. Sport in the post-*Sputnik* era became substantially more specialized and economically important, with the lines separating amateur from professional becoming less clear. A fitness renaissance occurred among middle- and upper-class adults. Women took part fully in the fitness movement for the first time.

24. In school physical education, the post-*Sputnik* years were dominated by curricular innovations such as movement education, adventure education, cooperative games, the discipline movement, and expanded opportunities for girls and for people with disabilities.

25. The academic-discipline movement in colleges and universities changed the nature of academic programs and created a series of subdisciplines focusing on specific academic areas of physical education.

DISCUSSION QUESTIONS

1. What do the pictures and discussions of "gymnastics" classes tell you about the early models of physical education?

2. Why do you think that sport had such a difficult time becoming part of physical education during the "gymnastics era"?

3. How did you react to the stories of early abuses in collegiate sport? Were they worse than abuses today?

4. What type of philosophy would you say supported the physical education that you experienced in middle or high school?

5. How did the popular view of fitness change during the time period examined in this chapter?

6. What were the significant events between 1900 and World War I that influenced physical education?

7. How did the Great Depression affect the development of sport and physical education?

8. How did World War II change our views of fitness, sport, and physical education?

9. What factors seem to make fitness more or less important and/or popular among the American public?

10. How has the physical-education curriculum changed in the past 100 years?

11. What factors have made collegiate and professional sport so popular?

CHAPTER 3

Changing Philosophies for Sport, Fitness, and Physical Education

Running, then, is my discipline, my speciality, my secret. And these golden days of perfection on the road are the wholeness that results. . . . In those moments my philosophy becomes, "I run, therefore I am." And from that point I view all creation.

Dr. George Sheehan, physician, elite age-group runner and foremost philosopher of the running movement, 1982

LEARNING OBJECTIVES

- To describe the philosophies underlying gymnastic systems, muscular Christianity, Arnoldism, and amateurism and to assess their impact

- To analyze the influence of nineteenth-century masculine and feminine ideals

- To describe how progressive education influenced the development of the new physical education

- To describe the education-through-the-physical approach

- To discuss human movement, humanism, play education, and adventure education as physical-education philosophies

- To describe the development of the wellness movement

As someone who aspires to a career in the sport, fitness, or physical education professions, you will be expected to examine issues in your field and make judgments about them. You certainly will have the technical expertise that comes with your professional preparation, but how you apply that technical expertise will reflect your philosophy about your field and the many, many issues that surround your practice in that field.

This chapter is not about the formal study of philosophy, but the discussion will involve all of the major categories of philosophy. As you express your views of the relationship between mind and body, you are in the field known as *ontology*. When, as a coach or athletic trainer or teacher, you try to instill certain values in your players, clients, or students, you are in the field known as *axiology*. When you respond with "That was beautiful" after viewing a particularly good performance, you are making an *aesthetic* judgment. When you are in a difficult professional situation and have to decide what is the right thing to do, you are making an *ethics* judgment. When you try to decide what the common good is for a team you coach, the department you administer, the fitness specialists with whom you work, or the students you teach, you are in the field of philosophy called *politics*. In all these situations, it will be helpful if you have thought carefully about your views, how you came to adopt them, and how you express them in your professional practice.

If you are a teacher, you will have a philosophy of what you consider to be the most important goals. You will look for a curricular model that reflects those goals. If you are a sport manager, you will have views about the values of sport, the right and wrong kinds of sport practices, and the common good to be achieved in the organization within which you work. If you are in a fitness profession, you will probably have definite opinions about the major benefits of fitness, the relative importance of various activities, and the right and wrong ways to interact with clients. This is philosophy in action.

A striking example of the influence of a coherent professional philosophy was that of the late George Sheehan, known internationally as the *runner's philosopher*. Sheehan was a physician and a long-distance runner who interpreted the running movement of the 1970s and 1980s to a generation of men and women who found meaning in training for and competing in road races. His books, which sold widely throughout the world, focused on finding meaning in running and on the role of running in a healthy lifestyle. Although not trained in philosophy, he became one of the most prominent sport–fitness philosophers of recent times.

Your professional philosophy is more than a collection of your opinions. It is more than wisdom gained solely from your own experience. To be effective, your philosophy has to be reasonable and coherent as well as connected to the evolution of philosophies in your field, whether it be sport, physical education, or fitness. You must also be able to think critically about diverse points of view. In developing your own philosophy, you will profit from finding out how philosophies within your field

have evolved and how they connect to the past and point toward the future. The remainder of this chapter offers you the opportunity to establish some of those connections.

PHILOSOPHICAL INFLUENCES IN EARLY AMERICAN SPORT, FITNESS, AND PHYSICAL EDUCATION

The nineteenth century was an extraordinary time for the developed world, especially for the United States. (See Chapter 2 for details about sport, fitness, and physical education in the nineteenth century.) Revolutions in France and America had created new forms of government. The Industrial Revolution had been triggered by breakthroughs in science and technology—and in turn had unleashed powerful changes in economics, population demographics, and social institutions. It was in the nineteenth century that the sport, fitness, and physical-education professions formed and began to mature.

The nineteenth century was just as important in the realm of ideas as it was in programs and institutions. The range of philosophical beliefs that vied for influence in sport, fitness, and physical education was extraordinary. The emergence in the twentieth century of physical education as a school subject, the acceptance of competitive sport into school programs, the development of intramural sport, the acceptance of fitness as a value in its own right, and the recognition of the role of play in childhood were all results of philosophical debates (see Focus On Box 3.1). Such is the power of philosophy and belief systems. What follow are brief descriptions of the more important philosophical influences on the development of nineteenth-century sport, fitness, and physical education.

The Gymnastic Philosophies

The gymnastic systems that influenced American physical education in the latter half of the nineteenth century were described in Chapter 2. The German and Swedish systems, though quite different in the

FOCUS ON	CHRONOLOGY AT A GLANCE—Changing Philosophies	3.1

Pre-1800	Puritanism, democracy, frontier spirit, individualism
1800–1850	European gymnastic philosophies introduced to United States
	Emerson's philosophy of self-reliance
	Muscular Christianity
1850–1900	*Tom Brown's Schooldays*
	British "fair play" ideals
	Arnoldism
	Battle of gymnastic systems and philosophies
	Masculinity–femininity ideals
	Institutionalization of sport
	European antecedents of progressive education
1900–1950	Reemergence of play philosophies
	The new physical education
	Progressive-education theory—John Dewey
	Faculty control of college sport
	Professionalization of sport
1950–1996	Human-movement philosophies
	Academic-discipline movement
	Humanistic education and physical education
	Fitness–wellness movements
	Lifespan-physical-activity movement

activities they comprised, were similar in the philosophies supporting them and the conditions from which they developed. The common force in Europe that gave rise to these systems was *nationalism*. Friedrich Jahn's entire life was devoted to unifying Germany and developing German patriotism. He admired the self-reliance and independence of the peasant farmers whose life was spent outdoors and for whom physical tasks were a part of daily life. His gymnastic system was designed to encourage those qualities. The motto he adopted for his gymnastic society (The Turners) was *"Frisch, froh, stark und frei, ist die Turnerei,"* which means "Gymnasts are vigorous, happy, strong, and free" (Gerber, 1971, p. 131). Similarly, Per Ling's great mission was to restore to the Swedish people the spirit and grandeur of the ancient Scandinavian race, particularly the glory that emanated from Norse mythology. Ling was first of all a

fencing master, who learned about gymnastics while training in Denmark. When he returned to Sweden, he developed the complex and multifaceted program that came to be known as Swedish gymnastics.

Both Germany and Sweden were at low points in their national histories when Jahn and Ling were developing their respective programs. Each of the gymnastic systems had goals for individual development, yet there was also a distinct group dynamic to the programs—one that lent itself particularly well to military training. Thus, the philosophy of gymnastic training, although clearly to the benefit of the individual participant, was also linked to the health and well-being of the state. A strong and morally upright state could develop only from the firm foundation provided to young men (and, to a lesser extent, to young women) by an education that included a substantial involvement in gymnastics.

The nationalism that provided the supporting philosophy for European gymnastic systems could not survive in America. In competition with emerging American systems of gymnastics, proponents of the European systems began to emphasize more strongly the physical and health benefits and the individual moral growth that were thought to be the product of regular participation in these programs. Still, if one examines physical-training programs in the armed forces, or the periodic national concerns about fitness among children and youth that tend to arise when the nation is at war, the spirit of nationalism can easily be seen.

Muscular Christianity

Much has been written about the *Puritanism* that pervaded early American history. It was indeed a stern view of human life, which left little room for physical activity that was unrelated to work and took a harsh view of anything that was playful. The new world of America was in many respects an inhospitable place, one that could be developed only through a strong work ethic and a climate in which codes of behavior were strict. Thus, Puritanism—a set of beliefs deriving from the stricter forms of religion that grew out of the Reformation—served a genuine purpose in the development of America. By the midnineteenth century, however, the eastern half of the nation was well developed, the Industrial Revolution was at hand, a middle class was emerging, cities were developing, and the once-strong hand of the Puritan philosophy was gradually losing its grip on the social life of the young nation. It was within this context that religion and sport reached an understanding through the philosophy that was to be known as *muscular Christianity*.

This philosophy was not necessarily associated with any one person or group or movement, but it was an idea whose time had come for America. One important force for the move away from Puritanism and toward muscular Christianity was the American philosopher Ralph Waldo Emerson. Greatly influenced by what he saw as the best in English education and life, Emerson developed an American philosophy of self-reliance and faith in human perfection. His philosophy granted sport and fitness a central place:

> Emerson reckoned that moral and physical courage were partly dependent on body fitness. "For performance of great mark," he said, "it (the body) needs extraordinary health." In his *The Conduct of Life*, Emerson noted that "the first wealth is health." He admired the great men of the past and urged young people to read their exploits. Yet sometimes youth does not take readily to books, he noted. "Well, the boy is right; and you are not fit to direct his bringing up, if your theory leaves out gymnastic training, archery, cricket, gun and fishing rod, horse and boat, all are educators, liberalizers." (Lucas & Smith, 1978, p. 88)

The idea that participation in sport had moral benefits was almost directly opposite to the Puritan philosophy—and, gradually, the idea took hold.

Muscular Christianity is the label given to the philosophy that physical fitness and sporting prowess were important avenues through which mental, moral, and religious purposes were developed and sustained. An important source for this philosophy was the educational ideals of aristocratic British education. Charles Kingsley, a prominent American cleric, greatly admired the combination of sport, fitness, and intellectual–moral training that boys received in elite British schools. He borrowed those combinations as he wrote and spoke about the new vision of the religious person in whom moral, intellectual, and physical characteristics were equally important (Lucas & Smith, 1978).

The philosophy of muscular Christianity spread quickly and was made even more popular through the novel *Tom Brown's Schooldays*, a best-seller in the 1850s. The book told the story of life at the Rugby School, an elite British boys' secondary school. The headmaster of the Rugby School was Thomas Arnold, a prominent figure in British philosophy and education. Arnold believed in an education that produced manliness, courage, patriotism, moral character, and team spirit as well as intellectual independence. Sport and fitness were considered to be important activities through which such goals were achieved. In the late nineteenth century in England, this philosophy was termed **Arnoldism**; it is virtually identical to what is described here as muscular Christianity.

The novel *Tom Brown's Schooldays* was a highly romantic book in which sport and fitness occupied a more important role than they did in the real life of the Rugby School. Nonetheless, this novel was read widely by educators, clergy, and common people, all of whom were influenced by the idea that competitive sport was an attribute of the virtuous, moral life. It was the general acceptance of those notions that allowed sport to develop so quickly in the last part of the nineteenth century in America.

Masculinity–Femininity Ideals

No examination of the philosophies that influenced the development of sport, fitness, and physical education in the nineteenth century would be complete without an examination of the then-prevailing views of masculinity and femininity. If the muscular Christianity movement allowed sport, fitness, and physical education to become more philosophically acceptable, it did so much more for boys and men than for girls and women.

The nineteenth-century views of masculinity and femininity were highly stereotyped. In England in that period, the Victorian era, women were raised to occupy narrow and circumscribed roles. The prevailing philosophy in the United States was much the same. Girls were socialized to the "feminine virtues"—piety, purity, submissiveness, and domesticity (Spears & Swanson, 1978). Although mild forms of "proper" exercise were thought to be useful for women, vigorous exercise and competitive sports were generally thought inappropriate, both because women were assumed to be genetically unfit for vigorous exercise (such activity would harm them) and because vigorous and competitive activities were presumed to promote behavior that was unladylike.

This narrow view of femininity changed very slowly, partly because of the companion views about masculinity. To be "masculine," one had to be virile; to express virility in one's behavior, one had to avoid behaving in ways that might be perceived as feminine. Men were supposed to be tough, physical, and aggressive. There were many Americans in the nineteenth century who believed deeply that American men were becoming too "feminine" and that these men needed to be more "masculine" for America to become a great nation. In one of his popular novels, the famous American writer Henry James had one of his characters express the prevailing beliefs—that Americans were suffering from "the most damnable feminism . . . the whole generation is womanized . . . the masculine character is passing out of the world" (Lucas & Smith, 1978, p. 288).

The cultural focus on masculinity and virility was evidenced in the most popular literature of the day—the series of stories and novels known as the *Frank Merriwell sagas*. In serial form in magazines and in popular novels, the character of Frank Merriwell became the prototypical American male, the ideal model for the age. Merriwell attended a prep school and then Yale. He was bright, wealthy, fit, skilled, and highly moral. In each new episode or novel, Merriwell would be confronted with some seemingly impossible obstacle to attaining his goal, which he would promptly overcome, most often through an act of physical skillfulness and courage. He typified all the manly virtues, and his high moral stature was intertwined with his virility.

Programs of sport, fitness, and physical education for girls and women did begin to develop during the nineteenth century, but they developed much more slowly than and in ways different from the programs for boys and men (Spears & Swanson, 1978). Girls' sport programs were controlled almost exclusively by physical-education departments. Games were designed to be less strenuous. Spectating was discouraged. Fitness programs were decidedly less vigorous. Sport had to be done "acceptably." Even so, there was much criticism during this time that programs for girls and women were too strenuous and thus were of potential physical harm and promoted unladylike behavior among participants. Such attitudes changed very slowly until more recently when the feminist movement and the federal law known as

Title IX began to bring some parity for girls and women in sport, fitness, and physical education.

Thus, even though the nineteenth century was a period of growth and importance for sport, fitness, and physical education, we must recognize that it was so for males more than for females. The prevailing stereotypes of masculinity and femininity would not allow for full participation for girls and women.

Amateurism, Fair Play, and the British Ideals

The philosophy of muscular Christianity brought religion, sport, and fitness together in a way that bred a new civil religion—one that, according to a British writer in the 1860s, "enjoined its disciples above all to fear God and run a mile in four and a half minutes" (Lucas & Smith, 1978, p. 139). Much of the growing American sense of sport behavior and preparation for sport also was influenced by British ideals. As sport grew in the latter part of the nineteenth century, it grew partially along the lines of amateurism and **fair play** that characterized much of British sport.

For the most part, amateurism in the late nineteenth century was the province of the wealthy, and being an amateur in sport typically meant that you were the son of a privileged family. It also meant that you did not train full-time for your competition and that you did not receive any real coaching. The notions of fair play and of the well-played game were part of the moral codes of the upper classes in England—and those values were adopted by the wealthy sports enthusiasts of America.

Nowhere can this code and all of its inherent meaning be seen more clearly than in the beginning of the modern Olympic Games in 1896. The French Baron Pierre de Coubertin wanted to revive what he saw as the pageantry and almost mystical meaning of the Olympic Games, but he revived the games on the model of amateurism and fair play that represented the nineteenth-century ideals. The now widely proclaimed motto of the Olympic Games—"The most important thing in the Olympic Games is not to win, but to take

The revival of the Olympic Games made sports such as gymnastics popular throughout the world.

part"—probably would have been considered silly in ancient Greece where only the winner of an Olympic contest received any prize.

The ideals of amateurism and fair play were taken seriously by emerging sport groups in America. The Amateur Athletic Union was formed in 1888 and quickly became the most powerful force in amateur sport in America (Spears & Swanson, 1978). Local clubs, such as the New York Athletic Club, were also in the vanguards.

Character Education Through Physical Challenge

In 1934 Kurt Hahn, a German Jew who had fled from his homeland to escape Nazi persecution, founded the Gordonstoun School in Scotland.

Hahn's primary educational goal was to train character rather than intellect. He was interested in action rather than reflection. Students (all boys at that time) at Gordonstoun were always active, starting with a 6:30 a.m. wake-up to take a cold shower and go for the morning run. They learned track-and-field, seamanship, and water-rescue skills. They were taught about appropriate character and were assessed on elements of character such as public spirit, sense of justice, persevering in the face of obstacles, and civic courage (Skidelsky, 1969).

Physical fitness was a high priority at Gordonstoun. Classroom activities were interrupted each morning for a 40-minute strenuous workout. Physical challenges were constantly presented to test the fitness of the students, their courage, and their willingness to persevere under difficult conditions.

Character education was generally important in England in the late nineteenth and early twentieth centuries. The philosophy of Arnoldism (see page 61) stressed courage, team spirit, and character. The YMCA movement, which began in England, quickly began to focus on training in discipline, obedience, health, and patriotism. These movements shared the belief that national weaknesses were related to character weaknesses in men. It should be noted that all these initiatives were focused on boys.

The YMCA movement was very successful with young boys but less so with youths. Kurt Hahn believed that youths needed education through adventure; that through expeditions focused on physical adventure, such as treks, mountain climbs, dangerous sailing expeditions, and the like, young men would develop character, experience important achievement, and form significant friendships. Thus was born the *Outward Bound* movement. Outward Bound courses were organized in several places throughout England and Scotland. Expeditions would typically last 4 days, present significant tests of courage and skill, and result, it was hoped, in a sense of accomplishment and confidence that would transform young lives. The belief that character could be developed through demanding physical experiences would remain strong in educational philosophy and, later in the twentieth

century, would find a home in experiential and adventure education, described later in this chapter.

This notion has recently been generalized to a current form of education redesign known as Expeditionary Learning Outward Bound (www.elob.org or www.aasa.org/reform/approach/explearn.htm). This is a whole-school reform model for which there is research evidence of improved student performance. Students pursue all subjects through a series of expeditions, a series of extended periods of study focused on single themes, which average 10–16 weeks to complete. Schools form into communities of learners in which there is shared decision making, and learning is assessed through real-world performances related to each theme. Citizenship and character are central to the model.

SCHOOL SPORT AND THE NEW PHYSICAL EDUCATION

When Thomas Wood presented his vision of a new physical education to the International Conference on Education in Chicago in 1893, his talk set the stage for the transition period from a gymnastics curriculum to the education-through-the-physical philosophy that was to dominate twentieth-century physical education. The philosophical basis for the new physical education was rooted in **progressive-education theory**. Because this philosophical rationale for sport, fitness, and physical education was so completely to dominate the profession in the twentieth century, it is important to trace briefly from where it came and how it came to be adopted.

The main figure in American progressive education was John Dewey, who was not only a premier educational thinker of the nineteenth century but also one of America's foremost philosophers. Dewey was educated at Johns Hopkins University at a time when the major new theoretical issues of the nineteenth century created a spirit of inquiry and experimentalism. Dewey took his newly formed ideas about education to the University of Chicago

The fact that children love to play was central to the development of progressive education.

where he opened a laboratory school to experiment with and further develop those ideas. In 1897 he published *My Pedagogic Creed*, followed in 1899 by his book *School and Society*.

Dewey's main agenda for education was social reform through a child-centered, natural education. One has to remember that in the 1890s, child labor was still rampant, sweat shops were everywhere, and common people suffered enormously, especially in cities. It was a time in American history when a collective social conscience began to form.

> To look back on the nineties is to sense an awakening of social conscience, a growing belief that this incredible suffering was neither the fault nor the inevitable lot of the sufferers, that it could certainly be alleviated, and that the road to alleviation was neither charity nor revolution, but in the last analysis education. (Cremin, 1961, p. 59)

Dewey believed passionately that the road to peaceful change in a democracy was through education and that education had to be viewed as lived experience in which students were active participants rather than passive recipients. In progressive education, *doing* was every bit as important as *knowing*. He also believed strongly in what he described as the *unity of man*, the notion that mental and physical could not be separated and that all educational activity had intellectual, moral, and physical outcomes. Because of those beliefs, activities such as natural play, sports, and games were valued by Dewey and his followers. Dewey was a firm supporter of physical education, especially when it was directed toward the achievement of social goals.

Dewey was, without question, the most important figure in the history of American education. In 1904 he left Chicago to be professor of philosophy at Columbia University where he stayed until his retirement. Thomas Wood had been appointed head of physical education at Teachers College, also at Columbia University, in 1901. He was joined there later by Clark Hetherington, another major interpreter of the education-through-the-physical philosophy. In 1924 Teachers College, in cooperation with New York University, started the first doctoral program in physical education. Thus, many of the early leaders in physical education received their advanced training at the institution that was the main center for progressive education and the education-through-the-physical philosophy.

Dewey's education philosophy had clear antecedents in European educational thought; because that history of thought is so important to sport, fitness, and physical education, we examine it briefly here.

The European Antecedents

The chain of influence that led to the development of both progressive education and the new physical education originated in the mideighteenth-century philosophy of *naturalism*, articulated most prominently by the French philosopher Jean-Jacques Rousseau. One of Rousseau's major works was *Emile*, which described his ideal of education for boys and girls. This book was considered to be so radical that it was banned in France, but it was quickly published and eagerly read elsewhere in Europe and later in the United States.

Simply put, Rousseau's argument was that children were born good and then were ruined by their contacts with society. His educational program was *natural*, designed to help children and youths grow up in perfect freedom. He strongly supported sensory experiences of all kinds and was particularly enthusiastic about physical activity, gymnastics, sports, and games. His views of the interrelatedness of mind and body foreshadowed the *holistic* view that became central to Dewey's philosophy.

Rousseau advocated having physical-education facilities in schools and promoted the use of games and sports because he believed that these activities were important in developing two major traits of character: cooperation and competition. Rousseau's philosophy had immediate and long-term influence on education through the work of educators who read and interpreted his philosophy:

- *Johann Bernhard Basedow* founded a school in Germany in 1744 that put the natural philosophy into practice in a real setting. Basedow advocated treating children as children rather than as miniature adults, thereby leading the movement to establish childhood as a distinct developmental stage. Physical activity was central to the curriculum in this school.

- *Johann Heinrich Pestalozzi*, perhaps the most influential of all European educational reformers, believed that all knowledge had a basis in action; thus, he made sensory learning and physical activity central to the school curriculum. The German physical educator Ludwig Jahn taught in a school inspired by Pestalozzi's educational theories.

- *Friedrich Froebel* believed in the unity of life and action, expressed in observing, creating, discovering, and exercising. He created the word *kindergarten* to express his belief in cultivating the natural talents of young children

just as gardeners tend to the natural growth of plants. He, too, believed that sports and games had the power to not only develop the physical talents of students but also strengthen intelligence and develop character.

Physical education could never have developed as it did as a school subject in America were it not for this chain of influence from Rousseau to Dewey, with the major European naturalist philosophers and educators acting as the links in the chain. Dewey extended this chain through his progressive-education philosophy, and it was within the context of progressive-education theory that Wood argued for a *new* physical education and Hetherington articulated the goals for education through the physical, bringing the philosophical basis for sport, fitness, and physical education clearly within the realm of progressive-education theory.

The Reemergence of Play as a Philosophical Concept

A fundamental concept in the aforementioned philosophical linkages is **play**. Rousseau recognized the value of natural play in the education of children. Basedow and Pestalozzi not only made room for natural play but also made formalized play, through games and gymnastics, a basic part of the school curriculum. It was Froebel, however, who was to make play the cornerstone of children's education. For Froebel, play was the most natural expression of childhood and therefore the most fundamental medium through which children learned about themselves and their world. Dewey made play in childhood a basic tenet of progressive education. Thus, as progressive education influenced more powerfully the course of American education, the notion that play was not only a legitimate but also indeed a fundamentally important education focus was widely accepted.

The concept of play and its role in education and life was central to many ancient philosophies. Our knowledge of ancient cultures and customs indicates that playful activities were often central to individual and community life. With the rise and spread of Christianity, however, the concept of play found disfavor with theologians and philosophers. This is not to suggest that people were less playful because it is now clear that people in all cultures and throughout history have found ways to play. It is only to suggest that, as a philosophical and educational concept, play began to be viewed negatively rather than positively. Work was the appropriate form of activity for virtuous women and men. Play was thought to occasion idleness and sinful behavior. This general philosophical trend gained strength in the Christian theologies of the Reformation.

Thus, for several hundred years, religious leaders tended to frown on playful activity. Even children at play were barely tolerated rather than encouraged. Play in the form of games and sports was often branded as anti-Christian behavior. The renaissance of the concept of play can be traced to important thinkers such as Rousseau, but it was in the nineteenth century that the concept was fully reborn as a positive human attribute. Froebel's work was important in recognizing play as a positive educational process.

Whereas Froebel helped reestablish play as a legitimate educational concept, it was the German poet-philosopher Friedrich von Schiller who helped make play a respectable concept in general philosophy and intellectual thought. Schiller did not focus only on child's play, nor was he concerned with leisure-time activity, nor, indeed, can his ideas be viewed simply as a reaction to the pervasive antiplay theology of the Reformation. Schiller argued that play was a basic, integrating mode of human behavior throughout life and across all cultures. He believed strongly that people experienced the wholeness of life most clearly when at play: "For to speak out once for all, man only plays when in the full meaning of the word he is a man, and he is only completely a man when he plays" (Schiller, 1910). Schiller's now-famous statement about play does not sound extreme in today's philosophical climate, but how radical it must have sounded in the early nineteenth century when people at work and people as pious creatures were the ideal models for human life!

By the beginning of the twentieth century, play had returned to respectability both as a central philosophical concept and as an educational theory. The manifestations of this perspective can be seen not only in American progressive education and in the rapid expansion of sport during that time but also in equally important yet less well-known movements such as the expansion of the playground movement in early-twentieth-century America and in the widespread adoption of sport and fitness activities by organizations such as the YMCA and the Catholic Youth Organization (CYO).

The idea of play is clearly evident in the work of Hetherington and of other prominent leaders of the new physical education. The education-through-the-physical approach utilized the medium of playful activity to accomplish its various goals, especially its social goals. We must understand that the program *utilizing* play could have developed only after the *concept* of play had been accepted in philosophy and education. Again, we see the power of ideas!

The Early Twentieth Century: Philosophies Come Together

The nineteenth century was an extraordinary period of development in both *ideas* about sport, fitness, and physical education and *participation* in those fields. Muscular Christianity allowed activity and competition to become not only acceptable but also favorable. Moral development began to be tied to sport and fitness. The ideal person was portrayed as fit, skilled, and moral. Education began to change from a narrow, academic view to a more child-centered view in which playful activity was seen to be central to an appropriate education.

Each of these philosophical forces developed from a different source, and each had somewhat different initial effects. In the early twentieth century, the forces began to coalesce into a unified philosophical position that was to undergird sport, fitness, and physical education for the next 50 years. People who were prominent in physical education were also influential in fitness movements, sport, and other areas such as the playground movement and the YMCA movement. Thus, because these people tended to adopt a common philosophy, all those areas were influenced in many of the same ways.

What an exciting and marvelous period that must have been for sport, fitness, and physical-education professionals! Just after the turn of the century, Theodore Roosevelt won the presidency and advocated the "strenuous life" for all Americans. Universal schooling was becoming more of a reality, and physical education was beginning to be seen as a necessary part of basic education. America was quickly becoming a major sport culture—more people were participating and more people were spectating. The long period of Puritanism was over, and America had begun to embrace fully the value of physical activity.

The major philosophy that undergirded the next 50 years was an amalgamation of many of the ideas described here. It was represented most clearly in the new physical education of Wood and was elaborated most articulately by Hetherington, Cassidy, Williams, and Nash (see Chapter 2). The philosophy, simply stated, asserted that participation in sport, fitness, and physical education was useful because of the contributions it made to intellectual, physical, social, and moral development.

Those contributions were thought to be extremely important in the lives of children and youths; thus, the inclusion of physical education and sport programs in schools was of major importance. Play was accepted as the mode of behavior through which children learned most naturally. Competitive sport, properly organized and administered, was thought to be an important educational experience.

Although activity forms and opportunities for women were still less than equal to those for men, this period also marked a dramatic change in what was considered appropriate for women in sport and physical education. In addition, participation during adulthood was considered to be an important recreational counterbalance to the demands of modern life. It was this unified philosophy that was widely accepted in the first half of the twentieth century, the period during which these professions developed and began to form an identity of their own, leading to the more recent periods of specialization.

PHILOSOPHICAL FORCES IN SPORT, FITNESS, AND PHYSICAL EDUCATION SINCE 1950

The period from 1900 to 1950 was one of unified professional consolidation and growth; the period from 1950 to the present was one of diversity and ferment. The education-through-the-physical philosophy, the dominant underlying belief system for the profession in the early twentieth century, was not seriously challenged until the 1950s. Then a series of societal and professional developments provided the context for a period of diversification, specialization, and accompanying philosophical ferment within sport, fitness, and physical education.

A more detailed description of the events underlying this new period of philosophical ferment

Skill themes give children opportunities to explore their movement potential in ways that are fun.

appears in Chapter 2. In summary, when cultural factors such as the post-1950 reformist movement in education, the civil rights movement, the fitness renaissance, and the era of specialization in universities all came together in a fairly short time span, they produced serious questioning of basic philosophical assumptions of the field. In one sense, much of the remainder of this text involves descriptions of the *effects* of that philosophical ferment. At this point, however, I describe briefly the major philosophical movements since midcentury.

Human Movement

The first serious challenge to a half-century of unified philosophical belief in physical education came during the 1950s with the development of the *human-movement philosophy.* First developed in England during the late 1930s by the German immigrant Rudolph Laban and foreshadowed clearly in the work of Rosiland Cassidy, the notion that a philosophy of human movement could underlie physical education took hold in England in the 1940s. After World War II, American physical educators began to learn about this philosophy and saw in it a more satisfying intellectual and emotional approach to their subject matter.

In 1948 Laban published *Modern Educational Dance,* an important and influential book not only for its curricular implications but also for its articulation of the underlying philosophy. In 1952 the British Ministry of Education produced a new curriculum syllabus in physical education for British schools titled *Moving and Growing,* which gave an official stamp of approval to the theoretical and curricular innovation called "human movement."

Exactly how and when human movement became an important concept in American physical education is difficult to determine. In the middle to late 1950s, the philosophy and its implications began to appear regularly in the American physical-education literature. Cassidy had identified movement as the "stuff" of physical education as early as 1937 (Caldwell, 1966). In 1954 Eleanor Metheny, one of the early and most important advocates,

published an article that provided a basic definition of the human-movement approach, a definition that would still find widespread acceptance today:

> If we may define the *totally educated person* as one who has fully developed his ability to utilize constructively all of his potential capacities as a person in relation to the world in which he lives, then we may define the *physically educated person* as one who has fully developed the ability to utilize constructively all of his potential capacities for movement as a way of expressing, exploring, developing, and interpreting himself and his relationship to the world he lives in. (Metheny, 1954, p. 27; emphasis in original)

In 1958 the physical-education faculty at UCLA began to define and develop an undergraduate curriculum for training professionals in human movement.

During the same period, physical education at the university level was also undergoing a revolution of sorts. Many departments were forced to justify the academic nature of their program—and they found it difficult to do so relying solely on the teacher-education program undergirded by an education-through-the-physical philosophy. Thus began the period of specialization that eventually led to the academic-discipline movement in physical education, which is a focus in Part 5 of this text. Areas such as sport psychology, sport physiology, and sport sociology began to develop. They needed a philosophical framework within which to relate to one another; they found that framework in the human-movement philosophy. In 1966 Warren Fraleigh called for adoption of the human-movement philosophy as the unifying theme on which the discipline of physical education should be built. In 1967 the influential journal *Quest* devoted an entire issue to this topic; it became clear that most professional leaders saw human movement as the most useful and relevant philosophy on which to develop the young academic specializations.

The philosophy of human movement was sufficiently strong and appealing that it was able to provide the framework for the early development of academic specializations in universities, the reworking of the undergraduate professional curriculum, and the beginning of change in school programs of physical education. At the school level, the philosophy of human movement advocated a more open, exploratory approach to teaching physical education, as compared with previous approaches. Equipped with a new vocabulary and a new curriculum, movement educators began to redirect the nature of physical education in schools, especially for children in elementary schools.

Movement education was the only serious challenger, as a curriculum philosophy, to the education-through-the-physical approach in the twentieth century. In its purest form, it was meant to be an entirely new approach, both to program development and to teaching.

> There is a fundamental distinction that must be made between the organizational structure of contemporary Physical Education and Movement Education. In the former, *the activity itself* (volleyball, track and field or folk dance) provides *the structured basis* for developing a curriculum. Skills within each area are arranged from the simple to the complex and presented to children in accordance with their physical maturity and general readiness.
>
> Within the organizational structure of Movement Education, the concepts and underlying principles of "body awareness," "space," and "qualities" of movement provide a basis for *understanding* all movement. In Movement Education, *all* activities are selected on the basis of how well they can foster and develop the concepts and movement principles described under *body awareness*, *space*, and *qualities* of movement. These concepts or *elements of movement* thus become the *framework of a Movement Education Curriculum.* (Kirchner, 1970, pp. 16–17; emphasis in original)

The movement curriculum began to be divided into educational gymnastics, educational dance, and educational games. The approach was through exploration and guided discovery. The climate was noncompetitive and success oriented. Most of the elementary texts in physical-education methods used in universities today reflect the rather substantial changes that occurred in physical education during the period from 1955 to 1975 as the

human-movement philosophy began to attract adherents. The philosophy of human movement continues to be a major influence in American physical education, especially in professional teacher education and in school programs.

Humanistic Sport and Physical Education

Philosophies in sport, fitness, and physical education often reflect ideas and ideals that are popular in the intellectual and social climate of the surrounding society. Nowhere is this more clearly seen than in the **humanistic philosophies** in sport and physical education of the 1960s and 1970s. One of the important factors in American culture in this period was *third-force psychology* or *humanistic psychology.* These ideas reached maturity as a popular movement in America during the social turmoil of the 1960s and 1970s. Third-force psychology focuses on the full development of individual potential through personal growth and self-development.

The two major educational movements of the post-1950 era were the renewed emphasis on science and mathematics and the humanistic-education movement. In education, this philosophy—really a set of loosely related philosophies—promoted open education, affective education, values clarification, and less emphasis on competition for grades and academic outcomes. The personal and social development of children was thought to be more important than—or at least as important as—their academic development.

In 1973 Donald Hellison published his influential book *Humanistic Physical Education*, setting forth the conceptual and theoretical basis for the emerging humanistic movement in physical education. This approach to physical education in schools stressed personal development, self-expression, and improved interpersonal relationships as primary goals for physical education.

During the same period, a companion movement developed within the world of intercollegiate and professional sport, fueled by the same societal factors that led to the humanistic physical-education movement. In 1969 Jack Scott published *Athletics for Athletes* and became an early leader in the movement. This text was followed by a series of popular books condemning abuses in sport, criticizing how athletes were treated, and advocating reforms that would allow sport to be more devoted to the personal development of the athletes. Typical of these books were Dave Meggyesy's *Out of Their League*, a strident criticism of Meggyesy's experience in football; Olympic medalist Don Schollander's *Deep Water*; Leonard Shector's *The Jocks*; and Glenn Dickey's *The Jock Empire*.

The proponents of humanistic sport and physical education were critical of then-current practices and were advocates of new forms of participation:

> Visualize a nation of sadistic people who get their kicks out of humiliating others or ensuring that others do not get what they want. I am fearful that this is what lies ahead unless we are capable of reversing the present direction of our contemporary games and lives. (Orlick, 1977, p. 33)

> In fact, the counterculture ethic reverses every value of the Lombardian ethic. Cooperation replaces competition, an emphasis on process replaces an emphasis on the product, sport as a co-educational activity replaces sport as a stag party, a concern for enjoyment replaces a concern for excellence, and an opportunity for spontaneity and self-expression replaces authoritarianism. (Scott, 1974, p. 159)

The humanistic movement had an enormous influence on many people while it was popular. Although it is no longer described in the terms used during its developmental period, this movement has some clear ties to several current philosophies in physical education. The work started by Donald Hellison has developed into a major curricular and pedagogical force within physical education, known now as "the personal and social responsibility" model (Hellison, 1984, 1995, 1996). Although it has been applied widely, especially in elementary-school physical education, it has manifested its strong social commitment most clearly in programs for at-risk urban youths.

Play Education and Sport Education

The traditional philosophy of physical education emphasized *using* activities to reach valuable educational goals—physical, mental, social, and moral goals. In the 1970s, some professionals began to argue that the activities of physical education were valuable *in and of themselves*. Metheny's (1954, 1970) influential work had long promoted this basic idea. A philosophy expressing this point of view was put forth by Siedentop (1972, 1976, 1980) as **play education**. The goal of play education was to help students acquire skills and develop an affection for the activities themselves. Play educators were to be seen as transmitters and transformers of valuable cultural activities:

> Play is the proper classification for physical education, both from a logical and psychological perspective. Classifying physical education as a form of play puts it clearly in perspective alongside other primary institutionalized forms of play—art, music, and drama. . . . This classification allows us to recognize that the activities of the weekend golfer or skier, the after-dinner tennis player, and the noon-time handball player are analogous to those of the painter, the member of the community theater, or the musician. Each is at play, at an institutionalized form of play, and it is only the play form that distinguished one from the other. (Siedentop, 1980, p. 247)

From the point of view of play education, physical education did not need to be justified by reference to outcomes beyond involvement in the activities:

> We must have the good sense and courage to stand up and defend our field on the basis of the personal and cultural meaning in our subject matter. . . . We do not have to *use* our activities. There is no doubt that they can be used, and often for quite legitimate and noble purposes. But those other purposes are of a different order than play education. In play education we can let our subject matter be just what it is—institutionalized forms of play that are of fundamental importance to the culture in which we live and grow. (Siedentop, 1980, p. 259; emphasis in original)

The philosophy of play education did not directly influence curriculum development in schools. Nonetheless, many physical educators began to argue more boldly that their subject matter (however defined) was valuable in and of itself and did not need to be justified by reference to external objectives or outcomes. Play education never became a reality because it was more a philosophy than a prescription for a program.

In 1986 a similar philosophical point of view was expressed as **sport education** (Siedentop, Mand, & Taggart, 1986). The purpose of sport education was to educate students in the skills, values, and attitudes of good sport so that they might enjoy and participate themselves and so that they would be active contributors to a healthier sport culture:

> The rationale for sport education rests on a few very basic and important assumptions. The first is that sport derives from play; that is, sport represents an institutionalized form of competitive motor play. The second is that sport is an important part of our culture and that sport occupies an important role in determining the health and vitality of the entire culture; that is, if more people participate in good sport, then the culture is stronger. The third assumption follows from the first two. If sport is a higher form of play and if good sport is important to the health and vitality of the culture, then sport should be the subject matter of physical education. The development of good sportspersons and the development of a better sports culture should be central to the mission of physical education. (Siedentop et al. 1986, pp. 188–189)

If play education lacked a clear program prescription, sport education did not. In sport education (Siedentop, 1994; Siedentop, Hastie, & van der Mars, 2004), students become members of teams for the duration of a season (unit), a schedule for competition among teams (or individuals, in the case of an individual sport) is established, a culminating event through which a seasonal champion can be determined is arranged, and records are kept that infuse the competition with greater interest and meaning for students and that begin to develop a sense of tradition in that sport in that school.

In sport education, students compete in modified games as members of a continuing team.

This of course was all to be done within the structure of the physical-education class. Students would learn skills, and they would still practice skills and strategies, but they would do so as a team. They would compete as a team for the duration of that season (unit). As the season (unit) progressed, less time would be devoted to skill practice and more time would be spent in competition and in preparation for it (strategy).

Experiential and Adventure Education

The emergence of character-education models in England in the 1800s (see pages 60–62) was a prelude to the current focus on experiential and adventure education. Much of what is done in experiential and adventure education grew from the Outward Bound movement. Note that the five core values of Outward Bound are consistent with much of adventure education (www.outwardbound.com):

- Adventure and challenge
- Compassion and service

- Learning through experience
- Personal development
- Social and environmental responsibility

Many school physical-education programs now include adventure activities, and it is not uncommon to see climbing walls and challenge courses on school sites. Adventure-education curricula have also led the way in moving physical education outside the regular class schedule and away from the normal facilities of schools. Day trips and weekend trips are common. Activities such as cycling, climbing, hiking, and canoeing are typical in adventure-education curricula.

Major assistance for adventure education in schools is provided by Project Adventure (www.pa.org), a nonprofit organization devoted to supporting adventure programs in schools and communities. Project Adventure provides curriculum materials for developing programs at all school levels and workshops to prepare physical educators to deliver adventure programs. They also have developed a number of products, including ropes courses, that schools can purchase to implement adventure-education programs.

THE FITNESS RENAISSANCE AND THE WELLNESS MOVEMENT

For more than 15 years now, fitness has been "in"! Most people who appear in advertisements are fit and active. The active lifestyle is portrayed as "the good life," not only for young people but also for adults and the older generations. Fitness is big, big business in America (see Chapter 8). The dilemma of our times, however, is that although fitness is seen as valuable and obtainable, we are in the midst of an epidemic of overweight and obesity, leading to increases in the several diseases for which those conditions are precipitators. Early historical periods where fitness became important occurred during wars or polio epidemics. The current fitness movement seems to have more staying power and is likely to become even more stable as the role of physical activity in developing and maintaining health becomes ever more apparent.

The fitness renaissance cannot be explained solely on the basis of health concerns. It's true that more is known about the degree to which lack of fitness can contribute to health problems, but all these problems together can't account for the degree to which the physically active lifestyle has become crucial to so many Americans. Fitness manifests itself in many different ways in the lifestyles of Americans—through walking, jogging, running, swimming, aerobics, Pilates, weight lifting, and cycling and through a host of "exercise machines" that can be found in schools, in fitness centers, and (increasingly) in American homes. The philosophy that supports this movement has much to do with health and living longer, but it also has very much to do with *living well*.

The recent popularity of fitness seems to coincide with a number of other movements in society that refocused popular attention on quality-of-life issues. For example, the fitness movement has developed in the same era as have the consumer movement, the ecology movement, the civil rights movement, and the human rights movement. Each, in its own way, focused attention on what living well meant and on what impediments to living well existed in modern American culture.

If there is a discernible philosophy underlying the fitness movement, it has been most clearly articulated by the health-education and allied medical professions. The relevant philosophical concept is *wellness*. Traditional definitions and views of health all related to *illness*. *Health* was viewed as the *absence* of illness. Ways of measuring health were to assess the "five Ds"—death, disease, discomfort, disability, and dissatisfaction (Edlin & Golanty, 1982). Like a washing machine or a refrigerator, your health was assumed to be good if your body and life were "working." You did not pay much attention to your health until it "broke down."

Wellness takes a much broader, more holistic, and more proactive view of health. The factors that define wellness include not only traditional criteria such as freedom from disease but also a number of positive criteria such as adaptability to cope with everyday stresses; feelings of accomplishment and personal growth; the spiritual component of the capacity for love, compassion, forgiveness, and altruism; the interpersonal component of having strong, mutually supportive relationships with people in our lives; and the capacity to think critically, be open to new ideas, and have a sense of humor (Fahey, Insel, & Roth, 2007).

A main feature of the wellness philosophy is that to achieve wellness you must work toward it—it will not "happen" to you. The holistic view suggests that physical, mental, and psychological problems are all related and that to achieve wellness you must make sure that your work, play, and social lives not only are positive in themselves but also are appropriately balanced.

The fitness and wellness movements have now evolved to incorporate the concept of lifespan physical activity as a main ingredient of a healthful lifestyle, leaving behind an older, more narrow concept of physical fitness. (See Chapter 7 for a discussion of this distinction.) Research has established physical activity as contributing positively to increased longevity, enhanced work capacity, a healthful lifestyle, and general well-being (Karvonen, 1996; Corbin, Welk, Corbin, & Welk, 2005). Regular involvement in moderate to intense physical activity is seen as a necessary component of achieving and maintaining wellness (Blair & Connelly, 1996). The movement now focuses on *lifestyle* changes that include nutrition, physical activity, useful and satisfying work, and recreation.

Fitness, wellness, and lifestyle-education programs have focused primarily on individuals and have been treated as matters of individual responsibility. More recently, the soaring cost for public health has focused attention on the collective concerns associated with a nation where too many people are inactive and eat unhealthy diets. The

Step aerobics is one of the many popular forms of aerobics.

publication of *Healthy People 2000* (U.S. Public Health Service, 1991) made it clear that diet and physical activity are *public-policy* concerns. The assessment of the 2000 goals and the setting of new goals in *Healthy People 2010* (U.S. Department of Health and Human Services, 2000) further emphasized that the nation's health was both an individual and a *collective responsibility.* Evidence suggests strongly (Siedentop, 1996c) that people in each socioeconomic group tend to be healthier than the people in groups below them and to be less healthy than the people in groups above them. In the United States, socioeconomic status also correlates strongly with racial/ethnic status. In nations where socioeconomic differences are less widespread or where they have been reduced over time, the health status of citizens tends to be better. This suggests that improved health and the achievement of physically active lifestyles are socioeconomic and political issues as well as medical and health issues (Siedentop, 1996c; Sparkes, 1991).

Although the fitness–wellness movement and the philosophy underlying it are often identifiable in school physical-education and health programs, this philosophy and the programs developed from it have spread mostly through the private sector in adult society. The wellness movement may develop further by taking into account the lifestyle of children and youths, with school and nonschool programs to promote wellness and to provide activity. If so, then the wellness philosophy and the movement representing it could form the underlying rationale for lifespan involvement in sport, fitness, and physical education.

Lifespan Involvement in Physical Activity: The New Visions

Traditionally, philosophies for sport, fitness, and physical education have focused primarily on children and youths and to a lesser extent on young adults. Currently, however, it is clear that physical activity and wellness are important concerns for working adults and retired adults, many of whom were part of the baby-boomer generation. The current generation, known widely as the "millennials" or "Generation Y" and their immediate predecessors, most often referred to as "Generation X," grew up in an increasingly technology-driven culture and were attracted to what are most typically referred to as extreme sports such as snowboarding, paintball, skateboarding, artificial-wall climbing, and in-line skating.

For most of the twentieth century, sport philosophies focused on the traditional values of cooperation, teamwork, character development, and healthy competition (Lauer, 2006). For many members of Gen X and Gen Y (the millennial generation), however, their sport experiences are better defined by individualism, risk taking, and even a sense of defiance against establishment sport. Lauer (2006)

argues that many young people participate in these activities to escape the authority and supervision of adults and the pressures too often brought by overzealous parents and coaches. Likewise, Coakley (2007) argues that youngsters gravitate toward extreme sports in order to exert their own control over rules, skills, and competitions. Like many innovations, however, extreme sports have begun to become institutionalized over the past decade. For example, they played a significant role in the last Winter Olympic Games and the X Games' competitions are widely televised.

Finally, it is clear that fitness has become a major focus for the retired and elderly generations. Retirement communities have increasingly marketed themselves by emphasizing the facilities for fitness, including walking trails, exercise facilities with the latest fitness machines, and classes especially designed for older adults. Retirement communities and recreation departments in towns and cities are focusing efforts on engaging adult and older citizens in fitness programs and in sport activities. The lesson to be learned by these generational changes is that physical activity is important both to health and a satisfying lifestyle, but the specific nature of the activities engaged in at various stages of the lifespan is likely to continue to change.

SUMMARY

1. Our use of the term *philosophy* refers to the set of values and principles that guide work in a professional field.

2. Professional philosophies should be coherent, reasonable, and connected to the evolution of the professional field.

3. The gymnastic philosophies of Europe promoted nationalism through formal programs of gymnastics aimed at physical, mental, and emotional development of the individual to produce and maintain a strong state.

4. *Muscular Christianity* broke down religious opposition to sport and fitness and endorsed the

belief that moral courage was related to physical courage and fitness.

5. *Arnoldism* was a philosophy that promoted an education in which physical activity had a central role in developing manliness, patriotism, moral courage, and intellectual independence.

6. Nineteenth-century philosophies and ideals emphasized masculine–feminine differences and relegated women to a lesser role in which physical activity was seen as unladylike and potentially harmful.

7. American sport and physical education were strongly influenced by British standards of fair play and amateurism, those ideals being highlighted with the rebirth of the Olympic Games in 1896.

8. The beginnings of an American physical-education philosophy borrowed heavily from progressive-education theory, which was directly traceable to a series of eighteenth- and nineteenth-century European philosophers and educators.

9. Philosophers, psychologists, and educators rediscovered the concept of play near the turn of the twentieth century and began to recognize its importance in the development of children and youths as well as in adult life.

10. The "new" physical education emphasized education through the physical as the philosophical basis for sport, fitness, and physical education, a philosophy in which activity was believed to contribute to physical, mental, social, and intellectual strength.

11. The education-through-the-physical philosophy dominated American professional thought for the first half of the twentieth century and remains today the most influential philosophy, even though it has more recently been challenged by several competing philosophies.

12. The philosophy of human movement emphasized the ability to move as a means for expressing, exploring, developing, and interpreting one's own self and one's relationship to the world.

13. Humanistic philosophies in the post-1950 era influenced both sport and physical education, focusing attention on abuses and emphasizing self-development, self-growth, and interpersonal relations.

14. Play education developed as a philosophy in which the activities of physical education were seen as culturally important in their own right, not needing justification by reference to educational outcomes. Sport education developed as a companion framework that offered a specific program through which the philosophy could be realized.

15. Experiential education and adventure education focus on academic and character education through challenge and responsibility.

16. The fitness and wellness movements were undergirded by a philosophy of holistic health that eschewed the traditional absence-of-illness model and replaced it with a proactive view in which people actively strove to produce a lifestyle through which positive physical, mental, and emotional health would result.

17. The physical-activity needs of the nation cannot be met by focusing solely on individuals but must include public-policy initiatives at local, state, and federal levels.

DISCUSSION QUESTIONS

1. Can you trace the origins of your professional philosophies? How coherently can you articulate these philosophical positions?

2. What current views reflect the influence of muscular Christianity, the gymnastic philosophies, or the British fair-play tradition? In what forms have these notions survived?

3. How have masculine and feminine ideals changed? What vestiges of the former views still linger?

4. What physical-education philosophy best represents your views? How would you describe the philosophy underlying the physical-education program in the high school that you attended?

5. To what extent does progressive education still dominate school aims and objectives? Is progressive education compatible with current educational reform?

6. How does the current wellness movement differ from the gymnastic philosophies? Will wellness supplant fitness as a primary concern?

7. Which philosophy seems to dominate professional sport? Which one dominates activity at a local fitness club? Which one dominates youth sport?

8. How will the activity choices of generations X and Y influence the sport and fitness culture in the future?

Sport

Most people who read this text have had a positive experience in sport. For many, like me, sport has been at the center of their lives and has helped form many of the fundamental experiences of their development as individuals. The sport culture in which we live is a dynamic, evolving enterprise. In many cases, the sport culture does well; in other cases, however, it does poorly. How will it evolve in the future? Who is responsible for helping sport to evolve in such a way that it will serve everyone in the future more fully than it serves us now?

These are important questions that we cannot answer without a thorough understanding of what sport is, how and by whom it is practiced, and the major problems and issues that specialists in this field must face and solve. The three chapters in Part 2 will increase your understanding of and critical thinking about sport.

CHAPTER 4

Basic Concepts of Sport

The very elaborations of sport—its internal conventions of all kinds, its cere-
monies, its endless meshes entangling itself—are for the purpose of training
and testing and rewarding the rousing motion within us to find a moment of
freedom. Freedom is that state where energy and order merge and all com-
plexity is purified into a simple coherence, a fitness of parts and purpose and
passions that cannot be surpassed and whose goal could only be to be itself.

A. Bartlett Giamatti, former commissioner of baseball
and president of Yale University, 1989

LEARNING OBJECTIVES

- To explain Novak's concept of sport as a natural religion

- To define the concept of play and to explain how it relates to sport

- To define the concept of a game, including the notions of primary and secondary rules

- To explain and provide examples of the game-classification system

- To discuss the several meanings of "competition"

- To analyze how sport becomes institutionalized

- To describe the aesthetic values of sport

- To discuss sport ethics

Sport has been a part of civilized societies throughout history. In some cases, as in Greece in the fifth century BCE, sport was of central importance to the culture. At other times, as during the repressive asceticism of the Middle Ages, sport was officially frowned on but still enjoyed by common people in villages and towns. At the height of the Roman Empire, athletes formed a strong labor union, bargaining for higher appearance fees and prizes and keeping out athletes who would not support the union. Sport even flourished in varied forms in early America despite the Puritan sanctions against it. Until recently, however, few people tried to examine and analyze sport—to understand what it is, from what human motivations it springs, and what role it occupies in culture.

Sport has been studied and analyzed by scholars in many disciplines since the 1950s—and increasingly since the mid-1970s when a national and world sport culture developed beyond what anybody could have imagined 100 years ago. The main argument in this chapter is that sport derives from the play impulse in human behavior, as do art, music, and drama. Yet few artistic or dramatic performances draw 80,000 spectators on an autumn afternoon, nor do musical events capture the national interest in the way the National Collegiate Athletic Association's annual basketball championship, known simply as "the Final Four," does. The extraordinary success of recent Olympic Games throughout the world foreshadows the development of a global sport culture that knows no boundaries of race, gender, ethnicity, or age. Understanding sport better and forming judgments about its role in culture are what this chapter is about.

Most people who read this text have had significant experiences in the world of sport. Many people who aspire to a career in the sport, fitness, and physical-education professions had childhood and youth experiences in sport that were the primary motivating factors in their choice of career. You probably *know* sport from an experiential point of view, having participated and been a spectator, perhaps having been an official or a coach. The purpose of this chapter is to provide a conceptual framework from within which you can understand your own experience of sport as well as that of the individual and the society.

By any measure, sport is important. The statistics on the number of people who spectate and who participate are impressive. The amount of money spent on sport is enormous. Sport heroes and heroines are used by corporations to advertise their products. Events such as the World Series, the Super Bowl, and the Final Four have become national celebrations, but these kinds of celebrations are also repeated endlessly in cities and towns everywhere during each of the sport seasons that together compose the sport year. For many people, young and old alike, sport has an almost religious significance.

SPORT: THE NATURAL RELIGION

Michael Novak (1976), in *The Joy of Sports*, argues that sport is a natural religion and that we must understand it as such to grasp its fundamental

The intensity of sport involvement is not defined by gender.

importance. He describes what it is like to be a *believer* among unbelievers:

> Faith in sports, I have discovered, seeks understanding. . . . Other believers know how hard it is to put into words what they so deeply and obscurely know. They have also argued with their wives and friends, and even in their own heads. All around this land there is a faith without an explanation, a love without a rationale. (Novak, 1976, p. xiii)

Novak's argument is not based on using a simple religious metaphor to explain sport, does not come from a sportswriter talking about the "sacrifice" of an athlete, and is not an athlete saying, "You gotta believe." His argument is based on qualities and characteristics fundamental to the sport experience and to the role that this experience plays in individual and social life:

> I am saying that sports flow outward into action from a deeper natural impulse that is radically religious: an impulse of freedom, respect for ritual limits, a zest for symbolic meaning, and a longing for perfection. The athlete may of course be pagan, but sports are, as it were, natural religions. (Novak, 1976, p. 19)

How is sport a religion? Sport is organized and dramatized in a religious way. There are rituals (for example, the coin toss and the opening lineups). There are costumes (or "vestments," to use the religious phrase). There is a sense of powers that are outside one's control (the ball bounces to the left, the wind blows at an inopportune moment). There are figures who enforce rules and mete out punishments (referees). Sport also can, when done well, teach qualities that are religious in nature, such as perseverance, courage, and sacrifice. In sport, athletes often strive for perfection just as many people do in religious orders. In sport, as in religion, there are heroes and heroines who provide models of perfection to strive for, who are admired for what they did, and who become almost saintlike. Such is the *religious* nature of sport.

Sport, like religion, can be intensely personal, yet in its fullest sense, it is *communal*. What we see and experience in sport takes us out of ourselves and lets us glimpse something more perfect than we know ordinary life to be. The late A. Bartlett Giamatti, former president of Yale University and former commissioner of baseball, argued that sport can do this for both participant and spectator, thus further enhancing its communal nature:

> To take acts of physical toil—lifting, throwing, bending, jumping, pushing, grasping, stretching, running, hoisting, the constantly repeated acts that for millennia have meant work—and to bound them in time or by rules or boundaries in a given enclosure surrounded by an amphitheater or at least a gallery is to replicate the arena of humankind's highest aspiration. That aspiration is to be taken out of the self. (Giamatti, 1989, p. 34)

Believers in sport should neither be ashamed of their beliefs nor be reluctant to defend those beliefs. Being better able to explain and defend your commitment to sport can be a source of personal satisfaction as well as a powerful professional tool. In addition, you should not have to tolerate having others make fun of sport.

> Sports are not merely fun and games, not merely diversions, not merely entertainment. A ballpark is not a temple, but it isn't a fun house either. A baseball game is not an entertainment, and a ballplayer is considerably more than a paid performer. No one can explain the passion, commitment, discipline, and dedication involved in sports by evasions like these. (Novak, 1976, p. 23)

It is clear that for many people—perhaps for you, too—sport participation provides a source of deep personal meaning. Eleanor Metheny (1970), one of America's leading physical-education scholars of the midtwentieth century, described how sport creates conditions within which people test themselves and find out a great deal about who they are in moments of self-revelation during competition:

> Or, as the competitors in the early Olympic contests put it, every man who would submit his own excellence to the test of sport competition must "stand naked before his gods" and reveal himself as he is in the fullness of his own human powers. Stripped of all self-justifying excuses by the rules of sport, he must demonstrate his own ability to perform one human action of his own choosing, and naked of all pretense, he must use himself as he is, in all the wholeness of his being as a man. (Metheny, 1970, p. 66)

Sport has the power to teach. As Wilfred Sheed (1995) points out, sport is not necessarily a force for good, but it is indeed a force. It is such a powerful force that it not only tells you much about yourself as an individual but also reveals a great deal about the society within which sport is pursued. There is good reason, then, for us to consider sport seriously.

LEISURE, PLAY, GAMES, AND SPORT

To understand sport, we have to examine the motivations from which it arises, the forms it takes, and the ways it has developed historically. We also have to understand four related concepts: *leisure, play, games,* and *competition.* We use the terms in our ordinary language when we discuss sport, but we also should understand their specific, technical meanings.

Leisure

Sport developed historically as a leisure-time activity. Leisure can be distinguished from work by examining the attitude of the person, the nature of the activity, and the time dimension of the activity.

1. **Leisure** can be viewed as an attitude of freedom or release from the demands of ordinary life. This is the subjective component of an understanding of leisure, indicating the great joy and satisfaction derived from leisure activities.

2. The notion of leisure as an activity shifts the focus from the person to the event and those who are responsible for providing the services the event represents—for example, going to a golf course to play a round of golf. Leisure activities are often distinguished from work activities, in that leisure is freely chosen and not obligatory.

3. Viewed as time, leisure has traditionally been the discretionary time left over after work, family, and personal maintenance commitments are handled. The time aspect of leisure shows the leisure–work distinction most readily because the leisure attitude can be found in work and because leisure and work activities are not always easily distinguishable. Some activities are work for some people but leisure for other people.

Leisure attitude, leisure activities, and leisure time are often thought to be related to play—that is, a playful attitude, play activities, and play time. It is in the linkage to the concept of play that we see the fundamental meaning of sport.

Play

Sport as a Form of Play   Most scholars agree that sport is a manifestation of play and that sports are institutionalized forms of play. Play is also thought to be the motivating impulse underlying the development of drama, art, and music. It was the Dutch historian Johan Huizinga who first conceptualized the role of play as a basic motivation in human activity. Huizinga defined play as follows:

> Summing up the formal characteristics of play we might call it a free activity standing quite consciously outside "ordinary" life as being "not serious," but at the same time absorbing the player intensely and utterly. It is an activity connected with no material interest, and no profit can be gained by it. It proceeds within its own proper boundaries of time and space according to fixed rules and in an orderly manner. It promotes the formation of social groupings which tend to surround themselves with secrecy and to stress their differences from the common world by disguise or other means. (Huizinga, 1962, p. 13)

Play, then, is different from ordinary life, different certainly from what we typically refer to as "work." Play does not produce the products that work does, yet it seems to absorb us at least as completely, and often more so. Play, anthropologists tell us, is something that all people everywhere do, in one form or another.

The French sociologist Roger Caillois (1961) refined Huizinga's definition. His characteristics of play are now most commonly cited when sport and play are discussed and analyzed. Caillois suggested that play is free, separate, uncertain, economically unproductive, and governed by rules or by make-believe. It is through an analysis of these characteristics of play that we can see how sport derives from play. Note that each characteristic represents a continuum; at one end is the most playful situation, and at the other end is the least playful situation.

1. *Free.* Sport is most playful when people enter into it voluntarily. To the degree that sport is required or that the player cannot choose when to participate, sport becomes less playful.

2. *Separate.* Sport is conducted in places where the time and space limits are fixed in advance. It is often conducted in places designed especially for that activity—for example, the soccer stadium, baseball field, golf course, or tennis court. The playful nature of the activity seems to be enhanced when the space for doing it is separate in this sense.

3. *Uncertain.* Sport is most playful when it is uncertain, when the contestants in a competition are evenly matched. Uneven competition is not fun for participants and is boring for spectators. Much effort is made in organized sport to ensure equal competition. Handicaps are provided as in golf. School competition is often grouped by size of school, wrestling by weight class.

4. *Economically unproductive.* Activity is most playful when it does not result in any new wealth being created (as opposed to work, where creating wealth is the main purpose of the activity). A game itself typically produces no wealth as a *contest* even though participants may be paid and much money may be made from other sources—television, concessions, parking, and so on. To the extent that new wealth is produced, the playfulness of the activity decreases.

5. *Governed by rules.* Play is almost always regulated. Even young children at play typically begin by creating rules. Sport, of course, is governed by rules that standardize the competition and are agreed to by all participants as necessary for the contest to proceed. Rules are typically established to define the activity, to ensure fairness, and to produce a winner. Further, rules in sport are completely arbitrary, which is one way that play differs from work where rules tend to make sense. Why three strikes? Why two serves in tennis but not in badminton? Why 10 yards for a first down? The point is that sport is a social agreement to compete within arbitrary rules—which makes it playful—and violating those rules denies the agreement and tends to destroy the playfulness (Giamatti, 1989).

6. *Governed by make-believe.* Play that is not rule governed is dominated by make-believe. Sport typically relies on the rule-governed characteristic of play whereas drama relies on the make-believe characteristic. Still, we can see in the sport play of young children the union of these two characteristics because the children often assume the identities of their favorite players as they take part in games.

It is in these ways that we can see sport as a form of play. Clearly, *sport does not have to be playful.* We can imagine forms of sport in which each characteristic is barely present—so much so that the sport activity is mostly devoid of the play element. Such sport forms seldom survive long; it appears that for people to want to continue in sport, the play element must be present. How to maintain the play element in sport is a major focus in Chapter 6.

It is in this sense that we need to think when we use *play* as a verb—that is, I *play* basketball, or let us go *play* a game of golf, or did you *play* racquetball last night? The term does not mean merely that you have participated. Instead, it means that you have *played.*

Play is viewed by most scholars as an irreducible form of behavior present in all animal life, finding its fullest expression in human behavior. Play, therefore, represents a fundamental category of behavior that needs no further explanation. People play. Why? Because play not only is fundamental to life but also is the mode of behavior through which some of life's most meaningful moments occur.

Play, then, is not a trivial concept. It is a concept rich with psychological, sociological, and historical meaning. It is also a sufficiently strong and rich concept to provide insight into what sport is, what sport means to people who play and watch it, and what role sport occupies in culture.

Child's Play and Adult Play   Most developmental psychologists believe that play is the most basic form of behavior in young children and that it is through play that children acquire much of their early knowledge about the physical and social world in which they live. Do adults play also? They say, "Let's play," but do they play as children do? Adults in a racquetball court, on a golf course, or in a football game certainly do not look the same as children do when they play. We have to recognize that there are *different ways of playing.*

Caillois (1961) has suggested that ways of playing can be placed on a continuum according to the degree of spontaneity, orderliness, and regulation present in the play form. At one end of the continuum is what we typically see in the play of young children: turbulence, gaiety, spontaneity, diversion. At the other end of the continuum is what we typically see when adults play their sports: calculation, subordination to rules, contrivance, and ritual.

This is not to suggest that one way of playing is necessarily *better* than the other way of playing. Each is appropriate at different times and for different purposes. Typically, as children grow and develop, they change their play activities toward the adult end of the continuum. It is this end of the continuum that is characterized by practice, training, rituals, costumes, skill, and strategy. That way of playing obviously appeals to the more mature person—it simply has more sustaining motivation. The appreciation for practice, strategy, skillfulness, ritual, and tradition is the main characteristic of mature involvement in play.

As play forms mature and as players mature in those forms (sport), it becomes necessary to create obstacles that must be overcome to achieve the goal of the play. The creation of new obstacles and the overcoming of them to produce a definite result are essential to continued motivation in play. Golfers, as they improve at the sport, continually look for new challenges in the courses they play. A good golf course, in this sense, is one that has obstacles that a player must overcome to shoot a good score. Thus, narrow fairways, sand traps, water hazards, and strategically placed trees all create obstacles that require strategy and skill to overcome. These obstacles make the play of golf more challenging and interesting, and they considerably increase the rewards of shooting a good score.

Sport, then, derives from the play instinct in human behavior and the play element in culture. When sport is most playful, it is most meaningful to the participants. When sport loses its playfulness, the meaning is lessened for the participants (but not necessarily for the spectators).

Games

Although the terms *game* and *sport* are often used interchangeably, there are important distinctions between them. One way to view sport is as a game occurrence—but sport can be viewed in other ways, too. Therefore, the two concepts are related in some ways but not in others.

A **game** is "any form of playful competition whose outcome is determined by physical skill, strategy or chance employed singly or in a combination" (Loy, 1969, p. 56). There are three important parts

Sport involvement often combines fun and seriousness.

of this definition. First, games derive from play. Second, games involve competition. Third, the outcome of the game is determined by use of physical skill, strategy, or chance. Not all games are sport, but sport is always a game. This is true even though we do not typically describe some sport involvement as game involvement; competing in a mile run is not described as "playing a game," but it does fit the definition. Some scholars differentiate games from contests and describe activities such as swimming or marathoning as contests rather than as games, but the activities are so similar that each can be referred to as a "game" in the sense defined here.

Competition is a defining characteristic of games and a fundamental quality of sport. The term *cooperative games*, which appears frequently in the physical-education literature, is a contradiction in terms. Without some element of competition, the activity ceases to be a game.

Sports are games that involve combinations of physical skill and strategy. Games that have outcomes determined primarily by chance—dice, for example—are not sports. Even though there clearly are *chance elements* in sport, such as weather changes or the errant bounce of a ball, these are not the primary determinants of outcomes. Games that involve strong elements of strategy but involve no physical skill are also not sports; bridge, chess, and other board games are examples.

Each sport game is different because each game poses a problem to be solved—what Almond (1986) termed the game's **primary rules**. The primary rules of a game identify how the game is to be played and how winning can be achieved. The primary rules of a game are what makes basketball basketball, not volleyball.

Games also have many **secondary rules**, which typically define the institutionalized form of the game, or what we might call the *parent* game. Secondary rules can be altered or modified to make the game more developmentally appropriate or different in some other way without changing the essential character of the game, which is defined by the primary rules. The 3-second zone rule and the 10-second half-court rule in basketball are examples of secondary rules. They can be changed without changing the essential elements that define the game as basketball. The primary rule of volleyball is to strike the ball over a net in a divided court in such a way that it either cannot be returned by opponents or hits the floor within their side of the court. Secondary rules include the height of the net, the size of the ball, the size of the court, and the number of hits per side.

Sport games can be categorized in several ways, but for our purposes, it will be most useful to examine a category scheme based on the similarities among the primary rules that define the games (Almond, 1983). This game classification has four categories: (1) territory or invasion games, (2) target games, (3) court games, and (4) sector games.

1. *Territory* or *invasion games* are defined by the problem of needing to invade the space of the opponent to score. Two types of territory-invasion games are those in which goals are used (basketball, ice hockey, soccer, team handball, lacrosse, water polo, and so on) and those in which lines are used (American football, Australian rules football, rugby, speedball, and so on). Territory-invasion games can be further subdivided according to whether the game involves the use of the hand with a ball (basketball), the foot with a ball (soccer), or a stick with a ball (hockey).

2. *Target games* are defined by the primary rules of propelling objects with great accuracy toward targets. Target games can be subdivided according to whether the opponents are directly opposed (croquet, horseshoes, curling, and so on) or indirectly opposed (golf, bowling). In the former, one plays directly against one's opponent, often hitting the other player's ball, for example. In the latter, one plays against the target (the pins, the par on the golf hole) and then compares scores with an opponent.

3. *Court games* are those in which an object is strategically propelled in such a way that it cannot be returned by an opponent. Court games can be subdivided according to whether the court is divided (badminton, tennis, table tennis, and so on) or shared (handball, squash, jai alai, and so on). Court-divided games typically use a net. Court-shared games typically rely on rebounds from walls.

4. *Sector games* are defined by primary rules that require one opponent to strike an object such as to elude defenders on the field. The shape of the field might differ somewhat (fan shaped or oval shaped), but the basic natures of the games are similar. Cricket, baseball, softball, and rounders are examples.

A knowledge of games—of their meaning and function—is fundamental to the person interested in understanding sport. New games develop all the time. Sometimes the new games become sports; sometimes they do not. Frisbee is a good example.

On any spring afternoon, you can see students throwing Frisbees in open spaces, but there is seldom a *game* going on, and no one would call it a *sport*. Yet Frisbee has developed into a sport/game called "ultimate Frisbee"—one for which there are rules and growing traditions. Frisbee as a sport is in the process of becoming *institutionalized*; that is, it is changing from an informal game to an institutionalized sport. To become institutionalized, a sport must be defined with standardized rules to which all players adhere, must have a governing body, and must encompass a growing sense of tradition that binds people to it.

Not all sports fit these categories of games. Track and field, swimming, wrestling, surfing, ski jumping, and bobsledding are all sports but are seldom referred to as games even though many of these sports are part of the Olympic Games or Pan American Games. An entirely new group of sports have developed over the past quarter-century, created mostly by young people, many of whom were associated with youth subcultures most commonly referred to as Generation X or, more recently, the millennial generation, known also as Gen Y. These sports are most commonly described as "extreme sports" and include skateboarding, in-line skating, snowboarding, skiing, and BMX racing. Many scholars associate the development of these sports as similar to the counterculture sport movement of surfing in the 1960s.

Many of these new sports combine high-level athletic skill along with high-level risk. Extreme sports also tend to encourage individual creativity that creates higher risk. Skateboarding hero Tony Hawk explained the motivation for participation in these new, risk activities: "I liked having my own pace and my own rules . . . and making up my own challenges" (Finger, 2004, p. 84). Participation in extreme sports was motivated by an individualism that was nearly opposite of the values espoused by youth and school sports—that is, the values of teamwork, cooperation, conformity, and character (Lauer, 2006). Many of these sports are in the process of becoming institutionalized as demonstrated by the creation of the X Games and the EXPN television channel.

Competition in Sport and Games

Sport and games involve competition. Without competition, there is no game. Yet competition is among the most seriously misunderstood concepts in sport, fitness, and physical education. Almost everybody has strong views about competition. Some people advocate competition at all costs as a positive virtue. Others view competition as inherently bad and want to make sports noncompetitive as though that were possible. Because competition is a controversial issue, it is necessary to examine the concept closely and to understand its different meanings in relation to the concepts of sport and games. Competition is almost always defined first as a rivalry in which opponents strive to gain something at the expense of each other. This kind of definition tends to emphasize the use of the term in economics and business. Far too often, competition in sport is defined exclusively in this economic sense. One form of competition, stemming from the world of economics, is **zero-sum competition**. In a zero-sum competition, whatever is gained by one competitor must necessarily be lost by the other competitor; that is, to the extent that I win, you must lose. One sometimes hears overzealous coaches state that "winning isn't the most important thing, it's the only thing" or "defeat is worse than death." Those kinds of remarks reflect a zero-sum view of competition.

The concept of competition is far richer than that—especially when used in reference to sport. There are three important and related meanings of the concept of competition (Siedentop, 1981). The first meaning is *to come together*, which denotes the festive aspects of competition. When the term is used as a noun (as in "Let's have a competition"), we can sense the notion of a festival. All the world's great sport competitions are clearly festivals—the Olympic Games, the Super Bowl, the World Cup in soccer. We find similar festivals, on a smaller scale, at high-school football games, children's soccer games, and adult equestrian competitions. This festive nature of sport is the clearest evidence of its communal importance.

Sport involves rituals and traditions. The *festive* nature of competition is where the rituals and traditions are most easily seen, and the festive nature of sport competition is one of its most appealing attributes.

A second meaning of the concept of competition is to strive to achieve an objective; it is what I call the *competence* meaning of the term. The words *compete* and *competence* derive from the Latin word *competere*. Competition provides a forum within which people strive to become competent, to become excellent. When rules and conditions are standardized, performances can be compared fairly, and competitors can learn about their strengths and weaknesses.

Many scholars believe the pursuit of competence—trying to get better—is a fundamental, sustaining motivation for sport involvement (Alderman & Wood, 1976; Coakley, 2007; Eitzen & Sage, 2003). This belief comes from evidence showing that young athletes rank wanting to get better as a primary motivation for their continued participation. They also rate being with friends and being part of a team (affiliation) as a strong motivation. It also should be noted that these motivations are ranked higher than the excitement of competition or beating another person or team.

The third meaning of the concept of competition is the one with which we are most familiar—to be in a state of *rivalry*. The opportunities for rivalry within sport are many and varied: team against team, individual against individual, individual against a record, individual against a previous best performance, individual against a physical barrier. Many of these rivalry motivations coexist in one contest. When 30,000 runners start the New York Marathon each year, it is difficult to describe their competitive motivation as a zero-sum rivalry. If that were true, there would be 1 winner and 29,999 losers! The fact is that few athletes view their own competition as a zero-sum phenomenon. Occasionally a coach does, or a parent, or a sportswriter.

Within the boundaries of a sport, individuals and groups compete, but seldom, if ever, is that competition a zero-sum arrangement. There are many ways to win and to lose within a competition, and the winning and losing have meaning only within the competition and, even then, only momentarily. If winning or losing has meaning that carries over from the competition to other aspects of life, then it clearly diminishes the play element in the competition.

Sport, therefore, can be understood as a game occurrence in which playful competition is the primary motivational force. The *players* can practice diligently, train seriously, prepare strategically, and compete vigorously yet still manifest the play element in its fullest. Factors such as unevenly matched opponents, required participation, economic consequences, and pressures for winning that carry over to real life outside the sport event seriously diminish the play element in sport.

THE INSTITUTIONALIZATION OF SPORT

Somewhere, sometime, someone thought of a new game to play. Rules were suggested, the goal of the game was explained, equipment was probably designed, and special space was acquired. The game was played and enjoyed. Perhaps it was enjoyed sufficiently that others wanted to play it. The rules were then written down, a sketch of the space (for example, field or court) was made, and the needed equipment was listed. Each time that the new game was played, it was no doubt changed slightly to meet local needs and interests and to accommodate local problems with equipment and facilities. Eventually, however, some *common form of the game* was needed because many people wanted to try the game. At that point, the game began to become institutionalized (see Focus On Box 4.1).

No doubt, something akin to this process happened for the several games invented in America in the late nineteenth century—basketball, softball, and volleyball. They started as local games for local purposes. Today, they are international

---

In the 1980s, when the term *extreme sports* first was used, it referred to adult sports such as skydiving, scuba diving, surfing, rock climbing, waterskiing, mountain biking, and hang gliding. The magazine *Outside*, with its focus on marketing outdoor clothing from The North Face and Patagonia, was a main resource. Competitions were mostly local. Also in the 1980s, young boys were increasingly drawn to activities that represented values (individualism, risk, a flair for creating their own performance clothing) that were nearly opposite of those espoused in youth and school sport (cooperation, teamwork, subordination to leadership, uniforms).

The label "Extreme Sports" was used by ESPN in 1995 in their planning for the initial Extreme Games (now the X Games). The X Games are now held each year. The 2008 Summer X Games 14 was held in Los Angeles; the 2008 Winter X Games 12 was held in Aspen.

The Summer X Games competitions are Freestyle BMX, MotoX, Skateboarding, Surfing, and Rallying. Within each of these competition categories are subcategory competitions; for example, the competition categories within Freestyle BMX are Vert, Park, and Big Air. The Winter X Games

competitions are Skiing, Snowboarding, Snowmobiling, and Snowskating. The competition categories within Snowboarding are Slopestyle, Snowboarder, SuperPipe, and Best Trick. In many categories, there are separate competitions for men and women.

The X Games are shown live on ESPN and ABC with videoclips available on ESPN.com. Nearly 40 million viewers tuned in to X Games coverage with the highest rating ever for young male viewers. Attendance has increased steadily, currently reaching near 150,000. Concurrent with the X Games competitions is the X Fest sports and music festival with live music and interaction with competitors.

The increasing difficulty of the "tricks" performed by X Games competitors has been assisted by innovations in technologies—for example, advances in ski design, rubber-soled climbing shoes, artificial climbing walls, and better-designed and lighter knee braces. Extreme sports are now competed throughout the world with the Planet X Games in Australia, the Asian X Games, the Latin X Games, and the Dubai X Games.

---

games with rules, traditions, rituals, governing bodies, and championships. When volleyball is played in a developing nation, it is essentially the same game as that played here and everywhere else. The game has a common form that is recognized internationally. It has become a fully institutionalized sport.

It is important to understand sport as a social institution. Most people who enter the various professions associated with sport can do so because sport is thoroughly institutionalized in developed societies. Think for a moment of the role that the following professionals occupy relative to sport:

- The orthopedic surgeon who is a sport-medicine specialist

- The sportswriter
- The radio or television sport commentator
- The sport manager
- The referee or umpire
- The sport administrator
- The coach
- The trainer
- The equipment specialist
- The sport promoter
- The sport strength coach

Conspicuously absent from that list is the sport performer! The sport performer is the *only* person necessary for sport to take place at a local level, at a level that is casually organized, flexible, and *not yet institutionalized.* (How many of these other sport types are necessary for a pickup softball game?) All roles other than participant develop as sport becomes more highly institutionalized to the point in some sports where all these sport specialists far outnumber the people who actually play the game.

The Codification of Rules

As a sport becomes institutionalized, it adopts certain characteristics. First, the rules governing the sport are *codified.* The same rules are supposed to govern all contests, and there is typically a system through which the codified rules are enforced and, from time to time, changed. How people are to play the game and what is expected of them within the game are defined primarily by the rules and secondarily by the traditions that develop within the sport as it becomes institutionalized. Why does the crowd get so quiet when a golfer putts, whereas in basketball the crowd makes extra noise when an opponent shoots a free throw? The answer cannot be found in the nature of the two skills or in the official rules of the two sports but only in the traditions of how the two games have developed over time.

The Role of the Referee

The codification of rules for a sport typically produces the need for trained officials and referees. The importance of a referee to a sport is misunderstood by the public and often by sportspersons, too. The nature of sport is to strive for victory within a set of rules and conditions that are similar for all contestants; that is, sport is meaningful only when it is a *fair* contest. The main role of the referee is to ensure fairness by seeing that all contestants honor the rules and that no contestants get an advantage that is disallowed by the rules. The more highly institutionalized a sport becomes, the greater is the need to train and supervise referees so that the contests are played as much in accordance with the rules as is possible.

The referee plays a crucial role in ensuring a fair contest.

The Genesis of Sport Organizations

As sport becomes more institutionalized, it is natural that those associated with the sport want to see whether they, or their teams, are the best for that particular sport season. It seems to be in the nature of sport competition to want to find out who is best at the moment. For people to find out who is best, certain conditions need to be present. First, of course, all participants and teams have to be playing the same game, using the same rules. After the game becomes standardized, there has to be a schedule of playing that allows individuals and teams to compete against others. Also, an agreement has to be reached for a means through which the best can be selected each season. This all requires organization—and these very motivations led to the formation of sport associations and sport conferences.

A group of local teams might form a league to arrange a predictable schedule and to determine a local champion at the end of a sport season. A city or a state might organize a competition that allows a champion to be determined at that level. A national organization such as the Athletic Congress or the NCAA organizes individual and team championships for its members nationwide. An organization has to be created to arrange these competitions, to schedule facilities, and to secure officials. At most local levels, these organizations can be staffed by volunteers. As the sport becomes more institutionalized, however, the organizations become more formal and require full-time workers. This creates the need for trained people to do these specialized jobs and leads to the development of professions such as sport management, sport promotion, and sport administration.

The Importance of Records

As soon as a sport begins to become standardized, records begin to be kept. Records are important to sport in many ways. Many people have argued that the central motivation in sport is striving for excellence. Records are one important way that excellence is defined and preserved. They provide standards against which participants measure their improvement and set their goals. They also provide items of great interest to those who follow the sport but do not necessarily participate in it.

Without standard rules and good officiating, records could not assume the importance that they do in sport. When we can be reasonably sure that the competition was fair, then the record produced becomes part of the legend of the sport. The records that are of most general interest are those describing the limits beyond which men, women, or teams have yet been unable to go (Weiss, 1969).

Think of the almost magical importance that new records create in the world of sport. My memories are of Michael Johnson obliterating the 200-meter sprint world record in the 1996 Olympics and Bob Beamon not only breaking the world record in the long jump at the Mexico City Olympics but also moving the record completely through the 28-foot barrier by jumping over 29 feet. I can recall Joe Dimaggio's 56-game-hitting streak and the first sub-4 minute mile run by Roger Bannister, Wilt Chamberlin's 100-point NBA game, as well as Wilma Rudolph's four gold medals at the Rome Olympics. You are more likely to remember the Chicago Bulls 72 regular-season games won in 1995–96, Michael Phelps's eight medals in swimming at the Beijing Olympics in 2008, Tiger Woods's domination of the PGA Men's Tour, or the Boston Patriots undefeated season of 2007–08. These memorable moments not only set new standards for athletes of the future but also give us a momentary glimpse of what is possible in human endeavor.

Records become standards through which young athletes define their improvement. Research has shown that for many young athletes the primary motivation for continued participation is increased *competence*, the desire to get better at some event or skill that has value in the sport culture. *Getting better* is most easily judged in reference to standards within the sport, and standards are typically records of past performances by others in similar age groups and settings. For example, most aspiring age-group swimmers know exactly what a new personal best time means for them. They know what the time means not only with respect to their local swim team and local competition but also compared with regional, state, and national norms for the same event and the same age group. Their progress and their potential will be defined and charted by those kinds of comparisons.

In other sports, the comparison of performance and the establishment of competence cannot be accomplished so neatly through records as it can in swimming or track and field. In sports such as basketball or baseball, the records are important—batting average, points per game, rebounds, strikeouts—but they are all established under slightly different conditions against different kinds of opponents. Thus, in sports such as these, it becomes necessary to test oneself directly against the competition to find out one's own limits.

Records, however, are not just benchmarks that provide goals that define excellence. Performing in record fashion or witnessing a record-setting performance is deeply important to the nature of sport, and it is one reason why people pursue sport, both as athletes and as spectators. Records play a vital role in sport. They provide much of the tradition of a sport. They define its heroes and heroines. They provide standards for measuring one's improvement. They provide goals for which to strive. For the aficionado who follows the sport, they provide endless hours of pleasure in reading, discussing, even arguing about the relative merits of one performance versus another, one performer versus another, or one team versus another.

The Public Nature of Institutionalized Sport

As sport becomes institutionalized, it assumes a public role. It becomes part of a culture, locally at first, then perhaps regionally, and, for some sports, nationally and even internationally. The general importance of the sport at any of these cultural levels is proportional to the number of people who are interested in following the sport—the more fan interest there is, the more public attention is devoted to the sport.

It is this facet of institutionalized sport that is responsible for sport journalism, sport broadcasting, and sport literature. The first two, at least, are historically recent phenomena, depending as they do on modern technologies. It is no simple coincidence that the late nineteenth century in the United States was not only the period of the emergence of organized sport as a major cultural phenomenon but also the time at which communications technologies began to emerge in their modern forms (see Chapter 2).

The invention of the telegraph in the 1840s made it possible to communicate sport results over long distances. By the 1880s, newspapers had begun to devote separate sections to sport in their daily editions. The emergence of radio allowed for immediate vicarious enjoyment of live sport events across great distances. Television, of course, completely revolutionized sport spectating and is probably mainly responsible for the recent, enormous growth

in sport. Now cable and satellite capabilities provide immediate worldwide access to endless numbers of different sporting events.

Sport is now big business as information and entertainment. Sport sections in newspapers have grown larger. The number of sport magazines in shops seems endless. Books on the techniques of various sports are widely available. DVDs for sport instruction have also become widely available. All of this sport-related information has created new jobs for persons who want a nonparticipant sport vocation. Sport literature and sport films have come of age. Books such as David Halberstam's *The Breaks of the Game* (basketball) and *The Amateurs* (rowing), Mark Harris's *Bang the Drum Slowly* (baseball), and W. P. Kensella's *Shoeless Joe*, from which the film *Field of Dreams* was made, provide a serious sport literature. When *Chariots of Fire* captured the Academy Award for Best Picture in 1981, it marked the start of an era of sport films that won critical acclaim and were box-office hits—for example, *Bull Durham, Tin Cup, A League of Their Own, The Legend of Bagger Vance,* and *Remember the Titans.* In 2005 *Million Dollar Baby*, a film about a female boxer, won the Academy Award for Best Picture.

All of this public attention has made sport a part of our everyday life in America. It has created a number of new sport professions, and it has contributed to the further institutionalization of sport—more rituals, more traditions, more attention to records. It has moved sport from the periphery of American culture, where it was in the 1850s, to the center—all in the relatively short period of one century.

SPORT SPECTATING

Sport spectating is among our most frequently mentioned leisure-time activities. Early in the twentieth century, watching sports was considered to be an inappropriate behavior, especially if done too often. The term used by physical-education professionals was *spectatoritis*, and its medical connotation was purposely chosen. It was thought to be like a disease.

Most of us enjoy watching sports on occasion. Many of us enjoy watching sports often. Are we wasting our time? Should we be using our time in a more productive way? We cannot completely understand sport without including sport spectating in the analysis.

The sport spectator is not just a fan who responds emotionally but not intellectually to sport. The sport spectator is also often a sophisticated, knowledgeable, and appreciative viewer. Fans watch sport not just to see the contest, not just to see who wins, but also to see athletes perform within a contest in which the standards are clear and rules are enforced so that the playing field is indeed "level." Modern television has created new generations of informed spectators. Instant replay, telestrators, slow-motion replay, and technical analysis by commentators have provided viewers with an in-depth education in the skills and tactics of the sport being viewed. The subtle nuances that show the individual excellence of players or the collective excellence of a team offensive or defensive maneuver are revealed immediately after an exciting moment during a contest so that the viewer not only participates in the excitement of the moment but also gets an immediate education in what produced that excitement.

Often, however, the sport spectator is not just a knowledgeable observer, a detached connoisseur who lacks emotion and passion about sport events. The sport spectator is also often a fan. Some sport events can be watched for the sheer pleasure of seeing grace in action, an excellent contest, or a well-played game, but other sport competitions must be viewed from one side or the other. How often have you sat next to a seemingly calm, mature person who at some point in a game was transformed into an exuberant, partisan fan? How often have you experienced the same transformation yourself?

Sport loyalties often run deep. Modern society is extremely mobile. People move often. Sport is one of the few cultural institutions that has provided a sense of enduring meaning and continuity in the midst of mobility and change. A person's allegiance to a local team, to a university team, or to a professional team can form a sense of belonging and permanence. This is one of the important meanings of being a fan. Fans *root* for their team. The choice of terms is important. A *root* is the attached or embedded part of any structure, the part that holds the structure in position, the essential or core part of the structure. To root for a team means to *be rooted* in the fortunes of that team:

> To watch a sports event is not like watching a set of abstract patterns. It is to take a risk, to root and to be rooted. Some people, it is true, remain detached; they seem like mere voyeurs. The mode of observation proper to a sports event is *to participate*—that is, to extend one's own identification to one side, and to absorb with it the blows of fortune, to join that team in testing the favors of the Fates. (Novak, 1976, p. 144; emphasis in original)

The behavior of the sport fan, then, is an important part of the sport; to understand what sport is and how it has become so important to us, we must consider the role of the fan. The term *fan*, short for *fanatic*, is related to the Latin word *fanum*, which translates as "temple" or "feast." The original relationships of these terms take us full circle to the religious nature of sport, where we began this chapter.

SPORT AESTHETICS

Have you ever watched a game or a sport performance and seen something done by an individual or a team that made you say, "That's beautiful"? If so, you have reacted to the aesthetic quality of sport, the beauty that sometimes seems so evident in sport performance. In that sense, sport is the people's art!

Sport and athletes have always been subjects for art. In early Greek culture, where sport was so fundamental to social life, artists often used athletes as subjects, creating sculpture and decorating vases with depictions of athletes in action. Throughout history, artists have been intrigued by the physical beauty of the athletic body and the visual beauty of athletic performance. The fact that sport and athletes have been the subjects for artists' portrayals, however, does not mean that sport itself has aesthetic value.

To understand the aesthetic value of sport, we must find beauty *in sport* rather than in paintings or sculpture. As sport became the object for intellectual analysis and investigation during the twentieth century, aestheticians, as well as historians, psychologists, and sociologists, began to consider it seriously. Their work has helped us understand the artistic dimensions and qualities of sport.

If sport *is* art, then it most certainly is a performing art—like music, dance, and drama. The beauty of the art is found in the performance itself, and it is through understanding the source of that beauty in performance that we can begin to appreciate the aesthetic qualities of sport. When considering **sport aesthetics**, we must divide sport into two categories: (1) form sports and (2) all other sports.

Aesthetics of Form Sports

In some sports, the physical form of the performance is the determining factor in the competition—diving, gymnastics, and figure skating are prime examples. In these sports, the performer consciously works toward achieving a physical form that is aesthetically pleasing, that is beautiful. These kinds of sport performances are typically decided by a judging system, and the judges look for aesthetic qualities in the performance.

The aesthetic qualities evident in **form sports** are harmony, form, dynamics, flow, gracefulness, rhythm, and poise (Lowe, 1977). *Harmony*, for example, refers to the correct relation of parts to a whole, the way in which a sequence of movements brings about a harmonious whole. The instructions in an international gymnastics handbook describe it this way:

> While in all exercises on the apparatus we are always involved with harmony, this concept and evaluation factor will have to be given even greater attention in the floor exercises, where handsprings, Saltos and kips are combined with pauses and gymnastic elements;

> where strength and movement have to follow in a harmonious manner, harmony will play an ever greater role. (Lowe, 1977, p. 176)

It is in form sport that the aesthetic qualities of sport are most easily seen and most often remarked on. Commentators, spectators, and sportswriters often use descriptive aesthetic language when talking or writing about gymnastics, ice dancing, synchronized swimming, and diving.

What is important to remember about form sports is that they are *sports*! The goal of a sport performance is to achieve victory, to strive to do the best you can to win. In other artistic performances, this competition element is less obvious. In form sport, the athlete wants her or his performance to look beautiful in order to gain a position as high as possible in the competition. Does this mean that in sports other than form sports the aesthetic quality is lost? I do not think so.

Aesthetic Quality of Other Sports

The beauty and artistry in figure skating or diving are easily seen, but what beauty can we find in a rugby match, a marathon run, or an ice-hockey game? Of course, games and contests do not have to be beautiful to be enjoyable for spectator and competitor alike. It is common, after a hard-won victory, to hear a coach or player say, "It wasn't pretty, but we got the job done." Nonetheless, both competitors and spectators feel enhanced enjoyment of sport when a good competition also has an aesthetic quality.

In what ways do we experience sport as beautiful? Carlisle (1974) has suggested four types of beauty present in sport:

1. *The beauty of a well-developed body in motion.* The high hurdler, the agile football running back, the field-hockey player winding between defenders, and the slalom skier all show efficient, graceful effort applied to solving a particular performance problem.

2. *The beauty of a brilliant play or a perfectly executed maneuver.* This quality combines the beauty of the physical performance with strong

One kind of aesthetic beauty is seen in form sports such as diving.

competitive intelligence in which decisions are made quickly and then well executed. This happens especially in team sports where all the players on a team move as if in some intricately choreographed series of maneuvers to achieve a competitive outcome. Bill Bradley described that beauty in this way: "In my Knicks days, there was no feeling comparable to the one I got when the teams came together—those nights when five guys moved as one. The moment was one of beautiful isolation, the result of the correct blending of human forces at the proper time and to the exact degree" (Bradley, 1998, p. 21).

3. *The beauty in a dramatic competition.* Sport is most aesthetically appealing when the outcome is uncertain. Competitions that ebb and flow in favor of one team or competitor, then the other, produce a dramatic tension that is among the most attractive of the aesthetic qualities of sport. This quality is experienced more strongly by the spectator who is involved, who roots for one team or the other, than by the more detached observer.

4. *The beauty in the unity of an entire performance.* No doubt, each of us can remember a game or competition that engendered high-level excellence for all competitors, in which the dramatic tension of competition produced a unified experience that is perhaps the ultimate beauty in sport. In outstanding sport events, such beauty is apparent from the outset through to the dramatic conclusion of the game or event.

Sport in which athletes exhibit some or all of these aesthetic qualities helps explain why sport is so popular and has achieved such a central role in culture: "If we wish to show that sport has aesthetic values comparable to those of art, then I think the qualities to be stressed, in the context of opposition, are swiftness, grace, fluency, rhythm, and perceived vitality—the qualities which in various combinations constitute beauty" (Elliot, 1974, p. 112). Despite the efforts of Elliot and others, as in many aspects of sport, the experience of beauty in sport is often better than the explanation.

SPORT ETHICS

Ethics is a branch of the subdiscipline of philosophy termed *axiology*, the study of values. Ethics, or *moral philosophy*, is concerned with how people *ought* to behave, particularly in situations in which there is potential for behaving well or poorly. For many reasons, sport has always been considered an important place in which to learn about ethical or moral behavior. The general term used to discuss and examine ethical behavior in sport is *sportsmanship* although a better, gender-neutral term is *fair play*.

Many people believe deeply that participation in sport builds character and that some of the character traits it develops predispose people toward ethical behavior. Coaches often ascribe this power to sport when they talk at banquets about the developmental experiences that youths get through sport. On the

Rhythmic gymnastics have a high aesthetic quality.

other hand, we do not need to have had much experience in sport, as either a participant or a spectator, to know that players sometimes cheat, that coaches bend rules, that fights occur, and that it is possible for youths to learn unethical behavior through sport experience. How, then, is sport related to ethics, and how is ethics related to sport?

Fair Play and the British Tradition

The concept of **fair play** encompasses how a sportsperson behaves not only during a contest but also before and after it. The notion of fair play means that one plays by the rules, does not take unfair advantage of an opponent even when the opportunity arises, treats the opponent with respect, and shows modesty and composure in both victory and defeat. Although elements of fair play can be seen historically in many sport cultures, it was the aristocratic British sport of the nineteenth century that elevated fair play to a way of life as well as a way of competing in sport.

As we noted in Chapter 3, the philosophy of fair play in nineteenth-century England was termed *Arnoldism* after the popular headmaster of the

Rugby School, an elite secondary school. Thomas Arnold believed that sport should be played fairly and vigorously with opponents always honoring one another, showing both moral character and team spirit.

Because American sport was strongly influenced by British sport, it is not surprising that the philosophy of fair play still permeates sport today, especially sport in schools. This philosophy not only prescribes how one ought to behave within sport but also uses sport as a metaphor for how life should be lived. It is the antithesis of a "win-at-all-costs" approach to sport competition. Within the tradition of fair play, the primary goal of sport is victory within the letter and spirit of the rules, but not victory at any cost.

> Honorable victory is the goal of the athlete, and, as a result, the code of the athlete demands that nothing be done before, during, or after the contest to cheapen or otherwise detract from such a victory. (Keating, 1973, p. 170)

Rules and the Nature of Games

Those who study the ethical nature of sport often focus on rules and how rules are related to the

Competitors are often bonded together in their quest for excellence.

purposes of games. The argument made is that the game is changed when the rules are bent, broken, or misused and, therefore, that it is not possible *really* to win unless the rules are kept:

> The end in poker is not to gain money, nor in golf to simply get a ball into a hole, but to do these things in prescribed (or, perhaps more accurately, not to do them in proscribed) ways: that is, to do them only in accordance with rules. Rules in games thus seem to be in some sense inseparable from ends. . . . If the rules are broken, the original end becomes impossible of attainment, since one cannot (really) win the game unless he plays it, and one cannot (really) play the game unless he obeys the rules of the game. (Suits, 1976, pp. 149–150)

The rule violations referred to in such an analysis are of course those done intentionally. Rules are often broken in games, and referees are there to notice the infractions and to apply the appropriate penalty so that the game may continue. The purpose of the penalty is typically to restore evenness to the contest, to provide for the offended player or team some measure that makes up for what was lost—a free throw in basketball, a loss of yardage in football, or time off the ice in hockey.

Considerable evidence shows that cheating in organized competitive sports is a growing problem (Morgan, 2007). What might be considered cheating ranges from a baseball catcher quickly making a slight movement of the caught pitch back into the strike zone to influence the umpire to call the pitch a strike or an offensive lineman anticipating the snap count to gain the edge on a blocking assignment to the use of performance-enhancing substances by athletes in a growing number of professional sports. Evidence over the past decade has shown that use of performance-enhancing drugs has moved into high-school sports as young athletes seek to gain athletic scholarships to major universities and the adulation and potential income that is earned by the small percentage that make it all the way to professional sport.

THE DEVELOPMENTAL POTENTIAL OF SPORT

Parents, educators, and youth-development specialists want children to become involved in sport programs because they believe that sport experiences make positive contributions to the development of children and adolescents. The developmental expectations include a healthier child due to regular involvement in the physical activity provided in sport programs and the social–psychological benefits of self-confidence, resilience, and capacity to work productively within a peer group, all of which contribute to a growing sense of self-efficacy (Policy Studies Associates, 2006).

The venues for sport as child/youth development include out-of-school community and agency programs that include sport and physical activity in their programs, community sport programs that provide age-group instruction and competition, private-sector programs that provide fee-for-service programs (particularly in sports such as gymnastics and ice hockey), and school physical-education, intramural, and interscholastic sports programs. Most of these programs are inclusive in the sense that all children/youths that want to participate are included, whereas interschool athletic programs are selective.

Most out-of-school programs (such as those administered by the Boys and Girls Clubs of America or local recreation departments) include physical activity and sport as part of their programming. There is substantial evidence that out-of-school programs, either community programs or agency programs, can contribute to child/youth resiliency. Evidence suggests that well-run programs improve school attendance and grades, lower dropout rates, and inspire higher aspirations. Indeed, evidence also shows that many of these programs use sport and physical activity as the "hook" to recruit and retain children and youths in their programs (Policy Studies Associates, 2006).

Does sport build character as so many sport enthusiasts have argued for centuries? Or does sport corrupt character, teaching children and youths how to cheat cleverly and take advantage of rules and opponents? The answer is, Sport teaches! It has the capacity to teach not only positive outcomes but also negative outcomes. Sport, when done well, teaches valuable lessons of perseverance, teamwork, and loyalty. Whether any sport experience is more likely to build character than to corrupt depends on those who plan, administer, and teach in the program.

SUMMARY

1. Sport has been a part of every civilized culture but has been taken seriously by scholars only in recent times—a fact that is surprising, given the amount of money and attention devoted to sport by people of all ages.

2. *Sport* has rituals, costumes, symbolic meaning, a striving for perfection, a system of rules, and a means for enforcing the rules—all the elements of a natural religion. These elements underscore the seriousness with which we should view sport.

3. Sport derives from play—activity that is free, separate, uncertain, economically unproductive, and governed by rules or make-believe. Although sport does not have to be playful, participants enjoy it most when it is.

4. *Play* is an irreducible form of human behavior that provides meaning in life and is thought to be a creative element in culture.

5. Child's play is characterized by spontaneity, exuberance, and gaiety; adult play is typically characterized by practice, training, ritual, skill, and strategy.

6. A *game* is a playful competition where outcomes are determined by combinations of physical skill, strategy, and chance. Games derive from play, and sports can be thought of as games or contests in which skill and strategy predominate.

7. Games are, by definition, competitive; a "noncompetitive game" would be a contradiction in terms.

8. Sport games have *primary rules*, which define the problem to be solved, and *secondary rules*, which give form to the game but can be altered without changing the essence of the game.

9. Sport games can be categorized as invasion games, target games, court games, and sector games.

10. *Competition* has three related meanings. First, it is a festival that provides a forum for contests and carries with it traditions and rituals. Second, it is a striving for competence within the rules of the forum. Third, it is a rivalry for victory.

11. Competition in sport is seldom a zero-sum arrangement in which losers must lose to the extent that winners win.

12. As sport becomes more institutionalized, an increasing number of professional roles develop. The process of institutionalization ranges from local to international.

13. Sport becomes more institutionalized as rules are codified, referees are specially trained, organizations form to manage and administer activities, records are kept formally, and public communication develops through radio, television, newspapers, magazines, books, and videocassettes.

14. Spectating is an important part of institutionalized sport. Sport spectators are among the most knowledgeable and sophisticated spectators for any cultural pastime.

15. Spectators are also often fans who have deep loyalties to teams and who contribute to the total meaning of the sport experience.

16. Sport has aesthetic value and can be viewed as an art form. Form sports, in particular, have high aesthetic value, in that performances are judged by the degree to which they achieve beautiful physical form and motion.

17. There are four types of aesthetic value in sport: the beauty of trained bodies in motion, the beauty of a brilliant play or performance, the dramatic tension produced by competition that is uncertain, and the unity of a well-played game or match.

18. *Sport ethics* is the study of values in sport. It focuses primarily on sportsmanship.

19. The fair-play tradition of British sport involves both how to compete and how to behave before, during, and after the competition.

20. Most of sport ethics focuses on rules and their violation because rules give the sport its form, and violations of them break the contract between opponents to compete fairly.

DISCUSSION QUESTIONS

1. How do important local sport events, such as a high school football game, show the characteristics of sport as a natural religion?

2. Can scholarship and professional athletes still be engaged in play when they are playing their sport? Explain your answer.

3. To what extent does the game-classification system depend on similarities and differences in primary rules?

4. How do views of competition among the general public differ from views among athletes themselves?

5. What kinds of rules and practices should be adopted in school sports to ensure that competition is as good as it can be?

6. What kinds of sport events or performances have you found to be aesthetically pleasing? What about them has caused you to react this way?

7. What personal experiences have you had that highlight controversial issues in sport ethics? How did you and other people involved react?

8. Are extreme sports a passing fancy, or are they here to stay?

9. How would you define cheating in the sports that you play?

CHAPTER 5

Sport Programs and Professions

Sports are the highest products of civilization and the most accessible, lived, experiential sources of the civilizing spirit.

Michael Novak, 1976

LEARNING OBJECTIVES

- To describe the dimensions of the sport culture
- To discuss issues related to leisure time
- To define and provide examples of the different kinds of sport participation
- To analyze youth sport, interscholastic sport, and collegiate sport
- To discuss issues related to coaching in youth, interscholastic, and intercollegiate sport
- To analyze the various ways in which sport is organized and implemented, from youth sport to professional sport
- To describe recent movements that have extended sport participation
- To describe nonparticipant sport vocations

Will historians and anthropologists of the future refer to our times as the "era of sport"? When you look at all the data about sport—data on participation, spending, and so on—you may get that impression. If you look through a listing of television shows for any weekend, you may get that impression. If you go out for a leisurely drive in many areas, seeing the various indoor and outdoor sport spaces and facilities, you may get that impression.

There was a time, not too long ago, when sport was primarily for youths and young adults. Children played, but they did not *do* sport. Older adults watched, but they did not *do* sport. Children now often begin sport participation by the age of 5 or 6. Young swimmers and gymnasts may undergo several years of intense training and competition before they reach puberty. In addition, many sports offer a large and growing number of masters-level or veterans competitions for people over age 40—competition graded in 5-year blocks all the way to age 70 and beyond. Most states now hold summer sport festivals that include competitors from young children to seniors.

How big is sport in our society? Very big! Are we the biggest sport culture in the world? We might be the largest in absolute size, but in relative importance of sport in a culture, you would get a real argument from an Australian, a Brazilian, or a German. Suffice it to say that in America and many developed countries sport has, in the second half of the twentieth century and the early part of the twenty-first, assumed unprecedented economic and cultural importance.

The purpose of this chapter is to describe what kinds of sport are done, who does them, what specialized roles have developed to support the sport culture, and what qualifications are necessary to work in those roles. First, however, we examine the assumption that a growing sport culture must be built on increased leisure time for participating and spectating.

UNTANGLING THE LEISURE MYTHS

The conventional wisdom about the relationship between leisure and work is that modern societies work less and have more leisure than counterparts in ancient societies. The fact is that, except for a relatively brief period during the industrialization of developed countries in the late nineteenth and early twentieth centuries, people in most cultures throughout history had substantially more leisure time than do modern Americans (De Grazia, 1962). The ancient Greeks and Romans, whose cultures shaped many of the practices of Western societies, had as many "festival" days (what we would now call vacation days) as they did workdays. Although our average workweek today is shorter than in the early twentieth century, it is likely longer than in most times during recorded history.

When one examines the availability and use of contemporary leisure time, it becomes clear that statistics that offer the *average* of work and leisure time among Americans and how we use that leisure time are likely to lead to misleading conclusions. The reliance on using averages masks the fact that

leisure time in America is going significantly up for some adults and significantly down for others (Scott, 2000). Thus, studies of the reporting of average time in the workweek have shown divergent results—some reporting longer hours with fewer vacation days (Cordes & Ibrahim, 2003) while others reporting (Robinson, 1997) shorter workweeks and more leisure and vacation days.

There is also the corresponding issue of how Americans use the leisure time they do have. Of particular interest to professionals in sport, fitness, and physical education is the amount of leisure time that is spent in exercise, sport, and recreation activities as opposed to other social pursuits, household activities, shopping, and organizational or civic activities.

CHILD AND YOUTH SPORT

There are many ways that children and youth participate in sport. The categories covered below are (1) informal game and activity participation, (2) out-of-school child and youth sport programs sponsored by local community agencies or recreation departments, (3) fee-for-service, sport-specialization instructional programs, (4) sport-specific, fee-for-service organizations that provide instruction and age-graded competition including "select" teams that travel widely, and (5) interscholastic sport sanctioned by state associations. Each of these will be considered individually.

The National Council on Youth Sports (www .ncys.org), a nonprofit organization representing 163 member organizations dedicated to advancing the values of participation and to developing and educating leaders, estimates that as many as 52 million American youths participate in at least one organized sport (that figure may include interscholastic sport participation), which means that about 65 percent of American children and youths participate in organized sport (Eitzen & Sage, 2003). Estimates are that 58 percent of those participate in agency-sponsored programs, while community-sponsored programs account for 36 percent of the participants, with the remaining 6 percent in private clubs.

Some of the best sport is not formally organized.

Extreme sports, popular with the millennial generation (Gen Y), often involve high-risk maneuvers.

Informal Participation

Many children and adolescents participate in sports that are organized and controlled by the players, what have been traditionally called "pickup games," in backyards, parks, school playgrounds, driveways, and even on streets. Stickball, basketball shooting games, and in-line skating contests would be typical of these activities. Coakley (2007) and his students have observed such activities over a number of years. What they have found is that children and youths who participate in these informal activities create games and competitions that emphasize four features: games that (1) have a lot of action, particularly scoring action; (2) optimize personal involvement; (3) are challenging and exciting, typically through close scores; and (4) allow participants to reaffirm their friendships with fellow competitors. The rules of these games and activities often resemble those of the "parent" game/activity but are modified to make these four features more likely. A primary goal is to keep the activity moving and to sanction actions that tend to disrupt the activity. Not all informal games and contests reflect these values. Sometimes equal participation is not tolerated as older or more skilled players dominate the action within the game/contest to the exclusion of less-skilled participants. There are no national data on the numbers of children and youth that participate in sport informally, although it is fair to speculate that the percentage of children/youth participating informally has gone down dramatically with the growing number of opportunities offered in community, private, and school programs.

Informal participation also includes the activity patterns of the Gen X generation and the current child/youth generation, referred to most often as the "millennial" generation (Gen Y). These activities are most frequently described as extreme sports and have been institutionalized in the X Games (see page 87). Activities such as skateboarding, in-line skating, and snowboarding are activities that no doubt have widespread informal participation. Data on participation rates in these activities are more difficult to capture, but most experts agree that these activities represent a generational change in child/youth activity patterns (Lauer, 2006). Many communities are now trying to provide facilities for some of these, particularly skateboarding.

The North Columbus Athletic Association (NCAC) was formed in 1966 to develop a softball program for children and youths in the neighborhoods of north Columbus, Ohio. In 1973 the NCAC purchased 25 acres of land to construct ball diamonds. In 1974 it added soccer, with 130 boys and girls participating. By the late 1970s, the programs had grown to serve over 2,000 participants. The original land was sold in order to buy a larger tract of 53 acres, which now includes soccer fields, ball diamonds, a concession stand, restrooms, a storage facility, and a shelter house.

The NCAC now has 1,200 children playing soccer on sixty-six recreational and twenty-one select teams each spring and fall. About 900 youths participate in the summer softball and baseball program. They play on twenty-one soccer fields of various sizes and on seventeen permanent ball diamonds. Children as young as age 3 can enroll in instructional activities. As a service to member parents, adult soccer and softball leagues were started in 1997. Fees are kept minimal, and parent volunteers perform much of the upkeep and administration of the organization. Participation and instruction are emphasized in the bulk of the activities, the select teams having more intense involvement and travel. No public monies are involved, but local businesses have been very supportive of the organization.

Out-of-School, Nonprofit Public or Community Sport Programs

Child and youth sport includes all the organized sport activities that take place outside of school under the sponsorship of nonprofit public or community organizations. Many of these begin as neighborhood projects and develop over the years into larger, more organized operations (see Focus On Box 5.1). Other local sport programs are affiliated with national organizations, the largest of which is Little League Baseball. Participation in Pop Warner football has nearly doubled in the last 15 years, from about 130,000 to 260,000 (Hilgers, 2006). Still other programs are developed and sustained through local recreation departments. Boys still represent the largest participant group, but girls' participation has increased markedly over the past two decades and now represents about 40 percent of the participation. Many national service organizations, such as the Optimist and Kiwanis clubs, have traditionally sponsored teams at the local level.

Children are beginning to participate at younger ages. Age-group gymnastics and swimming programs now enroll 3-year olds, and hockey, soccer, football, and T-ball, among others, enroll 4-year olds. Many parents, however, prefer that their children not start at such an early age, preferring that girls and boys begin participation closer to age 10. Dropout rates for youths increase steadily from ages 11 to 18 years, with the percentage of dropouts higher for girls than for boys. A significant factor in understanding this dropout rate is the fact that middle-school and high-school interscholastic sport have "limits" for team membership; that is, only those girls and boys good enough to "make the team" are allowed to participate. This problem is made more complicated by the fact that the increase in the number of boys' teams and girls' teams in most middle and high schools has inadvertently led to the diminution of middle- and high-school intramural sports programs, due to budget and facility constraints.

Fee-for-Service, Sport-Specialization Instructional Programs

Over the past 30 years, the cultural importance of sport has grown markedly. It can be seen in attendance, TV audiences, the importance of interscholastic sports, and the number of sport opportunities for youngsters in most communities. This cultural change has led to an increasing commercialization of sport; that is, entrepreneurs have learned that there is money to be made by offering sport-specific training for young children. Coakley (2007) argues that specialized training for young children is one of the major trends to develop during this period. This is especially true for "individual" sports such as gymnastics, tennis, and figure skating (see www.olympiadgymnastics.org and www.topflightsportscenter.com for two examples). Many of these centers market themselves as an educational and developmental program that aids physical development and socialization with an emphasis on fun. If, indeed, the programs are child friendly and do not expect year-around involvement, they can contribute to child development. If, however, they do involve year-around training in a single sport, they put children at risk.

Another aspect of this large and growing market for sport-specialization instructional programs is the summer sport-camp business. Mysummercamps.com lists 3,893 camps in forty-six sports, ranging from 424 equestrian camps to 2 squash camps. Key high-school sports—such as soccer (304), football (102), and basketball (290)—are among the most popular programs. Camps are either day camps serving boys and girls in a local community or residential camps where participants travel to and stay, typically for one week. Camps often offer other activities besides the primary focus on the sport.

In 2000 the American Academy of Pediatrics studied these issues from a number of different medical and developmental perspectives and published the following summary statement:

> Children involved in sports should be encouraged to participate in a variety of different activities and develop a wide range of skills. Young athletes who specialize in just one sport may be denied the benefits of varied activity while facing additional physical, physiologic, and psychologic demands from intense training and competition. (American Academy of Pediatrics, 2000)

Sport specialization has also become the norm for many high-school athletes. Football players are encouraged to use winter and spring for strength training instead of sport participation. Many parents and their high-school sons or daughters see the possibility of an athletic scholarship to a college or university, so they commit themselves to year-around participation,

with travel to summer camps where their skills can be more fully developed. In Chapter 6, we will address the problems of overuse injuries that often accompany year-around participation.

Sport-Specific, Fee-for-Service Organizations

Specialization in sports for children and youths is also available through local and national organizations. The sports where this is most fully developed are soccer and basketball. In soccer, it is now common for most metropolitan areas to have "clubs" that offer soccer instruction, age-group competition, and "select teams," which travel widely and often train and compete year-around.

Soccer clubs offer youngsters the opportunity to train year-around, coached by women and men with extensive playing and coaching experience in soccer; to participate in local competitions; and to travel widely as members of select teams. An example is the Lonestar Academy Soccer Club in Austin, Texas, that has over 550 players forming sixty-eight different teams to compete locally, regionally, and nationally. The club offers a youth-development program for U8–U10 (Under 8 through Under 10) boys and girls, as well as team membership for the U11–U18 age groups. The club has forty staff members, and all coaches are nationally licensed, with coaching experience at state, regional, and national levels. The club offers "college showcases," where players are showcased to college and university coaches, and has an online system designed to support individual players making themselves available to college recruiters. The club also arranges college visits to "expose the players within the club to the overall experience of playing at the next level" (www.lonestar-sc.com). Parents of club members often travel with their sons or daughters to local, regional, and national competitions. In this respect, the child's development in soccer becomes a focal point for the family and a considerable expense when one considers club fees, uniforms, and travel.

Another Austin, Texas, soccer club offers a somewhat different profile. The Austin United Capital Soccer Club serves nearly 3,000 students in three

Organized sport begins early for many children.

different programs and employs fifteen professional staff members. The Club offers three programs. The "Recreational" program serves 2,040 boys and girls from 4–18 years of age who want to learn soccer and have fun, whatever their skill level. Teams practice twice weekly and play a game on Saturday. Coaches are volunteer adults who must first participate in a coaching course. The "Academy" program serves over 100 boys and girls who qualify in the "preselect" U9 and U10 age groups. This program focuses on advanced technique training, tactical play, and fitness. The "Select" program offers local, regional, and national competition in Premiere, Division 1, Super 2, and Division 2 competitions for girls and boys from the U11 to U18 levels. Girls and boys are placed on teams through a try-out process. The club offers college-placement assistance for girls and boys who want to continue their soccer careers. The club also offers coed adult soccer.

Another example of sport-specific, fee-for-service programs is the girls' and boys' basketball programs sponsored by the Amateur Athletic Union (AAU). This program, built around local AAU clubs, offers basketball competition at the local, regional, and national levels. Competition for girls (www.aaugirlsbasketball.org) is offered for each age level starting with 8-under, then for each age group until 15-under, then junior girls, and open competitions. Competitions for boys (www.aauboysbasketball.org) start with 7-under,

then for each age group until 16-under, and then junior boys followed by senior boys. A smaller basketball is used for all competitions from 7-under to 12-under. Players are "attached" to AAU clubs when they participate in AAU-sanctioned competitions that involve two or more AAU clubs, which simply means that they are not allowed to change clubs. All players must be AAU members.

Funding for AAU basketball differs by club. Some clubs use a yearly/seasonal fee to cover basic costs. Others use separate fees for clinics, team membership, and the costs of participating in tournaments. A key marketing strategy for AAU basketball is "exposure," which means that players who make the teams are guaranteed to play in state and regional tournaments—and national exposure should teams be successful regionally. This exposure is meant to help players gain athletic scholarship to colleges and universities.

Organizations That Support Child and Youth Sport

The Youth Sport Coalition of the National Association for Sport and Physical Education (NASPE) has developed a "Parent's Checklist for Quality Youth Sports Programs" (NASPE, 1995c). The document provides a series of statements to help parents evaluate the developmental and educational benefits likely to accrue from children's and youths' participation in any sport program. The checklist is organized into six areas: philosophy of the program, organization and administration of the program, coach qualifications, parental commitment to child participation, children's readiness to participate, and safety. Each area has ten statements, which a parent can check off. The more statements checked off, the greater is the possibility of a high-quality experience.

A welcome addition to resources for child and youth sport is the Center for Sport Parenting (www.centerforsportsparenting.org), a program developed by the Institute for International Sport. This Web-based initiative offers practical guidance for parents to help their children/youths handle the psychological and physical challenges involved in

---

FOCUS ON — NAYS Standards for Youth Sport 5.2

The National Alliance for Youth Sports has developed a set of standards to guide organizations that sponsor sports programs for children and youth. Each standard has detailed implementation guidelines that together ensure a developmentally appropriate experience for participants.

1. *Proper sports environment.* Implementation guidelines include minimum play rules for all participants regardless of ability, programs organized in 2-year age group, no-cut rules, awards for participation only, and no league standings below age 9.

2. *Programs based on well-being of children.* Implementation guidelines include developmental programs for the 5–6 age group, sports introduction programs for the 7–8 age group, scores kept but standing de-emphasized for the 9–10 age group, and ability grouping for the 11–12 age group. There are weight and skill groupings in all age groups.

3. *Drug-, tobacco-, and alcohol-free environment.* Leagues prohibit use of drugs, tobacco, and alcohol by coaches, administrators, and game officials. Player and parent education programs are available.

4. *Part of a child's life.* Leagues adopt policies that encourage participation in a variety of youth activities, limit practices, and do not demand year-round involvement.

5. *Training.* Parents much insist that all coaches be trained and certified. The organization uses appropriate screening devices for selecting and assigning coaches.

6. *Parents' active role.* Parents are required to attend orientation meeting; teams have to have at least one team–parent meeting during the season; leagues encourage parent–child communication about the sport experience.

7. *Positive role models.* Leagues adopt a conduct code that includes unacceptable behaviors, and they communicate conduct expectations to parents, officials, and coaches.

8. *Parental commitment.* Parents must sign a parental code of ethics to have children participate.

9. *Safe playing situations.* Playing facilities and equipment chosen and inspected for safety, first-aid equipment and plans in place, no participation during unsafe conditions, and coaches required to take CPR and advanced first-aid training.

10. *Equal-play opportunity.* Implementation guidelines include nondiscrimination policy for all players, all youngsters able to play regardless of financial ability to pay fees, co-recreational programs through age 12, and affirmative action coaching-recruitment policy.

11. *Drug-, tobacco-, and alcohol-free adults.* Coaches, game officials, and league administrators refrain from use of these substances at youth sport events and encourage spectators to refrain. Enforcement plan in place for removing coaches, parents, and spectators who are under the influence of alcohol or illegal substances.

---

their sport experience. In March 2008, the center launched a new Web initiative, the Encyclopedia of Sports Parenting Social Network, that allows parents and others to interact online to discuss issues and solve problems. The Center's Web site offers advice from experts in the fields of sport psychology, health, nutrition, and sports medicine. The Center's main publication, *The Encyclopedia of Sports Parenting*, is sold in bookstores and online.

The nonprofit National Alliance for Youth Sport (NAYS; www.nays.org) offers programs and services for organizations that sponsor youth sports, including administrators, parents, volunteer coaches, and volunteer officials. NAYS has also developed a comprehensive set of standards to guide child/youth sport programs (see Focus On Box 5.2). Each standard is further defined by implementation guidelines. NAYS programs are offered through state park and recreation associations, national organizations such as YMCAs and CYOs, and community associations.

The NASPE Youth Sport Coalition has created a "Bill of Rights for Young Athletes" (NASPE, 1999), which are meant to apply to all sport and physical-activity programs that involve children and youth. These include the right to

- Participate in sports.
- Participate at a level commensurate with each child's maturity and ability.
- Qualified adult leadership.
- Play as a child and not as an adult.
- Share in the leadership and decision making.
- Participate in safe and healthy environments.
- Proper preparation for participation in sports.
- Be treated with dignity.
- Have fun in sports.

The question that sport educators must ask of themselves is, What kind of child/youth sport program will reflect those characteristics? As you look back on your early sport experiences, how many of the proposed "rights" were represented in the programs in which you took part? Which of the rights were most likely to be violated?

Coaching for Child and Youth Sport

There are probably as many as 7.5 million youth sport coaches in North America, the vast majority of whom have had no formal instruction in the educational, developmental, and health aspects of coaching children and youth (Eitzen & Sage, 2003). A half-million more can be described as paid or professional coaches, typically working in fee-for-service sport clubs focused primarily on the development of elite athletes. In some sports, there are now *sport academies* where youngsters can get top-level coaching and be with other young elite athletes as they live, train, compete, and go to school together. Many volunteer coaches played sports when they were younger, and many of them also watch a great deal of sport on television and in

Coaches are fundamental to success in all sports.

person, but that, of course, does not equip them with current knowledge from the fields of sport pedagogy, sport medicine, or sport psychology that would be useful in working with children and adolescents.

Child and youth sport programs are constantly changing, but as Coakley (2007) argues, the changes are too often functionalist in nature. Adults trying to "improve" child and youth sport programs typically focus on increasing the skill of the young athletes and making the organization more efficient. Although the typical changes that focus on training programs for coaches and regulating the behavior of parents and spectators are appropriate, these changes do not often enough include efforts to help coaches and parents make the experience more fun and meaningful for the youngsters.

Again, the situation for coaching is different in nations where the government has played a stronger role in developing and administering child and youth sport. Canada, Great Britain, New Zealand, Australia, and other nations have developed coach-education programs with different levels of training necessary for positions at different levels of competition—from a beginning level, necessary to work with local children's teams, to the highest level, necessary to coach a state or national team. The coach-education materials are often developed in conjunction with national sport

Coaching in specialized age-group sports is typically done with smaller classes and better equipment.

organizations and delivered through local recreation agencies. For example, a national volleyball organization might develop beginning coaching materials for volleyball, and local recreation agencies would use those materials to prepare volunteer coaches for youth volleyball.

The nonprofit NAYS includes as one of its main programs the National Youth Sport Coaches Association (NYSCA), which has trained over 1.2 million coaches since its inception in 1981. Its program is offered through state offices and local/regional chapters. The program focuses on developmental and safety considerations, physiological and psychological concerns, and sport-coaching techniques. Participants must pass an exam on the materials they have covered and sign a pledge

that they will uphold the association's code of ethics. Focus Box On 5.3 describes NAYS in more detail.

INTERSCHOLASTIC SPORT

The U.S. Constitution specifically designates education as a *state* function. Therefore, interscholastic sport is organized and regulated at the state level. Although the organization of school sport differs somewhat from state to state, the similarities in governance and structure far outnumber the differences. Interscholastic sport occupies a place in the American sport culture that is unlike that in any other nation.

The National Federation of State High School Associations (NFSHSA) is the national service and administrative organization for state high-school athletic associations. The mission of NFSHSA is to serve its fifty state associations members by providing leadership for and national coordination of the administration of high-school sport in ways that improve the educational experiences and reduce the risks associated with sport participation. NFSHSA publishes rules for sixteen sports competed in high schools, serving 18,500 high schools and more than 11 million students. Among its many service programs, NFSHSA regularly compiles data on participation in interscholastic sport throughout the nation (see Focus On Box 5.4).

During the 2006–07 school year, 7,342,910 boys and girls competed in more than forty-five different sports, compared to the first NFSHSA survey in 1971–72 when 3,960,932 boys and girls competed. It is fair to say that as a percentage of high-school enrollment sport participation has increased steadily over the past 30 years. The initial survey showed that girls' participation was 7 percent of the overall participation, while the most recent survey showed that girls' participation had reached 41 percent of the overall participation. The change in girls' participation was rapid after Title IX became law in 1972. If one discounts the more than 1.1 million boys participating in football, where

---

FOCUS ON   National Alliance for Youth Sports   **5.3**

Founded in 1981, NAYS sponsors nine programs that educate volunteer coaches, parents, youth sport program administrators, and officials about their roles and responsibilities in youth sports. NAYS programs are provided at the local level through partnerships with community-based organizations.

- The National Youth Sport Coaches Association trains volunteer coaches.
- The National Youth Sports Officials Association trains volunteer youth sport officials.
- The Academy for Youth Sport Administrators offers a 20-hour program to earn the Certified Youth Sports Administrator credential.
- The National Clearinghouse for Youth Sports Information provides the public with access

to a variety of materials pertaining to youth sports.

- Parents Association for Youth Sports provides materials and information to make parents aware of their roles and responsibilities in youth sports.
- Child Abuse and Youth Sports provides a comprehensive risk-management approach to building a protective shield around participants and programs.
- Hook a Kid on Golf™ helps communities develop comprehensive youth golf programs.
- Start Smart brings parents and children ages 3 years and over together in an instructional program that helps parents learn how to teach their children.
- Kids on Target is a team-oriented program for archery for youngsters ages 10–14.

SOURCE: www.nays.org.

---

team membership often includes forty to sixty players, the participation of girls is nearly equal that of boys. It should be noted that some students participated in more than one sport and are thus double- or triple-counted although the percentage of multisport athletes has likely subsided due to young athletes tending to specialize in one sport and training for that sport during the off-season.

The top-ten sports, in terms of number of participants, have remained stable over the past decade (see Focus On Box 5.4). Volleyball has increased steadily as a sport for girls but does not come close to making the top ten for boys. Soccer continues to grow as a favored sport by both girls and boys. The number of boys participating in football is nearly twice that of any other sport.

Organization of Interschool Sport

Most states have adopted a system of competition in which the number of students in a school determines the classification within which the school competes

(AAA, AA, and A; A, B, C, and D; or V, IV, III, II, and I). **Interscholastic sport** is typically governed by a state organization, which in many states is *not* a government agency but, rather, a private corporation that schools join. For example, the Ohio High School Athletic Association (OHSAA) is a private organization to which Ohio high schools belong by virtue of paid membership. The OHSAA organizes and administers sports for the high schools that belong to the organization, including establishing rules for participation, length of season, starting times for practice and conducting regional, district, and state championships in a variety of sports.

The financing of interscholastic sport also differs from state to state. In some states, interscholastic sport is considered a regular part of the educational program and is funded directly from tax revenues through regular school budgets. In other states, however, laws limit the amount of regularly budgeted tax funds that may be spent on extracurricular activities. Interscholastic sport, as an extracurricular activity, then has partially to pay for itself through gate

FOCUS ON Most Popular Interscholastic Sports 5.4

Ten Most Popular Boys' Programs

Schools		Participants	
1. Basketball	17,762	1. Football—11-player	1,104,548
2. Track and field—outdoor	15,709	2. Basketball	556,269
3. Baseball	15,458	3. Track and field—outdoor	544,180
4. Football—11-player	13,922	4. Baseball	477,430
5. Golf	13,541	5. Soccer	377,999
6. Cross-country	13,354	6. Wrestling	257,246
7. Soccer	11,066	7. Cross-country	216,085
8. Wrestling	9,445	8. Golf	159,747
9. Tennis	9,438	9. Tennis	156,944
10. Swimming and diving	6,358	10. Swimming and diving	106,738

Ten Most Popular Girls' Programs

Schools		Participants	
1. Basketball	17,458	1. Basketball	456,967
2. Track and field—outdoor	15,578	2. Track and field—outdoor	444,181
3. Softball—fast pitch	14,968	3. Volleyball	405,832
4. Volleyball	14,881	4. Softball—fast pitch	373,448
5. Cross-country	13,146	5. Soccer	337,632
6. Soccer	10,503	6. Cross-country	183,376
7. Tennis	9,678	7. Tennis	176,696
8. Golf	9,046	8. Swimming and diving	143,639
9. Swimming and diving	6,708	9. Competitive spirit squads	95,177
10. Competitive spirit squads	3,743	10. Golf	66,283

SOURCE: National Federation of State High School Associations, 2006–07, "Athletics Participation Study" (www.nfhs.org).

receipts and through fund-raising. It is in the latter area that high-school booster clubs have developed; such clubs often provide substantial financial support for athletic departments.

Many school districts suffering from budget shortfalls have recently instituted pay-to-play plans, which require a fee to be paid, typically by parents, for girls or boys to be on a sports team. Fees for varsity sports are typically more than for junior varsity or middle-school sports. This method of financing school sport has drawn national attention with the general concern that the impact will fall greatest on those least able to pay, therefore denying students the right to participate in a school-sponsored activity. This issue is described more specifically in the following paragraph and will be considered again in Chapter 6.

The Palo Alto (California) High School Boosters provides an example of the degree to which booster clubs become important to interscholastic sport programs (www.palysports.com). This booster club had been supporting the Palo Alto High School teams for many years, but in recent years as funding within the school district withered, the boosters assumed a more central role to the funding of the high-school program, now paying for 100 percent of the noncoaching costs of the program, including transportation, officials, uniforms, equipment, janitorial expenses, tournament fees, and awards. Nearly 40 percent of the high-school students participate in the sports program.

Participation fees paid by parents, what are typically referred to as "pay-to-play fees," are between $150–200, covering about 80 percent of the program expenses. Although the fees are not mandatory, families must address the fee in some way—that is, through partial payment, during the season. The remainder of the budget is paid through fund-raising of various kinds, including running the concessions at contests and selling clothing with school logos.

School Coaches

The number of coaches required to staff the nearly 200,000 interscholastic sport teams in America each year is substantial (DeRenne, Morgan, Hetzler, & Taura, 2007). Since the enactment of Title IX, as girl participant numbers have increased each year, the need for coaches has increased significantly. In some sports, it is not unusual to have assistant coaches. Most high schools have varsity and reserve teams, but larger high schools might have separate freshman, reserve, and varsity teams. We have also seen a consistent increase in the number of sports offered in interscholastic programs, with the NFSHSA now tracking participation in thirty-nine sports.

In the early 1960s, because there were fewer sports and girls' participation was severely limited, fewer coaches were needed. Nearly all of those coaches were certified teachers, and many of them were trained physical-education teachers. Another confounding issue is that many certified teachers do not have the time to coach, the result of the strong national focus on the improvement of school performance, which began during the *Sputnik* era and continues today with the legislation we know as No Child Left Behind. Thus, many high-school coaches are not certified teachers, and most of them have no specific preparation for coaching except their own experience participating in sports. As the number of sports and the number of participants have increased, there has been a consistent effort to address the issues surrounding the qualifications of coaches. The increase, however, has been so steady that many states have found it difficult to pass legislation requiring qualifications for hiring coaches or coaching-education requirements once hired. Remember that our federal constitution leaves the governance of education to the states, so the approach to establishing and applying standards or minimum requirements for coaching in school sport differs greatly from state to state.

In the early 1960s, the lack of educational requirements for coaching began to generate concern nationally, particularly among educational associations. The National Association for Sport and Physical Education (NASPE) was among the early leaders in this movement, partnering with various national associations to address issues related to hiring qualifications and advocating for coaching-education programs. In the early 1970s, Rainer Martens, a sport psychologist and physical-education professor, influenced by his research and the pioneering work of the Coaching Association of Canada, founded the American Coaching Effectiveness Program, which later expanded into the American Sport Education Program (ASEP) (www.asep.com). By 1981 the first ASEP courses in coaching philosophy and the basics of sport science were available through Human Kinetics. By 1986 ASEP had 1,400 certified instructors who had trained over 50,000 coaches. In 1990 the NFSHSA partnered with ASEP to offer Coaching Principles and Sport First Aid courses to high-school coaches. Gradually, ASEP expanded its coaching curriculum and began to offer courses online. ASEP now offers a Volunteer Education Program for beginning coaches

The national governing bodies (NGBs) of most Olympic sports have developed their own coaching-education programs. Many of them use ASEP or a similar entry-level program as the beginning program but then advance to levels of accreditation that are more specific to the sport sponsored by the NGB. The program below is for USA Volleyball.

USA Volleyball Coaching Accreditation Program (CAP)

- Level 1: ASEP Coaching Principles, skills, games, drills, basic systems, and practice management. Candidate must pass test and sign coaching code of ethics statement.
- Level 2: Team systems, blocking and setting development, problem solving, and social issues.

SOURCE: www.usavolleyball.org.

Candidate must attend or instruct one non-CAP volleyball clinic.

- Level 3: Instruction from peer coaches, critical thinking, outreach project.
- Level 4: Mentor with Cadre or National Team for 1 week. Candidate must complete three experiences from four categories of higher-level coaching and develop a publishable manuscript.
- Level 5: All current and previous national team coaches are considered honorary Level 5.

Accreditation at most levels lasts for 4 years, during which time the candidate must advance to the next level or complete an accreditation-renewal course.

---

of athletes 13 years of age and younger, plus courses for parents, officials, and sport administrators. ASEP's Professional Education Program consists of Bronze, Silver, and Gold levels. The Bronze level, for coaches of athletes 14 years of age and over, consists of a three-course program, which includes Coaching Principles, Sport First Aid, and Coaching (Sport) Technical and Tactical Skills. The Silver and Gold levels will cater to the more-specialized interests of coaches and are now in preparation.

A second coaching-education program that has made important contributions is the Program for Athletic Coaches Education (PACE), developed at the Institute for the Study of Youth Sports at Michigan State University (Seefeldt & Milligan, 1992). PACE is typically delivered without state organizations or universities, with materials that include a coach's guide and DVDs that simulate situations related to coaching. The NFSHSA has recently severed its relationship with ASEP and launched its own program, which includes a Fundamentals of Coaching and First Aid for Coaches

courses (NFSHSA, 2007). Twenty-four state athletic associations have so far adopted these courses. As with most coaching-education programs, these courses are offered online.

There is now a proliferation of coaching-education programs offered by a range of providers including universities and national sport-specific associations (see Focus On Box 5.5). It has been helpful to these organizations to have access to widely accepted standards that define broadly what the content of coaching-education programs should contain. The standards developed by the National Association for Youth Sports (see Focus On Box 5.2, page 104) focus primarily on age-group sports offered through community and agency programs while the NASPE's *National Standards for Sport Coaches* focuses primarily on interscholastic sports. These standards are helpful in defining the content that should be part of coaching-education programs.

Many state associations have either strongly suggested or made mandatory that coaches complete minimal coaching-education courses in order to

---

FOCUS ON   Maine's *Sports Done Right* Initiative   **5.6**

Funded by a federal Department of Education initiative and endorsed by Maine's governor and commissioner of education, the *Sports Done Right* initiative has provided a state model that has attracted the interest of more than thirty states.

As young athletes increasingly express concerns about unruly fans, overbearing coaches, and undue pressures to perform, the Maine initiative instills core principles and supporting practices to guide youth sport and school sport experiences. The initiative aims to increase opportunities for positive learning through sports, promote fair play over a win-at-all-costs ethic, and hold parents and community members to higher standards and behavior.

The initiative's important report, "Sports Done Right: A Call to Action on Behalf of Maine's Student Athletes," is serving as a model for other states to develop similar programs.

SOURCE: *Education Week*, August 10, 2005.

FOCUS ON   Montana's Innovative Coach Education Program   **5.7**

Montana is a rural state with 190 school athletic programs divided into AA, A, B, and C classes. The A schools have a student enrollment of over 900; the C schools enroll fewer than 129 students. The Montana High School Athletic Association (MHSAA) faced a severe logistical problem with schools so widely dispersed across the large, thinly populated state. Its approach to coaching education had to address delivery of up-to-date information in an economical and user-friendly format.

Under the leadership of Craig Stewart of Montana State University, the staff of MHSAA developed an online coaching-education curriculum and assessment program. Using the coaching standards developed by NASPE as a starting point, MHSAA engaged athletic directors across the state to rank its program's priorities in the seven domains identified by NASPE. An additional domain, "coaching the female athlete," was added.

The curriculum materials and online assessments for the eight domains were developed and piloted. MHSAA made the coaching-education process mandatory by the end of the 2002 school year. Coach candidates get a password to access the materials and assessments involved. Coaches can register for university course credit as part of the process. About 2,000 to 3,000 coaches a year complete all eight exams.

---

be hired or to retain their roles in school sport programs. In some states, legislation has been passed to require coaching education. Typical is the recent Coaching Education and Steriod/Performance-Enhancing Supplements bylaws passed by the California Interscholastic Federation (CIF), the governing body for interschool sport in that state. The new bylaw requires that by December 31, 2008, all coaches will be certified in the CIF Coaching Education program or its equivalent. The CIF program requirements can be met by completing either the NFSHSA Fundamentals of Coaching course or the ASEP Coaching Principles course; both are offered online or can be completed in local courses taught by certified CIF Coaching Education Instructors (for two other approaches see the Focus On Box 5.6 and Focus On Box 5.7).

Some universities offer coaching-education programs. West Virginia University offers an Athletic Coaching Education (ACE) in both bachelor's and master's degree programs. The ACE program is built on the eight domains of the NASPE's *National Standards for Sport Coaches*. The U.S. Sports Academy offers both certification programs and diploma programs in a variety of sports-related professions. Sport coaching is offered in continuing education, certification, and diploma programs.

The number of women coaching interscholastic sports teams has declined dramatically since its high-water mark just after Title IX was passed into law in 1972 (Pastore, 1994; Sisley & Capel, 1986). Several states have developed experimental programs to attract, train, and retain women in school coaching positions (Hasbrook, 1987; Schafer, 1987), but the shortage continues. A 1998 study in Ohio found that 33 percent of girls' teams had female head coaches, but a 1994 Illinois study found that only 25 percent of girls' teams had female coaches (Pastore, 1994).

The National Council for Accreditation of Coaching Education (NCACE) was established in 2000 to ensure that coaching-education programs are of high quality and to encourage continuous improvement of coaching education. The NCACE uses NASPE's *National Standard for Sport Coaches* to review programs that seek accreditation, requiring that programs comply adequately with the standards defined in the eight domains of the NASPE standards.

In 1994 a national summit on coaching standards was convened by NASPE. LeRoy Walker, then president of the U.S. Olympic Committee, opened the summit by stating that "it is time to move the idea of national coaching standards 'off the back burner.' We need a framework that will guarantee us that there is at least a minimum level of competence among these coaches who are affecting the lives of our young people" (*NASPE*, 1994, p. 1).

These national standards now exist. In 1995 NASPE introduced the thirty-seven standards grouped under eight domains. In 2006 NASPE gathered experts from various national governing bodies of sport (for example, U.S. Olympic Committee and NFSHSA) to review and revise the standards, with the new standards published in 2007. The forty new standards are grouped under eight domains:

- Philosophy and ethics
- Safety and injury prevention
- Physical conditioning

- Growth and development
- Teaching and communication
- Sports skills and tactics
- Organization and administration
- Evaluation

The standards are not meant to be a certification program but can be used by (1) coaching educators to develop targeted coaching-education programs and (2) sport administrators to develop evaluation protocols for the coaches in their programs.

The NCACE held its first meeting in the summer of 2000. The organization was formed by a variety of people interested in standardizing and improving coaching education at various levels. NCACE includes single-sport and multisport organizations, sport sciences and sport pedagogy organizations, and colleges and universities concerned about the availability of well-trained coaches at all levels of sport (NASPE, Spring 2001b). NCACE supports, facilitates the development of, and provides accreditation for coaching-education programs. It also offers workshops that address the eight domains of the *National Standards for Athletic Coaches* (NASPE, 1995). The 2008 National Coaching Educators Conference was held in Park City, Utah. The NCACE continues to provide accreditation services for college and university coaching-education programs as well as for coaching programs sponsored by national and state sport-specific organizations.

COLLEGIATE SPORT PROGRAMS

Intercollegiate Sport

In the post–World War II era, when America became a major sport culture in the world, a significant factor in the overall development of sport was the substantial growth in intercollegiate sport. To be sure, America had a significant history in intercollegiate sport dating to the late nineteenth century when student interest and pressure became so strong

Football grows in popularity at all levels.

that universities began to incorporate sport into their programs (see Chapter 2). Major intercollegiate rivalries had for years captured the interest of the entire nation—the Army–Notre Dame football game, for example. Between 1945 and 1960, intercollegiate sport still grew enormously in importance. It became more important as entertainment, more important economically, and more important on campus. The United States is still the only country in the world where sport and college or university education have become so completely linked.

Most colleges and universities offer extensive sport programs to their students. The advent of Title IX provided the impetus for the phenomenal growth of intercollegiate sport for women in the 1970s. Many colleges and universities have joined with similar institutions in their region to form athletic conferences—the Big Ten, the Western Athletic Conference, and the Michigan Intercollegiate Athletic Association, for example. These athletic conferences govern issues such as eligibility and organize competition for the member institutions, including championships.

Nationally, college and university sport is governed by individual institutional membership in private organizations. The two organizations that dominate the governance of intercollegiate sport are the National Collegiate Athletic Association (NCAA) and the National Association of Intercollegiate Athletes (NAIA). As with child and youth sport, state and federal government have not become involved in the administration of college and university sport in America.

The NCAA has three main divisions, based on level of competition and rules regarding financial aid to athletes. Focus On Box 5.8 shows the number of member institutions in each division and the participation rates for female and male athletes. Division I is subdivided into three divisions, again based on level of competition and rules for financial aid, but pertaining almost exclusively to football. Division I-A has 117 members, I-AA 118 members, and I-AAA 91 members. Division III is often referred to as the "college" division and is defined by not allowing athletic scholarships rather than by size of school. Indeed, some universities in Division III actually have larger enrollments than some in Division I.

The NCAA conducts yearly championships in each division—nineteen in women's sports and

FOCUS ON	NCAA Sport Participation by Division, 2005–06			5.8

Division	Men	Women	Total
I	86,600	70,437	157,037
II	50,463	34,469	84,932
III	87,863	63,677	151,540
Overall	224,926	168,583	393,509

SOURCE: www.ncaa.org.

twenty in men's sports. Nearly 100 athletic conferences are voting members of the NCAA, a major benefit of which is that conference champions automatically qualify for NCAA championship play.

In 1997 the NCAA completed a significant restructuring of its governance system. The restructuring gives each division greater autonomy and allows for more control over sport programs by the chief executive officers of the member schools, who are typically the presidents of the colleges and universities. An annual convention is held, at which all NCAA business is conducted. Each school and conference member has one vote on all issues before the convention.

In 2008 Title IX reached its thirty-sixth year. Female participation in high-school sports has increased by nearly 900 percent, but male athletes still receive 1.1 million more participation opportunities. Only three of the fifty-one directors of state high-school athletic associations are female. While women are 53 percent of the study body in Division I colleges, they represent only 41 percent of the athletes, 32 percent of the recruiting funds, and 36 percent of the overall operating budget (NAGWS, 2007). Women hold only 16.9 percent of the athletic director positions in higher education, only 12.3 percent of the sports information director positions, and 27.8 percent of the athletic trainer positions (Women's Sports Foundation, 2007). Nothing in Title IX requires colleges and universities to cut men's teams; indeed, a 2001 General Accounting Office study found that 72 percent of those colleges and universities that added women's teams did so without cutting any men's teams (NAGWS, 2007).

In terms of significant leadership positions, Richard Lapchick (2006), director of the Institute for Diversity and Equity in Sports, argues that Division I-A sports leadership is an "old-boys" network. Of the 119 presidents of the Division I-A institutions, 97 (94.1 percent) are white men. Of the 119 athletic directors, 101 (84.9 percent) are white men (8 are white women). The commissioners of all eleven conferences whose teams compete in Division I-A are white men. Only 5 of the 119 Division I-A football teams are coached by black men, in contrast to the 49 percent of the Division I-A football players who are black.

The NAIA, which was formed in 1940, has nearly 300 institutional members. It organizes championships for thirteen sports in Divisions I and II. NAIA membership is divided into fourteen regions serving North American colleges and universities. Thirty athletic conferences have official affiliation with the NAIA. NAIA institutions are typically smaller colleges and universities. Although they do not attract the national attention that the NCAA does, they do provide organized intercollegiate sports competition for a large number of women and men.

Many people work professionally within intercollegiate sport—coaches, assistant coaches, athletic directors, sport information directors, sport business managers, sport trainers, sport-medicine experts. Only in the medical area—trainers and physicians—are there any specific certification requirements that define entrance into those professional roles.

Coaching today relies heavily on technology.

College Recreational Intramural Programs

In addition to intercollegiate sport, college and university programs of recreation and intramural sports have grown tremendously in the recent past. Many institutions, seeking to attract and retain students, have built new recreation facilities that have all the amenities of upscale private health and fitness clubs. Programs include all the traditional sport competitions, yearly membership sport clubs, special events (weekend three-on-three basketball tournaments, for example), regularly scheduled fitness and aerobics classes, and drop-in activity for both sport and fitness. Weight-training rooms are typically crowded from early morning until late at night. Pools are filled with recreational and fitness-oriented swimmers.

Many of these programs offer additional opportunities for faculty and for the families of students, staff, and faculty. Recently, recreation and intramural departments have entered the lucrative business of offering summer-camp programs for youths. Recreation and intramural departments are typically staffed by trained professionals and have development programs for student employees. Programs are funded through some combination of subsidies from the university, direct student fees, user fees, and facility rentals (Noyes, 1996).

PROFESSIONAL SPORT

A main purpose of professional sport is to make money—professional sport is a business. The number of players involved in professional sport is remarkably small. The number of players in the NBA is only 250 to 300, whereas the number of boys competing in high-school basketball in a given year is typically greater than 550,000. More than 400,000 girls participate in high-school volleyball, but only a few compete in the Women's Professional Volleyball League. Looking at the figures from a different perspective, we can see that the odds for becoming a professional athlete are not good! There are about 3,000 professional athletes in the three major American professional sports for men—baseball, basketball, and football. Yet there are more than 110 million males in the country, which means that 1 out of every 42,000 makes it to the professional level. The number of players that can earn a good living from other sports is even less—the tennis player or golfer ranked as 250 is not getting rich from sport.

It seems as though, every day, we read on the sports page about an athlete who has signed a lucrative professional contract. We must remember, however, that the wealth in professional sport is distributed unevenly among the athletes. A few make the headline money; the more typical athlete makes considerably less. It is also important to understand that being a professional athlete seldom amounts to having a career. Although a few athletes remain in their sport for 10 to 20 years, the average length of stay is much shorter: 4.3 years for football, 4.2 years for basketball, 6.5 years for baseball, and 4.8 years for hockey.

Although professional sport is not a realistic goal for most young men and women who compete in child, youth, interscholastic, and collegiate sport, the emergence of professional sport (and big-time intercollegiate sport) has been accompanied by the development of nonparticipant sport professions, many of which are reviewed in the final section of this chapter. Suffice it to say that an NBA team, with its eleven or twelve players, also has three coaches, at least one trainer, a general manager, and a publicity or promotion director, as well as assistant managerial and promotional staff. That is, the number of nonparticipant professionals is equal to or greater than the number of participants!

Professional sport is organized and regulated through its parent organizations: NBA, NFL, LPGA (Ladies Professional Golfers Association), National Hockey League (NHL), and so on. Most sports have commissioners who oversee the establishment and governance of standards and rules within the sport. Remember, however, that professional sport is a business. *Owners* exert the most influence on the governance of the sport, typically through an owners' council.

There are no formal qualifications for entrance into professional sport in most participant and nonparticipant roles. Concepts such as certification and training of personnel, which are so important to the future of youth and school sport, are not issues at the professional level.

In the early 1990s, in response to media criticism, many professional sports began to develop specific recruitment and development programs to increase the number of minority persons in coaching/managing roles and in administrative roles. It appears that some professional sports have had beginning success in attracting minority candidates to both positions. In the NBA, 59 percent of the head coaches are black, and 30 percent hold general manager positions. In Major League Baseball, 30 percent of the managers are black or Latino, but only 6 percent hold high-level management positions (Lapchick, 2005). It seems clear that development programs are

needed at the interscholastic and collegiate level to encourage minority women and men, who might be interested in administrative roles, to pursue such roles and to assist them through support efforts that help them to succeed.

ORGANIZED RECREATIONAL SPORT

The scope of organized recreational sport in the United States is enormous. By *organized*, I mean that a regular competition is organized and governed by a sponsoring agency, records are kept, and officials are provided to ensure appropriate play. Most organized recreational sport in the United States is sponsored by community recreation departments; businesses or industries; service clubs, such as the Kiwanis or Rotary; and private community organizations, typically started and maintained by interested parents.

The range of sport involvement at this level is as broad as sport itself—golf leagues, road races, fishing tournaments, baseball leagues, tennis tournaments, horseshoe leagues, and the like. We would also expect to find some major regional differences in organized recreational sport participation—curling in the Dakotas, surfing in southern California, cross-country skiing in New England. The major involvement in organized recreational sport, however, has been and continues to be in the dominant sports of basketball, touch football, volleyball, soccer, and, most of all, softball.

Here is a breakdown of the participation figures for the City of Columbus, Ohio, Parks and Recreation Department sports program in a recent year:

Softball	195 leagues	1,621 teams	29,000 players
Basketball	38 leagues	308 teams	4,600 players
Volleyball	38 leagues	376 teams	4,500 players
Football	7 leagues	68 teams	1,300 players
Soccer	4 leagues	32 teams	500 players

In all there were 12,177 games played in these various leagues, with 7,806 umpires, referees, and scorekeepers employed. There were of course similar kinds of programs in the many suburbs surrounding the city and active programs in the other cities, suburbs, and towns in the state—and all across the nation. This level of participation makes a mockery of accusations that we are a nation of spectators.

Different kinds of sporting interests are accommodated in organized recreation programs because the programs are most often sensitive to the needs and interests of those they serve. In the softball program in Columbus, Ohio, there are slow-pitch leagues for men, slow-pitch leagues for women, fast-pitch leagues for men, fast-pitch leagues for women, and *co-rec leagues*, where men and women compete together. These differentiations allow people to participate in a way that is most challenging and enjoyable to them. Some participate primarily as a *social* experience; others participate primarily as a *competitive* experience.

Similar kinds of organized recreational-sport programs are implemented in most colleges and universities. Students can participate in a wide variety of sport activities throughout the school year. As with community programs, college and university programs frequently offer men's, women's, and co-rec competition.

Sport for People With Disabilities

One of the best features of recent sport history is the degree to which the benefits of sport participation have begun to be extended to people who historically have had difficulty finding ways to be involved in sport. I have mentioned many times the Title IX federal legislation, which opened the door to more equal opportunity in sport for girls and women. The next section considers the role of sport among older age groups. This section reviews sport opportunities for people with disabilities.

Should a physical or mental disability prohibit someone from participating in meaningful sport competition? No! Has it historically? Yes. Before World War II, there was virtually no opportunity for competitive sport participation for athletes with physical or mental disabilities (DePauw, 1984).

Since then, we have made major progress. That progress is associated with three specific pieces of federal legislation:

1. Public Law 93-112 (Rehabilitation Act—1973) specified that equal opportunity and access, including physical education, intramurals, and athletics, must be provided for people with disabilities.
2. Public Law 94-142 (Education for All Handicapped Children Act—1975) required a free and appropriate public education, including instruction in physical education, in the least restrictive environment possible, for children with disabilities.
3. Public Law 95-606 (Amateur Sports Act—1978) specifically included people with disabilities within the province of the law.
4. Public Law 105-117 (Individuals with Disabilities Education Act—1997) restructured the Individuals with Disabilities Education Act (IDEA) to become the primary law guiding treatment of children and youth with disabilities in schools, including a requirement that they must have access to the general education curriculum.

Support for persons with disabilities (a term more appropriate than the earlier term, *handicapped*) has extended to concerns about their recreational and sport involvement. The more than 500 million persons with disabilities around the world represent approximately 10 percent of the human population (www.paralympic.org). More than 54 million of these individuals are Americans. Sport opportunities for persons with disabilities have broadened considerably over the past 20 years, from local recreation to adapted physical education in schools, to interscholastic sport, and to national and international competitions.

While adapted physical education is now a regular part of school programs that serve students with disabilities (see Chapter 10), participation by students with disabilities in interscholastic sports is developing only slowly. In 1992 Minnesota State

Association became the first to sponsor adapted athletics for students with disabilities (Matter, Nash, & Frogley, 2002). Regular and postseason competitions are organized in adapted floor hockey, adapted soccer, and adapted softball. These students are eligible for athletic letters, letter jackets, and membership in school athletic clubs. Georgia has also been proactive in providing for adapted interschool sport competitions (American Association of Adapted Sports, 2008). Starting in 2001, the Georgia High School Association worked with the nonprofit American Association of Adapted Sports Programs (AAASP) to better provide for the interscholastic sports experiences for students with disabilities. Hundreds of participants now compete in six sports—wheelchair soccer, wheelchair basketball, power hockey, wheelchair football, track and field, and beep baseball. There

is a formal season in each sport, culminating with a state championship competition. The Alabama High School Athletic Association has recently partnered with AAASP to create and implement an interscholastic sports program for students with disabilities in their state. Legislation in New Jersey has recently required the New Jersey State Athletic Association to partner with AAASP to establish an interscholastic sports program for students with disabilities.

The many organizations that support sport for persons with disabilities are shown in Focus On Box 5.9. The development and spread of sport for persons with disabilities not only have expanded the opportunities for a fuller life for the participants but also have served as a source of inspiration and motivation for countless others.

FOCUS ON Sport Organizations for People With Disabilities   **5.9**

Alliance for Disability Sport and Recreation

American Athletic Association for the Deaf

American Blind Bowling Association

American Wheelchair Bowling Association

American Wheelchair Pilots Association

Amputee Sports Association

Blind Outdoor Leisure Association

Braille Sports Foundation

Cerebral Palsy International Sports and Recreation Association

Disabled Sportsmen of America

Disabled Sports USA

Dwarf Athletic Association of America

Eastern Amputee Athletic Association

52 Association for the Handicapped

Goal Ball Championships

Handicapped Scuba Association

International Coordinating Committee of the World Sports Organization for the Disabled

International Foundation of Wheelchair Tennis

International Paralympic Committee

International Sports Organization for the Disabled

International Wheelchair Aviators

International Wheelchair Road Racers Club

National Beep Baseball Association

National Disability Sports Alliance

National Foundation of Wheelchair Tennis

National Wheelchair Basketball Association

National Wheelchair Marathon Association

National Wheelchair Racquetball Association

National Wheelchair Shooting Federation

National Wheelchair Softball Association

North American Riding for the Handicapped Association

(continued)

FOCUS ON Sport Organizations for People With Disabilities *(continued)* 5.9

Paralyzed Veterans of America

Skating Association for the Blind and Handicapped

Ski for Light, Inc.

Special Olympics International

Tennis Association for the Mentally Retarded

USA Deaf Sports Association

U.S. Amputee Athletic Association

U.S. Association for Blind Athletes

U.S. Blind Golfer's Association

U.S. Cerebral Palsy Athletic Association

U.S. Deaf Skiers Association

U.S. Olympic Committee, Sports for the Disabled

U.S. Organization for Disabled Athletes

U.S. Quad Rugby Association

Wheelchair Athletes of the USA

Wheelchair Sports Federation

SOURCE: DePauw, 1984.

FOCUS ON The History of Special Olympics 5.10

The Special Olympics is perhaps the most remarkable and successful sport programs in world history. Here is a brief chronology of key developments in that history.

- 1962: Eunice Kennedy Shriver invites thirty-five boys and girls with intellectual disabilities to a day camp, intended to explore their capabilities in a variety of sports and physical activities, at her home in Rockville, Maryland.
- 1963: The Kennedy Foundation, founded in 1946, supports eleven similar camps around the United States.
- 1963–1968: More than 300 camps based on the Camp Shriver model are started within the United States. W. Freeberg, Chair of Recreation and Outdoor Education at Southern Illinois University, develops 1-week workshops to train professionals to plan and provide the camp program. One of the students is a teacher, Anne Burke, from Chicago.

- Anne Burke works with the Chicago Park District to plan a citywide track-and-field meet, modeled after the Olympic Games, and submits a proposal to Shiver. The proposal is accepted after Shriver suggests that more athletes from across the country be included.
- July 20, 1968: Shriver opens the First International Special Olympic Games with 1,000 athletes with intellectual disabilities from twenty-six states and Canada, competing in track and field, floor hockey, and aquatics.
- December 1968: Special Olympics is established as a nonprofit charitable organization.
- February 1977: The First International Special Olympic Winter Games are held in Steamboat Springs, Colorado, with more than 500 athletes competing. Major television networks cover the events.
- October 2007: In the Special Olympics Summer Games in Shanghai, China, 7,500 athletes compete.

The sport organization for persons with intellectual disabilities that is most familiar to the general public is the **Special Olympics** (see Focus On Box 5.10). There are more than 200,000 community-oriented Special Olympic programs in the United States, operated primarily by an extensive organization of 450,000 volunteers who provide instruction and conduct competitions in sixteen sports on a yearly basis. Any person with intellectual disabilities above 8 years of age may participate because the Special Olympics movement has been so popular that it works with adults also. The Special Olympics program has developed a number of instructional programs for use in training personnel to work in a sport environment with persons who have intellectual disabilities. More than 24,000 women and men have been trained as officials, instructors, coaches, and event directors.

Special Olympics now has more than 200 programs in 165 countries that serve 2.5 million children and youths with intellectual disabilities. Children and adults who participate in Special Olympics show improved fitness and motor skills as well as improved self-confidence. Special Olympics has transformed itself from a sports program to help children and youths improve their lives to an effective catalyst for social change throughout the world.

In 1989 the Special Olympics launched a new program called **unified sports** (www.specialolympics .org; James, 1995). The term *unified sports* refers to sporting events in which teams include athletes with and without intellectual disabilities. One of the many benefits of unified sports is that it allows Special Olympic athletes' families to participate on unified sports teams. Unified sports is a manifestation of the powerful movement toward inclusion so prevalent in American schools. Unified sports presently include basketball, bowling, cycling, distance running, soccer, softball, tennis, and volleyball. Unified sports have begun to spread at the local level through community recreation programs and through agency programs such as the Boys and Girls Clubs of America. Unified sports help schools meet the transition mandates imposed by IDEA.

A significant worldwide movement for athletes with disabilities is promoted and administered by the Paralympic Games organization (www .paralympic.org). Tracing its origins from the effort in 1948 to organize athletic competitions for World War II veterans with spinal cord injuries, the movement now has regular international competitions for summer and winter sport activities. The movement now accommodates athletes from six disability groups. The summer Paralympics first competed in 1960 after the Rome Olympic Games attracted 400 athletes from 24 countries. The most recent Paralympics, held in conjunction with the Athens Games, attracted 3,806 athletes from 136 countries. The International Olympic Committee and Paralympics have agreed that the games, both winter and summer, will be held together in the future.

The U.S. Paralympics, a division of the U.S. Olympic Committee, works with fifty member organizations to provide programs and services to develop athletes and coaches to participate in national and international competitions. U.S. Paralympics provides sport clinics, competitions, training and discussion forums, and the Paralympic Academy in Colorado Springs, Colorado.

The key legislative provision supporting increased access to sport for people with disabilities is Section 504 of the 1973 Rehabilitation Act (French, Henderson, Kinnison, & Sherrill, 1998). The language of this key provision states:

> No otherwise qualified handicapped individual in the United States, shall solely by reason of his handicap be excluded from participation in, be denied the benefits of, or be subjected to discrimination under any program or activity receiving Federal financial assistance or under any program or activity conducted by an Executive agency. (U.S. Public Law 93-112, 1973)

The phrase *otherwise qualified* is legal terminology that means that the person has the skills or abilities to participate in the sport after reasonable accommodation has been made. As people with disabilities use Section 504 to challenge denial of access to participation in sport, more and more opportunities will open to them. A number of states are passing laws in this area that are even stricter than the federal law. When state and federal law conflict, the more stringent requirement is used.

The major journal supporting sport, recreation, and physical education for persons with disabilities is *Palaestra* (www.Palaestra.com). For more than

Meaningful sport is important for everyone.

20 years, *Palaestra* has provided a wide range of historical, topical, and informational articles on sport, recreation, and physical education for persons of all ages who have physical and intellectual disabilities. The journal has played a key leadership role in uniting the various dimensions of the *sports for the disabled movement* in the United States (Beaver, 2004).

Masters or Veterans Sport

The historical approach to sport and aging was simple: Young people compete and older people watch. That too has changed. There is a growing movement for what, in the United States, is termed *masters sport* (in most of the world, the same movement is referred to as *veterans sport*). The general

proposition underlying this movement is that men and women can continue to find meaningful competition in sport throughout their lifetimes.

Masters sport has become the major competitive outlet for people who want to devote more time to training or to test themselves in a wider arena of competition than is available through organized recreational sport. Masters competition typically begins at age 40 years and is graded in 5-year age groups. At regional and national competitions, it is no longer unusual to find spirited competition in the 70- to 74-year age group.

Masters programs are most well developed in track and field, road racing, swimming, and bowling. There are more than 42,000 registered swimmers in the United States Masters Swimming organization (www.usms.org), which holds an annual convention and has a regular calendar of regional and national events. The World Association of Veteran Athletes (WAVA) was renamed the World Masters Athletics (WMA). The WAVA held its first world championships event in Toronto, Canada, in 1971 with 1,408 competitors. In Brisbane, Australia, in 2001, more than 6,000 athletes from seventy-nine countries competed in the WMA World Games. At the 2008 WMA Indoor World Championships held in Clermont Ferrand, France, nearly 3,500 athletes from fifty-two countries participated, organized in 5-year age groups starting with the 40–44 age group and going up to the 95–99 age group.

The World Masters Games is yet another age-group organization that holds regular national and international championship competitions. The first World Masters Games were held in Toronto in 1985 with 8,000 athletes from sixty-one countries competing in twenty-two sports. The 2005 Games were held in Edmonton with 21,600 athletes participating in twenty-five sports. The 2009 Games will be held in Sydney, Australia, featuring twenty-eight sport competitions with many events held in the Sydney Olympic Park.

Veterans and masters competitions in track and field use age-grading to adjust the athlete's performance according to age and gender. Age-grading tables, developed by the WMA, work by recording the world-record performance for each age at each distance, allowing older runners to compete on even terms with young runners. It also allows for athletes to compare their own performances over time and to identify their best-ever performance (www .runningforfitness.org).

The involvement of adults and senior citizens in sport has led to the creation of statewide sport festivals, the first of which was held in New York in 1978. A state sport festival typically involves competition in a large number of Olympic, national, and local sports across all age ranges but emphasizes adult and senior participation. Forty-four states have conducted state sport festivals over the past decade. These state games are good examples of the festive nature of sport competition, with goodwill and participation ranking as values equal to vigorous competition.

Like sport for people with disabilities, the growing availability of masters competition for older athletes not only enriches the lives of men and women who want to continue to train and compete in their sport but also serves as an important model for a healthy, active lifestyle, which has serious implications for fitness as well as for sport.

NONPARTICIPANT SPORT INVOLVEMENT

There are many ways to be involved in sport besides playing or coaching. As a sport becomes more highly institutionalized, a variety of roles are created that require professional expertise to be applied to the interests of the sport. Thus, sport vocations develop as a sport becomes more highly institutionalized. Organized sport at the local level, typically in communities, often operates primarily with part-time and volunteer help. To the extent that sport is more highly organized and more institutionalized, there is a need for full-time, professional services.

The following list of vocational opportunities is evidence of the diverse professional roles in the field of sport. Each listed vocation is followed by typical places of employment.

Athletic administration—high schools, colleges, pro teams, clubs

Sport administration—corporations, pro clubs, colleges

Sport leadership—recreation centers, industry, camps, churches, resorts, commercial centers

Sport broadcasting—radio, television stations

Sport journalism—newspapers, magazines, self-employed

Sport-facility design—corporations, government, self-employed

Sport camps—established camps, self-employed

Sport-facility management—government, pro teams, industry, universities

Sport medicine—hospitals, sport-medicine centers, universities, pro teams

Sport counseling—high school, colleges and universities, private practice

Athletic training—schools, universities, pro teams, sport-medicine centers

Sports officiating—schools, universities, pro teams, recreational programs

Sport psychologist—universities, pro teams, national teams

Sport scientist (physiology, biomechanics, and so on)—universities

Sport-equipment design—self-employed, industry

Sport studies (history, sociology, and so on)—universities

Sport fitness—universities, pro teams, national teams

Sport publicity—universities, pro teams

Sport promotion—universities, pro teams

Sport photography—newspapers, magazines, self-employed

Although many men and women earn their living within these vocations, this does not mean that they have been *specifically prepared* for that vocation. There are a few universities where a person can study sport photography, sport journalism, or sport broadcasting. The more typical route to these vocations is through the broader field of study: photography, journalism, or broadcasting. The physician specializing in sport medicine is exactly that—a *physician* who, after completing medical training, specialized in the application of medical science to sport.

In some of these vocational areas, one can study the vocation directly and proceed to work in that vocation. That is the case for sport psychology, the sport sciences, sport studies, and sport management and administration. Direct training in these fields, however, is not the only way to enter the vocation. Many sport psychologists were trained as psychologists and have a deep interest in sport. Many sport administrators were trained in business administration and have a deep interest in sport. These are areas where direct training *is* available, but that training is not *necessary* to enter the vocation.

The vocation of athletic training is one of the few in the list where specific training is needed to enter the vocation—and it is difficult to enter the vocation without that training because of the certification required to practice as an athletic trainer.

Thus, preparation for a career in a nonparticipant sport vocation, at the current stage of sport development in America, presents a flexible set of options. As sport becomes more highly institutionalized, we can expect that more specific preparation for nonparticipant vocational roles will be made available and that certification or licensing programs will be developed to ensure that people entering the vocational roles have the requisite skills and knowledge. Two such areas—sport management and administration and athletic training—are reviewed in this chapter. The sport sciences and sport studies are reviewed in Part 5.

Sport Management and Administration

One of the fastest-growing vocational specializations in sport, fitness, and physical education in recent years has been the area of **sport management** and administration. Sport-management programs currently attract large numbers of women and men who want a career in a sport-related field but have no interest in coaching or teaching. Many programs are now available. Some are undergraduate majors, providing a choice at that level for young men and women who traditionally might have majored in physical education. Other programs are at the master's-degree level, offering opportunity for further career development for students who have majored in physical education, business administration, or some other nonsport-related undergraduate subject.

The sport and activity industry can be divided into six segments (Miller, Stoldt, & Comfort, 2000). These are

- Professional sport entertainment (MLB, NFL, NASCAR, minor leagues)
- Amateur sport entertainment (college sport, high school sport, Olympics-related events)
- Sport services (agents, event management, resorts, cruises)
- Sport and activity participation, for-profit (golf courses, bowling alleys, fitness centers, martial arts centers)
- Sport and activity goods (manufacturers, distributorships, retail)
- Sport and activity participation, nonprofit (parks and recreation, YMCA, hospital fitness)

The number of professional roles in these industry segments is quite varied and includes athletic directors, ticket agents, human resource managers, risk management, marketing, public relations, facility management, and financing/accounting. A facility manager, for example, might be employed by a university, a professional team, a community recreation department, or a resort hotel. Nearly all of these industry segments require marketing and publicity personnel. The nonprofit organizations almost always require professionals to direct and manage fund-raising.

The job opportunities are not evenly divided across the industry. Sporting goods and health and fitness management jobs appear to be most prevalent, with sports media and college athletics in the middle tier and professional sport and recreation administration in the lower tier (Miller et al., 2000).

In 1993 the National Association for Sport and Physical Education (NASPE) joined with the North American Society for Sport Management (NASSM) to develop competency standards for sport-management curricula at the undergraduate, master's, and doctoral levels. The core undergraduate curriculum for students in sport management includes ten competency areas: sociocultural dimensions of sport, management and leadership in sport, ethics in sport management, sport marketing, sport communications, sport finance, legal aspects of sport, economics of sport, sport governance, and a field experience in sport management. Each of these ten areas has required content that defines the minimum coverage to achieve the standard. The competency standards for the master's degree include nine areas, many of which are similar to the areas included in the undergraduate standards. Courses that fulfill these standards can be in the major department or in other departments, such as business, law, or economics.

Degree programs in sport management are widely available, especially as part of an undergraduate-degree program (www.nassm.org). Degree programs are also available at the master's and doctoral levels. NASSM has a program approval process for degree programs at all three levels. There are 240 college and universities offering a sport-management major at the undergraduate level, with 50 of them having successfully passed the NASSM review. There are 120 at the master's level, with 34 of them approved. There are 20 universities offering doctoral programs in sport management, with 5 of them approved.

Programs in sport management and administration often include an internship in which the student actually performs the skills necessary for the various roles. These may range from assisting an athletic director or working in a ticket office to helping in the promotions department of a pro team. Sport-management and administration programs are popular with young men and women who want a career in a sport-related vocation that is not directly in the coaching field.

Athletic Training

The most highly developed sport vocation is that of athletic trainer. The National Athletic Trainers' Association is one of the strongest of all the sport, fitness, and physical-education associations. Although athletic trainers are employed primarily by interscholastic, intercollegiate, and professional sport teams, they also find outlets for their professional services in sport-medicine centers. A more detailed presentation of the purposes of **athletic training** and the requirements for certification can be found in Chapter 8 under the section "Sports Medicine and the Rehabilitative Sciences."

Nonparticipant Sport Vocations: By Whom?

Earlier in this chapter, reference was made to the degree to which women were underrepresented in leadership roles in intercollegiate and professional sports. The same is true for African American men, especially in intercollegiate sports. Data shown in this chapter support the assertion that participation opportunities for girls/women and minorities have improved. The exception to that optimistic finding is for young boys and girls in urban poverty neighborhoods where participation opportunities are few due to poor facilities, inadequate programs, and concerns about safety.

In 2004, 44 percent of the coaches of women's intercollegiate teams (all divisions) were women, which is close to the lowest representation of female head coaches of women's teams since Title IX became the law of the land. In the same year, nearly 18 percent of all NCAA athletic programs did not have a woman in the administrative structure of the athletic department. Despite the fact that women account for 40–50 percent of our Olympic teams, they have only 11 of the 115 active members of the

Athletic trainers have become commonplace in high-school and collegiate sports.

International Olympic Committee (Women's Sport Foundation, 2006).

Similar concerns have been expressed for women in officiating and in athletic administration at levels from interscholastic sport to professional sport. In response to media criticism, many of the organizations that control professional sports have developed specific recruitment and development programs to increase the number of women and minority persons in leadership and administrative positions.

When Title IX was passed in 1972, many women took coaching and administrative positions in newly expanded interscholastic and intercollegiate sport programs. In the 1980s, however, it became clear that the number of women in those roles had decreased substantially (Sisley & Capel, 1986).

A longitudinal study at the collegiate level conducted by Vivian Acost and Linda Jean Carpenter (www.aahperd.org/nagws) shows some promising results for athletes and some disturbing results for coaching.

- All three NCAA divisions show an increased number of sports offered to women.
- The average number of women's teams per school is 8.34.
- In the last several years, 885 new teams have been added.
- There are 8,132 head coaching jobs for NCAA women's teams.
- We now have the lowest percentage of female head coaches in history (44 percent).
- Women filled only 10 percent of the 361 new positions in 2002.
- Division I programs are least likely to have female head administrators (8.4 percent).

Similar concerns have been expressed for women in officiating and in athletic administration at both collegiate and interscholastic levels.

The low incidence of minority personnel in coaching and administrative positions has received substantial national publicity since the early 1990s. In response to media criticism, many professional leagues have developed specific recruitment and development programs to increase the number of minority persons in coaching and administrative positions.

Sport and Technology

Sport and technology have grown together since the early 1970s. Technology has been routinely used for years to improve athletic performance through computer simulations and comparison. The technology of strength development has changed the performance standards in most sports. Many elite athletes whose performance depends on optimum levels of strength and endurance are monitored daily through technology, and they adjust their workouts, sleep, and nutrition according to regular feedback, obtained through technology, from their bodily systems.

Newsgroups on the Internet and Web sites have created countless opportunities for gaining information about team and other sports. Professional basketball teams now typically have an assistant coach whose main role is to edit video clips of offensive and defensive play for immediate feedback during half-time at games and for scouting in preparation for future play. Data on coaching behaviors are collected from laptop computers that can produce instant profiles for coaches and their athletes (Partridge & Franks, 1996).

The largest bibliographic database on sport is available through SPORTDiscus, developed by the Sport Information Research Centre (SIRC) in Canada (www.sportdiscus.com). SPORTDiscus contains more than 500,000 references, 20,000 theses and dissertations, and 10,000 Web site addresses. Each month SIRC examines more than 1,200 magazines and journals, from practical to scholarly, to compile references related to sport, sport medicine, physical fitness, sport administration, coaching, physical education, sport law, physical therapy, and recreation. The system can be researched easily and quickly using keyword indicators to guide the search. SPORTDiscus is often available through university libraries or through a variety of fee-based services.

SUMMARY

1. The sport culture of America is one of the most highly developed in the world. It extends from children's sport through age-group competition in masters-level sport.

2. All statistics—those on participation, attendance, money spent on leisure, coverage in the media, equipment, and cultural norms—indicate the growing size and importance of sport in American culture.

3. The idea that leisure abounds in contemporary American culture is a myth. Especially among the professional and business class—the group that is most involved in sport—much less leisure time is available than during most periods in history.

4. Sport participation can be classified as recreational, amateur, nonprofessional, and professional, with distinctions based on the degree of institutionalization of the sport involvement and the relationship of the involvement to monetary gain.

5. Participation in organized, nonschool sport for children and youths has grown substantially since the mid-1950s with even stronger growth patterns for girls in the more recent past.

6. Organized sport for children begins as early as 3 years of age with an average early-entry age of 5.8 years and an average entry age of 11 years.

7. Child and youth sport has developed in the United States almost entirely in the local government and private-community sectors with major organizational entities at the state and national levels.

8. Child and youth sport tends to be exclusionary in the sense that opportunity for participation decreases as young adolescents grow into their teens.

9. Coaching for child and youth sport is mostly volunteer with little control or certification of people who coach.

10. Countries that have a stronger federal involvement in child and youth sport tend to have coach-certification programs at various levels.

11. Interscholastic sport is regulated at the state level and occupies a place in the American sport culture unlike that in any other nation with more than 7 million boys and girls participating annually.

12. Most states have adopted a classification scheme that grades competition based on school enrollment. Financing differs from state to state, from full funding out of tax revenues to a model wherein most athletic funds have to be raised by boosters or earned in gate receipts.

13. Few states require any coaching certification beyond a valid teaching certificate; some states do not have any requirements; and only a few states require special certification in coaching.

14. Intercollegiate sport is primarily an American institution. Colleges and universities typically form leagues and affiliate voluntarily with a national governing organization such as the NCAA or the NAIA.

15. College and university competition is classified by size of school and by the degree of funding available to athletes.

16. Professional sport actually involves a relatively small number of athletes, who typically have short careers and whose pay scales within a given sport are uneven.

17. Professional sport is organized through parent organizations typically run by a commissioner but with the real power retained by owners.

18. Organized recreational sport is implemented through recreation departments, businesses, service clubs, and private community organizations. The range and amount of participation are extremely diversified.

19. The enactment of federal legislation in the 1970s greatly expanded the sport opportunities for people with disabilities. The scope of these people's sport involvement now rivals that of people without disabilities. The best-known example of these programs is the Special Olympics.

20. Masters sport is organized in 5-year age groups for people over age 40 years. It has recently experienced substantial growth, especially in road racing, track and field, and swimming.

21. With the institutionalization of sport in the twentieth century, a number of nonparticipant sport vocations developed, some of which require special preparation and certification.

22. Sport management and administration is the fastest-growing nonparticipant sport vocation. Many undergraduate and graduate programs are available throughout the country.

23. Athletic training is the most highly developed sport-related profession. Specific undergraduate and graduate programs lead to certification, which is typically necessary for entry into the vocation.

24. Nonparticipant sport vocations are dominated by white males; women and minorities continue to be underrepresented.

25. Technology has an impact on sport by providing more access to information and by offering highly sophisticated analysis of physiology, fitness, competitive strategy, and many other aspects of sport.

DISCUSSION QUESTIONS

1. In what ways do participating and spectating positively and negatively influence each other?

2. What would be the benefits and liabilities of increasing local, state, and federal government involvement in child and youth sport?

3. What would school sport be like if it were based on an inclusionary, rather than an exclusionary, model?

4. If a program for coaching certification were to be required, what criteria would you want coaches to meet?

5. What opportunities are available for athletes between the ages of 18 and 23 years to continue to develop in their sport if they do not go to college and are not skilled enough to be hired as professional athletes?

6. How should school sport be financed? How should recreational sport be financed?

7. How does the sport experience differ for (a) the athlete with a disability, (b) the masters athlete, (c) the scholarship athlete, and (d) the child athlete?

8. In what ways will the quality of preparation for nonparticipant vocations in sport be related to the future development of sport?

CHAPTER 6

Problems and Issues in Sport

My high school coach forced me to run intervals until I vomited. I did both, exceedingly well, and after graduation turned my back on running for more than a decade. Not much has changed. Too many high school coaches still follow the same prescriptions.

James C. McCullagh, editor, *Runner's World*

My high school coach was short, white and out of shape—different than me. But he cared about me even though I wasn't the best player on our team. And it's a good thing too. Because nobody else was looking out for me then, and I needed his help more than once.

Former athlete and current school coach,
from Coakley (1994, p. 189)

Sports teach, it is their nature. They teach fairness or cheating, teamwork or selfishness, compassion or coldness.

Wilfred Sheed, 1995

LEARNING OBJECTIVES

- To analyze the manner in which cooperation and competition are important to good sport participation

- To describe features and practices that provide developmentally appropriate competition

- To discuss major issues related to child and youth sport, interschool sport, and intercollegiate sport

- To analyze equity issues in sport at all levels

- To describe different sport systems and discuss how each one's goals, organization, and finance are related

- To describe myths related to sport participation and analyze their validity

Chapter 4 explained the fundamental meanings of sport. It stressed the positive aspects of sport and the beauty that can be seen and the satisfaction that can be experienced through sport participation. It stressed that sport developed from play and was most meaningful when the sport experience was playful. Sport was described as a "natural religion" to which players and fans alike become committed.

Chapter 5 emphasized the degree to which sport has become central to American culture in the twentieth century and how it now extends from early-childhood sport opportunities to masters sport for women and men up to age 90. We also saw that sport has expanded not only in age range but also to previously underrepresented groups: women, minorities, and people with disabling conditions. The argument for the very positive potential of sport in the lives of all persons having been made, it is now time to examine the problems and issues that threaten sport, that have the potential to detract from and diminish sport's fundamental goodness. This task will not be difficult because as the abundant and widespread problems within sport have been widely publicized.

While most experts and laypeople still recognize and support the positive benefits of sport participation, we have also become much more cognizant of the myriad problems that have developed, particularly in the last few decades. In newspapers, magazine articles, and scholarly journals and on television, the problems in sports have been revealed and analyzed: parents misbehaving in youth sport, performance-enhancing drugs and supplements, abusive coaches, gender inequities, crippling injuries, illegal payments, and racism. If you are interested in a career in sport or physical education, it is important that you understand current issues and problems, are acquainted with the facts surrounding them, and are knowledgeable about current efforts to confront those problems and issues. If sport is to play a central, positive role in the development of children and youths, it is the values, knowledge, and skills of the adults in charge that will determine whether positive outcomes will be realized.

All the contemporary scrutiny of sport—of sport's purposes, practices, and accomplishments—has shown two things clearly. First, sport has become vitally important in the culture, for children, youths, and adults; unimportant issues do not attract the attention that sport generates in our daily lives. Second, to preserve and strengthen the sport culture for the next generation, there are problems in sport that we need to attend to. In this chapter, we review those major problems in sport at various levels with the primary goal of identifying practices that help make sport better for participants.

First, however, it is necessary to distinguish between what will be described as problems in sport from the many social problems in our society. Inevitably, some sport participants fall prey to those social problems. A basketball player dies from a drug overdose. A football player is arrested for participating in a robbery. A tennis player is arrested for driving while intoxicated. A baseball player is sentenced to jail for failing to pay child support. Many stories like these are reported on the sport pages of newspapers and on sport shows on television. The question is whether these are sport stories or stories about social problems that happen to involve sport participants. Most of the evidence suggests that children and youths who participated in sport are *less likely* to be involved in such problems as adults than are their nonparticipating peers. In this chapter, the discussion is confined to problems that are specific to sport.

CHILD AND YOUTH SPORT

If you plan to have a career in teaching or coaching, you need to be aware of issues in child and youth sport. Parents will ask you questions about local programs. It will certainly be within your professional role to work to ensure that children and youths who you serve in your professional role also have good sport experiences in the community, to contribute to creating and sustaining a positive youth sport culture in your local area.

Children need appropriate coaching and supervision as they learn sport.

Sport is an important part of the lives of many children and youths (and their parents!). Estimates suggest that over 35 million girls and boys between the ages of 5–16 years participate in nonschool sports, coached mostly by 4 million volunteer coaches, 90 percent of whom are parents of the children playing (www.coachingschool.org). That is the good news! The bad news is that estimates suggest that up to 70–80 percent of the participants drop out of organized sport activities by their early teen years. Most children and youths who drop out are much less likely to engage in an appropriate amount of physical activity, while others may instead switch to forms of extreme or action sports such as skateboarding, BMX biking, and the like. Other youngsters leave out-of-school sport activities because they become involved in school sport, often in the middle-school years. Interscholastic sport, which will be considered in the following section, is an *exclusionary* model; that is, only those girls and boys who are good enough make the team. For those who try out and do not make the team, there are fewer out-of-school programs available to them as they advance through their teen years.

It is also clear that many youngsters drop out of youth sport programs because they are not fun, most likely because there is an overemphasis on performance and winning. Others drop out due to

excessive pressure from coaches or parents. Others drop out because they find more interesting pastimes such as music, dance, or less-organized action sports such as in-line skating.

We should start by emphasizing the widespread agreement that sport participation, *properly conceptualized and properly delivered*, can be extremely valuable to the positive development of children and youths. Research has shown that substantial physical and psychosocial benefits are derived from child–youth sport involvement (Fraser-Thomas and Cote, 2007). Sport experiences enable children and youths to develop motor skills that serve as a foundation for lifetime involvement in physical activities. Sport participation provides physical activity that contributes to improved physical health, a particularly important outcome in an era when child and youth obesity has reached epidemic proportions. Sport participation also provides opportunities for children and youths to learn life skills such as cooperation, discipline, leadership, and self-control. Youth sport experiences correlate positively with adult career achievement (Larson & Verma, 1999) and correlate negatively with school dropout and delinquent behavior (Eccles & Barber, 1999). What we need to be aware of is that these positive outcomes do not occur automatically by enrolling children and youths in a local sport program; rather, they are achieved when the program is conceptualized and delivered in a way that is developmentally appropriate for the needs and capacities of the children and youths who participate.

In 2005 the Citizenship Through Sports Alliance (CTSA) convened a panel of youth sport experts to evaluate community-based youth sports in the United States. The panel reviewed evidence in five areas and gave each a grade (www.sportsmanship.org). The Child-Centered Philosophy area graded D, the Coaching area graded C−, the Health and Safety area graded C+, the Officiating area graded B−, and the Parental Behavior/Involvement area graded D. The panel reported that many programs had lost a child-centered focus and replaced it with an emphasis on winning. They also reported that too many parents behaved in ways that did not support the

---

FOCUS ON   National Standards for Youth Sports   6.1

1. *Proper Sports Environment* Parents must consider and carefully choose the proper environment for their child, including the age appropriate and development levels for participation, the type of sport, the rules of the sport, the age range of the participants, and the proper level of physical and emotional stress.

2. *Programs Based on the Well-Being of Children* Parents must select youth sport programs that are developed and organized to enhance the emotional, physical, social, and educational well-being of their children.

3. *Drug-, Tobacco-, and Alcohol-Free Environment* Parents must encourage a drug-, tobacco-, and alcohol-free environment for their children.

4. *Part of a Child's Life* Parents must recognize that youth sports are only a part of a child's life.

5. *Training* Parents must insist that coaches are trained and certified.

6. *Parent's Active Role* Parents must make a serious effort to take an active role in the youth sport experience of their child, providing positive support as a spectator, coach, league administrator, and/or caring parent.

7. *Positive Role Models* Parents must provide positive role models, exhibiting sportsmanlike behavior at games, practices, and home while also giving positive reinforcement to their child and support to their child's coaches.

8. *Parental Commitment* Parents must demonstrate the commitment to their child's youth sports experience by annually signing the Parent's Code of Ethics Pledge.

9. *Safe Playing Situations* Parents must insist on safe playing facilities, healthful playing situations, and proper first-aid applications, should the need arise.

10. *Equal-Play Opportunity* Parents, coaches, and league administrators must provide equal sports–play opportunity for all youths regardless of race, creed, sex, economic status, or ability.

11. *Drug-, Tobacco-, and Alcohol-Free Adults* Parents must be drug-, tobacco-, and alcohol-free at youth league sporting events.

SOURCE: National Association for Youth Sports. www.NAYS.org.

---

development of the children and that too many programs focused on sport specialization leading to burnout. Furthermore, the panel suggested that too many programs failed to do background checks on coaches and did not invest in any coaching-education assistance for the volunteer coaches. It is clear that the parents of girls and boys playing in youth sport programs must play a proactive role in ensuring that the programs in which they enroll their children are quality programs. Each of these issues is discussed in this chapter.

Although requirements for volunteer coaches and for parents who come to watch their children play sport are few, a major effort in the past decade has been to provide educational materials and guidelines for coaches and parents. The National Youth Sport Coaches Association (NYSCA) provides eleven guidelines for parents to help them choose the right programs for their children and then ensure that the program is being administered appropriately (see Focus On Box 6.1).

Cooperation and Competition

A major criticism of child/youth sport is that it is often too competitive. The truth is that children learn to be appropriately or inappropriately competitive through their early experiences in sport. These early experiences should involve a variety of sport activities, modified so as to be fun and exciting for the participants. These would include both organized sport activities modified to meet the beginning needs of the participants as well as informal activities organized by the children themselves.

FOCUS ON — Coaches Code of Ethics   6.2

I hereby pledge to live up to my certification as a NYSCA coach by following the NYSCA Coaches Code of Ethics:

- I will place the emotional and physical well-being of my players ahead of a personal desire to win.
- I will treat each player as an individual, remembering the large range of emotional and physical development for the same age group.
- I will do my best to provide a safe playing situation for my players.
- I will promise to review and practice basic first-aid principles needed to treat injuries of my players.
- I will do my best to organize practices that are fun and challenging for all my players.
- I will lead by example in demonstrating fair play and sportsmanship to all my players.

- I will provide a sports environment for my team that is free of drugs, tobacco, and alcohol, and I will refrain from their use at all youth sports events.
- I will be knowledgeable in the rules of each sport I coach, and I will teach these rules to my players.
- I will use those coaching techniques appropriate for the all of the skills that I teach.
- I will remember that I am a youth sports coach and that the game is for the children and not for adults.

Coach' Signature: _____

Date: _____

SOURCE: National Youth Sports Coaches Association.

Sport activities for younger children should be "small-sided" and intrinsically motivating, provide immediate gratification, and optimize enjoyment with their friends (Fraser-Thomas & Cote, 2007). All participants should get equal playing time. For these early activities to be successful, the participants must learn how to cooperate. The effects of winning or losing are momentary. Children especially do not like to be thrust into zero-sum situations where the only satisfaction comes from winning. The "fun quotient" is the more powerful motivator. See Focus On Box 6.2 for how the NYSCA's Coaches Code of Ethics reflects these goals.

This stands in stark contrast to many youth sport programs that are driven by a *performance ethic*; that is, the quality of the performance, typically measured against a standard, becomes the primary way to measure program effectiveness. Even during late childhood (8–11 years), children tend to define their own competence by comparing it to their close peers (for example, Billy knows that he can run faster than Michael) rather than in absolute terms (Billy can run 100 meters in 17.2 seconds). Young

athletes in performance-oriented programs are encouraged to define *fun* in terms of improving their performance, often in ways that are measured by performance outcomes (for example, a lower time in a swimming or executing a more difficult gymnastic skill) or by being moved from a "bronze" level to a "silver" level on a performance chart (Coakley, 2007).

Developmentally Appropriate Sport

There is also substantial agreement among researchers that young children (grades 1–4) should be involved in a variety of sport activities, some of which can be organized and some in free playtime. Most scientific experts and pediatricians agree that children should not begin organized sport competition before the age of 8 years. At about the 5- to 6-year-old age, children develop the capacity to compare themselves to others in order to understand their own competence. They tend to learn competition as a social motivation around age 7 years. What this means is that community sport activities below 8 years of age should be

---

FOCUS ON   **Children's Bill of Rights in Sport**   **6.3**

Children in sport should have the right:

- To participate regardless of ability level
- To participate at a level commensurate with their development
- To have qualified adult leadership
- To participate in safe and healthy environments

- To share in leadership and decision making
- To play as a child and not as an adult
- To receive proper preparation for participation
- To have equal opportunity to strive for success
- To be trained with dignity
- To have fun

SOURCES: Adapted from *Youth Sports Guide*, by J. Thomas, 1977; American Alliance for Health, Physical Education, Recreation and Dance.

Age-group sport training for youngsters is now commonplace.

reduced competition. Activities should involve a lot of physical activity and help develop skills that involve large-muscle groups as well as help participants learn how to cooperate and play fairly. Activities should also be organized in ways that participants can experience success; that is, the complexity of the activity and the skills needed to perform the activity are matched to the experience and skill levels of the participants. Program rules should ensure that all participants get equal playing time (see Focus On Box 6.3). Green (1997) describes a beginning program for young children, designed to help them learn soccer and

to enjoy the experience. This coed program had no formal competition, no league standings, no trophies, and no statistics. Coaches led the coed play groups through a progression of soccer games over the course of a season. Each game emphasized one or more soccer techniques and tactics while maximizing the number of opportunities for players to touch the ball. There were no drills and no scrimmages, just games. In this sense, the well-designed games, following a clear progression to develop techniques and tactics, became the teachers. The age-appropriate games also had a high fun quotient.

All sports for children should be modified to fit the developmental status of the participants. Teams should be organized to make the modified-game competitions as close as possible—the most exciting and fun games are those where the score is close throughout the game and both teams have a chance to win. Modifications are especially important in games that, in their parent forms, involve complex tactics. Anybody who has watched young children trying to learn soccer in an eleven per side game on a large soccer field will see most participants "swarming" to the ball, with no offensive balance and no sense of tactics. To be played well, soccer, like all invasion games, requires a fairly sophisticated understanding of offensive and defensive tactics. These are best learned through a series of small-sided, modified games through which techniques can be developed and tactics made gradually more complex.

If a child/youth sport program is defined primarily as a performance ethic rather than a "fun" ethic, many of the positive outcomes described earlier will less likely be achieved. If children and youths are in programs where the main focus is on performance improvement and winning in competition, evidence suggests that result for many will be a decreased sense of self-esteem and competence and an increased level of anxiety (Csikszentmihalyi, Rathunde, & Whalen, 1993). Inevitably, such negative outcomes lead to many participants dropping out of the programs.

Specialization

Not too many years ago, children and youths did not often specialize in a sport until they reached the college level, and even at that level, it was not unusual to find two-sport athletes. In high schools, many boys played on a team in at least two of the three sport seasons of the school year (girls typically did not have the opportunity, or they would have done so also!). That was then. Now it is rare to find a three-sport athlete in high school. What is more common is the *sport specialist*, the athlete who trains year-around for his or her sport, competes on the school team in that sport, and is likely part of a sport club in that sport during the off-season.

Early specialization has also become more common. Gymnasts and swimmers start training at an early age and train year-around. Hockey and soccer players get early training in sport-specialization clubs, and by the time that they are in their teens, are competing on select teams for their club in competition that is often of a higher grade than the local high-school competition. Ten-year-old hockey players play ninety games in a season. Young figure skaters train 30 hours per week. Soccer players finish their interscholastic season and move immediately to their club team where they continue to compete in local, regional, and national competitions. There is no doubt that advances in exercise science have made year-around strength and endurance training another part of sport specialization.

Not only do young athletes specialize in a single sport, but in some cases they also specialize in a single position within that sport—that is, a quarterback in football, a pitcher in baseball or softball, a backstroke specialist in swimming, or a goalie in soccer. The more talented the young athlete, the more likely will be the pressure to specialize and train year-around. Some of the pressure to specialize comes from parents and others who see a college scholarship and eventually a professional career for the young athlete as the preferred future. Is specialization inappropriate? For those who survive, there is little doubt that the process breeds talented elite athletes. Less is known about those who burn out during the process or suffer overuse injuries that derails their path to glory. There are few issues in child and youth sport about which there is more debate and less good evidence.

Child and Youth Sport Injuries

Accurate and reliable data on the extent and nature of injuries in child/youth sport are difficult to obtain (whereas data on injuries in interscholastic sport are readily available as you will see in the next section).

Acute injuries, referred to as *macrotrauma*—such as sprains of joint ligaments, strains of muscle tendon units, contusions involving muscle tendon units and their overlaying soft tissue, and fractures of the long bones and axial skeleton—are estimated to result in 4 million emergency-room visits every year (Micheli, Glassman, & Klein, 2000). What is clear is that the incidence of injuries is sufficient to cause some hospitals to open pediatric sport-medicine clinics. The more serious injuries are the overuse injuries that sometimes develop when children/youths specialize in a sport (Micheli et al., 2000). Overuse injuries are seen more often in younger children because of the softness of their bones and the relative tightness of their ligaments and tendons during growth spurts. What is known as "Little League elbow" is the result of damage to the growth cartilage of the elbow joint. Other common overuse injuries occur in the knee and ankle.

The current generation has seen a growing involvement of children and youths in various kinds of extreme or action sports such as skateboarding, BMX biking, and in-line skating—activities that are inherently risky. Indeed, risk is one of the attractions. Very little data exist on the nature or severity of injuries in these activities. Some, like handlebar injuries in BMX stunt-biking, are so serious that some government health units are beginning to release warnings to media to alert parents to the potential dangers. Handlebar injuries can result in ruptures of the spleen, liver, kidneys, and bowel, sometimes so severely that organs have to be removed (Media Release, 2007).

Duquin (1988) suggests that what she calls "sado-asceticism" has too frequently crept into child/youth sport. Too many adults, coaches and parents, support a "no pain, no gain" ethic for practice, training, and competition. Duquin, however, argues that the wisdom of the body and the wisdom of childhood are to avoid pain, that "no pain is sane," and that children typically quit when they get hurt. The asceticism she describes as having crept into organized child/youth sport in recent years is to redefine pain as discomfort and to encourage young athletes to work through the discomfort. As she so eloquently states, "Adults may choose to sacrifice their bodies for their perceptions of truth. In youth sport, the 'truths' are those of adults, the sacrificial bodies are those of children" (Duquin, 1988, p. 35).

Coaching Child and Youth Sport

The vast majority of the volunteer coaches for community child/youth sport are parents of participants. Typically, they coach for as long as their child or children are involved in the sport at that level, which is typically no longer than 3 years. Most community-based sport programs have difficulty attracting a sufficient number of coaches, so they have few requirements. Increasingly, however, programs are requiring background checks to ensure that volunteer coaches have no police record that would disqualify them from coaching children/youths. Many states and communities are encouraging volunteer coaches to take part in courses or workshops that provide at least a beginning understanding of coaching techniques that are appropriate for child/youth sport and, of course, those techniques that are inappropriate. The NYSCA has developed a code of ethics that describes the qualities and competencies that volunteer coaches should have or develop to optimize the potential of sport experiences for children/youths. The code of ethics is described in a "pledge" form that coaches sign before they begin their child/youth sport coaching assignment (see Focus On Box 6.2, page 132).

Research on volunteer coaches is sparse, but what has been done shows that they too often behave in ways that are not productive for young athletes—too much evaluation, too much criticism, too few supportive interactions (Eitzen & Sage, 2003). Research in the 1970s showed that volunteer coaches can change when they are helped through a modest educational program (Smith, Smoll, & Curtis, 1978). Out of that research grew a model for preparing volunteer coaches called "Coach Effectiveness Training" (Smoll, 1986), which has influenced many of the coaching-education programs now in use throughout the United States. The philosophy of that program was built on

---

FOCUS ON   What Kids Want to Tell Parents and Spectators   **6.4**

- Don't yell out instructions—then I can't concentrate on what the coach says.
- Don't put down the officials—that embarrasses me.
- Don't yell at me or the coach—that takes away from my fun.
- Don't put down my teammates—that hurts team spirit.
- Don't put down the other team—you're not being a good sport.
- Don't lose your temper—that embarrasses me too.
- Don't lecture me after the game—I've messed up, I already feel bad.
- Don't forget the things I did well—I'm proud of them.

- Don't forget it's just a game—I need to be reminded of that sometimes too.

Resources for Positive Spectating and Parenting in Sport

- Positive Coaching Alliance—www.positivecoach.org
- National Alliance for Youth Sports—www.nays.org
- Gatorade's "Playbook for Kids"—1-877-PLAYKIDS
- Character Counts Sports—www.charactercounts.org
- The Center for Sports Parenting—www.sportsparenting.org
- Citizenship Through Sports—www.sportsmanship.org

SOURCE: Gatorade's "Playbook for Kids: A Parent's Guide to Help Kids Get the Most Out of Sports."

---

notions such as winning is an important goal but not the only goal, that losing does not imply failure, that success can be achieved in many ways including but not exclusive to winning, and that success is related as much to effort as it is to outcome. This approach stands in stark contrast to the "winning is the only thing" ethic that pervades so much of elite sport.

A risk for volunteer coaches is for them to adopt what Coakley (2007) describes as a "techno-science" approach that values improvement in techniques and tactics more than the developmental aspects of maturing children and youths. Many volunteer coaches have watched sport on television, with instant replay and with commentators making constant assessments on the technical and tactical decisions made by coaches. Although learning techniques and tactics is important, it must be done in a way that is gradual and is combined with at least equal focus on helping youngsters develop as competent, autonomous, and responsible people.

Impact of Sport on Family Life

During the years in which their young children participate in sport, many families have to totally alter their lives (Harrington, 1998). That is particularly true for parents whose sons or daughters are skilled enough to make the "traveling" or "select" team. Participation costs can become substantial, especially for sports that require indoor facilities (for example, winter soccer and ice hockey). Summer camps have become the norm rather than the exception. Some parents put 40,000 miles on the family car taking sons or daughters to away competitions. There are early mornings and late nights. The family seldom is able to have a meal together. Parents can get very intense about the participation and performance of their sons or daughters and their team (see Focus On Boxes 6.4 and 6.5). Although most parents willingly support all those endeavors because they believe them to be beneficial to the development of their children, there is no doubt that severe dislocation of family life can occur.

FOCUS ON   Problematic Parents   **6.5**

Most parents support their children/youths in their sport endeavors, whether in community sport or interschool sport. Still, there are parents who create problems for coaches. Shown below are the kinds of confrontation most commonly experienced by coaches.

- An angry parent confronts you immediately after a game.
- A parent blocks you from reaching your car in the parking lot after a game.
- A challenging parent schedules what you know will be a contentious meeting.
- A parent makes an unreasonable demand (such as taking away the MVP award just

presented and giving it instead to his/her son/daughter).

- A parent makes disparaging comments about you and your program behind your back.
- A parent challenges your decision about who you assign to the starting lineup.
- A parent angrily criticizes you about playing time of his/her son/daughter.

Coaches need to keep program directors or school athletic directors informed of such incidents. Using e-mail provides a time and date of the information.

SOURCE: Hoch, 2007.

Unequal Access Based on Socioeconomic Status

Opportunity to participate in child and youth sport in the United States is not offered on a level playing field. Opportunity is strongly tilted toward the daughters and sons of the middle and upper socioeconomic classes. The Carnegie Council on Adolescent Development (1992) found that boys and girls from lower-social-status communities were seriously underserved in all forms of childhood and youth services, including sport opportunities. They concluded that "young adolescents who live in low-income neighborhoods are most likely to benefit from supportive youth development services; yet they are the very youth who have least access to such programs and organizations" (p. 12). The Center for the Study of Sport in Society at Northeastern University (www.sportinsociety.org) estimates that 15 percent of urban children and youths participate in youth sport programs, as compared with 85–90 percent of their suburban counterparts. That makes a mockery of the concept of a "level playing field" in child and youth development.

If we believe that appropriately planned and conducted sport experiences for children and youths are

developmentally and educationally valuable, and the evidence strongly supports that belief, then we must all work to see that such experiences are available to all youngsters, whether they are rich or poor. (See Focus On Box 6.3, page 133.)

Trends in Child and Youth Sport

Sport for children and youths continues as an important part of the lives of many families in America, and there have been some positive recent improvements: the availability of coaching-education materials, the increasing requirement for background checks for volunteer coaches, a vast array of materials available for parents to better educate them about developmentally appropriate sport, and a better understanding of likely injuries that might occur through overtraining and sport specialization. At the same time, however, there are some developing trends are troublesome. Sport sociologist Jay Coakley (2007) has described five trends that are disturbing:

- Declining publicly funded child/youth sport programs due to federal and state tax cuts that create local budget crises

FOCUS ON   The Benefits of Interscholastic Sport   6.6

As we examine problems in interscholastic sport, it is important to show that there is good evidence that school sport has benefits for many participants and for the school:

- Better grades
- Better self-concept
- Higher educational aspirations
- Stronger sense of personal control
- More likely to eat healthy diet
- Less likely to used banned substances

There is also descriptive and anecdotal evidence that interschool sports can indeed create what we traditionally have called school spirit.

"Interschool sports competition, then, is a means of unifying the entire school. Different races, social classes, fraternities, teachers, school staff, and students unite in a common cause. . . . An athletic program sometimes keeps potentially hostile segments from fragmenting the school. The collective following of an athletic team can also lift morale, thereby serving to unify the school" (Eitzen & Sage, 2003, p. 93).

- Increased privatization of youth sports favoring families who can afford club and facility fees
- Segregation of programs by socioeconomic status, race, and ethnicity
- Decreasing opportunities for children in low-income families and communities
- More children seeking alternatives to adult-controlled organized sports

Will these trends continue? If so, what will child/youth sports look like in another decade? It is important that all sport, fitness, and physical-education professionals be aware of these issues and commit themselves to work toward a child/youth sport culture that is developmentally appropriate and equally available to children/youths throughout the nation.

INTERSCHOLASTIC SPORT

Interscholastic sport for girls and boys plays a significant role in the American sport culture. The American model for interscholastic sport is unique in the world. Interscholastic sport often begins in the middle school, but it's most robust presence is at the secondary-school level. In high schools that have adequate funding and a significant enrollment, it is common to find teams at the freshman, junior varsity, and varsity levels. Smaller schools or schools where school funds are inadequate may have only junior varsity and varsity teams. Likewise, school size and school funding determine the number of sports that are offered.

Many people are rightfully proud of the interscholastic sports model in the United States, the opportunities that it provides girls and boys to grow in their sports, and the cohesive force it creates in both the school and community (see Focus On Box 6.6). In many communities, high-school teams and their falling or rising fortunes provide a focal point around which the entire community coalesces. Like other parts of the sport culture, however, interscholastic sport is not without problems. In this section, we address the following problems and issues:

- Exclusion and the varsity model
- Youth and interscholastic sport injuries
- Eligibility and pass-to-play rules
- Specialization
- Performance-enhancing supplements
- Coaching issues
- Funding through pay-to-play plans and booster clubs

Exclusion and the Varsity Model

If you examine participation in child and youth sport in America, you see a triangle with broad-based participation at the bottom (that is, child and youth sport) and less participation in interscholastic sport (ages 14 to 18). As we have noted, sport for children is programmed primarily through community sources and is widely available. Sport for high school–aged youths is programmed mostly through the school and is *decreasingly* available as the youths get older. This tendency to make participation less available (or available only to the better players) is known as the **varsity model** of competition, and it is the dominant feature of American school sport.

Many children in communities across the nation play soccer or baseball when they are young, often continuing their competition until they are 12 or 13 years of age. Even small communities have a soccer league or a Little League Baseball competition involving many children. Each of these same communities, however, has only *one* school team—or perhaps one reserve team and one varsity team. What happens to the further participation of all of those soccer and baseball players? The answer in most communities is *very little*!

The nature of an *exclusionary* model of sport development is that the entire system acts to identify and eventually cater to the more highly skilled player. Those players who are excluded have few opportunities to continue to develop in a sport, at least not until they are old enough to take part in more adult-oriented recreational sport. Adolescence is the time when boys and girls develop many, varied interests. Thus, we should not expect that they all will necessarily want to continue to develop within a certain sport or to try a new one. The issue here is *opportunity*, and unless a child is good enough for a varsity team, she or he has little opportunity to continue to develop in a sport in the current varsity model.

The varsity model used in the United States is quite different from school sport throughout the world. In most European countries, some school sport is available but is "low-key" compared to the United States. Instead, adolescents use the widely available *club system* for their continuing participation in sport. In sport clubs, boys and girls can compete at a level commensurate with their skills. If a

The high-school varsity model produces elite athletes but excludes most students from the opportunity to participate.

soccer club or basketball club has enough interest among the 14- to 18-year-old group, they will organize a series of teams that compete against other clubs with similar groupings. In club sport, children join a club at a young age and can continue to compete for that club throughout their lifetime. The club system is *inclusionary*. The A team for each club would be analogous to an American varsity team in that it would have the best players, but in the club system, practice and competition would also be available for B, C, and D teams in the same age group if there was sufficient interest.

New Zealand has, perhaps, the most inclusionary system in the world. Any high-school student who wants to compete in a sport can do so. Many more sports are offered than is typical in the United States. Students can compete both for their high school and their club. In New Zealand, it would be typical that 70–80 percent of students in a particular high school would be competing in school sport in a typical year. Teams typically practice 2 days a week and have one competition per week. For example, if girls' badminton is the sport, competitions typically involve two singles and a doubles team (four girls). If the high school has forty-eight girls on the badminton team, the competition would involve 12 four-girl teams that are

FOCUS ON An Inclusionary High-School Sport Model 6.7

Tawa High School in New Zealand enrolls 1,389 students, 638 girls and 751 boys, with 91 teachers. It competes primarily with other high schools in and around Wellington, which is New Zealand's second largest city. What follows is a snapshot of its interscholastic sports program for 2007–08:

- Seventy-nine percent of all students compete in at least one sport, and many participate in three to four sports.
- Ninety-one sports are offered.
- The most popular sports and number competing for girls were net ball (161), soccer (66), and badminton (56).

- The most popular sports for boys were soccer (123), rugby (109), and cricket (85).
- Other popular sports and number of boys and girls competing were basketball (90), field hockey (64), and track and field (51).
- Other sports offered included water polo, softball, tennis, road racing, indoor bowls, cross-country, field hockey, golf, squash, touch football, and rowing.
- Nearly 30 percent of the teachers coach teams.

No athlete is "cut" from a team. Teams typically practice 2 days per week and compete once per week.

SOURCE: Personal Communication, S. Smith, Tawa High School, Wellington, NZ (2008).

organized by skill levels. No players are "cut" from the team. Focus On Box 6.7 provides a snapshot of the participation rates for girls and boys in one New Zealand high school.

Youth and Interschool Sport Injuries

Despite the documented health benefits of participation in interscholastic sports (for example, weight management, improved self-esteem, and increased strength and endurance) there is continuing concern about injury prevention and treatment. Until recently, there was no way to document either the extent of sport-related injuries for high-school athletes or the seriousness of the injuries. The Centers for Disease control sponsored a national study of sport injuries during the 2005–06 school year (MMWR Weekly, 2006). Nine high-school sports were studied with reports made by athletic trainers in the 425 participating schools. The data allowed researchers to conclude that high-school athletes account for an estimated 2 million injuries, 500,000 doctor visits, and 30,000 hospitalizations yearly.

Nearly 1.5 million injuries occurred for the nine sports studied in the sample schools. Injuries for both practice and competition were 2.44 injuries per 1,000 athlete exposures. Football had the highest injury rate, followed by wrestling, boys' and girls' soccer, and girls' basketball. For all sports, injury rates were higher in competition than in practice. The most common injuries were sprains, contusions, fractures, and concussions. Eighty percent of the injuries reported were new injuries rather than recurrences of previous injuries. The severity of injury, measured by days lost from play, varied by sport. Overall, about half of the injuries reported resulted in less than 7 days lost. Football, girls' basketball, and wrestling had higher proportions of injuries resulting in more than 7 days lost. Fortunately, surgery was required for only 2.4 percent of the cases in football, 2 percent in wrestling, and 1.4 percent in field hockey.

Using data available from previous studies of injuries in interscholastic sports, the investigators estimated that injury rates have likely dropped by more than 50 percent over the previous decade. They attributed this reduction in injury rates to better equipment and better conditioning for the athletes.

Data on youth sport injuries is considerably more difficult to gather. A recent study on youth football sheds some light on the issues (Dompier, Powell, Barron, & Moore, 2007). Current estimates suggest that 28 percent of the 5.5 million youths aged 5–14 years who participate in various forms of youth football are injured each year, with an estimated 187,000 emergency rooms visits. The study focused on 779 youth football players, ranging in age from grade 4 to grade 8. Injuries were categorized into time-loss injuries (TL) and nontime-lost injuries (NTL). Injury data collected by athletic trainers showed that 36.5 percent of the players sustained an injury during the season, with nearly 15 percent reporting more than one injury. Injury rates tend to increase by grade level. Cumulative NTL injury rate was 10.5 per 1,000 exposures, and TL injury rate was 7.4 per 1,000 exposures. What this suggests is the importance of coaches and officials having first-aid certification.

Eligibility and Pass-to-Play Rules

In almost all high schools, students have to meet eligibility standards to be on a school team. Many athletic-eligibility standards go well beyond criteria a student is required to meet to stay in school. In recent years, many states have instituted new *pass-to-play* eligibility standards, producing even more stringent requirements for athletes to maintain their eligibility.

In some cases, these more stringent eligibility standards have been legislated because of abuses in school sport. The issue is not whether abuses should be tolerated. The issue is how abuses should be remedied. The more fundamental issue in eligibility rules, however, has little to do with abuses. Instead, it has to do with one's basic view of the educational importance of school sport.

If school sport is an extracurricular activity, a privilege to be earned, then eligibility rules are clearly appropriate. If, however, school sport has basic educational value, then why deny the experience to anybody who is legitimately a student at a school? If being on a team provides an important set of experiences for personal and social development, then why should that opportunity for development be denied to some students?

As you can see, this argument is also related to the exclusionary issue discussed previously. The same logic prevails. If school sport is such a strong developmental experience for adolescent boys and girls, why not make it more widely available so that more students can benefit? It is true that there are important economic issues here also. Could we afford—or, more accurately, would we be willing to pay for—a greatly expanded school sport program? Despite the economic overtones, however, some important philosophical issues are at stake in this debate.

Specialization

The problem of specialization was discussed in the section on child and youth sport. The issue is similar for school sport, with one added dimension. Athletes in high schools do specialize much more today than they did even as recently as the mid-1980s. Many athletes compete in one sport only and train for that sport in the off-season, sometimes attending a specialized summer camp. Sport specialization at the high-school level seems to be related to two important developments in the American sport culture in recent years.

First, the value and importance of weight and endurance training have been widely recognized. For many school athletes, an off-season spent in the weight room is more important than training for and competing in another sport. Many coaches promote this view—some directly demanding it, others more tacitly encouraging it. Second, many high-school athletes have hopes for an athletic scholarship to a college or university. The number of scholarships available has increased dramatically since the mid-1980s. To be as competitive as possible in the scholarship area, many high-school athletes forgo multisport competition in favor of specialization.

Is specialization good or bad? There are few issues in sport about which there is more heated debate—and for which there is less solid evidence. At this time, at least, the debate is more philosophical than scientific.

Performance-Enhancing Supplements

In 2004–2005, the performance-enhancing-drug scandals in organized sport became front-page news. The accusations about steroid use among high-profile baseball players was the most prominent of those scandals, resulting in hearings in the U.S. Congress and new rules for steroid testing and stricter penalties for steroid use in baseball and other professional sports. Just several years earlier, the focus had been on the dietary supplement *creatine* and its alleged use by home-run slugger Mark McGwire.

For our purposes, however, the more disturbing problem is one that attracted national attention when the December 20, 2004, cover of *Newsweek* showed a high-school football player with the heading "Steroids and Kids: How Sports Doping Hits Home." Another article followed on March 7, 2005, describing admitted steroid use by nine football players at Heritage High School in Texas. Although this one high school was the main focus of the article, it was clear that steroid use among young athletes had spread nationwide and become a major problem.

Steroid use among adolescents is inherently dangerous. Steroid use can hasten the process in which skeletal growth ends in adolescence, shutting down growth prematurely. Although steroids promote muscle growth, the tendons that attach muscles to bones are not strengthened, increasing the risk of injury. Steroids lower the level of "good" cholesterol and raise the level of "bad" cholesterol markedly. Steroid use can become toxic to the liver (Adler, 2004).

Creatine is produced naturally in the body; it can also be obtained from diet and stored in the body (Bowers, 1999). Supplements are marketed on the basis that they can increase the availability of the substance to use in muscular performance. The effects, particularly the long-term effects of such supplements on young athletes, are largely unknown. Some experts feel that prolonged use may be related to kidney dysfunction. Creatine and most other supplements are not approved by the Food and Drug Administration (FDA) and are largely unregulated as to quality of the product.

Concerns about the growing incidence of high-school athletes using performance-enhancing drugs and supplements have caused states to consider legislation designed to reduce and eliminate such practices. State legislators often confront this issue as a result of new evidence of the use of performance-enhancing drugs in their own state. For example, in June 2006, the *Dallas Morning News* published a multipart series on steroid use among high-school athletes in Texas. The series focused particularly on the 13,700-student Grapevine–Colleyville School District, north of Dallas. Soon thereafter, that district's school board passed a requirement for random testing of students who participate in sports and other extracurricular activities (LaFee, 2006). In early 2007, the governing body of interschool sports in Texas partnered with the Texas Association of School Administrators to develop a program to educate students about the dangers of using performance-enhancing supplements. By this time, 130 of the 1,300 high schools in Texas were already testing for steroid use. In 2007 the Texas House of Representatives voted 140 to 4 to support legislation requiring random drug testing of high-school athletes in Texas. When the governor signed the bill, Texas joined New Jersey and Florida as states requiring random testing. Other states have passed legislation allowing school districts to choose to do drug testing, while other states have passed legislation that allows for voluntary student drug testing.

In a sport environment where young athletes are striving to improve their performance, hoping to get an athletic scholarship to college, and are socialized into a view of sport that accepts the use of steroids and ergogenic aids in the form of nutritional supplements, it is no surprise that many young athletes use supplements. Coaches, athletic trainers, and parents need to play a stronger educational and supervisory role so that these young athletes do not use questionable substances that may prove harmful to them in the long run.

The School Coach as Teacher-Coach

In Chapter 5, details of coaching certification (or the lack thereof) were provided. In Chapter 12, the problem known as teacher–coach role conflict is addressed. That well-documented problem is straightforward. Men and women who fill both teaching and coaching roles over a period of years tend to spend more of their energies in coaching than they do in teaching because that is where the real and perceived rewards are found. The United States has chosen to program the largest part of its sport culture for adolescents through the school. That means, theoretically at least, that the coaches of school sport teams are *teachers*.

The involvement of *teachers* in *school* sport is no mere convenience or coincidence. An important philosophical issue is represented in that arrangement—namely, that sport is educational and should be conducted in an educationally sound manner. I have mentioned that few states require coaching certification and that many states do not require teaching credentials for their coaches. Thus, the philosophical principle underlying the system is not always followed.

In most school districts, coaching is compensated on a supplemental contract, both for teachers and for nonteachers. In 2006 a Pittsburgh high school with a teacher contract of $56,000 earned $18,000 additional in supplemental contracts: $8,700 for football, $6,200 as a fitness coach, and $2,900 as a senior class sponsor (Strecker & Young, 2007). Coaches who do not have a teaching license typically have to go through a background check and have completed a first-aid course. A continuing issue is whether school districts hire teachers, first and foremost, for their potential as a classroom teacher or physical-education teacher, and then secondarily for their desire and qualifications to coach in the interscholastic program. This is obviously the preferred approach, but some coaches are hired first and foremost for their record as a coach and then only secondarily for their record as a teacher.

Parental Pressures and Booster Clubs

Parents, coaches, and townspeople often care about the sport performance of local school teams and athletes in ways that *differ* from the ways that athletes care about them. Parents, coaches, and townspeople are adults, spectators, fans, and enthusiasts. The adolescent athletes are participants. The differences in points of view can sometimes create pressures that are counterproductive to the development of the athlete and of school sport in general (Focus On Box 6.8).

Dress an adolescent in a uniform, have him or her play in front of spectators who include peers, parents, and friends, under the gaze of a coach who looms as an important person in the athlete's immediate future in the sport, with the results written about in school and local newspapers and talked about among people in the town—and what do you have? Pressure! That kind of pressure is often important to the development of the adolescent, important in a positive way. The major point here, however, is that it is a great deal of pressure in and of itself. Additional pressure is unnecessary.

When parents put undue pressure on their sons and daughters, when coaches put too much pressure on their athletes, and when the expectations of administrators and parents put too much pressure on coaches, then the conditions are such that the sport experience can rapidly become less enjoyable and rewarding than it should be. In states where support for school sport has to come from booster clubs and gate receipts, the conditions that might create undue pressures on coaches, athletes, and programs are even more likely to occur.

With the growing importance of sport generally and with the specific focus in local communities on the success of the high-school teams, there is enormous pressure on school coaches, especially those in the high-profile sports of football and basketball. Increasingly, coaches quit their "coach" job or are dismissed. The major sources of pressure for high-school coaches are parents, fans in the community, and boosters (Miller, Lutz, Shim, Fredenburg, & Miller, 2005). Principals report that the major

On July 5, 2000, a parent watching his son at a youth hockey practice session assaulted the man supervising the practice and beat him so severely that he went into a coma and eventually died (Nack & Munson, 2000). That tragic event brought to the attention of the nation what appears to be widespread instances of parents and even coaches out of control in youth sport.

- In an Illinois state soccer playoff game, a coach is accused of striking a referee.
- In Florida, a parent walks out of the stands and head-butts a referee.
- In Pennsylvania, police are called to quell a riot involving fifty parents after a football game for 11- to 13-year-olds.
- In a California Little League Baseball game, a man coaching his son's team assaults and beats the manager of the opposing team.

SOURCES: Meadows, 2003; Nack & Munson, 2000; Sutton, 2000.

- In Ohio, the father of a soccer player pleads no contest to the charge of assaulting a 14-year-old boy who had scuffled for the ball with the man's 14-year-old son.

Community and agency sport groups are beginning to take a more proactive stance to prevent such incidents. In Jupiter, Florida, for example, a community sport organization now requires that

- Parents take a class that includes a video on the responsibilities of parenting a young athlete.
- Parents sign a code of ethics pledging to behave at youth sport contests—if they don't sign, their kids don't play.
- Parent behavior is monitored at games. For a first offense, they review the video and sign another pledge.
- The parent and child are sent home after a second offense and are not allowed to return.

reasons for dismissal of high-school coaches are poor player–coach relations, lack of coaching skill, and failure to win (Scantling & Lackey, 2005).

Pay-to-Play Plans

School districts in many states have had enormous difficulties raising monies through local tax initiatives to fund the continuing expenses of education. As a result, many districts have begun to charge user fees for many extracurricular activities offered by the schools. *User fees* are a form of direct taxation; that is, those who use the services pay an additional tax for those privileges.

Pay-to-play plans have been declared illegal in California and New York on the basis of the discriminatory effects of such plans; that is, students who can't afford the fees should not be denied access to what is an approved school program (Swift, 1991). The National Federation of State High

School Associations has also come out against such fees, arguing that interschool sport programs have documented educational value and that students should have access to them as part of the regular school program.

Still, pay-to-play plans are springing up all over the country. At least thirty-four states indicate that some school districts now charge students to play sports. In several states, the number of school districts that now charge fees for participation in school sports has doubled in recent years (Brady & Glier, 2004). In some cases, the fees are not charged by school districts but instead are handled by parent groups or booster clubs which in turn use the funds to support the school sport programs. In Michigan, more than half the school districts now charge fees for participation in school sports (Martin, 2003).

It is spring as I write this, and the suburban school district in my immediate area is full into the spring sports schedule. The track teams in the three high schools in the district have a long tradition of successful competition in their league and at the state level. This year, however, it costs $425 for a student to participate in track and field at the three high schools. In one high school, 49 girls and boys participate under the new fee structure. Last year, the track team had 125 members. Another of the high schools is down from 60 track-and-field athletes a year ago to 33 this year. One can just imagine what would happen to school sports in urban school districts if pay-to-play plans were imposed.

It is curious that pay-to-play programs have developed at the same time that state courts all over the United States have begun to force states to fund schools more equitably—that is, to ensure that schools in financially strained districts have per-pupil budgets that are similar to those in schools in wealthy districts. The basis for such decisions is always a clause in a state constitution that ensures an equal and appropriate education to all children and youths in public schools. If pay-to-play plans become the norm, then it is certain that youths in financially strained districts will have fewer sport opportunities than their counterparts in wealthy districts and that their equipment and training facilities will be inferior.

INTERCOLLEGIATE SPORT

Intercollegiate sport in the United States has become big business for some schools, especially in Division I schools in the National College Athletic Association (NCAA). Yet big-time intercollegiate sport occupies an important niche in American sport culture. Events such as the Rose Bowl and the Final Four are truly national in scope. Intercollegiate sport provides a common ground of loyalty among alumni, students, and friends. Division I NCAA sport provides entertainment to millions via radio and television.

At the Division III level of the NCAA, thousands of student-athletes take part in competition that seems an appropriate extension of school sport. No scholarships are given for athletic prowess at this level. Athletes' commitments within and outside the boundaries of the season are more limited. There is less commercialism. Nobody expects the sports to pay for themselves.

Thus, when we talk about problems and issues in intercollegiate sport, we must keep in mind that there are major differences between big-time university sport and the kind of competition we might typically find at a local college. The major problems and issues in intercollegiate sport are the following:

1. Recruiting violations and pressures
2. Drugs used to enhance performance
3. Economic disparities among top powers
4. Economic pressure for winning
5. Treatment of athletes at the university

Recruiting Violations and Pressures

Each year, the NCAA puts several university athletic programs on *sanctions* because of recruiting violations. The recruiting of athletes to play on university teams is governed by rules established by the NCAA. The rules are intended to protect the athlete and to ensure reasonably equal competition among schools trying to influence young athletes to attend their universities.

What is sad and alarming about many recruiting violations is that they are done with the help and (in some cases) at the insistence of influential alumni and friends of the universities, who are often in positions of prestige, trust, and power within the community. Recruiting violations occur because the pressures to attract the best athletes are so strong. Those pressures are so strong because pressures to have a winning program are immense. The pressures to have a winning program exist because of economic factors and because of the status that accrues to those associated with winning programs at universities—particularly alumni and friends of the university.

Coaches sometimes succumb to those pressures. In other situations, coaches sometimes initiate the cheating themselves because they want so badly to win or to advance their careers. Direct cash payments, cars, high-paying jobs that require little or no work, and sexual favors have all been used to lure young athletes.

Drugs That Enhance Performance

Drugs are a problem for many college-age youths. For athletes, however, there is a special set of problems that have to do with drugs taken to improve performance. Evidence (USA Today, 1988) indicates that the use of *anabolic steroids* (male hormones that help increase strength and allow athletes to perform more work in training) has begun to show up even at the junior high-school level! The use of these drugs in certain sports, such as track and field and football, is thought to be widespread at elite levels of competition.

Most of the increased size of weight-event athletes in track and field and of linemen in football is the result of more scientific application of weight-training principles. There is widespread fear, however, that some of it is also due to the regular use of anabolic steroids. Drug testing has become a major issue in the NCAA. Student athletes at NCAA championship events are regularly tested for drugs that might affect performance. The issue of drug testing has caused a national debate that still persists. The debate hinges on the right to privacy of the athlete (or the worker, if in a business) and on whether such testing is constitutional under the prohibition of *unreasonable* search and seizure in the Fourth Amendment to the U.S. Constitution.

Economic Disparities Among Top Powers

For a few universities, the sports of football and basketball generate most of the revenues that support all the rest of the sports in the program. The presence of 80,000 fans for every home football game or of 15,000 for every home basketball game means income for the athletic program. In addition, the monies earned from televised games or for bowl-game appearances can be even more important than the gate receipts. Nonetheless, the vast majority of NCAA Division I athletic programs do not even break even with their football and basketball programs, let alone provide support for other sports.

In big-time collegiate sport, the rich tend to get richer. If you have a winning program and, for example, are consistently ranked in the top twenty in football or basketball, more fans come to your games, you are offered a large local television contract, you have more regional and national television appearances, and you play more postseason games. More people see your team play. More young athletes see your team play—and the better ones are easier to recruit as a result. Of course, some universities not in this inner circle would like to get in! The difficulties in doing so are enormous. Thus, the temptation is there to cheat in recruiting to overcome the natural advantage enjoyed by the established programs.

In professional football and basketball, there is a yearly player draft in which teams at the bottom of the yearly standings get to pick first, a system designed specifically to promote more even competition over time. No such system exists for university sport, so over time the same teams tend to dominate the top rankings. Remember, big-time sports are a losing proposition economically for most universities. Still, the temptations created by hoping to improve that situation are substantial.

Economic Pressure to Win

The economic disparities that exist in big-time collegiate sport produce strong pressures to win simply because it is through winning over a period of years that university athletic programs either remain in the elite economic group or break into that group. The economic consequences of making it are substantial. Programs that do not make it still have to build stadiums, put Astroturf on their fields, erect fancy scoreboards, and pay for equipping and training 100 football players. Without the economic power that accrues to the elite programs from gate receipts and television, these other institutions are left with huge bills that they must pay from regular funds.

FOCUS ON — Do College Athletes Need a Bill of Rights?   6.9

Many people close to Division I college athletics believe that too many athletes are exploited and that a bill of rights is needed to protect their interests. How do you react to the following possible provisions of a bill of rights?

- The right to transfer to a different college without having to lose eligibility
- The right to a 4-year scholarship rather than one renewable at the discretion of the institution
- For those who compete for 3 years, the right to scholarship support until they graduate

- The same rights to protection from physical and mental abuse and the right of free speech that other university students have
- The right to consult with agents concerning their future in sports
- The right to be compensated for endorsements, speeches, and appearances
- The right to adequate insurance to totally cover current injuries and problems that arise from them

What can you add? What would you delete?

SOURCE: Adapted from Eitzen & Sage, 2003.

Learning to work together for a team goal is an important experience.

Of course, there are always the alumni and friends who would like the athletic program to be as good as those at the few universities with the largest gate receipts, television contracts, and visibility. The issue here is status. The combined pressures that result from the search for status and for economic gain through big-time collegiate sport are at the heart of most of the abuses within the system.

Treatment of the Student Athlete

There are many student athletes in sport programs in American colleges and universities who fit well

the best possible image of how sport and academic life can be combined such that each is enriched by the other for a better total college experience. There are others, however, for whom the term *student athlete* is badly misused. This is often not so much their fault as the fault of the institution that is *misusing* the young athlete.

What is the quality of life for an elite, scholarship athlete at a major university? Although there are surely as many answers to that question as there are individual athletes, there are some disturbing signs, to say the least. The NCAA commissioned a study of more than 4,000 athletes from forty-two Division I schools (Wrisberg, 1996) (see Focus On Box 6.9). The major findings were as follows:

- Student athletes focus most of their attention on their sport. They miss more classes and participate in fewer other university activities than their student peers.
- Basketball and football players perform less well than student peers on every measure of academic performance, even though there are substantial academic support services provided for them.
- Many suffer from frequent or chronic injuries and, despite better access to good health care,

feel pressure to practice and perform despite injuries.

- Most elite-scholarship athletes suffer from chronic fatigue.
- These athletes tend to attribute actions to external influences more than do nonathletes; that is, they report less of a sense of personal control.
- These athletes report having little opportunity or time to participate in personal-development activities on campus.

The picture that emerges from this study "offers little evidence of a high level of life quality by any definition or measuring standard" (Wrisberg, 1996, p. 397). It should be noted that the NCAA has used the results of this study to foster changes in Division I athletic programs that are aimed at reversing these trends.

Some sport scholars have long argued that scholarship athletes are badly exploited by the system (Sack, 1977). Scholarship athletes can receive nothing more than tuition, room, board, fees, and books—at least, not legally. The total cost of this package differs depending on the costs at the university, but even at the most expensive university, when one divides the number of hours of work that the athlete devotes to his or her sport by the total value of the scholarship, the pay per hour is low. Clearly, few athletes *feel* exploited. Most are happy to be where they are, and many feel extremely lucky to have been awarded the scholarship. The charge of exploitation comes from the huge financial rewards the institution can achieve, which are not shared in any way with the athlete.

EQUITY ISSUES IN SPORT

Many issues in sport have a central theme—*equity*. Historically, much of organized sport has been the special province of wealthy, white males. When the first Olympic Games were held in ancient Greece, the competition was available only to male citizens of the Greek city-states. Citizens were males of privilege. The menial labor of the day was done by slaves. Not only were women disallowed from competition—they could not even watch!

When the Olympic Games were reborn in 1896, the tradition had not changed very much. The new games were much like the old games in that males dominated and wealth was assumed—the games were, after all, for *gentlemen* athletes. You were not a gentleman if you came from the working class or if you really trained hard for the competition. Much has changed since those days, particularly since the 1970s. Nonetheless, the traditions of inequity in sport still linger and need continually to be addressed. Women's issues and minority issues are two such areas.

Women's Issues

Access to training and competition in sport has historically been denied to women. The nineteenth-century "feminine virtues" of piety, purity, submissiveness, and domesticity were alien to sport competition. The philosophy of muscular Christianity from which twentieth-century sport and physical education emerged was, above all, a *masculine* philosophy. Clearly, those views have changed in recent years. The passage of Title IX made equity for girls and women in sport the law of the land. Since then, girls have had access to more sports, their participation has increased dramatically, and scholarships for them have become more widely available. Moreover, there have been some notable successes by women in elite and professional sport. In 1984 women were finally allowed to compete in the marathon at the Olympic Games, and Joan Benoit showed extraordinary athletic prowess in winning the event. In Barcelona, in 1992, it became clear that Jackie Joyner-Kersee was the greatest multievent track-and-field athlete of all time, regardless of gender.

In sport, compliance with Title IX focuses particularly on equal provision of equipment and supplies, practice and game times, travel, compensation of coaches, publicity, tutoring and other such services, locker rooms, medical and training facilities, housing

Women's competition in Olympic swimming
is followed worldwide.

and dining facilities, and financial aid (Fox, 1992)
(See Focus On Box 6.10 on page 150.). These are
easily identifiable factors, and discrimination against
girls and women on the basis of these factors should
be easily discernible. Yet problems related to these
factors still exist in many schools and universities.
The more subtle forms of discrimination—negative
stereotyping, poor media coverage, underrepresentation in coaching and administration, and lack of female role models—will be more difficult to confront
and correct (Fox, 1992).

Title IX became law in 1972. After a brief period
of increased opportunity for women in coaching and
administrative positions, the 1980s saw a decrease in
the percentage of women in those roles. In 1984
Grove City College in Pennsylvania brought suit,

charging that, because college athletic programs receive no direct federal support, Title IX did not
apply to college athletics. The U.S. Supreme Court
agreed. That decision led to a concerted lobbying
effort in the U.S. Congress by advocates for
women's sport and others interested in civil rights.
Their efforts were rewarded when the Civil Rights
Act of 1987 was passed with much stronger provisions for Title IX (Motley & Lavine, 2001). Thus,
from the mid-1980s through the 1990s, we witnessed what might be called the first true "Title IX
generation" of girl and women athletes. All fifty
states offered state championships for girls' sports,
and the NCAA sanctioned seventeen national championships for women.

Still, as we noted in Chapter 5, recent data show
that the percentage of women in coaching, administrative, and training positions remains low and shows
few signs of improving dramatically in the near future. Women athletes receive only 30 percent of the
scholarship dollars in intercollegiate sport, 23 percent of the athletic operating budgets, 17 percent of
the recruiting dollars, and 35 percent of the participation opportunities (Motley & Lavine, 2001). Programs to attract, train, and place more female
coaches have generally failed (Pastore, 1994), with
the exception of a Colorado program that has increased the percentage of female coaches in school
sport programs in that state. Male officials still dominate important women's sports such as basketball
and softball (Casey, 1992). It is uncommon to see a
woman as head athletic director at any level. In 2002
there were 3,210 administrative positions in NCAA
women's athletic programs. Women held only 40
percent of those jobs. Acosta and Carpenter (1994,
pp. 117–118) have summarized the issues well:

> With the increase in women's participation in inter-
> collegiate athletics has come a decrease in women's
> leadership opportunities at the administrative and
> coaching levels. If the women who currently enjoy
> collegiate athletics are to have the opportunity to re-
> main in college athletics and exert leadership over
> the activities they enjoy, we must recognize the pat-
> terns of exclusion that presently exist in women's ath-
> letics and work to reverse this undesirable trend.

FOCUS ON The Three-Point Test for Title IX Compliance 6.10

In 1979 compliance with Title IX was determined to be acceptable if institutions passed one of the three criteria listed below. In 1996 the Office of Civil Rights described the first criterion (the proportionality criterion) as the safest way for an institution to be in compliance.

1. The number of male and female athletes at a school must be in proportion to the overall student body. If women are half the school's population, half of its athletes should be women.

2. A school must demonstrate that it has increased opportunities for women, mostly by adding women's sports.

3. A school must continue to show that its existing athletic programs meet the interests of women on campus.

About one-third of schools that have had compliance complaints use the proportionality criterion to pass the inspection.

Few schools use the adding-sports criterion to gain compliance.

Nearly two-thirds of schools use criterion 3 to show compliance.

The proportionality criterion continues to be the most controversial.

SOURCE: Coffin, 2002.

When interscholastic and intercollegiate sport budgets get tight, as they have in many places in recent years, it is now common to hear the requirements for gender equity in sports blamed for the reduced support for boys' and men's programs (Stourowsky, 1996). A men's volleyball program is eliminated at a university, and the reason given is the need to provide more support for the new women's tennis program—a zero-sum argument is forwarded suggesting that gains for women occur only at the expense of men. This is what Sage (1987) and Stourowsky (1996) refer to as "blaming the victim" strategy; that is, the fault is found in the group that has the least amount of power while the focus is deflected from the main issue, which is providing resources that are sufficient and equitable.

Another barrier that girls and women are now contesting is the barrier to participation in contact and strength sports traditionally thought to be appropriate only for males. Participation for high-school girls in football, wrestling, ice hockey, and weight lifting has increased steadily over the past few years. For 2007, 1,073 girls participated in football, 7,010 in wrestling, 7,350 in ice hockey, and 7,110 in weight lifting. Athletic directors and coaches need to be sensitive to create conditions that are supportive of girls' participation, and their sensitivity can be increased through appropriate educational programs. The good news is that young girls and their support groups have continued to confront the stereotypes that have heretofore hindered their participation.

What seems clear is that the status of women in sport will not improve without vigorous advocacy by sport and physical-education professionals. The National Association for Girls and Women in Sport (NAGWS) has adopted a strategic plan to remediate problems that exist for women because of unequal opportunity in sport and lack of compliance with Title IX (Hester & Dunaway, 1991). This plan includes advocacy for full participation both in athlete roles and in indirect roles in administration, training, officiating, and the like; recruitment, development, and promotion plans to help women assume leadership positions; and the initiation of new programs and enhancement of existing programs for females of all ages, races, economic levels, and ethnic origins.

Although the ideal of the athletic woman has become much more accepted today—even for substantial profit in advertising—the old conceptions linger in more subtle ways. We still hear male sports announcers describing a female athlete as "pretty, too" when "prettiness" or "attractiveness" has nothing to do with the competition. (When was the last time you heard a male announcer talk about a handsome baseball or football player?) Research indicates that adults frown on girls' participation in activities considered to be normal for boys and that signs of assertiveness typically reinforced in young boys are often not accepted in young girls (Elias, 1983). All of this indicates that the nineteenth-century views still linger in many ways—and that as long as they do, equity for girls and women in sport will not be complete.

Minority Issues

If sport in America has been typically male dominated, it has also been "lily white." Blacks and other minorities have always participated in sport but were denied access to mainstream sport competition in schools, universities, and professional sport. The *color barrier* in major professional sport was not broken until Jackie Robinson played for the Brooklyn Dodgers in 1947. The integration of top-level collegiate sport did not come until much later, especially in the South. Although integrated schools were first mandated in 1954 (*Brown v. Board of Education*), school sport was not fully integrated until lawsuits were decided during the civil rights movements of the 1960s and 1970s.

Today, black and Hispanic players are abundant in some professional sports—particularly baseball, football, and basketball. Yet it is still rare to see a minority athlete on the tennis court or on the professional golf circuit. Minority athletes have been traditionally stereotyped by position in many sports (Loy & McElvogue, 1981), and they are seriously underrepresented in coaching and administrative positions in all sports (Coakley, 2007).

Many coaches and athletic administrators are former players. It has been more than 60 years since the color barrier was broken in professional baseball and more than a quarter-century since the implementation of Title IX, but gender and race inequalities are still prevalent in hiring and promotion practices in both intercollegiate and professional sport.

Recent studies show a small increase in the numbers of minority persons and women as head coaches, assistant coaches, and athletic directors in athletic programs at Division I and Division I-A universities (Lapchick, 2007). Still, the issues for minorities and women in high-level intercollegiate sport are substantial. In 2007,

- 82 percent of athletic directors were white males.
- 655 of faculty athletic representatives were white males.
- All Division I-A conference commissioners were white males.
- 93 percent of head football coaches were white males.
- 87 percent of offensive and defensive coordinators were white males.
- 45 percent of student-athlete football players were white males.

Thus, at the top level of athletic management and coaching in collegiate football, minorities are substantially underrepresented.

In our coverage of the various aspects of sport, it has been made clear that child/youth sport has enormous potential to contribute to the development of girls and boys. Yet, we have also seen that child/youth sport has problems, and one of them is the cost involved for a family to keep their children involved in youth sport. For many minority families and others living in disadvantaged communities, the opportunities for quality youth sport experiences for children/youths are considerably less available. School physical-education programs and community recreation programs in disadvantaged communities are typically underfunded and cannot provide comprehensive programs. These issues are most problematic for minority girls, who have been shown to be most at risk for physical inactivity and obesity.

Urban schools typically schedule less time in physical education, provide less opportunity for intramural sports, and offer fewer opportunities in interscholastic sports. Urban communities typically have fewer opportunities for child/youth sport participation. What is most disturbing is that there is good evidence that minority children/youths who do get the opportunity to participate in community and school sport are more resilient and more motivated to do well in school (Hawkins & Mulkey, 2005).

Problems of race in sport tend to interact with problems that are socioeconomic in nature. The idea of "sport for all," an ethic of access and participation, is being achieved much less in cities than in suburbs, much less among nonwhite children and youths than among white children and youths, much less for the poor than for the wealthy. Although these issues represent problems that institutionalized sport can help combat, we also need to recognize that the problems are manifestations of *structural* inequities in our society.

SPORT SYSTEMS

The sport system of the United States is composed of diverse elements: child and youth sport, school sport, university sport, professional sport, and recreational sport. Some features of this system are distinct in the world sports community. Nowhere is school or university sport as important to a sport culture as in the United States. Nowhere is government support for and regulation of sport less than in the United States. The combination of youth, school, and university sport that serves youths and young adults as they develop in sport is primarily an *exclusionary* model, one in which a few skilled sportspersons get to continue in the system, whereas those who are less skilled have little access to continued training and competition in their sport.

In most of the rest of the world, the overall sport system of countries is guided and funded by government. The sport-club system is the primary vehicle of training and competition from youth sport through to elite sport. Coaching is more often certified at all levels. Which system is better? The question is relevant only if we have previously agreed to the purposes and goals the systems should serve. Sport systems serve different goals and reflect different political and economic systems. The systems thus are most often not directly comparable.

Alternative Goals for Sport Systems

What goals should a sport system serve? In what order of priority should those goals be arranged? These are useful questions to consider because there are real choices to be made as to how limited resources are allocated in sport.

To what extent should Olympic development programs dominate a sport system? Some countries keep national teams and athletes training year-round in a national training facility. Many countries have full-time national coaches. Should more resources be allocated to the continued training of elite athletes who are beyond their university years, especially in sports for which there is no way to earn a living in relation to those sports, or should resources be allocated more for increased participation at the recreational level?

Still another choice is whether to expand the opportunities for sport at the child and youth sport levels, providing better coaching and more developmentally appropriate sport forms and extending those opportunities to *all* children rather than just to sons and daughters of the middle and upper classes. It would be nice if there were sufficient resources to do all the sport development implied in these questions. Resources are always limited, however, and choices must be made. What is interesting to consider is the means by which those choices are made in the United States. Do we need an overall national sport policy or a state-level policy? Instead, are we better off continuing to develop sport primarily through the private sector, with decisions made mostly on the basis of *consumer demands*?

Sport in Perspective

In this chapter, we have focused on issues and problems in sport at all levels. To conclude the chapter, we need to reflect that in many instances sport is still just sport, an experience to be enjoyed and from which people derive substantial meaning for their lives. Sport does have problems. Sport can and often does provide substantial benefits to participants. In 1995 Nike (White & Sheets, 2001) developed a now famous television commercial featuring adolescent girls engaged in various sports. In each scene, a girl athlete began by speaking the same phrase, "If you let me play sports," which was followed by one of the following statements:

- I will like myself more.
- I will have more self-confidence.
- I will suffer less depression.
- I will be 60 percent less likely to develop breast cancer.
- I will be more likely to leave a man who beats me.
- I will be less likely to get pregnant before I want to.
- I will learn what it means to be strong.

All these claims are backed by evidence, and the commercial was a powerful argument for increasing opportunities for girls in sport.

Compelling as the above argument is, we need to keep in mind that those are probably *not* the reasons why girls want to play sports. Robin Marantz Henig is a writer from the pre–Title IX generation. Her daughter, Sam, is an athlete, and watching Sam and her teammates compete caused Ms. Henig to argue that although all those claims of benefits for girls are good and true, "sports is not birth control" (Henig, 1999). Because Ms. Henig was raised in a pre–Title IX era, she never came to view herself as an athlete, even though she was physically active. This is what she concluded as she watched her daughter compete:

> It is against this background that I find myself watching with great pleasure, as Sam plays basketball each winter—just as I love watching her play soccer in the fall and spring, and softball in the summer. I love the idea that she thinks of herself as an athlete and as a member of a team. When I join the other parents on those hard bleachers every Sunday afternoon of basketball season, we are all reveling in our daughters' freedom to dance a dance that was never really available to the mothers among us. Whether or not it keeps them out of harm's way, for these hours at least, basketball turns them into something quite remarkable: a group of graceful, agile, self-confident young women taking pride in their bodies, not for who or what they can attract, but for what they can accomplish.

The deepest meaning of sport is always in the moment. What the many moments do or do not do for any of us in other aspects of our lives is important, but it should never diminish our understanding or appreciation of sport as experience.

Do not be dismayed by the problems presented in this chapter. Take heart in the many organizations that are working diligently to make sport better for athletes at all levels. Some of these organizations were created by athletes for athletes. Among these are Athletes for a Better World, the Collegiate Athletes Coalition, the National Alliance of African American Athletes, the International Association of Athletes Against Drugs, and the National Student Athletes' Rights Movement (see the list of Web sites near the end of this chapter). All of these organizations and others cited in this chapter work to make the sport experience more educational and more fun for all involved.

SUMMARY

1. Traditionally, sport enthusiasts have ascribed almost mystical and miraculous qualities to sport participation; more recently, many of these myths have been questioned seriously.

2. Cooperation among athletes is essential to high-quality sport and is a fundamental aspect of the sport experience.

3. Appropriate competition—developmentally sound and psychologically suited to the participants—should be the goal, rather than less competition or noncompetitive activities.

4. Children lack the social and psychological abilities to benefit from organized sport before age 8 years.

5. Epiphyseal injury due to year-round specialization or weight training is the most dangerous, common injury in children's sport.

6. Sport for children and youths needs to be developmentally appropriate; equipment, space, and rules should be modified accordingly.

7. Early specialization increases the risk of physical injury and psychological burnout.

8. Children and youths from relatively low socioeconomic areas have much less opportunity to participate in appropriately conducted sport, compared with their wealthier peers.

9. Coaches in child and youth sport often behave in ways that are unproductive for player development, but evidence suggests that coaches can change easily once appropriate behaviors are made known to them, as is done in many coach-effectiveness training programs.

10. Children will play to win and then move on to the next interesting part of their daily life; inappropriate pressures to win are most often imposed by adults.

11. The large, diversified interscholastic sport program is unique to the American high school.

12. The interscholastic model is basically exclusionary in that opportunities are available to fewer and fewer athletes as they advance. This model differs markedly from the European sport-club approach.

13. Injury in school sport is not a major problem with the exception of injury in football. There, injury to the knee continues to be the biggest problem.

14. Eligibility for school sport continues to be a major issue. Legislation promoting pass-to-play practices is becoming more common.

15. Athletes tend to specialize more now than they did previously, with strength and endurance training occupying their off-season.

16. In most instances, school sport teams are coached by teachers; the problems associated with hiring teacher-coaches are substantial.

17. Pressure from parents and booster clubs is a potential source of problems for the adolescent athlete.

18. Pay-to-play plans are making access to interschool sport a socioeconomic issue.

19. Recruiting violations continue to be the major problem in intercollegiate sport, often resulting from economic pressures to win.

20. Performance-enhancing drugs have become a major problem in many sports.

21. Economic disparity among top powers and economic pressures to produce winning programs are responsible for many of the violations and abuses in intercollegiate sport.

22. Equity issues in sport are seen in the underrepresentation of women and minorities among athletes, coaches, and sport administrators. Furthermore, we are witnessing decreasing access to sport in low-income areas because of the shift of sport instruction and participation to the private sector.

23. Sport systems around the world differ markedly because they serve different goals, resulting in different resource allocation and different models for participation.

)) GET CONNECTED to Sport Web Sites

Children and Youth Sport

National Alliance for Youth Sports	www.nays.org
The NAYS Web site will also connect you to:	
National Youth Sport Coaches Association	
Parents Association for Youth Sports	
Academy for Youth Sports Administrators	
Start Smart Sports Development Program	
National Council on Youth Sports	www.ncys.org
National Youth Sports Safety Foundation	www.nyssf.org
Youth Sports Foundation	www.youthsportsfoundation.com
Center for Sports Parenting	www.sportsparenting.org
Institute for the Study of Youth Sports	http://ed-web3.educ.msu.edu/ysi/
Positive Coaching Alliance	www.positivecoach.org
Sport for All	www.s4af.org
Character Counts Sports	www.charactercounts.org
Citizenship Through Sports	www.sportsmanship.org
American Sport Education Program	www.asep.com
Urban Youth Sports	www.sportinsociety.org/uys
Youth Sport Network	www.myteam.com
Mom's Team: Youth Sport Parenting Information	www.momsteam.com
North American Youth Sports Institute	www.naysi.com
Youth Sport Trust	www.youthsporttrust.org
Youth Sport Coalition	connect through www.aahperd.org/naspe

Interscholastic Sport

National Federation of State High School Associations	www.nfhs.org
Through the NFHS Web site, you can also connect to:	
National Federation Coaches Association	
National Federation Officials Association	
National Federation Interscholastic Sport Association	
National Interscholastic Athletic Administrators Association	
NFHS Coaches Education Program	

Intercollegiate Sport

National Collegiate Athletic Association	www.ncaa.org
National Association of Intercollegiate Athletics	www.naia.org
National Junior College Athletic Association	www.njcaa.org
Canadian Interuniversity Athletic Union	www.cisport.ca
National Association of Collegiate Directors of Athletics	www.nacda.com
National Association of College Women Athletic Administrators	www.nacwaa.org

(continued)

Get Connected to Sport Web Sites (continued)

Social Concerns for Athletes

Athletes for a Better World	www.abw.org
Collegiate Athletes Coalition	www.cacnow.org
International Association of Athletes Against Drugs	www.adcd.org/iaad/eng/inicial.htm
National Alliance of African American Athletes	www.naaaa.com
National Student Athletes' Rights Movement	www.studentathletesrights.org

Sport for People with Disabilities

American Association of Adapted Sports Programs	www.aaasp.org
Special Olympics	www.specialolympics.org
Athletes Helping Athletes	www.athleteshelpathletes.com
Paralympics	www.paralympic.org
Disability in Sport	www.sportinsociety.org/vpd/dis.php
National Disability Sports Alliance	www.ndsaonline.org
Disabled Sports USA	www.dsusa.org
National Beep Baseball Association	www.nbba.org
United States Quad Rugby Association	www.quadrugby.com
USA Deaf Sports Federation	www.usdeafsports.org
United States Association of Blind Athletes	www.usaba.org
Wheelchair Sports USA	www.wsusa.org
U.S. Paralympics	www.usparalympics.org

Masters Sports

United States Masters Swimming	www.usms.org
International Masters Games Association	www.imga.ch
Masters Track and Field	www.masterstrack.com
World Masters Athletics	www.world-masters-athletics.org

State Games and Sport Festivals

National Congress of State Games	www.stategames.org
Inner City Games	www.lainnercitygames.com

Women in Sport

National Association for Girls and Women in Sport	www.aahperd.org/nagws
Women's Sports Foundation	www.womensportsfoundation.org
Women in Sports Careers Foundation	www.WiscFoundation.org
Empowering Women in Sports	www.feminist.org/research/sports2.html
Title IX—Equity Online	www.edc.org/womensEquity
Title IX—National Women's Law Center	www.nwlc.org
Title IX—Office of Civil Rights	www.ed.gov/offices/OCR
Women in Sports	www. Makeithappen.com/wis/

Get Connected to Sport Web Sites (continued)

Other Relevant Sites

Amateur Athletic Union	www.aausports.org
International Amateur Athletics Federation	www.iaaf.org
United States Olympic Committee	www.usoc.org
National Association of Sports Officials	www.naso.org
North American Society for Sport Management	www.nassm.org
Active Americans	www.activeusa.com
North American Society for Sport Management	www.nassm.org
European Association for Sport Management	www.unb.ca/sportmanagement/easm
National Association of Police Athletic Leagues	www.nationalpal.org

DISCUSSION QUESTIONS

1. In what ways can poor cooperation destroy competition? In what ways can inappropriate competition destroy cooperation?

2. Do the ways in which child and youth sport are practiced in your area reflect developmentally appropriate forms of competition?

3. What kind of coaching-education program would you suggest for volunteer youth sport coaches in a local recreation department?

4. Do eligibility rules for sport participation in school discriminate against less talented students?

5. How early should athletes specialize? What are the benefits and the problems of specialization at the high-school level?

6. If you were making policy for the NCAA, what policies would you suggest for (a) drug abuse, (b) recruiting violations, and (c) academic progress of athletes?

7. How should youth and school sport be financed? What influences are exerted by differing approaches to financing sport?

8. Should America have a more developed national sport policy? Should it have a national sport system? How might such a system be structured?

Fitness

Fitness has periodically been a concern in America since early in the 20th century, when World War I draft rejects produced a national fitness crisis. Fitness then was defined as strength, flexibility, and speed, tested by push-ups, sit-ups and sprints, and was focused on children through young adults.

In mid-century fitness again became a national concern as new evidence showed the importance of fitness for health throughout the lifespan. In the late 1960s, the concept of cardiovascular fitness first swept the nation, fueled by Kenneth Cooper's book "Aerobics." Fitness became important throughout the lifecycle and many adults began to strive to achieve the "fit" look.

In recent years, the obesity crisis among children, youths, and adults produced a national concern about health costs related to treating diseases associated with obesity. In this part of the text, we examine the various ways in which fitness is now defined, the components of fitness, the variety of fitness programs available at all ages, the breadth of the fitness professions, and the current issues related to fitness.

CHAPTER 7

Basic Concepts of Fitness

Scientists and doctors have known for years that substantial benefits can be gained from regular physical activity. The expanding and strengthening evidence on the relationship between physical activity and health necessitates the focus this report brings to this important public health challenge. Although the science of physical activity is a complex and still-developing field, we have today strong evidence to indicate that regular physical activity will provide clear and substantial health gains. In this sense, the report is more than a summary of the science—it is a national call to action.

Audrey Manley, surgeon general
of the United States 1996

LEARNING OBJECTIVES

- To discuss various approaches to defining fitness

- To distinguish between and explain health fitness and motor-performance fitness, as well as cosmetic fitness

- To discuss major concepts and issues in the dose–response debate

- To describe the health benefits of a physically active lifestyle

- To describe the social gradient in health and fitness and discuss its implications

- To describe fitness-training principles

- To describe and discuss differences among various kinds of fitness training

- To discuss major issues associated with the measurement of fitness

- To discuss major issues associated with the measurement of physical activity

In 1996 the U.S. surgeon general issued a landmark report titled *Physical Activity and Health* (U.S. Department of Health and Human Services, 1996). That report, as the quotation at the start of this chapter indicates, not only presented the most convincing case ever for the relationship between physical activity and health but also served as a national call to action to increase physical activity among children, youths, and adults of all ages, especially among the many Americans who live essentially sedentary lives.

The importance of physical activity and its relationship to health at all ages became a major national issue as evidence of the alarmingly increasing rates of overweight and obesity among children, youths, and adults became apparent. Over the past 25 years, the prevalence of overweight and obesity

FOCUS ON — Determining Overweight and Obesity Rates   7.1

The prevalence of overweight and obesity in the population is most often estimated by use of body mass index (BMI), which is calculated by the individual's body weight divided by the square of his or her height multiplied by 703. This calculation is used because an individual's height and weight are easy to measure and are always parts of medical records and school records, thus inexpensive compared to other methods. For children and teens, the BMI figure is plotted on the CDC BMI-for-age growth charts for girls or boys to obtain a percentile ranking, indicating the relative position of the child's BMI among children of the same gender and age.

Weight Status Category	*Percentile Range*
Underweight	Less than the 5th percentile
Healthy weight	5th percentile to less than 85th percentile

Weight Status Category	*Percentile Range*
Overweight	85th to less than 95th percentile
Obese	Equal to or greater than the 95th percentile

For adults, overweight and obesity ranges are determined by dividing body weight (in kilograms) by the square of your height (expressed in meters).

BMI	*Classification*
<18.5	Underweight
18.5–24.9	Normal
25.0–29.9	Overweight
30.0–39.9	Obese

BMI is used to broadly categorize population groups. Its accuracy can be distorted by factors such as muscle mass, bone structure, and fitness level.

SOURCE: Centers for Disease Control, *Defining Overweight and Obesity*, 2008.

among children and youths reached epidemic proportions, more than doubling in the 6–11 year age group and tripling in the 12–19 year age group (Koplan, Liverman, Kraak, & Wisham, 2006). Current estimates suggest that 19 percent of children and 17 percent of adolescents are obese (Wang & Beydoun, 2007). Overweight and obesity rates for adults have increased from 15 percent in 1980 to 32 percent in 2004 (Levi, Segal, & Juliano, 2006). What this shows is that future rates of overweight and obesity for adults will increase markedly unless efforts are made to reduce the incidence of overweight and obesity among children and youths (see Focus On Box 7.1).

Overweight and obesity are associated with a range of significant health problems during childhood and adolescence as well as being important early risk factors for adult health problems. Among the medical problems associated with overweight and obesity among children/youths are high blood pressure, hypertension, type II diabetes, orthopedic problems, and psychological/behavioral problems (American Academy of Pediatrics, 2003). Nearly 60 percent of overweight children 5–10 years of age have elevated blood pressure and increased insulin levels, both risk factors for heart disease (Wilkinson, Eddy, MacFadden, & Burgess, 2002). Among adults, overweight and obesity are known risk factors for diabetes, heart disease, stroke, hypertension, gallbladder disease, osteoarthritis, sleep apnea, and some forms of cancer (Weight-control Information Network, 2006).

The health and economic costs of overweight and obesity are substantial. The United States spends more than $1.5 trillion on health care each year, a figure that has doubled over the past 5 years and is expected to double again within 6 years. The Centers for Disease Control (CDC) has determined that obesity is now the second leading cause of death in the United States and the surgeon general estimates that direct and indirect costs (costs due to lost workdays and the like) come close to $1.2 trillion annually (Senate Report 108-345, 2006). This is why fitness and physical activity have become so important to national health goals.

FOCUS ON Key Definitions 7.2

- *Aerobic* The process of metabolizing body fuels through exercise in the presence of oxygen
- *Anaerobic* The process of metabolizing body fuels through exercise without oxygen
- *Body Composition* The relative amounts of muscle, fat, bone, and other vital body parts
- *Cardiovascular Endurance* The ability of the circulatory and respiratory systems to supply fuel during sustained exercise
- *Exercise* Leisure-time physical activity conducted with the intention of developing physical fitness
- *Health* A state of being associated with freedom from disease and illness, including the positive component of wellness

- *Healthy Lifestyles* Presence of appropriate physical activity, nutrition, and stress-management behavior patterns
- *Hypokinetic Diseases* Conditions related to physical inactivity or low levels of habitual activity
- *Leisure Activity* Physical activity undertaken during discretionary time
- *Physical Activity* Bodily movement that is produced by skeletal muscle and substantially increases energy expenditure
- *Wellness* A state of positive biological and psychological health in the individual, exemplified by quality of life and a sense of well-being

SOURCES: Corbin, Pangrazi, & Franks, 2000; Costill, 1986.

Many still use the term *fitness* in a global sense, encompassing physical, social, moral, mental, and spiritual fitness. Although that use of the term might be sufficient in everyday language, it is not specific enough to guide policy or programs. Others have said that fitness is an adequate amount of strength and endurance to meet the needs of everyday life, but that too is very misleading. What are the needs of daily life? Whose life? Some women and men sit at a desk all day and watch TV in their leisure. They have enough strength and endurance to do that, but they are probably unfit.

A CONTEMPORARY UNDERSTANDING OF FITNESS

Research in exercise science, medical sciences, and health has led to a changing concept of physical fitness—one that is not only more meaningful but also more useful in providing directions for sport, fitness, and physical-education professionals as they implement programs designed to help children, youths, and adults of all ages improve their fitness. The first step in this contemporary understanding

was to recognize that the umbrella concept of fitness had to be understood in relation to a large number of related concepts (see Focus On Box 7.2).

Fitness is currently viewed as a series of components, each of which is specific in its development and maintenance. Typically, fitness components are divided into two basic categories: those essentially related to health and those related to motor-skill performance. An additional category, cosmetic fitness, will also be considered because of its importance in the culture.

The distinction between these two fitness categories is quite important. **Health fitness** is important for the prevention and remediation of disease and illness leading to a better quality of life. **Motor-performance fitness** is essential to performing well in sports and work that requires physical skill, strength, and/or endurance. The components of health fitness are general in the sense that they apply to everybody; that is, each person should strive to develop and sustain a reasonable level of health fitness to enjoy a better quality of life (see Focus On Box 7.3). Motor-performance fitness is more functional and specific to the task or activity that enables the performer to do well. A football tackle, a sprinter, a tennis player, and a swimmer

FOCUS ON   Components of Health Fitness   7.3

Body Composition: The body's relative amount of fat and fat-free mass (muscle, bone, and water).
Assessment
Underwater weighing: Person is weighed out of water and underwater, with correction made for amount of air in lungs when underwater.

Skinfold measures: Half of the body's fat is located just under the skin. Calipers are used to measure skinfolds (two thicknesses of skin and the fat just under the skin) at various places around the body.

Body mass index: BMI is calculated by dividing body weight (in kilograms) by the square of the individual's height (in meters).

Body circumference measures: Use of various height, weight, waist, thigh, and hip measurements to estimate body fatness.

Bioelectric impedence analysis: Electrodes placed on body with low doses of current passed through the skin. Muscle has less resistance to current, making possible an estimate of body composition.

Cardiovascular Endurance: The ability of the body to perform prolonged, large-muscle, dynamic exercise at moderate to high levels of intensity.
Assessment
Laboratory test of maximal oxygen consumption: Person runs on a treadmill, and the air inhaled and exhaled is analyzed while the person exercises to exhaustion.

1-mile walk test: For person who meets criteria for safe exercise but have low levels of fitness. Calculate (1) time it takes to complete a brisk 1-mile walk and (2) exercise heart rate at end of the walk.

3-minute step test: The individual steps continuously at a steady rate for 3 minutes; then heart rate during recovery is calculated.

1.5-mile run–walk test: A time test; faster times indicate a greater capacity to consume oxygen.

Flexibility: The ability to move a joint through its full range of motion.

Assessment
Because flexibility is specific to each joint, there are no general assessments of flexibility. No evidence exists to establish norms for flexibility. Too much flexibility may be as problematic as too little.

Sit and reach test: Most common flexibility test. Person is seated with knees fully extended and feet flat against a measuring device. Keeping knees extended, person reaches as far forward as possible.

Range-of-motion assessments: Flexibility in any joint can be measured by a goniometer, which provides the degrees of motion capable at that joint.

Muscular Endurance: The ability of a muscle or muscle group to remain contracted or to contract repeatedly for a long period of time.
Assessment
Dynamic curl-up: Sit on mat with legs bent more than 90 degrees so that feet remain flat on floor and arms extended at sides with palms down and fingers extended. Two tape marks 4.5 inches apart are placed on floor so that fingers touch the first tape mark. Curl head and shoulders forward so that fingers touch second tape mark. Repeat curl every 3 seconds until exhaustion.

Dynamic push-up: Support body in push-up position from the toes with hands just outside the shoulders and back and legs straight with toes tucked under. Lower body until upper arm is parallel to floor or until elbow is bent at 90 degrees. Do one push-up every 3 seconds until exhaustion.

Strength: The amount of force a muscle can produce with a single maximum effort.
Assessment
Muscular strength can be assessed by taking one-repetition-maximum (1RM) tests for various muscle groups. Upper-body strength is best tested by 1RM effort on a seated press machine or a bench press machine. Lower body is best tested by a 1RM effort on a leg press machine.

SOURCES: Fahey, Insel, & Roth, 2008; Corbin, Welk, Corbin, & Welk, 2008.

Although historically an important competitive sport, running is often pursued now for its cardiovascular benefits.

The major difference in athletic performance today is increased levels of sport-specific fitness.

need different amounts of each of the motor-performance components; that is, the training for motor-performance fitness is functionally related to the goals of each activity. Health fitness, on the other hand, is not related to shooting baskets more accurately or to jumping farther. It is related to living better, being more resistant to diseases, and even perhaps living longer.

Health fitness is an important component of **wellness**, which is often referred to now as the overall goal for healthy individuals. Historically, health has been thought of primarily as the absences of disease and illness, but wellness not only relies on a positive emphasis of factors but also includes aspects of living beyond physical health. Wellness is considered to be a dynamic process of change and growth rather than a static state (Fahey, Insel, & Roth, 2007). The components of

wellness are physical wellness, emotional wellness, intellectual wellness, spiritual wellness, interpersonal and social wellness, and environmental wellness. These dimensions are not separate but interact to develop and sustain the state of being described as wellness. For example, the self-esteem that comes with emotional wellness is likely associated with better eating habits and a more regular physical activity program, all working to produce a better quality of life (Fahey et al., 2007).

Health Fitness

Health fitness is important for the prevention and remediation of **hypokinetic diseases**, the most serious of which have been those related to the heart and vascular systems and, more recently, to the several conditions specifically related to obesity, particularly type II diabetes. We have lived through 30 years of emphasis on aerobic exercise—road racing, marathons, triathlons, aerobics of all kinds (low-impact, water, and so on), cycling, and power walking. In that time, people have learned that regular aerobic exercise of the right intensity and duration can help control weight, reduce the percentage of fat in body composition, improve circulatory function, control blood-glucose levels, increase insulin sensitivity, and reduce stress and depression (Blair, Kohl, & Powell, 1987; Fahey et al., 2008).

Aerobic work contributes primarily to cardiovascular fitness, which consists of a fit heart muscle, a fit vascular system, a fit respiratory system, and fit muscle tissue capable of using oxygen efficiently (Corbin et al., 2008). Cardiovascular activities increase heart health by increasing the blood and oxygen supply and decreasing the work and oxygen demand on the heart, thus increasing its efficiency (Fahey et al., 2007). This does not mean that to develop and sustain a healthy cardiovascular system you need to become a daily distance runner! What it does mean is that you need to engage in an aerobic activity three to five times per week at a sufficient intensity to develop and sustain an appropriate level of cardiovascular fitness. This can be accomplished through walking, jogging, cycling, swimming, and using fitness machines such as treadmills and elliptical trainers. If you want to improve your cardiovascular fitness, then you need to gradually increase the intensity of the exercise in ways that raise the heart rate sufficiently to produce a training effect.

In recent years, it has become clear that core strength and flexibility is an important ingredient in health fitness. Many youths and adults suffer from health problems that originate with lack of strength, stability, and flexibility in the core musculature of the back. Core stability is achieved through strengthening the muscles that stabilize the spine. Core strength is achieved through strengthening the muscles that bend, extend, and rotate the spine (Corbin et al., 2008). The most well-known "system" for achieving core strength and flexibility is Pilates, developed early in the twentieth century by German gymnast and boxer George Pilates (Fahey et al., 2007). Pilates focuses on strengthening and stretching the core muscles of the back. Exercises are done on mats, with bands, and with training balls (www.pilatesmethodalliance.com).

Physical activity in the form of resistance training has many benefits (Fahey et al., 2008; Pollock & Vincent, 1996; Westcott, 1993). These include positive effects on bone-mineral density, body composition, muscular strength, glucose metabolism, serum lipids, maximal oxygen consumption, and basal metabolism. We have just begun to understand that resistance training, especially when done with lighter weights and increased repetitions, can improve aerobic capacity. Not only is metabolic rate increased during a strength workout, but also, as a result, it is increased slightly throughout the day. Although our cultural perception of strength training is typically muscular young men in weight rooms, it is clear that regular resistance work is important for women and men, both young and old. Indeed, some regular resistance work is especially important as people get older.

The recent national attention focused on the problems of obesity in the population, especially the increase in obesity among children, has given new urgency to our awareness of the need for physical activity among children and youths. Obesity is typically defined as an excessive amount of body fat relative to fat-free body mass (Fahey et al., 2008). Individuals with a BMI of 25–29.9 are considered overweight, and those with a BMI of 30 or more are considered obese. Estimates suggest that 65 percent of American adults are currently overweight or obese. Today there are nearly twice as many overweight children as there were in 1980 and almost three times as many overweight adolescents (Dietz, 2004), with the rate of increase higher for African American and Hispanic children and youths (Ogden, Flegal, Caroll, & Johnson, 2002). The relationship between obesity and diabetes has produced a new term, *diabesity* (Kaufman, 2005). The concerns about the increase in obesity are due partially to the estimated $117 billion a year spent on health costs related to that condition (www.healthyamericans.org). In 2003 the United States Senate passed the Improved Nutrition and Physical Activity Act, which is aimed at reducing obesity among children and adolescents.

Gains in health fitness are not permanent! The body systems adjust to lower levels of physical activity in the same way they adjust to higher levels (Fahey et al., 2008). When you stop exercising, you are likely to lose up to 50 percent of fitness improvements in just 2 months. Not all fitness gains reverse at the same rate, however. Cardiovascular

FOCUS ON	**Components of Motor-Performance Fitness**		**7.4**

Agility	The ability to move the body accurately and rapidly in different directions. Shown in activities such as skiing, wrestling, and soccer.	*Power*	The ability to transfer energy into force at a fast rate. Shown in activities such as shot put and blocking in football.
Balance	The maintenance of equilibrium while moving or stationary. Shown in activities such as balance beam and skating.	*Reaction Time*	The time elapsed between stimulation and the onset of movement in response to that stimulation. Shown in sprint starting or change of possession in invasion games.
Coordination	The ability to use body parts to perform motor skills smoothly and accurately. Shown in activities such as kicking, batting, dribbling, or shooting a ball.	*Speed*	The ability to perform a skill in a short period of time. Shown in sprinters, wide receivers, and base stealers.

SOURCE: Corbin et al., 2008.

gains are quick to reverse; strength gains are slower. Strength gains can also be sustained with less frequent workouts, whereas maintaining cardiovascular gains typically requires regular workouts. The lesson here is straightforward: To maintain health fitness you have to "keep on keeping on!"

Motor-Performance Fitness

When people today talk about physical fitness, they are likely to mean health fitness. When someone asks "Are you physically fit?" the question probably relates to health fitness. Fitness classes in schools and fitness centers are most likely to have a health-fitness focus. This does not mean that motor-performance fitness is not important—it simply means that it is different.

The goal of motor-performance fitness is to perform a motor skill better, typically a sport skill. Focus On Box 7.4 defines the six components of motor-performance fitness. Every sport, and even different roles or positions in sports, requires a different combination of these components. Obviously, the training

for tennis would be dramatically different than the training for being a lineman in football, but each of those training programs would include some focus on each component. Even within a sport, the training would be different depending on the role or position played within the sport; that is, the speed that a defensive lineman needs in football is different from the speed needed by a wide receiver or running back, and their training for increasing and maintaining their speed would be different.

If walking, jogging, and aerobics are the most visible methods of developing and sustaining aerobic fitness, then activity in the weight room has become the most visible sign of motor-performance fitness. There is no doubt that power plays a central role in sport performance at any level and in virtually every sport. Power is functionally related to a specific motor activity, and the training to increase power will be different depending on the activity; that is, the power to put the shot is developed differently than the power needed to increase the speed of the serve in tennis. The same tends to hold true for the other components of motor-performance fitness. Many athletes work to improve their agility, balance, reaction time, speed, and coordination, but the specific training activities that they use are designed to increase each of those components in ways that are specific to their use in the sport. For example, a defensive back in football needs to react quickly to an offensive play and move quickly—either forward, backward, or sideways—to be in the position to defend successfully. The components of reaction time, agility, and speed would likely be combined in training activities to improve play at that position. The increased understanding of motor-performance fitness and the important role that it plays in sport has led to a new profession, most commonly referred to as "strength trainer" or "strength and conditioning coach."

COSMETIC FITNESS

It would be a mistake not to recognize that for many people, youths and adult, looking good is an important outcome of fitness activities. One of the significant shifts in public perception over the past several decades is the change in what is considered to be an attractive physical appearance. It was not too many years ago that a man with well-defined muscular features was often described as "musclebound"—and was not necessarily admired for looking that way. If a girl or a woman had well-defined muscular features, she might have been socially ridiculed. Not so today!

Looking fit is in—and looking strong is an important part of looking fit. This is true for both men and women:

> Perhaps the most prevalent and least understood reason people train with weights is to add quality to their lives. Many people engage in strength training simply because they look better and feel better when they do. They find the training process enjoyable, and the training product well worth the effort. For most people, controlled physical exertion is a satisfying experience, and increased muscle strength is a gratifying accomplishment. Something about becoming stronger enhances a person's self-image. (Westcott, 1982, p. 4)

If **cosmetic fitness** is not confused with health fitness, then it can be a positive addition to the overall fitness movement. The more that our culture encourages adoption of an active lifestyle, the better off future generations will be. There is, however, a downside to some aspects of the motivation to "look better." The incidence of eating disorders among youths and young adults is far too high. Television and magazine advertising have made the slim, athletic look the preferred body shape to sell products. This has produced what the Australian physical educator Richard Tinning (1985) called "the cult of slenderness." In some cases, the quest for cosmetic fitness leads to inadequate consumption of nutrients, leading to a diminished appetite that puts the health of the person at substantial risk.

The fact is that people come in all shapes; that is, their genetic endowments play a significant role in determining their body shape. Whatever that body shape may be, it can be enhanced by regularly engaging in health-fitness activities. If people engage in these activities to "look better" and "feel better about themselves" that is appropriate, but if they carry that too far, they put their health at risk.

THE DOSE–RESPONSE DEBATE

Current investigations and discussions, referred to here as the "**dose–response debate**," are about what is needed to generate health benefits—that is, how much of what kind of activity, at what intensity, for how long, and how frequently (Pate, 1995). Put simply, what "dose" of exercise is necessary to achieve the beneficial health "responses"? The dose–response debate developed since the late 1980s as a new, specialized field of scholarship called "exercise epidemiology" began to present evidence on the relationship of physical activity to all causes of mortality (Blair, Kohl, Paffenbarger, Cooper, & Gibbons, 1989). Dividing activity patterns into five groups, from low activity to high activity, researchers found that men in the least-fit category were 3.44 times more likely to die during the follow-up period than

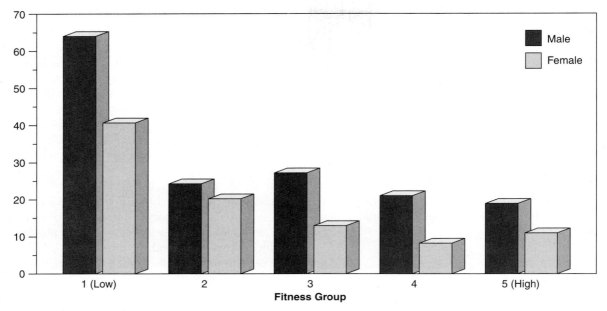

FIGURE 7.1 Age-adjusted death rates (all causes) per 10,000 person-years of follow-up for men (10,000+) and women (3,000+) in the Aerobics Center Longitudinal Study.

NOTE: *Subjects were apparently healthy at baseline, physical fitness was assessed by maximal exercise testing on a treadmill, and the average length of follow-up was slightly more than 8 years. Rates are based on 240 deaths in men and 43 deaths in women. Data for this figure were taken from Blair et al., (1989).*

those in the most-fit category, and the least-fit women were 4.65 times more likely to die than the most-fit women (Blair, 1992). Figure 7.1 shows these data and indicates clearly that the most impressive improvements in mortality are between groups 1 and 2—that is, between the least active group and the group that gets some activity regularly. There are some additional modest improvements as people move to the more and more active groups, but clearly the major problem is in the sedentary group, and the major gain to be achieved is by modest increases in physical activity as part of lifestyle.

In a more recent summary of research related to dose–response issues, Rankinen and Bouchard (2002) concluded that ample evidence supports the assertion that regular physical activity has beneficial effects on all health outcomes. They also asserted that "there is strong suggestion of an inverse and linear relationship between regular physical activity and rates of all-cause mortality, total CVD [cardiovascular disease] and coronary heart incidence and mortality, and incidence of type 2 diabetes mellitus" (p. 6).

Fitness improves when the amount of exercise is gradually increased—a principle often referred to as *progressive overload*. Most fitness professionals use a dose formula based on the frequency, intensity, duration (time), and type of activity (FITT). *Frequency* is related to the need for body systems to recover and rebuild. The FITT recommendations for aerobic activity would of course be different from that for strength training. The examples shown here are for aerobic activity. Many joggers, cyclists, and swimmers work out most days of the week. If their exercise intensity and duration are within their capacity, their bodies will adapt and recover sufficiently to sustain that level of frequency. The American College of Sports Medicine (ACSM) recommendation is three to five times per week.

FOCUS ON   Calculating Your Target Heart-Rate Zone   7.5

Your target heart-rate zone should be between 65 and 90 percent of your maximum heart rate (MHR).

1. Estimate your MHR by subtracting your age from 220.
2. Multiply your MHR by 0.65 and also by 0.90 to calculate your target heart-rate zone.

For example, a 21-year-old would calculate her target heart-rate zone as follows:

MHR = 220 − 21 = 199 beats per minute (BPM)
Lower range of zone = 199 × 0.65 = 129 BPM
Upper range of zone = 199 × 0.90 = 179 BPM

Fitness benefits are gained when the heart rate stays within the parameters of the zone. Unfit people or people just starting an exercise program should use the lower end of the range for their threshold.

Intensity refers to the level of exercise stress that is progressively increased to produce the desired outcome. For aerobic exercise, intensity is typically calculated by subtracting your age from 220 (maximum heart rate for a well-trained young person) and then multiplying that figure by an appropriate percentage related to previous training (Focus On Box 7.5). The ACSM recommendation for intensity is 60–90 percent of maximum heart rate. *Duration* refers to the amount of time that you engage in aerobic activity. The ACSM recommendation is between 20 and 60 minutes or more. For purposes of improving aerobic fitness, the *types of activities* recommended are jogging, cycling, brisk walking, aerobic dancing, and swimming. Of course, aerobic activity can also be done in fitness centers using elliptical trainers, stationary bicycles, or treadmills.

For strength training, the FITT recommendations would be somewhat different. For frequency, it is often recommended that hard workouts be alternated with easy workouts to allow for recovery and to prevent injury. For intensity, exercise bouts would gradually increase the amount of weight resistance. For strength training, time or duration refers to the number of sets (consisting of eight to twelve repetitions) that are done for each muscle group as part of the total workout. For type of activity, the most common approaches are through free weights or machines.

An alternative method to using a dose–response approach to training, either for health purposes or

for improvement in a specific activity, is the concept of "training effects." This may be especially important for people, young or old, who are trying to improve their fitness either for health purposes or for specific improvement in performing an activity. One of the biggest problems in our nation's health is the number of people—women and men, young and old—who are badly out of shape. For them, the main issue is to get started in a modest fitness program and to see some immediate results—that is, to see the training effects that can be achieved very early in a fitness program. For example, some very modest aerobic training will lower resting heart rate. Some modest strength training will show a capacity to perform daily tasks better. When people undertake a beginning effort in fitness that results in modest exercise done at least several times per week, they will experience improvement. They will be able to walk for a longer period of time without tiring and can begin to walk a longer period of time. They will be able to lift a weight with less effort and can begin to lift a heavier weight. As Figure 7.1 shows, the most important improvement in age-adjusted death rates occurs between the least-fit and the next least-fit groups, showing that modest improvements in health-related fitness can be very important. Having people focus on key training effect indicators can be a major motivational influence to keep them involved in their fitness effort.

The dose formula for exercise prescription that has developed from this research suggests that substantial health benefits will accrue to people who *accumulate* about 30 minutes of activity per day in 10-minute bouts doing activities at least equal to a brisk walk (Pangrazi, Corbin, & Welk, 1996). This dose formula was approved in 1996 by a consensus panel convened by the National Institutes of Health (Rankinen & Bouchard, 2002). Engaging in 30 minutes per day of moderate-intensity physical activity, in at least 10-minute bouts, accumulates 210 minutes per week, which is now the suggested baseline exercise prescription.

The prescription for children and adolescents is different from that for adults. In 1998 the National Association for Sport and Physical Education (NASPE) issued guidelines suggesting that adolescents should be physically active daily for at least 30 minutes in some kind of planned exercise in the context of work, play, exercise activity, or sport. They should also engage in three or more sessions per week that last at least 20 minutes per session and require moderate to vigorous levels of activity (Corbin, Pangrazi, & Le Masurier, 2004). Then, in 2004, NASPE issued new physical-activity guidelines for children, suggesting that they accumulate at least 60 minutes and up to several hours per day in age-appropriate physical activity. This should include moderate and vigorous activity with the majority of time spent in activity that is intermittent in nature (NASPE, 2004a).

The current evidence relating physical activity to health and mortality variables has created a new sense of health-related activity, what many now refer to as moderate-to-vigorous physical activity (MVPA) (Simons-Morton, 1994). MVPA takes into account a broader range of physical activities than did health-related aerobic fitness, particularly activities that are near the moderate end of the range, such as brisk walking.

Which of the two dose formulas is correct? One appears to be anchored in the concept of fitness, albeit health-related fitness. The other is clearly anchored in health, particularly related to reductions in all causes of mortality. We have much to learn in both approaches, and it is impossible at this time to determine which is preferable. Blair and Connelly (1996, p. 194), in reviewing studies

from both traditions, have suggested a holistic view that makes sense at this time:

> Most of these projects used the standard exercise prescription described by the ACSM as the training stimulus, although others have evaluated various combinations of frequency, intensity, and duration. It is still common, however, for scientists and clinicians to consider two somewhat competing views of the effects of physical activity: one on the role of physical activity in promoting health and the other on physical activity to improve fitness. We disagree with this approach of categorizing physical activity as contributing to health or fitness. We think physical activity works through multiple biological pathways to improve both health and function.

The Physical Activity Pyramid shown in Figure 7.2 reflects this holistic view. Some combination of strength training, flexibility work, aerobic conditioning, and MVPA is the way to achieve a level of physical activity that contributes significantly to health and well-being.

The introduction of MVPA has also greatly influenced how we think about fitness for children and youths. NASPE now suggests that the overarching goal for school physical education is for students to "adopt and value a physically active lifestyle." If this goal is considered seriously, then fitness in physical education will likely mean less about exercises and fitness testing and more about helping students find activities that they enjoy and helping them to get better at those activities so that they will voluntarily participate in those activities outside of school and in the future.

THE SOCIAL GRADIENT IN HEALTH AND FITNESS

This review of basic concepts of fitness related to health would be incomplete without noting how social and economic status within a society affects health and longevity. We know that the proximal causes of degenerative diseases—commonly referred to as "risk factors"—are physical inactivity, smoking,

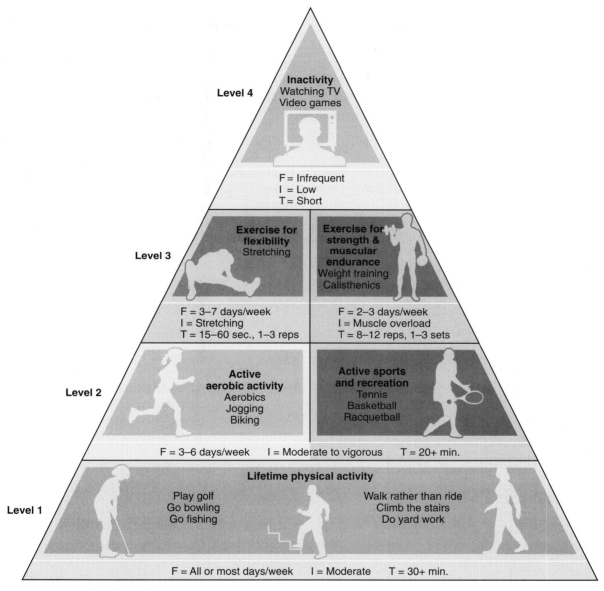

FIGURE 7.2   The Physical Activity Pyramid.
SOURCE: *Corbin et al., 2008.*

a high-fat diet, and the like. These risk factors, however, are not distributed normally across populations within societies. The fact is that as we move our lens *down* the social-class structure of developed nations, we see that risk factors and health problems increase, resulting in increased mortality (Siedentop, 1996c).

This socioeconomic impact on health and fitness is what health epidemiologists refer to as the **social gradient** in health; that is, the health status of a particular class within a nation is typically better than that of the classes below it and worse than that of the classes above it (Hertzman, 1994). The social-gradient hypothesis argues that relative social and economic deprivation within societies accounts for better or poorer health. Hertzman (1994) suggests that "one's place in the social hierarchy and the experiences which follow from it appear to be powerful determinants of the length and healthfulness of life" (p. 169). Note that the term *determinants* is used purposely because that relative deprivation "influences life-style choices and differential access to high quality social environments" (Marmot, 1994, p. 213).

Traditionally, fitness has been viewed nearly totally as an *individual* responsibility (Tinning, 1990). When people are unfit or less fit than might be desirable, the less-than-optimally fit people get the blame for their condition. A **socioecological view**, on the other hand, looks to the social contexts within which people live their lives as partial explanations for their levels of health and fitness:

> Health is increasingly understood to be a social commodity, much like other social commodities such as housing and education. Some get more of it, some get less, and those at the top of the social stratification tend to do better than those at the bottom. Too many are, in current government parlance, underserved. For this reason, new strategies for empowerment, social support, and community-based services are advocated as broad and powerful strategies for health. (Vertinsky, 1991, p. 83)

The socioecological view is supported by evidence showing that in nations where income inequality is less, life expectancy is higher (Wilkinson, 1994). Also, increases in life expectancy have been shown in countries that have reduced income inequality in the current generation.

People in lower socioeconomic groups have less access to nutritious food and to information about nutrition—and the foods high in fat are among the least expensive. Urban areas are in decay and are typically unsafe for outside physical activity. No infrastructure is available to support and

sustain involvement in physical activity for children, youths, or adults. Although individual responsibility remains an important and compelling concept in the effort to improve the health and vitality of our nation, we must also realize that there are structural problems that have profound impact on individual motivation and responsibility.

If society is to become healthier and if a more fit citizenry can help achieve that public health goal, then we need this new approach to understanding the social complexities of fitness and activity across the variety of groups within our society. We must view fitness as both an individual and a social issue—and we must attempt to develop a society in which more people have access to safe, affordable, and inclusive opportunities to pursue a physically active lifestyle.

FITNESS-TRAINING CONCEPTS AND PRINCIPLES

In the 1970s and 1980s, aerobic exercise and cardiovascular health were the main emphasis in health fitness. We have already considered the notion of a cardiovascular heart-rate training zone and the frequency, intensity, and duration recommended for cardiovascular exercise. Muscle strength and flexibility were much less prominent in exercise prescriptions and discussions about the health benefits of regular exercise. Muscles make up more than 40 percent of body mass (Fahey et al., 2008), and they are the place where a substantial portion of the metabolic-energy reactions in the body take place. This section further considers some of the principles associated with aerobic activity and also emphasizes the principles and benefits associated with resistance training.

When you train properly, the muscles and the energy systems that fuel those muscles become more efficient and stronger. This is true whether the muscles in question are the heart and leg muscles of a marathon runner or the arm and shoulder muscles of a javelin thrower. In that sense, the basic mechanisms underlying fitness training are the same for health fitness, motor-performance fitness, and cosmetic fitness.

When you train appropriately, the muscular system *adapts* to the training stresses; that is, when the training *load* increases, muscles are stressed and they adapt and improve their function (Fahey et al., 2008; Westcott, 1982). For aerobic fitness—or for endurance activities such as distance running, cross-country skiing, and cycling—it is important that individuals be able to use oxygen efficiently. That is why aerobic (with-oxygen) conditioning is so central to health fitness. To use oxygen efficiently, a person must have a fit heart muscle that is capable of pumping large amounts of blood. The blood, too, must be fit in that it must be capable of carrying large quantities of oxygen (which it does through hemoglobin). The arteries must be fit in that they must be free from elements that prevent the flow of blood. Finally, the muscles that the blood flows to must be fit so that they are capable of using the oxygen brought by the blood to energize them for activity.

General Training Principles

The human body adapts to meet the demands that are placed upon it. Short-term adaptations, when done repeatedly, gradually translate into long-term improvements. The FITT (frequency, intensity, time, type) and type of activity principles described earlier in this chapter form the primary basis for planning an individual fitness program. The FITT formula, however, needs to be applied with great **specificity**, which means that to produce a desired effect, exercises must be related to the bodily component in which improvement is sought. Improvement via aerobic conditioning requires that the FITT formula be used with aerobic activities such as running, cycling, treadmill, and elliptical trainer. If you want to improve your arm and shoulder strength, then you have to apply the FITT formula to the muscles of the arms and shoulders.

Fitness training also should respect the principle of **progressive overload**, which means that the "load" or exercise chosen must be done at a level

that produces a conditioning effect. If the load is too small or light, then the effect is not achieved. If the load is too large or too small, then the required amount of exercise will not be able to be accomplished. But if you gradually increase a modest load, then small increments of improvement over time will eventually lead to significant improvement.

A final training principle is to allow for appropriate **recovery time**. The muscular system needs time to adapt to training stresses because the physiological and biochemical mechanisms responsible for gains in fitness operate during the rest intervals between exercise bouts. The frequency that one can exercise with safely varies with the fitness component being developed and the level of fitness that the person has in that component. After some beginning work, most people can engage in aerobic work every day as long as all-out efforts are avoided. Most strength-training guides recommend that at least one day of rest be taken between strength workouts for the same muscle groups.

These principles of training are relevant to health fitness, motor-performance fitness, and cosmetic fitness. Each should be applied somewhat differently, depending on the kind of fitness a person is trying to achieve.

Health-Fitness Training

People interested in health fitness typically engage in some form of aerobic training. The more faithfully that they adhere to a workout schedule that represents the intensity, duration, and frequency required for cardiovascular improvements, the more likely they are to achieve those improvements. Other people prefer more moderate physical activity and perhaps walk for 30 minutes before or after dinner each night. Still others achieve their health-fitness goals through a form of workouts known as "interval training" in which more intense exercise periods are alternated with rest periods to allow for recovery.

In recent years, it has become clear that a total health-fitness program needs to include regular attention to core strength and flexibility. Twenty-nine muscles attach to the body's core: the abdomen, pelvic floor, sides of the torso, back, buttocks, hip, and pelvis (Fahey et al., 2007). Core muscles not only stabilize the spine but also assist in transferring force between the upper and lower body. Core training typically focuses on holistic movements and exercises that work on groups of muscles rather than isolating muscles, such as isolating the biceps in a biceps curl exercise. Most core training uses whole-body exercises that force the core muscles to stabilize the spine. The most famous approach to core training is *Pilates*, an exercise program that focuses on strengthening and stretching the core muscles to create a solid base of support for whole-body movement (www.pilatesmethodalliance.com).

The frequency of exercise patterns depends on which of these approaches people choose; that is, the moderate-activity approach typically requires daily exercise, whereas the continuous-aerobic and interval-aerobic approaches can achieve results with three to five workouts per week.

Current evidence for the long-term benefits of health fitness suggest that activity of moderate intensity is appropriate. If infrequent, high-intensity fitness activities are imposed on children and youths, as they often are during infrequent fitness-testing days in physical education, these children and youths are likely to become averse to involvement in fitness programs.

Continuous and Interval Training

Two kinds of aerobic training are used both for health-fitness purposes and by athletes training for endurance events: continuous and interval exercise. Walkers, joggers, and cyclists typically favor the continuous form of training, engaging in sustained exercise with their heart rate at or above the threshold level. More serious runners and many swimmers tend to favor interval training where exercise bouts are interspersed with rest periods.

There is no doubt that both continuous training and interval training are sufficient to build and maintain high levels of health fitness. Continuous exercise is probably the better form for beginners simply because it is less intense and can be adjusted easily and done almost anyplace. **Interval training** tends to be more intense (that is, intense exercise periods, followed by rest periods) and typically needs a measured distance to be done appropriately—for example, a 25-meter swimming pool or a 400-meter running track. The great value of interval training is that it allows you to do more work during any given exercise period. The exercise period can be more intense because it is followed by a rest period that allows for some recovery before the next exercise period begins.

The minimum continuous program for achieving and maintaining health fitness would involve exercising so as to lift the heart rate to the target threshold level and to maintain it there for 30 minutes (15 minutes would be an absolute minimum to achieve any training effect). This should be done three to five times per week. The same outcomes could be achieved through an interval program in which the trainee exercised at 80 percent of the maximum heart rate for a 2- or 3-minute period, then walked or did some mild jogging for the same length of time, and then repeated the work–rest intervals.

Anaerobic Training

Anaerobic exercise is short-duration exercise completed without the aid of oxygen (which distinguishes it from aerobic exercise). Anaerobic exercise builds muscle mass. It has some health-related benefits in that it positively affects resting metabolic rate, enhances bone density, and may contribute to long-term weight control (Gutin, Manos, & Strong, 1992). The main functional outcome of anaerobic exercise, however, is to move quickly and deliver great force, which is why anaerobic training is highly relevant to sprinters, wrestlers, football players, gymnasts, and other athletes who must move explosively or deliver a substantial amount of force in a short time. Common anaerobic training activities are sprinting, weight lifting, plyometrics, and running stairs.

The threshold for building and maintaining anaerobic fitness is much higher than that for aerobic training. Athletes must perform at near-maximum

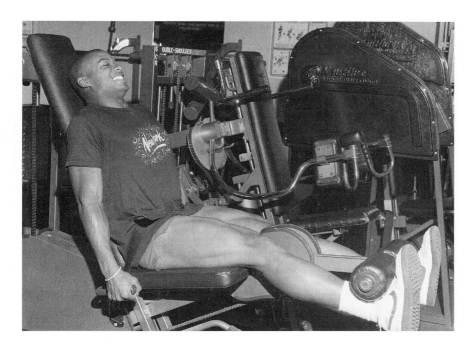

Strength training is often done on sophisticated weight machines.

effort for short distances or time periods, then allow a sufficient rest for nearly complete recovery before repeating the effort. Thus, virtually all anaerobic training is of the interval variety with much longer rest intervals than in aerobic training.

Strength Training

Strength training, the primary component of motor-performance fitness, is best done through some form of exercise against resistance, typically through weight training. In this form of fitness training, there are four primary variables to be considered (Fahey et al., 2008; Westcott, 1982):

1. Amount of resistance (weight) per lift
2. Number of repetitions of each lift (a set)
3. Number of sets per workout
4. Number of workouts per week

The phrase used most commonly among strength-training enthusiasts is *repetition maximums*, or *RMs*; for example, "5RM" means a "five-repetition maximum,"

and "10RM" means a "ten-repetition maximum." Thus, a 5RM load is the most weight you could lift five times in succession, and a 10RM load is the most weight you could lift ten times in succession.

In strength training, there is a direct corollary to the aerobic–anaerobic distinction made earlier. To build muscle *endurance*, one would perform numerous repetitions against a fairly low resistance. To build muscle *strength*, one would perform few repetitions against a much higher resistance. As in aerobic–anaerobic training, the results are highly specific to the nature of the exercise stress. The benefits of strength training are substantial.

Weight-training experts generally agree that weight loads at or exceeding 75 percent of one's maximum lifting capacity are most beneficial for developing and maintaining strength. (A 10RM weight load is generally thought to be about 75 percent of maximum for most individuals.) The five general training principles of specificity, progressive overload, recovery time, intensity, and duration apply to strength training just as they do to aerobic and anaerobic training. As the person gets stronger, the weight load gradually is increased even though the basic workout program remains the same.

The rest interval in resistance training is a function of the amount of resistance used. With less resistance—in a program to develop endurance and strength for purposes of wellness—a rest period of 1–3 minutes between sets is appropriate. For higher levels of resistance—to build maximum strength for some specific activity or for cosmetic purposes—a rest period of 3–5 minutes between sets is appropriate.

Strength training is done most often using either free weights or an exercise machine such as a Universal Gym or Nautilus equipment. Any of these approaches offers sufficient variety to exercise what most people consider to be the ten major targets for a complete program (chest, back, shoulders, triceps, biceps, quadriceps, hamstrings, lower legs, forearms, and neck). The degree to which each of those areas is included in a strength program, however, is highly specific to the desired outcomes of the program. Sprinters will have a strength program very different from that of discus throwers, and each of those will be substantially different from a program for basketball or volleyball players. You can be sure, however, that any athlete who is trying to get better at his or her sport will be involved in a strength-training program of some kind.

Flexibility

Physical activity is crucially important to maintaining good health. Activity requires movement. Movement is not possible without an adequate level of the fitness component commonly called *flexibility. Static flexibility* refers to the linear or angular measurement of the limits of the range of motion at a joint. *Dynamic flexibility* refers to the rate of increase in tension in a relaxed muscle as it is stretched.

Increased flexibility allows for easier and more efficient performance of exercise activities. As we grow older, our flexibility decreases, and that inhibits our capacity to move efficiently. Regular flexibility work is now a key component of most exercise

programs. Like other training modalities, flexibility work is defined by frequency, intensity, and duration.

Flexibility work should be done at least three times per week after moderate or vigorous activity. Four to five stretches for each major muscle group are recommended, typically during the cooling-down period after exercise. Muscles should be slowly elongated and held for 30 seconds with low levels of force. Flexibility work before exercise, when muscles are not yet warmed up, is not recommended.

THE MEASUREMENT OF FITNESS AND PHYSICAL ACTIVITY

The measurement of fitness and physical activity continues to be a source of considerable debate in the fitness, health, and physical-education professions. The debate focuses on the measurement of health fitness and physical-activity behavior. Motor-performance fitness has one primary assessment, which is the outcome of the performance itself; that is, fitness to jump higher in track and field is best assessed by the height achieved in competition. Fitness training for basketball involves training to jump higher, to run up and down the floor quickly without tiring, and to be more agile to defend opponents better. The fact that a basketball player can bench press 200 pounds will not mean much unless it translates directly into better performance in the game.

Likewise, there is no useful way to measure the effects of a strength program that is undertaken for cosmetic purposes. Do you think you look better? Do you feel better about yourself? Do other people think you look better? If so, then the program is a success.

In health fitness, however, the consequences of measurement are substantially more important, and the strategies for measuring health fitness are considerably more varied, thus causing a certain amount of controversy. Two approaches dominate the current fitness-measurement scene: (1) fitness tests and (2) direct measures of **cardiovascular fitness** and body composition.

Fitness testing is done frequently in school programs. A health-fitness test battery typically includes measures of body composition, back flexibility, abdominal strength, upper-body strength, and cardiovascular capacity. In the National Children and Youth Fitness Study II (Ross, Delpy, Christenson, Gold, & Damberg, 1987), these parameters were measured as follows:

- Body composition—triceps, subscapular and medial calf skinfolds
- Back flexibility—sit-and-reach test
- Abdominal strength—bent-knee sit-ups
- Upper-body strength—modified pull-ups
- Cardiovascular capacity—1-mile walk/run for children 8 years and older, ½-mile walk/run for children under age 8

This test is similar to a number of fitness tests currently used in fitness centers and schools. The two most widely used tests are the FITNESSGRAM® battery, developed at the Institute for Aerobics Research, and the Physical Best battery developed by American Alliance for Health, Physical Education, Recreation, and Dance (AAHPERD).

Fitness testing always involves the reporting of results. A measure is obtained from a test, and that measure must be interpreted and reported. The traditional method is to test a large number of subjects and then report *norm-referenced scores*—that is, a score that tells you where you stand relative to the performance of the larger group. If you are in the 50th percentile, then you are average for that group. A more recent approach has been to interpret and report scores on the basis of criteria that are thought to produce a health benefit or indicate a reduced risk for a specific health problem, a method of scoring and reporting known as **criterion-referenced health (CRH) standards** (Corbin & Pangrazi, 1992).

CRH standards have two distinct advantages. First, they assess fitness or physical activity against absolute standards that indicate minimum levels necessary to achieve health outcomes (Cureton,

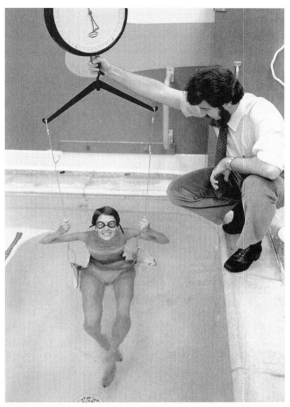

Hydrostatic weighing provides the most accurate estimate of body composition.

1994). Second, they provide immediate diagnostic feedback about whether performance is adequate to promote health. Cureton (1994) argues that separate CRH standards should be used for physical fitness and physical activity and that children and youths should be encouraged to meet both sets of standards. There is also a strong consensus now that any award system associated with fitness or physical-activity programs should be related to CRH standards rather than norm-based performances.

Another possibility is to reduce standards to "zones of interpretation" (Whitehead, 1994). An *interpretation zone* allows people to use fitness-performance or physical-activity data to understand whether they are (1) at risk for hypokinetic disease, (2) at a level that will contribute to health, or

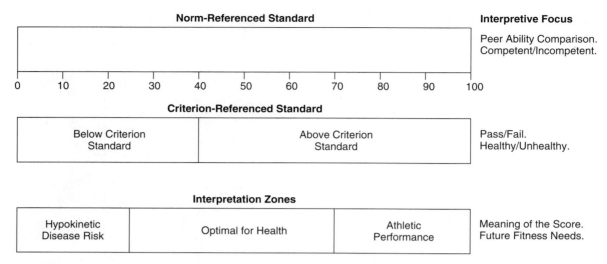

FIGURE 7.3 Three methods for interpreting the results of fitness assessments.
SOURCE: *Adapted from Whitehead, 1994.*

(3) at a level necessary for some athletic performance. Figure 7.3 shows the differences among norm-referenced standards, CRH standards, and interpretation zones.

Body composition is also considered to be an important measure of health fitness. A high percentage of body fat relative to bone and muscle has been shown repeatedly to be a predictor of risk for a wide range of degenerative diseases (Ross & Pate, 1987). Body composition is a much better measure of health fitness than is body weight. Many people who begin to take part in health-fitness programs do not lose weight quickly. What happens is that the composition of their body changes as the percentage of fat decreases and the percentage of muscle increases—with weight staying level or declining only slightly.

In fitness tests, technicians estimate body composition by taking skinfold measurements at two or three places (triceps, subscapular, and medial calf, in the National Children and Youth Fitness Study [NCYFS] II), and using the sum of these to estimate body fat. This method is relatively inexpensive and, if done carefully, can provide a sufficiently accurate gross measure of body composition to note changes

that occur with training. Exercise-science laboratories, however, use a more accurate method of estimating body composition: hydrostatic or underwater weighing. Briefly, this method involves weighing the body on land and under water to estimate body density. Fat is lighter per unit volume than is water (Costill, 1986) and therefore floats—people with a higher percentage of body fat have a lower density and therefore are good floaters.

Measuring Moderate-to-Vigorous Physical Activity

There are many problems associated with the measurement of physical activity, particularly moderate-to-vigorous physical activity (**MVPA**). For example, what activities count as "moderate" or as "vigorous"? One study might consider sustained walking moderate, and another study might label it vigorous. Walking, of course, can range from quite leisurely to intensely active (as in power or race walking). Researchers have had difficulty getting reliable data on the amount of time a person spends in MVPA (Lee & Paffenbarger, 1996). Heart-rate monitors and accelerometers are two

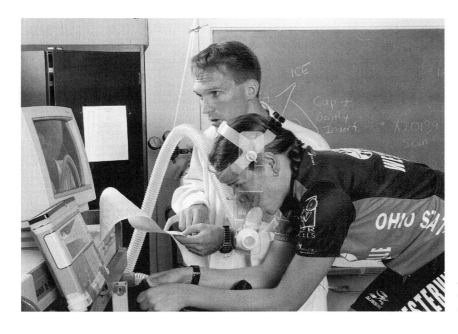

A bicycle ergometer test is one good way to measure cardiovascular function.

FOCUS ON — Pedometer Target Zones   7.6

Category	Steps/Day
Sedentary	< 5000
Low active	5,000–7,500
Somewhat active	7,500–9,999
Active	10,000–12,500
Very active	> 12,500

SOURCE: Based on values from Corbin, Welk, Corbin, & Welk, 2008.

---

kinds of devices that have been used to provide more reliable information on MVPA (Beighle, Pangrazi, & Vincent, 2001). Heart-rate monitors can be calibrated to estimate energy expenditure but tend to be influenced by factors such as age, mode of exercise, and body size. Accelerometers can store data that allow for assessment of the frequency, intensity, and duration of physical activity, and they can detect the intermittent activity of young children, which is an important variable in estimating MVPA. A major problem with

accelerometers is that they are expensive. It appears now that the most cost-effective and widely accessible devices for measuring MVPA are pedometers, which measure the number of steps taken during activity. Although they are not sensitive to some forms of activity, such as cycling, they do allow for a valid assessment of the amount of daily activity. They are also very useful for teachers and parents who want to help children and youths develop active lifestyles. The goal for adults is typically set at 10,000 steps per day (see Focus On Box 7.6).

It is also possible to calculate the number of calories expended each day from the step count. Pedometers are not overly expensive and can be used in a number of ways to help people learn more about the amount of activity that they need and how they can get it through modest changes in their lifestyles.

The Cooper Institute has also developed an ACTIVITYGRAM, an assessment tool for recording physical-activity data and interpreting those data relative to standards related to healthy lifestyles. In schools, ACTIVITYGRAM assessment is conducted over 2 school days and 1 non-school day (weekend or holiday). Students record their physical activity for each 30-minute period between the hours of 7:00 a.m. and 10:30 p.m. Entries include the time of day, the number of minutes in activity, the intensity level of the activity, and the type of activity (chosen from an Activity Pyramid). Information for each student is entered into a computer so that a summary analysis can be provided to students and parents. The report summarizes the 3-day activity and provides recommendations on how to increase or maintain physical activity based on guidelines developed by the Council for Physical Education for Children (COPEC), a division of NASPE.

Another promising method of informally measuring fitness is to estimate caloric expenditure of various activities. The unit of measurement used for this purpose is called a **MET**, or metabolic equivalent (Corbin & Pangrazi, 1996). METs are designed to estimate the metabolic cost of activity. One MET equals the number of calories expended at rest (resting metabolism). Activity that is twice that intensity measures 2 METs. Activities such as slow walking, slow stationary cycling, and bowling are typically 3 METs or less and are considered to be light activities. Activities that reach a level of 6 METs are labeled moderate, such as brisk walking, tennis, or mowing the lawn with a power mower. Activities that are 7 METs or higher are considered to be vigorous, such as jogging, fast cycling, mowing the lawn with a hand mower, and many sports.

AAHPERD has developed a functional-fitness test for older adults (Darby & Temple, 1992). The test measures agility, hip flexibility, muscular strength and endurance, coordination, and an endurance walk. The test is useful for formal programs in which adults seek to develop higher levels of cardiovascular fitness and motor-performance fitness that allows them to have greater flexibility and mobility.

Informal Measurement of Fitness

Most adults are not interested in formal tests of fitness although they do often want to monitor their fitness levels informally. This is particularly true for cardiovascular fitness. A simple way to do this is to regularly take your own heart rate during exercise and as you recover from exercise: Check your pulse rate, either at the carotid artery in the neck or at the radial artery in the wrist; count beats for 10, 20, or 30 seconds; multiply that total by 6, 3, or 2 to calculate the rate per minute that your heart is beating.

As we saw earlier in this chapter, the method of calculating your target heart rate for maximum benefit in aerobic activity is to take a maximum heart rate of 220, subtract your age, and multiply by 0.65 and 0.90. Thus, if you are 35 years old, the lower range of your target heart-rate zone would be $220 - 35 = 185 \times 0.65 = 120$. The upper range of your target heart-rate zone would be $185 \times 0.90 = 167$. This is the threshold heart rate you would need to reach during exercise to gain maximum aerobic benefit. It should be noted, however, that you can do aerobic exercise at a heart rate below the target rate and still gain substantial benefit.

Another use of pulse rate as an informal measure is to assess your capacity to recover from exercise in which the pulse rate is elevated. The more-fit person will recover the resting pulse rate more quickly. People have different resting pulse rates. One way to calculate the resting pulse rate is to take it immediately upon awaking in the morning. If you keep a record of your morning resting pulse rate, you will be able to see clear signs of improvement in fitness as that pulse rate lowers. A second way is to take your normal resting pulse rate while standing before you begin to exercise. The time it takes to return to that rate after exercise is a good measure of fitness; that is, the more quickly you recover the preexercise heart rate, the better your fitness level.

Yet another way to monitor aerobic conditioning is to keep track of distance and time for the same kind of exercise. Thus, if you do brisk walking as a main aerobic exercise, you can walk measured distances and simply know the total time it took to complete the distance. Walking further in the same amount of time is a good measure of improved cardiovascular fitness.

We should expect that further improvements will be made in measuring and monitoring MVPA. Fitness of all kinds has captured the attention of a large portion of the public, and the clear relationship between physical inactivity and a host of health problems will keep fitness high on the public-policy agenda for some time. In the next chapter, we will consider how various forms of fitness and physical activity get done, where physical activity happens, and who implements programs.

SUMMARY

1. The health benefits of fitness and physical activity are better known now than ever before.
2. Early definitions of fitness were too broad and failed to distinguish between fitness characteristics related to health and those related to motor performance.
3. Current definitions of fitness distinguish between *health fitness*, with cardiovascular efficiency as the main component, and *motor-performance fitness*, with strength as the main component.
4. The major benefits of health fitness include a stronger heart, better circulatory function, increased oxygen-carrying capacity of the blood, more favorable body composition, and reduced levels of fat in the blood.
5. Motor-performance fitness is directly related to improved performance in physical skills.
6. Moderate and high levels of regular physical activity are associated with decreases in all causes of mortality and morbidity as well as with other health benefits.
7. The dose–response debate contrasts a view that is anchored in health-related fitness and cardiovascular functioning and a view that is anchored in health alone, particularly with regard to reductions in all causes of mortality.
8. Cosmetic fitness can be important to psychological well-being and is part of today's focus on an active, healthy lifestyle.
9. The social gradient in health and fitness reveals that socioeconomic status is strongly related to better or poorer health and fitness.
10. Muscles adapt to training by becoming more efficient and stronger, enabling people to do more intense or longer-duration work or to do the same work with less effort.
11. Five general training principles for fitness are exercise specific to the fitness component where improvement is desired, progressive overload of the exercise stress, adequate recovery time between bouts, appropriate intensity within bouts, and appropriate length of the bout.
12. Health fitness is achieved through aerobic training with exercise bouts of sufficient intensity, duration, and frequency.
13. To improve and maintain aerobic fitness, a person must reach a threshold of training, sustain it for 15 to 20 minutes, and repeat this exercise three to five times per week.
14. Aerobic fitness can be achieved through continuous exercise at or just above the aerobic threshold or through interval training, in which shorter, more intense exercise bouts are interspersed with rest periods.
15. Anaerobic training requires nearly maximum effort for short periods, followed by long recovery periods.

16. Strength-training factors include the amount of resistance per lift, the number of repetitions per set, the number of sets per workout, and the number of workouts per week.

17. *Endurance* strength training uses lower resistances with more repetitions; *power* strength training uses higher resistances with fewer repetitions.

18. A typical power-strength training program involves five or six repetitions with a 5RM or 6RM workload, two to four sets per workout, and three workouts per week.

19. Motor-performance fitness is best measured through improved performance in the activity for which the fitness training is used.

20. Health fitness is typically measured through physical-fitness tests or through direct measures of cardiovascular functioning and body composition.

21. Criterion-referenced fitness standards have distinct advantages over norm-referenced standards, and zones of interpretation allow for people to understand their level of risk for hypokinetic disease.

22. The measurement of physical activity, especially MVPA, can be done informally through a variety of approaches that typically include self-monitoring of frequency, duration, and intensity of activity and attention to heart-rate measures and more formally with programs such as the ACTIVITYGRAM.

DISCUSSION QUESTIONS

1. Should health fitness become a major, independent goal of school physical education? Why or why not?

2. To what extent are the differences in kinds of fitness misunderstood by the public? How can the public become better educated?

3. For which population groups might cosmetic fitness be more important than health fitness? How can that emphasis be changed? Should it be changed?

4. Give one example of how each of the training principles is violated. Which principle is violated most often?

5. How can aerobic fitness be developed and maintained in everyday life? How can strength fitness be developed and maintained?

6. How fit are you? Answer in terms of your health and motor-performance. What factors in your life have contributed to your fitness or to your lack of fitness?

7. What fitness programs have you enrolled in? Which appealed to you? For what reasons? Which did not appeal to you? For what reasons?

8. To what extent do youths and adults suffer from the societal pressures to look fit?

9. How will the focus on moderate levels of physical activity affect fitness programs?

CHAPTER 8

Fitness Programs and Professions

Promotion of physical activity for children, adolescents, young adults, the middle-aged, and older adults is one of the most effective means of improving health and enhancing function and quality of life. All governments of the world should initiate policies to increase individual participation in physical activity by creating an environment that will encourage an acceptable level of physical activity in the whole population. This will require cooperation of governmental agencies, scientific and professional bodies, the private sector, and other community groups.

from Consensus Statement of the International Scientific Consensus
Conference on Physical Activity, Health, and Well-Being, Québec City, 1995

LEARNING OBJECTIVES

- To describe the purpose and goals of *Healthy People 2010* and outcomes related to those goals

- To describe fitness levels among children and youths

- To describe activity patterns among children and youths

- To describe fitness levels among adults

- To describe activity patterns among adults

- To describe and discuss school fitness and activity programs

- To describe AAHPERD efforts to promote fitness

- To describe and discuss worksite fitness programs

- To describe certification and preparation for fitness professions

In Chapter 7, we established the increasingly strong scientific evidence relating physical activity and fitness to positive health, mortality, and quality-of-life outcomes. We also indicated that motor-performance fitness has become increasingly important to success in sports and is important for quality-of-life outcomes among elderly people. It is also clear that many people engage in fitness activities to develop and maintain the kind of appearance that helps them feel good about themselves. In this chapter, we review information about fitness levels in the population, fitness programs, and career opportunities in the various professional fields that support the fitness movement.

From a national policy perspective, it is clear that health fitness is the most important aspect of the entire fitness movement. The U.S. government has brought the issue to the nation's attention through a series of goals and reports that began in 1979 with the publication of *Healthy People: The Surgeon General's Report on Health Promotion and Disease Prevention.* That was followed in 1990 by *Healthy People 2000* (U.S. Public Health Service, 1991), which established more than 300 health objectives in twenty-two priority areas, the first of which was "physical activity and fitness." Data related to achievement of the objectives are tracked and reported (Spain & Franks, 2001). No one thought that all the target goals could be reached in a single decade. One of the goals—increasing the number of worksite fitness programs—has been met, and we got close to meeting a few of the other goals. For example, the death rate from coronary heart disease declined, nearly achieving the target goal; and 16 percent of people 18 years and older engaged in vigorous physical activity 3 or more days per week for at least 20 minutes per session (the target was 20 percent). For other goals, however, the picture was bleak. Overweight and obesity indicators rose rather than fell. The proportion of adolescents in grades 9–12 who participate in daily physical education fell precipitously (from 42 percent in 1991 to 27 percent in 1997; the target was 50 percent).

Early in 2000, *Healthy People 2010* (U.S. Department of Health and Human Services, 2000) was published, starting the second chapter in the nation's effort to become healthier. *Healthy People 2010* has two overarching goals: to increase the years of healthy life for all people and to eliminate health disparities based on race, gender, and income. *Healthy People 2010* has four primary enabling goals: to promote healthy behavior, to protect health, to achieve success in quality health care, and to strengthen community prevention. For our purposes, our main interest is goal 22: Improve health

fitness and quality of life through daily physical activity. Table 8.1 describes that goal.

Many states have now developed state-level healthy-people plans and programs. The only way to progress toward achievement of those goals is through widely accessible and inclusive programs with competent leadership. It is the purpose of this chapter to examine programs and the kinds of leadership that professionals bring to the fitness and physical-activity movements. In the following chapter, we will review problems and issues related to fitness and physical activity.

FITNESS LEVELS AMONG CHILDREN AND YOUTHS

In the mid-1950s, data from comparative fitness tests (Kraus & Hirschland, 1954) of European and American children set off the first large-scale, national children's fitness movement. Most tests and surveys of child and youth fitness since then have produced information that is discouraging, to say the least. The popular media have again focused attention on the low levels of fitness among children and youths. *U.S. News and World Report* (Levine, Wells, & Knopf, 1986) and *Time* magazine (Toufexis, 1986) featured stories on child and youth fitness, and the conclusions were gloomy indeed. The *Time* feature suggested that children were "getting an F for flabby."

It is difficult to make historical comparisons of child and youth fitness because fitness tests have historically emphasized motor-performance items rather than health-fitness items. Another complicating factor is the recent emphasis on the accumulation of moderate-to-vigorous physical activity (MVPA), which is even more difficult to monitor and quantify, and still more difficult to compare with more traditional fitness measures such as the 1-mile run.

In 1985 the results from the National Children and Youth Fitness Study (NCYFS I) were released. This nationwide study assessed the degree to which

TABLE 8.1	*Healthy People 2010* Goal 22 for Fitness and Physical Activity

22-1   Reduce the proportion of adults who engage in no leisure-time physical activity. (Baseline is 40 percent of adults 18 and older engaged in no leisure-time activity.) Target is 20 percent.

22-2   Increase the proportion of adults who engage regularly, preferably daily, in moderate physical activity for at least 30 minutes per day. (Baseline is 15 percent of adults 18 years and older who now engage at that level.) Target is 30 percent.

22-3   Increase the proportion of adults 18 years and older engaged in vigorous physical activity 3 or more days per week for 20 or more minutes per session. (Baseline is 23 percent of adults 18 years or older who now engage at that level.) Target is 30 percent.

22-4   Increase the proportion of adults who perform physical activities that enhance and maintain muscular strength and endurance. (Baseline is 18 percent of adults aged 18 and over who perform such activities 2 or more days per week.) Target is 30 percent.

22-5   Increase the proportion of adults who perform physical activities that enhance and maintain flexibility. (Baseline is 30 percent of adults aged 18 and older who do stretching activities regularly.) Target is 43 percent.

22-6   Increase the proportion of adolescents who engage in moderate physical activity for at least 30 minutes 5 days per week. (Baseline is 27 percent of students in grades 9–12 who engaged in moderate physical activity for at least 30 minutes on 5 of previous 7 days.) Target is 35 percent.

22-7   Increase the proportion of adolescents who engage in vigorous physical activity 3 or more days per week for 20 or more minutes per occasion. (Baseline is 65 percent of students in grades 9–12 who engaged in vigorous physical activity 3 or more days per week for 20 or more minutes per occasion.) Target is 85 percent.

22-8   Increase the proportion of public and private schools that require daily physical activity for all students. (Baseline is 17 percent for middle schools and 2 percent for high schools.) Targets are 25 percent for middle schools and 5 percent for high schools.

22-9   Increase the proportion of adolescents who participate in daily school physical education. (Baseline is 29 percent of students in grades 9–12 who participated in daily physical education in 1999.) Target is 50 percent.

22-10   Increase the proportion of students in grades 9–12 who spend at least 50 percent of their school physical education class time being physically active. (Baseline is 38 percent of students in grades 9–12.) Target is 50 percent.

22-11   Increase the proportion of adolescents who view television 2 or fewer hours on school days. (Baseline is 57 percent of students in grades 9–12 who viewed TV 2 or fewer hours.) Target is 75 percent.

22-12   Increase the proportion of public and private schools that provide access to their physical-activity spaces for all people outside school hours. This is a developmental goal for which there is no baseline and no target.

22-13   Increase the proportion of worksites offering employer-sponsored physical-activity and fitness programs. (Baseline is 46 percent of worksites with fifty or more employees that offered programs in 1999.) Target is 75 percent.

22-14   Increase the proportion of trips made by walking. (Baseline for trips of 1 mile or less is [a] 17 percent by adults and [b] 31 percent by children and adolescents.) Target is for 47 percent improvement for (a) and 68 percent improvement for (b).

22-15   Increase trips made by bicycling. (Baseline for [a] trips of 5 miles or less for adults is 0.6 percent and [b] trips by children and adolescents of 2 miles or less is 2.4 percent.) Targets are 2 percent for (a) and 5 percent for (b).

SOURCES: Adapted from Spain & Franks, 2001; see also U.S. Department of Health and Human Services, 2000.

Fun and challenging physical activities are important for children.

fifth- through twelfth-graders were fit and active. Because our understanding of what fitness is and of how it should be measured had improved greatly by the early 1980s, the NCYFS was the most rigorous study of youth fitness ever conducted in the United States. The investigators tested 8,800 boys and girls and completed surveys regarding the youths' activity habits.

The two results that are most alarming are the measure of **body composition** (skinfold test) and the cardiopulmonary measure (1-mile run–walk). The skinfold test data indicated that the average score for both boys and girls was in the moderately high range, indicating some risk for problems associated with too much body fat. The average scores for the 1-mile run–walk showed that many girls did more walking than running and that many boys and girls could do no better than slowly jogging for that distance.

A similar fitness study (Milverstedt, 1988) in 1985, the National School Population Fitness Survey, examined a large number of elementary and secondary students on six fitness items and compared

the results with national norms. Of the 9,678 boys tested, only 11 reached the 85th percentile on all six items! Thus, we should be concerned not only about the *average* scores on fitness tests but also about the low number of high scores.

In 1987 the results of NCYFS II were released. This study examined the fitness levels and activity patterns of 6- to 9-year-old children (4,853 in the sample). The tests were similar to those in NCYFS I.

The low fitness scores were alarming, leading to the concerns voiced in the national media. The body-composition data indicated that the 6- to 9-year-olds in the study carried more body fat than the children tested 20 years earlier (Ross & Pate, 1987). The general picture of these major, national tests seems clear. Children carry more body fat than is healthy. Between 1980 and 1994, the percentage of overweight children doubled, and data today indicate that this trend is continuing (Koplan, Liverman, Kraak, Wisham, 2006). The percentage of youths who are overweight has more than tripled since the mid-1970s (Pangrazi, 2003). Children typically do not have well-developed cardiopulmonary capacity. Children, especially girls, perform poorly in tests of upper-body strength.

The general notion that children are not fit has been argued in both the professional and the popular literature since the 1970s. In the 1990s, the accuracy and fairness of that perception began to be questioned (Corbin & Pangrazi, 1992). Blair (1992) argued that we have been looking at the fitness data through the wrong set of lenses. He argued that physical activity that results in a particular level of energy expenditure per day is associated with important health benefits. (The figure is calculated to an energy expenditure of 3,000 calories per 1,000 grams of body weight per day, or 3 Kcal/kg of body weight.) Blair recalculated the NCYFS II data and concluded that 77 percent of the boys and girls tested had met that standard, a finding that does not support the common perception of a nation of unfit children.

The effort to produce an accurate, reliable picture of the fitness levels of children and youths has also been hindered by the widespread use of

The World Health Organization estimates that 30–45 million children worldwide are obese and 155 million are overweight. Although the two key elements in any plan to reduce obesity and over-weight involve caloric intake and energy expendi-ture (physical activity), restricting food intake in young children is generally discouraged because children need nutrients to grow and develop. For the first time in history, a generation of children has the misfortune to live a completely sedentary lifestyle. Many children get transported rather than transporting themselves. Television, video games, and the computer occupy far too much of their discretionary time; their recreation is attending to multimedia rather than being active. Research in Canada has shown that children who live a lifestyle more representative of previous generations are leaner, stronger, and more aerobi-cally fit than children who live a "modern" lifestyle. The differences are mostly attributable to the presence of regular physical activity among children whose lifestyle is more representative of a previous generation.

SOURCE: Trembal, Barnes, Copeland, & Esliger, 2005.

norm-referenced scores to gauge fitness levels, a measurement problem discussed in Chapter 7. Re-call that a norm-referenced score places any single child or youth in relation to all the other children or youths who took the tests when the norms were es-tablished. What do you know if you are a 12-year-old girl and you rank in the 70th percentile on the 1-mile run? You know only that you ran a time that was faster than about 69 percent of those tested and slower than about 30 percent of those tested. This outcome tells you nothing about whether the time that you ran is a good indicator of your fitness level.

In most important tests, norm-referenced re-porting has been replaced by criterion-referenced health (CRH) standards. CRH standards compare performances to criteria that indicate *potential risk* where amounts of activity may be inadequate to contribute to health benefits. Thus, a performance score is immediately comparable to a standard re-lated to health risks rather than to the performance of other children or youths.

Scientific evidence supporting the link between health-fitness indicators and adult hypokinetic disease and mortality grows stronger with each pass-ing year. Children who are low on fitness measures in elementary school tend to remain at risk during adolescence. Young children who are obese tend to become obese adolescents and then obese adults. On the other hand, children who are active and healthy tend to remain so as adolescents and into adulthood. Thus, measures of childhood physical ac-tivity and health are predictive of adolescent and adult patterns. This underscores the importance of strong programs of physical education and physical activity for young children. The children who need help can be identified, and there are intervention programs to help them (Bouchard, Shephard, & Stephens, 1993; Corbin, 2002; Sallis & McKenzie, 1993).

Traditionally, concerns about improving physi-cal fitness or achieving healthier lifestyles have been considered to be matters of personal re-sponsibility. Recently, however, it has become clear that child/youth obesity has become a public health epidemic and many have argued that to ad-dress the causes of the epidemic and improve the situation we must shift our view of obesity away from the medical model, focusing on individuals, to a public health model, focusing on the popula-tion (Schwartz & Brownell, 2007) (see Focus On Box 8.1). While personal responsibility will no doubt remain a significant issue in programs to prevent obesity, an equal effort must be focused on the environmental issues that are considered to be precipitating factors of the epidemic. These would include foods that have a higher caloric value, more dietary fat, and higher caloric density. Consumption of such foods is related to less in-home cooking, greater reliance on take-out food, more fast-food meals, and eating in restaurants. Foods served at school breakfasts and lunches and in-school vending machines have tended to include nonnutritious ingredients (Levi, Segal, & Juliano, 2006).

Reduction in physical activity is caused by a number of factors primarily related to what is now commonly referred to as the "built environment." Factors such as communities designed to foster driving rather than walking/biking, lack of public transit, and an increase in commuting reduce opportunities for physical activity. Children and youths tend to spend more time watching TV, using the computer for games, or connecting with the Internet than they did a generation ago, thus reducing physical activity (Siedentop, 2007). The federal legislation, No Child Left Behind, has caused a 14 percent reduction in time for physical education in schools (Jennings, 2006). The fact that most students are bused to and from school reduces participation in after-school programs that include physical-activity opportunities. Parents report five primary barriers to their children's participation in physical activity: transportation problems, lack of opportunities for physical activity in the immediate area, expense, parents' lack of time, and concerns about neighborhood safety (CDC, 2003).

These are issues that must be confronted with social policy, legislation, and community efforts as well as with greater personal responsibility. For example, the 2004 federal legislation renewing the National School Lunch Act required all schools that receive federal support for school lunches to establish nutrition guidelines ensuring that only healthy foods will be available in school during the school day (Senate Report 108-345, 2006). The same legislation required schools to develop "wellness councils" to improve nutrition and physical activity within the school day. In 2005 the federal Department of Transportation created the national Safe Routes to School Program with an initial appropriation of $54 million, primarily to improve the infrastructure so that

more students could walk or bike to school. Many states have since developed "walk to school programs." In Chapter 10, we will revisit this issue with legislative and policy actions to increase physical education and physical activity for children and youths.

Many states have adopted the Centers for Disease Control's Coordinated School Health Program, a model that consists of eight interactive components including health education; physical education; health services; nutrition services; counseling, psychological, and social services; a healthy school environment; health promotion for staff; and family/community involvement. The model allows for issues such as physical-activity promotion to be considered and dealt with throughout the school program and by developing relationships with community agencies.

ACTIVITY PATTERNS AMONG CHILDREN AND YOUTHS

Participation in physical activity among children and youths is difficult to assess because information is typically obtained from self-reports, diaries, questionnaires, and reports from parents, and these reporting mechanisms often are not reliable. The NCYFS II survey found that nearly 85 percent of 6- to 9-year-old children participate in some activity through a community organization, typically public park and recreation programs, community-based sport programs, church programs, YMCA/YWCA programs, scouting groups, and private health clubs (Ross & Pate, 1987). The same survey found that children watch just over 2 hours per day of television during the week and 3.5 hours per day on weekends; these figures are substantially lower than those from many other national surveys.

The following conclusions can be reached regarding evidence of activity patterns among children and youths (American Sports Data, 1999; Rosenbaum & Leibel, 1989; Sallis, 1994; Sallis &

Children are more likely to be active if activity is supported by their parents.

McKenzie, 1993; U.S. Department of Health and Human Services, 1996):

1. The self-reports of children indicate that 90 percent or more are active at a level required for health benefits.

2. Studies monitoring the heart rates of children throughout the day show that most children are sufficiently active to meet the American College of Sports Medicine's (ACSM, 1990) recommendations for adult activity levels.

3. A large proportion of children do not get regular physical education from a specialist teacher.

4. When activity in physical-education classes is monitored, it is not uncommon for children to have as little as 2 minutes of vigorous activity in a 30-minute lesson.

5. More than 34 percent of American children and youths can be classified as overweight or obese. Girls are more likely to be obese than boys. African American and Hispanic children and youths are obese at nearly twice the rate of non-Hispanic whites.

6. Only about one-half of American young people (ages 12–21 years) regularly participate in vigorous physical activity. One-fourth report no vigorous physical activity.

7. Only 21.3 percent of all adolescents participate in school physical-education programs 1 or more days per week in their schools.

8. Data assessing *Healthy People 2000* goals show that 41 percent of ninth-graders participate in physical activity on a daily basis, but the figure declines to 13 percent by the twelfth grade.

9. About 50–60 percent of high-school boys and 38–43 percent of high-school girls participate on a school sport team each year. About 45 percent of boys and 25 percent of girls participate on sport teams run by nonschool organizations.

10. The participation data are all higher for males than for females. Because girls appear to be less active than boys, special programs may be needed to motivate and sustain their participation.

11. In the 1990s, the fastest-growing age group in frequent activity participation were children 6–11 years of age, and the steepest decline of all age groups was found in the 12–17 age bracket.

As children develop into their adolescent years, two things seem clear. Too many children reduce their physical activity substantially. It also appears that the "rich get richer and the poor get poorer"; that is, highly active children tend to develop habits that persist into adolescence, and those who are less active and less successful in physical activity tend to do less and less.

All evidence indicates that participation in sport and physical activity among youths reaches a peak at or about age 11 years and declines markedly through the teen years (Athletic Footwear Institute, 1990; Coakley, 2007; Sallis, 1994). In some cases, this decline occurs because opportunity to participate is reduced (for example, the varsity model). In other cases, this decline is a reaction against how the sport is organized and conducted (many youths say it is no longer "fun"), and in still other cases, sport becomes less attractive when compared with other opportunities (work, dating, computers, and so on). It may be that some youths begin to participate in physical activities (recreational swimming, skate-boarding, in-line skating, and the like) that are not typically classified as sports and are difficult to monitor in terms of participation. Many have argued that youths are currently motivated by the adult model of fitness participation in clubs rather than by informal, recreational sports. Children are typically motivated by enjoyment, companionship, and adult approval of their activity participation. Adolescents are more likely to be motivated by seeking to influence their body shape, to control stress, to respond to peer influence, and to increase their sense of control over themselves and their lives. Attention to those factors is necessary to reduce the age-related decline in activity participation (Sallis, 1994).

Another new entry into the world of fitness for children and youths are interactive video games that provide a range of fitness activities. Typical of these are the interactive video games provided through GenerationFit (www.generation-fit.com). Interactive video activities for movement, fitness, dance, and rhythmic music are provided with separate activities for grades 3–5, 6–8, and 9–12. Often, learning activities are also incorporated with the movement and fitness activities.

Lack of participation among youths is a serious problem simply because the teen years are when adult habits begin to emerge. Because a large majority of children are active, adolescence must be the period most related to the high incidence of inactivity that is commonly found among adults. That relationship makes the reduction of physical activity among youths a major national problem, which must be solved if a healthier adult population is the goal.

FITNESS LEVELS AMONG ADULTS

It is difficult to obtain reliable and valid information about adult fitness levels. Whereas fitness testing of children and youths can be done in schools, no such opportunity exists for adults. Both public- and private-sector agencies have tried to estimate levels of fitness and physical activity among adults, but these estimates come most frequently from surveys and questionnaires and are extremely variable: Some show that as much as 78 percent of the population has an active lifestyle, and others show that as little as 15 percent does (Blair, Kohl, & Powell, 1987). The best estimate we have is from the documentation for *Healthy People 2010* (see Figure 8.1), which shows estimated activity levels for women and men related to the 2010 goals.

Those figures seem surprising in an era that has been described as a renaissance of fitness. There is little doubt that the fitness boom, at its outset, was primarily a "yuppie" phenomenon; that is, it was primarily confined to young, middle- and upper-class people, particularly those in professions. Television and magazine advertisements catered to that group because they had more disposable income. In 1990 there were 51.5 million frequent fitness participants in the United States, a significant increase since the 1950s (Lauer, 2006). The baby boomers and yuppies are now older, and much of our attention is devoted to the health and

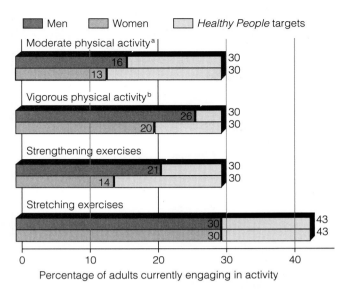

FIGURE 8.1 Current levels of physical activity among American adults

SOURCES: *National Center for Health Statistics. 2004;* DATA2010: The Healthy People 2010 Database, January 2004 Edition (*http://wonder.cdc.gov/data2010; retrieved April 6, 2004*).

[a]Moderate physical activity for 30 or more minutes on 5 or more days per week
[b]Vigorous physical activity for 20 or more minutes on 3 or more days per week

activity problems of our younger generation, most often referred to as the "millennial" generation (Generation Y).

Another way to estimate participation in healthy physical activity is to focus on the facilities and programs that have been developed to accommodate health-related physical activity. Health-club membership in 2004 reached 41.3 million, 138% higher than the 17.4 million in 1987 (Lauer, 2006). In 2004, 6.2 million Americans used the services of a personal trainer, up 55 percent since 1999. The Curves for Women franchise, initiated in 1995, uses a 30-minute exercise routine that combines strength training and sustained cardiovascular activity using hydraulic resistance. In the first 5 years, Curves had 1,000 locations and over 9,000 in 10 years. Today, Curves for Women operates over 10,000 locations serving more than 4 million women annually. In Chapter 11, you will see how fitness and physical-activity programs and facilities to support them have become important in American high schools. The significant growth of college and university health and fitness centers, cited in Chapter 1, shows how important regular physical activity is becoming to

that generation. The senior population also has more access to facilities and programs that support physical activity. Home fitness rooms are now big business for builders and those who remodel homes. Fitness rooms typically include both cardiovascular and strength-training equipment, along with a television set. Most retirement communities and senior-citizen centers now have facilities and programs that encourage physical activity among their residents and attendees.

Another way to look at fitness levels among adults is to examine risk factors that indicate a high degree of risk for cardiovascular disease (CVD). The data in the Focus On Box 8.2 show that inactivity is the most prevalent CVD risk factor. Adults over the age of 60 who have higher levels of cardiorespiratory fitness live longer than those with lower levels, regardless of their levels of body fat (Sui, 2007). Previous data had shown that inactive adults are twice as likely to die of CVD as are active adults (Sallis & McKenzie, 1993). These data support the notion that activity levels rather than fitness-test data are more important indicators for public health purposes.

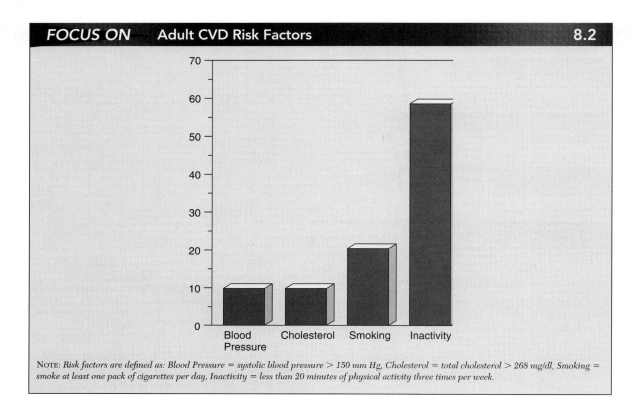

FOCUS ON   Adult CVD Risk Factors   8.2

NOTE: *Risk factors are defined as: Blood Pressure = systolic blood pressure > 150 mm Hg, Cholesterol = total cholesterol > 268 mg/dl, Smoking = smoke at least one pack of cigarettes per day, Inactivity = less than 20 minutes of physical activity three times per week.*

A national movement that focuses more on regular activity and less on body composition is Health at Every Size, sponsored by the Wellness Councils of America (www.welcoa.org). The Health at Every Size program has three major components. The component of self-acceptance affirms the worth of human beings irrespective of differences in weight, physical size, and shape. The component of physical activity supports increasing social, pleasure-based movement, and the component of normalized eating disavows externally imposed rules for eating and seeks a more peaceful relationship with food by re-learning to eat in response to physiological hunger and fullness cues.

The image of an active lifestyle may be quite different than the reality of an active lifestyle. Initiated in 1987, the American Sports Data in the *Superstudy of Sports Participation* (Lauer, 2006) suggests that the fitness boom reached its apex in 1990. Since the 1990 survey, the number of frequent (100 + days/year in an activity) fitness participants has dropped from 51 million to 50.9 million in 2002 (Lauer, 2006). Among children/youths, ages 12–17 years, the drop is 41 percent. Focus On Box 8.3 shows the 1998–2004 changes in various forms of fitness-exercise participation.

What is clear is that more people of all ages are becoming better educated about health fitness and the importance of regular physical activity. Evidence seems clear that more adults and children/youths have been made more aware about the benefits of physical activity and the health risks associated with inactivity. As Chapter 9 will show, however, the access to and the financial resources to support healthy lifestyles are not distributed evenly across our population. The broadening of the fitness movement to include older Americans is an important trend, especially when one considers that the large population segment known as the baby boomers are moving into that age group.

Mass exercise sessions take on the atmosphere of a festival.

FOCUS ON — Changing Styles of Exercise*   8.3

Exercise Type	1998	2000	2004	Change (%)
Pilates		173,900	1,100,541	+506.2
Stationary cycling	1,076,500	2,879,500	3,143,100	+2.8
Weight machines	1,526,100	2,518,200	3,090,300	+102.5
Free weights	2,555,300	4,449,400	5,205,600	+130.8
Treadmill exercise	439,600	4,081,600	4,746,300	+979.7
Fitness walking	2,716,400	3,798,100	4,029,900	+48.4
Running/jogging	3,713,600	3,615,200	3,731,000	+0.5
Aerobics	2,122,500	1,732,600	1,576,700	−25.7
Fitness swimming	1,691,200	1,454,200	1,563,500	−7.5
Home gym exercise	390,500	757,700	934,700	+139.4

*U.S. population 6 years and older.
SOURCE: Lauer, 2006.

Exercise plays an important role in cardiac rehabilitation.

Adult women and men often participate together in group exercise.

FITNESS AND ACTIVITY PATTERNS AMONG OLDER ADULTS

No age group incurs greater public health costs than older citizens do. We live in a "graying America." Baby boomers (those born between 1946 and 1964) are entering the senior-citizen age range, and it is clear that they will live longer than previous generations (Mathieu, 1999). Not only has life expectancy increased steadily over the past 100 years, but the fastest-growing age group in America are also those 75 years old and older.

All signs indicate that older citizens are becoming more active. Perhaps this is due to the increased knowledge that the benefits of regular physical activity to health and well-being are nowhere more clear than among older citizens (Mathieu, 1999). One study classified elderly walkers into three groups. The study showed that those in the least-active walking group were more than twice as likely as those in the other groups to suffer a heart attack or some other coronary event, even when differences in risk factors (such as age, hypertension, and cholesterol levels) were taken into account (Physical Activity Today, 1999). Even for older people who have become

sedentary and are seriously at risk for hypokinetic diseases of various kinds, the benefits of becoming more active are typically quick to appear and are tremendously important to improving lifestyle.

Thirty years ago, the common perception was that weight lifting was an activity for young men. No more! Resistance exercise may well be to the next generation what aerobic conditioning was to the previous one. The number of older citizens who regularly use strength equipment nearly doubled in the 1990s (American Sports Data, 1999). For older citizens to maintain their mobility and avoid the risk of broken bones associated with falling and osteoporosis, they must maintain an adequate level of muscular strength. Even terribly frail older adults can quickly realize important lifestyle gains through regular resistance exercise.

And the increasing evidence that exercise is a good antidote to depression is especially important for older citizens, who suffer more frequently from this mental illness. All new evidence points to the conclusion that appropriate exercise can reduce and in some cases reverse the adverse effects of biological aging and also have significant psychological benefits (Duda, 1991; U.S. Department of Health and Human Services, 1996).

All this good news needs to be tempered by a few sobering facts. Of those over 65 years of age, 85 percent have at least one chronic health condition (National Blueprint on Physical Activity Among Adults Age 50 and Older, 2000). Of women over age 70, 35–50 percent have difficulty with general mobility tasks such as walking a few blocks or climbing stairs in a home. Of people over age 50 who have hip fractures, 24 percent die within a year. Physical inactivity is not distributed evenly across the population. Inactivity is more frequent in lower-income groups and among minority populations.

Fitness and physical activity for seniors will be an important research field for the future and is already an important new direction for fitness professionals. In 2001 a coalition of forty-six national organizations released the *National Blueprint: Increasing Physical Activity Among Adults Age 50 and Older* (www.agingblueprint.org), designed to promote physical activity among America's aging population. We must remember that most women and men who are now seniors grew up in an era when very little was known about the specific health benefits of exercise. Indeed, most norms for that era suggested that older people, especially women, should not be active. To overcome this early socialization and to establish patterns of effective participation require both education and well-planned and accessible programs.

FITNESS AND PHYSICAL-ACTIVITY PROGRAMS FOR CHILDREN AND YOUTHS

Most parents would like their children to learn about fitness at school and develop and maintain an adequate level of fitness through school physical-education programs. The federal government agrees with that view, having two decades ago cited fitness development and maintenance as a fundamental goal for the nation's elementary and secondary schools (Bennett, 1986). The Centers for Disease Control and Prevention (1997) developed the policy guidelines through which this agenda should be pursued. These guidelines for school and community programs to promote lifelong physical activity among young people are shown in Focus On Box 8.4. What will be clear as you review the guidelines is that the concept of "program" extends beyond physical-education classes to the entire school and out to the local community.

In Chapter 7, the minimum guidelines for child and youth engagement in physical activity were presented. The key elements of those suggestions are as follows (NASPE, 2004a: Sallis, 1994):

- Children should accumulate at least 60 minutes, and as much as several hours, in physical activity on most if not all days.

- Daily participation for children should include moderate-to-vigorous activity, with several bouts lasting 15 minutes or more, with the majority of time spent in activity of an intermittent nature.

- Activities for children should be age appropriate.

- Extended periods of inactivity for children are discouraged.

- Adolescents should be physically active daily for at least 30 minutes.

- Adolescents should engage in three or more sessions per week of activities that last a minimum of 20 minutes and require moderate-to-vigorous levels of exertion.

It is not possible for these guidelines to be met solely through physical-education classes. Thus, activity programs for children and youths must be available after school, on weekends, and in the community or at home. Nonetheless, the health imperative for the nation suggests strongly that school physical education should be strengthened not only by allotting

FOCUS ON

Youth Physical-Activity (PA) Recommendations by the Centers for Disease Control

8.4

1. Establish *policies* that promote enjoyable, lifelong PA.
   - Require daily physical education K–12.
   - Require health education K–12.
   - Commit adequate resources for PA instruction and programs.
   - Hire professionally trained people.
   - Require that PA programs meet the needs and interests of children.

2. Provide physical and social *environments* that encourage PA.
   - Provide access to safe spaces/facilities in school and community.
   - Prevent PA-related injuries/illness.
   - Provide time in the schoolday for unstructured PA (to accumulate a significant percentage of weekly PA requirements).
   - Do not use PA as punishment.
   - Provide health promotion for school faculty.

3. Implement planned and sequential *physical education (PE)* curricula that emphasize participation in PA and that encourage students to develop the knowledge, attitudes, motor skills, and confidence needed to adopt physically active lifestyles.
   - Make PE curricula consistent with national standards.
   - Impart knowledge of PA to students.
   - Develop students' positive attitudes toward, motor skills for, and confidence in participating in PA.
   - Promote participation in enjoyable PA in school, community, and home.

4. Implement planned and sequential *health education (HE)* curricula that encourage students to develop the knowledge, attitudes, and behavioral skills needed to adopt physically active lifestyles.
   - Make HE curricula consistent with national standards.
   - Promote collaboration among PE, HE, and classroom teachers for PA instruction.
   - Develop students' mastery of behavioral skills needed to adopt and maintain positive lifestyle behaviors.

5. Provide *extracurricular PA programs* that meet students' needs and interests.
   - Provide a diversity of developmentally appropriate PA programs for the largest number of students.
   - Link students to community PA programs, and use community resources to support extracurricular PA programs.

6. Include *parents and guardians* in PA instruction and extracurricular PA programs, and encourage them to support their children's participation in enjoyable PA.
   - Encourage parents to advocate for high-quality PA instruction and programs for their children.
   - Encourage parents to support their children's participation in appropriate, enjoyable PA.
   - Motivate parents to be role models for PA and to plan family activities that include PA.

7. Provide PE, HE, recreation, and health-care professionals with *training* that imparts the knowledge and skills needed to effectively promote PA among youths.
   - Through higher education, provide preservice training for education, recreation, and health-care professionals.

FOCUS ON   Youth Physical-Activity (PA) Recommendations by the Centers for Disease Control *(continued)*   **8.4**

- Teach educators how to deliver PE that provides a significant percentage of each student's weekly PA.
- Teach active learning strategies needed to develop knowledge about, attitudes toward, skills in, and confidence in PA.
- Create environments that enable youths to enjoy PA instruction and programs.
- Qualify volunteers who coach sport and recreation programs for youths.

8. Provide *health services* that assess PA among youths, reinforce PA among active youths, counsel inactive youths and refer them to PA programs, and advocate for PA instruction and programs for youths.

- Regularly assess PA, reinforce active youths, and refer inactive youths.

- Advocate for school and community PA instruction and programs.

9. Provide a range of developmentally appropriate, noncompetitive *community sport and recreation programs* that are attractive to youths.

10. Regularly *evaluate* school and community PA instruction, programs, and facilities.

- Conduct process evaluations to determine how policies, programs, and training are implemented.
- Conduct outcome evaluations to measure students' achievement of PA knowledge, behavioral skills, and motor skills.

SOURCE: Adapted from *Guidelines for School and Community Programs to Promote Lifelong Physical Activity Among Young People*, Centers for Disease Control and Prevention, Public Health Service, U.S. Department of Health and Human Services, 1997.

---

more time to it but also by finding creative ways to extend the physical education program beyond that provided in the regular school schedule.

It should be noted that some research suggests that parents are not always aware that their children are overweight or obese (He & Evans, 2007). The tendency is for parents to underestimate the degree to which their children are overweight or obese. The factors accounting for these misperceptions were the children's sex and ethnicity, the mothers' weight status, and the level of the family education and income. This of course creates problems for teachers, health workers, and physicians who attempt to deal with cases of childhood overweight and obesity.

Following are examples of how creative and persevering physical educators have developed and sustained fitness and physical-activity programs in their schools. These examples should be considered together with the information on child

and youth sport presented in Chapter 5 to form a comprehensive view of activity opportunities and programs.

1. *Schoolwide programs at the elementary level.* Some schools have adopted a schoolwide approach to programming for fitness. At a certain time of the day, for example, all classes might take a 15-minute jog or do various other kinds of aerobic activities.

2. *Fitness clubs.* At the elementary- and middle-school levels, many physical educators have successfully developed fitness clubs that provide incentives for students to engage regularly in fitness activities outside physical-education class time. For example, students might chart the course of a cross-country bicycle trip on a map by carefully keeping track of the miles that they ride their bicycles each week.

3. *Fitness-remediation programs.* Some physical educators have focused on students who are

particularly at risk in health fitness. After initial diagnosis with a health-fitness test, at-risk students and their families are informed of the problems, and the children are enrolled in a remedial program. A special fitness class is developed for these students, and progress is monitored until the children have improved sufficiently to move out of the at-risk category.

4. *Daily fitness programs.* Daily fitness first appeared on a national scale in Australia (Siedentop & Siedentop, 1985). *Daily fitness* is a program that separates fitness programming and goals from physical-education instruction. Each day, classroom teachers take 20 minutes to work with their children in aerobic activities. Fitness materials are provided, eliminating the need for extensive planning by the teacher. The children also get physical-education instruction, but the goals and activities of the two programs are kept separate.

5. *Fitness courses.* Many schools, particularly middle and high schools, have instituted a required fitness course, often at the ninth-grade level. The purpose of the course is to educate students about fitness, test them, help them to plan personal fitness programs, and teach them the kinds of activities that will help them maintain an adequate level of health fitness. The assumption is that after completing the course, students will be more able and more likely to develop and maintain a personal fitness program.

6. *Fitness elective courses.* Many high schools have started to offer a variety of fitness elective courses, ranging from aerobics to weight training to body shaping. These courses typically focus on the range of fitness outcomes—aerobic, motor performance, and cosmetic.

7. *Fitness centers.* Some middle and high schools have developed fitness centers that accommodate both classes and drop-in activities. Hoover High School in San Diego, California, operates a 2,800-square-foot fitness center (Samman, 1998) used for physical-education classes, sport teams, staff members, and the community. An after-school fitness club is open to all students.

8. *A complete high-school fitness program.* West cott (1992) described a high school in which physical education is required all 4 years, and a fitness focus defines the program. Students take a series of wellness courses, all of which have a fitness-related focus. They also choose from a series of activity courses that emphasize different approaches to fitness, including lifetime sports, fitness walking, aerobics, weight training, and the like.

9. *A state-requirement approach.* Florida requires all ninth-grade students to complete a semester of physical-education credit in personal fitness (Johnson & Harageones, 1994). A state syllabus has been prepared and staff development programs are offered to teachers to help them prepare to teach the course, which involves both classroom and gymnasium sections. The course has three objectives: to develop a healthy level of fitness, to understand fitness concepts, and to understand the significance of lifestyle to health and fitness.

The CDC guidelines make it clear that to fully serve the physical-activity needs of children and youths, educators and community leaders must take a comprehensive approach that goes beyond regularly scheduled classes to build a *physical-activity infrastructure* that links school, home, and community to help all citizens stay active. Physical education alone cannot achieve the nation's goals for physical activity. Schools alone can't do it. These objectives can be achieved only by developing and sustaining the physical-activity infrastructure, a concept that was introduced in Chapter 1. Chapter 13 will describe in detail the elements of such an infrastructure and provide information on how states and communities are moving to build and sustain such an effort.

FITNESS AND PHYSICAL ACTIVITY FOR PEOPLE WITH DISABILITIES

Historically, programs for physical activity and fitness for people with disabilities has been framed in a medical rationale and strongly focused on rehabilitation. Physical activity was focused on activities of daily living such as dressing, ambulating, or lifting items (*PCPFS Research Digests,* 1999). The new paradigm for active, healthy lifestyles for people with disabilities is one of inclusion and integration. For the most part, people with disabilities gain similar benefits from physical activity as do people without disabilities.

To participate fully in physical activity, children, youths, and adults with disabilities have many barriers to overcome. People with mobility problems confront many architectural barriers that make it difficult to sustain activity. Many people with disabilities deal with health problems caused by living sedentary lifestyles. People with learning disabilities and mental retardation are less likely to have access to recreational and fitness activities. People that have inefficient movement patterns and poor body alignment due to a disability expend more energy doing simple, normal tasks, leaving them too fatigued for leisure-time physical activity. Regardless, people with disabilities can derive health benefits from activity in much the same way as do people without disabilities.

People with disabilities need to develop cardiovascular fitness, muscular strength, and flexibility just as do people without disabilities. With some conditions, heart-rate formulas need to be adjusted to compensate for the disability. For people with conditions that affect capacity to participate in cardiovascular exercise, a rating of perceived exertion may be a better indicator that a heart-rate formula. Most people with disabilities can gain marked benefits from participating in activities to increase muscular strength. The specific nature of some disabilities require special assistance in resistance training, such as a spotter, and the resistance training should be designed specifically for his or her disability. For example, people who use wheelchairs should develop the muscle groups that counterbalance those used for daily ambulation. Flexibility exercises, specifically designed relative to the disability, should be done at the outset of a training session and again at its conclusion. Problems of overweight and obesity are no different for people with disabilities than for those without disabilities. Here, the

issue is to increase the levels and duration of activity so as to reduce the percentage of body fat.

As shown in Chapter 5, there is increasing participation in sport for people with disabilities. Public Law 94-142 ensured that children and youths with disabilities would be placed in the least restrictive environment in schools and should have access to a physical-education program that meets their needs and helps them improve their fitness levels.

AAHPERD EFFORTS TO PROMOTE PHYSICAL ACTIVITY AND FITNESS

AAHPERD (American Alliance for Health, Physical Education, Recreation, and Dance), the main professional organization for sport, fitness, and physical-education professionals (now most commonly referred to as "the alliance"), has a long history of promoting physical fitness and continues to play a central role in national efforts to promote physical activity and fitness. AAHPERD has developed and promoted a series of fitness testing and motivational programs since the 1970s. In 1993 AAHPERD joined with the Cooper Institute for Aerobic Research (CIAR) in a partnership to develop educational materials, an assessment program, and an incentive program—which is called the "Physical Best-FITNESSGRAM®" program.

In 1999 AAHPERD joined the Cooper Institute and Human Kinetics Publishers to form the American Fitness Alliance (AFA) (www.american fitness.net). The AFA produces a number of materials that are widely used in schools and elsewhere.

- *Physical Best* provides the educational component of a comprehensive health-related fitness-education program, supplying curriculum materials, activity guides, and teacher certification.
- The *FITNESSGRAM* test for evaluating K–12 students' physical fitness includes a test-administration manual, software, and related

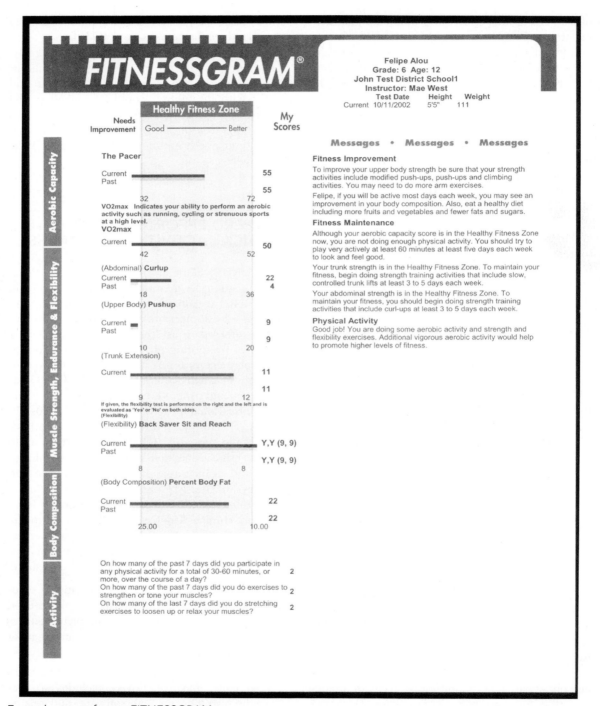

FITNESSGRAM®

Felipe Alou
Grade: 6 Age: 12
John Test District School1
Instructor: Mae West

Test Date	Height	Weight
Current 10/11/2002	5'5"	111

Healthy Fitness Zone

Needs Improvement | Good ——————— Better | My Scores

The Pacer

Current: 55
Past: 55

32 ——— 72

VO2max Indicates your ability to perform an aerobic activity such as running, cycling or strenuous sports at a high level.

VO2max

Current: 50

42 ——— 52

(Abdominal) Curlup

Current: 22
Past: 4

18 ——— 36

(Upper Body) Pushup

Current: 9
Past: 9

10 ——— 20

(Trunk Extension)

Current: 11
11

9 ——— 12

If given, the flexibility test is performed on the right and the left and is evaluated as 'Yes' or 'No' on both sides.
(Flexibility)

(Flexibility) Back Saver Sit and Reach

Current: Y,Y (9, 9)
Past: Y,Y (9, 9)

8 ——— 8

(Body Composition) Percent Body Fat

Current: 22
Past: 22

25.00 ——— 10.00

On how many of the past 7 days did you participate in any physical activity for a total of 30-60 minutes, or more, over the course of a day? — 2

On how many of the past 7 days did you do exercises to strengthen or tone your muscles? — 2

On how many of the last 7 days did you do stretching exercises to loosen up or relax your muscles? — 2

Aerobic Capacity
Muscle Strength, Endurance & Flexibility
Body Composition
Activity

Messages • Messages • Messages

Fitness Improvement

To improve your upper body strength be sure that your strength activities include modified push-ups, push-ups and climbing activities. You may need to do more arm exercises.

Felipe, if you will be active most days each week, you may see an improvement in your body composition. Also, eat a healthy diet including more fruits and vegetables and fewer fats and sugars.

Fitness Maintenance

Although your aerobic capacity score is in the Healthy Fitness Zone now, you are not doing enough physical activity. You should try to play very actively at least 60 minutes at least five days each week to look and feel good.

Your trunk strength is in the Healthy Fitness Zone. To maintain your fitness, begin doing strength training activities that include slow, controlled trunk lifts at least 3 to 5 days each week.

Your abdominal strength is in the Healthy Fitness Zone. To maintain your fitness, you should begin doing strength training activities that include curl-ups at least 3 to 5 days each week.

Physical Activity

Good job! You are doing some aerobic activity and strength and flexibility exercises. Additional vigorous aerobic activity would help to promote higher levels of fitness.

Example report from a FITNESSGRAM.

ACTIVITYGRAM®

Hank Williams
AGRAM 123 - 08/01/2002
Sandra District School1

MINUTES OF ACTIVITY

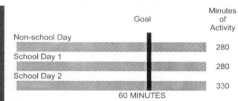

	Minutes of Activity
Non-school Day	280
School Day 1	280
School Day 2	330

60 MINUTES

Messages • Messages • Messages

The chart shows the number of minutes that you reported doing moderate (medium) or vigorous (hard) activity on each day. Congratulations, your log indicates that you are doing at least 60 minutes of activity on most every day. This will help to promote good fitness and wellness. For fun and variety, try some new activities that you have never done before.

TIME PROFILE

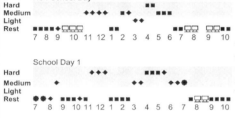

Legend ◆ Most of the time(20 minutes)   ■ All of the time (30 minutes)
        ● Some of the time (10 minutes) 🖥 TV/Computer Time

The time profile shows the activity level you reported for each 30 minute period of the day. Your results show that you were active both during and after school and that you were also active on the weekend. Keep up the good work.

ACTIVITY PROFILE

Participated in these types of activities

Did not participate in these types of activities

The activity pyramid reveals the different types of activity that you reported doing over a few days. Your results indicate that you participated in regular lifestyle activity as well as some activity from the other levels. This is great! The variety in your program should help you stay active.

ACTIVITYGRAM provides information about your normal levels of physical activity. The report shows what types of activity you do and how often you do them. It includes information that you reported for two or three days during one week.

ACTIVITYGRAM is a module within FITNESSGRAM 7.0 software. FITNESSGRAM materials are distributed by the American Fitness Alliance, a division of Human Kinetics. www.americanfitness.net

©The Cooper Institute for Aerobics Research

Example report from an ACTIVITYGRAM.

tools. The software includes an ACTIVITY-GRAM option, which allows students to enter up to 3 days of physical-activity data and assess their own progress toward goals.

- *The Brockport Physical Fitness Test*, a national test developed especially for youths with disabilities, has features and tools similar to FITNESSGRAM.

- The *FitSmart* test is designed to assess high-school students' knowledge of concepts and principles of fitness. It includes a test manual and software.

- The *You Stay Active* recognition system is a program for setting goals and recognizing achievement of those goals. It includes a manual and incentive awards.

In 1995 AAHPERD joined the ACSM and the American Heart Association (AHA) to form a National Coalition for Promoting Physical Activity (*Update*, 1995). The coalition focuses on communication and education about physical activity and its relation to health and acts as a physical-activity advocate to federal and state governments, concerning relevant policy and legislation; to corporations such as insurance companies, which might provide incentives for people to become and stay active; and to foundations that fund relevant research and development programs.

The alliance has also initiated, with the AHA, a program called Jump Rope for Heart. This program has both educational and fitness-development objectives. It also serves as a major fund-raiser for both the AHA and the AAHPERD. Children solicit pledges and then engage in continuous rope jumping to demonstrate the value of aerobic fitness activity, as well as to raise money.

In March 2001, NASPE launched a new program called *Sport for All*, intended to increase quality physical activity for children. The program includes three modules: SportFun for ages 3–5, SportPlay for ages 5–7, and SportSkill Basic for ages 8–10. Each module includes Activity Card Packets (available from Human Kinetics Publishers). Individuals can

Strength-training stations are increasingly common at worksites, schools, and fitness centers.

train as *Sport for All* program leaders through NASPE. *Sport for All* is intended to be used in camps, recreation centers, after-school programs, and day-care centers.

WORKSITE FITNESS AND WELLNESS PROGRAMS

Worksite fitness and wellness programs have become increasingly common over the past 25 years. According to the Wellness Councils of America, 81 percent of businesses with fifty or more employees have some form of health-and-fitness promotion program (www.welcoa.org). Companies develop and sustain worksite fitness and wellness programs because they reduce health-care costs, increase productivity of employees, and reduce absenteeism (http://prevent disease.com). For example, after the first year of implementing a worksite wellness program, Johnson & Johnson Corporation saw a 9 percent decrease in sick leave. Absenteeism among Bonne Bel Corporation employees declined by 50 percent after the second year of implementing an employee wellness/fitness program. Prudential Insurance Company reduced health-care costs by $1.93 for every $1 they spent to support their employee wellness/fitness program.

Employees who are more fit and healthy work more productively, are absent less often, and cost companies less in insurance claims. The more risk factors that employees have (smoking, high blood pressure, inactivity, and the like), the higher are the medical costs incurred by the company. There is also considerable support for the notion that company-supported wellness/fitness programs increase employee morale, reduce employee turnover, and prove helpful in recruiting new employees. The Wellness Councils of America is a national, nonprofit membership organization dedicated to promoting healthier lifestyles, especially through health-promotion initiatives at worksites. They also act as the national clearinghouse and information center for worksite wellness.

A worksite fitness and wellness program is typically made up of some combination of the following items (www.fitresource.com):

Fitness

- Personalized fitness programs
- Fitness testing
- Employee fitness facilities
- Organized classes and activities

Nutrition

- Healthy-heart programs
- Nutritional guidance
- Weight management

General Health

- Health-risk appraisal
- Healthy-back programs
- Blood pressure screening
- Cholesterol testing
- Smoking cessation
- Stress management
- Health-education programs

The Adolph Coors Company has won a number of national awards for helping their employees adopt and value healthy lifestyles. The company operates a large wellness center, gymnasium, clinic, and counseling center for its employees. Participation in the fitness/wellness programs is voluntary, but workers who do take part receive a 5 percent reduction in their insurance payments. The program includes a testing program to determine what aspects of wellness and fitness that employees most need to improve, a range of activity programs that include specific rehabilitation programs such as cardiac rehabilitation, sports, and a wide variety of fitness activities. Many of these activities are offered with a "club" concept so that members who enjoy the same activities can participate together, thus increasing the motivation to continue participation. The entire effort is seen as a "win-win" for both employees and the company.

Shephard (1999) reports that companies support worksite fitness programs to attract employees with good attitudes toward health, reduce absenteeism, increase productivity, and reduce health-care costs. Companies not only provide facilities for exercise but often form company sport teams or provide breaks for calisthenics during the day. Larger companies often provide a health-assessment area near their fitness facility. Some companies charge a fee for using facilities, but the fee is much less than the cost of membership in a community or commercial fitness facility.

Although worksite fitness and wellness programs are becoming more widely available, it is not clear that the majority of employees participate, particularly on a regular basis. As health fitness has become a major issue in public health—and for corporations, too—the research field of exercise adherence has developed to investigate why people stay in fitness programs or leave them (Dishman, 1988). Lack of time, lack of suitable facilities, poor leadership, and inadequate programs are key reasons why employees do not participate (Shephard, 1988). Personal factors such as income, education, perceived vulnerability, positive motivation, and strong sense of self-efficacy are positively related to participation (Landers, 1997).

This high-tech exercise system allows a person to swim in place against a current.

There are good reasons for worksites to involve themselves more in employee health-promotion and fitness programs. The savings in reduced absenteeism and health-related insurance costs are substantial. Also, a healthy and physically fit workforce is likely to be more productive and happier than a less fit or less healthy workforce. Although such outcomes are less direct and more difficult to measure, they may prove to be even more important than other benefits in the long run (Baun & Bernacki, 1988).

NATIONAL EFFORTS TO PROMOTE FITNESS AND PHYSICAL ACTIVITY

Historically, the federal government's concern with fitness has been in response to high rates of military draft rejects during wartime or in response to national health epidemics such as the severe polio epidemic of 1916. In the mid-1950s, a "fitness crisis" occurred in the United States, the result of a series of tests showing that American children were much less fit than European children (see Chapter 2). In 1955 President Dwight Eisenhower, an avid golfer, convened a national conference of experts to examine fitness problems. Soon thereafter, the president suffered a heart attack, after which he spoke out even more vigorously about federal involvement in the nation's fitness. In 1956 an executive order created the President's Council on Youth Fitness, which was eventually to become the President's Council on Physical Fitness and Sport.

President John F. Kennedy continued this emphasis and published a much-discussed article in *Sports Illustrated* (1960) titled "The Soft American." Since then, the number of federal agencies involved in promoting and investigating fitness and physical activity has increased considerably. In 1978 the U.S. Department of Health, Education, and Welfare produced a major report that listed exercise as one of the twelve categories of behavior that are important determinants of health status (Blair et al., 1987). The federal government then established national objectives in the area of healthy lifestyle and fitness, known as the 1990 Objectives because they were articulated as goals to be met by the year 1990. Of the 226 specific objectives defined, 34 were related directly to physical fitness and health.

The President's Council on Physical Fitness and Sport (PCPFS) serves to encourage and motivate citizens of all ages to become physically active and to participate in sport. The PCPFS advises the president and the secretary of Health and Human Services on how to encourage more Americans to be physically fit and active. The PCPFS consists of twenty members appointed by the president and is currently headed by John Burke, president of Trek Bicycle Corporation. The vice chair is Dr. Dot Richardson, an Olympic gold medalist in softball and an orthopedic surgeon.

The PCPFS collaborates with public- and private-sector sponsors to conduct its programs and to produce public information materials. Among these programs and materials are the following:

- *The President's Challenge Physical Activity and Fitness Awards* program, a recognition program for school-aged children administered by teachers and others who work with youths
- *The Presidential Sports Award* for Americans aged 6 and above who participate regularly in one of over sixty sports and fitness activities and who meet criteria defined by the governing body for each sport/activity
- *Web site* www.fitness.gov, a gateway Web site to access programs and publications of the PCPFS
- *PCPFS Research Digest,* a quarterly publication, summarizing scientific research about topics related to physical activity and fitness
- *State Champion Award,* an annual award program for schools, conducted in collaboration with state departments of education
- *National School Demonstration Program,* conducted in coordination with state departments of education to recognize exemplary elementary-, middle-, and high-school physical-education programs

Both the 1996 publication of the U.S. surgeon general's *Report on Physical Activity and Health* and the 1997 recommendations from the CDC, which focused on policies and strategies for increasing physical activity and healthy lifestyles among children and youths, have placed the importance of fitness and physical activity more

squarely in the public view than ever before. With increasing evidence of an obesity epidemic widely publicized, the campaign for activity and fitness has grown stronger, and the federal government is increasingly involved. In 2000 the secretary of Health and Human Services released *Promoting Better Health for Young People Through Physical Activity and Sport* (U.S. Department of Health and Human Services, 2000). This report included strategies for families, after-school programs, youth sports and recreation programs, and community support. It was followed in 2001 by "Increasing Physical Activity: A Report on Recommendations of the Task Force on Community Preventive Services" (Centers for Disease Control and Prevention, 2001). This report focused on the crucial roles that communities can play in supporting physical activity, including community campaigns, school physical education, and the creation of infrastructure to support activity.

Will these policies and programs help improve the nation's fitness and physical activity? It is clear that the federal government is playing a proactive role in emphasizing the importance of activity. As we show in the next chapter, programs and infrastructures are needed, especially for those in the population who are most at risk. Now it remains to be seen whether the infrastructure and programs can be developed and sustained at the local level (see Chapter 13).

LEGISLATIVE EFFORTS TO IMPROVE CHILD AND YOUTH FITNESS

In the past several years, a number of efforts have been made at the federal level to combat the child/youth obesity epidemic and to improve fitness opportunities for school-aged children. Earlier in this chapter, we cited the reauthorization of the federal School Lunch Act that required school districts that receive federal funding for school lunch programs to create school wellness councils to address nutrition, nutrition education, and physical activity. Most states have now passed legislation to further define, for the respective states, the requirements that local school districts will have to meet in the areas of school lunches, school breakfasts, foods sold in vending machines, foods sold in school stores, and time requirements for physical education, recesses, and physical activity outside of physical education or recess. Also cited was federal legislation to support developing infrastructure to encourage students to walk or bike to school.

More recently, HR 3257 introduced the Fitness Integrated With Teaching Kids Act (FIT Kids Act) as a proposed amendment to the No Child Left Behind legislation. The key elements of this legislation would require schools to report multiple measures of the performance of their physical-education programs, including progress toward achieving the national goal of 150 minutes/week for elementary physical education and 225 minutes/week for high-school physical education. It would also require school districts to support professional development for their physical-education teachers.

The Personal Health Investment Today (PHIT) legislation has also been introduced in the House of Representatives. This legislation would change federal tax law to allow for the use of pretax dollars to cover expenses related to sports, fitness, and other physical activities. Citizens could invest up to $1,000 annually to pay for physical-activity engagement by investing money in existing pretax Flexible Spending Accounts, Health Saving Accounts, Medical Savings Accounts, and/or medical reimbursement arrangements.

The Carol M. White Physical Education Program (PEP) was passed by Congress in 2001 with a $5 million appropriation. In 2007 the level of support had increased to $73 million. PEP grants are awarded to local school districts to purchase equipment and train teachers in physical-education methods, with particular attention to health- and wellness-based physical-education programs. The National Coalition for Promoting Physical Activity, a consortium of seventeen national organizations, is a key organization in supporting legislation to improve opportunities for children and youths (www.ncppa.org).

PHYSICAL-FITNESS INSTRUCTION: BY WHOM?

The evidence in this chapter shows that fitness and physical activity are pursued by children/youths and adults in many different places—at home, in schools, and in health spas, fitness centers, sport clubs, and weight-training centers. Fitness facilities and equipment are now commonly found not only in fitness centers of various kinds but also in homes, workplaces, public and private schools, colleges and universities, community facilities, and country clubs. While walking for exercise remains the most widely used form of physical activity for adults, it is clear that many families use the fee-for-service health-club industry. In 2006 there were 29,069 health clubs in the United States, serving 41.3 million members and 23.6 million nonmember patrons—that is, those who pay a daily fee or gain access to a health club via a hotel, hospital, or worksite facility (Active Marketing Group, 2007).

The largest of the health-club chains is Curves with 10,000 locations serving 4.2 million members, followed by Gold's Gym, Lady of America, Health Fitness Corp, Bally Total Fitness, and 24-Hour Fitness World Wide. The largest group of members is the 18- to 34-year age group, accounting for 36 percent of the total club membership, with 32 percent membership among the 35–54 age group, and 19 percent among the 55+ age group. Fifty-seven percent of the membership is female, and 50 percent of the membership has a household income of at least $75,000.

The difficulty in answering the question raised in this section—"by whom?"—is that there is no *national* certification for fitness instructors. Many organizations offer certification for various roles in the fitness professions, such as the American College of Sports Medicine, the Institute for Aerobics Research, the National Strength and Conditioning Association, the International Dance Exercise Association, and the Aerobics and Fitness Association of America. Many fitness centers now require certification as a condition of employment, and having certification certainly can be a factor in securing a job within the fitness industry. Still, there are fitness centers where fitness "leaders" and "advisors" have no certification.

Another crucial issue for anyone aspiring to a career as a fitness professional is the value of various certifications. Currently, there are at least fifty organizations nationally offering more than 400 different certifications (Pierce & Herman, 2004). The issue here is straightforward: Not all certifications are alike! Many organizations offer their certification process online. They sell study materials, and then eventually, you take a certification exam online. Other organizations require that you attend classes and seminars, and then eventually, you sit for an exam under the proctoring of the organization. Students interested in entering the fitness professions and physical-education teachers who want to add a fitness certification to their resumé should be very careful to thoroughly investigate the organization from which they will obtain certification. When you move into the job market, employers will probably know the differences among the various certifying agencies and be more likely to employ women and men who have obtained their certifications from reputable national organizations that require rigorous study and examination to achieve the certification.

The National Board of Fitness Examiners (NBFE) was formed in 2003 to begin to move toward a national standard for fitness trainers (http://nbfe.org). The NBFE is in process of creating a national examination to ensure an approved level of competency for instructors in the health-and-fitness industry. Part 1 will be a written examination, and Part 2 will be a hands-on performance assessment where each candidate will be presented with eight to ten "client interactions" to test the candidate's readiness to provide safe and expert instruction for clients. It seems clear that as the fitness industry continues to expand providers will want to employ women and men who have obtained their certifications from reputable national organizations.

SPORT MEDICINE AND THE REHABILITATIVE SCIENCES

The material in this chapter and others makes it clear that sport and physical fitness are pursued by people of all ages and in many different venues—schools, health clubs, weight-training centers, parks, sports venues, and the like. Child and youth sport, interscholastic sport, collegiate sport, professional sport, and recreational sport have all experienced substantial growth in the past quarter-century. That growth has been accompanied by a parallel growth in the professions that serve these many participants, both by providing instruction about fitness and safety and by providing professional services in the care and prevention of sport- and fitness-related injuries.

Sport medicine is a generic term used to encompass many areas of specialization related to physical performance and injuries related to physical performance.

A sport-medicine team is required to provide health care to athletes and to those who are regularly involved in fitness work and may incur injuries. Key to this team are athletic trainers and physicians. Medical specialists who can often be found in sport-medicine centers include family-practice physicians, orthopedists, neurologists, internists, ophthalmologists, and pediatricians. One is also likely to find dentists, podiatrists, nutritionists, and physical therapists in some way related to the sport-medicine team. Nurses, physician's assistants, and other health-care professionals are also involved.

Athletic Training

The most highly developed sport vocation is that of athletic trainer. The National Athletic Trainers' Association (NATA) is one of the strongest of all sport, fitness, and physical-education associations. The mission of NATA is "to enhance the quality of health care for athletes and those engaged in physical activity, and to advance the profession of athletic training through education and research in the prevention, evaluation, management and rehabilitation of injuries" (www.nata.org). Increasingly, where there are well-developed sport programs, you will find athletic trainers. More and more high schools and universities are hiring athletic trainers as full-time personnel. Athletic trainers work closely with sport physicians in the prevention and rehabilitation of sport-related injuries.

The chief function of NATA is to supervise and control the certification of athletic trainers through its education program and its board of certification (NATABOC). All athletic trainer students complete a rigorous major program at a college or university. The program includes substantial study in basic and applied sciences, along with extensive professional content including risk management and injury prevention. The program also requires a minimum of 2 years of academic clinical education through which students gain clinical experience with a variety of patient populations (www.NATA.org). These clinical experiences are under direct supervision of qualified clinical instructors who are certified athletic trainers or other health-care professionals. NATA also offers certification through a master's-degree program that typically takes a minimum of 2 years of study.

Athletic trainers are certified through a rigorous examination process that is developed and controlled by a board of certification. The examination assesses candidate knowledge in areas of prevention, clinical evaluation and diagnosis, immediate care, treatment, rehabilitation and reconditioning, organization and administration, and professional responsibility. A committee of athletic trainers prepares questions, and a panel of independent judges validates the questions. Exams are scored by an independent, professional testing organization. In addition, the candidates must pass a Competency Evaluation Checklist from a certified athletic trainer and present proof of certification in standard first aid and cardiopulmonary resuscitation. Those who successfully complete the examination process become Certified Athletic Trainers, a certification typically required for employment.

More high schools are hiring full-time athletic trainers, partially in response to the problems of liability and to research showing that the injury rate in schools without full-time trainers is much higher than in schools with such services (Rankin, 1989). The employment potential for athletic trainers is good, and the profession they enter is obviously well controlled, perhaps being a model for other sport and fitness vocations to emulate. Specific skills are identified and specific programs are arranged to help young men and women acquire those skills. Meaningful, supervised experience is required. Then, entrance to the field is controlled by examination and presentation of a skills checklist.

ACSM Fitness-Instruction Certification

The mission of the American College of Sports Medicine (ACSM) is to promote and integrate scientific research, education, and practical applications of sport medicine and exercise science to maintain and enhance physical performance, fitness, health, and quality of life (www.acsm.org). ACSM is the nation's largest professional organization of exercise scientists, physicians, physiologists, physical educators, and fitness instructor/managers interested in the implementation of fitness programs.

ACSM offers different levels of certification within two specific tracks. The Health and Fitness certification track offers three certification levels for individuals who work in settings where the exercise participants are apparently healthy and exercising for health maintenance. The Clinical track offers three certifications for those who work with low- to moderate-risk individuals or patients with acute or controlled diseases in hospital-based or medically supervised settings.

ACSM is also heavily involved in the continuing education of the professionals it serves. ACSM endorses more than 180 conferences a year in which those professionals can get continuing education credit or continuing medical-education credit. Since most professional organizations now require a certain level of continuing education to maintain certification, these conferences are often heavily subscribed.

Strength and Conditioning Coach Qualification

The National Strength and Conditioning Association (NSCA) is an international nonprofit association with 30,000 members in fifty-two countries. NSCA's primary goal is to support and disseminate research-based knowledge to improve athletic performance and fitness. NSCA has created a registry of qualified members who have been certified as strength and conditioning specialists. To qualify, one must have current NSCA membership and current certification as an NSCA Certified Strength and Conditioning Specialist. Candidates must have a bachelor's degree in exercise science or a related field, CPR certification, and a minimum of 2 years full-time employment in a collegiate or professional setting or 2 years as a graduate assistant in strength and conditioning at an institution recognized by NSCA as a Graduate Recognition program. Candidates must also main an average of two NSCA approved continuing education credits per year when employed as a strength and conditioning professional.

In 2002 NSCA released new professional standards and guidelines for strength and conditioning specialists. The standards and guidelines document is designed to identify areas of liability exposure, increase safety standards, and decrease the likelihood of injuries that might lead to legal claims. The standards and guidelines concentrate on athletic preparticipation screening, personnel qualifications, program supervision, facility and equipment inspection, emergency planning and response, record keeping, youth participation, and the use of supplements, ergogenic aids, and drugs (NASPE, 2002).

AFPA Certification

Fitness in America has become big business. It is therefore understandable that for-profit organizations that prepare workers for the fitness industry have developed. The American Fitness Professionals and Associates (AFPA) has certified over 60,000 personal trainers and fitness instructors, using a distance-education format. AFPA currently offers certifications in twenty-three specializations (http://afpafitness.com), ranging from Personal Trainer, to Pre/Postnatal Exercise Specialist, to Senior Strength Training Specialist. Two levels of Yoga Instructor certification and three levels of Pilates Instructor certification are also offered.

All courses require that applicants seeking certification order textbooks and DVDs that provide the course materials. The DVD also typically can be used to print movements and exercises that can be used in practice. Applicants then must complete a written certification examination that typically includes multiple-choice questions and discussion questions. A passing grade is 90 percent or better correct. Applicants may retake the exam once. Certification course materials and testing costs range from $500 to $800.

The AFPA also provides continuing education courses, conferences, a monthly newsletter, and access to job listings and career enhancement tools.

ACE Certification

The American Council on Exercise (ACE), a nonprofit organization, has certified more than 40,000 fitness professionals in 107 countries (www.acefitness.org). In 2003 ACE was granted accreditation by the National Commission for Certifying Agencies for its Personal Trainer, Group Fitness Instructor, and Lifestyle & Weight Management Consultant certification programs. ACE also offers a Clinical Exercise Specialist certification program and an Advanced Health & Fitness Specialist certification.

To be eligible for any of these certifications, candidates must be at least 18 years of age and have a current adult CPR certification. For the Clinical Exercise Specialist certification, candidates must also have completed a 4-year bachelor's degree in an exercise science or related field or a current ACE Personal Trainer Certification. For the Advanced Health + Fitness Specialist certification, candidates must also have a 4-year bachelor's degree in exercise science or related field, a current ACE Personal Trainer Certification, and at least 300 hours of work experience designing and implementing exercise programs for healthy individuals and/or high-risk individuals.

Students in an ACE certification program begin with self-study materials and then schedule and take an ACE exam review course. They then take an online diagnostic practice test prior to taking the certification exam at an ACE site. The certification exam is followed by ACE practical training programs.

Physical Therapy

Physical therapists work in a variety of contexts including rehabilitation, community health, industry, and sports. Although they often work as members of a health-care team in hospitals, they increasingly work in private physical therapy practices, community and corporate health centers, sport facilities, rehabilitation centers, and the like. The American Physical Therapy Association is the main professional organization for physical therapists (www.apta.org).

Physical therapists do therapeutic exercise, range-of-motion exercise, cardiovascular training, relaxation training, therapeutic massage, biofeedback, and a host of other therapies that help people recover from illness or injury. This is a highly specialized field requiring extensive training.

Most physical therapy preparation and certification is done at the graduate-school level. To prepare for physical therapy, undergraduates often major in one of the sciences; more and more, they are majoring in exercise science or kinesiology. Certification for physical therapy is controlled at the state level, so students interested in a physical therapy career should inquire at a university or the state licensing board about specific requirements. After graduating from an accredited physical therapy program, candidates must pass a state-administered national exam.

Physical therapists can become certified as clinical specialists in seven areas: pediatrics, geriatrics, sports physical therapy, cardiopulmonary, clinical electrophysiology, neurology, and orthopedics. Specialist certifications in these areas are controlled by the American Board of Physical Therapy Specialties.

Bachelor's Degree in Adult Fitness

There are many universities where it is now possible to obtain an undergraduate bachelor's degree in a fitness-related subject—adult fitness, corporate fitness, or fitness programming. There are also many universities where students can major in exercise science, but this undergraduate degree is more often designed to prepare students for entrance into graduate school than for employment in a professional role in the fitness world.

The nature of the requirements for the undergraduate degree in fitness differs somewhat at each university, depending on the emphasis within the program. The typical program includes core courses similar to those taken by other students studying for undergraduate degrees in physical education: foundations of physical education, exercise physiology, kinesiology, biomechanics, sport psychology, sport sociology, tests and measurements, and some activity-oriented courses such as aquatics, gymnastics, individual sports, and team sports.

Beyond this core, the fitness major takes further courses in exercise science, such as analysis of cardiopulmonary function and graded-exercise testing. In addition, the fitness major takes supportive scientific courses in areas such as nutrition and injury prevention/care. Because much fitness programming is done in the private sector, the fitness major is often likely to take courses focusing on the business aspects of fitness, such as marketing and administration. Often these courses are offered by a department of business administration.

The undergraduate fitness major should have intern experiences where knowledge and skill can be used and refined. These often take place in campus fitness programs but can also occur in local hospitals or fitness centers. This internship comes toward the end of the program and serves a function similar to student teaching in the teacher-certification program.

Many undergraduate fitness programs also encourage their students to achieve certification under the ACSM guidelines. In that way, the student graduates with not only a bachelor's degree in fitness but also certification. This student is equipped both to seek employment in the fitness field and to attend graduate school for further study and experience in the adult fitness field.

Master's Degree in Fitness

Master's-degree programs are widely available in a number of fitness-related areas: adult fitness, fitness programming, cardiac rehabilitation, strength development, fitness management, corporate fitness, and exercise physiology. The exact requirements for each degree depend on the specific focus for the master's program. Most programs include ACSM certification of one kind or another.

Although these degree programs differ in the specific course required for graduation, they do have much in common (Hall & Wilson, 1984). Because they are *graduate* programs, the entrance criteria are those common to the graduate program at the institution offering the degree. The criteria typically include at least a 2.75 to 3.00 undergraduate grade point average (GPA), a certain level of performance on the Graduate Record Examination (GRE) or a similar test, and a background in the core sciences related to fitness.

Specific prerequisites for entrance most often involve previous coursework in anatomy, physiology, and exercise physiology. Some programs also require coursework in chemistry, mathematics, physics, kinesiology, and measurement. The degree programs themselves combine advanced coursework, acquisition of the technical skills associated with fitness (for

example, testing), practical experience within the program, and, often, an internship in an agency dealing with fitness (for example, corporation, hospital, or fitness center). Most programs take from 12 to 24 months to complete. In some programs, students must complete a thesis to graduate.

These programs require that candidates have a good background in science courses, and they emphasize the underlying scientific basis of fitness. A student who aspires to a career in a fitness-related profession should thus be sure to acquire the appropriate scientific expertise.

SUMMARY

1. It is clear that inactivity is a risk factor for hypokinetic disease.

2. Youth fitness testing indicates that boys and girls in the fifth through twelfth grades rank poorly in tests of body composition and cardiopulmonary efficiency.

3. Similar testing among children in the 6- to 9-year-old group indicates alarmingly high percentages of body fat and inadequate cardiopulmonary functioning.

4. Some experts feel that when activity is considered rather than fitness testing, children and youths are more fit than reports indicate.

5. Research on activity patterns among children is uneven but indicates that too few get regular physical education and that those who do are less active within physical education than they should be.

6. Participation in sport declines dramatically as children approach adolescence.

7. There is often insufficient time within school physical-education classes to develop and maintain health fitness, which has led to a national movement to provide daily physical education that emphasizes health fitness.

8. A number of different effective fitness programs have been developed in school physical education, including schoolwide elementary

programs, fitness clubs, remediation programs, daily fitness programs, fitness courses, and a strong fitness focus within the physical-education class.

9. AAHPERD has promoted fitness strongly through testing and incentive programs such as the FITNESSGRAM® and Jump Rope for Heart.

10. Although reliable data on fitness levels of adults are difficult to obtain, the best estimates are that 20 percent of adults get sufficient health-fitness exercise, 40 percent get some but not sufficient benefits from exercise, and 40 percent are sedentary.

11. The recent fitness boom is mostly a young-adult, relatively upper-income phenomenon in which the *appearance* of fitness participation seems more pervasive than actual participation.

12. Surveys of activity patterns among adults and seniors indicate that exercise decreases with age and is relatively higher among males, in suburban communities, among professionals, among high school and college graduates, and among whites.

13. Most fitness professionals expect the fitness movement to continue to expand because of increased media exposure, discretionary income, acceptability among women, influence of elite sport, and emphasis within the health and medical professions.

14. Worksite fitness programs are becoming increasingly available but are strongly influenced by the availability of facilities.

15. The federal government has become heavily involved in promoting health fitness and has developed specific objectives for the nation to achieve in the twenty-first century.

16. Most fitness programs are developed and led by uncertified personnel although several organizations, such as the ACSM, NSCA, and ACE, have well-developed certification programs.

17. Many universities now offer bachelor's degrees in fitness-related subjects—adult fitness, fitness programming, or corporate fitness. These curricula typically require core coursework, special training in exercise science and testing, an internship, and some courses in business.

18. Many universities now offer master's-degree programs in fitness that combine advanced training in exercise science with training in the skills needed to work professionally within the fitness area. These programs typically require an internship and, sometimes, a thesis.

DISCUSSION QUESTIONS

1. Why is it that the fitness boom has been primarily a young-adult, upper-income phenomenon?

2. What can be done to promote regular fitness habits among children?

3. How fit are you? What either motivates you to maintain or prevents you from maintaining an adequate level of fitness?

4. What were fitness programs like when you were in elementary and high school? Were they effective?

5. What can communities do to promote fitness? Who should pay for community-based programs?

6. Why is it in the interest of corporations and businesses to promote fitness among their employees?

7. Will specializing in fitness become more of a profession with increasing certification and preparation? Would such a trend be good?

CHAPTER 9

Problems and Issues in Fitness

For years we have tried the same fitness philosophy; that is, trying to achieve fitness goals by compelling children to exercise. We should realize that it is time to try something different. As professional physical educators we must recognize that "getting children fit" (by itself) is not the answer if children and youth do not develop the lifetime habits of physical activity.

Charles Corbin, 1987, speaking of perennial
problems in the fitness curriculum

LEARNING OBJECTIVES

- To discuss the costs and the benefits to society of fitness and lack of fitness among various populations
- To analyze and discuss strategies that support or prevent the development of lifetime commitment to physical activity
- To discuss issues related to public information and misinformation about fitness
- To discuss equity issues in fitness and physical activity
- To describe issues related to certification for fitness professions
- To describe the role of fitness in an aging population
- To describe and discuss the role of fitness in physical education
- To discuss research issues in fitness and physical activity

- To describe how a physical-activity infrastructure is related to physical-activity lifestyles

Physical activity and physical fitness are more important to our national health agenda than at any time during our history. All experts realize that physical activity and fitness can be achieved in a number of ways—through child and youth sports, interscholastic sports, recreational sports for adults, participation at fitness and health centers, membership in a worksite wellness program, informal recreational activities, and regular physical activity done within and outside the home. Chapter 7 introduced you to the differences among health-fitness, motor-performance fitness, and cosmetic fitness. Each of these is of different importance to those who participate.

Most clearly, health fitness is important to life itself, both to living well and to living free from degenerative disease. That kind of importance has both personal and social significance. Motor-performance fitness is important, too. For the high-school volleyball player, jumping higher and hitting more strongly is of immediate short-term importance. The strength and endurance of an Olympic athlete are important not only to him or her but also to each of us who roots for the athlete and takes pride in his or her accomplishments. Cosmetic fitness has a different kind of importance; it enhances self-esteem and builds confidence, qualities that may be important to achievement in school, at work, and in social relationships. Therefore, although we tend to focus more on health fitness, we should not forget the importance of motor-performance and cosmetic fitness in the lives of people for whom those qualities are central to success.

Life expectancy for Americans has increased with each generation. Life expectancy for males is now over 75 years and for females over 80 years. Retirees now represent a larger proportion of our population than ever before. Health costs for an aging population are extraordinary. Senior citizens who maintain an adequate level of health-related fitness not only have a better quality of life but also help reduce national health-care costs. Experts, however, have cautioned that, unless we can deal successfully with the current epidemic of overweight and obesity among children and youths, the current young generation may be the first in American history to have shorter life expectancy than their parents (Daniels, 2006)!

The vast majority of modern occupations are mostly sedentary. The requirements of daily life in a mostly urban society are insufficient to develop and maintain an adequate level of heath fitness. What most experts now describe as the "built environment" tends to discourage rather than encourage physical activity. Generations ago, the hours now spent watching television, working at a computer, or playing electronic games were spent in some sort of physical activity. Healthy foods are now more expensive than unhealthy foods. Eating in fast-food restaurants and taking home carry-out food has dramatically increased over the past quarter-century.

Put simply, it is easier and less expensive to eat unhealthy foods than to eat healthy foods. All these factors have contributed to the crisis of overweight and obesity. Americans, for the most part, are increasingly aware of these issues. More than $35 billion is now spent annually on weight-loss related products and services (Levi, Segal, & Gadola, 2007). It is to the effects of these societal developments that we now turn.

THE COSTS OF INADEQUATE HEALTH FITNESS

Traditionally, health and fitness were seen nearly exclusively as issues of personal responsibility. Today, although that point of view is still seen as important, it has become clear that the costs of inadequate fitness in the population constitute a major national problem that must be dealt with through programs designed to reach specific segments of the population. The costs associated with inadequate levels of health fitness now represent a substantial proportion of the yearly gross national product (Pritchard & Potter, 1990).

Among the medical problems related to overweight and obesity among children and youths are high blood pressure, hypertension, type II diabetes, orthopedic problems, and psychological/behavioral problems. Nearly 60 percent of overweight children 5–10 years of age have elevated blood pressure and increased insulin levels, both risk factors for heart disease (Wilkinson, Eddy, McFadden, & Burgess, 2002). Among adults, overweight and obesity are known risk factors for diabetes, heart disease, stroke, hypertension, gallbladder disease, osteoarthritis, sleep apnea, and some forms of cancer (U.S. Department of Heath and Human Services, 2006).

The increased prevalence of overweight and obesity among children and youths has convinced many in the health professions that the future costs of health care will be catastrophic if we can not combat the epidemic in the near future (Barrett, 2008).

Researchers have predicted that if the current trend in child/youth overweight/obesity is not curtailed, the prevalence of coronary heart disease will increase by 16 percent by 2035, and that pediatric obesity will likely shorten life expectancy.

The United States spends more than $1.5 trillion on health care each year, a figure that has doubled over the past 5 years and is expected to double again within 6 years (Siedentop, 2007). The Centers for Disease Control (CDC) has determined that obesity is now the second leading cause of death in the United States, and the surgeon general estimates that the direct and indirect costs (costs due to lost workdays and the like) of obesity come close to $1.2 trillion annually (Senate Report 108-345, 2006). Workers' compensation claims for low-back pain cost employers more than $400 million annually. A one-pack-per-day smoker is estimated to cost his or her employer nearly $1,000 per year in otherwise avoidable health costs.

The point is that inadequate levels of health-related fitness is not simply an *individual* issue. The problem also has economic and social implications that affect us all. Moreover, the people who are most often at risk for health problems due to lack of health-related fitness are those for whom fitness information and opportunities for physical activity are least accessible. Thus, issues of socioeconomic status, race, and gender need to be understood and factored into proposed programmatic solutions. This is not to suggest that individual responsibility is of no consequence in these matters but rather that the social structures of society also contribute to these problems and that solutions will not be successful without addressing those structural inequities.

Precipitating Factors Related to the Overweight and Obesity Crisis

Overweight and obesity stem from the imbalance created when energy intake exceeds energy expenditure. This imbalance develops over time when caloric intake through eating and drinking patterns exceeds energy expenditure through physical activity.

Currently, children and youths in the United States consume more energy-dense foods and are less physically active than they were 25 years ago (Levi, Segal, & Juliano, 2006). In food consumption, the primary factors are higher-caloric intake, more dietary fat, higher-caloric density of foods, and larger portions (Levi et al., 2006). These factors in turn have been related to less in-home cooking, greater reliance on take-out food, more dietary fat, and larger portions. Spending in fast-food restaurants has increased from $6 billion to $18 billion over the last 30 years. Foods served in school breakfast and lunch programs, school vending machines, and school stores have included too many nonnutritious ingredients. Schools have increased revenues through contracts with vendors who sell nonnutritious snacks and drinks and advertise those products on school property (Molnar, Garcia, Boninger, & Merrill, 2006).

Another factor associated with these current health issues related to physical activity is what experts now refer to as the *built environment*, which encompasses the range of physical and social elements that make up the structures of communities (Papas et al., 2007). Factors such as commuting time, communities designed to foster driving rather than walking/biking, and lack of public transit reduce physical activity. Forty years ago, more than half of all children in the United States walked or cycled to school, while today only 10 percent do (ncdot.org). The average American adult takes 42 percent fewer walking trips than a generation ago (Wilkinson et al., 2002). Research has shown that physical activity is substantially higher among people living in high-walkable communities compared to low-walkable communities (Sallis & Kerr, 2006). Access to parks and recreation space has been limited, including the lack of safe, accessible indoor facilities for physical activity during periods of inclement weather. Physical activity among children and youths has decreased while time spent on video games, electronic games, watching TV, and connecting to the Internet has increased. Historically, schools have been embedded within communities and have served as centers for community activity, accessible to most children, youth, and adults by walking or cycling. More recently, larger schools are built in more remote locations that are accessible primarily through driving, an issue particularly prevalent with middle and high schools (Beaumont & Pianca, 2002).

Since the federal No Child Left Behind (NCLB) legislation, schools have increased their focus on language arts, English, and math, leading to a reduction in time allotted for other subjects. Most notably, for purposes here, is a reported 14 percent reduction in time for physical education (Jennings, 2006). Financial strains on schools have also contributed to reduced time allotted to recess and after-school programming.

Suburban sprawl and urban decay both contribute to decreased physical activity among persons of all ages. Parents cite five primary barriers to their children's participation in physical activity: transportation problems, lack of opportunities for physical activity in the immediate area, expense, parents' lack of time, and concerns about neighborhood safety (CDC, 2003).

FITNESS BEHAVIOR: SHORT TERM AND LONG TERM

There is no doubt that the public is becoming more aware of the importance of health-related fitness. Most current polls show that as many as 90 percent of Americans *believe* that regular exercise is important to health and well-being, but many Americans do not exercise regularly.

A major issue in improving the health fitness of our society is determining how to confront this difference between belief and behavior. Why do people who *know* that regular exercise is important still fail to exercise regularly? Coming to grips with this problem and finding workable solutions to it may be the most important advancements of all.

Another issue preventing many adults (and adolescents) from engaging in health-related fitness activities is the attractiveness of alternative activities,

such as watching a game or a movie or playing an electronic game. One approach to these problems is to start with lower-intensity activity such as walking or cycling. Starting a walking program and gradually increasing both the pace of the walk and the distance walked has helped many adults to not only improve their health but also prepare them for participation in physical activities that have a heavier workload. This is referred to as *lifestyle physical activity* and would also include gardening, climbing stairs, doing housework, or engaging in light-to-moderate sports such as table tennis, bowling, and golf (Corbin, Welk, Corbin, & Welk, 2008).

When a person has engaged regularly in lifestyle physical activity for some time, he or she will have a sufficient base to begin to engage in aerobic activities and more active forms of sport and recreation. Using the physical-activity dose formula of 30 minutes per day of moderate-to-vigorous physical activity (MVPA) to a total 210 minutes per week is an alternative strategy to reach health-fitness goals. Brisk walking for 30–40 minutes a day, in addition to sound nutrition and absence of risk factors such as smoking, will lead to health benefits that are very similar to those achieved through more vigorous health-related fitness activities. What is crucial to each, however, is the commitment to sustained involvement; that is, activity has to become a part of lifestyle.

In the past few years, it has become clear that the overarching goal for school-based physical education is for children and youth to *adopt and value a physically active lifestyle*. This issue will be addressed more completely in Chapters 10–12, but it should be abundantly clear that this is a long-term goal. Short-term approaches such as an obligatory 5 minute fitness session at the start of each physical-education lesson and using antiquated fitness testing that has little to do with health-related fitness likely works against the achievement of that goal for many girls and boys.

Getting people to exercise in ways that are fun and satisfying is a first step. Helping them to become fit (in the health-fitness sense) is a second step, but it is unfortunately the step at which many

Many young adults are serious about their fitness workouts.

fitness programs stop. To achieve a commitment to lifetime fitness, programs must also help their participants (whether third-graders or adults in a recreational center) establish patterns of exercising that fit their recreational interests and needs. The program must also teach them how to evaluate their own fitness and how to solve problems related to fitness; thus, a sound knowledge base with a variety of ways to address fitness problems must be included.

Research is beginning to show that fitness programs that have this *lifestyle* emphasis tend to produce *commitment*; that is, those who complete such a program tend to think and behave differently *in the long term* (Rider & Johnson, 1986; Slava, Laurie, & Corbin, 1984). Programs that emphasize lifestyle not only teach people about fitness and help them to

exercise regularly but also teach them self-testing skills, fitness-planning skills, consumer information, and related information, such as sound nutritional planning.

Motivation is, of course, the key to getting children, adolescents, and adults into activity programs and keeping them involved in those programs. It is clear that programs for children and adolescents must address three major motivations if those programs are to be successful (M. Weiss, 2000). First, boys and girls want to develop and demonstrate physical competence through skills, fitness, or appearance. Second, they want to be accepted and supported within a peer social group, including appreciation and support from significant adults. Third, they want to have fun, which means that activity experiences have to be positive and that potentially negative aspects of the experience have to be minimized. Fitness experts, physical educators, recreation personnel, and sport coaches all need to keep those motivations in mind as they implement sport, recreation, and activity programs.

It would be interesting for you, along with classmates or other friends, to consider how the fitness programs that you experienced as a student or an adult compare with what has just been described as a lifestyle approach to health fitness. What were they like? What effect do you think they had on your long-term commitment to fitness?

DEVELOPING A FITNESS-EDUCATED PUBLIC

A major step forward in any national effort to improve the health fitness of citizens will be taken when the general public becomes well educated about fitness issues. This means that the *average* person on the street will know about the different kinds of fitness, what needs to be done to develop and maintain health fitness, and what fitness products and services are appropriate to fitness goals. We are certainly a long way from being able to take that step forward.

Fitness instructors focus on appropriate postures for workouts.

Part of the problem associated with educating the public is that the popular media—through advertising and promotion of products—create false impressions that make it even harder for the general public to understand the *real* issues about fitness. Skinner (1988) has identified three general media-related problems:

1. The media image of a fit person is typically someone who has a young, hard, thin, and beautiful body. That kind of body is neither necessary for health fitness nor attainable by most people, no matter what they might do!

2. The impression left by the media is that fitness miracles can occur quickly and often without any real effort on the part of the person undertaking the

fitness program. The media goal seems to be to get people started in a program by buying products (a diet book, a workout video, a piece of exercise equipment). Whether you stay in that program is not the main interest of the company whose product is being promoted.

3. The media seem to create instant experts who have celebrity status but who may have no training in exercise science and who may actually know very little specific information about fitness.

Making sure that citizens, young and old, have appropriate, accurate knowledge about fitness and fitness activities is fundamentally important to improving the nation's health. Have you recently seen youths or adults doing the hurdler's stretch, the quadriceps stretch, or the standing toe touch? All are contraindicated by research as inappropriate and potentially dangerous. Have you seen children, youths, or adults doing straight-leg sit-ups, deep knee bends, or double leg lifts as strengthening exercises? Again, all are contraindicated by research as potentially dangerous, and each has a safer, more appropriate exercise. Have you seen youths or adults who decide to start a fitness program and on the first day try to run for 60 minutes at what they think is an appropriately brisk pace? If so, they don't understand the principle of progressive overload and moving gradually in small increments in any fitness activity, whether for strength, flexibility, or cardiovascular improvements.

Accurate information about the various aspects of health fitness is widely available in books, in magazine articles, and on the Internet. The best venue through which the public will become better educated about health fitness and motor-performance fitness is school health and physical education—at least it should be! The American Public Health Association has long noted the importance of school programs that are available to all children and youth:

> The school, as a social structure, provides an educational setting in which the total health of the child during the impressionable years is a priority concern. No other community setting even approximates the magnitude of the grades K–12 school education

enterprise. . . . Thus, it seems that the school should be regarded as a . . . focal point to which health planning for all other community settings should relate. (McGinnis, Kanner, & DeGraw, 1991)

If school physical education continues to dwindle and private health clubs continue to grow, then future generations will learn about fitness and have access to fitness programs more and more as a result of the socioeconomic status (SES) of their parents. The fitness gap between rich and poor will grow. Fitness will continue to be seen primarily as an individual issue, even though the costs to the public of an unfit society will be enormous.

EQUITY ISSUES IN FITNESS AND ACTIVITY

Gender, race, and SES are key factors in understanding differences in health, fitness, and activity participation in the United States. National data on physical-activity participation (National Center for Health Statistics, 2004) show that in all age groups females were less active than males and blacks and Hispanics were less active than whites. Black males typically fared as well as white males, but black females fared much worse than white females). It is also clear that young people from lower-income families tend to be less active than those from middle- and upper-income families. This reflects the social gradient in health and activity described in Chapter 7, which means simply that socioeconomic groups are typically healthier than the groups below them and less healthy than the groups above them.

Currently, 66 percent of adults are overweight or obese, and 50 percent of all children and adolescents are overweight or obese (Wang & Beydoun, 2007). Gender, race, and socioeconomic factors all influence the prevalence of overweight and obesity. Obesity rates for high-school males are 15.2 percent for non-Hispanic whites, 15.9 percent for non-Hispanic blacks, and 21.3 percent for Hispanics. For high school females, the rates are 8.2 percent for non-Hispanic whites, 16.1 percent for non-Hispanic blacks, and 12.1 percent for Hispanics (American

Heart Association, 2007). It is clear that the SES of individuals and families is partially related to the incidence of overweight and obesity (Wang & Beydoun, 2007). Obesity is more prevalent among adults below the poverty line (34.7 percent) than among adults above the poverty line (28.7 percent) (Levi et al., 2007). Urban and rural children are somewhat less likely to be active and more likely to be overweight and obese. There is no reason to suggest that this is based on genetic differences; indeed, the evidence strongly suggests that the main determinants are environmental rather than genetic.

Physical activity and obesity are obviously related. Research has shown that minority children and youths are more at risk than whites, that girls are more at risk than boys, and that minority girls are the most at risk (Kimm et al., 2002; Strauss & Pollock, 2001). In the last decade of the twentieth century, overweight increased significantly among all children and youths, but the rate of increase among African American and Hispanic children was nearly twice that for whites. Research has also shown that participation in physical activity declines markedly among girls during adolescence, with the largest declines among black girls. From ages 8–9 to 18–19, the decline was 64 percent for white girls and 100 percent for minority girls. By the ages of 16 to 17, 31 percent of white girls and 56 percent of black girls reported no regular leisure-time physical activity. The long-term health implications of these data for this age cohort of girls are substantial.

Only recently have physical-activity and fitness studies begun to focus on girls' and women's issues. Traditionally, most physical-activity and fitness research has been conducted on males (Wells, 1996). Currently, there are three important trends in girls' physical-activity participation (Tucker Center for Research on Girls and Women in Sport, 2007). First, girls are participating in sports in record numbers, from youth sport to interscholastic sports, extreme or action sports, and Olympic sports (see Focus On Box 9.1). Second, girls' participation in MVPA outside of organized sports is declining. Third, girls' participation rates in all types of physical activity lags consistently behind

---

FOCUS ON **Helping Girls Become and Stay Involved in Physical Activity and Sport** **9.1**

- Girls should be encouraged to become involved in sport and physical activity at an early age.
- Practices that enhance girls' opportunities to be physically active must be developed and supported.
- Recreational activities, physical education, and community sport programs are ideal ways to facilitate health-related fitness and the acquisition of skills.
- Involvement in sport and physical activity has great potential to enhance a girl's sense of competence and control. Leaders should incorporate cooperative as well as competitive opportunities in nonthreatening environments.

- Parents, coaches, and teachers should be aware that girls' motives for participating are not only to be competitive but also to socialize, improve skills, be with friends, and have fun.
- Coaches and physical educators should provide equal access and attention for girls.
- When adults observe girls being treated inequitably, they should intervene.
- Involvement in physical activity and sport promotes psychological well-being and is an anxiety reducer for adolescent girls, thereby acting as a natural, cost-effective mental health program.

SOURCE: President's Council on Physical Fitness and Sport (1997).

FOCUS ON **Helping Young Girls Get and Stay Healthy** **9.2**

In 2002 the Department of Health and Human Services' Office on Women's Health launched a new Web site (www.4girls.gov) to encourage adolescent girls to choose healthy behaviors.

Young girls (12–16), especially minority girls, are particularly at risk for physical inactivity and all the problems associated with inactivity.

One section of the Web site deals with being "Fit for Life" and provides girls with the tools to develop exercise plans that are safe, enjoyable, and long-lasting. That section also provides education about strength training, eating outside the home, and maintaining a healthy weight. A fitness questionnaire can be filled out to help girls understand their own needs.

The site also includes a parent/caregiver section that can be used to help address issues that adolescent girls face.

SOURCE: www.fitness.gov/4girls press release.html.

---

those of boys and the dropout rates from sport are also higher than for boys. Exercise has been shown to reduce the risk of breast cancer (Physical Activity Today, 1996), and its benefits for combating problems associated with osteoporosis are well known. It is also clear that participation in physical activity and sport has important psychological and social, as well as physiological, benefits (Bunker, 1998). It becomes increasingly important that programs specifically designed to reach and assist girls and women be developed and implemented (see Focus On Box 9.2).

Residents of lower socioeconomic neighborhoods in urban areas are particularly at risk for health problems associated with physically inactive lifestyles. In urban areas, there is crime in the streets, high-density housing with few open spaces, working parents with little time for supervision of outdoor activity, relatively few recreation facilities, and little adult leadership (Sallis, 1994). The Carnegie Council on Adolescent Development (1992), in a landmark study of discretionary time among youths, concluded that "young adolescents who live in low-income neighborhoods are

---

FOCUS ON — Dealing With the Obesity Epidemic: Complex Relationships   9.3

In 2004 Julie Gerberding, director of the CDC, said, "If you looked at any epidemic—whether it's influenza or plague from the Middle Ages—they are not as serious as the epidemic of obesity in terms of the health impact on our country and our society" (Trust for America's Health, 2004). The statistics are clear. Sixty-five percent of American adults are overweight or obese. One in every seven children is either overweight or obese. Sport, physical-education, and fitness leaders have to provide leadership in dealing with these issues.

When dealing with children or youths, it is particularly important to understand that obesity is a complex social and psychological problem as well as a physical problem (Berger, 2004). Fitness and physical-education professionals who deal with these problems as though they were solely about more activity and better diet will probably fail to

achieve desired goals. Short-term weight loss without a long-term plan for lifestyle change nearly always results in some short-term improvement followed by a rapid return to the lifestyle habits that produced the problems in the first place. The worst scenario is a fitness or physical-education professional trying to move obese children or youths to some "ideal" body composition and form. We know that it is possible to be *reasonably fit* and at the same time to be overweight in terms of body composition (a BMI of 25–29.9).

Physical-activity, exercise, and fitness programs should focus on helping children and youth improve their health rather than primarily on losing weight (AAALF, 2003). This takes patience and understanding as well as activity programs where children and youths can be successful and have fun.

---

most likely to benefit from supportive youth development services; yet they are the very youth who have least access to such programs and organizations" (p. 12).

Opportunity for physical activity and fitness is not a level playing field in the United States. Those who have had restricted opportunity and support have become the most at risk for a number of health problems related to physical inactivity. Thus, whether one views this problem primarily as a social–moral issue or chiefly as a cost–benefit issue from the standpoint of health costs, the solution is the same—namely, to remove barriers and to target supportive programs at those among us whose opportunities have been most restricted (see Focus On Box 9.3). This is a *structural* problem requiring public policy and programs for its solution. Exhorting people to show more individual responsibility may be an element in this solution, but in and of themselves, such exhortations are unlikely to change anything.

CERTIFICATION OF FITNESS LEADERS

At the moment, most people who are in positions of leadership in adult-fitness groups are not certified in any way to occupy that position. This is not to suggest that they are not competent in many cases. It only shows that the mechanisms are not present to *ensure* that exercise leaders have undergone a certain kind of training.

The number of different kinds of aerobic-conditioning programs at the national level is substantial. In many cases, a person needs no specific certification to put an advertisement in the paper or a sign in a window and to enroll people in aerobics classes. Many of these programs do certify their instructors, but the certification is sometimes available through the mail, and the requirements for obtaining it are minimal. The certification programs provided by the American College of Sports

Medicine (ACSM) (see Chapter 8) are examples of other efforts to upgrade the qualifications of exercise leaders.

This problem of certification for exercise leaders is tied to the problem of public education about fitness. The more that the public knows about fitness, the more likely people are to demand appropriate leadership in fitness classes and to be able to discriminate between good and bad practices. In the final analysis, an informed public might create such widespread consumer awareness that inappropriate fitness leadership would be driven from the market. Still, requiring exercise leaders to obtain certification by an agency such as the ACSM would represent another major step forward in the fitness movement.

FITNESS TESTS OR ACTIVITY ESTIMATES?

As epidemiological data on exercise related to mortality have become available, it has become clear that inactivity is a serious risk factor but that moderate activity is nearly as valuable as a preventive measure as is vigorous activity (Blair, 1992). This has led some fitness experts to argue for measures of activity in children and youths as more valid estimates of health fitness than fitness tests themselves (Freedson & Rowland, 1992).

The notion is quite simple. A healthy lifestyle includes activity. Moderate activity is sufficient to serve public health goals, and many of the kinds of activities that people enjoy most are moderate in nature—that is, walking, recreational cycling, gardening, and the like. Earlier in this chapter, we noted that fitness education must focus on long-term goals and that changes in lifestyle are the main long-term outcomes. If that is so, then one must at least give serious consideration to the argument that measures of daily activity are, from this perspective, valid indicators of fitness.

In contrast to measures of activity, mass fitness testing with students competing against one another is typically counterproductive to fitness and

activity goals. This does not mean that fitness testing has no place in school or agency programs. Pate (1994) suggests the following guidelines for fitness testing:

- Testing should be used to identify at-risk children, but their privacy should be respected in both testing and remediation.
- Award systems should be based on criterion-referenced standards, not norm-based tables.
- Accumulated activity, as well as performance on fitness tests, should become part of the evaluation strategy with children and youths.
- Self-testing can reduce some of the unfortunate side effects of mass fitness testing in physical-education classes.
- The primary purposes of fitness testing should be diagnosis, providing feedback, setting goals, and charting improvements.

FITNESS AND AGING: CHANGING VIEWS AND EXPECTATIONS

The American population is graying! Not only are there more older citizens than ever before, but our senior citizens have become one of our largest population groups. Every day, more than 4,000 Americans celebrate their sixty-fifth birthday. This population group has traditionally viewed vigorous physical activity as inappropriate. Increasingly, fitness for older Americans will become a major issue in the sport, fitness, and physical-education professions.

The dimensions of the problems associated with an aging population are substantial. The post–65-year-old group will soon be the dominant social and political group in America. Most people who retire at age 60 or 62 can expect to spend 20 years or more in retirement. As of the year 2000, approximately 100,000 Americans were over the age of 100!

The most important issue resulting from all of this is not necessarily how to increase life expectancy further. Rather, it is how to help older

Golf is an activity enjoyed by people of all ages.

citizens maintain their productive living capacity and better enjoy their later years. A pertinent corollary of this issue is reducing national health-care costs.

The benefits of activity in later years are beginning to be understood. Along with appropriate diet, exercise appears to be a key factor in controlling the effects of aging. It now seems that many of the so-called signs of aging (hearing loss, hair loss, reduced heart and lung function) are not as much signs of aging as they are signs of inactivity and poor nutrition (Kotulak & Gorner, 1992). Exercise programs do increase physical and physiological function among the elderly, thus having major effects on physiological aging and quality of life (Shephard, 1996). Quite elderly and even bed-ridden people have dramatically improved their physical status through planned exercise and nutrition interventions.

One of the most common ailments of senior citizens is depression of various kinds and intensities. The fact is that the declines that often accompany aging tend to produce depression and lower self-esteem. Studies, however, have shown that sedentary seniors who participate in regular physical-activity programs experience long-term psychological benefits (News, 2001). This is all more proof of the prophylactic and remedial benefits of regular activity.

Contemporary surveys of activity participation among the post–65-year-old age group are encouraging. It is clear that activities such as walking, cycling, aerobics, and calisthenics are popular with and doable by women and men in this age group. It is also clear that SES is strongly related to activity in later years. Women and men who can afford to retire in retirement communities or care centers have access to planned activities and to easily accessible exercise facilities that cater to older adults.

We are just now beginning to investigate and understand the problems associated with motivating older adults to incorporate regular physical activity into their lifestyles (Duda, 1991). Educating older people about the importance of physical activity must emphasize the personal meaning of the activity and the personal investment that the individual makes when entering an activity setting. It will take a great deal to overcome the traditional myth that people slow down because they get older. It appears that the opposite is more nearly true—that is, people get older because they slow down!

FITNESS ISSUES IN PHYSICAL EDUCATION

Many children first encounter physical fitness in their school physical-education program. These children will be in school for their formative years of childhood and the crucial years of adolescence. Therefore, what their physical-education classes teach them is likely to be of major importance in the formation of habits and attitudes that might last a lifetime.

The issues and problems associated with fitness programs within physical education are complex and not amenable to simple solutions. Nonetheless, to neglect them would be a serious mistake.

Leaders in the fitness movement have been particularly critical of school physical-education programs. In 1986 Kenneth Cooper, the physician who made the nation aware of aerobics, commented that fitness among children was so poor

Extreme sports have become popular among the "millennium" generation.

that we may "see all the gains made against heart disease in the past 20 years wiped out in the next 20 years" (*ARAPCS Newsletter*, 1986, p. 4). More recent evidence estimating children's physical activity, rather than their performance of fitness tests, has reduced that concern but not changed the clear fact that too many children are obese and inactive and that during adolescence, many youths become much less active.

The elementary-school years are particularly crucial in forming habits and predispositions among children. To be fair, one should consider the frequency and duration of physical-education time as a "dose" and the outcomes with children as a "response." What is clear over the past decade is that many schools have reduced the amount of

time allotted to physical education in order to focus more on reading and math. In many states, the classroom teacher is also the physical-education teacher and may not be sufficiently prepared to plan and deliver a physical-activity or fitness program to children that will not only help them to become more fit but, just as important, help them enjoy physical activity so much that they seek it out in nonattached time.

In 1994 Pate and Hohn suggested that the primary goal of physical education should be to promote lifelong physical activity and fitness. In the same year, Simons-Morton (1994) suggested that this goal would be accomplished through a "health-related physical education." The National Association for Sport and Physical Education recently published the second edition of *Moving Into the Future: National Standards for Physical Education* (NASPE, 2004). The overall goal is stated as physical activity is critical to the development and maintenance of good health. Focus On Box 9.4 shows how sport participation impacts health behaviors. The goal of physical education is to "develop physically educated individuals who have the knowledge, skills, and confidence to enjoy a lifetime of healthful physical activity." We should note that the overarching goal is not about fitness but about healthy physical activity. In 2007 the Trust for America's Health conducted a survey among chronic disease directors and state directors of health promotion and education to find out what these experts believed are the most important strategies for obesity prevention and reduction (Levi et al., 2007). The strategy that gained the most support from the experts was "increasing physical education and activity in schools, including before and after school programs" (p. 89).

Fitness in physical education used to mean push-ups, sit-ups, jumping jacks, and running. Many teachers "tested" fitness at least once each year, but students often had little preparation, except for the obligatory 5 minutes of "exercises" at the start of class. Most students endured it, but if it taught them anything it was to dislike what they

---

FOCUS ON   Sport Participation and Healthy Behaviors   9.4

A study of 14,221 female and male American high-school students from three ethnic groups showed that sport participation among high-school students is strong and that numerous positive health behaviors are associated with sport participation.

- 70 percent of males and 53 percent of female students reported participating on one or more sport teams.
- Sport participants were less likely to report not eating fruits or vegetables regularly.
- Sport participants were more likely to report participating in three or more vigorous physical-activity sessions in the past week.
- Female sport participants were less likely to report having sexual intercourse in the past 3 months.

- Both African American and Hispanic participants were somewhat less likely to be associated with positive health behaviors and somewhat more likely to be associated with negative health behaviors.
- Among males, sport participants across all three ethnic groups were less likely than nonparticipants to report cigarette smoking, illegal drug use, steroid use, or attempts to lose weight.
- Among females, sport participants across all three ethnic groups were less likely than nonparticipants to report cigarette smoking, illegal drug use, sexual intercourse, or contemplating or attempting suicide.

SOURCE: Pate, Trost, Levin, & Dowda, 2000.

---

had learned as fitness activities. Today, one is more likely to see a physical-education teacher who helps students learn how to use a pedometer, to chart courses to walk/run around their neighborhood, to establish realistic goals, and to record activity to reach those goals. Currently, there are many varied and attractive approaches to health-related fitness and physical activity in physical education. Specific examples of such programs are presented in Chapter 11.

Many physical educators believe that the major problem in achieving more in fitness and activity is the lack of time. If one looks at time only in terms of scheduled class time, the concern is well founded. Most elementary specialist teachers see children 1 or 2 days a week. Middle-school physical education is often 3 days per week, and the norm for high-school physical education is 5 days per week for 1 year in the ninth grade. Physical educators need to expand their horizons beyond class schedules. Physical-education programs should include attractive, inclusive, invitational programs for children and youths in nonattached school time.

School physical education should also be the place where children learn about community programs, are encouraged to participate, and are helped to gain access to such programs, especially those that are after-school, weekend, or summer programs (see Chapter 13).

The guidelines recommended by the CDC (1997) clearly indicate that fitness and physical activity are *schoolwide* responsibilities. For children and youths to build habits that lead to a lifetime commitment to activity, we must develop activity as a *social norm* in the school. This can be done only if the entire school believes in and supports that norm, particularly through the development of attractive programs that include all children and youths. The guidelines also suggest that the school is the hub of a school–family–community connection that supports physical activity for children and youths. In this sense, the physical education of children and youths becomes the responsibility of not only the physical-education teacher but also the other classroom teachers, the principal, the parents, and the community leaders.

RESEARCH ISSUES IN FITNESS AND PHYSICAL ACTIVITY

Although much has been learned about fitness and physical activity in the past several decades, there is much still to be learned. Some of these issues involve basic research, and others involve finding solutions to problems of delivery and exercise maintenance through applied research. The following are some of the more intriguing questions for research (Blair, Kohl, & Powell, 1987; U.S. Department of Health and Human Services, 1996):

- What is the relationship between exercise and the body's immune response system? Can exercise help make us more resistant to infectious disease?
- What important features or combinations of features of physical activity (intensity, duration, frequency, cumulation, type of activity) are related to specific health benefits?
- What protective effects might physical activity have on lifestyle characteristics and disease-prevention behaviors?
- What type of exercise best preserves muscle strength and functional capacity among the elderly?
- What are the determinants of physical activity among various population subgroups (for example, age, sex, race/ethnicity, SES, geographic region)?
- What is the relationship between the amount and kind of physical-activity involvement in children and youths and their later adult habits?
- What interventions are most likely to promote adoption and maintenance of a physically active lifestyle at various stages of the life cycle?

As you can see, there is a great deal to be learned as we continue to know more, to be able to do more. Achieving a lifespan commitment to physical activity for a larger proportion of our population, regardless of age, sex, race/ethnicity, handicapping condition, or SES remains the major problem to be solved.

A CONCLUDING THOUGHT

The national goals for helping motivate and sustain a more active citizenry, from early childhood through old age, cannot be achieved by sport, fitness, and physical-education professionals working alone. The concept of a *physical-activity infrastructure* was introduced in Chapter 1 and has been referred to at other points throughout this text. Chapter 13 will provide a detailed examination of what that infrastructure might contain and what is being done at the national, state, and local levels to develop and support it.

SUMMARY

1. Health, motor-performance, and cosmetic fitness are important both to individuals and to society. However, the demands of everyday modern life are typically insufficient for the development and maintenance of fitness.

2. The costs to society of inadequate health fitness are substantial; they include the costs of expensive health insurance, rehabilitation, reduced productivity, and lost workdays.

3. The immediate consequences of aerobic activity are often aversive, and the benefits are often delayed. To maintain health fitness, a person must make appropriate activity a regular part of her or his lifestyle.

4. Fitness programs that affect lifestyles incorporate education, activity, planning skills, and consumer information in a comprehensive effort to produce permanent changes in exercise behavior.

5. Media images of fitness are often misleading. A national fitness-education effort would help

)) GET CONNECTED to Fitness Web Sites

Fitness for Children and Youths

Healthy Schools   www.healthyschools.net
President's Council on Physical Fitness and Sports   www.fitness.gov
Project Fit America   www.projectfitamerica.org
Health and Fitness for Kids   www.howtobefit.com/kid-fitness.htm
Shaping America's Youth   www.shapingamericasyouth.com
Fitness for Youth   www.fitnessforyouth.umich.edu
Physical Activity for Youth with Disabilities   www.hhs.gov/od/physicalfitness.html
President's Challenge   www.presidentschallenge.org

Fitness for Adults

Worksite fitness programs   www.fitwellinc.com
Active   www.active.com
Project Fit America   www.projectfitamerica.org
Senior Fitness Association   www.seniorfitness.net
Fifty-Plus Fitness Association   www.50plus.org

Fitness-Related Professions and Organizations

Healthy People 2010   www.healthypeople.gov
National Athletic Trainers' Association   www.nata.org
American Physical Therapy Association   www.apta.org
National Strength and Conditioning Association   www.nsca-lift.org
American College of Sports Medicine   www.acsm.org
American Council on Exercise   www.acefitness.org
American Occupational Therapy Association   www.aota.org
Fitness Management   www.fitnessworld.com
Cooper Institute   www.cooperinst.org
President's Council on Physical Fitness and Sport   www.fitness.gov
Aerobics and Fitness Association of America   www.afaa.com
American Fitness Professionals & Associates   www.afpafitness.com
Aquatic Exercise Association   www.aeawave.com
National Association for Health and Fitness   www.physicalfitness.org
National Coalition for Promoting Physical Activity   www.ncppa.org
United States Water Fitness Association   www.uswfa.com
Canadian Fitness & Lifestyle Research Institute   www.cflri.ca
Get Active America   www.getactiveamerica.com

curb the amount of fitness misinformation and help the public make wiser choices about personal fitness.

6. The social gradient in health and activity results in highly inequitable access to activity programs and facilities.

7. Many exercise leaders have no certification. Others have only mail-order credentials. Certification, especially for adult-fitness leaders, would help ensure that appropriate fitness testing and prescriptive programs are utilized.

8. The size of the senior population is growing, and seniors are living longer. Many seniors have many misconceptions about fitness and do not engage in activity that is as vigorous as it could be. Fitness in old age is important both for maintaining functional capacity and for improving quality of life.

9. Physical education has been strongly criticized for its lack of appropriate fitness programming, but fitness is just one of many objectives that physical educators attempt to reach.

10. Fitness programs at the national, state, district, and local levels have been successful, but no single pattern has emerged. Lack of sufficient time for activities that meet minimum health-fitness requirements appears to be the biggest problem.

11. Health-related fitness among schoolchildren and youths will not be given appropriate attention until it becomes a schoolwide objective rather than an objective for physical educators alone.

12. Although substantial fitness research has been completed in the past several decades, much remains to be done at both the basic and the applied levels.

13. To achieve national goals in health and physical activity, we must develop a physical activity infrastructure of accessible programs and facilities.

DISCUSSION QUESTIONS

1. Of what should fitness education consist if the goal is to incorporate regular fitness into the student's lifestyle?

2. Have the media advanced or hindered the goals of fitness education? How could the media be used more effectively to promote those goals?

3. Should fitness be a required school subject? Should students have to meet fitness standards on a regular basis?

4. Should physical education have fitness as its most important goal? Why or why not?

5. How can fitness be made important for *all* segments of the national population? Will it remain a mostly upper-middle-class movement?

6. If the children of today are unfit, will the adults and seniors of tomorrow also be unfit?

Physical Education

Physical education has been an accepted part of the curriculum of American schools for about a century. Even in the midst of current educational reform, physical education is still described as a necessary subject that has the potential to contribute a great deal to the education of children and youths. Yet there is also a substantial amount of "fizz-ed bashing," both in the serious literature of education and in the popular media. Think for a moment about how the physical-education teacher is typically portrayed in contemporary films!

School is still one institution that touches us all—and that touches us at crucial periods of our development as individuals. It is vitally important that physical education thrive as a well-taught, well-accepted subject in our schools. What is physical education? What activities are acceptable? How can the subject be improved? What kinds of programs seem to work? The three chapters in Part 4 are designed to help you examine these issues and to reach conclusions that are informed by evidence and thoughtful argument.

CHAPTER 10

Basic Concepts of Physical Education

Modern physical education with its emphasis upon education through the physical is based upon the biologic unity of mind and body. This view sees life as a totality. Correct in their appraisement that the cult of muscle is ludicrous, those who worship at the altar of mental development too frequently neglect the implications of unity. "Socrates with a headache" is always preferable to a brainless Hercules, but the modern spirit in physical education seeks the education of man through physical activities as one aspect of the social effort for human enlightenment.

Jesse Feiring Williams, 1930

LEARNING OBJECTIVES

- To discuss definitions of physical education

- To analyze education-through-the-physical and multiactivity programs

- To describe and discuss alternative curriculum influences

- To describe the development of and issues in adapted physical education

- To analyze the influences of liability and Title IX on physical education

- To formulate your own view on the central meaning and preferred focus of physical education

Physical education has been a school subject in America for more than 100 years. For most of that time, it was a "minor" subject, seldom attracting attention of educators or the public. The times when physical education did attract national attention were always times when the lack of fitness among American youths became an issue. This was true for a polio epidemic in the early part of the twentieth century, the number of draftees rejected for fitness reasons in World War II, and during the mid-1950s when a research study showed that 60 percent of American children/youths failed a test of minimum muscular fitness compared to only 9 percent of European children, leading President Eisenhower to form the President's Council on Youth Fitness.

The recent epidemic of child/youth overweight and obesity has once again brought physical education into the national spotlight. Curiously, this national focus on increasing the physical

| FOCUS ON | Historical Influences on the Development of Physical Education | 10.1 |

1. Concerns about health and fitness and character development were at the heart of the early formal gymnastic systems. Concerns about fitness have occurred periodically as reactions to rejection of draftees for military service and to epidemics such as polio.

2. Progressive-education theory focused on the development of the whole child and led to the developmental perspective known historically as education through the physical, which is still the

most widely accepted approach to articulating goals for physical education.

3. The continuing development of sport in the twentieth century merged with the developmental approach to make physical education largely a sport-based curriculum.

See Chapter 2 for a full discussion of these developments.

---

activity of children and youths developed during the same period when time for physical education in America's schools had diminished due to the federal No Child Left Behind legislation, which caused schools, especially at the elementary level, to devote more time to reading and mathematics (Jennings, 2006). As you will see in this chapter and the next, many physical-education programs have changed to better respond to this current health crisis.

A physical-education program is defined both by the content to be learned and the manner in which it is taught; that is, programs are defined both by their curricular choices and the pedagogy used to deliver those curricular choices. The programmatic approaches to physical education described in this chapter will show different choices of activities and different approaches to teaching those activities. The various programmatic approaches are described with as little bias as possible so that you can decide which approach seems most able to help children and youths in today's schools become physically educated people.

THE PRIMARY TWENTIETH-CENTURY INFLUENCES ON MODERN PHYSICAL EDUCATION

The most important influence on physical education in the twentieth century was what has become known as the developmental model (see Chapter 2),

often referred to as "education through the physical" or the "new physical education." This model was wholly consistent with progressive-education theory, which dominated ideas about schooling and learning in the first half of the twentieth century (Focus On Box 10.1).

In 1910 Clark Hetherington earned the title of "father of modern physical education" with his landmark paper "Fundamental Education." Hetherington described both the scope and the categories of the *new* physical education.

This paper aims to describe the function and place of general neuromuscular activities, primarily play activities, in the educational process. . . . To present the thesis four phases of the education process will be considered: organic education, psychomotor education, character education, and intellectual education. (Weston, 1962, p. 160)

Hetherington's four phases became the four primary objectives of the new physical education. For the better part of the twentieth century, these objectives were used to explain and justify the presence of physical education in the school curriculum. Although the objectives were explained somewhat differently by different leaders and organizations, the differences were minimal. Charles Bucher, a leading midcentury American physical educator, suggested the following goals a half-century after the Hetherington goals were formulated. One can't help but notice the similarity to the Hetherington goals.

1. Physical development objective: The objective of physical development deals with the program of activities that builds physical power in an individual through the development of the various organic systems of the body.
2. Motor development objective: The motor development objective is concerned with making physical movement useful and with as little expenditure of energy as possible and being proficient, graceful, and aesthetic in this movement.
3. Mental development objective: The mental development objective deals with the accumulation of a body of knowledge and the ability to think and to interpret this knowledge.
4. Social development objective: The social development objective is concerned with helping an individual in making personal adjustments, group adjustments, and adjustments as a member of society. (Bucher, 1964, p. 155)

A typical physical-education lesson included fitness, skill development, knowledge, and social development. Lesson plans organized around the four objectives quickly became the standard in the physical-education curriculum in schools.

A corollary feature of this developmental model for physical education was the establishment of the **multiactivity-curriculum** approach to program design. For *full* development to be ensured, people believed, each child had to experience a *variety* of activities. Because physical education sought a diversity of physical, mental, and social goals and because each child was unique in her or his own development, a wide variety of activities was needed to fulfill the promise of this developmental model; team sports, individual sports, adventure activities, fitness activities, and dance all found acceptance within the multiactivity framework.

In 1927 the multiactivity model was officially sanctioned by a national committee. The idea and guidelines to use this model were published as a monograph, "The Physical Education Curriculum,"

Can physical education begin to engender the same enthusiasm among students that school sport does?

in 1938 and eventually were revised through seven editions. This was as close to a *national* curriculum for physical education as we have ever had. The primary feature of this curriculum model was a *block* or *unit* plan. Across a school year, students would experience a fairly large number of activity units, some sports, some fitness, some dance. This unit model with the multiactivity approach became the main programmatic feature of American physical education, and it remains so today in most places.

In 1971 the American Alliance for Health, Physical Education, Recreation, and Dance (AAHPERD) launched the Physical Education Public Information (PEPI) project, designed to inform the public about the goals of physical education (Biles, 1971). PEPI's five primary concepts showed that Hetherington's four objectives were alive and well

---

FOCUS ON   NASPE Content Standards in Physical Education   10.2

A physically educated person:

1. Demonstrates competency in motor skills and movement patterns needed to perform a variety of activities.

2. Demonstrates understanding of movement concepts, principles, strategies, and tactics as they apply to the learning and performance of physical activities.

3. Participates regularly in physical activity.

4. Achieves and maintains a health-enhancing level of physical fitness.

5. Exhibits responsible personal and social behavior that respects self and others in physical-activity settings.

6. Values physical activity for health, enjoyment, challenge, self-expression, and/or social interaction.

SOURCE: National Association for Sport and Physical Education, 2004b.

---

in physical education:

1. A physically educated person is one who has knowledge and skill concerning her or his body and how it works.

2. Physical education is health insurance.

3. Physical education can contribute to academic achievement.

4. A sound physical-education program contributes to development of a positive self-concept.

5. A sound physical-education program helps an individual to attain social skills.

Can you see Hetherington's influence? The language is different, but the emphasis on fitness, skill, knowledge, and social development remains.

NASPE'S MOVE TOWARD NATIONAL GOALS AND STANDARDS

In the 1990s, the National Association for Sport and Physical Education (NASPE), a main affiliate of AAHPERD, began to develop a set of national goals and standards for physical education. The first part of this initiative was called the "Outcomes Project," and it sought to answer the question "What should students know and be able to do as a result of physical education?" In 1992 NASPE published its first outcomes statement, which established a set of national standards for physical education. In 2004

NASPE (NASPE, 2004b) revised the outcome standards to those shown in Focus On Box 10.2. The outcomes project and the resulting standards provided, for the first time, a national consensus that defined the physically educated person. Each of the 2004 standards is further delineated by *student expectations* that are defined for grades K–2, 3–5, 6–8, and 9–12. What is expected of the student is then still further delineated by examples of performance outcomes for that standard at each of the grouped grade levels. Some of the performance expectations are shown in Focus On Box 10.3.

The NASPE standards and performance outcome suggestions represented the first national effort (1) to define what physical-education programs in schools should attempt to achieve and (2) to provide examples that define outcomes. It should be noted, however, that this initiative did not specify the activities that should be taught at each grade level; that is, it does not prescribe an activity curriculum. Outcomes at each grade level could be achieved using very different activities. Physical-education teachers, even in school districts that have adopted the NASPE standards, are typically free to choose the activities that compose their yearly curriculum at each grade level. One can even imagine that a physical-education teacher could choose to use dodgeball as a regular activity in the physical-education yearly schedule and argue that it met NASPE standards, even though that activity is widely viewed as inappropriate for physical education.

FOCUS ON — Samples from NASPE Performance Outcomes 10.3

Motor skill and movement patterns

- K–2   Skips, hops, gallops, slides using mature form
- Demonstrates a smooth transition between locomotor skills in time to music
- 3–5   Performs a tinikling step to 3/4 time
- Dribbles then passes a basketball to a moving receiver
- 6–8   Places the ball away from an opponent during a tennis rally
- Designs and performs gymnastics or dance sequences
- 9–12   Uses a variety of ground stroke placements to keep opponent moving during a tennis match
- Dribbles a soccer ball at moderate to fast speeds, while maintaining control of the ball, evading opponents, and shielding the ball

Understanding of movement concepts, principles, strategies, and tactics

- K–2   Corrects movement errors in response to feedback
- Identifies body planes correctly
- 3–5   Describes how heart rate is used to monitor exercise intensity
- Accurately recognizes the critical elements of a catch made by a fellow student and provides feedback to that student
- 6–8   Describes basic principles of training and how they improve fitness
- States the biomechanical reason to extend elbow in striking skills
- 9–12   Develops realistic short-term and long-term personal fitness goals
- Explains appropriate tactical decisions in a game of softball

Participates regularly in physical activity

- K–2   Engages in moderate to vigorous activity on an intermittent basis

- Participates in chasing and fleeing activities outside of school
- 3–5   Participates in organized sport activities in local community
- Monitors his or her physical activity by using a pedometer
- 6–8   Sets realistic physical-activity goals and strives to attain them
- Participates in health-enhancing activity during and outside of school
- 9–12   Accumulates a recommended number of minutes of MVPA outside of PE class five or more days per week
- Demonstrates effective time management skills to allow opportunity for PA to be created or found during the day

Achieves and maintains a health-enhancing level of physical fitness

- K–2   Engages in a series of locomotor activities
- Increases arm and shoulder strength by traveling hand-over-hand along a horizontal ladder
- 3–5   Runs the equivalent of two laps around a regulation track without stopping
- Meets the age- and gender-specific health-related fitness standards defined by FITNESSGRAM
- 6–8   Self-assesses heart rate before, during, and after vigorous PA
- Maintains heart rate in target zone for a minimum of 20 minutes
- 9–12   Develops a personal fitness profile based on fitness assessment results
- Maintains appropriate levels of cardiorespiratory endurance, muscular strength and endurance, flexibility, and body composition

Exhibits responsible personal and social behavior that respects self and others in PA settings

- K–2   Shows compassion for others by helping them
- Accepts all playmates without regard to personal differences

FOCUS ON   Samples from NASPE Performance Outcomes (*continued*)   10.3

- 3–5   Cooperates with class members by taking turns and sharing equipment
- Assesses and takes responsibility for his or her own behavior without blaming others
- 6–8   Shows self-control by accepting a controversial decision by a referee
- Seeks out, participates with, and shows respect for a peer with lesser skill ability
- 9–12   Invites less skilled students to participate in a warm-up activity prior to class
- Shows leadership by diffusing conflict during competition

Values physical activity for health, enjoyment, challenge, self-expression, and/or social interaction

- K–2   Willingly tries new movements and skills

- Exhibits both verbal and nonverbal indicators of enjoyment
- 3–5   Selects and practices a skill on which improvement is needed
- Chooses to participate in group physical activities
- 6–8   Sees learning new activities and skills as challenging
- Invites all students, regardless of ability, to participate in activities
- 9–12   Enjoys working with others in a sport activity to achieve a common goal
- Identifies reasons to participate in PA

SOURCE: NASPE, 2004b.

IMPORTANT CURRICULUM AND INSTRUCTION INFLUENCES

Views of what physical education *should be* often involve a philosophical point of view within which there is a strong value orientation (Jewitt & Bain, 1985). The education-through-the-physical model started with optimal individual development within a democratic social framework as its primary value orientation. From that value orientation, physical educators set goals and chose activity experiences to meet those goals, thus creating a physical-education curriculum that is taught to students using an instructional process that reflects those values. A *curriculum* is not just a group of activities; rather, it is a sequence of activities taught from a particular *instructional* perspective, leading to outcomes that reflect a value orientation. The purpose of this section is to introduce you to important curriculum and instruction models that are prominent within American physical education.

Skill Themes

In the 1960s–1970s, many American physical educators, especially those focused primarily on elementary-school physical education, were influenced by innovations in British physical education that had developed from the work of Rudolph Laban, whose influence in the movement arts, especially dance, was widespread in Europe. Prominent American physical educators such as Eleanor Metheny and Rosiland Cassidy began to articulate a human-movement philosophy for physical education. The movement-education curriculum was organized around three areas: educational dance, educational gymnastics, and educational games. Movement education was innovative in both teaching method and curriculum design. Teaching methods emphasized problem solving, guided discovery, and exploration. The curriculum was defined by movement concepts, such as absorbing force or striking, rather than games or sports. The aesthetic dimension of performance was highly valued. Competition was kept to a minimum.

FOCUS ON — Skill Themes*   10.4

Locomotor Skills	Nonmanipulative Skills	Manipulative Skillls
Walking	Turning	Throwing
Running	Twisting	Catching/collecting
Hopping	Rolling	Kicking
Skipping	Balancing	Punting
Galloping	Transferring weight	Dribbling
Sliding	Jumping and landing	Volleying
Chasing, fleeing, dodging	Stretching	Striking with rackets

*Examples of skills taught in skill theme elementary-school physical-education programs. The list is not all-inclusive but provides examples of skill themes.

SOURCE: Graham, Holt-Hale, & Parker, 2007.

The movement-education approach gradually evolved into the skill theme model, mainly through the influence of the Canadian physical education and dance educator Sheila Stanley and the American physical educator Kate Barrett. The most prominent advocates of the skill theme model today are George Graham, Shirley Holt-Hale, and Melissa Parker who suggest that "skill themes are fundamental movements that form the foundation for success in sports and physical activities in later years. Initially they are studied in isolation (one skill at a time), and then in later grades they are combined with other skills and used in more complex settings, such as those found in dance, games, and gymnastics" (Graham, Holt-Hale, & Parker, 2007). See Focus On Box 10.4 for examples of skill themes.

Teachers who use the skill themes model focus on helping young children learn to perform a variety of locomotor, nonmanipulative, and manipulative motor skills such as throwing, catching, volleying, dribbling, balancing, striking with implements, and dodging. They also learn movement concepts such as location (self-space and general space), directions (such as up/down, forward/backward, and right/left), levels (such as low and high), pathways (such as straight, curved, and zig-zag), and extensions (such as large/small and far/near) (Graham et al., 2007).

The skill theme model typically has all children involved in activity all of the time during class sessions, also ensuring that a fair portion of that time is devoted to moderate-to-vigorous activity (MVPA), thus meeting fitness expectations. Teachers are constantly observing students and providing feedback. As a result, children learn how to assess their own progress and how to provide assistance to classmates by observing their efforts and providing feedback. Student progress proceeds through four generic levels of skill proficiency (Graham et al., 2007). Most students begin at the precontrol level where responses are often awkward and repeated movements in succession cannot be done. They advance to the control level where correct skill movements appear more frequently. Students then can move to the level where the skill is used in combination with other skills in less predictable situations. Finally, they achieve the proficiency level where they can focus outward, on the goal or larger dimensions of the activity, while performing the skill without having to pay attention to the critical elements of the skill. This final stage is important because achieving proficiency allows children to participate successfully in a number of game, sport, dance, and gymnastic activities.

Children can help one another as they learn.

The progress that students make is of course determined to a large degree by the amount of time that they have to learn. If K–5 physical education occurs only once per week, then teachers can achieve only limited outcomes. If, however, children in the K–5 grades have daily physical education, they can develop a through repertoire of skills that are useful in a large number of game, sport, dance, outdoor, and gymnastic activities. If children reach middle school without reasonable proficiency in a number of skills, they are unlikely to be able to participate successfully in the activities typically included in middle-school physical-education programs. Many physical-education advocates have become convinced that the greatest investment schools can make in physical education is sufficient time in the K–5 grades.

The Health-Related Physical-Education Model

Over the past decade, data on the increasing rates of overweight and obesity among American children and youths have led to a flurry of reports and recommendations to increase the amount of time that children and youths participate in physical activity, particularly physical activity that is of a moderate-to-vigorous nature. Thom McKenzie, in his 2007 Dudley A. Sargent Commemorative Lecture, described the problem in clear terms:

> Sedentary living is a serious global public health problem that is associated with numerous preventable diseases. Schools are in a position to be the most cost-effective public resource to combat inactivity. In schools physical educators are positioned to be the strongest advocates for a healthy, active lifestyle. To effectively promote physical activity on school campuses and to encourage it in communities beyond the school day, physical educators will need to develop skills that are not typically stressed in undergraduate physical education teacher education programs. (McKenzie, 2007)

What is typically referred to as health-related physical education (HRPE) has as its primary goal that children and youths develop and value a physically active lifestyle. The HRPE approach also seeks to ensure that schools provide adequate daily physical activity for students, including an appropriate amount of MVPA. In HRPE models, physical educators typically have an expanded role that goes beyond their responsibilities to plan and teach the physical-education classes. HRPE models typically aim to engage students in physical activity not only in physical education classes but also in recess, in classroom breaks, at the start of the school day, and through programs that involve students in physical activity outside of school hours. HRPE models also help students learn ways of managing and motivating their physical-activity behavior through planning, goal setting, self-monitoring, self-reinforcement, and resisting negative influences that prevent engagement in physical activity.

Many advocates of HRPE support an ecological approach that emphasizes the multiple levels of influence and the role of various environments that affect the physical activity of children and youths (Ward, Saunders, & Pate, 2007). This model suggests that

- Physical-education instruction be designed to increase the enjoyment of physical activity.
- Physical-education activities allow students to interact socially while being physically active.
- Physical activity outside of school is promoted.

- Students learn behavioral skills such as goal setting, overcoming barriers, and seeking support.
- Physical-activity homework incorporates family members in physical activity.
- Schools engage with community agencies to provide after-school physical-activity opportunities.
- Schools support physical-activity breaks in classrooms and physical-activity sessions to start the school day.

Physical educators and school leaders who are interested in developing an HRPE program in their school or district can gain access to a number of programmatic approaches that have been used throughout the United States. Some of these are described briefly:

- SPARK (Sports, Play, and Active Recreation for Kids) is a nationally tested program that is available for pre-K, K–2, 3–6, middle-school, high-school, and after-school versions (www .sparkpe.org).
- M-SPAN (Middle School Physical Activity and Nutrition) was the first HRPE program to focus especially on middle-school students (www.sparkpe.org/programMiddlePE.jsp).
- PEforLife is a national nonprofit organization promoting middle- and secondary-school physical-education programs that focus on developing lifetime physical-activity habits (www.PE4life.org).
- Take 10! is a classroom based physical-activity program for elementary schools that integrates grade-specific academic materials with MVPA in 10-minute segments in the classroom (www.take10.net).

The HRPE model has become very popular at the high-school level. In some high schools, the primary space for physical education looks very much like a community fitness center—and, in many cases, it is exactly that! Schools join forces with their communities to develop and sustain a fitness center at the high school that is used by students during the school day and is also accessible for community members during after-school and weekend hours. Most of these HRPE models include information about nutrition and healthy lifestyles, along with the physical-activity portions of the program.

Fifty years ago, physical-education programs that emphasized fitness would have students doing jumping jacks, push-ups, sit-ups, sprints, and distance running, typically with the whole class participating in unison following commands from the teacher. It is fair to say that for the majority of students this was not exciting or fun. It is also fair to say that this model for fitness probably turned more students away from a healthy lifestyle than toward a healthy lifestyle.

In many physical-education programs today, fitness is still either a unit in the yearly activity plan or a small focus in each lesson throughout the year. The new concerns about overweight and obesity and the illnesses and health costs associated with those issues are bringing physical activity (of a certain intensity and a certain duration—for example, MVPA) into the spotlight for physical educators at all levels. The HRPE goals can be achieved by any program that (1) contributes adequately to the amount of MVPA that students get in their physical-education classes and (2) influences them to lead a more physically active lifestyle. What HRPE has done is to take those as primary goals and to focus on them throughout the entire physical-education program.

The Academic-Integration Model

In the 1960s and 1970s, the academic discipline of kinesiology emerged, extending and deepening the knowledge base in what were increasingly referred to as the subdisciplines of kinesiology: motor behavior, biomechanics, exercise physiology, sport sociology, sport psychology, sport humanities, and sport pedagogy (see Chapters 15 and 16). In the 1980s, some high-school physical-education programs moved to a "concepts curriculum" (Siedentop, Mand, & Taggart, 1986) in which knowledge of the kinesiology subdisciplines was blended with activity programs that split time between the classroom and the gymnasium. Lawson and Placek (1981) defined this model as "a unique blend of performance skills and experience in sport, exercise, dance, and contests with that knowledge about performance which is derived from the disciplinary foundations of our field" (p. 6).

In the 1980s, AAHPERD published a series of booklets entitled *Basic Stuff*, which focused on important concepts in exercise physiology, kinesiology, motor learning, motor development, sport humanities, and the psychosocial aspects of sport. This series sought to provide physical-education teachers with information and strategies to incorporate disciplinary knowledge into their physical-education classes.

The academic-discipline model gradually gave way to an emphasis on *integration*. The integration model suggests that knowledge and skills traditionally taught in gymnasiums and those traditionally taught in classrooms can be integrated. A Russian folk dance might be taught in a fifth-grade social studies unit, the early Olympic Games taught in a ninth-grade history class, or the concept of force in a ninth-grade science class might be illustrated by how force is generated to put a shot or high jump. Likewise, physical educators could easily teach environmental knowledge and skills in outdoor education units and incorporate many scientific principles in a middle-school track-and-field unit.

Integration seems to be most popular in elementary and middle schools where subjects such as language arts can be integrated easily with physical education or outdoor adventure skills can be easily integrated with a classroom focus on environmental education. Integration has been a major goal of schools that are often referred to as *magnet* or *alternative schools*. An excellent example was an alternative elementary school where adventure education was the integrating force for the entire school curriculum (Stroot, Carpenter, & Eisnaugle, 1991).

The academic-integration model, however, has seen reduced use in elementary and middle schools in recent years as education reform in the wake of No Child Left Behind Act has caused schools to focus on increasing the time devoted to subjects included on yearly state tests. These tests typically focus on basic knowledge in reading, mathematics, and science; that is, the application of how that knowledge is integrated into more practical settings is less often tested.

It should be noted that the academic-integration model has become very popular in elective physical-education programs in the eleventh and twelfth grades of high school in Australia, New Zealand, and England (Macdonald & Leitch, 1994). Often these programs offer beginning preparation for careers in athletic training, physical therapy, and sport management.

The Personal and Social Responsibility Model

An important educational influence of the 1960s–1970s was the humanistic-education movement that focused on treating students as individuals and focusing primarily on personal growth and social responsibility rather than solely on academic achievement. In physical education, this approach has been developed and articulated consistently by Donald Hellison (1973, 1978, 1983, 2003).

The personal and social responsibility model (PSRM) is designed to help young people cope better with a complex social world, to achieve a higher degree of control over their own lives, and to contribute more positively to the small social worlds of which they are a part. The primary medium through which these goals are sought is physical education: the gymnasium, the weight room, and the playing field. The PSRM is well tested and has been used successfully in a variety of settings. In the 1990s, problems associated with youths became a major issue in American life (Carnegie Council on Adolescent Development, 1992); vandalism, dropout rates, teen pregnancy, violence, and drug use drew national attention. Many physical-education teachers in urban schools, particularly middle and high schools, feel that cooperation, social development, and responsibility are as important outcomes as skill and fitness (Ennis, Ross, & Chen, 1992). For these teachers and for many others, PSRM continues to be a useful curricular and pedagogical approach, either in its full form or as a supporting pedagogical strategy in the physical-education curriculum.

Many physical-education teachers, especially elementary specialists, have used aspects of the PSRM to assist with maintaining appropriate behavior in class and to help children learn to be more responsible. For example, many elementary-school physical-education teachers create a simple system for students to gauge their own behavior during physical-education class. A four- to five-level chart is used for students to assess their own behavior in cooperating, helping, and avoiding harm to other students during class. As student leave the gymnasium, they touch the "level" on the chart that represents their social and behavioral performance during the class. If the teacher disagrees with the choice made by a student, it creates the opportunity for the teacher and student to discuss their differences in perceptions of behavior for that day.

The PSRM does not specify particular activities but does create a particular pedagogical approach. Hellison (1995) developed a five-level progression of personal and social development (see Focus On Box 10.5). Level 1 focuses on respect for others; level 2, on demonstrating effort within class; level 3, on self-direction as a learner and class member; level 4, on helping others; and level 5, on demonstrating those qualities outside the physical-education setting. The levels are viewed as a progression; that is, students have to learn to control themselves and show respect for the rights and feelings of their classmates before they can focus on self-motivation and persistence in the learning setting.

The Sport-Education Model

A more recent entry into the physical-education curriculum and instruction literature is sport education (Siedentop, 1994; Siedentop, Hastie, & van der Mars, 2004). Although sport education was created as a way of helping students learn and enjoy various

sports, it has also been used for a large number of activities such as dance, cycling, outdoor adventure activities, and various fitness activities.

Within this model, sport, dance, and fitness activities are organized as *playful competitions*, thus deriving its main conceptual focus from what has been described in physical education as "play education" (Siedentop. 1980). The model has five defining characteristics that distinguish it from more traditional forms of physical education:

1. Sport education is divided into *seasons* that are longer than typical physical-education units in a multiactivity program. Elementary-school seasons last ten to twelve class sessions; middle-school seasons, twelve to fifteen class sessions; and high-school seasons, fifteen to twenty-two class sessions.

2. Students are organized immediately into teams, and they retain that *affiliation* throughout the season.

3. Seasons are built around a series of *competitions* that grow increasingly complex as students master the techniques and tactics involved in the activity for that season.

4. The season ends with a *culminating event* that not only determines the seasonal champion but also provides a festive way to conclude the experience.

5. Records are kept throughout the season so that students and teams can mark their progress.

In sport education, teams are organized so that each team has a mixture of more- and less-skilled students. A great deal of the responsibility for ensuring a successful season falls on the team members. Each team member has a role to play in ensuring that the team performs well and that the season is a success. The roles are determined partially by the nature of the activity; that is, in a sport activity, each team would have a coach, manager, statistician, trainer, and the like, or in a dance activity, each team would have a coach, manager, choreographer, costume designer, music manager, and the like. Each

---

FOCUS ON Hellison's Responsibility-in-the-Gym Model   **10.5**

Major focus: Put kids first! Teachers have to care about students as whole persons. The teacher–student relationship is fundamentally important. Teachers have to respect students' struggles, individuality, and capacity for growth.

Purpose: To help students take responsibility for their own well-being and learn to be sensitive and responsive to the well-being of others.

Responsibility Levels	Instructor Values
1. Respect for others' rights and feelings	Respect for students, equity, and empowerment
• Control temper and mouth	
• Right to be included	
• Peaceful conflict resolution	
2. Effort	Self-paced task mastery, task variation, competitive choices
• Explore effort and new tasks	
• Self-motivation	
• Learn persistence	
3. Self-direction	Empowerment
• Independence	
• Goal-setting progressions	
• Resisting peer pressure	
4. Helping	Well-being of others
• Sensitivity and responsiveness	
• Leadership	
• Group welfare	
5. Outside the gym	Values transfer
• Trying levels in other settings	
• Being a role model	

SOURCE: Adapted from Hellison, 1995.

---

student on each team would also have a role ensuring that the competitions are run smoothly and appropriately; that is, each team member would act as a referee and/or scorekeeper for competitions during the season. Most sport-education seasons use a three-team model so that the competition would be team 1 versus team 3 with team 2 acting as the *duty team*, providing the referees and scorekeepers and managing the transition between competitions.

As students gain experience in sport education, their roles can be expanded. Each team might have a

publicist, and the three students acting in that role for their teams would together decide how to publicize the season and the performances of teams and individuals. In one middle-school model, the team publicists together created a weekly column in the school newspaper that featured the standings and highlights of the sport-education seasons. In a national trial of sport education in New Zealand, one high school added the role of trainer to the model. The trainer had to be knowledgeable about the kind of injuries likely to occur in the activity for the season, have a

Being a member of a team can produce several benefits.

training kit ready to assist if a student were injured, and provide assistance to the teacher in such a case.

The sport-education model is based on the assumption that *good* competition is both fun and educationally useful. The model developed from the view that students should be able to compete against other students of reasonably equal abilities and that the games, sports, and activities should be *small-sided* so that all players are in the action continuously. Thus, in a volleyball season, a 3 v 3 competition would be preferable to the standard 6 v 6. In a elementary-school soccer season, a series of competitions might begin with a 2 v 2 competition, then move to 3 v 3, and culminate with a 5 v 5 competition. The model also encourages teachers to modify the conditions of play to help students acquire techniques and tactics—that is, lower baskets in basketball or a lower net and friendlier ball in volleyball.

The sport-education model has been used at all levels from third grade through high school (Bell, 1998; Jones & Ward, 1998; Siedentop, 1994). Teachers have found the model to be an excellent vehicle for helping students to assume more responsibility for their own sport involvement. The team-membership feature produces situations that require students to work together to achieve team goals. The various roles of sport education (coach, referee, scorer, trainer, statistician) require responsible performance for the season to move forward. Teachers also report that sport education produces excitement among students and encourages them to seek other sport opportunities outside the school (Grant, 1992).

The sport-education model can accommodate a host of activities other than traditional team and individual sports. For example, it has been used for a weight-lifting and strength-training season for high-school girls (Sweeney, Tannehill, & Teeters, 1992) in which students were judged both on the weight lifted and on lifting technique. It has also been used for a dance season (Graves & Townsend, 2000) in which students learned and performed dances from the 1960s to 1990s (see Focus On Box 10.6). It has also been used for an elementary-school level bicycle-safety season in which students learned cycling skills and safety skills, a season that culminated with a synchronized team bicycle ride (Sinelnikov, Hastie, Cole, & Schneulle, 2005).

Sport education is now used widely in New Zealand, Australia, England, Korea, and Japan where reports from teachers are promising and enthusiastic. Sport education has also been investigated more thoroughly than most curriculum and instruction models. Two national reviews in Australia indicated that students preferred the sport-education model to their previous experiences in physical education. Of special interest was the finding that lower-skilled students and typically nonparticipating students gained the most from the sport-education experience (Carlson, 1996). Wallhead and O'Sullivan (2005) reviewed twenty-eight research studies and concluded that the model's emphasis on persistent team membership promoted student personal and social development

FOCUS ON	A Sport-Education Dance Fever Unit	**10.6**

Day 1	Introduce dance skills, explain dance fever competition, assign students to dance troupes.	Day 17	Dance fever competition, 1970s.
		Day 18	Dance fever competition, 1980s.
Days 2–7	Introduce dances of various eras; practice dance techniques; dance troupes assign members to various roles; introduce dance-judging techniques.	Day 19	Dance fever competition, 1980s.
		Day 20	Dance fever competition, 1990s.
		Day 21	Culminating event and awards.

Student roles: choreographer, fitness trainer, disc jockey, master of ceremonies, dance judge

Days 8–12	Dance troupes learn dances from 1950s to 1990s.
Days 13–15	Dance troupes choose and practice dances for competitions.
Day 16	Dance fever competition, 1950s–1960s.

Possible dances: Twist, Mash Potato, Funky Chicken, Swim, Disco Duck, Hustle, YMCA, Saturday Night Fever, Break Dancing, Moonwalk, Robotics, Cabbage Patch, Macarena, Electric Slide, Line, Men in Black

SOURCE: Based on Graves & Townsend, 2000.

through improving student responsibility, cooperation, and trust skills. Not only does sport education provide typically nonparticipating and lower-skilled students a more equitable learning environment, but results also show that learning opportunities for all students are increased both in quality and in quantity. Articles showing teachers how to use the model at various grade levels have become more available (Alexander, Taggart, & Luckman, 1998; Bell, 1998; Jones & Ward, 1998; Siedentop et al., 2004).

The Adventure-Education Approach

Two major trends together have led to the development of **adventure education** in physical education. First, the idea that adventure activities—particularly risk activities in the natural environment—have potential for education and character development has grown consistently in educational philosophy throughout the twentieth century and into the twenty-first. Second, public interest in outdoor recreation has increased substantially in the past several decades. Taken together, these two trends have made it possible for physical educators to conceptualize and

implement an adventure-education curriculum within physical education.

Adventure education often includes areas of interest such as wilderness sports and outdoor pursuits. Activities such as backpacking, kayaking, scuba diving, and caving take place in natural environments and often involve some risk. Adventure education includes not only these *natural* activities but also activities created for specific educational purposes. Thus, a high-ropes course or an initiatives course is designed and built so that students can experience the challenge inherent in the design. A *high-ropes course* is a series of obstacles that the student must overcome from 20 to 40 feet in the air, on ropes strung between trees in a wooded area. Although students are secured by a harness, there is no net underneath them as they climb, crawl, and jump through the ropes course. In *initiatives*, eight to twenty participants work together to solve an unusual task such as how to get all members of a group over a 12-foot-high wall.

There are two sets of goals within adventure-education programs. The first set of goals is to gain skill, to participate safely, and to gain utmost satisfaction from participation—for example, to ski well

Adventure education, such as a high-ropes course, provides exciting challenges.

enough to do it safely and to be excited about doing it again and again. These kinds of goals are traditional and are not unlike those in other physical-education curriculum models (Siedentop et al., 1986).

A second set of goals, however, has more to do with problem solving, self-concept, and personal growth. These goals are typically emphasized in the *adventure* portion of the program, in activities where obstacles are designed to produce some risk, with the assumption that the risk produces anxiety and stress for the participant. When the participant learns to deal with the stress and to overcome the anxiety to solve the problem created by the obstacle, then personal growth is assumed to occur. Because this is often done within the context of a *group*, the interactions among members of the group also become an important educational focus.

Adventure education can also be taught successfully in gym classes, using the grounds around the school, and at outdoor camps. Climbing walls are increasingly common in schools at all levels. Some schools develop spaces in the immediate school area that accommodate learning outdoor

skills. Beginning skills in orienteering, for example, can be taught using maps of school grounds. Many adventure activities can be modified to teach in regular school facilities. Indeed, some of the best adventure units in schools are taught within regular school facilities. Some schools develop outdoor adventure-education units at school to provide students with introduction to skills and activities, following it with an adventure-education trip to an outdoor facility. In this model, students spend extended periods of time together, sharing meals and staying overnight. The group fosters a sense of involvement and intimacy that is difficult to recreate in regular physical-education classes at the school site.

Physical educators interested in adventure education have a national resource in the nonprofit organization *Project Adventure*. This organization has published helpful curriculum materials to assist physical educators in implementing adventure education at elementary-, middle-, and high-school levels (www.pa.org). Project Adventure also is a source of much of the equipment needed to do adventure activities and provides workshops specific to different kinds of adventure activities. Many physical-education teachers have become Project Adventure–certified and have implemented semester-long courses in high schools, as well as integrating adventure education into elementary- and middle-school physical-education curricula.

The purposes of adventure education show both similarities to and differences from more traditional physical-education goals (Siedentop et al., 1986, p. 215):

1. To learn outdoor sports skills and enjoy the satisfaction of competence
2. To live within the limits of personal ability related to an activity and the environment
3. To find pleasure in accepting the challenge and risk of stressful physical activity
4. To learn mutual dependency of self and the natural world
5. To share this experience and learning with classmates and authority figures

Teaching within this model is obviously different from meeting classes at an appointed hour in a gymnasium. More time is needed. Instruction often takes place in small groups. Risk is involved, so safety becomes a paramount concern. Because travel and longer, more intimate time with students are often features of such programs, teachers must have skills for interacting with and guiding students in such situations. Also, particularly with wilderness sports, the teacher must have some substantial experience and skills in the activity being taught.

Teaching Games

In 1986 British physical educators Rod Thorpe, David Bunker, and Len Almond published a book entitled *Rethinking Games Teaching*. The book called into question the traditional approach to teaching games; that is, begin by teaching skills, and after skills were learned to a certain level, then teach how to use the skills in games. They call their approach "teaching games for understanding" (TGFU) and argue that students first have to understand the

tactical problems posed by games in order to see how the skills should be used. TGFU (sometimes also referred to as the "games sense approach") has now become a prominent international movement among physical educators who subscribe to this point of view and want to learn more about how to implement it in elementary-, middle-, and high-school physical education. Many physical-education teachers have suffered through the frustration of teaching a sport unit by beginning with isolated skill drills with some modicum of success shown by students, only to see them unable to use the skill appropriately in even a modified-game environment.

This movement is as much about pedagogy as it is about curriculum, but it has given a strong boost to those physical educators who still see games and sports as fundamental parts of the physical-education curriculum. In America it is common to hear this approach described as a "tactical games approach" to teaching sport skills (Griffin, Mitchell, & Oslin, 1997). A valuable addition to this movement toward better teaching of sports and games came in 2001 with the publication of Australian Alan Launder's book entitled *Play Practice: The Games Approach to Teaching and Coaching*. In this book, Launder uses the term *technique* as a substitute for what traditionally had been called a *skill*; that is, passing in volleyball, jump shooting in basketball, and fielding ground balls in softball are techniques. Launder argues that techniques + tactics = skill. He offers a number of examples of how teachers could develop techniques and tactics together using small-sided and tactically simplified minigames, then gradually increasing the complexity of the game as student techniques and tactical understandings improved—what he calls the development of "game sense."

What the teaching games movement has achieved is a much stronger sense of how to organize games units for a physical-education curriculum. Small-sided games with simple rules in smaller spaces with modified rules are used to teach both techniques and tactics so that students understand how the nature of the tactical situation determines what techniques are needed to be successful.

It should be noted that in many parts of the world, the teaching games movement, originally brought forward in physical education, has begun to be adopted by national sport organizations as the preferred approach to use in developmental programs in junior sport. The Australian Sports Commission, for example, has developed a series of game sense–coaching resources for junior sport.

The Eclectic Curriculum

Most school districts require that a curriculum be developed for each subject matter taught in the district. For physical education, it is most common that the district curriculum begins with the NASPE standards and then lists all the activities that can be taught in the district. In many, if not most districts, the list of activities taught in physical education is very large because of the liability issues that would come forward if a physical-education teacher was using an activity that was not on the approved list and a student was injured during class, leaving the teacher liable. Likewise, the instructional strategies used by physical-education teachers within a school district might vary widely because specific requirements for instructional strategies are typically not included in district requirements. Traditionally, American teachers have been free to choose the instructional strategies that they use in their classes. Over the past decade or so, this tradition has begun to change somewhat as concerns over the low reading scores of young children have led to the development of K–3 reading curriculum and instruction models that are typically adopted at the district level; that is, all K–3 teachers in a district are trained to teach reading through a particular approach to the reading curriculum and using particular instructional strategies suggested by the curriculum developers. Recent Texas legislation required all school districts to adopt one of four state-approved health- and physical-education curriculum models for elementary schools, each of which includes suggestions for instructional practices.

Still, in most school districts the choice of activities and the instructional strategies used to teach those activities are left to the individual physical-education teachers. Many of these programs still reflect the multiactivity model that has been historically prominent in America—that is, short activity units with modest amounts of instruction. In some states—Florida for example—a one-semester course on health and fitness is required, typically in the ninth grade. These courses typically involve both classroom instruction and fitness activities in the gymnasium or fitness center. It should also be noted that it is common that students who are involved in school sport, cheerleading, or drill teams are exempted from the fitness-course requirement.

The differences between the models described in this chapter and the multiactivity approach are substantial. Teachers can't do skill themes, sport education, health-related physical education, adventure education, or the personal and social responsibility model without devoting substantial time to the content of the model and without using the pedagogical approach recommended by the model. Offering a large variety of activities in a program does not, in and of itself, ensure a good program; indeed, the multiactivity approach typically ensures that students will be unlikely to develop sufficient skill in the activity to pursue it outside of the class.

What Is the Subject Matter of Physical Education?

This chapter began with the assertion that it is more difficult to define *physical education* than to define either *sport* or *fitness*. The review of curricular options shows how valid that assertion is in contemporary physical education. Within these various curricula, one might see small children moving creatively to a poem, ninth-graders rappelling down the outside wall of their gymnasium, fifth-graders working hard as members of a soccer team engaged in a championship match, tenth-graders working out personal-fitness programs as part of a self-control exercise, and third-graders using different implements to hit different kinds of objects as part of a movement-education lesson on striking.

A stranger, viewing all such scenes and asking what is going on, might be told, "This is physical education!" If this stranger is middle-aged and has experienced a traditional form of physical education, it is easy to understand why she might ask, "What's going on?" It is also easy to see why the answer—"This is physical education!"—might be surprising: The activities look so different from the traditional stereotype of "fizz-ed."

Each curriculum model has a different view of the subject matter of physical education. What *is* physical education? Is it education in sport? Is it fitness education? Is it social development? Is it development through risk and adventure? Is it movement? Instead, is it all these things—and maybe more? A subject matter so loosely defined that it excludes very little is inevitably going to include activities that are hardly useful or defensible by any criteria. The question then becomes "If physical education encompasses everything, can it ever stand for something specific and important?" Before answering that question, I turn to two contemporary aspects of physical education: educating students with disabilities and responding to current issues such as state requirements.

Physical Education for Students With Disabilities

The roots of what we now refer to as adapted physical education go back to the 1920s when the parents of children who had been paralyzed in the 1915–1917 polio epidemic were ready to begin the children's public schooling (Sherrill, 2004). These children suffered from structural defects of the spine and lower extremities that were treated with corrective exercises—thus was *corrective physical education* born. The main foci of this new field were strength, balance, and flexibility exercises to correct postural and structural defects and medical/remedial exercises to relieve health problems.

The next stage of development began during and shortly after World War II when thousands of service personnel needed both rehabilitation from injuries and special activity programming through which they could enjoy leisure. The field grew slowly and began to use the term *adapted physical education* to describe the work done primarily in schools. In the early 1960s, the work of the Kennedy and Shriver families provided new impetus to expand the field to include sports and recreation, which eventually led to creation of the *Special Olympics* and the field took on a broader agenda as *adapted physical activity* (Stein, 2004). The information in Chapter 5 shows clearly the enormous growth of sports and physical activity for persons with disabilities.

The field continued to grow and captured the increasing attention of federal legislators, culminating in an extraordinary series of federal laws (DePauw, 1996):

- 1968 PL 90-170, Elimination of Architectural Barriers Act
- 1973 PL 93-112, the Rehabilitation Act, prohibiting discrimination on the basis of disability
- 1975 PL 94-142, Education of All Handicapped Children Act, which requires a free and appropriate education for all children and youths with disabilities, including specifically physical education
- 1978 PL 95-606, Amateur Sports Act, which recognizes athletes with disabilities as part of the U.S. Olympic movement
- 1990 PL 101-476, Individuals with Disabilities Education Act (IDEA), extending provisions to young children and incorporating provisions of previous laws
- 1990 Americans With Disabilities Act, which extended the broad protection of the Civil Rights Act of 1964 to people with disabilities

The key legislation that catapulted adapted physical education into a new era was **Public Law 94-142** simply because it singled out physical education and intramurals as important school activities and required that they be made available to students with special needs. A key provision of PL 94-142 was the goal of placing students in the *least restrictive*

Elite athletes come in all forms.

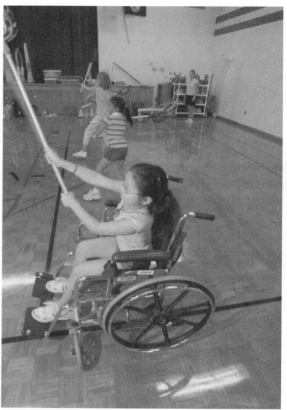

Children with disabilities can take full part in physical-education classes.

environment (LRE) to meet their needs and making every effort to ensure that they eventually become *mainstreamed* into regular classrooms that "qualify" as the LRE. This led to the movement most frequently referred to as **inclusion** with its emphasis on adapted physical education not being strictly a placement but a system of services with sufficient supports to enable most students to receive their education as part of the regular classroom population (Sherrill, 2004). Inclusion represents an alternative philosophy to LRE, with the goal that all students with disabilities should be in regular classrooms. It needs to be pointed out, though, that LRE is the law. Although there are many arguments, pro and con,

about inclusion, proponents tend to rest their case on the ethical position that any segregation of students with disabilities is inherently unequal. The key provisions of PL 94-142 were incorporated into the IDEA legislation, which was reauthorized in 2004.

The field of adapted physical education encompasses three main types of programs: adapted, corrective, and developmental (Jansma & French, 1994). An *adapted program* focuses on the modification of regular activities to enable individuals with disabilities to participate safely and successfully. A *corrective program* focuses on the rehabilitation of functional postural and body-mechanics deficiencies. A *developmental program* focuses on basic fitness and motor-skill training to raise students' skills and abilities to the point where they can participate with peers.

Adapted physical activity is the broad label used throughout the world to describe a profession, a scholarly, interdisciplinary field of study, and the delivery of services to persons with disabilities so as to facilitate their lifelong active, healthy living (Sherrill, 2004). Within that field, adapted physical education (APE) has become a robust area of teacher preparation, research and scholarship, and the delivery of services. The Adapted Physical Activity Council is part of the new American Association for Physical Activity and Recreation of AAHPERD. The *Adapted Physical Activity Quarterly* is the primary research journal for the field, publishing articles that continue to advance our understanding of the issues faced by those who deliver services to persons with disabilities and enabling APA practitioners to improve those services. Many universities now have master's-degree and/or doctoral-degree programs to prepare future APA specialists.

State Requirements for Physical Education

There is no federal law that requires physical education to be taught in schools. States vary widely in the degree to which they mandate physical education as part of the state education system (NASPE, Fall 2001). States typically set *minimum standards* for physical education, but individual school districts interpret those standards somewhat differently and of course can exceed them if they so desire and have the resources to do so. Some states delegate authority for what is taught in schools to the local school districts.

The objectives for physical education in the federal policy described in *Healthy People 2010* (U.S. Department of Health and Human Services, 2000) include the following:

- Increase the proportion of the nation's public and private schools that require daily physical education.

- Increase the proportion of adolescents who participate in daily school physical education.
- Increase the proportion of adolescents who spend at least 50 percent of school physical-education class being physically active.

A review of state requirements for physical education shows substantial variation (NASPE, 2006). Thirty-five states mandate elementary-school physical education, thirty-three states mandate middle-school physical education, and forty-two states mandate high-school physical education. High-school requirements range from seven semesters in Illinois to no specific credit requirement in Oklahoma. The median high-school requirement is two semesters. Sixteen states allow for exemptions to physical education (for example, band, ROTC, school sports). Nearly all states have adopted NASPE standards. Thirty-eight states have a physical-education coordinator in the State Department of Education. Twenty-two states require that physical-education grades be reported to parents. Fifteen states require some form of assessment in physical education.

The recent national concern about child/youth overweight and obesity has resulted in many states increasing their requirements for physical education. California was the first state to receive an A in the University of Baltimore's yearly review of state legislation to stem the childhood obesity epidemic (Siedentop, 2007). California law now requires a minimum of 200 minutes of physical education for every 10 school days in grades 1–6 and a minimum of 400 minutes of physical education for every 10 school days in grades 7–12. The new legislation also required that physical education must be taught by a credentialed physical-education teacher. Each school district must administer a physical-fitness test annually to all students in grades 5, 7, and 9 during the months of February to May. Student involvement in sports, band, ROTC, drill teams, and the like cannot be substituted for meeting the physical-education requirement. The state budget for 2006 included $40 million to hire more physical-education teachers.

Now, here is the rub! California, like most states, has little oversight and accountability for

An accessible environment is important.

school districts to enforce the physical-education requirements. A recent study sponsored by the California Endowment (2008) showed that 48 percent of elementary schools and 24 percent of middle and high schools were noncompliant with the physical education–minutes requirements. Class sizes, especially in urban schools, are so large (for example, 70 students per class) that no real outcomes can be expected. Many districts have chosen to allow for substitutions for the high-school physical-education requirement. Pass rates for the FITNESSGRAM fitness tests are low. Fewer than 30 percent of students meet all six health-related fitness standards in grades 5, 7, and 9. The pass rate for African American and Latino students is well below that of white students. None of this is intended to demean the state of California where state legislators have successfully passed important legislation. What is true for California is true for most states: There is very little oversight and accountability at the state level for districts to comply with whatever physical-education requirements are demanded by state law.

South Carolina has established itself as a national leader in physical education by adopting state standards and putting into practice the nation's first state assessment system for outcomes in physical education (Rink & Mitchell, 2003). Recent school wellness legislation in South Carolina requires that students in grades K–5 complete an average of 150 minutes per week in physical education and physical activity (60 minutes in physical education and 90 minutes in physical activity) with a student-to-teacher ratio of no more than 28:1 (Siedentop, 2007). All high-school students are required to complete 2 credits of health and fitness courses. The legislation also requires the phase-in of student-to-certified-physical-education-teacher ratios so that in 2008 the ratio for elementary schools is 500:1, which means that elementary schools with more than 500 students will have to employ more than one physical education teacher. Schools in South Carolina are required to report yearly the number of minutes in physical education and the minutes of additional physical activity weekly. These measures are all designed to hold districts accountable for fulfilling the requirements of the legislation.

Ample evidence shows that students who engage in regular physical activity of appropriate intensity and duration are better students. More physically active students earn better grades and achieve higher test scores. Physically active students are also more attentive and have enhanced concentration (California Endowment, 2008). Aerobic activity increases blood flow to the brain and speeds recall and reasoning skills. There is increasing evidence that for elementary-school students physical-activity sessions prior to school and physical-activity breaks during school increase attention and performance. There is also evidence that No Child Left Behind has reduced the amount of time spent in physical education. It is important that the physical-education leadership at state and district levels work to develop state rules that hold districts accountable for issues such as class size and number of minutes in physical education. The evidence is clear that without state-level accountability, state regulations can be routinely ignored at the district level.

DOES PHYSICAL EDUCATION HAVE A CENTRAL MEANING?

What does physical education mean? How should the field's content be defined? Is it physical activity? Is it fitness? Is it sport? Is it skill? Is it social development? Is it risk and adventure? Is it all those things together? What follows are scenes that can be seen in physical education today:

- Young children move to the sounds of a drum, each carrying a scarf. They change directions and change the level of their bodies as they move. The teacher, holding the drum, encourages them, from time to time or gives them new directions in the form of a problem question but does not tell them what to do.

- A coed group of ninth-graders works in a well-equipped Nautilus training room. They work in pairs, each carrying a chart on a clipboard. The teacher moves about, interacting with each pair, but provides no group cues or directions. Students move from machine to machine periodically.

- A group of fifty-five seventh-graders is receiving instruction from a teacher. The students are scattered in groups of four or five around a large gymnasium. Each group has a ball. The teacher gives instructions to the group and then signals for the group to begin practice. During practice, the teacher moves about, mostly watching to see that things are going smoothly. After several minutes, the teacher signals for attention, gives some feedback on what she has seen, and then gives new instructions for a slightly different task.

- Fifth-graders enter the gym and move into one of six areas to begin a group practice on soccer warm-up drills. At a signal, the groups form into teams. One member of each group leaves to pick up materials while two other members put on referee shirts. Shortly, three small-sided soccer games begin, with students acting as referees and coaches. On the gym wall, there is a soccer-season schedule and the standings for this soccer league. After 5 minutes, the game ends; within 3 minutes, a new game has begun, involving similar teams but made up of different children.

- Twenty-four helmet-wearing seventh-graders have harnesses around their waists. They stand beneath a clearing in a woods and look up to see a ropes course 40 feet above their heads, with different configurations of wood and rope at different places on the course. Their teacher is giving them instructions on belaying techniques, safety, and appropriate procedures for moving through the ropes course.

- A teacher sits with a group of ninth- and tenth-graders at the start of a lesson, describing what will be done that day. The teacher solicits comments on the students' feelings about their progress, talking about individual growth and responsibility. There is talk about levels, and students learn that today is a fitness day when they will work on their individually developed programs.

- A group of eleventh-graders have toured community health and fitness facilities as part of their assignment in physical education. They also have monitored their own activity and nutritional intake for 6 weeks. Based on their own data and what is available in the community, they each plan a comprehensive health-fitness plan for themselves, which they can easily do within their own community. They include their plans in a portfolio that they are building for evaluating their eleventh-grade physical-education experience.

- Twenty-four ninth-graders enter the gym. The teacher quickly organizes them into coed teams, and two basketball games start immediately. Each team has one substitute. The games begin and it is clear that there is little offensive or defensive strategy. Girls seldom touch the ball as boys dominate the action. The teacher sits in a chair working on some plans and occasionally monitoring the class action. Skilled players dominate and most girls and a few boys move up and down the floor but seldom pass or shoot.

All these scenes are part of today's physical education. You will recognize in these scenes the various models reviewed in this chapter, except for one that is! Does the last scene remind you of your physical education? As you look at the other scenes, can you recognize a common theme among them? Is there a common meaning that can be attributed to each of the scenes? Is it easy to see that the pedagogy of the first seven themes is different from the eighth scene?

When you think about physical education, you must think about both content and pedagogy. Whatever your goals for students may be, you will not accomplish them without blending content and pedagogy in ways that help you achieve your goals. A key to developing that capacity is to always think: What is it that *these* students need in terms of content, and how can I best deliver it to *them* (pedagogy) so that they will not only improve but also enjoy what they are learning? Teaching is

always specific to the students being taught, what their needs are, and the context in which you teach them.

SUMMARY

1. No single definition of *physical education* has gained widespread acceptance in contemporary professional circles.

2. Education through the physical was the dominant curricular philosophy for the first half of the twentieth century.

3. The fourfold objectives of physical education—physical development, motor development, mental development, and social development—dominated thinking in physical education for most of the twentieth century.

4. The multiactivity curriculum and the associated unit model for organizing activities became the standard for planning in physical education.

5. The skill-themes model is the most appropriate curriculum-instruction model for grades K–3.

6. Health-related physical education has developed as a response to public health concerns.

7. The academic-integration approach focuses on the emerging knowledge base in the subdisciplines of physical education. It has gained strength recently because of the emphasis on academic excellence in schools.

8. The personal and social responsibility model has emerged as a distinctive curricular option with a focused purpose.

9. The sport-education model is an inclusive approach to sport; it emphasizes appropriate competition and learning about multiple roles within sport.

10. Adventure education uses risk and challenge to develop personal and social skills through a variety of natural and contrived activities.

11. Most physical-education programs are conceptualized as an eclectic model that combines the approaches described in this chapter.

12. State requirements for physical education differ markedly and heavily influence physical-education programs in schools.

13. Adapted physical education has developed into a specialized area, which now focuses on inclusion.

14. It is still not clear what the central focus of physical education is.

DISCUSSION QUESTIONS

1. To what extent was your school program rooted in the education-through-the-physical philosophy? What were its main features?

2. Is the multiactivity approach useful? Can any real objectives be accomplished with short-term units? Is the variety engendered by this approach appropriate?

3. Which of the newer curriculum models most appeals to you? Which least appeals to you?

4. What are the requirements for physical education in your state? Did your school's program exceed them?

5. What was physical education like in your high school? Were the classes coed? Did boys and girls like or dislike it equally?

6. What kind of physical-education experience would adolescents have to have in order to influence their lifestyle choices about physical activity and health?

7. What do you believe should be the central focus of physical education at elementary-school, middle-school, and high-school levels? Can you develop a definition of physical education that accurately reflects that perspective?

CHAPTER 11

Physical-Education Programs and Professions

Whereas a high quality daily physical education for all children in kindergarten through grade 12 is an essential part of a comprehensive education: Now, therefore, be it resolved by the House of Representatives (the Senate concurring), that the Congress encourages State and local governments and local education agencies to provide high quality daily physical education programs for all children in kindergarten through grade 12.

House Concurrent Resolution 97, 100th Congress

LEARNING OBJECTIVES

- To discuss the narrow and broad views of physical education

- To discuss the effects of and prospects for high-quality, daily physical education

- To describe exemplary programs for a variety of curricular models

- To discuss the roles played by a physical educator

- To describe various certification models

- To describe the NASPE national standards for beginning teachers

- To describe how certification for adapted physical education is achieved

Physical education is best known as a subject offered in schools. Most people who prepare to become physical-education teachers complete a curriculum that culminates with not only a degree but also a teaching certificate. Does physical education take place *only* in schools? Here again, as we indicated at the beginning of Chapter 10, a problem of definition arises. If physical education is limited, *by definition*, to activities that occur in schools, then how do we describe programs that look similar to physical education in schools but are conducted in other places? All the curriculum models described in Chapter 10 could easily be implemented in places other than schools.

Adventure education is often done in summer camps and by private agencies such as Outward Bound. Fitness programs are conducted in health centers, spas, and family centers such as the YMCA and the YWCA. Children and youths learn and participate in sport (that is, they become *educated* in sport) in community programs. Movement skills

can be learned in preschools, gymnastic academies, and dance studios. Sport and fitness programs
with strong social-development goals can be found in
church camps, Police Athletic League programs, and
family centers such as a Jewish Community Center.
Are these all physical education?

How you answer that question will reflect how
narrow or broad your concept of physical
education is and how it affects the lives of children and youths. Most professionals tend to take
the broader rather than the narrower perspective.
Certainly, if you are serious about the notion of a
lifespan physical education—as advocated in
Chapter 1—then the broader perspective is
necessary.

Obviously, school physical education is important. School is still the one institution in our culture
that touches the lives of virtually all children and
youths. It is the institution to which we have dele-
gated a primary responsibility for passing on the
best of our culture and for trying constantly to
improve the culture. You do not have to be rich to
go to school, nor do you have to have special talents
to take part in the school curriculum. If the goal
of physical education for all—another position
advocated in Chapter 1—is ever realized, then the
school will have played the most important role in
achieving it.

The U.S. Congress declared its support for high-
quality, daily physical education in the 1987 Concurrent Resolution, a summary of which is shown on
the title page of this chapter. Can you imagine the
impact of such an idea? If every boy and girl, from
kindergarten through grade 12, received a high-
quality 30-minute daily physical-education lesson,
they would all accumulate nearly 1,000 hours of
quality physical education during their school years.
Many good outcomes could be accomplished if that
were a common commitment by local school districts. Is it really too much to ask? Not if you consider that a boy or girl who participates for 4 years
on a high-school basketball team would accumulate
more than 1,000 hours of practice, with a lower
student–teacher (coach) ratio, better equipment,
and much greater access to facilities!

On January 18, 2005, a headline for an Associated
Press story read, "Health Experts Say Schools Failing
Phys Ed." The article was critical of how physical education was taught (condemning the "throw out the
ball" approach) and also was critical of states and
school districts for not requiring more physical education and supporting better teaching. Indeed, in
2005, physical education was frequently addressed in
all media outlets, simply because of the startling data
about childhood and youth overweight and obesity
(see Chapters 1 and 7). The major solution to the
"obesity epidemic" is to provide more and better
physical activity for children and youths. All federal
guidelines specifically support more and better physical education, as well as after-school and community
physical-activity programs. Both the government
and our professional organizations have provided
specific guidelines about the duration, frequency,
and intensity of activity needed to secure the health
benefit. Yet only 8 percent of elementary schools, 6.4
percent of middle schools, and 5.8 percent of high
schools provide daily physical education or its equivalent for the entire school year in all grades in the
school (www.cdc.gov/nccdphp/dash/shpps/factsheets/
fs00_pe.htm). As you learn about exemplary programs in this chapter, keep in mind that physical education can be good, even in schools where facilities
are modest and time is less than adequate, but for
physical education to live up to its potential, the *state*
and the *school districts* must strengthen requirements for physical education and hold districts and
schools accountable for meeting those requirements.

EXEMPLARY PHYSICAL-EDUCATION PROGRAMS

As the next chapter shows, there are substantial
problems in contemporary physical education. In
this chapter, however, we focus on programs that
accomplish their goals. The programs described
are real, and each typically represents one or
several of the physical-education models described
in Chapter 10.

A Comprehensive Health-Related Elementary-School Model

Health-related physical education has developed in the wake of evidence strongly supportive of the health benefits of a physically active lifestyle in a time when health costs to the nation have become a major political issue. Virgilio (1996) has described a comprehensive healthy-lifestyles elementary-school program that grew from his work in developing the national Heart Smart fitness program (Virgilio & Berenson, 1988). A comprehensive model recognizes that children are unlikely to get sufficient physical activity in the time allotted to physical education in the elementary-school curriculum. The emphasis in this model is placed "on learning motor skills and participating in sport to stay physically active and develop lifelong movement skills" (Virgilio, 1996, p. 4). This physical-education program emphasizes learning lifelong skills and participating in high amounts of regular physical activity, utilizing many of the materials and programs from the Heart Smart program. According to this model, children develop their own personalized fitness portfolio, which they carry with them through their elementary-school years.

In addition, the model stresses a strong parent-education component, using newsletters, parent seminars, progress reports, parent–teacher conferences, PTA demonstrations, and a parent resource room. The progress reports include summaries of the child's fitness progress, physical-activity levels, and recommended areas for improvement. The parent resource room contains videos, computer software, cookbooks, cassettes, and educational games that parents can check out and use at home with their children. The model also involves parents in extending and improving participation in physical activity at school in nonattached time. Parents serve as aides in classes, monitor playground activity, help build or repair equipment, and participate in a committee that serves as an advocacy group for the goals of the program.

A home-based activity program is also a component of the model. Families are encouraged to

Classes that are well organized and well managed result in more activity.

commit to a family contract to exercise together, using a specific, family-developed schedule. Parents assist children in their fitness homework—for example, developing a fitness trail through their neighborhood and using it regularly. Parents are also encouraged to develop summer activity packets, which include activity plans, reading lists, games, and opportunities in the community. The nutrition component of the program is also extended to the home through the parent newsletter and through family activities designed to improve the nutritional content of family meals.

Classroom teachers include health, nutrition, and cardiovascular fitness in the classroom curricula. They are also asked to ensure that the children in their classes get at least 30 minutes per week of physical activity, excluding physical education and recess time. The school cafeteria is a component of the program. The parent committee meets with the school-lunch staff to ensure that school meals have reduced sodium, fat, and sugar levels. Cafeterias are decorated to promote healthy choices in food selection. If there is a school snack service, the service is encouraged to stock relatively healthy snack foods.

The physical-education teacher, in conjunction with the parent committee, seeks to develop links with community agencies that offer physical-activity programs for children. Efforts are made to get children into after-school activity programs or, if none exist in the community, to develop such a program at the school site. Special projects such as youth sport fairs and community health fairs are developed. The entire effort is designed to affect lifestyle choices, and the total environment of the child—school, home, and community—is enlisted in that effort

A High-School Healthy-Lifestyles Program

The Lake Park High School physical-education program—winner of the Blue Ribbon Award from the Illinois Association for Health, Physical Education, Recreation, and Dance—aims to "aid students in achieving their fullest potential through the acquisition of knowledge and skills necessary to attain healthy levels of well-being and to maintain active lifestyles throughout the lifespan." Students in the ninth and tenth grades take physical education one semester and health education for one semester. The ninth-grade physical-education program focuses on the knowledge and skills necessary for the maintenance and/or improvement of health-related fitness. All students learn about their own levels of fitness and, with the help of their teachers, plan for improvement or maintenance programs. They also learn to use technology to learn about and monitor different components of fitness. Facilities for the East Campus and West Campus include a life laboratory, weight room, cardio-fitness center, dance room, and strength-training center as well as gymnasiums. Other ninth-grade units are fitness basics, jump rope, volleyball, weight training, net games, and aerobic games.

The tenth-grade program starts with an introduction to fitness unit that includes an orientation to the Life Lab, health-related fitness components, skill-related fitness components, warm-up and cool-down procedures, and heart-rate targeting using heart-rate monitors. The tenth grade program starts with a fitness evaluation and review of healthy-lifestyles concepts, followed by units in tennis, badminton, weight training, aerobics, and volleyball.

In the eleventh and twelfth grades, students choose semester-long activities that include team activities, cross-training and aerobic wellness, strength and conditioning, introduction to dance arts, strength training, and personal wellness: nutrition and exercise. The program also offers a Leadership Training Fitness certification course and a Leadership Training Coaching certification course.

This program model is highly consistent with the current emphasis in physical education on preparing students to take active control of their health and physical activity as they move into adulthood. It is also exemplary in combining a basic program for all students in the ninth and tenth grades but allowing students a choice of activities in the eleventh and twelfth grades. If we want high-school students to begin to take responsibility for healthy lifestyles, we should provide programs that allow them some choice in what they pursue. This is typically achieved through providing students elective choices of courses within the requirement that they take physical education each of the 4 years in high school.

An Upper-Elementary-School Sport-Education Program

The upper-grades curriculum at Olde Sawmill Elementary School is based on the sport-education model described in Chapter 10 (Darnell, 1994). In grades 4–6, the curriculum is sport oriented. Students are placed on teams at the start of the school year and remain with their teams throughout the year as they work for points toward an all-sport award. Students select a name for the team and team colors. Captains and assistants are assigned and selected for each new sport season. A schedule of competition is arranged for each season.

Each day that the students have physical education, they do everything as members of their team. When they enter the gym, they have an assigned space where team members do their warm-ups together, led by their team captain. A period of skill practice follows, with captains again leading their teams through the assigned drills. As the season progresses, less time is allocated for team skill practice and more time is allocated for games.

In each sport season, students are players, coaches, referees, or scorekeepers. Simple records are kept for each game performance. Short-duration, small-sided games are used for team sport competition. Teams can earn points toward an overall championship in a number of ways, including winning games, practicing as a team at recess, behaving as good sportspersons, passing the knowledge tests, and exhibiting leadership.

In the soccer season, each class typically has three or four teams. Captains lead teams during the class and administer schedules and assignments between class sessions. The soccer season begins with a 2 v 2 (two players versus two players) round-robin competition in which games last 4 minutes. Captains must assign players from their team for each of the 2 v 2 games. Students not playing at any given time are involved as either referees or scorekeepers. Captains must have all these assignments completed and written out before the class begins.

After the 2 v 2 round-robin competition is completed, a 4 v 4 round-robin competition begins. Here the game is more complex, requiring more teamwork and careful execution of skills. Again, captains make all assignments, and all students are involved in some capacity during each game. At the end of the soccer season, an overall soccer champion is named for each class, based on points accumulated during game and practice time, as well as by good sportspersonship. At the end of the season, intramural time is used for interclass games at the same grade level.

The gymnastic season is done differently but still teaches gymnastics primarily as a competitive sport. The first part of the season focuses on compulsory competition, in which each team member must learn and perform a group of gymnastic skills. Students warm up and practice each day as a team, with captains not only leading during class but also handling administrative duties between classes. As part of learning the skills, students are also taught how to judge the performance of those skills. The compulsory competition is a routine involving the activities

being practiced. Students choose routines at three levels of difficulty. They then make up their own routine, following the guidelines for their level of difficulty.

Compulsory competition takes place over a number of class sessions, with students acting as judges. Students earn points, based on performance within their own level of difficulty. The team championship is determined by total points won in competition and for practicing.

An optional competition follows the compulsory part of the season. Now students choose one event in which to practice and compete. Each day there is an opportunity to practice and take part in at least one optional competition. Again, coaches have administered the assignment of students to events and have determined when each will compete. All individual performances count toward a team total. Students act as judges for the optional performances also. At the end of the gymnastic season, interclass competitions are arranged during intramural time. At the end of the season, an overall champion is determined, individual awards are presented for each event, and awards for sportspersonship and coaching are also presented.

By the end of a school year, all students will have learned to be a coach, a referee, a judge, a scorekeeper, and a record keeper. They no doubt will have been on some teams that lost, on some that won, and on some that finished toward the middle. They will have learned and experienced what makes any sport a sport and how the sport can be enjoyed from various perspectives.

A Districtwide Healthy-Lifestyles Curriculum

The 18,000 students in the Spokane School District experience a K–10 physical education program that is more like being a member of a health club than being in a traditional physical-education class (www.rwjf.org). Students both study a healthy-lifestyles curriculum and live it in their classes. Students take part in age-appropriate noncompetitive games and activities that have specific endurance and strength features. Students rotate through these games and activities, through fitness and activity stations, and through lessons on fitness and health. As in many current approaches, technology in the form of heart monitors, pedometers, and computer tracking of progress contribute to student interest and serve as a form of accountability. Students quickly learn what activities are appropriate for developing and sustaining muscular strength and endurance, cardiovascular capacity, flexibility, and body composition. Pop music can be heard in many classes, contributing to an atmosphere quite different from the "drills and skills" approach to physical education.

A Middle School Combining the Personal and Social Responsibility Model With Activities

The Marston Middle School in San Diego has been selected as a California Middle School Demonstration Program in Physical Education. The physical-education program has developed a variation of the personal and social responsibility model (PSRM) (see page 239) that is used in conjunction with an activity program that builds across the sixth- to eighth-grade years. In each year, the first 6 weeks emphasize responsibility; the second 6 weeks, accepting personal differences; the third 6 weeks, respect; the fourth 6 weeks, caring; the fifth 6 weeks, trust; and the sixth 6 weeks showing appreciation.

The theme for the sixth-grade activities is "working cooperatively to achieve a common goal" and includes orienteering, pretesting in the five components of fitness, games from around the world, tumbling, dance and rhythms, an introduction to track and field, and fitness posttesting. The theme for the seventh grade is "meeting challenges and making decisions." The activity schedule includes cooperative activities, fitness pretesting, lacrosse, combatives, volley tennis, fitness lab orientation, fitness training, fitness concepts, fitness

testing, track and field, dance, and swimming. The instructional theme for the eighth grade is "working as a team to solve problems." Activities include cooperative games, fitness pretesting, dance, track and field, strength and conditioning, soccer, leisure activities, flag football, lacrosse, and fitness posttesting.

As you can see, several activities, such as track and field, are repeated in each of the 3 years, thus allowing students to gradually build their skills and understandings of an activity. Fitness pre- and posttesting occurs each year with fitness activities of various kinds included in each year's activity program. The students are continuously confronted with situations where the yearly theme (for example, working cooperatively to achieve a common goal in the sixth grade) is incorporated with the PSRM goals for each of the 6-week sections of the year. Thus, in the fourth 6-week period of the sixth grade, students are working cooperatively to achieve the common goal of caring.

The three female and three male physical-education teachers at Marston Middle School have themselves worked to build a shared commitment to these curricular and instructional approaches. Their work has been rewarded with California's Physical Education and Health Education Exemplary School Award.

An Elementary-School Adventure Program

A portion of the physical-education curriculum at the Worthington Hills Elementary School focuses on adventure activities (Moore, 1986). Students learn sports and engage in fitness activities, just as many other children in elementary-school physical-education programs do, but what makes this program special is the manner in which risk, adventure, and cooperation are woven into the curriculum throughout the school year.

The regular activity program includes elements of adventure and cooperation throughout the year. For example, team sports are always introduced initially through cooperative games—for example, in volleyball, two teams work together to try to keep the ball in play. Skill instruction and practice for activities such as archery and orienteering are also done as part of the regular school curriculum.

For several weeks during the school year, special adventure activities become the focus of the curriculum. Climbing and rappelling are two skills learned by all students. The gymnasium contains three indoor climbing walls: a horizontal climbing course that traverses 60 feet along one wall and two vertical climbing courses of differing levels of difficulty. There are also several rappelling stations throughout the gymnasium. Each course has been attractively decorated, with the help of the art teacher, to look like a mountainous challenge. Climbing and rappelling are technical skills that have a strong element of perceived risk and challenge. (The tasks are in fact very low in actual risk when done properly.) Students are encouraged to extend themselves, improve their skills, and take new risks. Students reaching the top of one vertical course—where a snowy peak has been painted—can sign their names. At the top of another course, they can honk a horn while touching the golden egg depicted at the top of the beanstalk course.

Students get more opportunity to practice those and other adventure skills in the intramurals program. A final component of the adventure curriculum is a series of field trips. Sixth-graders go on a 3-day camping trip in which the adventure curriculum learned indoors is extended to natural settings. In addition, there are several 1-day trips to a nearby adventure center where students participate in a high-ropes course, group-initiatives courses, field archery, and orienteering, thus extending to a wooded, natural setting the skills learned originally at the school.

The goals and objectives of the adventure program described here have much in common with those of the social-development program described earlier. Both are concerned primarily with personal growth, cooperation, sharing, and responsibility. They differ primarily in the means through which those goals are achieved.

A High-School Fitness Emphasis

At Needham High School, students are required to complete sixteen quarters of physical education across their 4-year program (Westcott, 1992). The program's emphasis is on physical fitness from a personal perspective involving individual goals and lifestyle outcomes. The core of the program is a six-quarter series of wellness courses, ranging from fundamentals of fitness to nutrition to stress management. These courses involve extensive classroom work as well as activity involvement.

Needham students are also required to choose three fitness courses from a range of activity options, including aerobics, cross-training, fitness games, stretching, and weight training. The third set of requirements is in the lifetime sport category, again with an option to choose from a variety of offerings including archery, badminton, golf, jazz dance, tennis, and volleyball. The final four quarters of required physical education may be chosen from any of the three main areas: wellness, fitness, and lifetime sports.

All 1,000+ students at Needham High School get an individual fitness evaluation each year, focusing on the health-fitness factors of cardiovascular endurance, muscular endurance, muscular strength, flexibility, and body composition. Students receive a cumulative computer printout of their evaluation with specific information related to strengths and weaknesses.

The physical-education staff at Needham has worked diligently over a period of years to write grants to obtain the necessary activity equipment, testing equipment, and educational materials to run this exemplary program. Students leave the program knowing a great deal about fitness and their own strengths and weaknesses related to fitness. They also have had an excellent opportunity to develop lifestyle skills and commitments that will lead to a long-term commitment to personal health fitness.

A Research-Based National Elementary-School Program

Project SPARK (Sports, Play, and Active Recreation for Kids) originated as a 5-year national research study funded by the National Institutes of Health. Following the research phase, the program focused on dissemination through a nonprofit organization housed at San Diego State University (www.foundation.sdsu.edu/projects/spark/index). SPARK offers elementary-school physical-education curricula, staff development, and follow-up support to school districts, elementary-school physical-education specialist teachers, and classroom teachers nationwide. SPARK was validated by the National Diffusion Network of the U.S. Department of Education as an "Exemplary Program."

The program has several major goals. The first is to prepare children to be physically active through an emphasis on skills and play, along with learning how to manage their own behavior. SPARK also organizes lessons so that students are physically active for a large percentage of class time. SPARK also works with the school food service and classroom teachers to provide support for students to be active and make healthy choices in nutrition.

SPARK offers specific support for physical education in grades K–2 and grades 3–6, along with two levels of self-management (grades 4/5 and 5/6). It also provides support for after-school programs and nonattached time in the school day through its Active Recreation program.

Project SPARK is unique among physical-education programs in that it is based on extensive research that shows improvement in physical activity, fitness, academic achievement, motor-skill development, student enjoyment, improvement in body composition, and teacher acceptance of the program.

An Early-Elementary Skill Themes Program

A class of first-graders at Maryland Avenue School is spread out across the gymnasium space. Each

Basic skills are important early learning experiences.

student has a small racquet and a foam ball. The teacher periodically asks the students to try a new way to strike the ball with the racquet, most often in the form of a question: "Can you keep the ball up in front of you by hitting it softly?" A student occasionally loses control of his or her ball but retrieves it without interfering with the activity of classmates. It gradually becomes clear that the progression of activities is leading toward the development of striking skills that will be useful later in sports such as tennis, badminton, softball, hockey, and lacrosse. With each series of questions asked by the teacher, the children are carefully guided toward forehand, backhand, overhand, and underhand striking patterns. The children do not know—or care, for that matter—that eventually this will all lead somewhere. They are obviously enjoying the activity for what it is at the moment. There is no competition among the children. The learning is success oriented. The children often have to make decisions about what they will do in response to the prompts and questions from the teacher.

Skill themes use movement skills, rather than traditional sport skills, as organizing principles for activity. The children in this program will have units in striking, throwing/tossing, catching, and dodging. Later, in upper-elementary-school grades, they will use these skills in the more conventional games that dominate the curriculum.

Skill-theme curricula are most often divided into the areas of educational games, educational gymnastics, and educational dance. The themes from which curricular units are developed are movement themes rather than sport themes. In the educational-gymnastics portion of the curriculum, children have lessons that focus on balance, transferring weight, hanging and swinging, bearing weight on different body parts, and locomotion—both on the feet and on different body parts. Small apparatuses—such as boxes, benches, balance beams, bars, ropes, rings, and inclined planks—are used as aids in exploring movement possibilities.

This approach to physical education stresses the cognitive involvement of children, the development of positive self-concepts, and the establishment of a broad repertoire of movement skills (Siedentop, Herkowitz, & Rink, 1984).

The "New Physical Education" at a Middle School

Madison Junior High School is recognized nationally as a leader in developing a new approach to physical education that emphasizes preparing students for lifetime health and physical activity. Featured nationally on CNN and in *USA Today*, the program has influenced the direction of physical education in many parts of the nation. The Madison program (www.ncusd203.org/madison) was built on a limited set of clear goals (lifetime activity, understanding and being able to monitor and direct your own efforts), an innovative change in physical-education facilities, and a dramatic increase in the use of technology to support program goals.

Students at Madison have physical education 5 days a week. One day is spent in the "health club" working on cardiovascular and strength machines. (The health club looks much more like a community health/fitness center than a sport training facility, which is a real clue to what the goals are all about.) A second day is spent doing the weekly cardio run/walk. The other 3 days are spent in activities such as in-line skating, using the climbing wall, or participating in individual or team sports.

Technology is ever present. Students wear heart-rate monitors when working in the health club or doing their weekly cardio walk/run. In the autumn and again in the spring, they test and record their progress at a series of computer-aided fitness test stations. These stations measure flexibility, blood pressure, body composition, upper-body strength, and cardiovascular performance.

In 2001 the school district entered into a partnership with PE4life, (a national nonprofit organization dedicated to promoting quality physical-education programs nationally) to create the PE4life Institute so that teachers, administrators, and community representatives can attend programs where they can learn how to develop and sustain "New PE" approaches (www.PE4life.org).

PE4life launched its Center for the Advancement of Physical Education (CAPE) on National PE Day, May 5, 2004 (www.pe4life.org/cape.php). CAPE's mission is to build evidence on healthy-lifestyles approaches and delivery systems. A PE4life program is designed to

- Provide quality, daily physical education that meets the needs of all students.

- Provide a wide variety of health and fitness activities to promote a healthy lifestyle.

- Provide authentic, individualized assessment as a meaningful part of the learning process.

- Incorporate technology into physical education on a regular and continuing basis.

- Emphasize and provide support for the physical-education staff's continuing education.

- Continually communicate with parents, administrators, and other stakeholders.

- Meet or exceed the National Association for Sport and Physical Education (NASPE) standards for physical education.

CAPE used the FITNESSGRAM test to compare the ninth-grade students at Madison Junior High with non-PEforlife students in California. In all six categories, the PEforlife students far outpaced their California peers. Of the 1,500 ninth-graders at Madison, only 3 percent were found to be overweight or obese, compared to 32 percent of their California counterparts.

A High-School Program Emphasizing Community Linkages

Seattle's twenty-five high schools have embarked on a curriculum-development initiative to add interesting, challenging activities to their curricula and to do so by partnering with community, professional, and private-sector sport organizations (Turner, 1995). Each of the high schools was challenged to add a new alternative activity to its traditional list of offerings. Most of those alternative activities required partnering with a local agency or a national organization. For example, they have taken advantage of the U.S. Tennis Association's program of equipment, assemblies, and instruction as well as the "First Swing" golf program sponsored by the Professional Golfers Association. Locally, the Seattle Fire Department paramedics have taught CPR classes, and the Seattle Parks and Recreation Department, in cooperation with U.S. Rowing, has provided free rowing instruction. An added benefit of these efforts is the knowledge that students gain about where activities are done in the community, along with the skills to take part in them. The partnering allows for use of equipment and expertise that no single school could possibly afford.

A State Wellness Curriculum for High Schools

Kansas has created the *Physical Dimensions* curriculum for high schools. The development of this physical-activity and wellness curriculum was funded through the Kansas Health Foundation, and it aims to help adolescents build healthy lifestyles. The curriculum includes three dimensions: health-related fitness, lifetime physical activity, and health/wellness concepts (see Focus On Box 11.1). Students receive 3 weeks of instruction in each of the three dimensions every 9 weeks. Students who successfully complete the curriculum receive a certificate of achievement (the High School Ph.D.).

A Virtual High-School Physical-Education Program

Some students in Florida high schools fulfill their physical education requirements online (Brooks, 2003)! This fitness-focused program requires students to work out three to four times per week and report their workouts on the Web. Students also have reading assignments in fitness and nutrition and complete regular writing assignments. Students have choices about the form of exercise that they pursue to fulfill course requirements. Some jog and run, but others swim, dance, surf, cycle, or do yoga. Students are required to keep online logs of their workouts, including heart-rate numbers at various points during the workout. Physical-education instructors in Florida's Virtual School speak monthly with parents of students enrolled to make sure that students are actually doing their workouts. Some students select this approach to make their regular school schedule less crowded, whereas others seem to prefer it because it enables them to work out alone or with close friends.

A STATE APPROACH TO REVITALIZING HIGH-SCHOOL PHYSICAL EDUCATION

While much of the education community over the past several decades has focused on "reform," carrying with it the connotation that things have gone wrong and need to be corrected, North Carolina choose a different path (Veal, Campbell, Johnson, & McKethan, 2002). Key leaders from state professional organizations and state education departments came together to plan for the revitalization effort. A steering committee made up of high-school physical educators, higher-education faculty,

FOCUS ON   The Kansas Physical Dimensions High-School Curriculum   11.1

Dimensions

One	Two	Three
Health-Related Fitness	Lifetime Physical Activity	Health/Wellness Concepts and Skills

Outcomes

• Knowledge and skills to enhance cardiorespiratory endurance, muscular strength and endurance, flexibility, and body composition	• Skills development • Fitness reinforcement • Participation in a variety of physical activities with lifelong significance	• Analysis of health issues impacting youth and adults • Assessment of own health behaviors • Personal and social skills development to enhance health

Achieved Through

• Aerobics • Walking/Jogging • Strength and Conditioning • Orienteering	• Rhythms • Golf • Swimming	• Tennis • Badminton • Volleyball	• Nutrition and weight management • Stress management • Personal safety and conflict resolution • Preventing pregnancy, STDs, and HIV

Lifetime Wellness

This course is designed to provide young adults with the knowledge and skills needed to engage in a physically active, healthy lifestyle throughout life. There are three areas of focus in the course:

1. Health-related fitness
2. Lifetime physical activity
3. Health/wellness concepts and skills. The curriculum consists of four 3-week segments for each area. Students receive 3 weeks of instruction in each of three areas every 9 weeks.

Course Outcomes

As a result of participation in this course, students will be able to:

1. Interpret personal health/fitness status to design, implement, and evaluate a personal health/fitness plan to develop and maintain a physically active, healthy lifestyle.
2. Analyze current health issues impacting youths and adults.
3. Demonstrate effective use of personal and social skills to enhance health/fitness behavior.
4. Develop the motor competency to use a variety of physical activities to engage in a healthy lifestyle.
5. Display consideration and respect for differences among various individuals.

and a representative from the Department of Instruction was formed to create a long-range plan and to suggest ways to fund the effort. Their effort led to high-school physical-education teachers and university teacher educators joining together to create and implement the *Physical Education Partnership for Sport Education* (PEPSE). This project aimed to help selected high-school physical-education programs to re-create their physical-education learning environments with a focus on curricular revision and assessment. The project enabled physical-education teachers within high schools to build a shared vision, purpose, and sense of values. The idea was to allow teachers to come together to affect change from the "inside-out" rather than have change imposed from the outside.

The sport-education curriculum and instruction model was chosen because it had a strong assessment component, had been successfully implemented in research projects, and was compatible with NASPE standards. Eventually, all North Carolina public high-school physical educators were invited to participate in PEPSE. Ten schools from different regions within the state were selected to participate in the initial trial of the project. The teachers in these schools were paired with physical-education teacher educators from nearby colleges and universities. All participants met for a 3-day workshop so that strategies for implementation could be discussed. Model units using the sport-education approach were prepared in advance so that participants could discuss their implementation. Participants observed sample classes demonstrating how the model could be used.

All PEPSE-participating teachers then piloted the model in classes during the autumn of 2000. The teachers and their university partners collected data during these classes, using a variety of research instruments. The partnership reconvened in November 2000 to review the data and discuss the pilot experiences. Teachers rated the model as successful or very successful. Some teachers indicated that students in nonpilot classes asked why they could not have the model in their classes.

This effort in North Carolina is a model for how other states might attempt to reinvigorate high-school physical education. The North Carolina effort could be replicated using different models but having in common the strategy to engage high-school physical-education teachers in the opportunity to rethink the manner that

they provide content to students and the kind of instructional model that they use with students.

NASPE's STARS Project

NASPE developed the STARS project to identify and recognize quality physical-education programs. The STARS initiative recognizes two levels of achievement. The first level is for programs that exemplify NASPE's vision of excellence in teaching knowledge and skills of motor development and health-related fitness. The second level is called SuperSTARS, the highest achievement possible.

Frankfort Middle School in Ridgeley, West Virginia, earned a STARS level 1 award in 2005. The program was noted for its highly qualified teaching staff, good facilities and equipment, and the strength of its program. Students use daily fitness planners, keep a homework notebook and an activity log, and engage in outdoor/adventure activities. The program also includes opportunities for seventh- and eighth-graders to assist in teaching skills to elementary-school students. Students are encouraged to take part in lifetime fitness activities within the community.

Hortonville High School in Wisconsin earned a STARS level 2 award in 2007. The primary focus of the program is health-related fitness. Activities such as curling, wall climbing, snowshoeing, cross-country skiing, fly fishing, and archery are provided. "Workout Wednesday" is a key component of the program, addressing specific components of fitness each week. Results of 4 years of implementing this program showed that PACER (Progressive Aerobic Cardiovascular Endurance Run) test scores improved from 40 percent to 75 percent of the students achieving their "health fitness zone." A cardio room features treadmills, recumbent, bicycles, ellipticals, Airdyne bicycles, and Dance Dance Revolution pads. A weight room offers different strength-training equipment. The program also has other components to engage the community, including a 3K community walk and a walking club for faculty, staff, and community using pedometers to record activity levels.

Physical-Education Teachers as Physical-Activity Directors

In 2004 the U.S. Congress approved the reauthorization of the Child Nutrition Act that provides funds to support school breakfast and lunch programs. A provision of the reauthorization was that local school districts that receive funding under the program must create School Wellness Councils to establish school wellness policies that included "goals for nutrition education, physical activity, and other school-based activities that are designed to promote student wellness" (U.S. Congress, 2004). This legislation has not only encouraged many states to increase the time requirements for physical education but also has brought in the possibility for physical-activity programs that are in addition to time requirements for physical education. Some states—Kentucky, for example—have created legislation for total time requirements in physical education and physical activity and given schools some leeway in deciding how to allocate time to meet those requirements. Even in states where time requirements for physical education are strong, there is a movement toward including additional physical activity during the school day and after-school. In many states, the person on the local Wellness Council who is responsible for physical education and physical activity is called the physical activity director.

In elementary schools, classroom teachers are being encouraged to provide short "activity breaks" during the school day. The nationally available "Take 10!" program is a classroom-based physical activity program for grades K–5 students (www.take10.net). The Take 10! materials provide safe and age-appropriate 10-minute physical activities that integrate academic learning objectives with activity. Students do these activities within their classrooms. Many teachers are now more aware of the increasing evidence that supports the

idea that increased physical activity during the school day results in more attentive and more on-task student behavior. There is also a movement to ensure that time for recess is not reduced and that efforts are made to provide recess activities that keep children active throughout the 15-minute periods.

In Wake County, North Carolina, the school district has developed Wellness Academies and You (WAY)—a research-based obesity-prevention program focused on nutrition, wellness, and physical activity—implemented in elementary schools. The district has also expanded the number of high-school fitness centers and introduced "Hopsports," a multimedia fitness program in middle and high schools. All of this is in addition to the regular physical-education program.

The Madison Middle School Youth Development Program (Madison, Wisconsin) is supported by the school district in partnership with the community recreation department. Youth resource centers have been developed at seven middle schools, offering a variety of after-school, evening, and weekend programs. After-school clubs include riding, drama, music, bowling, dance, skiing, and canoeing. They also offer after-school sports for seventh- and eighth-graders and intramural sports for sixth-graders. Each middle school has a recreation counselor and a youth resource director.

The Coyote Ridge School District (Broomfield, Colorado) offers "Play It Again Gym" for 1.5 hours each Monday for students in grades 1–5. Students play a variety of games and activities that have been introduced in the physical-education program. The program focuses on being active, having fun, and making new friends. The program is free.

None of these efforts have reduced the emphasis on physical education in the school district. Indeed, it appears that many physical-activity programs being developed in response to the national imperative to increase physical activity for children and youths have attempted to reinforce and expand the opportunities for physical activity provided in the physical-education program.

What Makes These Programs Work?

The physical-education programs described in this section are not necessarily unique. There are many good programs in many places. Those described here represent different approaches to physical education, approaches that reflect the various models described in Chapter 10. What properties do they share? Are there features or characteristics common to all of these programs?

My own experience with reviewing these programs and many others (Siedentop, 1987) is that they do share several characteristics. First, in each program, a physical educator or a group of physical educators exerted substantial leadership to get the program started and to maintain it until it was sufficiently established.

Second, although each of these programs is obviously different, each stands for something *specific*. In each program, there is a main theme or focus—fitness, sport education, adventure, movement, personal growth, and so on. Good comprehensive programs tend to be either of two types. Either they have a main theme, which runs through the program, or they join two or three main themes.

Third, the programs not only look exciting but also, by all reports, tend to *be* exciting for the students who participate in them. Clearly, the teachers who have created and maintained them are excited about what they did. This excitement reflects a sense of purpose and a set of expectations that are no doubt communicated in many ways to students, fellow teachers, administrators, and parents.

Fourth, very few of the teachers who were responsible for these programs had major commitments in coaching interscholastic teams. The problem of role conflict that is suggested by this fact is reviewed in Chapter 12.

TECHNOLOGY IN PHYSICAL EDUCATION

Technology has made strong contributions to improving physical education in schools. Although too many schools cannot afford the kinds of technology described in this section, it is important to note how it is being used to improve the learning experience for students. Examples of technology in physical education are everywhere:

- Heart monitors enable students to track exercise patterns. The data can be downloaded into computers where they can be displayed graphically and used by students and teachers (Hinson, 1994).

- Students and teachers use the Internet to take part in newsgroups that address needs and interests related to physical activity and teaching (LaMaster, 1996).

- Teachers have access to a number of Web sites that can help them with lesson planning, assessment, promoting their program, and other issues. See PE Central Web site on page 269.

- An online technology newsletter for K–12 physical education keeps students and teachers up to date with the latest developments in the use of technology in physical education. See www.pesoftware.com/news.

- The Kinesiology Department at California State University at Northridge offers an online master's specialization program in Technology and Physical Education.

- Students and staff at Fargo, North Dakota, public schools get a complete fitness evaluation two times a year using the TriFIT 600 System, a portable fitness-evaluation system (www.polarusa.com/education/teachercorner/applicationExample.esp?ID=1).

- Pedometers are widely used to count steps per day in fitness evaluation. Students wear the pedometers throughout the day and compare their activity with national standards.

- Teacher educators and staff-development leaders use videotapes to help prospective and practicing teachers improve their practice by analyzing tapes (Everhart & Turner, 1995).

- GameBike is a plug-and-play video game controller in which movements on the screen can be controlled with body movement. The

GameBike works with a large number of racing games now available.

- Teachers and student-teacher supervisors use camcorders to help students and student teachers evaluate their performances.

A number of software programs are available for use in physical education and by physical-education teachers. Teachers have access to software programs that can be used for such teaching purposes as grading, banner and sign making, awards, and yearly calendars (Wilkinson, Hillier, & Harrison, 1998). Teachers can also use software programs to plan and analyze student learning activities such as workout programs, cardiovascular evaluation, health-risk appraisal, and diet analysis. One text on the sport-education model (Siedentop, Hastie, & van der Mars, 2004) includes an extensive CD-ROM that provides all materials that teachers need to plan and implement that model. The materials include tournament forms, banners, fair-play posters, seasonal planning forms, and posters for student roles (coach, referee, scorekeeper, manager, statistician, and the like). Teachers can download the forms, modify them, and use them in their classes, thus substantially reducing the planning time needed to implement the model.

Tutorials for fitness, interactive software for sport instruction, educational games, simulations for fitness and sport, and laboratory exercises for health and fitness are available directly for student use. Through these software programs, students can play a virtual racquetball game, discover how the heart works, or learn rules of and strategies for a variety of sports.

Telecommunications can also be used to enhance instruction and expand the student experience in physical education. Physical-education listservs can be created for each class or for a school physical-education program. This allows for e-mail messages to be sent and received. Bulletin boards are electronic-message systems by which individuals can post and read messages. Chat rooms can be created so that students may discuss issues related to their class work. Web pages can be created for physical-education programs to allow communication to students, parents, and the community. Links from Web pages can allow direct access to resources needed by students and their parents.

Technology can also be used to extend physical education in interesting ways. During winter and summer Olympics, many physical-education classes in the United States linked up with classes in the host countries to discuss issues involving the games. A junior high school in Nebraska used e-mail to organize a track meet involving seventeen schools around the world; the schools conducted similar meets and compared times, distances, and heights for each event. Overall results and standings were distributed to each school (Mills, 1997).

Using the Web has become second nature to most students and teachers. Key Web sites are listed throughout this text. A primary example of the success of Web sites in physical education is PE Central, developed under the leadership of George Graham and Mark Manross at Virginia Tech (see Figure 11.1). This comprehensive Web site includes pages for students, teachers, parents, administrators, and other professionals. The most popular sections of this Web site are lesson ideas, assessment ideas, top Web sites, the job center, and adapted physical education. It also includes links to other important sites, which is typical of how the Web works. In a recent 6-month period, PE Central averaged 95,000 unique visitors, many of whom no doubt visited the site frequently. In that same time period, more than 3.2 million pages of the site were accessed.

Another important site for physical educators at all levels is PELINKS4U (www.pelinks4u.org). A free monthly newsletter is available at this site. The newsletter includes sections on adapted physical education, coaching, elementary-school physical education, secondary-school physical education, and health, fitness, and nutrition. As the name of the site suggests, you can also find links to many other sites that are of interest to physical educators. A list of key Web sites for physical education can be found on page 295.

lunch in the teachers' lounge, usually more quickly than he should because the noon hour is when he has managed to squeeze in some intramural time for his students.

After intramural time, he has a planning period of 35 minutes—his only one during the week. Then, he sees three more classes before the gym helpers arrive at 3:30 to put away equipment and to prepare for the next day. Jay does some paper-work related to the day's lessons, checks in the office for any school messages or mail, stops to talk with the first-grade teacher, and then heads home at 4:15 p.m., where he does more school planning before he has dinner.

Joan leaves her home at 7:00 each morning for the short drive to the high school where she teaches and coaches. The school enrollment has grown, so classes now begin at 7:30. She has a plan-ning period during the first period, but she is ex-pected to be in her office when school officially be-gins at 7:30. She will teach six classes today, supervising the locker room before and after each class. Two of her classes will have a fitness orienta-tion, three will be on soccer, and one is a special elective class she started on weight training for fe-males. She has some lunch-supervision duties but manages to spend a pleasant 45 minutes in the teachers' lounge having lunch herself and chatting with her colleagues. Her last 50-minute class is over at 3:00, and she has a half-hour to prepare for her basketball practice.

The season has just started, so when practice is over at 5:30, she grabs a quick dinner on her way to scout the team that her school will play against the next weekend. She finally returns home at 9:30 p.m., works on her practice plans for the next day, and or-ganizes the scouting information she gathered at the opponents' game. She will need to be up at 6:15 the next morning to be at school by 7:30, to go through the routine again.

Only those who have taught or have observed a teacher for a full day can appreciate the intensity of these schedules. The coaching added to the full day of teaching extends the intensity longer in the day. When you teach and coach, you are *responsible* for the students in your care. If you try hard to do a good job of teaching and coaching, you are busy interacting with your students/players most of the time you are with them. All in all, the job of physical-education teacher is a demanding one that is often seriously underappreciated.

Teaching as Part of a Team Effort

Physical-education teachers at any individual school and within a district are part of a teaching team. This is especially true for large elementary schools and for nearly all middle schools and high schools. In these situations, there will be physical-education faculty who have to work together to make the school program successful. South Carolina is the first state to have not only physical-education standards for its K–12 schools but also state assessment of the degree to which schools are meeting those standards (Rink & Williams, 2003). With state assessment of student performance in physical education, it becomes possible to begin to make comparisons among schools in terms of their success (or lack thereof) in meeting those standards.

Castelli and Rink (2003) used data in South Carolina to compare high- and low-performing secondary-school physical-education programs. Their results show clearly that having an effective school physical-education *program* requires that physical-education teachers work as a team and that the team be supported by the school administration. The physical-education faculty in the high-performing schools in this study had regular and effective com-munication, clear teacher roles, high expectations and enthusiasm among the faculty, a department leader who served as liaison with school administra-tors, and an active school administration that was supportive of the team's effort. On the other hand, in the low-performing schools, the teachers tended to act as individuals, communicated only informally and mostly about procedures, lacked effective department leadership, and had a passive school administration.

Teaching physical education in schools, therefore, is not a "do your own thing" task. To be successful in accomplishing important goals, teachers have to work together, help each other, and be committed as a group to the school's goals for physical education—and they have to have the support of the school and district administrators.

PREPARING TO BECOME A PHYSICAL-EDUCATION TEACHER

As we noted earlier in this chapter, the primary way to become a physical-education teacher is to attend a college or university and to enter a teacher-preparation program. Some states have experimented with *alternative* routes to certification for teaching, but these all involve college graduation and, eventually at least, some specific teacher preparation. The purpose of this section is to describe the different ways in which teachers are prepared.

Because the U.S. Constitution leaves the responsibility for education to the states, the *rules* for teacher certification are made by state legislatures. Teacher education in the United States takes place almost exclusively at colleges and universities. Programs of teacher education in colleges and universities must adhere to *standards* that are devised by state legislatures or state departments of education.

Differences Among States

Because states differ markedly in their approach to teacher certification, what a student has to do to become certified as a physical-education teacher differs dramatically from state to state. Here are some of the ways in which states differ:

1. *Level of certification.* The three main kinds of certification in physical education are K–12, which allows you to teach at any grade level; K–6, which specializes training and restricts teaching to the elementary school; and 7–12, which specializes training and restricts teaching to the middle and secondary schools. Relatively few states have K–6 certification, whereas K–12 is the certification most commonly received by graduating physical-education majors.

2. *Number of teaching specialties.* States with many small, rural schools tend to require more than one teaching major or a teaching major with one or two teaching minors. Thus, the newly graduated teacher is certified in more than one teaching area (physical education and history, say, or physical education, general science, and health). This enables principals in small schools to use staff more effectively. In states with more consolidation and larger school districts, the trend has been toward certification in only one subject area.

3. *Amount of field experience.* There has been a strong trend in teacher education over the past several decades to increase the amount of contact that teacher candidates have with schools and students. This is typically done through what is called **field** or *school-based* **experience**. These experiences range from observation through full-scale teaching. Some states require extensive amounts of field experience before candidates start their official student teaching. Other states require none. Thus, first-year teachers may differ dramatically in the amount of teaching experience they have received in their preparation programs.

The actual curriculum that teacher candidates receive differs, depending on how the state in which they prepare creates standards reflecting the differences we have described. A student in a state that emphasizes K–12 certification and that requires two teaching majors but no field experience before student teaching receives a preparation very different from that of a student in another state who is working toward a K–6 certificate, where only physical education as a teaching area is required and where there is a strong emphasis on field experience. What does your state require or allow? How do its requirements differ from those of neighboring states? What do you think would be the best approach to preparing teachers in your state? These are all interesting questions, discussion of which will quickly get you deeply involved in feelings about teacher education and points of view relative to it.

National Standards for Beginning Physical-Education Teachers

Standards for initial teacher education in physical education were first published by NASPE in 1995 and then revised in 2001 (NASPE, 2001b). The teacher-education standards are meant to prepare students to deliver a physical-education program that is consistent with the NASPE content standards described in Chapter 10. Thus, the outcomes that define a physically educated person are aligned with the standards for preparing beginning teachers of physical education. The NASPE standards are shown in Focus On Box 11.2. Each standard is accompanied by a series of outcomes that more specifically define what the beginning teacher will know and be able to do.

Standards such as these will eventually influence the curriculum that students who want to be physical-education teachers take in their undergraduate years. Teachers are licensed at the state level in America, and each state differs somewhat in how it reviews teacher-education programs to grant them the right to prepare teachers. When national standards are adopted by a parent professional organization such as NASPE, they are quickly adopted at the state level also and used as the template through which accreditation teams periodically review each public and private institution approved to prepare teachers in that field. That is, to continue to be approved, the institution must successfully pass the state review. In this way, the standards quickly become the guidelines that individual institutions use to plan their physical-education teacher-education programs.

The highest credential an American teacher can achieve is to earn recognition from the National Board for Professional Teaching Standards (www.nbpts.org). To become a National Board Certified Teacher (NBCT) is to be recognized as having achieved the highest benchmark for teacher quality.

NBPTS certification takes between 1 and 3 years to complete and measures what accomplished teachers should know and be able to do. Teachers complete a rigorous portfolio and submit it to NBPTS to be evaluated. By the end of 2007, 1,139 physical-education teachers received this prestigious recognition (www.nbpts.org).

Certification for Teaching Adapted Physical Education

The Individuals with Disabilities Education Act (IDEA) mandates that children and youths with disabilities receive physical-education services and specially designed services (adapted physical education) from qualified personnel; however, the law does not specify what is meant by "qualified." Some states have interpreted the law to mean that teachers are certified in physical education, whereas others are more lenient and interpret the law to mean that personnel have teaching certificates in any field. Those states that have developed special requirements for adapted-physical-education teachers typically do so as an add-on validation or endorsement to a previously earned teaching certificate.

About one-third of the states now offer a validation/endorsement in adapted physical education. In 1995 the National Consortium for Physical Education and Recreation for Individuals with Disabilities (NCPERID) developed Adapted Physical Education National Standards (APENS) and a national certification examination to measure knowledge of those standards. The project to develop the standards and APENS examination was federally funded under the leadership of Luke Kelly at the University of Virginia (NCPERID, 1995). The APENS exam is for all teachers who consider themselves qualified and competent adapted physical educators. The minimum qualifications to take the exam are a bachelor's degree in physical education, a valid teaching certificate, 200 hours of experience providing adapted-physical-education services, and one 3-credit survey course in adapted physical education. It is hoped that the APENS examination process will serve as a motivation and a resource for

FOCUS ON NASPE Standards for Beginning Physical-Education Teachers 11.2

Standard 1: Content Knowledge

Physical-education teachers understand physical education and disciplinary concepts related to the development of a physically educated person.

Outcomes—Teacher Candidates Will:

1.1 Identify critical elements of motor skill performance and combine motor skills into appropriate sequences for the purpose of improving learning.

1.2 Demonstrate competent motor skill performance in a variety of physical activities.

1.3 Describe performance concepts and strategies related to skillful movement and physical activity.

1.4 Describe and apply bioscience and psychological concepts to skillful movement, physical activity, and fitness.

1.5 Understand and debate current physical education/activity issues and laws based on historical, philosophical, and sociological perspectives.

1.6 Demonstrate knowledge of approved state and national content standards and local program goals.

Standard 2: Growth and Development

Physical-education teachers understand how individuals learn and develop and can provide opportunities that support their physical, cognitive, social, and emotional development.

Outcomes—Teacher Candidates Will:

2.1 Monitor individual and group performance in order to design safe instruction that meets student developmental needs in the physical, cognitive, and socio-emotional domains.

2.2 Understand the biological, psychological, sociological, experiential, and environmental factors that impact developmental readiness to learn and refine movement skills.

2.3 Identify, select, and implement appropriate learning/practice opportunities based on understanding the student, the learning environment, and the task.

Standard 3: Diverse Students

Physical-education teachers understand how individuals differ in their approaches to learning and create appropriate instruction adapted to those differences.

Outcomes—Teacher Candidates Will:

3.1 Identify, select, and implement appropriate instruction that is sensitive to students' strengths/weaknesses, multiple needs, learning styles, and prior experiences.

3.2 Use appropriate services and resources to meet diverse learning needs.

Standard 4: Management and Motivation

Physical-education teachers use an understanding of individual and group motivation and behavior to create a safe learning environment that encourages positive social interaction, active engagement in learning, and self-motivation.

Outcomes—Teacher Candidates Will:

4.1 Use managerial routines that create smoothly functioning learning experiences and environments.

4.2 Organize, allocate, and manage resources to provide active and equitable learning experiences.

4.3 Use a variety of developmentally appropriate practices to motivate students to participate in physical activity inside and outside of the school.

4.4 Use strategies to help students demonstrate responsible personal and social behaviors that promote positive relationships and a productive learning environment.

4.5 Develop an effective behavior management plan.

Standard 5: Communication

Physical education teachers use knowledge of effective verbal, nonverbal, and media communication techniques to enhance learning and engagement in physical activity settings.

Outcomes—Teacher Candidates Will:

5.1 Describe and demonstrate effective communication skills.

5.2 Communicate managerial and instructional information in a variety of ways.

5.3 Communicate in ways that demonstrate sensitivity to all students.

5.4 Describe and implement strategies to enhance communication among students in physical activity settings.

Standard 6: Planning and Instruction

Physical education teachers plan and implement a variety of developmentally appropriate instructional strategies to develop physically educated individuals, based on state and national standards.

Outcomes—Teacher Candidates Will:

6.1 Identify, develop, and implement appropriate program and instructional goals.

6.2 Develop long- and short-term plans that are linked to both program and instructional goals, and student needs.

6.3 Select and implement instructional strategies, based on selected content, student needs, and safety issues, to facilitate learning in the physical activity setting.

6.4 Design and implement learning experiences that are safe, appropriate, relevant, and based on principles of effective instruction.

6.5 Apply disciplinary and pedagogical knowledge in developing and implementing effective learning environments and experiences.

6.6 Provide learning experiences that allow students to integrate knowledge and skills from multiple subject areas.

6.7 Select and implement appropriate teaching resources and curriculum materials.

6.8 Use effective demonstrations and explanations to link physical activity concepts to appropriate learning experiences.

6.9 Develop and use appropriate instructional cues and prompts to facilitate competent motor skill performance.

6.10 Develop a repertoire of direct and indirect instructional formats to facilitate student learning.

Standard 7: Student Assessment

Physical-education teachers understand and use assessment to foster physical, cognitive, social, and emotional development of students in physical activity.

Outcomes—Teacher Candidates Will:

7.1 Identify key components of various types of assessment, describe their appropriate and inappropriate use, and address issues of validity, reliability, and bias.

7.2 Use a variety of appropriate authentic and traditional assessment techniques to assess student understanding and performance, provide feedback, and communicate student progress.

7.3 Interpret and use learning and performance data to make informed curricular and/or instructional decisions.

SOURCE: NASPE, 2001b.

FOCUS ON — Recent State Legislation to Strengthen Physical Education — 11.3

In the wake of the federal legislation requiring local school districts to address school wellness issues, several states have passed legislation to strengthen physical education. Here are a few examples.

Arkansas

- created a statewide Child Health Advisory Council
- in 2007–08, K–12 students must receive 150 minutes/week of PE/PA
- maximum student to teacher ratio of 30/1

Washington

- created a comprehensive health/fitness curriculum with a minimum of 100 minutes/week in grades 1–8
- PE assessment strategies must be in place by 2008–09
- developing a statewide assessment of PE outcomes using a variety of assessment tools

Texas

- all districts must adopt the Coordinated School Health model
- requires 30 minutes daily or 135 minutes weekly of daily PE/PA in grades 1–8
- requires each elementary school to adopt one of four approved school health models

California

- requires a minimum of 200 minutes every 10 schools days in grades 1–6
- requires a minimum of 400 minutes of PE for every 10 school days in grades 7–12
- PE must be delivered by a credentialed PE teacher
- budgeted $40 million to support hiring of more PE teachers

---

those states that have not yet developed a validation/endorsement program.

The programs described in this chapter show that physical education can be done well and can contribute significantly to the education of all children and youths. Nonetheless, physical education in schools is beset by problems and by controversial, unresolved issues. Those problems and issues are explored in the next chapter.

Building a Vision for the Future

The programs described in this chapter, while different in certain respects, all seem to be focused primarily on helping students adopt and value physically active lifestyles. Some programs do it with a fitness/health-club approach whereas others do it with a recreational-activity focus. What does seem consistent across approaches is the manner in the pedagogical strategies that they develop. If you want girls and boys to *adopt* and *value* a physically

active lifestyle, you have to develop an instructional process and an instructional climate that is inviting, fun, and success oriented. Students need to know that you really care about their futures, are there to help them, and have the knowledge and commitment to help them achieve program goals. Many teachers also develop a pedagogical climate where students learn to respect and support each other, despite the differences in their native abilities or their different work ethics.

Obviously, it becomes difficult to accomplish lifestyle goals without sufficient time with students. What is clear in many of the programs cited here is the ways that they find to engage students outside of class time, with drop-in activities, after-school opportunities, physical-education homework, and the like. Physical education will prosper if more physical educators, working together in school districts, take the "Field of Dreams" approach; that is, "if you build it, they will come." The "it," of course, is an exciting program taught by teachers who care about and provide excellent instruction to their students.

It is also clear that a physical-education program in a school district needs to be conceptualized as a K–12 program. Teachers at elementary-, middle-, and high-school levels have to come together so that the goals and process of the program are consistent through the students' school years. When middle-school physical education builds on an excellent elementary-school program and high-school physical education builds still further on the middle-school program, then the likelihood of achieving a total programmatic impact on students is greatly increased.

What is your vision for the future? Which of these programs most appealed to you? When you go to look for a job as a newly certified physical-education teacher, what kind of program would you most like to join? This time that you are spending as an undergraduate should be used wisely to help you gain the skills that will enable you to compete successfully for a position in a program that emphasizes the programmatic elements that you think are necessary to achieve your vision.

SUMMARY

1. Although a broad view of physical education takes into account all the settings in which people learn, practice, and enjoy sport and fitness activities, the school is still the setting where physical education can best serve the majority of people.

2. High-quality daily physical education for all students is a hope for the future. It is necessary if we are to achieve fully the goals of physical education.

3. High-quality programs can and do exist with a broad range of curricular approaches including fitness, comprehensive-skill-grouped, sport-education, personal-growth, adventure-education, movement-education, and comprehensive elective programs.

4. Characteristics of exemplary programs include leadership by a qualified physical educator, a specific programmatic theme, a sense of excitement, and a teacher whose main interest is this program (as opposed to coaching).

5. Physical-education teachers earn certificates in the state in which they graduate from an approved teacher-education program.

6. The physical-education teacher plays a number of diverse roles including planner, manager, colleague, member of a profession, counselor, and representative of the school and school district.

7. Teachers lead intense daily lives in schools, teaching and supervising students. After-school coaching responsibilities can increase the length of the school day.

8. States provide different levels of certification, the most common being K–12, K–6, and 7–12.

9. NASPE's national standards for beginning teachers provide a mechanism for improving the quality of teacher preparation in physical education.

DISCUSSION QUESTIONS

1. What staff and facilities would an elementary school with 400 students require to implement a daily physical-education program? What would a high school with 1,000 students require?

2. Which exemplary program did you like most? Why? Which did you like least? Why?

3. Are there programs in your region that you think are exemplary? Which of the characteristics described in the chapter, if any, do they manifest?

4. Do you know people who are now teacher-coaches? Are their professional lives like those of the teachers described in this chapter? What roles do they occupy?

5. What certification is available in your state? If you are certified in your state, where else does that certification allow you to teach?

6. How does your preparation program compare with the NASPE standards?

CHAPTER 12

Problems and Issues in Physical Education

In the United States, physical education in schools continues, along with art and music, to be disposable: embraced when budgets are full and public outcries loud, restricted when money is scarce. Currently, finances are strained in most states, but the recognition of the value and importance of physical activity has never been higher. It is an interesting period in school physical education K–12 in the United States.

George Graham, 1990

LEARNING OBJECTIVES

- To analyze general issues related to time, class size, exemptions, liability, and gender equity

- To analyze issues related to elementary-school physical education, such as specialist teachers, facilities, curricula, and developmentally appropriate practices

- To analyze issues related to secondary-school physical education, such as main-theme curricula, coed participation, and role conflict

- To analyze issues such as assessment and accountability for physical-education outcomes

- To analyze issues related to skill equity

- To analyze issues related to good and bad competition

- To gauge what role physical education can and should play in the fitness and sport cultures

Chapters 10 and 11 described both the curriculum and instruction models that are currently used in physical education and provided examples for physical-education programs at elementary-, middle-, and high-school levels. This chapter focuses on problems and issues in physical education, some of which are issues across the K–12 spectrum and some of which are specific to elementary-, middle-, or high-school physical education. Some problems cannot be solved without stronger legislation at the state level whereas others are more specific to individual schools and can be solved with stronger leadership from administrators and stronger support from parents.

GENERAL PROBLEMS IN PHYSICAL EDUCATION

Some significant problems cut across the K–12 spectrum. Although they may not manifest themselves in exactly the same ways for the elementary-school program as they do for the middle- or high-school program, they are nonetheless endemic problems that seriously diminish the quality of instruction and seriously jeopardize the likelihood of achieving significant programmatic outcomes.

Time and Class Size

Lack of sufficient time and large class size may be the most serious problems that cut across K–12 physical education. When a high-school physical education teacher has seventy students that meet three days per week for a semester, it is difficult to imagine that significant outcomes can be achieved. When an elementary-school physical-education specialist has thirty-eight third-graders in a class that meets one day each week, it is equally difficult to imagine that significant outcomes will be achieved. As indicated earlier in this text, the recent national concern about child/youth overweight and obesity has resulted in many states increasing the time requirements for physical education. That is a positive step forward! However, it is also clear that few states have accountability mechanisms to ensure that time requirements are met by all school districts.

There is clear evidence that several school subjects (social studies, PE, etc.) have lost time in the school timetable as a result of the No Child Left Behind (NCLB) legislation. Elementary schools have been hit particularly hard because of the increased time devoted to reading and mathematics. Research has shown that since the inception of NCLB, time in physical education has been reduced by 14 percent (Jennings, 2006). Many school districts face financial problems and use reduced physical education to save resources that can be used to improve the core academic subjects, particularly reading and math. In some states, such as Kentucky, new legislation

increases the total school time that can be allotted for physical education and physical activity, but many districts choose to increase the time using physical-activity breaks with large numbers of students participating, with no increased time for physical education. This is not to suggest that physical-activity breaks are not useful! What it does suggest is that if 90 minutes per week in physical education/physical activity are required and 60 of those 90 minutes are in physical activity, then physical education is left with essentially one class period/week.

Class size is an equally difficult issue. The National Association for Sport and Physical Education (NASPE) suggests that class size for physical education be similar to that of other subject areas with a maximum ratio of 1:25 for elementary school, 1:30 for middle school, and 1:35 for high school. Classes that are larger than those ratios create significant problems for physical-education teachers. Management issues are more difficult and cut into instructional and practice time. The space and amount of equipment is often geared to the lower ratios, making students share equipment and space, thus reducing their opportunities to practice and be active. Large classes make it very difficult for teachers to individualize instruction. Large classes tend to increase the risk of injury and increase the amount of "off-task" behavior among students.

Certainly, skilled physical-education teachers find ways to deal with large class sizes by using strategies such as small-group work, cooperative learning, peer teaching, station work, and small-sided games. In these situations, however, the teacher finds himself or herself spending more time monitoring group activity and maintaining on-task behavior and less time providing individual attention and feedback.

What is most unnerving about these situations is that there is strong evidence to support the idea that more physical activity during the day improves student attention and engagement in the classroom!

Exemptions

Another feature of recent legislation to improve physical education has been to reduce or eliminate exemptions that allow students to count involvement in other activities as meeting the physical-education requirement. Still, many states allow exemptions, especially at the high-school level. Marching band, ROTC, drill teams, vocational training, cheerleading, and participation on a school sport team are all counted as exemptions for physical education in many states. Estimates suggest that 25 percent of middle-school students and as many as 40 percent of high-school students are exempted from having to meet the physical-education requirement of the school.

Why does this happen? The only explanation seems to be that school officials believe that what is accomplished in physical education can also be accomplished on a football team, in a marching band, or in ROTC. This has become a particularly difficult argument to make in an era when the primary goal for physical education is to help students adopt and value a physically active lifestyle! Perhaps the recent concern about child/youth overweight and obesity and the manner in which school physical-education programs are responding to the concern will lead to the elimination of exemptions.

Facilities

Traditionally, school physical-education facilities have been built as gymnasiums with the basketball court(s) as the main feature of the facility. In elementary schools, the gym is smaller than in middle or high school. In temperate climates, it is not unusual that 80 percent of elementary-school physical education is taught outside on school playgrounds. Even in colder climates, many children receive physical education in a multipurpose room or auditorium rather than a gymnasium.

We have seen evidence in this text that many high schools have refurbished facilities to create a health/fitness center and that others have developed new facilities build on the health-club model with strength- and cardio-training facilities as the main features. Inadequate facilities make good physical education difficult but not impossible. Great facilities make good physical education easier to achieve,

but the facilities in and of themselves are not sufficient to guarantee a quality program.

Liability

We live in an era where citizens have become increasingly assertive about prosecuting in courts of law to maintain their rights and to redress grievances. Physicians, for example, spend enormous amounts of money on malpractice insurance because of the number of lawsuits brought against them—suits in which patients try to hold them *liable* for alleged inappropriate or negligent practice of medical skills.

This era of liability has reached physical education. In the 1970s, it would have been fairly common to find trampolines used in physical education. Today, it is almost impossible to find one in schools. Why? There are simply too many safety issues that might lead to liability litigation for the teacher and school. The same is true for apparatus on elementary-school playgrounds. The newer approaches to outdoor play apparatus for elementary schools takes into full account the safety of the children.

Teachers today are more aware of liability issues. Adventure activities such as climbing and rappelling and the apparatus needed to pursue such activities are commonly found in schools today, but teachers are more aware of the safety issues, the safety equipment, and the instruction that needs to be provided for students to use the apparatus. They also carefully monitor student activity and are quick to remediate unsafe behavior. Issues of liability won't go away, but teachers today are much more aware of how to organize, teach, and manage students to create safe learning and practice environments.

Gender Equity

The issues of Title IX in sport were dealt with in Chapter 6. Many physical educators today don't realize the profound influence that Title IX had on physical education, starting in the 1970s. Because every public school in America receives some form of federal funding, all physical-education programs come under the aegis of the provisions of Title IX. In physical education, the most important specific influences of Title IX were (1) coeducational classes, (2) assignment of teachers according to skill rather than gender, (3) grouping based on ability rather than gender, and (4) equal access for girls and boys to the entire physical-education curriculum.

Physical education does not have a particularly admirable history with respect to gender equity. Girls have been denied access to learning and participating in certain sports. Female teachers have not always been able to teach those activities for which they are best prepared. Facilities and equipment has not been shared equally. Today, the effects of Title IX for physical education are mixed. Coed classes are the norm rather than the exception. In many programs, girls have access to the full range of activities offered. On the other hand, research has indicated that there has been a reduction of the percentage of female physical-education teachers in high schools (Hulstrand, 1990). In our own research (Siedentop & O'Sullivan, 1992), we have found that female high-school teachers are marginalized in their own departments and girls are getting fewer opportunities in physical-education classes and liking it less than boys do. Another study (Olafson, 2002) found that adolescent girls disliked their physical-education classes intensely and tried to find ways to avoid them. This kind of finding is particularly salient in an era when it is clear that adolescent girls are among the most at-risk population for overweight/obesity. We should all work toward the situation where girls and boys have the same access to all activities, learn together, and get equal opportunities to practice and improve and where teaching assignments are made on basis of competence and experience rather than gender.

ISSUES IN ELEMENTARY-SCHOOL PHYSICAL EDUCATION

One of the most important findings in education over the past decade has been evidence showing that boys and girls who reach the end of third-grade reading well below their grade level will likely have great difficulty being successful throughout grades 4–12. Reading well is essential to success in almost all school subjects. It has also become increasingly clear that children who reach the end of third grade and are overweight/obese will quite likely remain overweight/obese throughout their school years and into adulthood.

In the past two decades, prevalence of overweight and obesity among children in the United States has doubled and the prevalence among adolescents has tripled (American Academy of Pediatrics, 2003). Currently, nearly 16.7 percent of children and adolescents, are overweight, and 17.1 percent are obese (Koplan, Liverman, Kraak, & Wisham, 2006). Overweight and obesity are not distributed normally across the population. Low-income children and African American children have higher obesity rates. Twenty-three percent of teens from families living in poverty were overweight, compared to 14 percent of those not living in poverty (Meich, Kumanyika, Stettler, Link, Phelan, & Chang, 2006). In my home state of Ohio, recent data showed that 37.6 percent of third-graders were overweight/obese (Ohio Department of Health, 2006).

It has been abundantly clear that elementary schools in conjunction with community organizations and parents are primary battlegrounds to combat this epidemic of overweight/obesity. Why schools? Because they exist in all communities, are attended by nearly all children, provide safe environments, and have facilities, equipment, and trained personnel (McKenzie & Kahan, 2008). As noted previously, overweight/obese children who move beyond the third grade are likely to remain that way through adolescence and into adulthood. The most likely solution to this problem is for elementary schools to offer daily physical education, have active recess periods and activity breaks in classrooms, and work with community agencies and parents to provide physical activity in after-school and weekend programs. Unfortunately, for many schools the effects of the NCLB Act have resulted in less time in physical education, a reduction in recess time, and more interest in providing extra academic time than in extra physical-activity time—this despite the fact that there is substantial national agreement that children ages 5–12 should receive 60 minutes of moderate-to-vigorous physical activity daily (Strong et al., 2005). We know that the early elementary-school years are especially important for children to develop fundamental motor skills, to become comfortable when moving, and to enjoy moving in various activities. Children who reach third grade with only modest motor-skill development are less likely to enjoy and be successful in physical education throughout the remainder of their school years.

Elementary-School Specialist Teachers

The traditional elementary school is organized around the *self-contained classroom,* in which one teacher provides instruction in all the subjects. Over the years, specialist teachers have begun to relieve the classroom teacher of some of the instructional responsibilities in areas such as physical education, art, and music. Most states now certify specialist teachers in those areas.

States that have laws requiring physical-education instruction in the elementary school seldom specify that the instruction has to be done by a specialist teacher. However, the National Children and Youth Fitness Study II found that 83 percent of the children in grades 1–4 who were tested in the study had physical education at least once per week from a specialist teacher. That finding is higher than most estimates. Regardless of what the actual percentage might be, it is clear that many school districts hire elementary-school physical-education specialists even though they are not required by law to do so.

The issue here is clear. Most classroom teachers have had only one course in physical-education methods as part of their teacher preparation. They are not well prepared to teach physical education. The demands on their curricular time increase year by year. They cannot possibly do all the things expected of them—and physical education is too

often the subject that gets left out. The physical-education specialist has extensive training to do the job and has that job as his or her sole teaching interest. Children clearly benefit more from specialist teaching than from physical-education instruction given by the classroom teacher.

In many school districts, elementary-school physical-education specialists travel from school to school, often serving three or four schools each week. The specialist teacher teaches one lesson per week, and the classroom teacher follows up with a second and perhaps a third lesson that week. The specialist teacher is often responsible for providing lesson plans for the classroom teacher that build on what was taught during the specialist's one lesson with the children. Being a traveling specialist is a difficult job. Continuity is hard to achieve. The specialist sometimes does not feel that he or she is a member of any single school faculty. It is clear that elementary-school physical education will take a major step forward when *each* school has at least one specialist physical educator.

School districts that want children to have a daily period of physical education have one to three full-time specialist physical educators in each elementary school. The benefits of such an arrangement are clear. The school district obviously values physical education. Groups of specialist teachers can work together, each teaching in those activities for which he or she is best prepared. That this situation might someday become the norm for elementary schools everywhere is the hope behind the movement for high-quality, daily physical education.

Facilities

Have you seen a well-designed, fully equipped elementary-school gymnasium? What a bright, joyful, interesting place it is! How clearly it contributes to the potential of a program to accomplish program goals! Yet many children do not have the benefit of instruction within such a facility.

The facilities for physical education obviously affect what can be taught (choice of activities) and how it will be taught (teaching method). This is not to suggest that high-quality physical education cannot occur in an elementary school without a real physical-education facility. Of course it can! The issue here is providing appropriate facilities and equipment so that teachers can help children achieve the full range of benefits within a subject such as physical education.

Developmentally Appropriate Practices

Those who have studied effective elementary-school physical-education specialists have come away in awe of the manner in which they provide interesting, innovative, and **developmentally appropriate** experiences for a variety of children—some more skilled than others, some more fit than others, some more interested than others (Rauschenbach, 1992; Siedentop, 1989). In its continuing efforts to promote high-quality physical education for children, the Council on Physical Education for Children (COPEC), an affiliate of NASPE, published its position statement on "Developmentally Appropriate Physical Education Practices for Children" (NASPE, 1992).

COPEC has identified appropriate and inappropriate practices for twenty-six components in an elementary-school physical-education program. Some components—such as curriculum, cognitive development, and affective development—are broad and are intended to be general guidelines. Other components—such as not using fitness activities as punishment, forming teams, and measuring success rates—are quite specific. In each case, COPEC has provided a statement identifying appropriate practice and a companion statement identifying inappropriate practice.

School principals, parents, and policymakers can use the COPEC document as they evaluate and plan for elementary-school physical education. Teaching professionals also find the document beneficial as they attempt to continue to provide high-quality physical education for children.

Are parachute activities appropriate for physical education?

Curricular Issues

Another area of disagreement among physical-education professionals is the question of what constitutes the best curriculum model for elementary-school physical education. Is it the skill-theme model described in Chapter 10? Is it a health-related fitness model? Is it a lead-up games model? Should it be an age-appropriate version of a health-fitness model? Nearly every professional agrees that physical education for young children (grades K–3) should not be highly specific-skill practice and competitive games.

There seems to be increasing agreement that the K–3 years should focus primarily on issues of motor-skill development with the skill-theme model as the most appropriate and well-defined approach. There is also agreement that these early years in physical education should *always* be fun, what physical-education philosopher Scott Kretchmar describes as allowing children to "find their playgrounds" in a "joy-oriented" physical education (Kretchmar, 2008). He argues that joy-oriented physical education is grounded in meaning, what young children come to value and what it means to their lives, whereas health-related physical education is grounded, at least partly, in such mandates of efficiency as time on task and good heart rates. For students to *adopt and value a physically active lifestyle*, the overarching goal must pay attention to the meaning that children derive from their motor experiences because we are all more likely to adopt and value behavior patterns that provide us with joyful experiences. Joy-oriented physical education requires a very specific pedagogical approach. It seems, however, reasonable to argue that joy in movement activities is more likely when one is reasonably skillful. Thus, both these positions have merit, and finding ways to bring them together, especially in the K–3 years, would prove useful.

What does seem clear is that physical education in the K–3 years should not be watered-down versions of what we present to adolescent students. In the sport-education model, we have always argued that fourth grade is probably the best starting age to begin students in a curriculum and instruction model that involves working together, teamwork, specific activity–related technique and tactical-learning tasks, and age-appropriate competition formats. In grades 4–5, elementary-school students can begin to learn more institutionalized forms of motor activity, such as sports; adventure-education skills; and activities related to health-fitness such as strength-training, cardiovascular-training, and stretching techniques.

This kind of professional debate is very healthy but is not "won" in the sense of settling the issues. Elementary-school physical-education teachers are free to develop their own programs. District syllabi typically are defined so broadly that nearly any approach would be "in-bounds."

ISSUES IN SECONDARY-SCHOOL PHYSICAL EDUCATION

Concern about the quality and viability of physical education in many high schools has been expressed consistently in the professional literature and at conferences for over 20 years. One article described high-school physical education as an "endangered species" that will probably fail if it continues on its present course (Siedentop, 1987). Another talks about the "decline and fall of physical education" (Hoffman, 1987). Although many remain optimistic about elementary-school physical education, we should all be concerned about why high-school physical education appears to be so devalued by students. Possible explanations are explored in this section.

"Busy, Happy, and Good"

In 1983 Judith Placek investigated how teachers conceptualized successful teaching in secondary-school physical education. In the article reporting her findings, she coined a phrase that has become famous in the profession: She found that most teachers thought that keeping students "busy, happy, and good" (Placek, 1983) was the main gauge of their own success. If students are well behaved, fairly active in class, and reasonably happy, then teachers feel they have been successful. But what about significant learning? What about students getting excited about performing better or becoming more fit? As Griffey (1987, p. 21) argues, "The sense of mastering something important is denied most students in secondary physical education programs in this country." When students are busy, happy, and good, school administrators are usually quite satisfied. One of the keys to solving this problem is for school administrators to show more interest in a physical-education program focused on important learning outcomes. Instead, too many high-school classes can be honestly described as supervised recreation.

Multiactivity Curriculum

Many people who have assessed the problems of secondary-school physical education agree that the multiactivity curriculum contributes to the general lack of outcomes. Many high-school programs comprise a series of short-term units covering a wide variety of activities. (See Chapter 2 for the history of the multiactivity approach.) However, can 3- to 7-day units provide sufficient in-depth learning to produce lasting outcomes? Taylor and Chiogioji gave an answer that most experts would agree with:

> The generally accepted goals of physical education are to promote physical fitness, self-esteem, and cognitive and social development. However, the practice—the proliferation of and emphasis on teaching too many activities in too short a time—has made these goals more difficult to attain. The smorgasbord approach of requiring team sports, individual sports, dance, physical fitness activities, all within the space of one school year lessens those students' opportunities to master any one activity through which they can meet the stated goals. (Taylor & Chiogioji, 1987, p. 22)

Improvement, achievement, and mastery are themes that are neither readily apparent in multiactivity programs nor likely in programs that focus on keeping students busy, happy, and good.

There clearly *are* excellent high-school physical-education programs. It is interesting to note that some people believe that a dominant characteristic of such programs is that they have a main curricular theme:

> The (good) programs stood for something specific. We learned about good fitness programs, good social development programs, and good adventure programs. Each of the programs had a main focus that defined and identified the program. While many of these programs were multidimensional, each had a main theme that dominated the curriculum. (Siedentop, 1987, p. 25)

Main-theme curricula allow students to focus for longer periods of time on mastering content (Siedentop & Tannehill, 2000). Whatever the activity, it takes time for students to develop basic techniques, to understand the manner in which the activity is pursued or competed, to master tactics involved with the activity, and to engage in the activity for a long enough time to gain confidence and develop sufficient skill to enjoy the activity. When they enjoy the activity, students are more likely to continue to pursue it outside of school time. The curriculum-instruction models described in Chapter 10 and the examples shown in Chapter 11 all depend on allowing sufficient time for students to

Providing accurate feedback on students' performance is an important teaching skill.

become skilled and confident in the activity, thus allowing them to experience the enjoyment of performing the activity.

Examples of main-theme curricula for developmental physical education, adventure education, sport education, fitness and wellness, and integrated physical education can be found in Siedentop and Tannehill (2000). There is evidence from high-school reform models that a more focused curriculum improves student interest and achievement; thus, it may provide one way that high-school physical education can rescue itself from its current troubles.

Difficult Teaching Situations

If high-school physical education is in trouble, certainly part of the reason is the difficult situation that many of its teachers face. The difficulties involve combinations of class size and heterogeneity of skill levels as well as coed participation (addressed in the next section). In some schools, it is not uncommon to find fifty to seventy students in a physical-education class although classes in, say, English or algebra are considerably smaller. With that many students, there are always problems of classroom management, equipment, and space. Good teaching can be done in such situations, but it is difficult.

A second factor is the marked heterogeneity of the skill levels of a typical secondary-school physical-education class. Varsity-level athletes are scheduled in the same class as inexperienced, unskilled students. Whereas algebra teachers and chemistry teachers can expect their students to have a basic level of skill and understanding, physical educators have no such luxury. Physical educators must often accommodate enormously diverse levels of skills and interests in any given class, which makes effective teaching difficult. In programs where students *elect* classes and in programs where classes are based on progressions in skill (for example, Tennis I, Tennis II), this major problem is reduced substantially. The high-school program described in Chapter 11 used a fitness-skill testing procedure to place students in classes that were developmentally appropriate for them. Practices such as those enhance the quality of experience for the student and enable teachers to teach more effectively.

Coed Participation

Traditionally, boys and girls have been taught in separate classes in secondary-school physical education. When I was going to high school, before Title IX, it was generally known that the girls' physical-education classes were better taught and more interesting than the boys' classes. Title IX made coeducational classes mandatory, except in rare instances. It is true that in many places girls had less access to instruction, time, and equipment in physical education than did boys. It is not entirely clear that in the 31 years since Title IX, this particular provision of the law has "worked" as well as many hoped it would.

The assumption of Title IX was that sex-integrated classes would lead to more sex-equitable classes. Some coed classes surely do meet that assumption. Others do not. Some studies have shown that lower-skilled

girls are often marginalized in coed physical-education classes (Scraton, 1990; Siedentop & O'Sullivan, 1992). Recently, a study of adolescent girls in physical education found that many of them disliked their physical-education classes intensely and tried to find ways to avoid them (Olafson, 2002). Coed teaching is often difficult for teachers because of the wide range of abilities that they encounter, especially when invasion games are the focus of the curriculum, reflecting, no doubt, a history of girls having less opportunity to learn to excel in invasion games (basketball, soccer, and touch football, for example).

The issue of coed or sex-segregated physical education has also been addressed in other parts of the world. In England, as a result of extensive study of girls' participation in high-school physical education, Scraton (1990) recommended that a girls-centered physical education be developed that emphasized physicality, consciousness raising, and confidence building in physical-activity settings. Scraton believes in the ultimate value of coed physical education but believes also that, in most current situations, a girls-centered approach will increase the likelihood that young women will benefit from subsequent coed participation.

Australia developed a national policy for junior sport that speaks specifically to coed participation:

> Physical differences between girls and boys under the age of 12 are generally considered irrelevant to sporting ability. However, socialization may—and often does—prevent girls from developing sporting competencies equal to those of boys. Current evidence suggests that skill development in mixed groups is generally appropriate, but that competition should remain single-sex until it can be shown that girls will not be disadvantaged in mixed-sex contests. (Australian Sports Commission, 1994, p. 11)

The Australian policy provides a middle ground—that is, coed participation in skill development but separation for competition.

Most physical-education teachers have found that coed classes are fine for sports such as archery, bowling, and skiing. Where most problems develop are in invasion games such as touch football, basketball,

If children are to adopt and value a physically active lifestyle, they must have fun in their early learning.

and soccer. In many cases, some team and contact sports have been dropped from the curriculum to accommodate coed teaching (Geadelmann, 1981). Remember, this debate is not about the goal, which is a gender-equitable physical education. Rather, it is about the means to achieve that goal.

Treaner and her colleagues (1998) studied perceptions of coed physical education among middle-school students. Forty percent of boys and 33 percent of girls preferred same-sex classes, and 27 percent of boys and 30 percent of girls preferred a coed class structure. Both boys and girls reported that they performed skills better, played team sports better, and received more learning opportunities in same-sex classes. Boys tended to like physical education more than girls, and that difference increased from the sixth to the eighth grade. The study was possible because teachers had become frustrated by the challenges of teaching coed classes and wanted to experiment to see what differences occurred.

There are several approaches to solving the problems discussed in this section, problems that are most significant for middle- and secondary-school physical education. In middle schools, physical education is typically scheduled by class; that is, you go to physical education with the students who are with you for your other classes. With some activities, providing different groupings is quite easy. In a tennis unit, for example, students can learn and practice together, but competitions could be boys singles, girls singles, and coed doubles. Even in invasion games, where girls tend to be marginalized in coed competitions, this type of solution works especially well for large classes. These kinds of solutions do not violate the provisions of the Title IX legislation (Gabbei, 2004).

As described in the previous section, a quality coed physical education is much more easily achieved if students can elect the courses they take. In some cases, girls and boys might want to learn and participate together in a flag-football course or a fencing course. In other cases, girls might be more comfortable learning in a girl's flag-football course and boys in a boy's flag-football course. There is strong evidence (Prusak, Treasure, Darst,

& Pangrazi, 2004) that adolescent girls are more motivated and enjoy their physical-education experiences more if they have chosen the course.

Role Conflict

It is clear that many women and men become physical-education teachers partially, if not mostly, because they want to coach (Stroot, Collier, O'Sullivan, & England, 1994; Templin, Sparkes, Grant, & Schempp, 1994). Thus, the potential for role conflict exists from the outset of their careers. Not surprisingly, therefore, some evidence shows that some women and men who teach and coach suffer from **role conflict** (Chu, 1981; Locke & Massengale, 1978). Teaching is one role. Coaching is another role. Performing in both roles can produce role conflict and role strain. *Role conflict* exists when there are incompatible expectations for the different roles—for example, high expectations for coaching and lower expectations for teaching. *Role strain* exists when total role demands require more time and energy than a person has to give. The daily schedule, in and of itself, is sufficient to produce role strain over time. Role conflict also builds gradually, especially for head coaches, because the coaching role receives more attention than the teaching role, the expectations are higher, and the immediate rewards are greater. Coaching performance is very public and under the regular scrutiny of parents, administrators, and the community. Teaching is very private in comparison.

When role strain occurs, something eventually has to give. In some cases, the most likely casualty is quality teaching. That, however, is not inevitable! O'Connor and Macdonald (2002) found that some teacher-coaches manage the issues quite well, actually enjoy the dual responsibilities, and particularly like the differences in the student–teacher relationships in the two settings. There is also some evidence that some high-school physical-education teachers seek out responsibilities in school sport because it provides more challenge and satisfaction than they find in their teaching (O'Sullivan, Siedentop, & Tannehill, 1994).

The issue of role conflict among those who both teach and coach has been exacerbated during the last decade as high-school sports has taken on added importance. Many high-school athletes now specialize in one sport and train year-around to get better at it. A boy's football coach or a women's volleyball coach not only works many hours during the preseason and competition season but also often spends time and energy working with players during the off-season. Most high schools now have a strength-and-conditioning facility, and coaches often spend time with their athletes in that facility throughout the school year. The increased attention to and popularity of high-school sports has provided both a higher status for coaches within the community and greater demands that their teams perform well, all of which increases the chances of role conflict. Role conflict tends to increase when the role of coaching is supported more strongly than the role of teaching. As one coach put it, "I did not have any support for my teaching. They supported me as a coach, but as a teacher I could do anything or nothing at all. To sit on the bleachers and roll out the ball would have been fine" (Stroot, Faucette, & Schwager, 1993).

It is fair to point out that the recent national attention on child/youth overweight and obesity has made school boards and school administrators pay more attention to the nature and quality of physical education in their school districts. Many physical-education programs (see Chapter 11) have answered this call and brought forward innovative models that require planning and a renewed sense of good teaching for the district physical-education staff. Most of these efforts are *programmatic* in the sense that all teachers are meant to take part and do their fair share in implementing the new models. One might suspect that in districts that have renewed their effort in physical-education programming will pay more attention to the quality of new hires among the physical-education staff in the district. This will make it more difficult for a principal to hire a new physical-education teacher who happens to have great experience in preparation to be a defensive coordinator for the varsity football but whose credentials and commitment to physical education might be less robust.

There is no simple solution to this problem. Some people have suggested that coaching become part of the teaching assignment, thus allowing coaches to have a much lighter teaching load during their seasons. Some school administrators prefer to hire coaches who are classroom teachers, as opposed to physical-education teachers, thus avoiding this problem or, perhaps, shifting it to another group of people. Still others have suggested that a second teaching staff should be employed. Those people would begin their work in midafternoon and would continue through the evening hours, staffing recreational and community programs in schools as well as coaching. If secondary-school physical education is to thrive, this problem must be solved.

Rethinking Secondary-School Physical Education

There has been widespread discussion and debate about the possibility of rethinking how secondary-school physical education is conceptualized and delivered to youths (Locke, 1992; Siedentop, 1992; Vickers, 1992). These discussions have proceeded on the assumption that, in many places, high-school physical education is so sufficiently dysfunctional that it needs to be replaced rather than repaired—completely reinvented rather than improved.

Fortunately, there is evidence that such change can take place—and some interesting models have emerged. In New Zealand, more than 150 high schools have replaced a traditional multiactivity approach with the sport-education model in a drastically revised tenth-grade program (Grant, 1992). In Florida, a required fitness semester is followed by semester-long courses in a variety of activities (Graham, 1990). In many places, there have been experiments with health/fitness clubs in high schools, using an adult model of participation rather than the more compliance-oriented, regularly scheduled model common to most schools (Cohen, 1991). In other schools, physical educators have adopted a total-fitness perspective similar to the Needham High School program described in Chapter 11 (Westcott, 1992).

What is most needed at the moment is a better understanding of how such innovative programs get started and how they are sustained. They are exciting. They give us all hope for the future. Unfortunately, they too often have a way of not outliving the creative people who developed them.

Physical Education in Urban High Schools

Urban high schools often present difficult teaching situations. Physical-education facilities are typically old and inadequate, and class sizes are large. Many urban youths grow up in relative poverty and fail to develop healthy behaviors with regard to physical activity and good nutrition.

Urban play environments are inadequate, and those that do exist are typically unsupervised (Knop, Tannehill, & O'Sullivan, 2001). They are also typically dominated by skilled adolescent boys to the disadvantage of all others. Violence and the fear of violence too often pervade the lives of these adolescent boys and girls. For physical education to be successful in such settings, it must create trust through both sensitive curricular choices and appropriate teaching tactics, must build and sustain a sense of community so that students know they are cared for and feel some responsibility for the group, and must find multiple ways for students to be successful (Knop, 1998).

Two successful models for urban high-school youths are worth noting. The first is the social-development model created by Don Hellison (1995, 1996), which is described in Chapter 10. This model has been applied successfully in a number of urban high schools, using very different curricular approaches but maintaining the focus on the development of personal responsibility. A second model is the "sport for peace" curriculum (Ennis, Satina, & Solomon, 1999). This is a variation of the sport-education model described in Chapter 10, but with a strong focus on conflict resolution and good decision making during the sport season.

Physical education has much to offer in the form of positive youth development and physical fitness, both of which are important to the future of urban youth. Unfortunately, most urban schools are under extreme pressure to raise test scores in math, reading, and science, so most of their energies go to those parts of the curriculum.

The Intramural Program

Intramural activity is typically defined as activity beyond the regular instructional program but confined within the school. The traditional model for portraying the relationships among instructional physical education, intramurals, and interscholastic sport is a pyramid (see Figure 12.1). The base of the pyramid is the instructional physical-education program, which reaches all the students. The second tier in the pyramid is the intramural program, which provides activity opportunities for students who are interested in extending their skills and engaging in more competitive situations. The top of the pyramid reaches fewer students but is intended for those who are especially talented, providing them more practice and competitive opportunities. In the best of all worlds, **intramurals** would occupy a place of major importance in the school day. Many students would participate. A wide variety of activities would be available. Students could extend and refine the skills learned in the instructional program. Students could have an important competitive experience without making the daily commitment necessary to be on an interscholastic team. That ideal is seldom achieved. In fact, in many schools, the intramural program is virtually nonexistent, thus eliminating a major component in any complete physical-education program.

Intramurals suffer from a number of problems. Schools often do not have the resources to hire personnel to administer and conduct these programs. Teachers, with full class loads, are often not enthusiastic about the extra burden imposed by such an assignment. Facilities used in the instructional program are often taken over immediately after school by the sport teams. Students find it

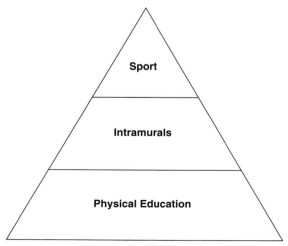

FIGURE 12.1 Traditional pyramid model for physical-education programs.

difficult to go home and then return to school for intramurals.

A major problem in sustaining intramural programs in middle and high schools is the fact that a great majority of students are bussed to and from school. Buses typically await students immediately after the last class period. As school districts have consolidated over the past 50 years, schools have tended to become larger with more students living farther from school facilities. Thus, students find it very difficult to stay at school for intramurals or to return to school for intramurals later in the day. With high schools typically starting earlier in the day, often with 7:30 a.m. classes, students finish the school day earlier. Intramurals would help fill the middle and later afternoon with useful and fun activities if problems of transportation and facilities could be mitigated. It is this very time in the afternoon that youth specialists throughout the nation have labeled as the most at-risk time for adolescents, time that should be filled with programs that appeal to their interests and make it less likely they would engage in problematic behaviors.

The immense popularity of intramurals in colleges and universities and the equally notable success of community recreation programs suggest strongly that boys and girls will take advantage of recreational sport and fitness opportunities that are available in reasonable facilities at reasonable times with reasonably competent staff. Intramurals have much to offer the secondary-school physical-education program and deserve to be done well.

CONCLUDING ISSUES

A few key issues that cut across K–12 physical education deserve our attention. It seems difficult to imagine that physical education can improve markedly without some forms of assessment and accountability. Likewise, we need to make sure that all students, regardless of their skill levels, get appropriate instruction and appropriate practice. Finally, because competition is inherent in many activities taught in physical education, we must consider the differences between good and bad competition.

Assessment and Accountability

Many physical educators have to regularly report grades. In some school districts, there is a grading format that must be followed and gives guidance to the physical educator. In other districts, physical-education teachers devise their own grading schemes and are required only to turn in grades at the end of each grading period. The "busy, happy, and good" approach described earlier in this chapter sometimes results in grading on the basis of attendance, dress, and participation; that is, to earn the top grade, students have to have good attendance, be dressed for class, and participate in activities with no serious behavior problems. Whether they actually know more or get better at an activity does not factor into the grade. Some teachers add "effort" to their grading scheme to differentiate between students who participate minimally and those who participate enthusiastically. In some districts, physical education may still be graded pass/fail, which strengthens the tendency to use attendance, dress, and participation as grading criteria.

At the national level, NASPE has made a substantial effort to define the attributes of a physically educated person and to develop content standards for physical-education programs (see Chapter 10). NASPE has also placed great importance on *assessing* student progress toward meeting content standards. Assessment refers to "tasks and settings where students are given opportunities to demonstrate their knowledge, skill, understanding, and application of content" (Siedentop & Tannehill, 2000, pp. 178–179). Assessment is mostly about supporting and encouraging learning and growth although the results of assessments clearly would provide a solid basis for grades also.

Physical-education teachers who use assessment do so primarily to motivate students and to help them learn more. They use skill tests, rating scales, checklists, portfolios, journals, written tests, and observations of game play to develop assessment profiles of their students. Some assessments are *formative*; that is, they are intended to provide feedback on developing skills, knowledge, and tactics. Other assessments are *summative*; that is, they provide a final judgment on outcomes achieved at the end of a unit.

The major focus of education reform currently is embedded in three related concepts: standards, assessment, and accountability. Physical education has a set of national standards (see Chapter 10) with benchmarks that are specific to grade-level outcomes. There are a variety of tools that teachers can use to assess student performance relative to the benchmarks and outcomes. The real issue yet to be addressed is, What use are standards and assessments if there is no accountability beyond that which the individual physical educator does for himself or herself? South Carolina is the only state that requires schools to report assessment data for physical education, thus creating a modest amount of accountability in that state.

There have been recent suggestions from within and outside the physical-education profession to provide greater accountability for outcomes in school physical education. One newspaper article addressed the issue by posing this question: "What if your children brought home a report card that said they were flunking fitness?" (Wier, 2004). There are two important ways to look at that quote. The first is that it recognizes that without stronger accountability physical education will continue to be done poorly in many schools. The second is that the quote suggests that the major—and perhaps the only—outcome in physical education is physical fitness. This is no doubt due to the strong national concern about the epidemic of overweight and obesity among children and youths in America. The same article quoted Dr. Judy Rink, a leader in the South Carolina state assessment project, to say, "We had a lot of administrators who called teachers in and said, 'What's going on here?' We recognized that we have to be a player. You've got to get people's attention. Right now there is no accountability, and without that we're just blowing in the wind."

Robert Pangrazi, a leading spokesman for physical education's contribution to healthy lifestyles, has argued that physical education should strive to be held accountable for increasing the amount and quality of physical activity for children and youths (Beighle, Pangrazi, & Vincent, 2001). He argues that through the use of pedometers and other measuring methods it is fairly easy to collect reliable data on physical activity, both in and outside of physical-education classes. Student logs can be kept and used as data for assessment and accountability purposes. The weekly cardio run/walk and computer-based records from the fitness-center work done 2 days per week by students in PE4life programs could provide similar kinds of data. These arguments, made by some of the strongest leaders in our profession, deserve to be considered seriously.

The debate about accountability is likely to continue and grow more heated in the near future. Many physical educators who provide extraordinarily good experiences for their students may be reluctant to jump on an accountability bandwagon for fear it will require them to attend to things they do not believe to be central to a good physical education. Many physical educators who practice a "throw out the ball" or "busy, happy, and good" model of physical education are likely to resist any form of accountability because it would jar them from their comfortable positions. There also is another threat—namely, that a sole focus on fitness or

physical-activity outcomes and accountability might backfire. Gard (2004) commented,

> There is a distinct possibility that a future funding body, say a national government, might decide that comprehensive physical education, complete with specialist teachers, syllabus documents, a varied curriculum and occupying a significant place in school timetables, is an appalling extravagance when all we are trying to do is to reduce body weight.

A 2000 report to the president of the United States from the secretary of Health and Human Services and the secretary of Education (A Report to the President, 2000) urged that a standardized assessment of student performance in physical education be developed so as to provide a means of holding physical-education programs accountable (www.cdc .gov/nccdphp/dash/presphsactrpt). The report also urged that physical education be included among the subjects on which students are tested as part of state education-assessment systems. If states were to enact legislation that put these recommendations into practice, one could expect that dramatic changes would occur in school programs.

Skill Equity

Another problem that occurs frequently in physical education is the inability to provide equitable learning experiences for less-skilled children and youths. Evidence suggests that less-skilled students typically get fewer opportunities to respond and have less success than do their more-skilled peers (Siedentop, 1991). When games are played, the less-skilled students sometimes get few real opportunities to take part in meaningful play. It is also clear that peers value competence in physical activity and sport; that is, one way in which children and youths can achieve better status among their peers is to be perceived as physically competent (Evans & Roberts, 1987).

Low-skilled students often don't try. They tend to have negative expectations for themselves because of their lack of success in physical education (Portman, 1995) and because they have received little assistance from the teacher or their classmates. They also are often the object of ridicule from

Children can help one another learn if they are taught how to do it appropriately.

classmates and criticism from teachers. It is no wonder that students like these try to find excuses to avoid participation or to be absent from physical education. The only fair description of what has happened to them is physical *mis*education.

Physical educators have the responsibility to provide equitable learning experiences for all children, regardless of skill level. Indeed, it is obvious that helping a less-skilled student to improve in ways that are recognized by peers not only is important in the physical domain but also produces benefits in the social and emotional domains.

Procedures for modifying activities to make them developmentally appropriate are available in our professional literature (NASPE, 1992; Siedentop, 1991). Physical educators must renew their commitment to helping less-skilled students experience success and improve in ways that contribute to the development of lifespan activity habits.

Good and Bad Competition

A continuing concern within physical education is the proper role and level of competition. Many of the abuses associated with organized sport (see Chapter 6) are assumed to be the result of an

overemphasis on competition, of a win-at-all-costs perspective. It is not uncommon for physical educators to advocate reducing competition, to replace competitive activities with cooperative activities, and to modify competitive activities in ways that reduce competitiveness. In its most extreme form, this kind of criticism within the physical-education profession suggests that competitive activities are harmful for children.

The issue can be viewed from another perspective (Siedentop, Mand, & Taggart, 1986). The issue is not whether competition is all good or all bad but, rather, how we can eliminate *bad* competition and emphasize *good* competition. Good competition creates a *festival* atmosphere, with all the attendant traditions, rituals, and celebrations. Good competition creates a *forum* within which children and youths can test themselves against accepted standards of excellence. Good competition involves *rivalry* but never the kind of rivalry in which one side can win only to the extent that the other side loses. Good competition also means *striving* within the rules and traditions to make the best effort possible—and then, when the competition is over, understanding that the winning or losing has little meaning outside the competition itself.

Bad competition, on the other hand, should be eliminated. Using the rules to gain an advantage, assuming that the only way to win is to have the best score, disregarding the traditions and rituals of the activity, and letting the outcomes affect the participants after the competition is over are all indications of inappropriate competition. Students in physical education should learn the differences between good and bad competition. The only way that they can do this is to have these things pointed out to them as they experience good competition.

Good competition is more easily attainable when individuals or teams are evenly matched. No one enjoys a competition that is terribly one-sided. The sport-education model (see Chapter 10) creates mixed-ability teams. For example, a class of thirty middle-school students would be divided into three teams, each of which would have ten players. Teams would be chosen or assigned to ensure that each

---

FOCUS ON   Expanding the Responsibility for Healthy Lifestyles   **12.1**

In October 2002, a national "Healthy Schools Summit" was held in Washington, D.C. Designed to bring together the nation's leading education and children's health and nutrition organizations, the summit was convened in an effort to improve children's health and educational performance through better nutrition and physical activity in schools.

The assumption of this summit was that the *responsibility* for developing healthy lifestyles in children belongs not only to physical-education teachers but also to the entire school and to families and the community as they connect with the school.

The summit focused on the obesity epidemic, on making nutrition and physical activity a priority for the whole school community, on marketing better nutrition and physical activity to children, on how to fund change, on coalition building, and on family and community involvement.

This is exactly the kind of total effort that is needed to achieve real gains in the health and well-being of children.

Source: www.actionforhealthykids.org.

---

team had a similar mix of less- to more-skilled players. When the first competition would take place—in 3 v 3 volleyball, for example—each team would have an A, B, and C team in the competition so that less-skilled teams and more-skilled teams would compete against each other, with each victory counting the same toward the seasonal championship. Small-sided teams of reasonably equal abilities can easily be created in a number of physical-education curriculum and instruction models. In tennis a teacher could have girl's singles, boy's singles, and coed doubles. In each competition, there would be A, B, and C level matches, again each match counting the same toward the final outcome.

PHYSICAL EDUCATION IN THE SPORT/FITNESS CULTURE

One of the most intriguing and disturbing issues facing physical education is the apparent lack of interest in and support for physical education as a school subject at exactly that point in our history when fitness and sport seem to be more popular than ever. Expenditures for fitness and sport in the private sector have increased steadily since the mid-1960s. The sport and fitness industries are booming, to say the least. Parents spend substantial amounts of money on lessons, clubs, and camps for their children—and a great deal of time and energy supporting community groups that sponsor sport and fitness activities for children and youths. Participation has increased, spending is up, and interest is higher than ever before.

How can school physical education be in decline in this era when fitness and sport are so popular? How can school physical education suffer from lack of support when the support is so willingly provided in the private sector? These serious and disturbing questions deserve to be carefully considered. There are no easy answers, but the fact remains that school is the one institution that touches the lives of *all* children and youths. The same cannot be said for the community sport program and most certainly not for the elite, private sport/fitness club.

Is school physical education an endangered species? Will it survive in this era of popular support for fitness and sport? If it is to survive and even to grow, what do we need to do to change how it is conceptualized and taught? How physical-education professionals answer the third question may indeed determine the answer to the first and second questions (see Focus On Box 12.1). If lifespan sport, fitness, and physical education are to become more of a reality in the future, then school physical education must begin to achieve its goals more completely.

GET CONNECTED to Physical-Education Web Sites

Teaching and Curriculum

PE Central	www.pecentral.org
PE Links 4U	www.pelinks4u.org
PE4Life	www.pe4life.org
PE Zone	http://reach.ucf.edu/~pezone
Action for Healthy Kids	www.actionforhealthykids.org
SPARK Physical Education	www.sparkpe.org
PE Digest	www.pedigest.com
Sports Media	www.sports-media.org
Physical Education Digest	www.pedigest.com

Adapted Physical Education

National Center on Physical Activity & Disability	www.ncpad.org
Motor Opportunities Via Education (Move)	www.move-international.org
National Consortium on PE and Recreation for Individuals with Disabilities	www.ncperid.org
American Association of Adapted Sports Programs	www.aaasp.org
Individuals with Disabilities Education Act (IDEA)	www.ed.gov/offices/osers/idea/index.html
Special Olympics	www.specialolympics.org
Palaestra	www.Palaestra.com

General Organizations and Associations

AAHPERD	www.aahperd.org
National Association for Sport and PE	www.aahperd.org/naspe
Society of State Directors of HPER	www.thesociety.org
National Board of Professional Teaching Standards	www.nbpts.org
Association for Supervision and Curriculum Development	www.ascd.org
International Council for Health, PE, Recreation, Sport, and Dance	www.ichpersd.org

SUMMARY

1. In elementary-school physical education, time allotted is often insufficient to achieve fitness and other instructional goals.

2. Too few schools require that elementary-school physical-education specialists be hired, and classroom teachers often do not actively teach physical education.

3. Facilities for elementary-school physical education are often inadequate, which can hamper program development.

4. Within the profession, there is disagreement about the nature of elementary-school physical education.

5. Too many secondary-school physical educators are content to keep their students busy, happy, and good, instead of focusing on learning and achievement.

6. The multiactivity program does not allow enough time in any one activity to realize important goals.

7. Large class size, heterogeneity of skill levels within a class, and the demands for coed

teaching have all made it more difficult to teach secondary-school physical education.

8. The dual demands of teaching and coaching often produce role strain and role conflict, with the result that teaching is sometimes relegated to a lesser status.

9. Intramurals should occupy a central place in the activity opportunities for high-school youths, but time, facilities, and staffing problems often cause them to be minimally important.

10. Many people believe that physical education has not yet been accepted as a subject of basic importance in the school curriculum.

11. Credibility can be earned only when real outcomes are achieved in physical-education programs and are then communicated effectively to the public.

12. Liability concerns have prompted teachers to pay more attention to instruction, curriculum, and supervision and have also resulted in some activities being deleted from the curriculum.

13. Physical education has a poor history regarding equity for girls; Title IX has begun to remedy that history of discrimination.

14. Skill equity requires that less-skilled students get equal opportunity and experience success.

15. There are important differences between good competition and bad competition, and these differences should be taught to students in physical education.

16. It is disturbing that physical education seems to be suffering during an era in which sport and fitness have assumed major cultural importance.

17. School physical education should provide the foundation for lifespan involvement in sport, fitness, and physical education, but to do so, it must begin to achieve its goals more completely.

DISCUSSION QUESTIONS

1. Were you taught by an elementary-school physical-education specialist? What was your elementary-school physical-education program like?

2. What was your high-school physical-education program like? Were you kept busy, happy, and good?

3. What would an ideal elementary- or secondary-school program be like? What facilities would be needed? What teacher–student ratio would be adequate?

4. Did your high school have intramurals? If so, what were they like? What role should intramurals play, relative to the instructional and inter-school-sport programs?

5. What credibility did the physical-education program have in the schools that you attended, among students and among teachers?

6. How were equity issues handled in schools that you attended? Did girls have equal access to facilities? Did they receive equal funding?

7. Why do you think that physical education is suffering during a time when fitness and sport are booming? How can that be changed?

Building a National Infrastructure to Support Physical Activity and Healthy Lifestyles

A multitude of initiatives in sport, fitness, and physical education are responding to the major national issues of developing healthy lifestyles, reducing the incidence of overweight and obesity, and child and youth development. Unfortunately, many of these initiatives are isolated rather than being connected within and among communities. We need efforts that connect initiatives developed in schools, communities, states, and the private sector. We need local, state, and national infrastructures that encourage young children to become physically active and start them on the road toward healthy lifestyles. We need connections across age groups so that children remain active and healthy as adolescents and into young adulthood. Then we need opportunities for lifetime involvement of adults and older citizens, regardless of gender, race, socioeconomic status, or disability.

To accomplish this, we also need the research and scholarship developed by the kinesiology subdisciplines, both the physical-science subdisciplines and the social-science subdisciplines. The four chapters in Part 5 provide information on policies and programs that can help to achieve these ambitious goals.

CHAPTER 13

Developing an Infrastructure to Support Physical Activity and Healthy Lifestyles

Our nation's young people are, in large measure, inactive, unfit, and increasingly overweight. In the long run, this physical inactivity threatens to reverse the decades-long progress we have made in reducing death from cardiovascular diseases and to devastate our national health care budget. Full implementation of the strategies recommended in this report will require the commitment of resources, hard work, and creative thinking from many partners in federal, state, and local governments; nongovernmental organizations; and the private sector. Only through extensive collaboration and coordination can resources be maximized, strategies integrated, and messages reinforced.

A Report to the President, 2000

LEARNING OBJECTIVES

- To describe the components of a physical-activity infrastructure

- To discuss the national blueprint for physical activity and healthy lifestyles

- To describe national efforts to support the physical-activity infrastructure

- To describe state-level efforts to support the physical-activity infrastructure

- To describe local efforts to support the physical-activity infrastructure

- To describe and discuss the role of allied fields

In Chapter 1, the concept of a physical-activity infrastructure was introduced. Sport, fitness, and physical-education professionals, along with colleagues from the health and recreation professions, need to work together to develop and sustain this infrastructure. A **physical-activity infrastructure** includes facilities, spaces, and programs enabling children, youths, and adults to become and stay physically active. The "enabling" provision requires that the infrastructure be attractive, accessible, and safe. Such an infrastructure exists in some locales (mostly upper-income communities), but in many other communities it is only partially developed, and in many rural and lower-income communities it is nonexistent. In a study of discretionary use of time among youths, the Carnegie Council on Adolescent Development (1992) suggested that "in a youth-centered America, every community would have a network of affordable, accessible, safe, and challenging opportunities that appeal to the diverse interests of young adolescents" (p. 77). We know that physical-activity infrastructures are not equally accessible to citizens from all socioeconomic groups, nor to all ages or both genders.

Currently, the environments in which young people grow from childhood through adolescence tend to make it easy to be sedentary and difficult to be active. Communities are typically designed around the automobile, which discourages walking and cycling and makes it more difficult for children to get together to play. In some communities, parental concerns about their children's safety severely limit the time and areas in which children are allowed to play outside. Electronic media in the form of computer games, video games, and cable and satellite television can occupy children and youths for hours at a time. As shown in Part 4 of this text, many states and school districts have reduced the amount of time that students spend in physical education, and large classes have become the norm rather than the exception. With budget problems facing many communities, funds for parks and community recreation centers are being curtailed. These situations all discourage activity for children and youths.

Research has been limited, but what evidence there is supports the view that a person's level of physical activity is influenced by aspects of the home, workplace, and community environment (www.cdc.gov/healthplaces/healthtopics/physactivity.htm). This means that the availability and accessibility of bicycle paths, hiking trails, exercise facilities and swimming pools play a role in determining the amount and type of physical activity that children, youths, and adults engage in. These are the kinds of facilities that together constitute the physical aspects of an activity infrastructure. When various community and private-sector organizations and physical-education, sport, health, and recreation personnel cooperate to develop and sustain attractive programs, the activity infrastructure becomes complete.

Many of the health problems that are increasingly common among children, youths, and adults are the result of inappropriate diets and lack of sufficient physical activity. As described earlier in this text, the overweight/obesity crisis among children and youths is related to a number of serious medical issues including diabetes, high blood pressure, and increased risk for heart disease. Although many efforts are being made to remediate the problems that overweight/obese young persons have, the more important long-term issue is to reduce the prevalence of overweight/obesity among children and youths through prevention programs that lead them toward healthy lifestyles. To accomplish this, we must develop and sustain attractive and inclusive physical-activity infrastructures that enable children and youths to become and stay physically active (Siedentop, 1996c). The infrastructure includes changes to the physical environment, development of facilities that attract young persons; physical-activity programs during school, after-school, on weekends, and over school-break periods; and personnel to develop and sustain those programs by making them attractive and inclusive. To achieve this, we must have policies, programs, and leadership at federal, state, and local levels. What follows in this chapter are highlights of policies and programs that are attempting to meet these important goals.

EFFORTS AT ALL THREE LEVELS OF GOVERNMENT

In June 2000, President Clinton directed the secretary of Health and Human Services and the secretary of Education to work together and report within 90 days on strategies to promote better health for our nation's youth through physical activity and fitness (A Report to the President, 2000). The resulting report, *Promoting Better Health for Young People Through Physical Activity and Sports* (U.S. Department of Health and Human Services, 2000), became the national blueprint for a physical-activity infrastructure. The report focused on the following six areas for which campaigns could be mounted to develop and sustain a more physically active life for children and youths.

- *Families* who model and support participation in enjoyable physical activity
- *School programs* that include quality, daily physical education, health education, recess, and extracurricular activities
- *After-school care programs* that provide regular opportunities for active, physical play
- *Youth sports and recreation programs* offering a range of attractive, developmentally appropriate activities
- *A community structural environment* that makes it safe for young people to walk, ride bicycles, and use close-to-home physical-activity facilities
- *Media campaigns* that increase the motivation of young people to be physically active

The report included ten implementation strategies that provide more specific guidance to further develop policies and initiatives in the six key areas. These strategies are shown in Focus On Box 13.1. You will see that these suggested strategies cover the full range of situations in which children and youths can become and stay physically active, as well as provisions for media campaigns and monitoring program and policy success at all levels.

Implementing a National Agenda for Physical Activity

Federal support for a national agenda to support physical activity is crucial, and there is also an important leadership role to be played by national organizations of various types. At a 1995 meeting of the American Heart Association, more than thirty health organizations discussed the possibility of forming a physical-activity coalition and quickly reached unanimous agreement that such a coalition should be created (www.ncppa.org). The American Heart Association (AHA), the American College of Sports Medicine (ACSM), and the American Alliance for Health, Physical Education, Recreation, and Dance (AAHPERD) agreed to create a coalition that in 1996 became the National Coalition for Promoting Physical Activity (NCPPA).

The NCPPA lead organizations include the three founding member groups plus the American Cancer Society, the National Athletic Trainers Association, the National Recreation and Park Association, PE4life, and the YMCA. The Division of Nutrition and Physical Activity of the Centers for Disease Control (CDC) and the President's Council on Physical Fitness and Sport serve as a federal advisory panel to the NCPPA.

The NCPPA has developed four strategic objectives to guide its work (www.ncppa.org):

- Champion public policies that reduce barriers to physical activity.
- Increase the adoption of activity-friendly community models.
- Promote incentives that result in greater adherence to recommended physical-activity behaviors through community, schools, and worksite environments.
- Influence policy and environmental changes for populations with low rates of physical activity.

The NCPPA has developed a policy platform to support these strategic priorities, convenes regular meetings to provide briefings on current and

FOCUS ON	Strategies to Develop and Sustain a Physical-Activity Infrastructure		13.1

Strategy 1	Include education for parents as part of youth physical-activity promotions.	Strategy 7	Enable youth sports and recreation programs to provide coaches and recreation staff with the training that they need to offer developmentally appropriate, safe, and enjoyable physical-activity experiences for young people.
Strategy 2	Help *all* children and youths receive quality, daily physical education.		
Strategy 3	Publicize and disseminate tools to help schools improve their physical education and other physical-activity programs.	Strategy 8	Enable communities to develop and promote the use of safe, well-maintained, and close-to-home sidewalks, crosswalks, bicycle paths, trails, parks, recreation facilities, and community designs featuring mixed-use development and a connected grid of streets.
Strategy 4	Enable sate education and health departments to work together to help schools implement quality, daily physical education and other physical-activity programs.		
		Strategy 9	Implement an ongoing media campaign to promote physical education as an important component of a quality education and long-term health.
Strategy 5	Enable more after-school programs to provide regular opportunities for active, physical play.		
Strategy 6	Help provide access to community sports and recreation programs for all young people.	Strategy 10	Monitor youth physical activity, physical fitness, and school and community programs in the nation and each state.

SOURCE: www.cdc.gov/nccdphp/dashprephysactrpt.

proposed federal and state legislation, monitors policy-change initiatives at the federal, state, and local levels, serves as a resource for state and local physical-activity coalitions, and is a major information resource for the physical-activity movement. Twice monthly the NCPPA publishes an electronic newsletter containing articles and information about the physical-activity movement.

If America is to build a sustainable infrastructure for physical activity, there must be policy and legislative efforts at all levels to develop the physical infrastructure, the program infrastructure, and the qualified personnel to deliver the programs. In 2001 the federal *Physical Education for Progress* (PEP) Act was passed, and the first funds of $5 million were distributed to eighteen programs whose applications were approved. The PEP grant program provides funds to initiate, expand, and improve K–12 physical-education programs. In 2007 more than 200 local school districts and community organizations received PEP grants totaling $74 million. The funds supporting PEP have remained fairly stable with 2008 funding at $75 million.

In June 2004, Congress passed Section 204 of Public Law 108-265, the Child Nutrition and WIC Reauthorization Act of 2004. Section 204 requires that "each local agency participating in a program authorized by the Richard B. Russell National School Lunch Act or the Child Nutrition Act of 1966 shall establish a local school wellness policy" (U.S. Congress, 2004). What this means is that schools that receive federal funding for school food programs must establish a wellness council. Among the issues that wellness councils are required to address are "goals for nutrition education, physical activity, and other school-based activities that are designed to promote student wellness" (Siedentop, 2007). This act has led nearly all states to introduce new legislation regarding student nutrition, physical education, and physical activity. In many cases, minutes for physical education have been increased, class sizes have been limited, requirements for credentialed physical-education instructors at the elementary-school level have been mandated, and substitutions for physical education have been disallowed.

The CDC, building on recommendations in the 2000 A Report to the President, created a *Kids Walk-to-School* program, the goals of which are to increase physical activity by encouraging children to walk or bike to schools in groups accompanied by adults. Forty years ago, more than half of all U.S. children walked or cycled to school, while today only 10 percent do (ncdot.org). The CDC encourages communities to make it easier for children to walk to school and provides information on how to initiate programs and develop local coalitions to make the program succeed. In 2005 new federal legislation allowed the federal Department of Transportation to support this initiative by creating a national *Safe Routes to School* program with an initial appropriation of $54 million. States were funded with requirements that at least 70 percent of the funds be used to support infrastructure projects such as sidewalks, pedestrian and bike paths, crosswalks, and traffic control. The remainder could be used for public awareness, bicycle safety, and funding for trainers and managers in state safe-routes-to-schools programs. Several states have now created state walk-to-school offices that add state funds to the federal initiative and begin to support "walkable environments" at the local level (Siedentop, 2007).

The CDC has also created *VERB*, a national, multicultural social marketing campaign that encourages young people ages 9–13 (the "tweens") to increase and maintain their daily physical activity. VERB uses paid advertising directed at tweens and engages the assistance of parents and other adults who are in positions to influence tweens, such as youth leaders, teachers, physical educators, health professionals, pediatricians, and health-care providers (www.cdc.gov/YouthCampaign).

Another national organization that promotes fitness, sports, and healthy lifestyles is the National Association for Health and Fitness (NAHF). NAHF is a network of state and governor's councils that promote physical activity at local levels in their states by supporting grassroots programs publicizing the need for and benefits of regular physical activity (www.physicalfitness.org). NAHF provides consulting services for states; a series of online tools that help organizations plan, evaluate, and build effective coalitions; and an electronic newsletter that offers information on successful approaches to increasing physical activity.

Shaping America's Youth (SAY) is another national organization that supports the development of physical-activity infrastructures. SAY is primarily a clearinghouse for information on state and local efforts. Through SAY's Program Registry, one can search specifically for local programs in specific states in a range of areas related to physical activity and healthy lifestyles. For example, the site enables you to look for programs that address both physical activity and nutrition in Ohio or any of the other states included in the registry (www.shapingamericasyouth.com).

Other national efforts to support healthier lifestyles for children and youth include the Healthy Kids Challenge (www.healthykids.org), Planet Health (www.harvard.edu/pre/proj_planet.htm), Take 10! (www.take10.net), and America on the Move (www.americaonthemove.org). The *Healthy Kids Challenge* provides instruction and support for preschools and elementary schools to improve the physical activity and nutrition within the schools and to support parents and caregivers in continuing the effort at home. *Planet Health* is an interdisciplinary curriculum focused on improving the health and well-being of students in grades 6–8 by linking classroom and physical-education activities. Classroom lessons are provided as well as "micro-units and FitChecks" for physical education, including tools for self-assessment. The *Take 10!* program provides teachers with information and activities to use as

10-minute exercise periods in classrooms. *America on the Move* works with states to introduce and develop statewide programs that rely on two small daily changes in lifestyle—taking more than 2,000 steps per day (about 1 mile) and eating 100 fewer calories per day. Colorado was the pilot state for this program. *America on the Move* provides resources to track physical activity, guides for reducing calorie intake, ways to develop and sustain support for the effort, special events to stimulate participation, and a bimonthly newsletter.

State-Level Efforts to Support Physical-Activity Infrastructures

The effort to create conditions that encourage children's walking to school was described in the previous section. Many states have developed programs with the help of the CDC's Kids Walk-to-School program.

- California has a Walk to School headquarters, which supports local communities' efforts to hold events that create interest in motivating kids to walk to school and has a "walkability checklist" to help families choose routes and help communities identify problem routes that can be improved (www.cawalktoschool.com). The program's overall aim is to help communities create permanent improvements that mean children walk more and walk safely.

- Oregon has a Walk+Bike To School Web site (www.walknbike.org). The Oregon program was initiated in 2005 at three pilot schools, encouraging children to walk, bike, blade, board, or scooter to school.

- In Nebraska the state Parent Teachers Association provides minigrants to communities to encourage adults to teach children safe pedestrian behaviors, identify safe routes to walk to school, emphasize the health benefits of walking, and have communities scrutinize the walkability of their neighborhoods and make improvements where necessary (www.nebraskapta.org).

- In Iowa where obesity doubled between 1990 and 2002, several state agencies joined together to create a health-promotion initiative called Lighten Up Iowa. This unique, low-cost initiative used friendly team competition (up to ten team members) to increase physical activity and improve dietary intake (Litchfield, Muldoon, Welk, Hallihan, & Lane, 2005). Teams could form at work, at schools, among families, in faith communities, or in civic organizations. Teams registered to compete for total accumulated physical activity and increased fruit/vegetable consumption, or both. The competition lasted 5 months. The sponsors kept in contact with teams through e-mails, and teams reported their progress. Winning teams accumulated the highest average activity per team member and highest percentage of weight loss. In 2003 Lighten Up Iowa engaged 12,000 Iowans across all counties. During the 5-month competition, 2.6 million miles of physical activity were logged, and 23.5 tons (47,000 pounds) of weight were lost!

The walk-to-school movement is an excellent example of federal leadership (CDC) helping states that in turn help local communities develop and sustain programs.

North Carolina is a good example of a state that is making vigorous efforts to support local communities in helping children, youths, and adults be more physically active and lead healthier lifestyles. *Be Active North Carolina* is a nonprofit organization (www.beactivenc.org) that aims to create change by (1) increasing public awareness, building grassroots advocacy, and assembling effective volunteer networks, (2) creating model statewide programs, and (3) advocating for policies that reduce barriers and create opportunities for physical activity. The organization grants funds to local programs and gives awards for model programs.

Another North Carolina program, *FitTogether*, has preventing obesity as a primary program focus (www.fittogethernc.org). This program has support from the medical and university communities in

North Carolina. The North Carolina Health and Wellness Trust Fund has partnered with Blue Cross and Blue Shield of North Carolina to establish twenty community-based and statewide obesity-prevention programs that receive assistance from Duke University Medical Center. Lessons learned from these programs will be converted into "best practices" to provide guidance for businesses, civic groups, and schools in creating local programs to support physical activity and healthy lifestyles.

The Physical Activity and Nutrition (PAN) Branch of the North Carolina Division of Public Health sponsors the *Color Me Healthy* program focused on children in day care, preschool, and kindergarten centers in North Carolina. The program provides training and materials to assist teachers, child-care workers, owners of day-care facilities, and Head Start personnel to create nutrition and physical-activity programs that improve the health and well-being of young children. The PAN Branch also provides *Eat Smart, Move More* grants to local communities to assist them in advancing the state's goals for more physical activity and healthier lifestyles (www.eatsmartmovemorenc.com).

In North Carolina, the state-level umbrella policy called *Healthy Active Children* supports the many state and local efforts described here. In June 2005, the State Board of Education approved a new addition to that policy, requiring that students accumulate 30 minutes of physical activity throughout each school day, whether in physical education, during recess, or in class. The physical-activity requirement complements but does not replace the school's physical-education program. The policy also recommends that schools move toward 150 minutes of physical education each week for elementary schools and 225 minutes for middle schools.

State-level policy and the legislation that flows from it are crucially important to achieving goals for more physical activity and healthier lifestyles. For example, the Oregon "Bike Bill" requires the inclusion of sidewalks and/or bike facilities any time a road or highway is built or rebuilt.

In 2001 the Texas legislature passed Senate Bill 19 recognizing the growing problem of children's health. The bill had three primary components: (1) 30 minutes daily or 135 minutes weekly in physical activity in grades 1–6, (2) the establishment of School Health Advisory Councils, and (3) the use in all districts of the CDC's Coordinated School Health model coordinating health education, physical education and activity, nutrition services, and parental involvement. Elementary schools in Texas are required to adopt one of four models to implement their local Coordinated School Health programs. The four models are the Coordinated Approach to Child Health (CATCH); Bienester, a model for schools with high Latino populations; Health Wise; and The Great Body Shop. Texas also has recently required the 135-minutes-weekly provision for middle-school physical education also.

South Carolina has established itself as a national leader in physical education by adopting standards for K–12 physical education and putting into practice the nation's first state assessment system for outcomes in physical education (Rink & Mitchell, 2003). School wellness legislation in South Carolina requires that students in grades K–5 complete an average of 150 minutes per week in physical education and physical activity (60 minutes in physical education and 90 minutes in physical activity) with a student to teacher ratio of no more than 28:1. Each elementary school must also appoint a physical-education teacher to serve as its physical-activity director to plan and coordinate opportunities for children that exceed the designated weekly time requirements. All high-school students are required to complete 2 credits of health and fitness. The legislation also required a phase-in of student-to-certified-physical-education teacher ratios, culminating in 2008–09 with a ratio of 500:1, which means that any elementary school with more than 500 students would be required to have two physical-education teachers.

California was the first state to earn an A on the University of Baltimore's yearly review of state legislation to stem to the childhood obesity epidemic. California's Senate Bills 12 and 965 defined the state's strategies for local school wellness councils and provided $40 million to hire more credentialed physical-education teachers and

$500 million for the purchase of physical-education, art, and/or music supplies and equipment. Activity requirements were increased to 200 minutes of physical education for every 10 school days in grades 1–6, a minimum of 400 minutes of physical education for every 10 school days in grades 7–12, and annual fitness testing in grades 5, 7, and 9. The state also required that all physical education be delivered by a credentialed physical-education teacher. What were lacking from this otherwise robust legislation were accountability measures to ensure that districts were implementing programs that met the requirements of the legislation. One study has shown that requirements for minutes were often not met and that class sizes, especially in urban middle and high schools, were often more than seventy students per class (California Endowment, 2008).

Local Efforts to Support Physical Activity and Healthy Lifestyles

Although national and state efforts to design policy, enact legislation, and provide support for physical activity and healthy lifestyles are essential, the programs are typically delivered locally, and the local government, organizations, school personnel, and recreation and health personnel must work together to develop and sustain the physical-activity infrastructure. What follows in this section is a sample of efforts that show the different approaches being taken at the local level throughout the nation.

The Escambia County Schools have a district-wide initiative that incorporates wellness throughout the curriculum and in the school environment (Samman, 1998). The program helps students, faculty, and staff develop healthy lifestyles, forms partnerships with the community to promote wellness for students, and involves parents in developing family wellness activities. School and community facilities have been upgraded to support this local physical-activity infrastructure, and both a wellness newsletter and an annual wellness fair help keep the initiative before the local citizens.

The community of Perry, Ohio, built a new high school that includes a comprehensive community sport and recreation center (Schmid, 1994b). This is a joint-use facility for students, faculty, staff, and community residents. The physical-education program and school sport teams use the facility, and it is also open to students and residents 30 hours a week for drop-in activity. The school district and community government share the cost of equipment, maintenance, and employee salaries. This sort of sharing enables communities to make better use of facilities and to avoid the cost of building and maintaining separate facilities.

In Centerburg, Ohio, the high school teamed up with the local YMCA to create and share an extensive fitness facility used by students and community members (Seymour, 2005). In Delaware, Ohio, the city council provided $50,000 to equip a new weight-training facility at the high school. The facility is a joint-use operation for both school and community.

In West Des Moines, Iowa, the school district developed an intramural program for seventh- and eighth-graders in conjunction with a local YMCA and the city Parks and Recreation Department (Samman, 1998). The students at three junior high schools are served by an extensive program headed by school intramural directors assisted by YMCA and Park District personnel, who organize adult volunteers to act as coaches, officials, and mentors. The program is jointly funded by the three partner organizations.

In Hawaii, a daily physical-activity program, *Getting Energized and Recharged* (GEAR), was developed in three schools (Maeda & Murata, 2004). This program requires collaboration between physical educators and classroom teachers. The purpose of the GEAR program is to have classroom teachers incorporate short bouts of physical activity into the daily schedule to supplement the physical-education program. Each short bout takes a minimal amount of time, yet it is sufficient to increase students' circulation after long periods of sitting and serves to help students regain their focus. Activities include performing locomotor-movement skills around desks or tables, moving rhythmically to children's aerobic videos, and using Speedstacks cups for cup stacking. These 5-minute GEAR bouts can be used two or three times daily, and teachers have responded enthusiastically, reporting that the effects on their students have been positive for both exercise and academic work.

In Waco, Texas, the *Lighted Schools* program was created to provide after-school, evening, and weekend services to elementary- and middle-school students, parents, and community members (www.financeproject.org). The program was developed with the involvement of nineteen local organizations, including the Waco Independent School District. The program operates in nine sites and serves six middle schools and three elementary schools with over 1,000 student participants. The McLennan County Youth Collaboration, a member organization of seventy-one youth-serving agencies, was the driving force behind the project. The program focuses on reducing crime rates and teenage pregnancy rates, along with providing academic and recreational services. It is funded from a number of state and federal grants, along with substantial in-kind support from local agencies.

Runn!ng for Life is an elementary-school program in Virginia that combines fitness with school subjects such as geography, language arts, and history (Davis, 2003). A single classroom, a combination of classrooms, or an entire school can participate. The program begins with the selection of an academic theme, featuring geography in conjunction with history and relevant local cultures. For example, in one year the focus was on the Lewis and Clark expedition. A large map of the area defined by the theme is created and posted in a central school location. On the map are routes that students can choose to follow. Teams are determined and identified by a name. The exercise in Runn!ng for Life is running and is measured in laps, which are converted into distances along the route selected and then depicted on the map. As students accumulate mileage in their "map run," classrooms study the geography, people, culture,

and history of the regions that they would encounter. The program is organized by having classrooms run three times per week around a 200-meter oval track (the shorter track allows students to pass the start line more frequently, thus accumulating more laps). At the end of each week, the laps and converted distances are accumulated and added to the map.

Since 1996 in Filer, Idaho, the Filer elementary school has sent its fourth-graders on a 50-mile walk to cap a school year spent learning the importance of meeting goals and enjoying exercise (Fanselow, 2004). The trek encourages lifetime fitness, and students spend the entire school year preparing for it. Because part of the route parallels the Oregon Trail, children keep journals similar to what pioneers did 150 years earlier. For 5 days, students walk 10 miles on back roads before being bused back home. The physical-education teacher reported that although fewer than 50 percent of her students can sustain a walk at a 4-mph pace at the start of the school year, by the time for the Big Walk Week they are all ready to walk at that pace. The last day of the walk is a 10-mile walk back to the Filer city limits where they are met by a police escort and the Filer school students and teachers.

The *Planned Approach to Healthier Schools* (PATHS) was first implemented in a rural high school and junior high school in Utah (Lounsbery, Gast, & Smith, 2005). The PATHS program includes a professional development and wellness program for faculty and staff, the development of school environmental supports, a parental awareness campaign, and an integrated physical-activity and nutrition curriculum, which also functions as a schoolwide intervention. Each teacher implements the PATHS curriculum in one class one time per week. Each 50-minute class contains a short lesson about the benefits of physical activity and nutrition, skills to help students become more physically active, environmental barriers to changing health behavior, or skills to encourage others to adopt healthier lifestyle habits. Students then divide into teams to create a plan to encourage the entire student body to be more active and "eat healthier." Tasks to complete the plan are identified and developed. Students then write in their PATHS log about what had happened and what their own contribution had been. This curriculum is designed to allow students to gain knowledge and to become *activists* for physical activity and nutrition in their own school communities.

AAHPERD's *School–Community Recognition* program is intended to honor exemplary programs of collaboration to promote healthy, active lifestyles. In 2005 the Bay Shore Middle School in New York and the Woodland Elementary School in Johnson City, Tennessee, were honored. The Bay Shore award was for forming a Wellness Alliance focused on changing behaviors of middle-school students. Local physicians and hospital workers became involved in helping develop the wellness program in the school with equipment donated by the community. A wellness/environmental walk was developed and was used both by students and by the community.

The Woodland initiative was based on a K–4 Growing Healthy program that was extended to six surrounding school systems. Local medical professionals, university faculty, and physical-education teachers created a community mapping project and activities for children using pedometers, maps, and compasses. The school now serves as a demonstration project for state and national political leaders.

The 2007 School–Community award winners were Broward County, Florida, schools for their *Commit 2B Fit* program; the Anchorage, Alaska, schools for their *Healthy Futures: Get Up & Go!* program; and the Waterville, Maine, school district for their *Waterville Kid Power! Collaborative*.

THE ROLE OF ALLIED FIELDS IN IMPROVING PHYSICAL ACTIVITY AND HEALTHY LIFESTYLES

This text has focused primarily on sport, fitness, and physical education. To build and sustain a national infrastructure to support physical activity and healthy lifestyles also requires the involvement of the allied fields of recreation, health, and dance. All of these fields moved from the early-twentieth-century umbrella field of physical education to establish professional and scholarly fields of their own. Obviously, the work of these allied fields is important to the future health and well-being of the nation's children, youths, and adults.

Recreation, health, and dance have made significant progress as independent fields. People who prepare for professional work within these fields frequently specialize to the point where they have little contact with the larger physical-education field from which they emerged in the 1940s. As Ellis (1988) has argued, it is less clear that those who seek activity, leisure, or health services recognize these specializations as distinct:

> The professions of health, education, physical education, and recreation, however, remain inextricably linked. All of them develop and deliver services that are part of the total health package. All contribute to the constructive use of leisure. If the boundaries between them are difficult for the professionals themselves to draw, they are impossible for the client. The client's body has multiple needs and possibilities, but the client lives and experiences these needs, and the connections between them, as a whole. (Ellis, 1988, pp. 5–6)

It can be further argued that most of the significant problems related to leisure, health, and activity cannot be solved except through collaboration by professionals within these fields. Thus, as the separate professions of recreation, health, and dance are described in this chapter, please keep in mind that for most consumers of these services, the separation is not apparent. Among professionals themselves, there is growing recognition that these separations need to be decreased.

Recreation

What is increasingly referred to as the *recreation and leisure-services industry* is a huge national industry, providing enormous and varied career

Cardiovascular workouts are often done indoors.

opportunities for women and men. This industry includes sports and games, travel and tourism, hobbies and the arts, various kinds of entertainment (theme parks, for example), fitness pursuits, and outdoor activities, as well as traditional recreation providers such as the YMCA, the YWCA, community recreation departments in towns and cities, state recreation departments, and federal parks and recreation (Kraus, 2002). Annual expenditures for recreation range from the U.S. Commerce Department's estimate of over $490 billion (U.S. Census Bureau, 2000, p. 253) to as high as $1 trillion a year.

Recreation providers are private and public, commercial and nonprofit. Together they constitute an enormous job market and create an increasing need for well-prepared professionals who seek a career in the industry. This diverse job market is best seen by perusing *Careers in Recreation*

(American Association for Leisure and Recreation, 2000), which describes more than twenty-five types of positions. Among them are jobs in municipal and community recreation programs, at ski resorts, at theme parks, at tennis clubs, at family recreation centers, in conservation areas, in state and national parks, at corporate recreation centers, at armed-services recreation centers, in university recreation and intramural programs, in camps of every imaginable variety, in therapeutic recreation programs, and in a host of other agencies for which recreation is a key component— YMCA, YWCA, Boy Scouts, Girl Scouts, 4-H, Police Athletic League, Boys and Girls Clubs, and so on. As this industry developed during and after World War II, it moved from a base of primarily public and service-organization offerings with many volunteer workers to a base of commercial/private/municipal services with paid workers.

Recreation has been defined as activities or experiences chosen voluntarily and done during leisure time for the satisfaction that they provide to the individuals and groups involved (Colfer, Hamilton, Magill, & Hamilton, 1986). The worthy use of leisure time by citizens has been a national concern since the cardinal principles of education were enumerated in 1918. An active, healthy leisure life is thought to have restorative power and is considered to be a necessary part of an overall high-quality lifestyle.

As a profession develops, more professional preparation is required for entry into its ranks, often through programs that must meet certification standards of one kind or another. The professional preparation of recreation and leisure-services personnel started after the 1930s (McLean, Peterson, & Martin, 1988). Yet, in this short time, a number of specializations have developed, and certifications for entry into professional roles are much more common. In the 1960s, a person would have been prepared as a general recreation specialist; today she or he is more likely to focus specifically on one aspect of the recreation and leisure-services industry— parks, resource management, recreation-program

Worthy use of leisure is a lifetime issue.

management, recreation and park administration, therapeutic recreation, outdoor recreation, camping, school recreation, youth-agency recreation, recreation-sport management, aging, corrections, commercial tourism, recreational planning, environmental interpretation, or research (McLean et al., 1988). Estimates in the 1980s indicated that even then as many as 550 institutions of higher education offered a curriculum that prepared students to enter the recreation and leisure-services industry (McLean et al., 1988).

A number of professional organizations exist within the field of recreation. The largest of these, the National Recreation and Park Association (NRPA), was formed in 1966. This association was created specifically to provide for a unified recreation profession and was formed by the merging of five professional groups: the American Recreation Society, the American Institute of Park Executives, the American Association of Zoological Parks and Aquariums, the National Conference on State Parks, and the National Recreation Association (Cordes & Ibrahim, 2003). The NRPA has an active citizen component in which laypeople interact with professionals to establish goals and programs. The

organization serves its members in many ways, through research, dissemination of program information, professional development, legislative policy information, field services to local groups, and publications including three major journals: *Parks and Recreation, Journal of Leisure Research*, and *Therapeutic Recreation Journal.*

Other professional organizations that serve this area directly are the American Association for Leisure and Recreation, which is the member organization for recreation in AAHPERD; the World Leisure and Recreation Association, which promotes professional interests at the international level; and the American Camping Association, which for many years has promoted camping as an educational and recreational experience for children and adults.

Leisure and recreation have become big businesses, so it is not surprising that the for-profit commercial enterprises have grown very rapidly in recent years. There is also increasing evidence that historically public and nonprofit enterprises (city recreation departments, YMCAs, and so on) are now creating partnerships to better meet the large demand for recreation services. The latest entry into the leisure field is electronic entertainment, which ranges in complexity from video games for home computers to video-game arcades to highly sophisticated virtual-reality experiences—for example, in skiing or golf.

The number of different occupations needed to keep the recreation and leisure-services industry going is staggering. Not all these occupations require *specialized* preparation, but many of them do. The trend in the recreation professions, as in any other professional group, is toward certification and licensing; typically, state legislation establishes the criteria for the certification. Thus far, recreation has not achieved widespread certification status although that is clearly the direction being taken within the profession. An intermediate step is *accreditation*, an approach in which institutions that train personnel have their programs approved by an autonomous body. Accreditation provides assurance to the public that personnel have competencies that ensure safety and appropriate programming for recreation services. Program accreditation now exists widely in the recreation and leisure-services professions.

The prospects for the recreation and leisure-services field are virtually limitless. Recreation is what Dunn (1986a) has described as America's "giant opportunity." As life in the modern age becomes more complex, stresses seem to increase, even to the extent that *stress management* has become a specialized field that tends to bring together the recreation and health professions.

This *restorative* goal for recreation will, however, be increasingly balanced by a newer view that sees recreation as a positive, preventive activity, as seen in the growing wellness movements in health. Corporations have begun to recognize that a healthy employee who has an active and satisfying leisure life is a more productive employee. Preparation for leisure continues to be recognized as a goal in school programs. Recreation for the increasingly large segment of the population in retirement is a growing field, filled with bright prospects and perplexing problems. Recreation for people with disabilities, for both regular and therapeutic purposes, is also a growing field. It is no wonder that

recreation specialists view the next few decades as being filled with possibilities.

A major issue in recreation now and for the future will be the reduction and elimination of constraints that interfere with access to and involvement in recreation (Henderson & Bialeschki, 1991). Historically, we have tended to think of constraints as limited time because of work and other obligations, inadequate skills for participation, insufficient discretionary income, poor facilities, and the like. Although those remain important, it is now clear that issues such as gender, age, disability, and socioeconomic status are also serious constraints (Cordes & Ibrahim, 2003). Of particular concern are the problems of adequate recreation for urban children, youths, and adults who live in relative poverty, especially compared with the typically abundant recreation opportunities in the suburbs. Inner-city communities have less public recreation land, fewer recreation staff, and minimal community volunteer support, and they must contend with the threat of gangs and violence (Cordes & Ibrahim, 2003, p. 275).

These inner-city problems led Kraus (1995) to argue that the growth of commercial recreation and the explosion of private-membership recreation groups, located primarily around city beltways and in suburbs, have divided American society into leisure haves and have-nots. Recreation is quickly becoming privatized. It is now common for residential developments to feature their own recreation facilities for which homeowners pay a yearly fee; programs are available only to those who live within the development.

Another key issue is that by 2020, more than 20 percent of the population will be over 65 years of age, living longer, in better health, and more in need of quality leisure and recreation experiences. Older people have traditionally been raised to think that active recreation is not something to aspire to, but it is clear that their attitudes are changing dramatically. We can expect that when the baby boomers reach 65 and beyond, they will fully expect to remain active and to participate in recreation activities.

Many kinds of competition engage us in our leisure time.

Recreation has always been closely allied to sport, fitness, and physical education. Historically, the fields had similar beginnings and strong relationships in programs and personnel. In the past several decades, however, each has tended to become more specialized, and interrelationships among the allied fields have weakened. That issue is addressed in the following chapter. Suffice it to say that if lifespan sport, fitness, and physical education are to become more of a reality for a larger percentage of the population, interrelationships among the fields will need to develop and strengthen.

Health

The healthy lifestyle is in! Americans, especially those in the middle- and upper-income brackets, have taken health more seriously in the past several decades than they ever did before. The health professions have gradually shifted from a primarily remedial or medical approach to a primarily preventive or wellness approach. Whereas remediating or preventing sickness and disease characterized the main agenda of the health professions early in the twentieth century, the notion of living well increasingly shared that agenda at century's end. Americans are living longer, and the senior population is becoming a strong political and social force in American society. For these senior citizens, access to health care and a healthy lifestyle have become important issues.

Traditionally, the primary focus of the health professions has been the education of children and youths. Thus, it is health education that has, historically, been the strongest force in the emerging health professions. Since the mid-1980s, however, that tradition has been modified substantially. We have witnessed the growth of the **health-enhancement**

industry and an explosion of interest in health-related issues pertinent to people of all ages:

> Lifestyle decisions concerning nutrition, drugs, safety, activity, stress management, and other related areas have been clearly identified as major influences on health and disease. The people's health needs are met by a complex web of service delivery systems—hospitals, clinics, health centers, counseling centers, fitness programs, advertising, health clubs—designed to enhance health as well as to eliminate disease. These systems exist in both the public and private sectors of our economy. They are created by individual action, by businesses for profit, by philanthropic organizations, and by the government. They employ a very large number of people and consume an enormous proportion of the nation's wealth even as they contribute to it. Together, they are known as the *health enhancement industry*, and they share a simple, common goal: improving people's health. (Ellis, 1988, p. 4)

When we consider the health needs of individuals, we most commonly think about the medical profession. Yet many health professionals work outside the area of direct medical care such as is provided in hospitals. They work both in the public sector, through community and government programs, and, increasingly, in the private sector, through a host of entrepreneurial and corporate programs.

One way to understand the broad parameters of the health-enhancement industry is to consider the many topics and issues that are now addressed within the field of health and health education: family living, sexuality, substance abuse, personal health, nutrition, weight control, first aid and safety, consumer health protection, and interpersonal relationships. Since the 1960s or so, these topical fields have been brought together under the concept of **wellness**, which conveys the broader meaning of a positive, vigorous, healthy lifestyle.

The services of the health-enhancement industry are delivered to people through five major components: school health education, government and community health programs, nonprofit health organizations, worksite health programs, and private-sector

Family-oriented activities are important to the wellness movement.

entrepreneurial programs. Health education has been historically linked with physical education and has long been an accepted part of the K–12 school curriculum. Originally referred to most commonly as *hygiene*, the school health-education program has grown steadily more important and increasingly separate from physical education. Many states have enacted laws requiring that health education be taught in schools, often specifying the grade levels at which it must be taught and the amount of time or the number of units to be devoted to it.

Health education in schools is likely to become increasingly important as more of the nation's wealth is devoted to health care and maintenance. School is still the only societal institution that reaches most children and youths; therefore, it makes sense for most health promotion and education for children and youths to be programmed through schools. Six categories of behaviors are strongly related to mortality and morbidity statistics, thus warranting attention in school health education and promotion (Kahn, Collins, Pateman, Small, Ross, & Kolbe, 1995):

1. Behaviors that contribute to injuries, such as carrying weapons or not wearing seat belts
2. Tobacco use (smoking or chewing)
3. Alcohol and other drug use
4. Sexual behaviors that contribute to sexually transmitted diseases and unintended pregnancies
5. Poor dietary habits
6. Physical inactivity

Most of these behaviors are established during late childhood and early youth, thus making them relevant targets for school-based interventions.

School health education and community health have traditionally been the two general areas of preparation for health professionals. Government and community health programs are varied in nature and widespread, ranging from direct intervention, such as in school lunch and breakfast programs, to educational efforts, such as the development of literature on subjects such as prenatal care. It is now common for city governments to develop senior-citizen centers where issues of health and recreation are dealt with through both education and direct intervention.

Nonprofit health organizations have become increasingly active in the health-enhancement industry—the American Heart Association and the American Lung Association are two good examples. The main purposes of nonprofit health associations are to generate financial support for research and program development in the particular areas that they serve, to educate the public about the central issues surrounding their focus, and to influence people to lead healthier lifestyles. Thus, these organizations not only solicit funds and produce educational materials but also promote healthy behavior. The AHA sponsors competitive

road races, fun runs, and walkathons, and the ALA each year sponsors the "Great American Smoke-Out," encouraging smokers to quit smoking. Perhaps most important, these organizations fund substantial research.

Health enhancement in the private sector has become big business with big profits to be made by entrepreneurs who cater effectively to the increasing demands of Americans for health-related activities, literature, and programs. Many of the private-sector programs described in Chapters 5 and 8 would qualify as health-enhancement efforts. The private sector of the health-enhancement industry is largely unregulated. Although many health professionals do have certifications and licenses, many do not. Most states allow people who have *not* completed a certified program or earned a license to continue to advertise their services as "counselors" or "specialists." Although many counselors are in fact either clinical psychologists or psychological counselors, which guarantees their training, many have no such preparation. Many consumers are anxious for quick results and are looking for miracle programs to improve their lives. This combination of loosely regulated services and consumers who are eager to improve but are not always well informed about the services has resulted in a certain amount of quackery in the private-sector health-enhancement industry.

School health educators are certified and licensed to teach in the same way as all teachers are: They complete an approved program of teacher education at a university or college, one that meets the standards established by the state. Health educators are typically certified as K–12 specialist teachers. There is no certification in community health programs although many colleges and universities have undergraduate-degree specializations in community health. A graduate degree, the Master of Public Health (MPH), is a widely sought and highly valued degree in the health professions. Criteria for accreditation of MPH programs have been established by the Council on Education for Public Health.

There are more than 300 professional preparation programs for health educators (Cissell, 1992). The task of creating and enforcing credentialing for such a diverse profession is substantial. Beginning in 1992, the National Commissions for Health Education Credentialing required professionals to complete an approved health-education program to become eligible to take an examination to qualify as a certified health-education specialist. Because the health-education field is so diverse, with individuals working in schools, communities, industry, and government, the direction of preparation for health specialists has been toward skills related to interaction between health professionals and their clients.

The contemporary emergence of healthy-lifestyle management as a positive force represents a major shift in perception among the public. The *possibility* and the *desirability* of involving individuals in the development and maintenance of a healthy lifestyle represent an important new value in American life. On the other hand, this revolution is mostly confined to young people with middle- or high-income levels. There is little evidence that people in lower-income brackets with little discretionary income have become involved in the wellness movement. The evidence on fitness levels and eating habits of children is so alarming that we cannot fairly say that this revolution is being passed on to the next generation.

Still, there is hope! Fewer people smoke. Smoking is prohibited in many transportation, office, commercial, and restaurant settings, making it more difficult for people who want to smoke to find a place where they are allowed to smoke. Although too many teens begin to smoke, and smoking, like many health-related behaviors, appears to be strongly related to social class, the nation has made important progress in this health-related behavior.

It appears that more people are exercising and have become more conscious of the nutritional values of the foods that they eat regularly. The advertising industry has obviously made the healthy person the centerpiece of advertisements selling a variety of products. People are portrayed as fit, active, and concerned about the health value of their lifestyles. Good information relative to the health benefits and liabilities of an increasing number of products, programs, and activities is now widely available.

Dance

Dance is a significant human activity in virtually every known culture. Dance can be a cultural art form, as are modern dance and ballet. Dance can be strongly educational, as are the creative-dance movement in schools and the educational dance portions of movement-education curricula. Dance can be used as a means of expression as when it is used as therapy. Dance has also become an important fitness activity; the growing aerobic-dance movement is an example.

Dance has always been an expression of the popular culture. What we now study as folk dance involves the popular forms of dancing from other cultures in other times. The traditional folk dance of the westward expansion of the United States was the square dance. Ballroom dancing has been a popular form of social dance for many years and is still taught in both schools and the private sector. The jitterbug and swing were the popular dance forms of several generations ago, and dancing to rock-and-roll music was the folk dance of the 1960s generation. Popular films such as *Footloose* and *Dirty Dancing* focused on the power of popular dance in the lives of young people.

The inclusion of dance in the physical education of children and youths is a product of the twentieth century. Margaret H'Doubler of the University of Wisconsin is generally credited with establishing dance as part of the school physical-education curriculum (Hayes, 1980). As physical education became a required subject in many states in the 1920s, dance was introduced into school programs. Within physical education, however, dance became severely restricted. As elementary-school physical education grew and prospered, many physical-education teachers included units on creative dance in their programs. Units on folk dance were also taught often with the help of the specialist music teacher. In middle schools and

Dancing is central to sustaining cultural traditions.

high schools, folk-dance units were common, but specialized teaching of jazz dance and ballet was infrequent, mostly elective, and chosen mostly by girls. Dance educators believe strongly that this typical scenario makes it impossible for any student to receive an education in dance (Posey, 1988). If young girls or boys wanted specific training in jazz, modern, or ballet dancing, they had to go to the private sector where dance schools have catered to those needs.

Physical educators often are required to take one or two dance courses as part of their certification programs. Many, however, do not like dance themselves, have insufficient training in it, and exclude it from their school programs if they have a choice. Thus, dance education in many places disappeared or was severely restricted to a unit on square dance.

In the 1970s, that picture began to change (McLaughlin, 1988). Dance, as an important cultural art form, began to be rediscovered. Established dance companies were revitalized. Important new companies were developed. Experimental forms of modern dance were well received. A growing national interest in dance precipitated renewed interest among children and youths. The federal and state governments made more money available to promote dance and dance education.

In the educational-reform climate of the 1980s and 1990s, arts education became a focus of school curriculum reform—and dance education became part of an integrated-arts approach in many elementary and middle schools. Physical education has played only a minor role in this new integrated-arts approach to school curricula. Schools and communities have begun to work together to bring dancers and other community artists into the schools.

Another significant development in arts education is the emergence of a movement known as **discipline-based arts education** (Posey, 1988). This movement focuses on art as technique—on learning to dance—but also has an equal emphasis on understanding the arts; on becoming an educated, literate consumer of the arts; and on being part of a knowledgeable arts audience. New curricula have been developed that stress the audience or consumer role in dance education. Students learn not only how to dance but also how to create dances, how to make decisions about what they see in dance, and how to enjoy dance as a member of a dance audience (Allen, 1988).

GET CONNECTED to Allied-Field Web Sites

Recreation

American Association for Leisure and Recreation	www.aahperd.org/aalr
American Trails	www.americantrails.org
American Hiking Society	www.americanhiking.org
American Recreation Coalition	www.funoutdoors.com
American Therapeutic Recreation Association	www.atra-online.com
National Recreation and Park Association	www.nrpa.org
Therapeutic Recreation	www.recreationtherapy.com
Wilderness Education Association	www.weainfo.org
League of American Bicyclists	www.bikeleague.org

Health

American Association for Health Education	www.aahperd.org/aahe
American College Health Association	www.acha.org
American Public Health Association	www.apha.org
American School Health Association	www.ashaweb.org
Department of Health and Human Services	www.os.dhhs.gov
National Institutes of Health	www.nih.gov
Society of Public Health Education	www.sophe.org
National Education Association—Health Information Network	www.neahin.org
Action for Healthy Kids	www.actionforhealthykids.org

Dance

National Dance Association	www.aahperd.org/nda
Folk Dance Association	www.folkdancing.org
American Dance Therapy Association	www.adta.org
Dance Vision	www.dancevision.com
DanceDanceDance	www.dancedancedance.com

Dance is one of the best vehicles for achieving goals in multicultural education, which is important and popular in many schools and agencies. For instance, dance, music, storytelling, and festivals are ways in which we come to understand both our own culture and other cultures (Monroe, 1995). The Full-house Children's Dance Company of St. Cloud, Minnesota, is a good example. By creating a multiracial dance company of children and by exploring cultural differences through dance, this company has contributed to significant social change in its local area (Leigh, 1994).

Many colleges and universities offer majors or minors in dance. Many of these departments are oriented toward performance and focus on preparing dancers for professional work as members of dance companies. Ballet and modern dance remain the two strongest dance forms in college and university departments. Few states offer teaching certification in dance. Thus, dance education is still embedded primarily within physical education. Although movement education and the emerging integrated-arts approach have made dance more important in elementary-school curricula, it is still viewed primarily as another activity unit in most school programs where it is taught by the physical educator. More intense and specific dance education takes place in the private sector, in dance schools. No certification is necessary, however, to teach dance in the private sector.

When the AAHPER was reorganized in 1974 to become the alliance, the Dance Division of the old AAHPER became the National Dance Association in the new alliance. In 1980 dance was added to the alliance name, which became AAHPERD. A *D* was also added to the major journal of the alliance, which became *JOPERD*. The National Dance Association continued to be an active member of the alliance and has worked hard to develop curricula and educational materials to foster the growth of dance education in schools.

Allied or Integrated?

Recreation, health, and dance are still nominally integrated with sport, fitness, and physical education. The AAHPERD umbrella still exists with each of these fields having major organizational representation within the alliance. Yet it is equally clear that each has established itself as an independent field with its own organizations and literature. Recreation has increasingly aligned itself with other aspects of the emerging leisure industry. Health has increasingly aligned itself with other allied medical fields. Dance has increasingly found a home with music and art within a unified- or integrated-arts perspective.

In one sense, the explosion of knowledge and interest in these various fields has required their development as independent professional areas. In 1900 it was possible for one person to acquire the basic knowledge, understanding, and skills to perform professionally as a physical educator, recreation educator, health educator, and dance educator. That is no longer true. Physical education has moved well beyond its limited gymnastics origins. Recreation has become a multidimensional enterprise. The health field has moved well beyond its historical emphasis on hygiene. Dance has also become a multifaceted discipline. It seems unlikely that any curriculum could be developed to prepare professionals to function well in all of the three areas. Thus, it seems unlikely

that the course of specialized development of these separate fields will reverse itself in the near future. Yet it also seems clear that some new integrative efforts will have to be made to satisfy the growing demand of people in the private sector for services that cut across these increasingly separate fields. That issue is discussed further in the next chapter.

SUMMARY

1. In 2000 *Promoting Better Health for Young People Through Physical Activity and Sports* became the national blueprint for a physical-activity infrastructure.

2. Various national organizations have formed to support physical activity across age groups, the most important of which is the National Coalition for Promoting Physical Activity.

3. State-level programs vary in their emphasis, but all seek to promote more physical activity with programs that support walking, cycling, and other forms of physical activity.

4. North Carolina has a strong state-level policy and many programs to support healthy lifestyles across age groups.

5. Local efforts that involve collaboration among schools, private-sector organizations, municipal organizations, and health providers are crucial to building and sustaining a local physical-activity infrastructure.

6. Recreation, health, and dance have all developed as independent fields, yet each has a significant contribution to make to physical activity and healthy lifestyles.

7. The number of occupations in the health, recreation, leisure-services, and dance industries is large. Some of these require certification, but others do not.

8. The health-enhancement industry provides an umbrella under which many health, recreation, and dance professionals can work together.

DISCUSSION QUESTIONS

1. Can you describe the physical-activity infrastructure in your local area?

2. What physical-activity programs exist for young children, youths, adults, and seniors in your local community?

3. Should public funds be used to build and sustain a physical-activity infrastructure?

4. How many of the many national, state, and local programs described in this chapter were familiar to you?

5. How would you see your professional future fitting into the notion of a physical-activity infrastructure?

6. What recreation, health, and dance opportunities for young persons and adults can be identified in your local community?

7. What is the balance between private and public opportunities in these fields in your local community?

8. Does your college or university provide certification/licensure programs in these fields?

CHAPTER 14

The Crucial Themes Defining Our Present and Future

My contention . . . is that we in health, physical education, recreation, and dance—that centaur known as HPERD—desperately need to widen and scrub off the windows through which we view the world. My belief is that our vision is too narrow and blurred, leaving us muddle-headed and exposed to the sharp edges of professional life.

John Burt, 1987

LEARNING OBJECTIVES

- To analyze issues and problems within and between the specialized professional and scientific groups

- To analyze problems between these groups and larger societal interests

- To analyze issues related to equity that cut across these professional groups

- To discuss public and private concerns about how sport, fitness, and physical education are delivered

- To evaluate unification and fragmentation as they are related to the future needs of lifespan involvement

The twenty-first century is here. Sport, fitness, and physical education traveled a long way in the twentieth century. In 1900 school physical education consisted largely of formal gymnastics. Physical fitness was a topic unknown to most people. School sport was virtually nonexistent. Intercollegiate and professional sport were in their infancies. Public health concerns centered primarily on infectious rather than degenerative diseases. Should the same amount of progress occur in the next 100 years, it is hard to imagine what sport, fitness, and physical education might look like in the early twenty-second century. We can, however, look carefully at the major themes that appear to be most salient for understanding the foreseeable future. How the issues and problems embedded within those themes develop and are resolved will determine the course of events for sport, fitness, and physical education for the first part of the twenty-first century.

The purpose of this chapter is to address the important common themes that have been identified throughout the text, to examine them critically, and to allow you to form a point of view regarding each of them. In each of the themes, I will take a clear position and provide an argument to support that position. You may disagree partially or wholly with some or all of these positions. That's fine! I want you to make your own argument, to form your own opinion on these issues. In Part 1 of the text, I argued that the ability to reflect critically on important issues is the hallmark of a professional. A professional philosophy is not an opinion but a coherent, defensible way of looking at your professional world and making judgments about future directions.

I began this text by arguing that the dominant characteristic of the era that we live in is the possibility and desirability of lifespan involvement in sport, fitness, and physical education. Will that *possibility* become more of a *probability* during the twenty-first century? Will that *possibility* be available to all or just to some? What do we need to do *now* so that sport, fitness, and physical education will be more available to more people with higher-quality services? How do we engage more of the population in lifelong learning related to physical activity? How do we educate children and youths so that they value physical activity enough to make it part of their adult lifestyle? These are the important questions that the themes identified in this chapter are meant to address. The themes explored are (1) meeting the public health challenge, (2) distributing sport, fitness, and physical education more equitably, (3) focusing on new populations, (4) gender equity in sport, fitness, and physical education, (5) the need for development of after-school programs for children and youths, (6) developing the physical-activity infrastructure, (7) the activity and leisure industries, (8) the movement toward an expanded physical education, (9) the movement toward an inclusive rather than exclusionary sport

culture, and (10) wellness as the center of lifestyle education.

THEME 1: MEETING THE PUBLIC HEALTH CHALLENGE

Since the late 1980s, the harmful effects of inactivity among the population have been documented scientifically. Engaging in regular physical activity has a host of health benefits, which in turn are strongly related to reducing the proportion of the nation's wealth that is spent on health care. The 1996 U.S. surgeon general's report clearly established the public health importance of regular physical activity and further established national policy related to improving the physical-activity involvement of children, youths, and adults (U.S. Department of Health and Human Services, 1996).

Most of our professional efforts have been directed toward changing individuals' behavior related to risk factors such as smoking, consumption of fatty foods, and physical inactivity. Our most typical strategy has been to offer risk-factor education and intervention programs aimed at individuals: smoking cessation, nutrition education, be-active ad campaigns, and the like. We have done much less to influence public policy in ways that might produce more systemic changes, particularly in influencing policy that is directed toward the establishment and maintenance of physical-activity infrastructures such as parks, facilities, bike trails, and activity programs.

Health, physical-education, recreation, and fitness professionals are now trained mostly in specialized programs. Although that enables them to be prepared at greater depth and breadth, it comes with a cost—namely, that they are less aware of one another's goals and problems and are less able to work together effectively. There is no doubt anymore that effective programs that will contribute to achieving the goals of *Healthy People 2010* require a broadly based, integrated approach. School personnel do not work with community professionals often enough to extend and sustain health and activity programs for youngsters. Exercise scientists know a great deal about the health benefits of activity but less about how to get people active and keep them active. To meet the public health challenge, we must create groups of specialized professionals who can combine their talents and knowledge to build and sustain programs that work.

It is clear that healthy lifestyles in general and physical activity in particular are not distributed equally throughout the population (Siedentop, 1996c)—what health epidemiologists have called the social gradient in health (see Chapter 7). Evidence shows that the health status of a particular socioeconomic class within a nation is typically better than that of classes below it and worse than that of classes above it (Hertzman, 1994). There is some evidence that in nations where socioeconomic distances have been reduced, relevant health-marker variables have improved (Wilkinson, 1994). These facts are clearly recognized now in federal health policy. One of the two overarching goals of *Healthy People 2010* is to eliminate health disparities based on race, gender, and socioeconomic status. This will be an enormously difficult task and will require strong and creative collaboration among the various health, fitness, recreation, and physical-education professions.

The health status of young children and older adults is a major factor in the amount spent on health care in the United States. If we can start with building healthy lifestyles for all young children and ensure that seniors have access to healthy, attractive recreational activities, the health costs to the nation would be considerably reduced. It also seems clear that their lives would be enriched as well.

THEME 2: DISTRIBUTING OPPORTUNITY MORE EQUITABLY

The public health challenge described in Theme 1 is not the only reason to hope that sport, fitness, and physical education will be distributed more equitably in the future. Adults who participate in all the

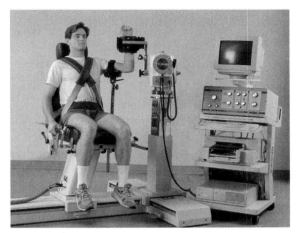

Exercise technology takes the guesswork out of exercise prescription.

various forms of physical activity—climb mountains, square-dance regularly as part of a social club, play golf each weekend in the same foursome, take long bike rides into the country, regularly compete in weekend distance-running events, or play in recreational volleyball leagues, for example—do so for many reasons, most of which have little to do with public health goals. The social and personal benefits of regular engagement in sport, recreation, or physical activity are tremendously important to what people think is meaningful in their lives. But a question remains: If the experiences are so important for so many reasons, shouldn't more people have a chance to take part?

This theme is directly related to Theme 7 because since the mid-1970s, the provision of health, activity, and leisure services has increasingly been performed by the private sector. This private-sector leisure-services industry is driven primarily by consumers who have discretionary income to spend on these services. The industry hardly touches the low-income families who live in the United States, who now represent 25–40 percent of the population. This is particularly true for programs aimed at children and youths; indeed, the children and youths who could most benefit from structured activity programs are the least likely to have access to them (Carnegie Council on Adolescent Development, 1992). Recreator Diana Dunn's description of this dilemma for recreation is equally true for sport, fitness, and physical education:

> If there is an overarching goal for American recreation in the last years of this century, it is the frustratingly familiar but increasingly urgent challenge to balance the continuum of available recreation opportunities to achieve social, political, and economic justice for both the haves and have-nots of America, wherever this dichotomy appears or however it is defined. (Dunn, 1986a, p. 35)

There are only two ways in which this problem can be addressed. One is to work within the political system to distribute income more equitably among people in America. This would require redistributing income through income-tax revisions and changing the economic structure of our society. There is little evidence that this will happen in the near future. A second solution is to work to have sport, fitness, and physical education distributed more through the *public* sector—through programs in schools, community recreation centers, public senior centers, and some form of publicly supported child care for infants and preschoolers.

A clear trend since the 1950s has been the **privatization** of leisure, recreation, sport, and fitness (Ellis, 1988; Kraus, 2002). User fees and pay-to-play plans have become more the norm than the exception. Public expenditures on sport, recreation, and fitness have decreased as this privatization has gradually spread. The real action in the sport, fitness, and leisure worlds is in the private sector.

If this trend continues, it seems clear that access to opportunity in sport, fitness, and physical education will increasingly be tied to personal wealth. To reverse this situation, programs to support children, youths, and adults in sport, fitness, and physical-education programs must be more readily available in the public sector through public child-care centers, schools, community recreation centers, public parks and recreation areas, and better and safe walking/biking routes in cities and rural areas.

THEME 3: FOCUSING ON NEW POPULATIONS

Sport, fitness, and physical education have tended to focus primarily on children and youths. School physical-education programs, youth sport, inter-school sport, and youth recreation have dominated the preparation of professionals in these areas and, subsequently, how these professionals plan and implement programs. The focus of our profession needs to extend in both directions, down below the kindergarten to infant and early-childhood programs, and up from college physical education and sport to adult activity and leisure, all the way to planning and implementing programs for senior citizens.

Two important trends mandate this expanded focus. First, it is becoming increasingly clear that early intervention and education in childhood are appropriate both from an educational point of view and, particularly, from an economic point of view. Young children can be more easily educated and more easily directed with respect to lifestyle than can adults, and at considerably less cost. Fitness and leisure habits are ingrained early in childhood, and once ingrained, they become difficult to change. Because adult habits are difficult to change, it tends to cost more to change them than to educate children to form good habits early. The saving to the nation in health costs and medical expenditures of a fitter, more active citizenry would be enormous.

The focus on children as a new population is made more difficult by the fact that children are the new poor in the United States. Estimates suggest that 30 percent of U.S. children live in poverty, representing a segment of the childhood population that is most at risk for health problems. These children and their parents and other caregivers have little access to health-care, nutrition-counseling, or physical-activity programs. They are most affected by the inequitable distribution of sport, fitness, and physical education described in Theme 2.

Eastern forms of exercise have a strong mental and spiritual component.

The second trend is equally clear. The average age of Americans is increasing. The baby boomers who so greatly expanded the school system in the 1960s and 1970s are now middle-aged and represent the largest age group in the population. Americans are also living longer. Thus, the older population groups wield major economic and political power. Their needs and interests in sport, fitness, and physical education must be taken into account.

An expanded focus for professional programs in sport, fitness, and physical education requires knowledge and skills different from those traditionally included in professional-preparation programs. We know a great deal about how to organize, teach, manage, and motivate captive children and youths in the context of schools. The typical sport, fitness, and physical-education professional knows much less about and has fewer skills relative to young children or older adults.

It also appears that much of the programming for these new population groups will take place in the private rather than the public sector, most typically in situations where consumers pay for services. This, too, means professionals will need knowledge and skills that are not typically included in current professional-preparation programs. Unless sport, fitness, and physical-education programs expand to include the knowledge and skills that allow people

to work effectively with the younger and older population groups, the market extending services to these groups will be captured by other people who are so trained.

THEME 4: GENDER EQUITY IN SPORT, FITNESS, AND PHYSICAL EDUCATION

In 1900 women could not vote. Being active and fit or engaging in vigorous sport was inconsistent with then-male-dominated views of femininity. Today's culture is different. When the American women won the world soccer championship, the entire nation celebrated. In 2002 Title IX became 30 years old. The high-school and intercollegiate participation data shown in Chapter 5 clearly indicate progress. Still, there is much to be done before gender equity is fully realized. Female athletes still struggle in many places for an equal share of facilities and budgets. Female coaches are seriously underrepresented in coaching and administrative positions. Old stereotypes too often linger.

Cultures tend to change slowly. Practices in and attitudes toward sport, fitness, and physical education have traditionally been shaped by males—they have typically been sexist. The male-dominated belief system has shaped a series of myths that have served to exclude girls and women from opportunity to participate (Coakley, 2007). These myths include prohibitions against strenuous activity because of supposed resulting problems in childbearing, damage to reproductive organs, and menstrual problems; because women were thought to have more fragile bone structures; because muscle development was deemed unattractive in women; because women were believed to be unable to perform endurance activities; and, most of all, because there was a perceived general threat to femininity for girls and women who actively involve themselves in fitness and sport. These socially invented myths served to deter young girls from becoming involved in sport and fitness, and habits developed young tend to persist in adulthood.

Do women's sports get the attention they deserve?

Ellis (1988) suggests that the activity and **leisure-services industry** is strongly influenced by the increased economic power of women in contemporary culture. He is optimistic about the future:

> However, the changes we have seen in sex roles have not been just economic. During the last two decades women have insisted upon, and have been granted, a fuller participation in all facets of American life. In sport, politics, and management particularly, and to a lesser degree in the male-dominated areas of trucking, maintenance, and construction, women have joined in and demonstrated clearly that they are equally capable. The process has not run its course, but it is clear that our society will continue to evolve in the direction that welcomes women into all areas of endeavor and achievement and breaks down sex-role stereotyping. (Ellis, 1988, p. 24)

Although there is good reason for optimism due to the increased involvement of girls and women in sport, fitness, and physical education, there are also continuing concerns. Many of the power structures in the educational, political, and economic structures of our society are still male dominated. Girls and women need not only equal opportunities in sport, fitness, and physical education but also visible support for fully exploring their potential in these areas. Sport, fitness, and physical-education professionals need to be advocates for girls and women—and they need to band together to develop and sustain advocacy programs that provide greater opportunity and support for girls and women.

THEME 5: CHILD AND YOUTH DEVELOPMENT: THE AFTER-SCHOOL HOURS

The responsibility for child and youth development has traditionally resided almost solely in families. Currently, however, that responsibility is shared with day care, preschool, school, and community agencies and programs. There are 39 million children between the ages of 5 and 14 in the United States. In most two-parent households, both parents work. Three of four mothers with school-aged children work, two-thirds of them full-time (Executive Summary, 1999). During the after-school hours, rates of juvenile crime triple, and many unsupervised youngsters experiment with alcohol, tobacco, drugs, and sex.

It is clear that children and youths have better developmental opportunities if they are in after-school programs supervised by caring adults. The sport, fitness, and physical-education professions have much to offer in this area as do the health, recreation, and dance professions. Of particular importance is the need to develop after-school programs for children and youths at risk for academic or social failure (Witt & Baker, 1997). There is ample evidence that organized academic, recreation, and sport programs for children and youths are useful in helping them progress toward becoming competent adults. Younger children and those in areas of poverty seem to gain the most from such programs, perhaps because they have less access to them. Teens who regularly engage in after-school programs achieve better academically and are less likely to engage in risky behavior than their peers who are not in such programs.

This national problem, however, cannot be solved by any single profession working alone. It is clear that collaborations among schools, community agencies, city government, and the private sector are necessary to develop and sustain successful programs. At the moment, it would be inaccurate to describe the United States as either a child-centered or a youth-centered nation. We need to make an investment in our children and youths, both in regard to their physical health and well-being and in regard to their personal and social development. Few national problems provide more opportunity for the sport, fitness, and physical-education professions to offer solutions.

THEME 6: DEVELOPING THE PHYSICAL-ACTIVITY INFRASTRUCTURE

Chapter 13 described the need for infrastructures consisting of the facilities, spaces, and programs that enable children, youths, and adults to become and stay physically active. It also gave examples of such infrastructures. If the infrastructure is truly to enable persons of all ages to be and stay active, it must be attractive, safe, and accessible. Parks, connected sidewalks within and between communities, jogging paths, cycling trails, recreation centers, fitness centers, and sport fields are some of the spaces and facilities recommended. Educational programs for young children, school-aged children, youths, young adults, and seniors are also needed to introduce them to the local physical-activity spaces, facilities, and programs through which they can become and remain physically active.

Policies that support the creation and sustaining of physical-activity infrastructures have to be developed at federal, state, and local levels. Federal legislation encourages action at the state level and helps fund it. State policy makes action at the local level possible, and it is at the local level where the action is particularly important. Schools, community agencies, hospitals, and local governments have to partner in ventures that create and sustain the local physical-activity infrastructure. This all requires a substantial investment of time and money, but the investment will more than pay for itself eventually in a healthier population that will substantially reduce the enormous burden of the nation's health costs. The physical-activity infrastructure cannot be developed and sustained without collaboration among professionals in sport, fitness, physical education, recreation, and health—and input from the scholarly disciplines that support these professions.

School physical-education and physical-activity programs must help students adopt and value a physically active lifestyle. This won't happen without states requiring more time in physical education and without programs that focus on physical-activity content and a pedagogy that helps students to so enjoy and value activity that they seek it out in discretionary time and, eventually, make it fundamental to their lifestyle. Local governments have to collaborate with local school districts to create attractive, affordable physical-activity programs and attractive and accessible indoor and outdoor facilities. Chapter 13 provides snapshots of how this is being done across the nation.

For the first time in history, Americans are facing an expectation of reduced life expectancy due to the large percentage of citizens who are overweight and physically inactive. The nation's health costs have become a major burden on federal, state, corporate, and family budgets. The imperative to build and sustain a physical-activity infrastructure is rooted within this set of national problems and is widely viewed as the most important strategy to reduce health costs and improve the quality of life for citizens of all ages.

THEME 7: THE ACTIVITY AND LEISURE INDUSTRIES

Ellis (1988) argues convincingly that activity and leisure services are being provided more and more in the *private* sector and that, increasingly, it is the adult client who pays for those services directly. The activity and leisure-services industry is made up of sections of the health-enhancement industry and sections of the leisure-services industry (see Figure 14.1). The defining characteristic of this new industry is activity, for both health and leisure purposes.

There is little doubt that this industry is *happening now*. Professionals in sport, fitness, and physical education who ignore it do so at risk of losing their influence and of losing substantial sources of income. At present, this industry is largely *unregulated*, except insofar as clients decide what programs they will support. This is a market-driven industry. It is easy to make money in it, but it is also easy to fail. We can expect more and more competition within this industry because of the substantial amounts of

How early should sport-specific training begin?

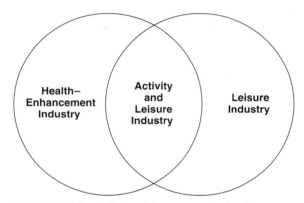

FIGURE 14.1 Relationship among the health-enhancement, activity and leisure, and leisure industries.
SOURCE: *Ellis, 1988, p. 5.*

money being spent on health- and leisure-related activity.

Except for programs in adult fitness and sport management and some in recreation, the sport, fitness, and physical-education professions have not responded quickly to the emergence of this new industry. The professions still prepare people more for the public sector and for occupations for which certification or accreditation is necessary.

Sport, fitness, and physical-education professionals bear some responsibility for helping shape the quality and direction of the activity and leisure industries. As long as these industries remain unregulated, there will be a continuing risk for fad activities that are not grounded in current knowledge about appropriate activities that serve healthy-lifestyle purposes and delivered with teaching strategies that are unlikely to help customers adopt and value a physically active lifestyle. Just as health educators have for some time included information about problems with "fad diets" in their classes and in their literature, so too can sport and physical-education professionals ensure that students are educated about the activities that contribute to various health-fitness goals, about the intensity and duration of those activities, and information about various "fad" activities that do not achieve the outcomes suggested by the advertising that promotes them. To become physically educated should mean that students have acquired knowledge about various activities and can make reasoned decisions about which ones can indeed contribute to their well-being.

THEME 8: TOWARD AN EXPANDED PHYSICAL EDUCATION

Physical education will remain a largely ineffective educational intervention as long as it is conceptualized as a school subject that is pursued in small bits of time in a regular school day and school week. Many of the effective physical-education programs described in this text have taken a much more expanded view of what the subject is and when children and youths are involved in the subject. Effective programs seem to break out of the box in which they have been confined—namely, as a school subject that meets in the elementary school for typically no more than two 30-minute periods per week or in the high school for a daily period of 50 minutes for two semesters in the ninth grade.

It seems abundantly clear that time for physical education in the school timetable should be increased! The national concern over the increased incidence of child/youth overweight and obesity has resulted in many states increasing not only the time

devoted to physical education but also ensuring that physical-education classes will have teacher-to-student ratios similar to other subjects, thus trying to eliminate what has long been considered to be the two most difficult issues in teaching physical education: not enough time and too many students.

It is also clear that we cannot meet the important goal of having children and youths adopt and value a physically active lifestyle simply by providing better programs during expanded class time. Effective programs find ways to get students physically active in nonattached school time and in out-of-school discretionary time. They do this by building links to the community and to the home and then by working with others to develop physical-activity programs that are attractive to children and youths and by supporting the development of outdoor and indoor facilities that are safe and accessible for informal physical activity in discretionary time.

The school is the hub of the developmental triangle—home, school, community—in which children and youths learn and grow. Physical educators not only provide appropriate and enjoyable activity experiences during class time but also develop recess, lunchtime, and after-school activities. They also need to build links to the community and to the homes of their students. Physical educators should build enduring links to the parents of their students, not only providing them with information about their sons' and daughters' progress but also encouraging them to help their children get and stay involved with informal and more programmatic physical-activity opportunities. Thus, the physical educator has important opportunities to be a key player in developing and sustaining a physical-activity infrastructure in the local community.

THEME 9: TOWARD AN INCLUSIVE RATHER THAN EXCLUSIVE SPORT CULTURE

The American sport culture has developed remarkably over the last 150 years. Chapters 4–6 described the size and importance of the sport culture in

American life. There are no signs that the public's attraction to sport is waning. Sport for children is widely available in many parts of the nation. School sport has expanded with girls having more access and the number of sports for which schools field teams. Colleges and universities field more teams and support more athletes. Professional sport has expanded in different ways; that is, indoor football in the "off-season," professional soccer, and the like.

Still, however, the sport culture, as it is currently constituted, is exclusionary in its developmental stages. Surely, youth sport has spread remarkably, and more children have access to it, but the increasing importance of "traveling teams" and the degree to which this excludes less-talented children/youths tends to make it exclusionary as children move into adolescence. This is the result of the "varsity model" that was adopted long ago in the United States and continues to dominate the developmental aspects of our sports culture. For adolescents and adults who were not good enough to make the varsity teams, little is available in the way of organized sport through which they can continue to develop and compete.

In many parts of the world, especially those influenced by the British model of youth sport, school sport developed with a very different model. Most girls and boys receive their early sport training and competition in local sport clubs—for example, the hockey club, the cricket club, and the basketball club. Children start in club sports and can continue practicing and competing for their club throughout their adolescent and adult years. No youths are "cut" from the club team. Rather, as the club attracts more adolescents, they simply create A, B, and C teams, all of which practice and compete the same amount of time; the only difference is that the competition is more likely to be against youths of similar skills in the clubs that they compete against.

School sport in these countries is also different. Typically, more sports are offered, and any student who wants to compete in a sport can be on the team; that is, no students get cut from the team. In New Zealand high schools, it is not uncommon to find six to eight basketball teams for boys and the same number for girls. The squads are smaller than in

Many new sports involve risk and are competed in individually.

American schools. Teams typically practice 2 days per week and have one competition per week. The squads are all graded by ability so that as players improve they can move up in the squad hierarchy. What this means is that many more girls and boys get to be on basketball teams and compete for their school.

This is a different model for sport development within the context of public schools. It certainly does not do as well as the American model in preparing elite athletes. In New Zealand, that is done primarily through sport clubs. What it does allow for, however, is much greater participation in organized school sport.

Much of the sport culture outside schools is becoming more inclusionary. Recreation and sport clubs often try to attract more participants. Because their programs are often fee-based, it is in the interest of the sponsoring group to attract more players. More adults are continuing their participation beyond their young-adult years. To be sure, this is a loosely coupled infrastructure, but at least it is a beginning.

THEME 10: WELLNESS AS THE CENTER OF LIFESTYLE EDUCATION

The concept of wellness was introduced in Chapter 1, and its philosophical and historical roots were described in Chapter 3. To reiterate, *wellness* is about getting and staying well—healthy and active. It is a *proactive* concept and movement rather than a reaction to illness or disease. Noted physical educator Celeste Ulrich was prophetic when in 1976 she described wellness as a "macrocosmic concept of fitness" (Ulrich, 1976, p. 151). Wellness is a valuable concept because it brings together the areas of nutrition, physical activity, psychological well-being, and stress management. Wellness is about *managing* your own lifestyle, hence the increasing use of the term *lifestyle management* for the effort to take control of your own well-being.

To achieve wellness, educational programs must focus on behavior change, not just information. Clearly, the school, the community, and the family must work together to form what has been appropriately called the *developmental triangle.* Knowledge about nutrition, physical activity, and stress management is important, but there must be an accompanying effort to influence the development of appropriate behaviors and habits. It is tremendously important that the behaviors that represent wellness be taught and reinforced in a number of different settings if they are to become part of a young person's lifestyle. This means that the collaborations referred to in Theme 6 must be taken seriously.

Wellness stresses the importance of lifestyle and encompasses work, leisure, and personal relationships. Wellness is viewed as a positive value with a primary emphasis on personal development. There is also widespread agreement that adoption of such a lifestyle by a larger percentage of the population can increase the productivity of workplaces and reduce the staggering costs of health and medical care. This is clearly why wellness has been so readily accepted by industry, as demonstrated by the development of worksite fitness programs (see Chapter 8).

Wellness cannot be viewed solely as an individual concern. Our nation has public health goals (Sallis & McKenzie, 1991) that should alert us to the important *collective* interest we have in wellness. The new socioecological view of health and fitness (see Chapter 7) suggests that wellness proponents need to examine the social structures that tend to prevent certain groups from gaining access to information, facilities, and programs that could improve their health and fitness. The costs of health care alone should motivate all of us to consider the wellness of all citizens, not just our own!

There is also a great need for consumer education. Dietary supplements, fitness fads, and so called "miracle" weight-loss programs are constantly advertised in magazines and on television, typically endorsed by very healthy and attractive-looking women and men. Wellness can become a positive force in lifestyle education, but it cannot achieve that goal based on information alone. Children and adolescents need good, accurate information, and they need to be introduced to and participate in appropriate health-fitness activities. These activities need to be reinforced in physical-education and health classes, at recess in elementary schools, in the school cafeteria at lunch time, and in school vending machines and school stores. They also need to be reinforced through communication with parents and by connecting school efforts with those in the community. Wellness can become a positive force in lifestyle education, but it requires timely, accurate information and a stronger focus on behavior change rather than information alone. Lifestyle education needs to begin with young children and is most important at the elementary- and middle-school years when habits form and children adopt activity and eating patterns that often last a lifetime.

SUMMARY

1. The public health challenge to achieve a healthier citizenry and reduce the nation's health costs will require cooperation among specialized professional and disciplinary groups.

2. Distributing sport, fitness, and physical education more equitably is made more difficult by the trend toward privatization.

3. Young children and older citizens have not traditionally been addressed by the sport, fitness, and physical-education professions, yet these age groups represent important populations with unique problems, especially children in poverty.

4. Gender equity in sport, fitness, and physical education needs to be promoted not only through legal means but also actively through education that breaks down stereotypes that have effectively denied girls and women equal opportunities.

5. After-school programs for children and youths need to be developed and staffed by caring adults. Few national problems provide more opportunity for the sport, fitness, and physical-education professions to offer solutions.

6. Federal, state, and local policies and programs must come together to build and sustain the physical-activity infrastructure.

7. An activity and leisure-services industry has emerged. We need to respond to it by creating new programs that combine knowledge and skill from health, recreation, and physical education.

8. It will be difficult for physical education to grow and prosper if it is confined to being a class subject within the school day. Ways of expanding opportunity and involvement for children and youths in nonattached time at school, in the community, and at home must become the focus of physical education.

9. The sport culture needs to develop new forms for children and youths that are inclusionary rather than exclusionary and that promote lifespan involvement in competitive and recreational activity.

10. Wellness can become the foundational concept undergirding lifespan sport, fitness, and physical education. Children need to start at an early age to attend educationally sound programs that emphasize behavior change.

DISCUSSION QUESTIONS

1. What school, home, and community interventions, taken together or separately, would increase the likelihood of achieving public health goals in the next generation?

2. What can be done to make the sport culture in your area less exclusionary and more lifespan oriented?

3. Can opportunities for activity throughout the lifespan be equitable and accessible if they are provided primarily through the private sector?

4. What does school physical education have to do to survive and prosper between now and 2020?

5. How will technology improve the activity lives of people? What are the risks that technology will worsen the inactivity problems so prevalent today?

6. Choose a specific activity problem in the area in which you live. How can the activity disciplines and the activity professions collaborate to solve this problem? What does each bring to the potential solution?

7. How can we integrate our efforts in schools, communities, and households to promote and sustain a more active citizenry?

8. When should wellness education begin? What might it look like for a first-grader, an eighth-grader, and a senior in high school?

9. Should activity be available to all income groups, through publicly supported programs, or should we adopt more of a pay-as-you-go philosophy where user fees fund programs?

CHAPTER 15

The Physical-Science Subdisciplines Supporting the Professions

The beginnings of the study of movement from a disciplinary perspective was a fragmented effort driven by the insight of a few individuals operating as individual scholars, practitioners of medicine, or aspiring academics in universities. Today, these various approaches to the study of movement have come under a single umbrella of Kinesiology. This is not to say that individuals in other disciplines or fields of study do not study movement, but rather that academic programs of Kinesiology in universities provide the structure and framework for the systematic study of the theory and practice of movement.

American Academy of Kinesiology and Physical Education

LEARNING OBJECTIVES

- To explain how the physical-science subdisciplines of exercise physiology, kinesiology, biomechanics, and motor behavior emerged
- To define each physical-science subdiscipline as a field of study
- To understand the research focus for each of the physical-science subdisciplines
- To understand the clinical-consulting focus of each of the physical-science subdisciplines
- To discuss current problems and issues in each of the physical-science subdisciplines

The field of kinesiology has developed rapidly over the past two decades. In 2006 the National Research Council included Kinesiology in its taxonomy of graduated programs to be ranked, a recognition that showed clearly the degree to which Kinesiology had become a rigorous, scholarly discipline (Clark, 2008). The Kinesiology subdisciplines reviewed in Chapters 15 and 16 also provide important information to a range of professions including physical education, dance, health education, sport management, adapted physical education, athletic training, recreation, and physical therapy. In this chapter, we review the physical-science subdisciplines of kinesiology that support these professions.

EXERCISE PHYSIOLOGY

Early physical education was preoccupied with health and fitness (see Chapter 2). Many of the great, early leaders in our profession were trained initially as medical doctors. It is not surprising, therefore, that many of the early scientific endeavors in our profession focused on exercise and fitness. Indeed, our primary scientific tradition has been the measurement and promotion of physical fitness. This tradition has developed into a formidable science known most widely as *exercise physiology*.

People today, young and old alike, are more knowledgeable about exercise physiology than about any other of the sport and physical-education sciences. Since the early 1970s, adults have shown an extraordinary explosion of interest in health and fitness. Evidence of this interest is everywhere: joggers, health spas, exercise centers, aerobics, television exercise shows, popular books about exercise and health, and a national concern about the health aspects of fitness. (See Chapters 7–9 for a full treatment of these phenomena.)

Exercise physiology was at the forefront of research on fitness and performance for all of the twentieth century. Results from this research field dramatically changed some common practices that were based on completely erroneous understandings, bordering on myths. For example, it was not very long ago that athletes were not allowed to drink water on hot days during practice, that girls were not allowed to compete in vigorous sports because of their supposedly weaker constitutions, that swimmers were cautioned not to work with weights, and that endurance work for children was prohibited for fear of developing what was then called the athlete's heart. Today, the athlete's heart is considered positively rather than negatively, women run marathons brilliantly, swimmers regularly lift weights as part of their training, and water is drunk in abundance at all practices and competitions where heat is a problem. Exercise physiology has made a difference!

Exercise physiology is now the largest and most popular of the Kinesiology subdisciplines. Much of the research conducted in this area is of great interest to scientists, professionals, and laypeople alike. Some typical questions investigated in exercise physiology are as follows:

- How can exercise prevent or retard the aging process?
- Can exercisers load up their muscles through diet to produce fuels used for short-duration, high-intensity exercise?
- How do muscle cells adapt to increasingly high exercise workloads?
- How do various energy systems contribute to performance?
- What levels of aerobic exercise are optimal for maintenance of cardiovascular health?
- How does heat (or cold) affect muscular performance?
- How does lung volume change as a function of exercise?
- How do different nutrients affect sustained exercise performance?
- At what age should children begin to engage in endurance exercise?

The answers to some of these questions are of interest primarily to exercise scientists, who then must translate their meaning for practical activity and communicate that practical meaning to professionals and to the public. The answers to other questions are of immediate concern to people in the fitness, sport, and physical-education professions. The answers to still other questions are of immediate interest to individuals concerned about their own health and to parents concerned about the development of their children. Thus, exercise physiology speaks to a scientific community, to a professional audience, and to the general public.

Definition of Exercise Physiology as a Field of Study

Physiology is the study of the functioning of plants and animals and of the activities by which life is maintained and reproduced, including the functioning of

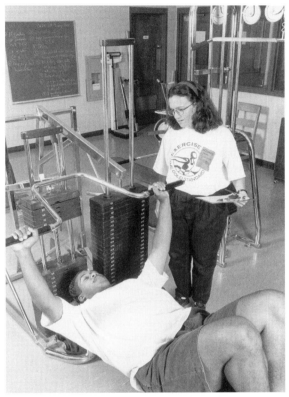

A thorough knowledge of exercise science leads to better exercise prescriptions.

and interrelationships among cells, tissues, organs, and systems such as the nervous and circulatory systems. *Exercise physiology* is the "study of acute physiological responses to physical activity and changes in physiological responses to chronic physical activity" (Haymes, 2000, p. 383).

There are two primary goals for exercise physiology (Brooks, 1994) and therefore two branches of the subdiscipline. One goal is to use exercise to further our understanding of human physiology. Those who emphasize this first goal tend to be basic scientists. Historically, this area has focused primarily on (1) how oxygen is utilized in the cardiovascular system and (2) what metabolic responses to exercise and training are—for example, exercise metabolism (Brooks, 1987). More recently, exercise biochemistry

has emerged as a specialization within the basic field. This new area of study was made possible by the development of the muscle-biopsy needle in Sweden in 1996 (Haymes, 2000), which enables investigators to study energy sources, muscle mitochondria, and muscle-fiber types.

The other goal is to use physiology to understand human exercise. Those who focus on the second goal tend to be applied scientists. Applied-exercise physiologists use physiology to understand aerobic exercise, strength development, sport performance, physical fitness, and the health benefits of physical activity. The field of **cardiac rehabilitation** is a more recent development from the applied side of exercise physiology. Cardiac rehabilitation involves the assessment of cardiovascular functioning and prescriptive work in preventing cardiovascular trauma or rehabilitating people who have experienced cardiac problems.

Development of Exercise Physiology

In the latter part of the nineteenth century, various European and American gymnastic systems of exercise battled for supremacy in the then-developing field of American physical education. Many claims were made for each system, and as the battle escalated when curricular adoptions in schools were at stake, the claims tended to become more outlandish. Into this battle stepped a physician who, at the young age of 37, was the president of the department of physical education of the National Education Association (Gerber, 1971). His name was George W. Fitz, and he is rightly described as the *father of exercise physiology.*

Fitz earned his medical degree from Harvard Medical School where he was no doubt influenced by Dudley Allen Sargent, a legend in American physical education, who was then director of the Hemenway gymnasium at Harvard. It was at Harvard that Fitz began the first exercise-physiology research laboratory in physical education, which quickly became a fundamental part of America's first degree program in physical education, the

Bachelor of Science in Anatomy, Physiology, and Physical Training (Gerber, 1971).

Brooks (1987) suggests that by the 1920s and 1930s *muscle physiology* and *exercise physiology* were virtually synonymous with *physiology* and *biochemistry*. The tradition begun by Fitz at Harvard continued and was strengthened. By the late 1930s and 1940s, the Harvard Fatigue Laboratory had become the world's major site for exercise-physiology research and the primary model for the development of other laboratories in America and throughout the world.

In the post–World War II period when physical education expanded rapidly in colleges and universities, exercise physiology became firmly entrenched as the scientific cornerstone of the field. In 1954 the American College of Sports Medicine (ACSM) was formed, linking the scientific endeavors within physical education with those in the larger medical and scientific communities. Many exercise-physiology textbooks were published, laboratories were built, and the study of exercise physiology became the main scientific focus of graduate study in physical education. The *Research Quarterly of Exercise and Sport* was a main outlet for research in this area until more recently when more specialized journals began to appear, such as the *American Journal of Sports Medicine*, *Medicine and Science in Sports and Exercise*, the *International Journal of Sports Medicine*, and *The Physician and Sports Medicine*.

As the role of exercise has become better understood, exercise physiologists have been able to attract substantial amounts of research money to expand further the knowledge base in this area. Thus, in many instances, the exercise-physiology programs have had the most success in securing research funding, increasing both the stature of the field within physical education and the number of graduate students who can be supported.

The substantial amount of interest in the field and the growing number of professional roles that derive from a study of exercise physiology have led to the development of undergraduate majors. Sometimes, these are majors in exercise science with a primary emphasis on scientific training. In other cases, they are majors in adult fitness with a primary emphasis on professional preparation. In still other cases, there is a common core with different tracks leading to the more scientific (research) specializations and to the more professional (applied) specializations.

Current Status of Exercise Physiology

To say that exercise physiology is alive and well is to make an understatement. Exercise physiology has been and continues to be the most popular and well known of the physical-education subdisciplines. Interest in health and fitness among the adult population has never been higher in America than it is today.

There certainly is *no* area in the Kinesiology subdisciplines where a popular literature (as opposed to a technical, scientific literature) exists to the same extent as in exercise and fitness. Much of the popular literature focuses on various self-proclaimed miracle approaches to diet and weight loss, but increasingly there is a corresponding focus on exercise, too. Bicycling, cross-country skiing, jogging, and walking are all fine aerobic activities, and each has a popular literature available. For example, most bookstores stock popular books that describe where to find good jogging or walking routes when you travel on vacation or business. There are also books describing bicycling routes that you can explore locally or as a vacation activity.

The extraordinary increase in sales of fitness equipment since the mid-1980s is also evidence of the current high status of this field. Although the increased interest in fitness might understandably result in increased sales of running shoes or bicycles, it is the rapid increase in sales of fitness equipment that is in many ways most remarkable. Weight-training systems, Nautilus equipment, rowing machines, bicycle trainers, and even complete home gyms are no longer uncommon household fixtures.

Our knowledge about the amount and type of fitness activity necessary to enhance life is changing. A new, specialized field of exercise physiology,

FOCUS ON	Areas of Study in Basic Exercise Science	15.1

Area	Questions Typically Asked	
Environmental effects on exercise	How does altitude affect exercise functions?	
	What kinds of pollutants most affect exercise functions?	
	What are the regulatory responses to exercise under conditions of high heat and humidity?	
Disease and health	How does exercise affect diseases such as diabetes, coronary artery disease, or cancer?	
	How is exercise related to blood pressure, appetite control, insulin sensitivity, and blood clotting?	
Cardiovascular system	How is blood flow regulated during exercise?	
	How is breathing regulated during exercise?	
	What factors limit aerobic capacity?	
	How do anaerobic and aerobic systems function under different exercise stresses?	
Exercise biochemistry	How is glucose homeostasis maintained during exercise?	
	How does exercise affect the aging process?	
	How does exercise affect obesity?	
Ergogenic aids	How does creatine supplementation affect strength development?	
	How does preexercise carbohydrate loading affect cycling performance?	

SOURCE: Adapted from Brooks, 1987; and Blair, Kohl, & Powell, 1987.

referred to as **exercise epidemiology**, has emerged. People in this field study the relationships between activity patterns and mortality. We are also in a period when the study of how exercise, or the lack thereof, affects aging is of great interest. This interest is due to findings suggesting that many typical signs of aging may be attributable to poor nutrition and lack of activity rather than merely to getting older.

The increased cultural attention to health and fitness is also apparent in the growth of interest in exercise physiology, both in the scientific study of basic exercise phenomena and in the clinical applications of that knowledge. In the scientific study of basic exercise phenomena, the areas studied and the kinds of questions typically asked within them are shown in Focus On Box 15.1.

As we have noted, exercise physiology has become the foundation on which a number of clinical, professional areas have developed. Cardiac rehabilitation, adult fitness, strength training, and athletic training are the most frequently cited clinical subdisciplines of exercise science. These areas have developed sufficiently to have their own professional organizations, journals, textbooks, and training programs. In some cases, certification is necessary to practice in these subdisciplines. Some of these fields may be categorized as "clinical exercise." The clinical-exercise fields use the information developed from basic exercise research and also have specific areas of study, as shown in Focus On Box 15.2.

Because not one of the questions in either of the Focus On boxes, has been answered fully, it is easy to see why research in basic and clinical-exercise

FOCUS ON	Areas of Study in Clinical-Exercise Science	15.2
Area	Questions Typically Asked	
Rehabilitation	What factors influence the exercise progression for patients who have had a heart attack?	
	How can a muscle best be rehabilitated after trauma?	
	What role does exercise play in treating depression?	
Prevention	What level of fitness is needed to lower cardiovascular risk?	
	How is exercise related to regulation of diseases such as diabetes?	
	What level of fitness is needed to resist the onset of high blood pressure?	
	How is children's fitness related to problems in their later years?	
Age-related	At what age should children begin fitness training?	
	How can exercise programs increase the quality of life for older people?	
	What role does exercise play in changes that occur in adolescence?	
	How can exercise deter traditional signs of aging?	

physiology continues to be important. The successful results of exercise-physiology research over the past several decades have begun to change the way in which many people protect their health through exercise. People are beginning to appreciate how exercise can be used as both a preventive and a rehabilitative instrument in the treatment of various kinds of medical problems. Obviously, much remains to be done.

What Do Exercise Physiologists Do?

Exercise physiologists are involved in research, teaching, and clinical service. In a narrow sense, the field of exercise physiology is confined mostly to colleges, universities, and laboratories. Exercise physiologists can be found in departments of sport sciences, Kinesiology, physical education, physiology, cardiology, general medicine, and veterinary medicine. They teach courses in exercise science, conduct research, train graduate students, and provide clinical services to an increasingly large number of diverse populations, ranging from elite athletes to patients who have had heart attacks.

In smaller departments, exercise physiologists typically focus on one of the three major approaches to exercise physiology: traditional cardiovascular and metabolic exercise physiology, exercise biochemistry, or applied exercise physiology (related to cardiac rehabilitation, athletic training, adult fitness, and the like). In larger departments, it is not uncommon to find all three represented.

Students who study exercise physiology at the master's-degree level are usually headed to one of the exercise and fitness professions and will be employed as athletic trainers, personal trainers, cardiac rehabilitation workers, leaders of worksite fitness programs, or strength and conditioning coaches. These fields are very popular with young women and men today, and exercise physiology is the foundation science for their professional work.

Thus, an exercise physiologist might test an elite athlete on a treadmill, obtain a muscle biopsy, analyze oxygen-consumption data with the help of a computer, direct a patient through a graded test on a bicycle ergometer, lecture an undergraduate class on basic cardiovascular functions, conduct an advanced seminar on recent research, or administer a large-scale fitness program.

Current Issues and Problems in Exercise Physiology

As in most fields that have a basic and an applied focus, the issues and problems of exercise physiology tend to be distributed between those related to the basic scientific investigation of exercise-related phenomena and the practical problems associated with clinical practice. Professionals in the clinical practice of exercise physiology do more applied research and would like the help of their more basic-oriented scientific colleagues to answer questions of immediate, applied significance. The basic researchers, on the other hand, feel strongly that theoretically oriented research pays higher dividends in the long run because it tends to focus on underlying mechanisms rather than on applied problems.

Another issue emerging within exercise science is the increasingly clear need for interdisciplinary approaches to investigate more fully issues in physical activity. Since the mid-1960s, researchers in the kinesiology fields have become more and more specialized in their graduate preparation and in their own fields of study as researchers and scholars. Now, it appears, there is recognition that to investigate the myriad phenomena that involve physical activity will likely require knowledge and research strategies from several of the Kinesiology subdisciplines—exercise physiology, biomechanics, and motor control, for example. In the near future, we may see a more concerted effort to prepare graduate students comprehensively in the physical-activity sciences rather than narrowly in one field of study.

Physical educator Janet Harris (1992) has argued that exercise physiology has largely ignored the social and political problems in which the field is embedded. In Chapter 7, the newer *socioecological* view of health and fitness was described, a view that focuses not only on individual responsibility for health and fitness but also on the social, political, and economic structures that prevent portions of the population from gaining access to information, facilities, and programs related to fitness and health. The fact is that a person's fitness status is related to her or his socioeconomic status and that solving

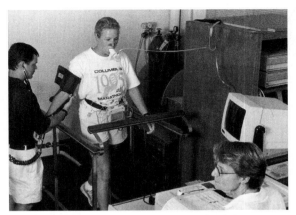

Exercise testing is an important step both in research and for prescriptive programs.

national problems related to fitness requires sensitivity to sociopolitical issues and programs designed to resolve sociopolitical problems.

The ACSM is the main professional and scientific association for this field, but it has grown large primarily because of the emergence of public interest in exercise and fitness. Large professional organizations can exert substantial power and can guide public policy, but they also become so diverse in their membership that the specific needs of exercise physiologists may get less attention.

The many important issues related to exercise, physical activity, and fitness were reviewed in Chapter 9. Needless to say, this is an active field with an important future, one that is exciting and attracts the interest of many talented women and men.

KINESIOLOGY AND BIOMECHANICS

Professionals in sport, fitness, and physical education have always been interested in how the body moves and in how more efficient and effective movement can be brought about. Sometimes, the goal is primarily educational as when a physical-education teacher helps children learn fundamental motor skills such as jumping and throwing. At other times, the goal is primarily competitive as when a coach seeks to fine-tune the technique of a hurdler in order to improve the athlete's speed. At still other times, the goal is safety as when a fitness instructor demonstrates proper lifting technique. Regardless of the specific goal, in each of these situations, the professional in charge must know a great deal about how the body is structured, how it moves, and what principles can be used to increase movement effectiveness. These areas constitute the realms of kinesiology and biomechanics.

The term *Kinesiology* has a broad meaning, in that it has become the most common umbrella term used to describe the discipline devoted to the study of physical activity and movement (I will use the uppercase spelling to denote the broad meaning). The term *kinesiology* has also historically been used to refer to the study of how the muscular system moves the bony structure of the body; indeed, most undergraduate programs in physical education, sport sciences, exercise science, or Kinesiology require at least one course in kinesiology. *Biomechanics* is the science that applies the mechanical principles of physics and engineering to the investigation of human movement and the structure and function of the human body (Simpson, 2000). Together, kinesiology and biomechanics form an increasingly important Kinesiology subdiscipline, which attracts the interest of scientists from diverse areas and which has many practical applications in the worlds of sport, fitness, and physical education.

Sometimes, biomechanical analysis *follows* advances made by athletes, providing an explanation for and an understanding of newly introduced techniques. The best modern example is the high-jump style popularized by Dick Fosbury in the mid-1960s. Fosbury won the Gold Medal at the 1968 Olympic Games in Mexico City and changed the course of high jumping with his flop style. Within 10 years, virtually all high jumpers in the world had switched from roll styles to the flop style. Biomechanists provided the explanations of why this new style was more effective.

In other cases, however, kinesiology and biomechanics have *led* changes in technique. The best example here is in swimming, where over a period of years in the 1960s and 1970s, kinesiologists working

Knowledge from biomechanics has revolutionized swim instruction and coaching.

with elite-level coaches determined that the traditional method of the arm pull in crawl swimming, based on drag forces for producing propulsion, was not as biomechanically efficient as an arm pull that produced lift forces (Adrian, 1983). Within 10 years, virtually every swim coach in the world had changed the techniques taught to swimmers in crawl events. This was an example of scientific investigation leading changes in practice rather than explaining changes in practice brought about through innovations by athletes.

Kinesiology and biomechanics are important sport sciences because they are so fundamental to the work of sport, fitness, and physical-education professionals and to that of other sport scientists. In areas as diverse as fitness, rehabilitation, equipment design, physical therapy, injury prevention, basic motor education, and improved sport performance, kinesiology and biomechanics have an important role to play. The kinds of questions asked in this subdiscipline show how both scientists and practitioners might find the answers interesting and useful in their work:

- How are muscle forces summated to produce power in the golf swing?

- How can joint flexibility be increased for rehabilitative purposes?

- What movement patterns do elite-level volleyball players use for spiking?

- What kind of shoe support can be developed to counter foot problems in distance running?

- How can tennis rackets be changed to produce better control?

- Which baseball-hitting technique is best for a singles hitter? Which is best for a power hitter?

- How does muscle use in throwing change as children develop skill?

The answers to those questions and to others like them have traditionally been based on experience, opinion, and, far too often, unwarranted assumptions and beliefs. A *scientific* answer to those questions comes only from improvements in scientific methodology that allow research to examine the issues systematically. Those scientifically derived answers can then form the primary information on which a sport, fitness, or physical-education professional bases judgments for intervention with clients, students, and athletes.

Definition of Kinesiology and Biomechanics as Fields of Study

As mentioned previously, *kinesiology* is the study of human motion, more specifically the study of how the muscles move the bony structure of the body. The human body consists of a bony structure—its anatomy—connected at the joints and moved and supported by muscles and tendons. The motions that humans are capable of are determined by the nature of the joints and of the muscles that move the bony structure at the joints. The knee joint, for example, is effective in flexion and extension movements whereas the shoulder is effective in rotational movements.

To understand human motion, we must have a complete command of the various actions of different joints and the muscles that contract and relax to move the bony structure at those joints. Thus, kinesiology has traditionally been the course that taught students to identify the actions of joints and the muscles that cause those actions. This kind of knowledge is fundamental to the practice of a profession such as *physical therapy* where a practitioner might have to provide graded exercise to restore the full range of motion at a shoulder joint following an injury sustained by a patient.

The study of kinesiology is often organized by joints or groups of joints in the same anatomical region of the body and subclassified by the type of movement at the joint. Thus, a primary grouping might include the foot and ankle, the knee, the hips and pelvic girdle, the spinal column, the elbow and wrist, and the shoulder girdle. The movements possible at each of these joints are determined by the nature of the joint and by the positions of the muscles around the joint. Some of these movement possibilities are *abduction* and *adduction* (movement *away from* and *toward* the midline of the body), flexion and extension, pronation and supination, inversion and eversion, medial and lateral rotation, and elevation and depression. This approach to the study of human motion is often referred to as *anatomical kinesiology.*

Biomechanics, often referred to as *mechanical kinesiology,* is the study of human motion from the standpoint of physics. In most cases, the study of kinesiology precedes the study of biomechanics because it is easier to understand the influence of various forces on human motion if you have a thorough knowledge of the motions that the body is capable of. *Mechanics* is the area of physics that studies how forces, both internal and external, affect the motions of objects, animate or inanimate (Brancazio, 1984). Biomechanics regards human motion from this mechanical point of view in which the body is divided into a collection of segments (shoulder, arm, wrist, and so on) connected to one another at the joints and moved by both muscular forces and externally applied forces. Biomechanics has developed into a highly sophisticated research field.

> The idea is to study the human body in action as it goes through some particular movement—swinging a golf club or throwing a javelin, for instance—in order to isolate the various individual motions that make up the activity, to measure the speeds of body segments and the forces that act on them, and in general to acquire accurate data on all aspects of the movement. The analysis can become quite complex—the golf swing, for example, involves nearly a hundred different forces acting on thirteen body segments—so sophisticated research equipment is a virtual necessity. (Brancazio, 1984, p. 18)

Biomechanists study how physical principles affect human motion and performance. If a subject uses an implement (for example, tennis racquet) or has to strike or receive an object (for example, kick a football), then the implement and the object also become part of the biomechanical analysis.

The fields of kinesiology and biomechanics form a coherent whole that represents a fundamental aspect of the emerging sport sciences. These fields are not only important in their own right but also are increasingly being used by researchers in other sport sciences in attempts to provide a more integrated investigation of sport and fitness phenomena.

Development of Kinesiology and Biomechanics

Kinesiology has been a traditional scientific field of study in physical education along with anatomy, physiology, and measurement. These subjects formed the core scientific training of physical educators during that time when health, fitness, recreation, and sport professionals all were educated under the umbrella of physical education. Historically, kinesiology has focused primarily on anatomical and structural issues with less focus on the mechanical factors that influence movement. To the

degree that mechanical factors were considered, they were investigated within the kinesiology course.

Biomechanics, as a specialized field of study, began to emerge in the mid-1960s as part of the development of the subdisciplines of physical education. Biomechanics developed as an international field of investigation. The First International Seminar on Biomechanics was held in Switzerland in 1967, and it was followed by similar meetings in Holland in 1969, Rome in 1971, and the United States at Pennsylvania State University in 1973. Research journals in medicine, engineering, sports, and exercise began to review biomechanics research (Adrian, 1983).

During the late 1960s and 1970s, growth was rapid. The International Society of Biomechanics was founded as was the American Society of Biomechanics, which also began to publish a new journal, the *Journal of Biomechanics*. Kinesiology texts had long been available in physical education, but the 1960s and 1970s witnessed the publication of a number of basic biomechanics textbooks as well as specialized biomechanical books. Two of the earliest and most influential were Councilman's (1968) *The Science of Swimming* and Dyson's (1964) *The Mechanics of Athletics*.

In the 1980s, there was sufficient research and development to warrant the formation of specialized organizations devoted to sport biomechanics. The International Society of Biomechanics in Sport was formed in 1982. Researchers and scholars in physics, many of them amateur athletes themselves, have begun to show interest in applying their knowledge of physics to sport. Many articles have appeared in the *American Journal of Physics*, a respected journal devoted to applications of physics in cultural life (Brancazio, 1984).

Like other subdisciplinary fields, biomechanics has both research and clinical subfields, and there is often a circular relationship between the two; that is, problems identified in the field are investigated, and research findings are put to use in the field. This circularity and the entire field of biomechanics were greatly enhanced with the initiation in 1982 of the Elite Athlete Project sponsored by the U.S. Olympic Committee (Hay, 1991). The

Digital video images can precisely compare differences in performance.

research and clinical activity spurred by this project has helped improve both research and methods and the delivery of services to athletes and coaches.

Biomechanics developed out of the traditional field of kinesiology. Recently, biomechanics has come to dominate the field. It is becoming more and more common for the field to be referred to as *sport biomechanics*. We can expect that label and the focus it implies to continue to dominate research and application.

Current Status of Kinesiology and Biomechanics

The explosion of interest in sport and fitness in the recent past has greatly increased interest in the work of biomechanics. Although technique has always been considered important in teaching and coaching, it is only recently that professionals and laypeople alike have become more knowledgeable and sophisticated about the mechanical aspects of technique and have learned how physical principles can be used to explain and improve performance.

There has also been a steady improvement of equipment, much of which is directly traceable to a better understanding of biomechanics. Pole vaulters continue to vault higher as poles provide more thrust and as the vaulters accommodate their technique to the new mechanical demands of the poles. Tennis players have been able to control their games better with bigger racquets. Distance runners avoid injury by wearing better-designed shoes.

Biomechanical research is carried out using a number of technical methods. High-speed photography has been a major tool in the development of biomechanics research methods. Whereas a standard movie camera records images at the rate of eighteen frames per second, specialized cameras can operate at thousands of frames per second, thus apparently slowing down the motion to the point where it can be analyzed in great detail.

Electromyography (EMG), a technique for recording the electrical impulses within muscles, has also been a favored research method. The impulses are translated into graphs or other representations so that the functions of muscles can be analyzed and compared. This kind of information can be used in many ways. For example, athletes have a certain rhythm to their performances that is detectable through EMG recordings. When they hit a slump, this is reflected by changes in their EMG patterns.

Transducers are used in clinical strength-measuring devices to quantify the force a subject can exert. Transducers are used in *force platforms* to assist in the measurement of force exerted by a performer. This kind of knowledge is used to evaluate footwear and is also useful in human-gait analysis (Simpson, 2000). Pressure devices are also placed in shoe inserts to provide analysis of pressures exerted on the foot during human motion. This kind of research is often a prelude to producing an *orthotic* (special shoe insert) that can provide correction and relief both to athletes and to individuals who experience foot problems because of structural or muscular abnormalities.

Technology has affected all the sport sciences but none more profoundly than sport biomechanics. Combinations of video, analog, and computer technology allow for viewing and analyzing the movement of athletes (www.peakfperform.com). Software programs calculate accurate kinematic measurements of linear and angular displacements, velocities, and accelerations that are necessary to analyze and improve technique. Movements can be viewed in two- or three-dimensional space. These technologies, of course, are also useful for the medical professions and for the media industries. The more general field that has developed from these technologies is referred to as "motion analysis."

Quantitative biomechanical analysis using these sophisticated techniques dominates the research field. Such methods are also being used more frequently as training aids for elite athletes. However, the ordinary coach or teacher has to depend more on *qualitative* biomechanical analysis if she or he is to provide the help that students and athletes need as they attempt to improve their performances. The regular, accurate application of biomechanical analysis in the gymnasium and on the playing fields remains the most important step forward to be made by the coaching and teaching professions. If this important step is to be accomplished, the field must be approached in terms of what physical educator Shirl Hoffman (1977) called a **"pedagogical kinesiology"**—that is, an approach to biomechanics that emphasizes recognition of the critical elements and common errors in sport-skill performance as it occurs in practical situations. Teachers and coaches must be able to *see* critical elements of sport-skill performance as it occurs in order to *detect* common errors being made and *respond* to the performer with accurate, relevant feedback.

Qualitative skill feedback depends on a teacher's knowledge of the skill.

Although sport biomechanics is emerging as an important sport science, this does not mean that sport is the sole or even the most important field of application for biomechanics knowledge. Areas such as physical therapy, occupational therapy, adapted physical education, and rehabilitative medicine have all used new knowledge from biomechanics directly in their professional practices. The major areas of study within kinesiology and biomechanics and the typical questions asked within them show the diversity of application within these fields (see Focus On Box 15.3).

The subdisciplines of kinesiology and biomechanics have a bright future because they have not only the ability to contribute important information to sport, fitness, and physical-education professionals but also a strong potential for contributing to areas such as medicine, rehabilitation, child development, and gerontology. In the field of sport equipment, too, we can expect continuing improvement based partially on contributions made by sport biomechanists.

What Do Kinesiologists and Biomechanists Do?

Kinesiologists and biomechanists work primarily in academic positions in colleges and universities although there are increasing employment opportunities in the private sector, particularly in the equipment industries. In the academic world, these

FOCUS ON	Areas of Study Within Kinesiology and Biomechanics	15.3

Area	Questions Typically Asked
Kinesiology	How does the wrist joint move when baseball pitchers throw curve balls?
	How does muscle potential differ between middle- and long-distance running?
	What range of motion should be achieved in rehabilitation of the knee after surgery?
	How do kicking motions change as children develop?
Quantitative biomechanics	How do forces summate most efficiently to produce maximum performance in the discus throw?
	What variables influence human tolerance to externally imposed stress, such as is inflicted in football tackling?
	What are the performance patterns of world-class spikers in volleyball?
Qualitative biomechanics	What are the critical performance elements of various sport skills?
	What are the most common errors made at various developmental stages in acquiring a sport skill?
	How can these critical elements and common errors be taught to teachers and coaches?
Equipment analysis	What is the optimal design of a golf club?
	How can shoes better prevent overpronation in running?
	What materials can best absorb shock in contact sports where protective gear is worn?

specialists are most often found in departments of physical education or sport science.

Like all academicians, kinesiologists and biomechanists teach, do research, and provide service to various constituencies. Much of the research is highly theoretical and has no immediate practical application. Some of the research, however, is designed to provide immediate answers to practical problems in sport and fitness.

The fields have become very technical, and biomechanics laboratories can cost a great deal to build. Kinesiologists and biomechanists who find work in the private sector are more typically involved in the practical problems of product design, testing, and evaluating. In some countries, sport biomechanists are finding employment with national sport teams or at national training centers where their work focuses mostly on helping elite athletes improve their performances.

Current Issues in Kinesiology and Biomechanics

The major issues within kinesiology and biomechanics are similar to those in other sport sciences. A continuing debate exists concerning the relative contributions made by quantitative analysis and qualitative analysis. The debate tends to be joined over the question of which approach should be emphasized in the typical undergraduate course for physical-education majors who are preparing to teach. Many professionally oriented people believe that the undergraduate course should emphasize qualitative techniques on a sport-by-sport basis. Others favor the teaching of principles that then can be applied to many sports. Still others favor the teaching of beginning quantitative techniques because that approach is the dominant research approach within the field.

Under what conditions do children best acquire sport skills?

These fields, as described earlier, have contributed research and information that is valuable to a variety of fields outside sport and physical education. Biomechanists often receive research monies from sources with concerns that are not at all related to sport and physical education. Thus, there is some danger that kinesiologists and biomechanists will become more and more distanced from sport and physical education.

MOTOR BEHAVIOR

Motor behavior is the subdiscipline of Kinesiology that focuses on how motor skills are acquired and controlled across the lifespan (Thomas & Thomas, 2000). This subdiscipline comprises three fields, which are distinct but highly related. **Motor learning** focuses on how motor skills are learned, particularly the conditions under which practice leads to improvement. **Motor control** focuses on the "neural, physical, and behavioral aspects of movement" (Schmidt, 1988, p. 17). **Motor development**

is the specialized aspect of the subdiscipline that focuses on how the acquisition, improvement, and control of motor skills change and vary across the lifespan.

People who practice in the sport, fitness, and physical-education professions have always been centrally concerned with helping people acquire and improve motor skills. Because a major portion of motor-skill learning occurs from infancy through adolescence, these same professionals have a keen interest in the developmental stages humans go through and how they affect motor learning, control, and performance. Faced with an aging population over the past half-century, professionals have also become increasingly concerned with motor-skill issues in older citizens.

Motor learning and control have formed a clear family of scientific interests since the early 1970s. Researchers in motor learning seek to understand the processes through which motor skills are developed and the factors that facilitate or inhibit skill development (Shea, Shebilske, & Worchel, 1993). Researchers in motor control seek to understand how motor skills are actually executed and what

Good physical education presents challenges that lead to real accomplishments.

factors lead to the breakdown of such skills. Motor development might be thought of as a first cousin. Researchers in motor development seek to understand the hereditary basis of motor development and the environmental factors that facilitate or inhibit such development.

How do children and youths learn motor skills? How are those skills executed? How do developmental processes interact with the learning and performance of motor skills? These are the questions that tend to make these scientific disciplines a family. The questions are particularly important in three developmental stages: childhood, adolescence, and old age. It is easy to recognize the importance of an integrated understanding of how children develop and execute motor skills and what factors facilitate or inhibit skill development and execution, but it is becoming increasingly important

to understand how the process of aging affects motor-skill development and performance.

Researchers in motor learning, motor control, and motor development work to provide good answers to these practical questions as well as to develop and refine theories within their fields. As with many fields, the link between theory and practice is not always strong or direct, a concern that periodically resurfaces within both the practitioner and the researcher communities. Nonetheless, the motor-learning, -control, and -development subdisciplines of physical education have grown and prospered since the early 1970s and are now firmly rooted within the sport, fitness, and physical-education sciences.

Motor learning and motor control tend to make up two branches of the traditional field of motor-skill acquisition. Motor development has had a separate history but remains linked to motor learning and control in fundamental ways. The kinds of questions asked within these three areas are obviously interrelated:

- Should practice trials be massed together or spaced over time?
- How does the quality of information in knowledge of results affect skill acquisition?
- How does a performer plan a complex, coordinated skill response?
- What stages does a child go through in learning to run?
- How does eye–hand coordination develop in children?
- Can mentally rehearsing a skill enhance performance?
- How can practice conditions best prepare an athlete for game play?
- How do performers visually track objects so as to catch or hit them?
- Are there gender differences in learning and performing skills?

To the extent that there may be definitive answers to those and other questions, the professional basis of teaching and coaching will be greatly enhanced. These areas have become part of the coursework typically done by teachers and coaches working toward certification—and it is easy to see why.

Definition of Motor Behavior as a Field of Study

Motor learning, control, and development have their historical roots in the discipline of psychology, defined broadly as the study of human behavior and development. Traditionally, psychology has been concerned with the effects of both heredity and environment on human development and behavior. The effects of the environment typically fall under the study of *learning*, which can be defined as a relatively permanent change in performance resulting from experience or practice (Kerr, 1982). Sport, fitness, and physical education are concerned primarily but not exclusively with the acquisition and refinement of motor or physical skills, defined as muscular actions directed toward the achievement of a goal. *Motor learning* is therefore a relatively permanent change in the performance of a motor skill, resulting from experience or practice. The motor skill can be as basic as a young child learning to climb and as complex as a highly trained basketball player performing intricate maneuvers in a constantly changing game.

Most motor-skill tasks initially involve perception of an object, especially visual perception (as in hitting a ball or striking an object). Thus, interest in perception accompanied the development of interest in skill acquisition. In fact, in many places, the field is referred to as *perceptual–motor learning*. The interest in the perceptual aspects of motor-skill learning and performance continue to the present day.

As psychology developed in the mid–twentieth century, it turned more and more of its attention to the underlying mechanisms associated with human behavior and development. Researchers in sport, fitness, and physical education began to focus on the processes underlying movement and

skill performance. Of major interest in this area is how the nervous system controls the muscular system to produce skilled movement. This focus has resulted in a strong emphasis on the cognitive basis of motor skill and on how the underlying cognitive processes are organized and used to control skilled movement. This relatively recent area is referred to as *motor control.* The emphasis here is still on learning but more on the underlying processes that accompany learning.

The field of motor development focuses on how the learning and performing of motor skills changes across the lifespan. Within motor development are both the study of how heredity influences motor development and performance and the study of how differences in motor development and performance may be explained among age groups.

Motor learning and motor control are fairly narrow fields of specialization conducted almost exclusively in universities in departments of physical education, sport science, or psychology. There are no direct, applied motor-learning practitioners. Indirectly, of course, teachers and coaches represent the applied practice of motor learning.

In motor development, the link between research and practical use of that research is closer. Elementary-school physical-education teachers, preschool specialists, and, increasingly, infant-stimulation specialists all directly apply knowledge generated in the research field of motor development. Motor-development knowledge is also of great importance to the professional in adapted physical education. Often, behavioral deficits of disabling conditions involve developmental delays in motor patterns. Thus, the adapted-physical-education specialist teaches basic motor patterns to individuals with disabilities.

Knowledge from motor development is used widely in the entire field of early-childhood development. During infancy and early childhood, a child's mental, physical, social, and emotional development are intimately related to and dramatically grounded in movement. A child's exploration of his or her world and the child's sensory development all depend on movement. Thus, cognitive and emotional development are intimately related to motor development in these early stages.

The rapid increase of participation in child and youth sport has also captured the attention of motor-development specialists. Even more recently, there have been attempts to devise systematic skill- and fitness-development programs for infants. Here, too, motor-development specialists have much to do in investigating such efforts and much to say about appropriate practices that respect what is known about developmental stages.

Development of Motor Behavior

When physical education developed as a full-fledged professional field in the early twentieth century, researchers began to show interest in how motor skills were learned and how the various developmental stages affected skill performance and fitness. Concepts such as general motor ability (GMA) were developed, researched, and widely discussed. Early research by physical educators often tried to relate GMA to motor-skill acquisition, much in the same way as educators attempted to link the intelligence-quotient measure to learning in schools (Sage, 1984). The major publishing outlet for this work was the *Research Quarterly*.

The period of most important growth for the field of motor learning was during and just after World War II. During that time, government agencies funded many projects aimed at better understanding of and training in a wide range of perceptual and motor skills. Those important wartime tasks had to do with sighting and identifying enemy planes at great distances, tracking quickly moving objects so as to shoot at them, operating the controls of airplanes, and designing display panels that would provide the necessary cues and information for quick, dependable responses from pilots, navigators, and gunners (Sage, 1984).

When the discipline of Kinesiology was created in the 1960s (see Chapter 2), motor behavior emerged as one of its subdisciplines. Two new journals, *Perceptual and Motor Skills* and the *Journal of Motor Behavior*, became primary outlets for research in the field.

During the 1970s, many researchers began to show interest in the underlying *processes* that accompany the more visible task attributes of motor learning. That was the beginning of the area now referred to as *motor control*. Rather than manipulate environmental variables, such as feedback, to investigate their effects on the task performance, motor-control researchers began to look instead at the underlying cognitive processes and at the nervous system's interaction with the muscular system to produce skilled movement.

To investigate aspects of motor control, researchers needed to extend their work beyond the traditional boundaries of psychology. Fields such as neuropsychology, neurophysiology, cognitive psychology, biomechanics, and computer science all contributed to the emerging field of motor control (Christina, 1987). Today, the fields of motor learning and motor control are equal partners in the general area of perceptual–motor development.

Motor development has always been a special area within developmental psychology. As physical education grew into a specialized, professional field in the early twentieth century, motor development slowly emerged as a focus within the field. Motor development is often divided into strongly related fields: (1) growth and (2) perceptual–motor development. Issues surrounding physical and motor growth have long held the interest of researchers from a number of fields. Longitudinal studies of growth and development are among the most famous and important in twentieth-century psychological and educational research. Following in that tradition, physical educators conducted similar studies. For example, the Wisconsin Growth Study focused on annual measurement of a variety of anthropometric, strength, and motor-performance items for boys and girls from ages 7–12 years; also, the Medford, Oregon, Boys Study followed a group of boys from ages 7–18 years (Clarke, 1986).

In addition to examining physical characteristics associated with development, researchers and practitioners have been interested in developing motor behavior such as walking, climbing, jumping, throwing, and catching. As physical education for elementary-school children became more widely available through specialist teachers, this aspect of the motor-development field became extremely important to practitioners, spurring new interest in the field. Teachers, coaches, and child-care workers need to know how best to help young children acquire and refine skills and build and maintain fitness. It is at this nexus that the fields of motor learning, motor control, and motor development come together to form a coherent subdisciplinary focus within physical education.

Current Status of Motor Behavior

Motor learning, control, and development are now distinct subject areas within the broad spectrum of the sport and physical-education sciences. Most teacher-certification programs in physical education require at least one course in motor learning and one in motor development. Motor control is typically treated within the motor-learning course. At the graduate level, motor learning, motor control, and motor development have emerged as distinct areas of specialization, particularly at the doctoral level.

Motor learning and motor control have developed into highly specialized research fields with strong ties to experimental psychology and neuropsychology. The links between research in these areas and the practices of teaching and coaching have weakened considerably since the mid-1980s. (See discussion of this issue later in this chapter.) Motor development, on the other hand, has strong, direct links to the practices of early-childhood education, elementary-school physical education, and adapted physical education. Much has been learned about the advantages of early-childhood education and the influence that early learning has on behavior throughout life. Many fitness problems among adults, for example, are traceable to problems that developed and habits that were established during early childhood. These links between experiences in childhood and lifestyles as adults have fostered growing interest in motor development.

Parents concerned about the early development of their children have also shown increased interest in popular literature on motor and physical development. As with all areas of popular interest, there is a high risk of fads and misinformation. Thus, researchers and professionals in motor development also have a strong interest in disseminating accurate public information, especially as it is related to proposed programs of infant stimulation and early-childhood motor and fitness training.

The major areas of study within motor learning, control, and development are broadly based. Some of those areas and associated typical questions are shown in Focus On Box 15.4. As the fields of motor learning, control, and development grow and mature, we should expect that they will be able to speak to wider audiences. Many of the topics shown in Box 15.4 are of interest to groups other than sport, fitness, and physical-education professionals. For example, the areas of physical rehabilitation, gerontology, architecture, industrial technology, and early-childhood education all might have reason to seek solutions to problems that fall within the scope of the motor-learning, -control, and -development subdisciplines. Professionals in physical rehabilitation need to understand motor-control information as they seek to help people regain full use of limbs and motor functioning. Gerontologists need to know how memory and motor-skill performance change in older people. The architect needs the motor-development specialist to design appropriate play spaces, and the industrial technologist needs him or her to develop play equipment.

The field of motor development may be beginning a period of substantial growth. Issues surrounding child care and early-childhood education are emerging as important political focal points in America. We should expect that major legislation supporting child care and early-childhood education will be enacted at both the federal and the state levels. When that happens, the expertise and information available in motor development will be widely sought, new programs will develop, and many new people will be attracted to the field.

FOCUS ON	Areas of Study Within Motor Behavior	15.4

Area	Questions Typically Asked
Motor learning	How do the frequency and timing of feedback influence skill acquisition and maintenance?
	How does skill performance change as it becomes more automatic?
	How does fatigue interfere with performance and learning?
	How does aging affect memory in motor-skill learning and performance?
Motor control	What series of cognitive steps does a beginner go through when acquiring a skill?
	How does the plan for executing a skill change from beginning to advanced levels of performance?
	What is the nature of the human information-processing system that stores and retrieves information for use in skill performance?
	How are verbal instructions for skill learning translated into images used by performers?
Motor development	At what age can a child safely benefit from cardiovascular training?
	What developmental stages do children go through as they learn to throw, catch, and strike objects?
	At what age or developmental status can young learners use mature motor forms?
	How is early motor stimulation related to the development of intelligence and thinking?

What Do Specialists in Motor Behavior Do?

Motor-learning and motor-control specialists work almost exclusively in academic positions in universities, usually in sport-science, physical-education, or psychology departments. Motor-development specialists are mainly employed in universities too, in similar departments, but there are increasing opportunities for them in private industry and in child care and early-childhood education.

Motor-learning and motor-control specialists typically teach and do research, performing little direct clinical application of their expertise. Motor-development specialists teach, do research, and provide clinical services through infant and early-childhood motor-development programs. Since the mid-1980s, motor-development specialists have also

become more involved in areas such as playground safety, playground design, and play-equipment design. It is also increasingly common to find university faculty positions that require expertise in both motor development and elementary-school physical education. Most students who seek advanced degrees specializing in elementary-school physical education or teacher education have cognate training in motor development.

Current Issues and Problems in Motor Behavior

Within any scientific discipline, there are numerous issues and problems related to questions of theoretical and methodological importance. These problems, however, are seldom of interest to people who are not members of the discipline. From a broad perspective, one major issue has always been present in motor learning: the relationship between research in motor learning and control and the practices of teaching and coaching.

Motor learning developed in physical education with a strong link to psychology. Most of the language and concepts of early motor learning were drawn from psychology. As the field developed, it turned quickly to psychology for its theoretical direction, its concepts, and the language it used to discuss issues. From the inception of the field as a subdiscipline, questions were raised about its relevance to teaching and coaching. Responding to a research paper in 1969, psychologist Robert Simon spoke directly to the issue:

> Certainly we know quite a lot about information feedback, and certainly Bilodeau and Jones know more than most of us. And, yet, if I try to look at their paper through the eyes of a physical education teacher or coach, I find very little there which I would be able to apply in teaching someone a particular athletic skill. (cited in Smith, 1970, pp. 24–25)

Five years later in 1975, the same problem was addressed by motor-learning expert Robert Wilberg, who suggested that the field had completely lost track of its professional counterparts in physical education and sport and that the language of motor learning had become "so filled with 'jargon' that the less well informed professional members have no idea about what we are doing, what we are saying, and where we are going" (Wilberg, 1975, p. 215).

As research and theory in motor learning and control have grown more sophisticated, the problem of application to sport coaching and physical-education teaching has grown more rather than less severe. Recently, however, motor-learning scholars have begun to rethink their relationship to sport and physical education not only because of the problem of applying the findings from their research but also because they recognize that in sport and physical education they may be able to build better theories.

It would appear that the favored approach now is to develop principles in the laboratory setting and then test them in applied settings.

In the field of motor development, debate continues concerning the degree to which heredity or environment can be linked to developmental changes. The nature–nurture question is difficult to answer satisfactorily; in trying to answer it, however, researchers and practitioners have found many effective new ways to help children develop more completely.

We should expect that in the future the field of motor development will focus more on aging populations where decrements in motor performance will become the main focus. What causes these decrements to happen? How can they be forestalled? These are important questions in a nation where the aging population continues to grow both because of new members and because of longer lifespans.

SUMMARY

1. The physical-science subdisciplines were the initial kinesiology subdisciplines to emerge in the last quarter of the twentieth century.

2. The subdisciplines eventually grew into the discipline called *Kinesiology*.

3. Exercise physiology is the oldest of the subdisciplines.

4. The physical-science subdisciplines have a strong research focus but also a growing consulting–clinical focus.

5. Some of the physical-science subdisciplines are housed in colleges of the arts and sciences; others are housed in professional colleges.

6. Beginning courses in the physical-science subdisciplines are often required for students seeking professional degrees and teaching licenses in physical education.

7. In many physical-science subdiscipline faculties, there is tension between faculty who want to do basic research driven by theory and faculty who want to do applied research to improve performance.

GET CONNECTED to Physical-Sciences Subdiscipline Web Sites

Exercise Physiology

American College of Sports Medicine	www.acsm.org
American Medical Society for Sports Medicine	www.amssm.org
American Orthopaedic Society for Sports Medicine	www.sportsmed.org
American Osteopathic Academy of Sports Medicine	www.aoasm.org
International Federation of Sports Medicine	www.fims.org
American Sports Medicine Institute	www.asmi.org
Gatorade Sports Science Institute	www.gssiweb.com
Institute for Preventive Sports Medicine	www.ipsm.org
SportsMedicine.com	www.sportsmedicine.com
The Physician and Sports Medicine Online	www.physsportsmed.com
American Society of Exercise Physiologists	www.asep.org
British Association of Sport and Exercise Sciences	www.bases.org.uk
Canadian Society of Exercise Physiologists	www.csep.ca

Kinesiology and Biomechanics

American Society of Biomechanics	www.asb-biomech.org
International Society of Biomechanics	www.isbweb.org
International Society of Biomechanics in Sports	www.uni-stuttgart.de/External/isbs
International Sports Engineering Association	www.sportsengineering.co.uk
Biomechanics Magazine	www.biomech.com

Motor Behavior

Canadian Society for Psychomotor Learning and Sport Psychology	www.scapps.org

DISCUSSION QUESTIONS

1. What are the separate spheres of study for each of the physical-science subdisciplines?

2. What are the clinical or consulting roles for faculty who work in the physical-science subdisciplines?

3. What options exist in universities in your area for students to prepare at undergraduate and graduate levels for the physical-science subdisciplines?

4. Which of the physical-science subdisciplines most appeals to you? For what reasons?

5. In what ways can faculty in these subdisciplines work together to study and find solutions to complex problems in sport, fitness, and physical education?

6. What courses have you taken that represent knowledge generated in each of the physical-science subdisciplines?

16

The Social-Science Subdisciplines Supporting the Professions

But games, I have argued, are fundamental and fundamentally human activities. They are in our blood and bones. Long ago, when we got too smart as a species, we found games. And games have been our rather constant companion ever since. . . . Nevertheless, it is too much to expect games in this imperfect world to be perfect. And this is one place where research from sociology, political philosophy, and economics comes in. . . . As so many scholars have already noted, our games reflect the ageism, sexism, nationalism, racism and all other "isms" that happen to be current at the time. Thus, we need to be vigilant critics of our games, seeing them as the imperfect human construction that they are.

R. Scott Kretchmar, 1989

LEARNING OBJECTIVES

- To explain how the social-science subdisciplines of sport sociology, sport and exercise psychology, sport pedagogy, and the sport humanities emerged

- To define each social-science subdiscipline as a field of study

- To understand the research focus for each of the social-science subdisciplines

- To describe how each of the social-science subdisciplines influences practices in sport, exercise, and physical education

- To discuss current problems and issues in each of the social-science subdisciplines

SPORT SOCIOLOGY

You probably grew up with an interest in sport and tend to take sport for granted. Sport is a basic part of your life, and you would have difficulty imagining what everyday life would be like without it. Most people in Western industrialized societies take sport for granted. It is just *there*, part of the fabric of daily, weekly, and seasonal life. As sport sociologist Ricky Gruneau has

Cultural differences in sport are topics for sport sociologists.

explained, sport is to be lived and enjoyed but not often analyzed:

> They (people in Western societies) live in a world where exposure to sport in one form or another is inescapable, but they rarely question sport's existence or see it posing problems which require anything more than superficial explanations. Sport is something that may be enjoyed, played, worked at, discussed or even disliked, but it is not something that is systematically analyzed, criticized or understood in its broader context. (Gruneau, 1976, p. 8)

Even in academic communities, this lack of interest in the deeper meanings of sport has been the norm. From time to time, scholars have attempted to examine and analyze sport, but those rare efforts have not been well received in academic communities and are virtually unknown to the public.

In the 1960s and 1970s, this traditional neglect of sport as a subject of inquiry and analysis began to change. One development that brought about this change was the emergence of the field of sport sociology. In the 1960s and 1970s, scholars within physical education and sociology began to ask questions using the research strategies of sociology. The questions in the realm of sport sociology are often of substantial interest not only to specialists but also, increasingly, to sport fans.

- Does participation in sport build character?
- Do minority athletes become more fully integrated into the dominant culture than do their nonathlete peers?
- How are children socialized through sport?
- How does the structure of professional sport affect participation?
- How does television affect sport institutions?
- How do various sport subcultures differ?
- How has increased sport opportunity affected the social and economic status of women?

The answers to questions such as these are of interest both to sport sociologists and to coaches, administrators, parents, and teachers, among others. As the disciplines of physical education and sport emerged in the 1960s, sport sociology quickly became one of their most important components.

Definition of Sport Sociology as a Field of Study

Sociology, an accepted scholarly field for more than 100 years, is a discipline that focuses primarily on social organization, social practices, and social behavior. Sport sociology focuses on "shared beliefs and social practices that constitute specific forms of physical activity (for example, sport, exercise)" (Harris, 2000, p. 209). Sport sociologists examine basic social units, such as individuals, groups, societies, and cultures. Coakley (2007) stresses that sports and physical activity have to be examined as social constructions; that is, "aspects of the social world that are created by people as they interact with one another under the social, political, and economic conditions that exist in their society" (p. 12). Sport sociologists study social processes such as socialization, social control, stratification, social conflict, and social changes (McPherson, 1981).

The subdiscipline of sport sociology has historically focused primarily on sport, but more recently there has been a growing interest in social phenomena in the area of exercise, particularly how society views and influences perceptions of the body and how it should look. Thus, it is not uncommon for sport sociologists to consider the fitness room or the health club, not just the playing field or the coaching office, as places to do research.

Sport sociologists conduct their investigations in the real worlds of sport and exercise. They study player–coach relations or aerobic exercise not in a laboratory but in the places where those things occur in society. They do so through surveys, interviews, thematic analysis of materials such as newspapers or the content of television coverage of sport, long-term observation in places where sport and exercise occur (called ethnography), theoretical analysis of trends in society, and historical analysis of changes in trends (Harris, 2000).

Sport sociology is typically defined, analyzed, and investigated within those definitional boundaries. Yet there is a broader sense of sport sociology, too. In the twentieth century, people recognized that sport is fundamental to the cultural fabric of organized, industrialized societies. Thus, not only was a sociology of sport created, but sport also was recognized more frequently in the larger analyses of basic social processes. In other words, sport not only became the main focus of a group of scholars known as sport sociologists but also began to be mentioned as an important factor when sociologists investigated and explained fundamental cultural processes. Sport is simply too important to be ignored in analyses of culture, and most scholars have come to recognize that fact.

Sport sociology is therefore typically defined within boundaries that derive from the parent discipline of sociology; however, laypeople's interest in topics that would typically fall within the parameters of sport sociology develops from their experience of sport, both as participants and as spectators. People recognize that sport is a social phenomenon and that it is part of a society—not a hypothetical society, but a particular society. Thus, to understand high-school football in Texas or ice hockey in Minnesota or ocean sports in Australia, one has to understand them in the context of the particular culture.

Competitors sometimes lose the play element in sport.

Although the term *sport* is used in the label of this subdiscipline, the actual focus of study is considerably broader than laypeople might assume. In fact, sport sociologists have been among the leaders, along with sport philosophers, in helping to clarify a group of related terms that, together, better define this area of interest: *play*, *games*, and *sport*.

The concept of *play* is of major importance in sport sociology, as it is in a number of related fields. What is play? How is it related to games and sport? Child's play is typically spontaneous, carefree, loose, and changeable; it is governed by rules, even though the children constantly change them. Adult play, on the other hand, is more typically rule governed and requires more preparation and training.

Games are structured, organized, rule-governed forms of play that have a specific purpose and a means for attaining that purpose. French sociologist Roger Caillois (1961) developed a model for games that is widely used in sport sociology and based on the fundamental playful motivation in the game. He recognized (1) *competitive games* such as football, chess, and racing; (2) *games of chance* such as roulette, poker, lotteries, and betting; (3) *games*

Play   (Unorganized, unstructured, spontaneous)
                            (Development of rules)
                         (Systematization, regulation)
Games
                          (Codification, transmission)
Institutionalized Games
                           (Formalization, records)
Sport
                              (Governing bodies)

FIGURE 16.1   Relations among play, games, and sport.
SOURCE: *Adapted from Gruneau, 1976.*

American football is not the only popular form of football in the world.

involving mimicry or pretense such as theater, imitations, and the wearing of masks; and (4) *games that stress vertigo* such as skiing and playing on a teeter-totter. Games can be loosely organized and flexible with rules changing often, or they can become more institutionalized with rules generally adhered to by all players.

Sport is typically seen as a physically active, competitive game that has become highly institutionalized. Sport has rules, histories, records, and governing bodies. Sports are games and can be participated in playfully—thus the relationship among these three concepts. Gruneau (1976) has placed these concepts on a continuum that helps show the definitional relationships among them (see Figure 16.1).

How the play, games, and sport of a culture affect the participants and the culture are the main topics that define sport sociology.

Development of Sport Sociology

Sport sociology was one of the earliest subdisciplines to emerge during the 1950s through the 1970s, when the discipline of physical education began. There was some interest in the sociological aspects of sport before that time, and there were a few publications of note, but the topic of sport was hardly of major interest in sociology. Sport sociologist George Sage (1979) reported that in surveys undertaken by the

American Sociological Association in 1950 and again in 1959 so few sociologists listed sport as an area of teaching or research that it was not classified as a topic in that field.

By the 1970s, however, all that had begun to change. The International Committee on Sport Sociology had formed in 1964; by 1968 it had acquired representatives from twenty-seven countries. International conferences were held, attracting the interest of both sociologists and physical educators. The *International Review of Sport Sociology* began in 1966, later to become a quarterly journal in 1973. In 1968 the Big Ten Symposium on Sport Sociology was held; in 1969 an initial, major textbook appeared: John Loy and Gerald Kenyon's *Sport, Culture, and Society.*

The sociology of sport started quickly and attracted many adherents. Early leaders in the field were typically sociologists with an interest in sport or physical educators trained in departments with strong science emphases (McPherson, 1981). In the 1970s, courses in sport sociology appeared in most universities, and specialized graduate training programs developed in a few. The second generation of sport sociologists prepared primarily in those young programs. In the early and middle 1970s, the number of books published in the area increased, and several important journals appeared—namely, the

Review of Sport and Leisure, the *Journal of Sport and Social Issues*, *Leisure Sciences*, and the *Journal of Sport Behavior.*

In the 1970s, the social dimensions of sport became, for the first time in America, a topic of considerable interest to the general public. Popular magazines, such as *Sports Illustrated*, published features on problems and issues in sport—for example, on gambling, the plight of the black athlete, and recruiting violations in collegiate sport. Popular books by and about athletes and sport began not only to be published but also to sell—Pete Axthelm's (1970) *The City Game*, David Meggyesy's (1971) *Out of Their League*, Harry Edwards's (1969) *The Revolt of the Black Athlete*, Larry Merchant's (1971) *And Every Day You Take Another Bite*, Don Schollander's (1971) *Deep Water*, and Glenn Dickey's (1974) *The Jock Empire*, to name a few. In 1976 the noted American author James Michener wrote a social critique of sport entitled *Sports in America*, indicating clearly the degree to which sport had become of interest to the general public.

This explosion of interest in sport as a topic for social analysis created a vast literature and a climate within which sport sociology prospered as an academic field of study in the late 1970s and early 1980s. The American Alliance for Health, Physical Education, Recreation, and Dance (AAHPERD) formed a Sport Sociology Academy, national and international scientific congresses always include sections related to this area, and publishing opportunities continue to expand. Sport sociology remains today a vital part of the sport sciences.

Current Status of Sport Sociology

Sport sociology has emerged as a social science of sport. Some undergraduate programs in physical education (or Kinesiology) require at least one course in this area although it might be a sport-and-social-issues class rather than one defined by the discipline itself. Most programs reflect the belief that because sport plays an important role in culture students need to understand how people are socialized in and through sport, how sport affects culture, and how an understanding of sport sociology can inform disciplinary education in kinesiology and professional practice in physical education. Specialization in sport sociology is typically limited to graduate programs, mostly at the doctoral level.

Problems in sport and the public's awareness of those problems increased markedly during the 1990s. People are genuinely concerned about issues such as the overemphasis on winning in youth sport, the forces that produce anorexia among too many young female athletes, the use of steroids to build strength, the use of drugs among professionals in sport, the recruiting scandals in collegiate sport, and the lack of minority representation in sport management. Clearly, these problems can be analyzed in a number of ways through the sport sciences, and sociological analysis is one way that seems most important to many interested sportspersons.

Since the early 1990s, a number of prominent sport sociologists have been influenced by the emergence of **critical theory**, a viewpoint that focuses on structural inequities in society and works to eliminate them through action-oriented programs known as *praxis*. Sage (1991), for example, argues that the enhancement of performance among elite athletes has largely ignored the athlete and his or her own life agendas. Harris (1991) offers a series of suggestions about how the sport-training fields can be more sensitive to athletes by examining the social and ethical issues within which training and competition decisions are made.

The major areas of study within sport sociology have remained fairly consistent throughout the years. A list of those areas of study and of some typical related questions is shown in Focus On Box 16.1.

Sport sociologists make an important contribution by "taking on" issues that are controversial and getting to the root of certain problems of social organization and social identity in modern cultures. Their consistent attempts to analyze issues such as gender relations, racial discrimination, ethnicity, and social and personal views of exercise and the body have resulted in a deeper understanding of these important issues and an increased willingness

FOCUS ON	Areas of Study Within Sport Sociology	16.1

Area	Questions Typically Asked
Social class and sport involvement	How does social class affect sport participation?
	How does sport participation affect social mobility?
	How are social class and spectating related?
Team dynamics	How is team cohesiveness related to success?
	How are coach–player relationships related to player success and satisfaction?
	What are the characteristics of leadership on teams?
Sport and education	What role does sport play in school dynamics?
	Are school athletes better students than their peers?
	To what extent do athletes get preferential academic treatment?
Sport and social processes	How do integrated sport teams affect player relationships and team success?
	How is spectating affected by economic swings?
	How do different sports socialize children differently?
Sport and social problems	How is aggressiveness treated in different sports?
	To what extent can sport participation decrease delinquency?
	Do professional sports stack athletes in positions by race?
Gender relations and sport	How does sport influence our views of male and female bodies?
	How do the media portray female bodies in sport?
	How does sport socialize boys and girls differently?
Global/national relations	To what extent is a global sport culture emerging?
	How does sport change national identity?

to discuss them. Inevitably, much of this research and commentary deals with societal inequities that are rooted in differences of race, ethnicity, gender, and wealth. In one sense, it is fair to say that the field of sport sociology has acted as a "conscience" for the discipline of Kinesiology.

Current Issues and Problems in Sport Sociology

As with most other specialized fields, the problems and issues confronting sport sociology fall into two groups: those within the field and those between the field and its publics. Within the field of sport

sociology, several persistent issues continue to be debated—namely, the degree to which scholarship can or should be value-free and the degree to which sport sociology should focus on basic research or applied research, and the combination of sport sociology and sport psychology.

From the beginning, many sport sociologists have suggested that research and scholarship within the field should be *value-free*. Pioneering sport sociologists Gerald Kenyon and John Loy, in an important and influential early article, emphasized that scholarship in this new field should be fundamentally different from the professional tradition in physical education from which it developed:

"The sport sociologist is neither a spreader of gospel nor an evangelist for exercise. His function is not to shape attitudes but to describe and explain them" (Kenyon & Loy, 1965, p. 38). This position, which reflects the traditional posture of scientific inquiry, has been questioned seriously by other scholars in the field (Sage, 1979), who suggest that all methods and positions have value implications and that these should be dealt with specifically rather than the ability to achieve value-free research being assumed.

A second issue within the field is the extent to which sport sociology should be theory oriented or action oriented. In traditional academic life, it has been sufficient to produce knowledge and build theory. More recently, however, a number of approaches have emerged, the most prominent being *critical theory*, which emphasizes action and change in the social structures of society to bring about a more equitable and humane society. This debate affects both what is studied in the field and what is done with the results of research.

A related question, more typical of other fields, is whether sport sociologists should investigate research questions that arise systematically from theory or whether they should answer questions that arise from the practice of sport. Both types of research occur, of course, and each has its own particular value. The issue is one of emphasis. Traditionally, in most universities and scholarly fields, the emphasis has been on theoretically derived research rather than on practical research.

The problems and issues for sport sociology that tend to exist between the field and its many constituents (such as coaches, physical educators, sport commentators, and sport journalists) have to do with problems in sport rather than in theory. The expectation here is that the sport sociologist will act as a social critic and even a social reformer. The many problems of youth sport, school sport, university sport, and professional sport (see Chapter 6 for a discussion of these problems) are of substantial interest to both the sport sociologists and the professional groups that might use their work. These professional groups look to sport sociology for viewpoints and even answers to problems that are sometimes complex.

SPORT AND EXERCISE PSYCHOLOGY

Myths and superstitions about sport and exercise performance almost always have a psychological basis: A male player shaves his head before every contest as long as the team continues to win; a weight lifter trains by rotating through the workout in exactly the same pattern each day; sportscasters attribute changes in the ebb and flow of a contest to the teams being "up" or "down" or to the "momentum" having shifted.

Research and common sense agree that athletes and exercisers perform best when they are in an optimal performance zone, but how do they get there? What psychological strategies are helpful in achieving and sustaining peak performance? Sport and exercise psychology has been an active research field since the early 1970s. The field has also developed a substantial *consulting* capacity to individuals and teams. Its findings and techniques are even becoming better known to the general public through popular books that are meant to help weekend golfers or age-group swimmers. Indeed, much of what has been developed in sport and exercise psychology is also proving useful in the world of work as corporations and businesses try to help employees work better as teams or deal with stresses that inevitably accompany pressure situations, as they do in sport. Issues such as the following are of common interest to many:

- What is the optimal relationship between "getting up" (arousal) and performance?
- What techniques best help athletes to concentrate?
- How can *choking* (being so gripped with fear that performance falters) be treated?
- How can imagery be used to improve performance?

- What strategies are best to help injured players cope with rehabilitation?
- What effects does good sport and exercise performance have on self-esteem?

Both laypeople and professionals in physical education, sport, and exercise have long been interested in answers to questions like these. Many coaches, athletes, and trainers believe that the psychological aspects of training and competition are as important as the physical aspects. It is therefore no surprise, that sport and exercise psychology has grown into one of the most popular of the subdisciplines of Kinesiology. We should also note that the knowledge and strategies developed in sport and exercise psychology have many applications other than elite sport. The elementary-school physical educator, the fitness trainer, the youth sport coach, and a host of others deal with the psychological issues of their students, clients, or players.

Definition of Sport and Exercise Psychology as a Field of Study

Broadly speaking, *psychology* is the study of human behavior. A dominant focus of psychology has been the mental aspects of behavior; indeed, the field of *cognitive psychology* has become a strong subfield of the general field of psychology. *Sport psychology* is the application of psychology to issues and problems in the world of sport. A companion field, *exercise psychology*, has developed and is devoted to issues and problems in the fields of fitness, exercise, and physical activity.

The manner in which sport psychology and exercise psychology have developed indicates that there are two major approaches to the fields: the academic study of sport and exercise psychology and how the knowledge from the fields can be applied to those who are engaged in sport and exercise, typically through a consultant relationship. Psychologists who complete rigorous preparation programs in clinical psychology are licensed by states to do clinical practice in the field of psychology. Sport and exercise psychologists, on the other hand, are not licensed but in some cases can earn certification. Thus, it is appropriate to describe theirs as a consultant role rather than a clinical-practice role. The distinction is important. Certified sport psychologists can help athletes learn to do mental rehearsal, visualization, and goal setting, but when they encounter issues such as eating disorders or substance abuse, they should usually refer athletes to a physician or a licensed psychologist for other professional assistance.

The consulting sport psychologist uses psychological interventions to improve the performance of athletes and to increase their psychological well-being. Many national, international, professional, and collegiate sport programs now employ full-time staff sport psychologists, and many others retain sport psychologists on a part-time consulting basis. A national team in track and field, for example, might travel to an international competition with coaches, managers, trainers, strength specialists, a sport-medicine physician, and a sport psychologist. Some licensed clinical psychologists become sport psychologists. Sport psychologists may be trained originally in counseling psychology, but many are prepared in sport psychology and work in a consulting relationship with the team and athletes.

Some sport psychologists tend to focus primarily on the mental aspects of sport performance. They use imagery, mental rehearsal, and other such techniques with athletes. Other sport psychologists prefer to deal directly with the behavior of athletes, using techniques from the field of applied behavior analysis. These consultants focus on actual physical rehearsals, behavior-shaping strategies, and behavior-modification approaches. Many, of course, use techniques from both perspectives.

In the 1990s, sport psychology and exercise psychology began to come together. This convergence will eventually result in changes in both curricula and clinical experiences in graduate programs, emphasizing health- and medicine-related topics, in addition to the more traditional sport-related topics.

Successful coaches often have strong psychological skills.

Given the current importance of public health policy and agendas in the nation, it will not be surprising if exercise psychology becomes more dominant as a potential professional field for those seeking ways to combine their interests in psychology and in physical activity.

In one sense, the academic and consulting approaches to sport psychology should work together with each informing the other. One group is interested in *why people behave as they do* in sport settings. The other group is interested in *helping people behave more effectively* in sport settings. There is no doubt that the two groups interact, often productively. As this chapter later shows, however, there is also tension between the two groups and

concern that their interactions are not always as productive as they could be.

Development of Sport Psychology

In 1925 the University of Illinois hired Coleman Griffith, a psychologist, to help coaches improve the performance of their players (Williams & Straub, 2001). Griffith wrote *Psychology of Coaching* in 1926 and *Psychology of Athletics* in 1928. He is rightfully considered to be the grandfather of sport psychology in America. Between that time and the 1960s, however, very little occurred to develop the field. The early history of sport psychology is closely related to that of motor learning (see Chapter 15) because people with a background in psychology could understand work in each of those developing fields. Whereas in Europe the two are still tightly intertwined, in the United States they have become distinct subdisciplines.

We could argue that the field of sport psychology was born in Rome in 1965 at the first International Society of Sport Psychology (ISSP), held just after the Rome Olympic Games. It was for purposes of organizing and administering that congress that the ISSP was founded. Three years later, the membership of the ISSP had reached 1,400 representing forty-seven nations (Antonelli, 1970).

The 1968 Olympic Games were held in Mexico City. Because of political and civil strife in Mexico at that time, it was decided that the second International Congress of Sport Psychology should be held in the United States, in Washington, D.C. To organize that meeting, the North American Society for the Psychology of Sport and Physical Activity (NASPSPA) was formed. This organization embraced the then still intimately related subdisciplines of motor learning and sport psychology.

The formation of NASPSPA marked the emergence of the first generation of sport psychologists in North America (Harris, 1987). Most of the professionals who were responsible for developing this field held doctoral degrees in physical education but had special interests in psychology and motor performance. Many of them had taken psychology courses as part of their doctoral training. It was this group that began to develop courses, and later programs, of sport psychology in North American universities.

In 1985 the Association for the Advancement of Applied Sport Psychology (AAASP) was formed to promote applied research and to advance the idea of establishing qualifications and certification for sport psychologists (Williams & Straub, 2001). Another significant milestone in the development of the field came in 1987 when the large and influential American Psychological Association (APA) created Division 47, devoted to sport psychology. In 1991 AAASP created criteria for minimum professional training. Preparation to be a sport psychologist is

strictly at the graduate level, and programs are now available in a number of universities. Students who meet the AAASP criteria and successfully undergo an extensive review process earn the designation "Certified Sport Psychology Consultant." Those with such certification and membership in AAASP and APA are approved to work with Olympic athletes and national teams and are listed on the U.S. Olympic Committee registry.

In the 1980s, *exercise psychology* developed as a companion field to sport psychology. The main focus of exercise psychology is to explain the "antecedents and consequences of exercise behavior" (Buckworth & Dishman, 2001). With the enormous interest in public health generated by the surgeon general's report (see Chapters 1 and 7), it is no surprise that academics and professionals in the field of psychology would want to investigate both the conditions under which people do or do not exercise regularly and the effects that physical activity has on psychological well-being. Buckworth and Dishman (2001) suggest that research currently coalesces in four areas: exercise and mental health, anxiety and depression, sleep, and self-esteem. We should expect that sport psychology and exercise psychology will converge to a certain extent and that both graduate school curricula and clinical experiences will change as a result to accommodate interests in both areas.

Current Status of Sport and Exercise Psychology

Sport and exercise psychology is a healthy field with a bright future. The emerging coupling of sport psychology and exercise psychology should serve to enhance that future and make the field even more attractive for both research and clinical practice. Still, that coupling has not yet been realized in many places, so the field is still described here primarily in terms of its sport-related focus.

There is no doubt that the field is currently divided into people who *study* the psychological aspects of sport performance and people who *work with athletes* in the capacity of sport psychologists.

| FOCUS ON | Topic Areas and Questions in Sport Psychology | 16.2 |

Topic Area	Questions Typically Asked
Psychophysiological approaches	Can teaching cognitive skills to athletes help them to regulate physiological responses?
	What happens physiologically during mental-imagery practice?
	What physiological effects does anxiety have on novice and expert performers?
Psychobiological approaches	What causes a person to feel good during exercise?
	What occurs physiologically during the "runner's high"?
	Can sport exercise help to replace chemical dependency?
Self-regulation	Can athletes learn to be aware of and to control their internal systems?
	Can stress be controlled and used to improve performance?
Social psychology	What factors control role modeling in sport?
	How are cooperation and aggression related?
Exercise psychology	How does strength training affect body image and self-concept?
	Are exercise programs an effective intervention for people experiencing depression?

The former are *academic sport psychologists*; the latter are *consulting sport psychologists*. A person does not have to be exclusively one or the other. Many sport psychologists work directly with athletes and still contribute to the emerging knowledge base through their research and scholarship.

No field can develop and improve without an expanding knowledge base that is built on sound research and constantly improved theories. The development of a knowledge base through research and the continued refinement of theory are the province of the academic sport psychologist. This work is done predominantly in university settings in departments of physical education or of psychology.

Sport psychologist Dan Landers (1983) has argued that research in sport psychology can be divided into three stages. The first stage (1950–1965) was dominated by research on how the personalities of athletes were related to performance. Questions such as the following were researched: Do elite athletes have personalities

different from those of average athletes? Do athletes in contact sports have personality traits different from those of athletes in noncontact sports? Can a winning personality be identified?

The second stage (1966–1976) was dominated by the borrowing of then-current theories from mainstream psychology, to test them in the sport setting; by the development of interactional approaches; and by the formulation of operant-conditioning models for sport. The third stage (1976 to the present) has focused more on developing information and theory directly derived from sport and on developing and refining psychological skills and strategies to enhance sport performance. Focus On Box 16.2 shows the topic areas and typical questions that are being investigated in academic sport psychology.

Since the 1970s, it has become increasingly clear that sport psychologists can help teams and individuals improve their performance. Thus, professional teams and athletes, as well as national and international amateur teams and athletes, have employed

Athletes need different types of precompetition preparation.

people who can provide those services. When a national team travels, a practicing sport psychologist is likely to accompany it.

The consulting sport psychologist often plays two roles although the roles can be played by different individuals. One role uses psychological strategies with athletes to improve performance directly—the *performance-enhancement role*. Within this role, the sport psychologist might teach the athlete to relax during competition, to overcome fear of competition, to cope with competitive stresses, or mentally to rehearse positive performances.

The second role, the *counseling role*, is less direct; it involves counseling athletes to help them overcome problems, adjust to situations, and deal with stresses in their lives. Counseling an athlete to help that person adjust to and cope with a personal problem might affect her or his performance, but the relationship is indirect.

In these two primary roles, the consulting sport psychologist focuses on distinct areas of assistance to coaches and athletes. One area is the immediate improvement of performance—for instance, by using mental imagery just before competition. A second area is helping athletes cope with the pressures of competition—for instance, using one of several relaxation strategies. A third area is assistance with injury rehabilitation, helping athletes deal with both physical rehabilitation and the psychological stresses of not being able to participate.

Focus On Box 16.3 lists the kinds of psychological interventions in sport psychology, with descriptions and examples of each. These techniques have typically been well researched and have been shown to have significant effects with athletes.

Athletes are often young people who are going through important developmental stages within their own lives. This means they must cope with stresses related to family, school, work, and relationships as well as those related to being athletes. Sport psychologists can often function as counselors to help athletes deal with these personal problems, thus allowing athletes to devote their full attention to the athletic performance.

A second area in which the counseling function is important is enhancing the relationships among athletes on a team and between athletes and their coaches. Here, too, the sport psychologist can play an important counseling function. First, the sport psychologist can observe interpersonal situations that seem to be developing inappropriately and can intervene carefully to alter those situations before they become problems. Second, when problems do arise, the sport psychologist can counsel athletes, suggest solutions, and provide support for the parties involved.

With an aging population of baby boomers and with the current concern about the incidence of overweight and obesity among children and youths, the field of exercise psychology has become more important, both in terms of research and clinical/consulting practices. Many degree programs, especially at the master's and doctoral levels now provide choices for students; that is, they can focus on sport psychology or focus on exercise/health psychology. In both cases, there is a track toward research and a track toward clinical practice.

In exercise-psychology programs, students focus on the relations between physical activity and public health, the sociological and psychological factors associated with adopting and maintaining exercise programs, the role of exercise related to body image,

FOCUS ON	Psychological Interventions Used With Athletes	16.3

Intervention	Description and Examples of Use
Relaxation training	Teach athletes to feel tension in muscles and to learn how to control release of tension.
	Example: Relax between events
Cue-controlled relaxation	Tie relaxation strategy to a word cue; allows the athlete to say the word to himself or herself to induce relaxation.
	Examples: Preparation for diving, free-throw shooting, putting in golf
Desensitization	Gradually reduce anxiety caused in specific competitive situations by teaching athletes to relax while imaging a series of increasingly aversive competitive situations.
	Examples: Fear of hitting head on platform in a back dive; fear associated with heights in climbing
Mental imaging	Teach athletes to rehearse successful performance mentally just before beginning the performance.
	Examples: High jump, swim races, wrestling
Coping strategies	Predict what events might intrude in preperformance time and during performance, and help athletes to develop and rehearse behavioral strategies to cope with and overcome those incidents.
	Examples: Rehearsing the specific procedures to follow when going to compete in a foreign land—how to cope with language, security, time, and food incidents; practicing what to do during an event if certain situations arise
Covert modeling	Teach athlete to imagine a model doing a particular performance as a means to help the athlete acquire that skill or ability.
	Example: Helping an athlete become more competitive in tense situations

eating disorders and other psychological states, and the influence of various levels of fitness on psychological systems. Exercise psychologists would also provide training in some of the same strategies used by sport psychologists—that is, relaxation training, coping strategies, and the like.

Current Issues and Problems in Sport Psychology

The two main issues in sport psychology currently are the split between academic and consulting sport psychologists and the related issue of licensing. In the mid-1980s, a definite split occurred in American sport psychology. Concerns were expressed that sport psychology had become too academic, too theory oriented, and not sufficiently grounded in the practice of sport. In 1985 the AAASP was started; shortly thereafter, a new journal, the *Journal of Applied Sport Psychology*, appeared. As in many other fields, people who practiced sport psychology were concerned that their academic counterparts were not studying events and phenomena that would prove to be directly useful in their practices.

This general concern is also debated strongly within academic sport psychology. The issue tends to be to what extent academic sport psychology should use theory and research from the parent discipline of psychology, as opposed to developing its own theory and research from the field of sport.

Since the late 1980s, sport psychology has moved to more applied work. Having firmly established their field as an academic subdiscipline, many sport psychologists have engaged in more practice-oriented research and have devoted more time to clinical services. This has resulted in increased tension between those who have taken this route and those who believe that the theoretical research base of the field should remain the primary focus.

A consensus seems to be emerging within sport psychology that the field needs to be more firmly anchored in the sport and exercise sciences. This trend toward embedding sport psychology more firmly in the sport and exercise sciences is being further enhanced by the emergence of exercise psychology as a companion field. Indeed, the funds available for exercise-psychology research and the demand for professionals in exercise psychology will probably soon outpace the funding availability and job demands for sport psychologists, resulting in pressures to bring the two fields together. We can expect that the future sport and exercise psychologist will be more broadly prepared in areas such as nutrition, exercise physiology, and sport biomechanics.

As sport psychology has emerged, the athletes and institutions that have felt the need to receive psychological services have tended to be in the elite category—professional golfers, Olympic-level teams, professional teams, and the like. These athletes and institutions have the resources to employ sport psychologists. Because of this financial incentive, many sport psychologists, and subsequently the field itself, have tended to focus on elite performance (Gill, 1991). There has been increasing debate within the field on this issue with arguments that sport psychology needs to focus more on the individual athlete's total well-being than on performance enhancement and more on children and youths, or recreational participants, than on elite athletes.

Another important issue for the future of the field is the degree to which evidence supports claims that sport-and-exercise-psychology interventions are actually responsible for performance gains and other important outcomes. Recent reviews have shown that in forty-five studies employing sport-and-exercise-psychology interventions and training programs to enhance performance in competitive sport settings, 85 percent have found positive performance outcomes (Weinberg & Williams, 2001). What appears to be important in the successful studies is that the intervention must be individualized and systematic, carried out over time, as part of a total package. These very positive findings will enhance the further development of the field.

SPORT PEDAGOGY

People are not born with sport skills. They may be genetically equipped to be stronger, taller, or faster, but those qualities in and of themselves will not enable them to succeed in sport. Somewhere, sometime, they must *learn* sport skills and the sport strategies that result in satisfactory participation in sport and competitive success. In most cases, young people learn sport skills and sport strategies from people who are designated to teach those things—physical-education teachers and coaches. Virtually all cultures, once they get beyond the subsistence stage of development, consider sport and physical education to be sufficiently important that they arrange programs for the young people in the culture to acquire the skills and strategies of sport in their childhood and youth and to improve those sport skills through practice and competition.

In most school systems, the areas of sport and fitness are considered to be of such importance that special courses are arranged and people with special credentials are employed to teach within those courses. The course of study is most often called "physical education," and the person designated to teach it is a physical educator.

The general field within which all this happens is **sport pedagogy**. In the United States, this field is also termed *teacher education* or *curriculum and instruction*. The questions that are the province of sport pedagogy are of obvious importance to all people in the sport-and-fitness culture who teach or coach:

- What teaching techniques are most effective at different stages of learning?
- What teaching techniques are most effective with different age groups?
- How can large groups of students be managed effectively to produce the most time for learning?
- What content knowledge do teachers need to teach effectively?
- How can teachers plan lessons so that students engage in moderate-to-vigorous physical activity at least 50 percent of the lesson time?
- What curricular activities are most important in grades K–3?
- How can the progression of activities within a unit be planned so that students become sufficiently successful to enjoy participation games/sports/fitness activities?

These questions have been studied and debated within professional physical education for more than 100 years. Answers to them continue to be refined and are of obvious importance to the culture of sport and fitness. Since the early 1980s, these questions have become more the special province of sport pedagogy as it has emerged as a full-fledged member of the sport and exercise sciences.

Definition of Sport Pedagogy as a Field of Study

Sport pedagogy is the study of the processes of teaching and coaching, of the outcomes of such endeavors, and of the content of fitness, physical-education, and sport-education programs. *Sport pedagogy* is a term used widely in international physical education and sport sciences. The field of sport pedagogy, as it is defined internationally, encompasses both school programs of physical education and community-based and club programs of sport and fitness. The term *sport pedagogy* is

Plastic pipe javelins allow the learning of important track-and-field skills.

beginning to be used more frequently in the United States and appears to be the term that will define this field in the future. Therefore, it is the term used to define and describe the field in this chapter.

Sport pedagogy is a broad field concerned with the content, processes, and outcomes of sport, fitness, and physical-education programs in schools, community programs, and clubs. The term **pedagogy** refers to teaching but should be taken in its broadest context; for example, it encompasses not just the *act* of teaching, as important as that is, but also the development of an instructional program, the plan for the implementation of that program, and an assessment of the outcomes of the program. The term *sport* should also be taken broadly to include not only competitive sport but also leisure activities and fitness. This is how the term *sport* is used in most of the world, and it is the same broad meaning that underlies the *Sport for All* movements prevalent throughout the world.

One of the best reasons to use the term *sport pedagogy* rather than *teacher education* is that the former clearly encompasses both teaching in schools and teaching and coaching in community and club programs. As we saw in Chapter 1, individuals now have the opportunity for lifelong involvement in sport, fitness, and physical education. They can learn for a lifetime, participate in many ways, and compete for a lifetime if that is their desire. If sport pedagogy is restricted to what goes on in school programs of physical education, then it will have defined itself far too narrowly.

Sport pedagogy can be divided into two main areas: instruction and curriculum. The teaching-versus-coaching distinction, with a somewhat different emphasis within each field, tends to cut across those two areas, as does the setting within which the activity takes place—for example, school, community, sport club, or workplace. Within sport pedagogy, there are people whose main task is to do research about instruction or curriculum, to provide knowledge about current practices, and to investigate potentially better practices. These sport pedagogists are involved in the *creation* of the new knowledge that helps us understand and improve the field. Other people, the practitioners of sport pedagogy, are charged with using the knowledge discovered in sport-pedagogy research in other sport-science fields in order to provide the best sport and fitness programs possible for children, youths, and adults in schools, communities, and clubs.

The field of *instruction* within sport pedagogy examines issues such as planning, teacher–student interaction skills, the activities of students or players that contribute to learning, the assessment of performance and learning, the comparison of different teaching or coaching methods, and the management and discipline issues associated with teaching and coaching. Most of the research in instruction is done by faculty members in universities, typically those involved in programs in which teachers and coaches are prepared and certified—for example, in departments of physical education.

The field of *curriculum* within sport pedagogy focuses more on the content of programs, the goals to which programs are or should be devoted, the manner in which programs are implemented, and the outcomes achieved within programs, especially as they relate to program goals. Some work within curriculum is highly theoretical, focusing on models for physical-education and sport programs. Other work is highly practical, focusing on what actually goes on in programs and how consistently programs achieve their stated goals.

The fields of instruction and curriculum are of course not totally separate. People with primary interests in instruction also are interested in curriculum, and vice versa. Those people who actually practice sport pedagogy—teachers and coaches—have a vital interest in both areas; for them, the distinctions between the two fields are not so clear-cut.

Development of Sport Pedagogy

Sport pedagogy is the youngest of the sport sciences. The emergence of a discipline of physical education in the 1960s and 1970s was in many ways a reaction to the low status of teacher-education programs in physical education in those days (see Chapter 2). Many education professionals and university administrators had become concerned about the perceived low quality of university education departments. Teacher-education programs were often viewed as being low quality, lacking a research foundation, and out of step with the directions of a modern university.

In this sense, sport pedagogy developed partially as a reaction to the development of subdisciplines such as sport sociology and sport biomechanics. Before the 1970s, virtually every physical educator who held a doctoral degree considered himself or herself to be a teacher educator! That was true simply because the major mission—and, in many cases, the sole mission—of most undergraduate programs in physical education was to prepare teachers. In the 1970s, all that changed.

Not only did the development of subdisciplines in physical education change the manner in which people and programs were defined, but also an impending oversupply of teachers in schools caused physical-education departments to experiment with *alternative career programs* for their students. Whereas before the 1970s, nearly all undergraduate physical-education majors were preparing to teach; during the 1970s, programs developed in areas such as sport management, adult fitness, sport journalism, and sport studies. This specialization occurred at the graduate level in the form of the subdisciplines and at the undergraduate level in the form of alternative career programs. Eventually, teacher education became more specialized, too.

Unlike most of the other subdisciplines, sport pedagogy has not developed its own national organization. Professionals interested in sport pedagogy have tended to maintain affiliations with the major national physical-education organization, AAHPERD. AAHPERD has several member organizations within which sport pedagogy has been able to play an important role: the National Association for Sport and Physical Education (NASPE) the Council of Physical Education for Children (COPEC), and the Curriculum and Instruction Academy.

An important milestone in the development of sport pedagogy as a specialized area was reached when the *Journal of Teaching in Physical Education* (*JTPE*) was first published in 1981. This journal publishes research and commentary on topics in instruction and curriculum in physical education.

Since the mid-1980s, sport pedagogy has grown rapidly, holding a number of specialized conferences. It is regularly included as one of the sections at Olympic Scientific Congresses. Internationally, sport pedagogy is well represented by an International Committee of Sport Pedagogy, jointly sponsored by four major international organizations: the Association Internationale d'Education Superior d'Education Physique (AIESEP), the Federation Internationale d'Education Physique (FIEP), the International Association of Physical Education and Sport for Girls and Women (IAPESGW), and the International Society on Comparative Physical Education and Sport (ISCPES). Each of these organizations publishes newsletters and sponsors conferences in which sport pedagogy is a major focus.

Research in sport pedagogy has begun to change the content of textbooks used in teacher-education programs in physical education. When we compare recent texts with those of a generation ago, it is clear that issues such as classroom management, discipline, and instruction are handled differently. Those differences most often represent knowledge gained from research and scholarship within sport pedagogy.

Current Status of Sport Pedagogy

During the 1970s and early 1980s, school enrollments dropped and a serious oversupply of teachers resulted. Jobs in teaching were scarce. Enrollments in teacher-education programs at universities were reduced drastically. Subsequently, there were few jobs for young professionals newly qualified as specialists in sport pedagogy. All of that has begun to change. Many faculty members who joined the university ranks in the 1960s, during the major expansion period in American educational history, are reaching retirement age, and we are now in another period of expansion in school enrollments. The demand for teachers rose each year during the 1990s. Enrollments in teacher-education programs have increased.

Thus, the need for new teacher-education faculty at the university level has increased. When a teacher-education position is created or a position becomes vacant upon the retirement of the incumbent, the job description is likely to be specialized in the area of sport pedagogy. Research and scholarship in sport pedagogy continue to develop. The general areas most often investigated and the questions typically asked are listed in Focus On Box 16.4.

The success of sport-pedagogy research and the dissemination of research findings, particularly in textbooks, have begun to change the content of teacher- and coach-preparation programs, the content of in-service education for practicing teachers, and, subsequently, the manner in which physical educators and coaches teach and coach. The area of classroom management has been greatly influenced by this body of knowledge. Teachers and coaches now know more about developing managerial routines, keeping managerial time short, developing clear rules and consequences for breaking rules, and using positive interactional strategies to support appropriate student or player behavior.

Instructional strategies have also been influenced. Teachers and coaches are more aware of the definition and progression of instructional tasks, the quality of learner responses, and the specificity of the feedback provided. They understand more

FOCUS ON	Areas of Study Within Sport Pedagogy	16.4
Area	**Questions Typically Asked**	
Teacher behavior	What kinds of feedback do teachers provide?	
	Do elementary teachers behave differently than secondary teachers?	
	How much time do teachers spend in various teaching activities?	
	How does the behavior of teachers differ from that of coaches?	
Student behavior	Do students enjoy and value physical education?	
	How do students spend their time in classes?	
	How many good learning opportunities do highly and poorly skilled students get during a class?	
	How do children behave in youth sport?	
Teacher effectiveness	What differentiates effective from ineffective teachers and coaches?	
	What teaching methods are most effective?	
	How do teachers cope with the problems encountered during their first year?	
	What characteristics make a coach effective?	
Teacher issues	To what extent is there role conflict in individuals who both teach and coach?	
	How do teachers cope with burnout?	
	What goals do teachers have for their students?	
Curriculum	What is the ideal physical-education curriculum?	
	How do teachers' values affect curriculum decisions?	
	To what extent do teachers achieve their goals?	
	How can fitness best be programmed?	
	What outcomes occur in youth-sport programs?	

clearly how important it is to provide for as many good learner responses as possible in each lesson or practice. The old phrase "practice makes perfect" is more clearly understood as "good practice makes perfect."

Work in the area of curriculum has also progressed rapidly. Whereas physical education 30 years ago would have looked similar from school to school, it is more likely to look distinctive today, as a variety of new curriculum models have appeared. Chapter 11 described a number of these newer curriculum models, including adventure education, social-development physical education, sport education, fitness education, movement education, and the more traditional multiactivity program.

Current Issues and Problems in Sport Pedagogy

Many of the major concerns within sport pedagogy are reflections of major concerns with the general fields of physical education and coaching. (See Chapters 6, 9, and 12 for complete descriptions of problem areas.) For instance, should there be a national physical-education curriculum? How can teacher–coach role conflict be lessened? How can schools develop effective fitness programs without taking all their allotted instructional time to do so? What can be done to prevent teachers from burning out or to help those who have burned out? How can youth-sport coaches be better prepared to

Equipment should be modified to be developmentally appropriate for instruction and practice.

deal effectively with young athletes? What activities should be included in a modern secondary-school physical-education program? These are typical questions debated within physical education, fitness, and youth sport; they are also widely discussed in sport pedagogy.

In addition, there are questions more specific to the field of sport pedagogy, many of which relate to the preparation of teachers because teacher education is a primary mission of sport pedagogy. For example, how much sport-skill training should prospective teachers have? Should sport-skill training be oriented to performance, to learning about the activity, or to learning how to teach the activity? How can teaching skills be acquired most effectively and efficiently? Are on-campus clinical experiences as effective as off-campus field experiences?

There are parallel issues in the field of instruction. How can teachers best plan for high-quality learning experiences despite the diversity of talents within a typical school class? How should tasks be sequenced within a lesson and throughout a unit? How can teachers best communicate tasks to students? As research and scholarship within this young discipline become more sophisticated, some

of these questions will be answered, and new questions will arise.

Two key concepts in sport pedagogy are *content knowledge*, which means knowledge of the content taught to students, and *pedagogical content knowledge*, which means knowledge of and skill in teaching a particular content to a particular group of students. If physical-education curricula consist primarily of games, sports, dance, adventure activities, and various forms of fitness, then, clearly, teachers must have knowledge of those forms of physical activity. For example, to teach a volleyball unit to a group of seventh-graders with the goal of having the students become sufficiently proficient in the techniques and tactics of volleyball so that they can play three-versus-three games skillfully, the teacher must have sufficient knowledge of the techniques and tactics of volleyball to teach the students. These teachers, however, must have some depth of pedagogical content knowledge to plan teaching strategies for the unit, strategies that reflect the students' previous experiences with volleyball and with other court-divided games that might share tactical similarities.

Our understanding of content knowledge and pedagogical content knowledge has been greatly enhanced with recent work in the area of teaching games. It is now common to distinguish between teaching techniques (for example, the pass in volleyball or the cross-over dribble in basketball) and tactics (for example, how best to attack a 2–3 zone in basketball or how attackers combine with teammates to keep possession of the ball and score in soccer). Skill in sports and games is the adequate ability to execute appropriate techniques and tactics (Launder, 2001). Sport pedagogy has also made significant strides in better understanding of how to teach games. Games are now typically categories as invasion games, court-divided games, and sector games. What is now referred to primarily as the "tactical approach" to teaching sport techniques and tactics uses modified, small-sided games/activities to assist students in mastering both the techniques and tactics of specific games/sports and how to transfer knowledge from one sport to another within the game category—that is, attacking tactics in invasion games such as soccer, basketball, and European handball (Mitchell, Oslin & Griffin, 2006).

One might assume that students in physical-education teacher-education programs bring a certain amount of content knowledge to their program but would also have a substantial part of their program devoted to broader and deeper content knowledge and substantial knowledge of pedagogical content knowledge related to various activities. Students who are dance-education or music-education majors typically get 40–50 credit hours devoted exclusively to content knowledge and pedagogical content knowledge (Siedentop, 2007). In math-education or science-education programs, students would typically be required to complete 45–65 hours of content knowledge. In physical-education teacher-education programs, however, the amount of content knowledge in the program is seldom more than 20 credit hours. Some have argued that the courses in the subdisciplines of Kinesiology count as content knowledge courses, but that cannot be true unless the physical-education program in schools consist of units such as exercise physiology, motor control, and sport sociology. This is not to suggest that courses in

those areas cannot inform the preparation of physical-education teachers. There is much pedagogically relevant information in the Kinesiology subdisciplines, but it is information that is more relevant to pedagogical content knowledge than to content knowledge.

Another emerging issue in sport pedagogy has been magnified greatly by the current issue of child/youth obesity and the national focus on having a revitalized physical education contribute to helping children/youths be more physically active. Indeed, the most common overall goal for physical education has become to help children/youths adopt and value a physically active lifestyle. That goal has significant implications for the pedagogy used in physical-education programs. It is one thing to have lots of physical activity in physical-education lessons and another thing to so influence the habits and predispositions of children and youths that they voluntarily seek out and enjoy physical activity on a regular basis in their leisure time. The kind of pedagogy needed to achieve that kind of influence has to emphasize a substantial amount of caring by teachers, a physical-education climate that is supportive and understanding, and activities through which students can find both satisfaction and joy. Sport philosopher Scott Kretchmar argues persuasively for a joy-oriented physical education where students can discover their own playgrounds:

> Joy-oriented physical education typically requires patient nurturing during those times when meaning and playgrounds grow conjointly, sometimes quickly, other times very slowly. Patient nurturing is needed because some movement play spaces need to be cultivated and grown . . . Likewise, no law says that joy-oriented physical education cannot promote cardiovascular health and weight reduction. (Kretchmar, 2008, p. 163)

Many national health and education organizations have called for a revitalization of physical education as a necessary element to combat the child/youth obesity epidemic. Recent research and development in sport pedagogy has defined new ways to better engage students in learning activities and better ways to develop a curriculum that leads

Runners on the beach evoke the memory of the Academy Award–winning film *Chariots of Fire*.

to meaningful learning outcomes. It will be interesting to see if these developments find their ways into day-to-day practice in schools.

THE SPORT HUMANITIES

When *Chariots of Fire* won the Academy Award for Best Picture of 1981, it became clear that the old argument—that sport was not suitable for popular and serious literary consideration—was no longer true. The film was a historical study of athletes competing in the Olympic Games in track and field in the early part of the twentieth century. Major philosophical themes—such as fair play, amateur versus professional, and the meaning of competition—were woven throughout the story. It was a *good* story, well acted, and enjoyable to all who viewed it. For people involved in the sport, fitness, and physical-education professions, it was not only enjoyable as theater but also a literary vehicle through which sport could be examined

historically and philosophically. The film is a good example of the contemporary impact of the **sport humanities**.

Nearly everyone who has participated in a fitness, sport, or physical-education program has at some point wondered about the field's meaning. Why do people do these activities? From where do these activities come? How do games develop, and why are people devoted to them? Why is sport "this way" rather than some "other way"? Most people who participate in or enjoy watching sport have a deep interest in it that goes beyond the competition itself. Many are concerned about some of the problems and excesses associated with sport, from children's involvement to the most elite levels. What is fair in sport? What are appropriate practices? Many of these kinds of questions are addressed in the sport humanities.

The fields of sport history, sport philosophy, and sport literature constitute the sport humanities. The *humanities*, as a general field, include those branches of learning concerned directly with human thought and relations. In general education, the humanities include literature, philosophy, the fine arts, and history. The study of the historical and philosophical aspects of sport, fitness, and physical education has a long tradition within professional physical education. The study of sport literature as an organized field is much more recent. Because the roots of these three areas are to be found in humanistic studies, rather than in the sciences, they are treated together in this chapter.

The full development of the sport humanities seems to have accompanied the explosion of interest in sport within Western culture in general and American culture in particular that started in the early 1970s. The degree to which sport is now a part of everyday life is truly extraordinary. Fifteen to 20 percent of newspaper space is devoted to sport information. Endless hours of television coverage are provided. Sport has become part of nightly local television newscasts. International events such as the Olympics occupy the major share of television for extended periods. A major national event such as the Super Bowl or NCAA basketball finals seems to fascinate the nation. The sport and fitness magazine sections in bookstores are likely to be among the largest, with specialized magazines in numerous sport and fitness activities, as well as comprehensive, weekly coverage in magazines such as *Sports Illustrated*. It is no surprise, then, that the philosophical, historical, and literary aspects of sport have also prospered in this era. Because sport seems to affect so many people and often in so fundamental a way, it is highly appropriate that philosophical, historical, and literary investigations have been undertaken to help us understand what all of this means from both an individual and a collective point of view.

Although the search for understanding that derives from philosophy, history, and literature differs somewhat across these fields, the questions each considers not only cut across the three areas but also interest the general public:

- How have sport and religion affected each other?
- How and for what reasons has youth sport developed?

- What changes have occurred in opportunities for girls and women?
- What has been the sport experience for African Americans?
- What values does professional sport promote?
- In what ways can competition be understood?
- What does *fair play* mean? What should it mean?
- In what ways is sport portrayed in films?
- How has the sport hero been treated in novels?

Definition of the Sport Humanities as Fields of Study

The sport humanities comprise three related fields, each of which has its own organizational structure, its own methodologies, and its own scholarly literature. *History*, as a field of study, is more than just descriptions of past events:

> Although when we use the word history we instinctively think of the past, this is an error, for history is actually a bridge connecting the past with the present, and pointing the road to the future. (Nevins, 1962, p. 14)

History, therefore, not only chronicles the past but also interprets the past, relates the past to the present, and provides guidelines to what might be expected or what courses might be taken in the future.

Sport history tends to fall into two categories based on the goals of the scholar conducting the investigation. One approach is to identify and describe patterns of change and stability in sport in particular societies or cultures during specific time periods (Harris, 2000). The second is to not only identify and describe patterns but also analyze them in terms of their relationships and the events that influenced the patterns. This is essentially the same distinction made by Adelman (1969), who separated sport history into narrative-descriptive history and interpretive-comparative history.

Some history books are written for popular consumption and may be read widely. An example is John Feingold's *A Season on the Brink*, a chronicle of one season of Indiana basketball and Coach Bob Knight. Some are written for a much narrower audience and are more scholarly in nature. A classic example is H. A. Harris's *Greek Athletes and Athletics*, which is the most authoritative source of information about sport in ancient Greece and what purposes it served.

As sport came to be taken more seriously by the general public, books about sport that were more seriously written found acceptance in the general literary culture. Two shining examples of quality literature in sport history are Roger Kahn's poignant history of the fates of the 1958 Brooklyn Dodgers in *The Boys of Summer* and David Halberstam's chronicle of elite rowers preparing for the Olympic games in *The Amateurs*.

Philosophy is a formal field of study that includes four main areas. *Metaphysics* is the branch of philosophy that addresses questions about the nature of reality. *Axiology* is the study of values. How knowledge is acquired is the focus of *epistemology*, and how ideas are related composes the study of *logic*. Many people, however, are interested in what are popularly called "philosophical issues" although these differ from the concerns of formal philosophy.

Bressan and Pieter (1985) have referred to this distinction as "first-order" and "second-order" philosophy. Philosophy as a *first-order activity* is a discipline with a unique set of problems that are classified within the four primary philosophical branches and several subdisciplines. Like other disciplines, philosophical investigation is highly technical and has a language and a concept system that people must master to take part in the discipline. Philosophy as a *second-order activity*, however, includes thinking creatively and logically about problems that belong to areas outside philosophy itself. Virtually every professional person in sport, fitness, and physical education has a philosophical point of view about what he or she does and for what reasons.

Harris (2000) suggests that the first goal of philosophy of sport is to clarify thinking about sport, play, games, and dance, including the relationship between body and mind. The second goal, she argues, is to encourage people to use their insights about sport and the relationship between body and mind to improve people's lives. The first goal is consistent with most views of the purpose of philosophy of sport, but the second moves into actually using insights to improve sport and the lives of people involved with sport. The idea that philosophers of sport and those who use the literature of the philosophy of sport would engage in activities directly intended to improve sport and the sport experience is very close to the *critical theory* branch of sport sociology where programs designed to improve the sport experience are referred to as *praxis*.

In the past 25 years, there has been a very strong literature in the philosophy of sport. Some books, such as Howard Slusher's *Man, Sport and Existence*, have been read mostly within the profession. Others, such as Paul Weiss's *Sport: A Philosophical Inquiry* and Michael Novak's *The Joy of Sports*, were written by people outside the field of sport philosophy and have been widely read both within the profession and by the general public. When famous and serious people take sport seriously and write about it, the public listens. Such was the case when A. Bartlett Giamatti, former president of Yale University and commissioner of Major League Baseball, wrote *Take Time for Paradise*, a philosophical and historical analysis of sport and play.

Literature, in the sense used here, refers to prose, poetry, and films that have a permanent value because of their excellence of form, their emotional effect, and their ability to provide insights about the human condition. Literature, in this sense, has literary value and is often contrasted with scientific writing, ordinary newswriting, and general nonfiction writing such as in textbooks. Sport literature is a recent and welcome addition to the sport humanities. It has arisen as a field because of the marked increase since the early 1970s in serious literary work that focuses specifically on sport or using sport themes as vehicles through which to examine basic human dilemmas and situations.

Sport literature is dominated by sport fiction with a lesser emphasis on sport poetry. Increasingly, films that are about sport or that use sport as a theme to examine important human questions have been included within sport literature. Some film scripts have been adapted from novels such as Bernard Malamud's *The Natural*, Mark Harris's *Bang the Drum Slowly*, and Pete Gent's *North Dallas Forty*. A few novels that have sport as a main theme or context have achieved critical acclaim *and* have become best-sellers—John Updike's *Rabbit Run* is perhaps the best example. Many more novels, although not achieving best-seller status, have received good critical reviews and have sold moderately well. Good examples are W. P. Kinsella's *Shoeless Joe*, Eric Rolfe Greenberg's *The Celebrant*, and Tom McNab's *Flannagan's Run*.

Of course, a number of books have been written about celebrities and sport teams. Each new hero or heroine, each new big winner, and each new major championship team seems to precipitate a large number of books, often ghostwritten or written in collaboration with a local sportswriter. Many of these books sell well, but they are very seldom considered to have literary merit in the sense defined here. They constitute the fringe of sport literature, but they are nonetheless an important vehicle through which sport is interpreted and made available to the public.

Sport films are becoming more and more popular and are likely to increase in importance in the field of sport literature. Historically, most films in which sport was a main theme could not be described as taking sport seriously or making a serious comment about sport and its role in the lives of women and men. In the past 25 years, however, sport films that have been very good entertainment have also made serious statements about sport. Primary examples are *Bull Durham*, *Field of Dreams*, and *A League of Their Own*, just to mention a few in which baseball was the sport focus. *Field of Dreams* had a strong philosophical focus, and *A League of Their Own* had more of a historical focus. More recently, *The Legend of Bagger Vance*, a philosophical treatise about golf and the game of life, found success both as a

Sport fans become deeply involved with the ups and downs of their heroes.

novel and as a popular film. In 2005 *Million Dollar Baby*, a film about a female boxer, won the Academy Award for Best Picture.

Development of the Sport Humanities

Within the profession of physical education during its development as a field from 1850 to 1950, the history and philosophy of physical education were always areas of interest to professionals. Chapter 3 reviewed the changing historical philosophies that accompanied the development of American physical education. At least one course in these areas has typically been included in teacher-training programs. Many of the most important early leaders in the field were best known for their contributions to a developing philosophy of physical education (using the term *philosophy* here in its broadest, professional sense).

The fields of sport history, sport philosophy, and sport literature are of more recent origin, being part of the general trend toward a discipline of

Kinesiology. (See Chapter 2 for a historical overview of this movement.) Historical interests in sport and physical education coalesced formally in 1973 with the first meeting of the National Society for Sport History (NSSH). This organization publishes the *Journal of Sport History*; that publication and the *Canadian Journal of History of Sport and Physical Education* have become the main publishing outlets for scholars working in the field.

Although philosophy, in the general sense, has always been important within physical education, there is little evidence that academic philosophers took sport seriously until the 1970s. As the physical-education subdisciplines developed, it was logical that a philosophy group would form—and it did. In 1973 at the annual meeting of the American Philosophical Association, a group of philosophers interested in sport joined with a group of physical-education specialists interested in philosophy to form the Philosophic Society for the Study of Sport (PSSS). The first president of PSSS was Paul Weiss, then Sterling Professor of Philosophy at Yale University. The society published its first issue of the *Journal of the Philosophic Society for the Study of Sport* in 1974.

The field of sport literature did not emerge until the 1980s. Physical-education faculty members and professors of English joined to form the Sport Literature Association (SLA) in 1982. In the autumn of 1983, the first issue of *Arete: The Journal of Sport Literature* appeared. In the summer of 1984, the association held its first meetings. The SLA continues to be a joint venture of professionals in physical education and in English. Its major focus has been and continues to be sport with only minor attention paid to either physical education or fitness.

Current Status of the Sport Humanities

The sport humanities continue to make important contributions to our understanding of sport, fitness, and physical education. However, changes in direction in undergraduate and graduate preparation in

physical education have constrained the growth of these fields. During the late 1970s and early 1980s, the demand for teachers for our nation's schools fell quickly as school enrollments dropped. That caused a reduction of interest in teacher-education programs in general and in physical-education programs in particular because physical education was one of the school subjects for which there was a serious oversupply of teachers. As applications to teacher-education programs dwindled, many college and university departments of physical education began to look for different curricula to attract students.

One model with which several universities experimented was a new undergraduate major in *sport studies*. This major had a strong emphasis in the sport humanities but did not specifically prepare students for jobs. It was more of a liberal-arts approach—and it did not fare too well. Many other universities began to experiment with alternative career curricula such as sport journalism, but these tended to be too narrow with few jobs awaiting graduates. The only new curricula, other than teacher education, to survive widely have been those in adult fitness and sport management, each of which tends to be vocationally oriented.

Thus, the sport humanities have not grown because there are few programs that emphasize them and the trend has been toward vocationally oriented programs rather than toward those emphasizing a liberal-arts approach. Because people who specialize in the sport humanities tend to be employed almost exclusively as college and university faculty and because there has been no strong need for more professors in these areas in undergraduate programs, the number of universities offering graduate specializations has not grown.

There is little evidence that the sport humanities are gaining ground as a coherent field of study in which people prepare at the graduate level to become teachers and researchers. This is not to suggest that the topics covered in sport humanities have not gained ground. Many sport-oriented humanities courses have developed in college and university curricula, but they typically are dispersed in the

FOCUS ON Areas of Study in the Sport Humanities	16.5

Area	Questions Typically Asked
Sport history	What causes certain sports to be more popular or less popular at certain times?
	How has sport been changed by television?
	How has Title IX changed participation by girls?
	How is sport changing as a social force in culture?
	How did the Olympics change in the twentieth century?
Sport philosophy	Does competition mean something different to spectator and competitor?
	How is the play element in sport changed as the sport competition becomes more highly organized?
	How does feminist philosophy interpret sport?
	What should "fair play" mean in elite sport?
	How do coach and athlete philosophies differ?
Sport literature	How are coaches portrayed in films emphasizing sport?
	How is the "sport hero past his or her prime" treated in sport fiction?
	How are failure and success treated in sport novels?
	What ideas and values are being expressed in sport poems?
	What role does sport play in fiction that focuses on adolescent development?

departments belonging to the parent disciplines—that is, sport-literature courses in English departments, sport-history courses in history departments, and sport-philosophy courses in philosophy departments. These are typically taught by people trained specifically in the parent discipline who happen also to have a strong interest in sport. Thus, the sport humanities have become a dispersed discipline, loosely held together by some common journals and associations but without a firm structural base in the university. Regardless, the serious study of sport from a humanities perspective continues to grow. The major areas of study and the questions typically asked are shown in Focus On Box 16.5.

Many people preparing to enter the sport, fitness, and physical-education profession find it difficult to understand why they should study the sport humanities. Issues of historical, philosophical, or literary merit seem often not to be immediately relevant to their preparation—but that view is shortsighted. Study within the sport humanities not only stimulates interest but also promotes one's ability to think critically about the work one does, and it extends one's appreciation for the importance and complexity of that work.

Current Issues and Problems in the Sport Humanities

There is little doubt that the main problem within the sport humanities is that they are too small and are not sufficiently represented in undergraduate and graduate curricula in teacher education and the sport sciences. There are too few graduate programs emphasizing the sport humanities. This underrepresentation creates a situation in which the fields are in constant jeopardy of losing more courses, more faculty, and, subsequently, more graduate programs. With the current focus on the sport sciences, it has been difficult for people in the sport humanities to hold their own in terms of faculty positions, budgets, and courses.

Gender issues in sport represent an active field of study in the sport humanities.

Sport celebrities often endorse products.

A second area of concern is related to the first. There is a widespread belief among specialists in the sport humanities that sportswriters and sport commentators in newspapers, magazines, radio, and television are often ignorant of the historical, philosophical, and literary issues that surround the sport events they report and comment on. You no doubt watch the sport news on a local television station from time to time. How well educated in the sport humanities do you think that the local television sport reporter is? How educated is the local sportswriter?

The concern here is that these people provide the commentary on and interpretation of sports, sport events, and athletes to the general public. When they comment on an event, the behavior of an athlete, or the importance of what has happened in sport, we would hope that their commentary would be informed by some specific knowledge of sport history, sport philosophy, and/or sport literature. How often is their commentary so informed? "Seldom" is probably the fair answer.

A final problem transcends all three of the specializations in the sport humanities. Each of these specializations has tended to focus more and more exclusively on sport. Fitness and physical education get only cursory treatment, if any. The names of the specializations clearly show their main interest—sport. It will be interesting to see whether this narrow focus continues or whether there is some broadening of focus to include the related areas of fitness and physical education.

SUMMARY

1. The social-science subdisciplines emerged somewhat later than the physical-science subdisciplines.

2. From the beginning, the social-science subdisciplines focused on critiquing and improving practice in sport, exercise, and physical education.

3. The social-science subdisciplines focused on sport, play, games, and exercise from their different research perspectives.

)))》GET CONNECTED to Social-Science Subdisciplines Web Sites

Motor Behavior

Canadian Society for Psychomotor Learning and Sport Psychology	www.scapps.org

Sport Sociology

American Sociological Association	www.asanet.org
North American Society for the Sociology of Sport	www.nasss.org
Center for the Study of Sport in Society	www.sportinsociety.org
Centre for Research on Sport and Society	www.le.ac.uk/crss
International Sociology of Sport Association	www.issa.otago.ac.nz

Sport and Exercise Psychology

Association for the Advancement of Applied Sport Psychology	www.appliedsportpsych.org
International Society for Sport Psychology	www.issponline.org
North American Society for Psychology of Sport and Physical Activity	www.naspspa.org
Athletic Insight	www.athleticinsight.com
Mental Skills	www.mentalskills.co.uk

Sport Pedagogy

National Association for Sport and Physical Education	www.aahperd.org/naspe
National Board for Professional Teaching Standards	www.nbpts.org
International Association of Physical Education in Higher Education (AIESEP)	www.aiesep.com
American Educational Research Association	www.aera.net

Sport Humanities

International Society for the History of Physical Education and Sport	www.ishpes.org
North American Society for Sport History	www.nassh.org
International Society for Comparative Physical Education and Sport	www.iscpes.org/
British Society of Sport History	http://bssh.mcs-creations.com
International Society of Olympic Historians	www.olykamp.org.isoh
Sport Literature Association	www.isoh.org
Sport Literature	www.h-net.org/~arete
Canadian Center for Ethics in Sport	www.cces.ca

4. Some faculty in departments of psychology, history, literature, sociology, and education have shown an interest in conducting research and teaching courses in the social-science subdisciplines of Kinesiology.

5. Each of the social-science subdisciplines has an organization of its own and scholarly journals of its own in which it publishes specialized research.

6. Sport psychology has developed into a field in which there are both university-based researchers and consulting sport psychologists working directly with teams and athletic departments in collegiate and professional sport.

7. Paths to careers in these fields are diverse. Some students start within the specialization (in an undergraduate sociology major, for example) and complete graduate work in the specialization. Others earn undergraduate physical-education degrees and then move to more specialized graduate preparation.

DISCUSSION QUESTIONS

1. What are the separate spheres of study for each of the social-science subdisciplines?

2. What clinical or consulting roles exist for those who work in these subdisciplines?

3. Are there practicing sport psychologists for the teams at your college or university?

4. What role can each of the sport-humanities areas play in helping the public to understand, value, and improve sport, fitness, and physical education?

5. How are sport, fitness, and physical education portrayed in books, films, and television shows that you have read or seen?

6. How good or bad were the physical-education programs in your elementary, middle, and high schools?

7. What role does sport play in the local culture in which you grew up?

8. How would you describe the culture of a fitness center?

Bibliography

AAALF Active Voice (2003). Fit versus fat: Can a person be both? 8(2), 8. American Association for Active Lifestyles and Fitness.

Acosta, R., & Carpenter, L. (1992). As the years go by: Coaching opportunities in the 1990s. *Journal of Physical Education, Recreation, and Dance, 63*(3), 36–41.

————. (1994). The status of women in intercollegiate athletics. In S. Birrell & C. Cole (Eds.), *Women, sport and culture* (pp. 111–118). Champaign, IL: Human Kinetics.

Active Marketing Group. (2007). *Health club industry review.* San Diego: The Active Network, Inc.

Adelman, M. (1969). The role of the sports historian. *Quest, 12,* 61–65.

Adler, J. (2004). Toxic strength. *Newsweek,* December 20, 45–52.

Adrian, M. (1983). Biomechanics: Theory into practice. *Proceedings of the National Association for Physical Education in Higher Education, 4,* 37–50. Champaign, IL: Human Kinetics.

Albany Times Union. (1992, July 22). Empire State Games special section.

Alderman, R., & Wood, N. (1976). An analysis of incentive motivation in young Canadian athletes. *Canadian Journal of Sport Sciences, 1*(2), 169–176.

Alexander, K. (1994). Developing sport education in Western Australia. *Aussie Sport Action, 5*(1), 8–9.

Alexander, K., Taggart, A., & Luckman, J. (1988). The sport education crusade down under. *Journal of Physical Education, Recreation, and Dance, 69*(4), 21–23.

Allen, B. (1988). Teaching training and discipline-based dance education. *Journal of Physical Education, Recreation, and Dance, 59*(9), 65–69.

Almond, L. (1983). Reflecting on themes: A games classification. *Bulletin of Physical Education, 19*(1), 33–36.

————. (1986). Primary and secondary rules in games. In R. Thorpe, D. Bunker, & L. Almond (Eds.), *Rethinking games teaching.* London: Esmonde.

Almond, L., Bunker, D., & Thorpe, R. (1983). Games teaching revisited. *Bulletin of Physical Education, 19*(3), 3–35.

American Academy of Pediatrics. (2000). Intensive training and sports specialization in youth athletes. *Pediatrics, 106,* 154–157.

American Academy of Pediatrics. (2003). Prevention of pediatric overweight and obesity, committee on nutrition. *Pediatrics, 112*(2), 424–430.

American Association for Adapted Sports. (2008). Model state. www.adaptedsports.org.

American Association for Leisure and Recreation. (2000). *Careers in recreation.* Reston, VA: AAHPERD.

ACSM (American College of Sports Medicine). (1990). The recommended quantity and quality of exercise for developing and maintaining cardiorespiratory and muscular fitness in healthy adults. *Medicine and Science in Sports and Exercise, 22,* 265–274.

American Sports Data. (1999). *Tracking the fitness movement.* North Palm Beach, FL: Fitness Products Council.

Anderrson, M., Williams, J., Aldridge, T., & Taylor, T. (1997). Tracking the training and careers of graduates of advanced degree programs in sport psychology, 1989–1994. *The Sport Psychologist, 11,* 326–344.

Anderson, P., & Butcher, K. (2006). Childhood Obesity: Trends and potential causes. *The Future of Children, 16*(1), Spring.

Antonelli, F. (1970). Opening address. In G. Kenyon (Ed.), *Contemporary psychology of sport* (pp. 3–9). Chicago: The Athletic Institute.

ARAPCS Newsletter. (1986). Our kids are out of shape, getting flabby. *ARAPCS Newsletter, 3*(1), 4.

A Report to the President (2000). Promoting better health for young people through physical activity and sports. *A Report to the President from the Secretary of Health and Human Services and the Secretary of Education.*

Arnheim, D., & Prentice, W. (2000). *Principles of athletic training* (10th ed.). New York: McGraw-Hill.

Athletic Footwear Institute. (1990). *American youth and sports participation.* North Palm Beach, FL: Athletic Footwear Institute.

Australian Sports Commission. (1994). *National junior sport policy.* Canberra, Australia.

Barrett, J. (2007). The price of childhood obesity. www.newsweek.com/id/73892.

Battagliola, M. (1993). Indian industries takes aim at employee health. *Business and Health*, 11, 12.

Baun, W. (1995). Culture change in worksite health promotion. In D. Dejoy & M. Wilson (Eds.), *Critical issues in worksite health promotion*. Boston: Allyn & Bacon.

Baun, W., & Bernacki, E. (1988). Who are corporate exercisers and what motivates them? In R. Dishman (Ed.), *Exercise adherence* (pp. 321–348). Champaign, IL: Human Kinetics.

Beaumont, C. E., & Pianca, E. G. (2002). *Why Johnny can't walk to school: Historic neighborhood schools in the age of sprawl*. Washington, DC: National Trust for Historic Preservation.

Beaver, D. (2004). Editor's corner, *Palaestra*, 20(1), pp. 4, 15.

Becker, D. (1996, January 18). More women athletes head for Atlanta. *USA Today*, p. 12C.

Beighle, A., Pangrazi, R., & Vincent, S. (2001). Pedometers, physical activity and accountability. *Journal of Physical Education, Recreation, and Dance*, 72(9), 16–19, 36.

Bell, C. (1998). Sport education in the elementary school. *Journal of Physical Education, Recreation, and Dance*, 69(5), 36–39.

Bennett, W. (1986). *First lessons: A report on elementary education in America*. Washington, DC: U.S. Department of Education.

Berg, K. (1988). A national curriculum in physical education. *Journal of Physical Education, Recreation, and Dance*, 59(8), 70–75.

Berger, B. (2004). Subjective well-being in obese individuals: The multiple roles of exercise. *Quest*, 56, 50–76.

Biddle, S. (1995). Exercise and psychosocial health. *Research Quarterly for Exercise and Sport*, 66(4), 292–297.

Biles, F. (1971). The physical education public information project. *Journal of Health, Physical Education, and Recreation*, 41(7), 53–55.

Blackledge, S. (1994, October 7). Pay-to-play takes toll at Big Walnut. *The Columbus Dispatch*, D-1.

Blair, S. (1992). Are American children and youth fit? The need for better data. *Research Quarterly for Exercise and Sport*, 63(2), 120–123.

Blair, S., & Connelly, J. (1996). How much physical activity should we do? The case for moderate amounts and intensities of physical activity. *Research Quarterly for Exercise and Sport*, 67(2), 193–205.

Blair, S., Kohl, H., III, Paffenbarger, R., Jr., Cooper, K., & Gibbons, L. (1989). Physical fitness and all-cause mortality: A prospective study of healthy men and women. *Journal of the American Medical Association*, 239–240, 262.

Blair, S., Kohl, H., & Powell, K. (1987). Physical activity, physical fitness, exercise, and the public's health. *The Academy Papers*, 20, 53–69.

Block, M. (1995). Americans with disabilities act: Its impact on youth sports. *Journal of Physical Education, Recreation, and Dance*, 66(5), 28–32.

Bookwalter, K., & Vander-Zwaag, H. (1969). *Foundations and principles of physical education*. Philadelphia: W. B. Saunders.

Bouchard, C., Shephard, R., & Stephens, T. (1993). *Physical activity, fitness and health: Consensus statement*. Champaign, IL: Human Kinetics.

Boucher, A. (1988). Good beginnings. *Journal of Physical Education, Recreation, and Dance*, 59(7), 42.

Bowerman, W., & Harris, W. (1967). *Jogging*. New York: Grosset & Dunlap.

Bowers, C. (1999). The creatine debate. *Strategies*, 12(6), 5–8.

Bradford-Krok, B. (1994). Citrus county fitness break: Funding and developing fitness videotapes. In R. Pate & D. Hohn (Eds.), *Health and fitness through physical education* (pp. 205–210). Champaign, IL: Human Kinetics.

Bradley, B. (1998). *Values of the game*. New York: Artisan.

Brady, E., & Glier, R. (2004). To play sports, many U.S. students must pay. *USA Today*, July 29. www.usatoday.com/sports/presps/2004-07-29-pay-to-play_x.htm

Brancazio, P. (1984). *Sport science: Physical laws and optimum performance*. New York: Simon & Schuster.

Bressan, E., & Pieter, W. (1985). Philosophic process and the study of human moving. *Quest*, 37(1), 1–15.

Brooks, G. (1987). The exercise physiology paradigm in contemporary biology: To molbiol or not to molbiol—that is the question. *Quest*, 39(3), 231–242.

———. (1994). 40 years of progress: Basic exercise physiology. In *40th Anniversary lectures*. Indianapolis, IN: American College of Sports Medicine.

Brooks, S. (2003, August 12). Virtual PE makes a splash. *USA Today*, 50.

Browder, K., & Darby, L. (1998). Individualizing exercise: Some biomechanical and physiological reminders. *Journal of Physical Education, Recreation, and Dance, 69*(4), 35–44.

Bryant, C., & Peterson, J. (1999) Prescribing exercise for healthy adults, *Journal of Physical Education, Recreation, and Dance, 70*(6), 31.

Bucher, C. (1964). *Foundations of physical education* (4th ed.). St. Louis: Mosby.

Buckworth, J., & Dishman, R. (2001). Exercise psychology. In J. Williams (Ed.), *Applied sport psychology* (4th ed., pp. 497–518). Mountain View, CA: Mayfield.

Bunker, L. (1998). Psycho-physiological contributions of physical activity and sports for girls. *President's Council on Physical Fitness and Sports Research Digest,* 3(1), 1–6.

Caillois, R. (1961). *Man, play and games.* New York: Free Press of Glencoe.

Caldwell, S. (1966). Conceptions of physical education in twentieth century America: Rosalind Cassidy. Doctoral dissertation, University of Southern California, Los Angeles.

California Endowment. (2008). *Physical education matters: A full report.* Los Angeles: California Endowment.

Carlisle, R. (1974). Physical education and aesthetics. In H. Whiting & D. Masterson (Eds.), *Readings in the aesthetics of sport* (pp. 21–32). London: Lepus Books.

Carlson, T. (1996). "Now I think I can." The reaction of eight low-skilled students to sport education. *ACHPER Healthy Lifestyles Journal, 42*(4), 6–8.

Carnegie Council on Adolescent Development. (1992). *A matter of time: Risk and opportunity in the nonschool hours.* New York: Carnegie Corporation.

Casey, A. (1992). Title IX and women officials: How have they been affected? *Journal of Physical Education, Recreation, and Dance, 63*(3), 45–47.

Castelli, D., & Rink, J. (2003). A comparison of high and low performing secondary physical education programs. *Journal of Teaching in Physical Education, 22,* 512–532.

Centers for Disease Control and Prevention. (1991). *Healthy People 2000,* www.healthypeople.gov

Centers for Disease Control and Prevention. (1997). Guidelines for school and community programs to promote lifelong physical activity among young people. U.S. Department of Health and Human Services, Centers for Disease Control and Prevention.

Centers for Disease Control and Prevention. (2000). *Healthy People 2010,* www.healthypeople.gov

Centers for Disease Control and Prevention. (2001). Increasing physical activity: A report on recommendations of the Task Force on Community Preventive Services. MMWR 2001, 50(No. RR-18), 1–14.

Centers for Disease Control and Prevention. (2003). Physical activity levels among children aged 9–13 years—United States, 2002. *MMWR, 52*(33), 785–788.

Centers for Disease Control and Prevention. (2006). Sports-related injuries among high school athletes—United States, 2005–06 school year. *MMWR, 55*(38), 1037–1040.

Centers for Disease Control and Prevention. (2008). Defining overweight and obesity. www.cdc.gov/nccdphp/ dnpa/obesity/defining.htm

Christina, R. (1987). Motor learning: Future lines of research. *The Academy Papers, 20,* 26–41.

———. (1989). Whatever happened to applied research in motor learning? In J. Skinner et al. (Eds.), *Future directions for exercise science and sport research* (pp. 411–422). Champaign, IL: Human Kinetics.

Chu, D. (1981). Functional myths of educational organizations: College as career training and the relationship of formal title to actual duties on secondary school employment. In V. Crafts (Ed.), *Proceedings of the National Association for Physical Education in Higher Education* (pp. 36–46). Champaign, IL: Human Kinetics.

Cissell, W. (1992). Health educators as professionals in the year 2000: A prediction. *Journal of Physical Education, Recreation, and Dance, 63*(5), 27.

Clark, J. (2008). Kinesiology in the 21st century: A preface. *Quest, 60,* 1–2.

Clarke, D. (1986). Children and the research process. *The Academy Papers, 19,* 9–13.

Coakley, J. (1982). *Sport in society* (2nd ed.). St. Louis: Mosby.

———. (1994). *Sports and society: Issues and controversies* (5th ed.). St. Louis, MO: Mosby.

———. (2004). *Sports in society: Issues and controversies* (8th ed.). Boston: McGraw-Hill.

———. (2007). Sports and society: *Issues and Controversies* (9th ed.). New York: McGraw-Hill.

Coffin, J. (2002, September 9). Football a focal point in the Title IX debate. *Golfweek,* 22.

Cohen, A. (1991). The children's crusade: In pursuit of youth fitness. *Athletic Business*, 15(10), 24–28.

———. (1995). Fitness equipment: The next generation. *Athletic Business*, 19(3), 26–36.

Colfer, G., Hamilton, K., Magill, R., & Hamilton, B. (1986). *Contemporary physical education*. Dubuque, IA: Brown.

Columbus Dispatch. (2005, March 17). Obesity threatens life expectancy, p. A-5.

Comstock, R., Nox, C., Yard, E., & Gilchrist, J. (2007). Sports-related injuries among high school athletes— United States, 2005–06 school year. *MMWR Weekly*, 55(38), 1037–1040.

Cooper, K. (1968). *Aerobics*. New York: Bantam Books.

Corbett, D., & Calloway, D. (2006). Physical activity challenges facing African-American girls and women. *President's Council on Physical Fitness and Sport Newsletter*, Winter, 1–5.

Corbin, C. (1981). First things first, but don't stop there. *Journal of Physical Education, Recreation, and Dance*, 52, 36–38.

———. (1987). Physical fitness in the K–12 curriculum: Some defensive solutions to perennial problems. *Journal of Physical Education, Recreation, and Dance*, 58(7), 49–54.

———. (2002). Physical activity for everyone: What every physical educator should know about promoting lifelong physical activity. *Quest*, 21(2), 128–144.

Corbin, C., Dowell, L., Lindsey, R., & Tolson, H. (1974). *Concepts in physical education* (2nd ed.). Dubuque, IA: Brown.

Corbin, C., & Lindsey, R. (1983). *Fitness for life*. Glenview, IL: Scott, Foresman.

———. (1999). *Concepts of physical fitness* (10th Ed.). New York: McGraw.

Corbin, C., & Pangrazi, R. (1992). Are American children and youth fit? *Research Quarterly for Exercise and Sport*, 63(2), 96–106.

———. (1996). How much PA is enough? *Journal of Physical Education, Recreation, and Dance*, 67(4), 33–37.

———. (1998). *Physical activity for children: A statement of guidelines*. Reston, VA: NASPE Publications.

Corbin, C., Pangrazi, R., & Franks, B. D. (2000). Definitions: Health, fitness, and physical activity. President's Council on Physical Fitness and Sport. *Research Digest*, 3(9), 1–8.

Corbin, C., Pangrazi, R., & LeMasurier, G. (2004). Physical activity for children: Current patterns and guidelines. *Research Digest*, 5(2), 1–8.

Corbin, C., Welk, G., Corbin, W., & Welk, K. (2008). *Concepts of physical fitness: Active lifestyles for wellness* (14th ed.). Boston: McGraw-Hill.

Cordes, K., & Ibrahim, H. (2003). *Applications in recreation and leisure* (3rd ed.). Boston: McGraw-Hill.

Costill, D. (1986). *Inside running: Basics of sport physiology*. Indianapolis: Benchmark Press.

Councilman, J. (1968). *The science of swimming*. Englewood Cliffs, NJ: Prentice-Hall.

Cremin, L. (1961). *The transformation of the school: Progressivism in American education*. New York: Knopf.

Csikszentmihalyi, M., Rathunde, K., & Whalen, S. (1993). *Talented teenagers: The roots of success and failure*. Cambridge, MA: Cambridge University Press.

Cureton, K. (1994). Physical fitness and activity standards for youth. In R. Pate & D. Hohn (Eds.), *Health and fitness through physical education* (pp. 129–136). Champaign, IL: Human Kinetics.

Daniels, S. R. (2006). The consequences of childhood overweight and obesity. *The Future of Children*, 16(1), 47–67.

Darby, L., & Temple, I. (1992). A research project that combines research, teaching and service. *Journal of Physical Education, Recreation, and Dance*, 63(8), 65–67.

Darnell, J. (1994). Sport education in the elementary curriculum. In D. Siedentop (Ed.), *Sport education in physical education*. Champaign, IL: Human Kinetics.

Davis, K. (1999). Giving women a chance to learn: Gender equity principles for HPERD classes. *Journal of Physical Education, Recreation, and Dance*, 70(4), 13–14.

Davis, R. (2003). Runn!ing for Life. *Journal of Physical Education, Recreation, and Dance*, 74(4), 11–13, 19.

De Grazia, S. (1962). *Of time, work and leisure*. New York: Twentieth Century Fund.

DePauw, K. (1984). Commitment and challenges. *Journal of Physical Education, Recreation, and Dance*, 55(2), 34–35.

———. (1996). Students with disabilities in physical education. In S. Silverman & C. Ennis (Eds.), *Student learning in physical education: Applying research to enhance instruction* (pp. 101–124). Champaign, IL: Human Kinetics.

DeRenne, C., Morgan, C., Hetzler, R., & Taura, B. (2007). A state analysis of high school certification requirements for head baseball coaches. *The Sports Journal*, 10(3).

Dietz, W. (2004). The effects of physical activity on obesity. *Quest*, 56, 1–11.

Dishman, R. (Ed.). (1988). *Exercise adherence.* Champaign, IL: Human Kinetics.

————. (1989). Determinants of physical activity and exercise for persons 65 years of age or older. *The Academy Papers*, 22, 140–162.

Dompier, T., Powell, J., Barron, M., & Moore, M. (2007). Time-loss and non-time-loss injuries in youth football players. *Journal of Athletic Training*, 42(3), 395–402.

Duda, J. (1991). Motivating older adults for physical activity: It's never too late. *Journal of Physical Education, Recreation, and Dance*, 62(7), 44–48.

Dugas, D. (1994). Sport education in the secondary curriculum. In D. Siedentop, *Sport education: Quality PE through positive sport experiences* (pp. 105–112). Champaign, IL: Human Kinetics.

Dulles, F. R. (1940). *America learns to play.* New York: Appleton-Century.

Dunn, D. (1986a). An introduction. *Journal of Physical Education, Recreation, and Dance*, 57(8), 34–35.

————. (1986b). Professionalism and human resources. *Journal of Physical Education, Recreation, and Dance*, 57(8), 50–53.

Duquin, M. (1988). Gender and youth sport: Reflections on old and new fictions. In F. Smoll, R. Magill, & M. Ash (Eds.), *Children in sport* (pp. 31–41). Champaign, IL: Human Kinetics.

Dyson, G. (1964). *The mechanics of athletics.* London: University of London Press.

Earls, N. (1981). Distinctive teachers' personal qualities, perceptions of teacher education and the realities of teaching. *Journal of Teaching in Physical Education*, 1(1), 59–70.

Eccles, J., & Barber, B. (1999). Student council, volunteering, basketball, or marching band: What kind of extracurricular involvement matters? *Journal of Adolescent Research*, 14, 10–43.

Edlin,G., & Golanty, E. (1982). *Health and wellness.* Boston: Science Books International.

Eitzen, S., & Sage, G. (2003). *Sociology of North American sport* (7th ed.). Boston: McGraw-Hill.

Elias, M. (1983, November 17). We frown on girls who play rough. *USA Today*, p. 1A.

Elliot, R. (1974). Aesthetics and sport. In H. Whiting & D. Masterson (Eds.), *Readings in the aesthetics of sport* (pp. 107–116). London: Lepus Books.

Ellis, M. (1988). *The business of physical education.* Champaign, IL: Human Kinetics.

Ennis, C., Ross, J., & Chen, A. (1992). The role of value orientations in curricular decision making: A rationale for teachers' goals and expectations. *Research Quarterly for Exercise and Sport*, 63(1), 38–47.

Ennis, C., Satina, B., & Solomon, M. (1999). Creating a sense of family in urban schools using the 'sport for peace' curriculum. *Research Quarterly for Exercise and Sport*, 70(3), 273–285.

Evans, J., & Roberts, G. (1987). Physical competence and the development of peer relations. *Quest*, 39(1), 23–35.

Everhart, B., & Turner, E. (1995). Computer feedback for improved teacher training. *Journal of Physical Education, Recreation, and Dance*, 66(9), 57–60.

Ewing, M., & Seefeldt, V. (1997). Youth sports in America: An overview. *President's Council on Physical Fitness and Sports Research Digest.* 2(11), 1–12.

Executive Summary. (1999). When school is out. *The Future of Children*, 9(2), 1–4.

Eyler, M. (1965). Sport historians. *Proceedings of the National College Physical Education Association for Men*, 57–60.

Fahey, T., Insel, P., & Roth, W. (2007). *Fit and well* (7th ed.). Mountain, View, CA: Mayfield.

————. (2008). *Fit and well* (8th ed.). New York: McGraw-Hill.

Faigenbaum, A. (2001). Strength training and children's health. *Journal of Physical Education, Recreation and Dance*, 72(3), 24–30.

Fain, G. (1983). Introduction. *Journal of Physical Education, Recreation, and Dance*, 54(8), 32–33.

Fanselow, J. (2004, March 21). With every mile they grow stronger. *Parade*, 5.

Faucette, N., Nugent, P., Sallis, J., & McKenzie, T. (2002). "I'd rather chew on aluminum foil." Overcoming classroom teachers' resistance to teaching physical education. *Journal of Teaching in Physical Education*, 21(3), 287–308.

Feltz, D. (1987). The future of graduate education in sport and exercise science: A sport psychology perspective. *Quest*, 39(2), 217–222.

Finger, D. (2004). Before they were next. *ESPN the Magazine*, 7(12), 83–86.

Flegal, K., Carroll, M., Ogden, C., & Johnson, C. (2002). Prevalence and trends in obesity among US adults, 1999–2000. *Journal of the American Medical Association, 288,* 1723–1727.

Fox, C. (1992). Title IX at twenty. *Journal of Physical Education, Recreation, and Dance, 63*(3), 33–35.

Fraleigh, W. (1985). Why the good foul is not good. In D. Vanderwerken & S. Wertz (Eds.), *Sport: Inside out* (pp. 462–466). Fort Worth: Texas Christian University Press.

Fraser-Thomas, J., & Cote, J. (2007). Youth sports: Implementing findings and moving forward with research. *Athletic Insight: The Online Journal of Sport Psychology, 3,* 1–12.

Freedson, P., & Rowland, T. (1992). Youth activity versus youth fitness: Let's redirect our efforts. *Research Quarterly for Exercise and Sport, 63*(2), 133–136.

Freeman, W. (1982). *Physical education and sport in a changing society* (2nd ed.). Minneapolis: Burgess.

French, R., Henderson, H., Kinnison, L., & Sherrill, C. (1998). Revisiting section 504, Physical Education and Sport. *Journal of Physical Education, Recreation, and Dance, 69*(7), 57–64.

Gabbei, R. (2004). Achieving balance: Secondary physical education gender-grouping options. *Journal of Physical Education, Recreation, and Dance, 75*(3), 33–39.

Gard, M. (2004). An elephant in the room and a bridge too far, or physical education and the "obesity epidemic." In J. Evans, B. Davies, & J. Wright (Eds.), *Body knowledge and control: Studies in the sociology of physical education and health* (pp. 68–82). London: Routledge.

Geadelman, P. (1981). Co-educational physical education: For better or worse. *NASSP Bulletin, 65,* 91–95.

Gensemer, R. (1985). *Physical education: Perspectives, inquiry, applications.* Philadelphia: Saunders.

Gerber, E. (1971). *Innovators and institutions in physical education.* Philadelphia: Lea & Febiger.

———. (1974). *The American woman in sport.* Reading, MA: Addison-Wesley.

Giamatti, A. B. (1989). *Take time for paradise.* New York: Summit Books.

Gill, D. (1991). Social psychological contributions to performance enhancement. *The Academy Papers, 25,* 117–121.

Gober, B., & Franks, B. (1988). The physical and fitness education of young children. *Journal of Physical Education, Recreation, and Dance, 59*(7), 57–61.

Goetzel, R., Sepulveda, M., Knight, K., Eisen, M., Wade, B., Wong, C., & Fielding, N. (1994). Association of IBM's "A plan for life" health promotion program with changes in employees' health risk status. *American College of Occupational and Environmental Medicine, 36,* 1005–1009.

Gorman, J., & Calhoun, K. (1994). *The name of the game: The business of sports.* New York: Wiley.

Gough, D. (1995). Specialization in youth sport. *Coaching Clinic, 34*(3), 5–6.

Government of South Australia. (2007). Handlebar injuries causing life threatening "mega-trauma." *Children, Youth, and Women's Health Science.*

Graham, G. (1990). Physical education in U.S. schools, K–12. *Journal of Physical Education, Recreation, and Dance, 61*(2), 35–39.

Graham, G., Holt-Hale, S., & Parker, M. (2007). *Children moving: A reflective approach to teaching physical education.* New York: McGraw-Hill.

Grant, B. (1992). Integrating sport into the physical education curriculum in New Zealand secondary schools. *Quest, 44*(3), 304–316.

Graves, M., & Townsend, J. (2000). Applying the sport education curriculum model to dance. *Journal of Physical Education, Recreation, and Dance, 71*(8), 50–54.

Green, J. (1997). Action research in youth soccer: Assessing the acceptability of an alternative program. *Journal of Sport Management, 11,* 29–44.

Griffey, D. (1987). Trouble for sure: A crisis perhaps. *Journal of Physical Education, Recreation, and Dance, 58*(2), 20–21.

Griffin, L., Mitchell, S., & Oslin, J. (1997). *Teaching sports concepts and skills: A tactical games approach.* Champaign, IL: Human Kinetics.

Gruneau, R. (1976). Sport as an area of sociological study: An introduction to major themes and perspectives. In R. Gruneau & J. Albinson (Eds.), *Canadian sport: Sociological perspectives* (pp. 3–7). Reading, MA: Addison-Wesley.

Gutin, B., Manos, T., & Strong, W. (1992). Defining health and fitness: First step toward establishing children's fitness standards. *Research Quarterly for Exercise and Sport, 63*(2), 128–132.

Hall, L., & Wilson, P. (1984). Industrial fitness, adult fitness, and cardiac rehabilitation graduate programs. *Journal of Physical Education, Recreation, and Dance, 55*(3), 40–44.

Harageones, M. (1987). Impact of educational reform: The quality of Florida's high school physical education programs. *Journal of Physical Education, Recreation, and Dance, 58*(6), 52–54.

Harrington, M. (1998, April 27). Families driven to keep competitive in sports. *USA Today*, 6D.

Harris, D. (1987). Frontiers in psychology of exercise and sport. *The Academy Papers*, 20, 42–52.

Harris, J. (1991). Modifying the performance enhancement ethos: Disciplinary and professional implications. *The Academy Papers*, 25, 96–103.

———. (1992, April). Using kinesiology: A comparison of applied veins in the subdisciplines. Amy Morris Homans Lecture, National Convention of the American Alliance for Health, Physical Education, Recreation, and Dance, Indianapolis.

———. (2000). *Sociology of physical activity*. In S. Hoffman & J. Harris (Eds.), pp. 207–240. Champaign, IL: Human Kinetics.

Hasbrook, C. (1987). Interscholastic coaching and officiating: Programs designed to increase the number of women involved. *Journal of Physical Education, Recreation, and Dance*, 58(2), 35.

Hastie, P. (1998a). The participation and perception of girls during a unit of sport education. *Journal of Teaching in Physical Education*, 18(2), 157–171.

———. (1998b). Applied benefits of the sport education model. *Journal of Physical Education, Recreation, and Dance*, 69(4), 24–26.

Hastie, P., & Sharpe, T. (1999). Effects of a sport education curriculum on the positive social behaviors of at-risk rural adolescent boys. *Journal of Education for Students Placed at Risk*, 4, 417–430.

Hawkins, R., & Mulkey, L. (2005). Athletic investment and academic resilience in a national sample of African American females and males in middle grades. *Education and Urban Society*, 38(1), 62–88.

Hay, J. (1991). Reaction to performance feedback: Advances in biomechanics. *Quest*, 25, 33–37.

Hayes, E. (1980). History of dance in the Alliance. *Journal of Physical Education, Recreation, and Dance*, 51(5), 32.

Haymes, E. (2000). Physiology of physical activity. In S. Hoffman & J. Harris (Eds.) *Introduction to kinesiology* (pp. 381–412). Champaign, IL: Human Kinetics.

He, M., & Evans, A. (2007). Are parents aware that their children are overweight or obese? Do they care? *Canadian Family Physician*, 53(9), 1493–1499.

Hellison, D. (1973). *Humanistic physical education*. Englewood Cliffs, NJ: Prentice-Hall.

———. (1978). *Beyond balls and bats: Alienated youth in the gym*. Washington, DC: AAHPERD.

———. (1983). Teaching self responsibility (and more). *Journal of Physical Education, Recreation, and Dance*, 54(7), 23.

———. (1984). *Goals and strategies for teaching physical education*. Champaign, IL: Human Kinetics.

———. (1990). Teaching PE to at-risk youth in Chicago: A model. *Journal of Physical Education, Recreation, and Dance*, 61(6), 38–39.

———. (1995). *Teaching responsibility through physical activity*. Champaign, IL: Human Kinetics.

———. (1996). Teaching personal and social responsibility in physical education. In S. Silverman & C. Ennis (Eds.), *Student learning in physical education: Applying research to enhance instruction* (pp. 269–286). Champaign, IL: Human Kinetics.

———. (2003). *Teaching responsibility through physical activity* (2nd ed.). Champaign, IL: Human Kinetics.

Henderson, K., & Bialeschki, M. (1991). Girls' and women's recreation programming: Constraints and opportunities. *Journal of Physical Education, Recreation, and Dance*, 62(1), 55–58.

Henig, R. (1999, January 21). Girls enjoy sports—isn't that enough? *USA Today*, 15A.

Henry, F. (1964). Physical education: An academic discipline. *Journal of Health, Physical Education, and Recreation*, 37(7), 32–33.

Hertzman, C. (1994). The lifelong impact of childhood experiences: A population health perspective. *Daedalus*, 123(4), 167–180.

Hester, D., & Dunaway, D. (1991). NAGWS: Paths to advocacy, recruitment, and enhancement. *Journal of Physical Education, Recreation, and Dance*, 62(3), 30–31.

Hetherington, C. (1910). Fundamental education. *American Physical Education Review*, 15, 629–635.

Hilgers, L. (2006). Youth sports drawing more than ever. CNN, Web article. July 5.

Hinson, C. (1994). Pulse power: A heart physiology program for children. *Journal of Physical Education, Recreation and Dance*, 65(1), 62–68.

Hirschhorn, D., & Loughead, T. (2000). Parental impact on youth participation in sport: The physical educator's role. *Journal of Physical Education, Recreation, and Dance*, 72, 41–46.

Hoch, D. (2007). Strategies for problematic parents. *Coaches' Quarterly*, Summer.

Hoffman, S. (1977). Toward a pedagogical kinesiology. *Quest*, 28, 38–48.

———. (1987). Dreaming the impossible dream: The decline and fall of physical education. In J. Massengale

(Ed.), *Trends toward the future in physical education* (pp. 121–135). Champaign, IL: Human Kinetics.

Hoffman, S., & Harris, J. (2000). Discovering the field of physical activity. In S. Hoffman & J. Harris (Eds.), *Introduction to kinesiology* (pp. 1–33). Champaign, IL: Human Kinetics.

Houlihan, S., & DeBrock, L. (1991). Economics in sport. In B. Parkhouse (Ed.), *The management of sport* (pp. 198–209). St. Louis: Mosby.

Huizinga, J. (1962). *Homo ludens: A study of the play element in culture.* Boston: Beacon Press.

Hulstrand, B. (1990). Women in high school PE teaching positions: Diminishing in number. *Journal of Physical Education, Recreation, and Dance,* 61(9), 19–21.

Jack, H. (1985). Division of recreation. *Journal of Physical Education, Recreation, and Dance,* 56(4), 97–98.

James, M. (1995). Unified sports gains momentum at '95 World Games. *Exceptional Children,* 25(6), 56–57.

Jansma, P., & French, R. (1994). *Special physical education.* Englewood Cliffs, NJ: Prentice-Hall.

Jennings, J. (2006). *Ten big effects of the No Child Left Behind Act on public schools.* Washington, DC: Center for Education Policy.

Jewett, A., & Bain, L. (1985). *The curriculum process in physical education.* Dubuque, IA: Wm. C. Brown.

Johns, E. (1985). Division of health education. *Journal of Physical Education, Recreation, and Dance,* 56(4), 105–106.

Johnson, D., & Harageones, E. (1994). A health fitness course in secondary physical education: The Florida experience. In R. Pate & D. Hohn (Eds.), *Health and fitness through physical education* (pp. 165–176). Champaign: IL: Human Kinetics.

Jones, D., & Ward, P. (1998). Changing the face of secondary physical education through sport education. *Journal of Physical Education, Recreation, and Dance,* 69(5), 40–44.

Kahn, L., Collins, J., Pateman, B., Small, M., Ross, J., & Kolbe, L. (1995). The School Health Policies and Programs Study (SHPPS): Rationale for a nationwide status report on school health programs. *Journal of School Health,* 65(8), 291–302.

Kaman, R. (1995). Costs and benefits of corporate health promotion. *Fitness in Business,* 5, 39–44.

Kantrowitz, B., & Joseph, N. (1986, May 26). Building baby biceps. *Newsweek,* 79.

Karvonen, M. (1996). Physical activity for a healthy life. *Research Quarterly for Exercise and Sport,* 67(2), 209–212.

Kaufman, F. (2005). *Diabesity.* New York: Bantam Books.

Keating, J. (1973). The ethics of competition and its relation to some moral problems in athletics. In R. Osterhoudt (Ed.), *The philosophy of sport* (pp. 157–175). Springfield, IL: Thomas.

Kennedy, J. (1960). The soft American. *Sports Illustrated,* December, 15–23.

Kenyon, G., & Loy, J. (1965). Toward a sociology of sport. *Journal of Health, Physical Education, and Recreation,* 36, 24–25, 68–69.

Kerr, R. (1982). *Psychomotor learning.* Philadelphia: Saunders.

Kimm, S., Glynn, N., Kriska, A., Barton, B., Kronsberg, S., Daniels, S., Crawford, P., Sabry, Z., & Liu, K. (2002). Decline in physical activity in black girls and white girls during adolescence. *New England Journal of Medicine,* 347(10), 709–715.

Kirchner, G. (1970). *Introduction to human movement.* Dubuque, IA: Brown.

Kleinman, S. (1987). On the edge (of oblivion). *American Academy of Physical Education Papers,* 20, 109–114.

Knop, N. (1998). Reconstructing physical education in an urban secondary school to create a more democratic environment. Teaching as praxis. Unpublished doctoral dissertation, Ohio State University, Columbus.

Knop, N., Tannehill, D., & O'Sullivan, M. (2001). Making a difference for urban youth. *Journal of Physical Education, Recreation, and Dance,* 72(7), 38–44.

Knoppers, A. (1988). Equity for excellence in physical education. *Journal of Physical Education, Recreation, and Dance,* 59(6), 54–58.

Knudson, D., Magnusson, P., & McHugh, M. (2000). Current issues in flexibility fitness. *Research Digest* 3(10), 1–8. President's Council on Physical Fitness and Sport.

Koplan, J., Liverman, C., Kraak, V., & Wisham, W. (Eds.). (2006). *Progress in preventing childhood obesity: How do we measure up?* Washington, DC: Institute of Medicine of the National Academies.

Kotulak, R., & Gorner, P. (1992, January 12). Diet, fitness proven keys to long life. *Columbus Dispatch,* p. 6F.

Kraus, H., & Hirschland, R. (1954). Minimum muscular fitness tests in school children. *Research Quarterly,* 25, 178–185.

Kraus, R. (1995). Play's new identity: Big business. *Journal of Physical Education, Recreation, and Dance,* 66(8), 36–40.

———. (2002). Careers in recreation: Expanding horizons. *Journal of Physical Education, Recreation, and Dance,* 73(5), 46–49, 54.

Kretchmar, S. (1989). On beautiful games. *Journal of the Philosophy of Sport*, 16(1), 23–32.

Kretchmar, S. (2008). The increasing utility of elementary school physical education: A mixed blessing and unique challenge. *The Elementary School Journal*, 108(3), 161–170.

LaFee, S. (2006). Steriods: To test or educate? *The School Administrator*, 6(63).

LaMaster, K. (1996). Go on-line: Get new ideas from newsgroups. *Strategies*, 9(5), 18–20.

Landers, D. (1983). Whatever happened to theory testing in sport psychology? *Journal of Sport Psychology*, 5(2), 135–151.

———. (1997). The influence of exercise on mental health. *President's Council on Physical Fitness and Sport Research Digest*, 2(12), 1–8.

Lapchick, R. (2005). *2004 racial and gender scorecard*. Orlando: Institute for Diversity and Ethics in Sport, University of Central Florida.

———. (2006). *Division IA conference leadership study*. Orlando: Institute for Diversity and Ethics in Sport, University of Central Florida.

———. (2007). *The buck stops here: Assessing diversity among campus and conference leaders for Division IA school in 2008*. Orlando: Institute for Diversity and Ethics in Sport, University of Central Florida.

Larson, R., & Verna, S. (1999). How children and adolescents spend time across the world: Work, play, and developmental opportunities. *Psychological Bulletin*, 125, 701–736.

Lauer. H. (2006). The new Americans: Defining ourselves through sports and fitness participation. American Sports Data Inc.

Launder, A. (2001) *Play practice: The games approach to teaching and coaching*. Champaign, IL: Human Kinetics.

Lawson, H. (1994). Toward healthy learners, schools, and communities. *Journal of Teacher Education*, 45(1), 62–70.

Lawson, H., & Placek, J. (1981). *Physical education in the secondary schools: Curricular alternatives*. Boston: Allyn & Bacon.

Lee, I.-M., & Paffenbarger, R., Jr. (1996). How much physical activity is optimal for health? Methodological considerations. *Research Quarterly for Exercise and Sport*, 67(2), 206–208.

Lee, M., & Bennett, B. (1985a). 1885–1900: A time of gymnastics and measurement. *Journal of Physical Education, Recreation, and Dance*, 56(4), 19–26.

———. (1985b). 1930–1945: A time for affiliation and research. *Journal of Physical Education, Recreation, and Dance*, 56(4), 43–51.

Leigh, D. (1994). Dance for social change. *Journal of Physical Education, Recreation, and Dance,* 65(5), 39–43.

Leonard, F., & Affleck, G. (1947). *A guide to the history of physical education*. Philadelphia: Lea & Febiger.

Leonard, G. (1974). *The ultimate athlete*. New York: Viking Press.

Levi, J., Segal, L., & Gadola, E. (2007). *F as in Fat: How obesity policies are failing in America*. Washington, DC: Trust for America's Health.

Levi, J., Segal, I., & Juliano, C. (2006). *F as in Fat: How obesity policies are failing in America*. Washington, DC: Trust for America's Health.

Levine, A., Wells, S., & Knopf, C. (1986, August 11). New rules of exercise. *U.S. News and World Report*, 52–56.

Lister, V. (1993, December 9). More opportunities open, but roadblocks still there. *USA Today*, p. 9C.

Litchfield, R., Muldoon, J., Welk, G., Hallihan, J., & Lane, T. (2005). Lighten up Iowa: An interdisciplinary, collaborative health promotion campaign. *Journal of Extension*, 43(2), 1–13.

Locke, L. (1992). Changing secondary school physical education. *Quest*, 44(3), 361–372.

Locke, L., & Massengale, J. (1978). Role conflict in teacher/coaches. *Research Quarterly*, 49(2), 162–174.

Logsdon, B., Barrett, K., Broer, M., McKee, R., & Ammongs, M. (1977). *Physical education for children: A focus on the teaching process*. Philadelphia: Lea & Febiger.

Lopez, M. (2006). Participation in sports and civic engagement. *Circle fact sheet*. College Park: The Center for Information and Research on Civic Learning and Engagement, School of Public Policy, University of Maryland.

Lounsbery, M., Gast, J., & Smith, N. (2005). The integrated curriculum of "Planned Approach to Healthier Schools," *Journal of Physical Education, Recreation, and Dance,* 76(3), 34–37.

Lowe, B. (1977). *The beauty of sport: A cross-disciplinary inquiry*. Englewood Cliffs, NJ: Prentice-Hall.

Loy, J. (1969). The nature of sport: A definitional effort. In J. Loy & G. Kenyon (Eds.), *Sport, culture and society* (pp. 23–32). New York: Macmillan.

Loy, J., & McElvogue, J. (1981). Racial segregation in American sport. In J. Loy, G. Kenyon, & B. McPherson (Eds.), *Sport, culture and society: A reader on the sociology of sport* (pp. 103–116). Philadelphia: Lea & Febiger.

Lucas, J., & Smith, R. (1978). *Saga of American sport.* Philadelphia: Lea & Febiger.

Macdonald, D., & Leitch, S. (1994). Praxis in PE: The senior physical education syllabus on trial. *New Zealand Journal of Physical Education, 27*(2), 17–21.

Maeda, J., & Murata, N. (2004). Collaborating with classroom teachers to increase daily physical activity: The GEAR program. *Journal of Physical Education, Recreation, and Dance, 75*(5), 42–46.

Maloney, L. (1984, August 13). Sports crazy Americans. *U.S. News & World Report,* 23.

Marmot, M. (1994). Social differentials within and between populations. *Daedalus, 123*(4), 197–216.

Martens, R. (1986). Youth sport in the USA. In M. Weiss & D. Gould (Eds.), *Sport for children and youths* (pp. 27–33). Champaign, IL: Human Kinetics.

Martin, T. (2003). More kids paying to play sports. *Lansing State Journal* (www.lsj.com).

Mathieu, M. (1999). The surgeon general's report on leisure services for older adults. *Journal of Physical Education, Recreation, and Dance, 70*(3), 28–31.

Matter, R., Nash, S., & Frogley, M. (2002). Interscholastic athletics for student-athletes with disabilities. *Palaestra, 18*(3), 32–38.

McCloy, C. H. (1936). How about some muscle? *Journal of Health and Physical Education, 3*(4), 22–24.

McCubbin J., & Zittel, L. (1991). PL 99–457: What the law is all about. *Journal of Physical Education, Recreation, and Dance, 62*(6), 35–37, 47.

McGinnis, J., Kanner, L., & DeGraw, C. (1991). Physical education's role in achieving national health objectives. *Research Quarterly for Exercise and Sport, 62*(2), 138–142.

McKenzie, T. (2007). The preparation of physical educators: A public health perspective. *Quest, 59*(4), 345–357.

McKenzie, T., & Kahan, D. (2008). Physical activity, public health, and elementary schools. *The Elementary School Journal, 108*(4), 171–180.

McKenzie, T., Nader, P., Strikmiller, P., Yang, M., Stone, E., Perry, C., Taylor, W., Epping, J., Feldman, H., Luepker, R., & Kelder, S. (1996). School physical education: Effect of the child and adolescent trial for cardiovascular health. *Preventive Medicine, 25*(4), 423–431.

McKenzie, T., & Sallis, J. (1996). Physical activity, fitness, and health-related physical education. In S. Silverman & C. Ennis (Eds.), *Student learning in physical education: Applying research to enhance learning* (pp. 223–246). Champaign: IL: Human Kinetics.

McLaughlin, J. (1988) . A stepchild comes of age. *Journal of Physical Education, Recreation, and Dance, 59*(9), 58–60.

McLean, J., Peterson, J., & Martin, W. (1988). *Recreation and leisure: The changing scene* (4th ed.). New York: Macmillan.

McMillin C., & Reffner, C. (1998). *Directory of College and University Coaching Education Programs.* Morgantown, WV: Fitness Information Technology.

McPherson, B. (1981). Past, present and future perspectives for research in sport sociology. In J. Loy, G. Kenyon, & B. McPherson (Eds.), *Sport, culture and society: A reader on the sociology of sport* (pp. 10–22) Philadelphia: Lea & Febiger.

Meadows, K. (2003, February 16). Parents have to play nice before kids can play sports. *Columbus Dispatch,* p. D1.

Mechikoff, R., & Estes, S. (2006). *A history and philosophy of sport and physical education: From ancient civilizations to the modern world* (5th ed.). Boston: McGraw-Hill.

Meich, R., Kumanyika, S., Stettler, N., Link, B., Phelan, J., & Chang, V. (2006). Trends in the association of poverty with overweight among U.S. adolescents. *Journal of the America Medical Association, 295*(20), 24–31.

Metheny, E. (1954). The third dimension in physical education. *Journal of Health, Physical Education and Recreation, 24*(3), 27.

———. (1970). The excellence of Patroclus. In H. Slusher & A. Lockhart (Eds.), *Anthology of contemporary readings: An introduction to physical education* (pp. 63–66). Dubuque, IA: Brown.

Micheli, L., Glassman, R., & Klein, M. (2000). The prevention of sports injuries in children. *Clinics in Sports Medicine, 19,* 821–832.

Mihalich, J. (1982). *Sports and athletics: Philosophy in action.* Totowa, NJ: Littlefield, Adams.

Miller, G., Lutz, R., Shim, J., Fredenburg, K., & Miller, J. (2005). Dismissals and perceptions of pressure in coaching in Texas high schools. *Journal of Physical Education, Recreation, and Dance, 76*(1), 29–33.

Miller, L., Stoldt, G., & Comfort, G. (2000) Sport management professions. In S. Hoffman & J. Harris (Eds.), *Intoduction to kinesiology* (pp. 525–552). Champaign, IL: Human Kinetics.

Mills, B. (1997). Opening the gymnasium to the World Wide Web. *Journal of Physical Education, Recreation, and Dance,* 68(8), 17–19.

Milverstedt, F. (1988). Are kids really so out of shape? *Athletic Business,* 12(1).

Mitchell, S., Oslin, J., & Griffin, L. (2006). *Teaching sports concepts and skills: A tactical games approach* (2nd ed.). Champaign, IL: Human Kinetics.

Mohr, D., Townsend, J., & Bulger, S. (2001). A pedagogical approach to sport education season planning. *Journal of Physical Education, Recreation, and Dance,* 72(9), 37–46.

Mokdad, A., Bowman, B., Ford, E., Vinicor, F., Marks, J., & Koplan, J. (2001). The continuing epidemics of obesity and diabetes in the United States. *JAMA,* 286(10), 1195–1120.

Molnar, A., Garcia, D., Boninger, E., & Merrill, B. (2006). *A national survey of the types and extent of the marketing of foods of minimal nutritional value in schools.* Commercialism in Education Research Unit, Arizona State University.

Monroe, J. (1995). Developing cultural awareness through play. *Journal of Physical Education, Recreation, and Dance,* 66(8), 24–27.

Moore, G. (1986). Elementary physical education: Involving outdoor adventure activities. *Journal of Physical Education, Recreation, and Dance,* 57(5), 61–63.

Morgan, W. J. (2007). *Ethics in sports.* Champaign, IL: Human Kinetics.

Morrow, J., & Gill, D. (Eds.) (1995). The academy papers: The role of physical activity in fitness and health. *Quest,* 47(3).

Motley, M., & Lavine, M. (2001). Century marathon: A race for equality in girls' and women's sports. *Journal of Physical Education, Recreation, and Dance,* 72(6), 56–59.

Mullan, M. (1986). Issues. *Journal of Physical Education, Recreation, and Dance,* 57(6), 18.

Nack, W., & Munson, L. (2000). Out of control *Sports Illustrated,* 93(4), 86–95.

NAGWS (National Association for Girls and Women in Sports). (2007). Title IX quick facts. www .aahperd.org/nagws.

Naisbitt, J. (1983). *Megatrends: Ten new directions transforming our lives.* New York: Warner Books.

NASPE (National Association for Sport and Physical Education). (1992). *Developmentally appropriate physical education practices for children.* Washington, DC: AAHPERD.

———. (1995). *National Standards for Athletic Coaches.* Washington, AAHPERD.

———. (1995a). *Moving into the future: National standards for physical education.* St. Louis: Mosby.

———. (1995b). *National standards for beginning physical education teachers.* Reston, VA: NASPE.

———. (1995c). *Parent's checklist for quality youth sport programs.* Reston, VA: NASPE.

———.(1999). *Bill of rights for young athletes.* Reston, VA: NASPE.

———. (2002). *2001 Shape of the Nation Report.* Reston, VA: American Alliance for Health, Physical Education, Recreation, and Dance.

———. (2006). *Shape of the nation report: State of physical education in the USA.* Reston, VA: AAHPERD.

———. (2006). *National standards for sport coaches,* (2nd ed.), Reston, VA: NASPE.

NASPE News. (1994, Summer). National summit on coaching standards, *NASPE News,* 39, 1, 9.

———. (1998, Winter). Shape of the Nation Report, *NASPE News,* 50 (1), 14.

———. (2001, Spring). Quality sports begin with quality coaches. *NASPE News,* 56(6), 1.

———. (2002, Spring). Standards developed for strength and conditioning professionals. *NASPE News.* 60, 6.

———. (2004a). *Physical activity for children: A statement of guidelines for children ages 5–12* (2nd ed.). Reston, VA: NASPE Publications.

———. (2004b). *Moving into the future: National standards for physical education* (2nd ed.). Reston, VA: NASPE Publications.

———. (2004c). *Standards for initial programs in physical education teacher education.* Reston, VA: NASPE Publications.

———. (2004d, Winter). Congratulations, national board certified teachers. *NASPE News,* 65, p. 8.

National Blueprint on Physical Activity among Adults Age 50 and Older (2000). Princeton, NJ: Robert Wood Johnson Foundation.

National Center for Health Statistics (2004). www.cdc .gov/nchs/about/major/nhis/released 200212/.

National Coalition for Promoting Physical Activity. (2002). A play for physical activity leadership, pp. 1–8. www.ncppa.org.

National Federation of State High School Athletic Associations. (2007). *2006–07 Athletics participation study.* www.nfhs.org.

NCPERID (National Consortium for Physical Education and Recreation for Individuals with Disabilities). (1995). *Adapted physical education national standards.* Champaign, IL: Human Kinetics.

Nevins, A. (1962). *The gateway to history.* Garden City, NY: Anchor Books.

Newell, K. (1990a). Physical education in higher education: Chaos out of order. *Quest, 42*(3), 227–242.

———. (1990b). Kinesiology: The label for the study of physical activity in higher education. *Quest, 42*(3), 269–278.

News. (2001). Active seniors less susceptible to depression. *Journal of Physical Education, Recreation, and Dance, 72*(1), 9–10.

———. (2002). Texas reinstates physical education. *Journal of Physical Education, Recreation, and Dance, 73*(5), 5.

Newsletter. (1996). NIH panel links activity to improved cardiovascular health. Washington, DC: President's Council on Physical Fitness and Sports, 96(1), 6.

NFHS (National Federation of High Schools). (2007). Available courses. www.nfhs.learn.com.

Novak, M. (1976). *The joy of sports.* New York: Basic Books.

Noyes, B. (1996). The program. *Athletic Business, 20*(4), 29–35.

NSRE (National Survey on Recreation and the Environment). (2000). *Summary report #1 from the National Survey on Recreation and the Environment: Outdoor recreation participation in the United States.* U.S.D.A. Forest Service & N.O.A.A., 1–9.

———. (2007). National survey on recreation and the environment. U.S. Department of Agriculture, Washington, D.C.

O'Connor, A., & Macdonald, D. (2002). Up close and personal on physical education teachers' identity: Is conflict an issue? *Sport, Education and Society, 7*(1), 37–54.

Ogden, C., Flegal, K., Caroll, M., & Johnson, C. (2002). Prevalence and trends among overweight U.S. children and adolescents, 1999–2000. *Journal of the American Medical Association, 288*(14), 1728–1732.

Ohio Department of Health. (2006). *A report on the body mass index of Ohio's third graders, 2004–2005.* Columbus: Division of Family and Community Health Services, School and Adolescent Health Section.

Ohio State University. (2008). "Summer 2008 Fitness Class Descriptions." http://recsports.osu.edu/fitness_programs.asp.

Olafson, L. (2002). "I hate Phys. Ed.": Adolescent girls talk about physical education. *The Physical Educator, 59,* 67–74.

Olsen, E. (1986). Your number's up. *The Runner, 8*(8), 40–47.

Olson, J. (1995). Sports participation: Efforts to involve minorities, females prove fruitful in Madison schools. *Interscholastic Athletic Administration, 22*(2), 4–5.

Orlick, T. (1977). Cooperative games. *Journal of Physical Education, Recreation, and Dance, 48*(7), 33–36.

———. (1986). Evolution in children's sport. In M. Weiss & D. Gould (Eds.), *Sport for children and youths* (pp. 169–178). Champaign, IL: Human Kinetics.

O'Sullivan, M., Siedentop, D., & Tannehill, D. (1994). Breaking out: Codependency of high school physical education, *Journal of Teaching in Physical Education, 13,* 421–428.

Pacific Mutual Insurance Co. (1978). *Health maintenance* (Survey conducted by Louis Harris and Associates, Inc.). San Francisco: Author.

Page, C. (1969). Reaction to Stone. In G. Kenyon (Ed.), *Aspects of contemporary sport sociology* (pp. 17–19). Chicago: Athletic Institute.

Pangrazi, R. (2003). Physical education K–12: "All for one and one for all." *Quest, 55*(2), 105–117.

Pangrazi, R., Corbin, C., & Welk, G. (1996). Physical activity for children and youth. *Journal of Physical Education, Recreation, and Dance, 67*(4), 38–43.

Papas, M., Alberg, A., Weing, R., Helzlsouer, K., Gary, T., & Klassen, A. (2007). The built environment and obesity. *Epidemiologic Reviews, 29*(1), 129–143.

Partlow, K. (1992). American Coaching Effectiveness Program (ACEP): Educating America's coaches. *Journal of Physical Education, Recreation, and Dance, 63*(7), 36–39.

Partridge, D., & Franks, I. (1996). Analyzing and modifying coaching behaviors by means of computer assisted observation. *The Physical Educator, 53*(1), 8–23.

Passer, M. (1986). A psychological perspective. In M. Weiss & D. Gould (Eds.), *Sport for children and youths* (pp. 55–58). Champaign, IL: Human Kinetics.

Pastore, D. (1994). Strategies for retaining female high school head coaches: A survey of administrators and coaches. *Journal of Sport and Social Issues, 17*(2).

Pate, R. (1994). Fitness testing: Current approaches and purposes in physical education. In R. Pate & D. Hohn (Eds.), *Health and Fitness through Physical Education* (pp. 119–128). Champaign, IL: Human Kinetics.

————. (1995). Physical activity and health: Dose–response issues. *Research Quarterly for Exercise and Sport,* 66(4), 313–317.

Pate, R., Davis, M., Robinson, T., Stone, E., McKenzie, T., & Young, J. (2006). Promoting physical activity in children and youth. *Circulation American Heart Association,* 114, 1214–1224.

Pate, R., & Hohn, D. (1994). A contemporary mission for physical education. In R. Pate & D. Hohn (Eds.), *Health and fitness through physical education* (pp. 1–8). Champaign, IL: Human Kinetics.

Pate, R., Trost, S., Dowda, M., Ott. A., Ward, D., Saunders, R., & Felton, G. (1999). Tracking of physical activity, physical inactivity, and health related physical fitness in rural youth. *Pediatric Exercise Science,* 11, 364–376.

Pate, R., Trost, S., Levin, S., & Dowda, M. (2000). Sports participation and health-related behaviors. *Archives of Pediatric Adolescent Medicine,* 154, September, 904–911.

Paul, P., & Cartledge, G. (1996). Inclusive schools—the continuing debate. *Theory into Practice,* 35(1), 2–3.

PCPFS Research Digests. (1999). Physical activity and fitness for persons with disabilities: A paradigm shift. President's Council on Physical Fitness and Sport, March.

Physical Activity Today. (1996). Exercise shown to lower breast cancer risk! *Physical Activity Today,* 2(1), 1.

Physical Activity Today. (1999). Elderly walkers miles ahead of inactive peers. *Physical Activity Today,* 5(3), 1.

Pierce, P., & Herman, S. (2004). Obtaining, maintaining, and advancing your fitness certification. *Journal of Physical Education, Recreation, and Dance,* 75(7), 50–54.

Pifer, S. (1987). Secondary physical education: A new design. *Journal of Physical Education, Recreation, and Dance,* 58(6), 50–51.

Placek, J. (1983). Concepts of success in teaching: Busy, happy and good? In T. Templin & J. Olson (Eds.), *Teaching in physical education* (pp. 46–56). Champaign, IL: Human Kinetics.

————. (1996). Integration as a curriculum model in physical education: Possibilities and problems. In S. Silverman & C. Ennis (Eds.), *Student learning in physical education: Applying research to enhance learning* (pp. 287–312). Champaign, IL: Human Kinetics.

Policy Study Associates. (2006). *Everyone plays!: A review of research on the integration of sports and physical activity into out-of-school time programs.* Washington, DC: Policy Study Associates.

Pollock, M., & Vincent, K. (1996). Resistance training for health. *President's Council on Physical Fitness and Sports Research Digest,* 1–6.

Portman, P. (1995). Who is having fun in physical education classes? Experiences of sixth-grade students in elementary and middle schools. *Journal of Teaching in Physical Education,* 14, 445–453.

Posey, E. (1988). Discipline-based arts education: Developing a dance curriculum. *Journal of Physical Education, Recreation, and Dance,* 59(9), 61–64.

Powell, J., & Barber-Foss, K. (1999). Injury patterns in selected high school sports: A review of the 1995–1997 seasons. *Journal of Athletic Training,* 34(3), 277–284.

President's Council on Physical Fitness and Sport. (1973, May). National adult physical fitness survey. *Newsletter,* 1–27.

Pritchard, R., & Potter, G. (Eds.) (1990). *Fitness, Inc.: A guide to corporate health and wellness programs.* Homewood, IL: Dow-Jones-Irwin.

Prusak, K., Treasure, D., Darst, P., & Pangrazi, R. (2004). The effects of choice on the motivation of adolescent girls in physical education. *Journal of Teaching in Physical Education,* 23, 19–29.

Quain, R. (1990). Community based sport. In J. Parks & B. Zanger (Eds.), *Sport and fitness management* (pp. 57–62). Champaign, IL: Human Kinetics.

Rankin, J. (1989). Athletic trainer education: New directions. *Journal of Physical Education, Recreation, and Dance,* 60(6), 68–71.

Rankinen, T., & Bouchard, C. (2002). Dose–response issues concerning the relations between regular physical activity and health. *Research Digest,* 3(18), 1–6.

Rarick, L. (1967). The domain of physical education as a discipline. *Quest,* 9, 50–59.

Rauschenbach, J. (1992). Case studies of elementary physical education specialists. Unpublished doctoral dissertation, Ohio State University, Columbus.

Richmond, J. (1979). *Healthy people: The surgeon general's report on health promotion and disease prevention* (DHEW Publication No. 79–55071). Washington, DC: U.S. Government Printing Office.

Rider, R., & Johnson, D. (1986). Effects of Florida's personal fitness course on cognitive, attitudinal, and physical fitness measures of secondary school students: A pilot study. *Perceptual and Motor Skills, 62*(2), 548–550.

Rink, J., & Mitchell, M. (2003). Introduction: State level assessment in physical education: The South Carolina experience. *Journal of Teaching in Physical Education, 22*(5), 471–472.

Rink, J., & Williams, J., (2003). Developing and implementing a state assessment program. *Journal of Teaching in Physical Education, 22,* 474–493.

Robert Wood Johnson Foundation. (2001). *National blueprint on physical activity among adults age 50 and older.* Princeton, NJ: Robert Wood Johnson Foundation.

Robinson, J., & Godbey, G. (1997). *Time for life: The surprising ways Americans use their time.* University Park, PA: Penn State Press.

Rosenbaum, M., & Leibel, R. (1989). Obesity in childhood. *Pediatric Review, 11*(2), 43–55.

Ross, J., Delpy, L., Christenson, G., Gold, R., & Damberg, C. (1987). Study procedures and quality control. *Journal of Physical Education, Recreation, and Dance, 58*(9), 57–62.

Ross, J., & Pate, R. (1987). A summary of findings. *Journal of Physical Education, Recreation, and Dance, 58*(9), 51–56.

Rowe, P. J., & Miller, L. (1991). Treating high school sports injuries: Are coaches/trainers competent? *Journal of Physical Education, Recreation, and Dance, 62*(1), 49–54.

Sack, A. (1977). Big time college football: Whose free ride? *Quest, 27,* 87–96.

Sage, G. (1979). The current status and trends of sport sociology. In M. Krotee (Ed.), *The dimensions of sport sociology.* West Point, NY: Leisure Press.

———. (1984). *Motor learning and control: A neuropsychological approach.* Dubuque, IA: Brown.

———. (1987). Pursuit of knowledge in sociology of sport: Issues and prospects. *Quest, 39*(3), 255–281.

———. (1991). Beyond enhancing performance in sport: Toward empowerment and transformation. *The Academy Papers, 25,* 85–95.

Sallis, J. (1994). Determinants of physical activity behavior in children. In R. Pate & D. Hohn (Eds.), *Health and fitness through physical education* (pp. 31–44). Champaign, IL: Human Kinetics.

Sallis, J., & Kerr, J. (2006). Physical activity and the built environment. *Research Digest, 7*(4), 1–6.

Sallis, J., & McKenzie, T. (1991). Physical education's role in public health. *Research Quarterly for Exercise and Sport, 62,* 124–137.

———. (1993). Physical education's role in public health. *Research Quarterly for Exercise and Sport, 62*(2), 124–137.

Sallis, J., McKenzie, T., Kolody, B., Lewis, M., Marshall, S., & Rosengard, P. (1999). Effects of health-related physical education on academic achievement: Project SPARK. *Research Quarterly for Exercise and Sport, 70,* 127–134.

Samman, P. (1998). *Active youth: Ideas for implementing the CDC physical activity promotion guidelines.* Champaign: IL: Human Kinetics.

Scantling, E., & Lackey, D. (2005). Coaches under pressure: Four decades of studies. *Journal of Physical Education, Recreation, and Dance, 76*(1), 25–28.

Schafer, S. (1987). Sport needs you. The Colorado model. *Journal of Physical Education, Recreation, and Dance, 58*(2), 44–47.

Schiller, F. (1910). Letters upon the aesthetic education of man. In C. Eliot (Ed.), *The Harvard Classics* (Vol. 32). New York: P. F. Collier & Son.

Schmid, S. (1994a). Campus showpiece. *Athletic Business, 18*(1), 47–50.

———. (1994b). Community asset. *Athletic Business, 18*(3), 20.

Schmidt, R. (1988). *Motor control and learning: A behavioral emphasis* (2nd ed.). Champaign, IL: Human Kinetics.

Schor, J. (1991). *The overworked American: The unexpected decline of leisure.* New York: Basic Books.

Schwartz, M., & Brownell, K. (2007). Actions necessary to prevent childhood obesity: Creating the climate for change. *Journal of Law, Medicine & Ethics, 35*(1), 78–89.

Scott D. (2000). Tic, toc, the game is locked and nobody else can play. *Journal of Leisure Research, 32,* 133–137.

Scott, J. (1974). Sport and the radical chic. In G. McGlynn (Ed.), *Issues in physical education and sport* (pp. 155–162). Palo Alto, CA: National Press.

Scraton, S. (1990). *Shaping up to womanhood: Gender and girls' physical education.* Buckingham, England: Open University Press.

Seefeldt, V., & Milligan, M. (1992). Program for Athletic Coaches Education (PACE): Educating America's public and private school coaches. *Journal of Physical Education, Recreation, and Dance, 63*(7), 46–49.

Senate Report 108–345. (2006). *Wellness initiative.* Departments of Labor, Health and Human Services and Education, and Related Agencies, Appropriation Bill 2005.

Seymour, S. (2005, January 9). Schools sharing their exercise facilities. *Columbus Dispatch,* B6.

Shea, C., Shebilske, W., & Worchel, S. (1993). *Motor learning and control.* Englewood Cliffs, NJ: Prentice-Hall.

Sheed, W. (1995, Winter). Why sports matter. *Wilson Quarterly,* 11–25.

Sheehan, G. (1982). Viewpoint. *Runner's World,* 27(7), 14.

Shephard, R. (1988). Exercise adherence in corporate settings: Personal traits and program barriers. In R. Dishman (Ed.), *Exercise adherence* (pp. 305–319). Champaign, IL: Human Kinetics.

———. (1995). Physical activity, health, and well-being at different life stages. *Research Quarterly for Exercise and Sport,* 66(4), 298–302.

———. (1996). Habitual physical activity and quality of life. *Quest,* 48(3), 354–365.

———. (1999, February). Do work-site exercise and health programs work? *The Physician and Sportsmedicine Online.*

Sherman, N. (2001). Tracking the long-term benefits of physical education. *Journal of Physical Education, Recreation, and Dance,* 72(3), 5.

Sherrill, C. (1993). *Adapted physical activity, recreation, and sport* (4th ed.), Dubuque, IA: Brown & Benchmark.

———. (2004). A celebration of the history of Adapted Physical Education. *Palaestra,* 20(1), 20–24, 45–47.

Siedentop, D. (1972). *Physical education: Introductory analysis.* Dubuque, IA: Brown.

———. (1976). *Physical education: Introductory analysis* (2nd ed.). Dubuque, IA: Brown.

———. (1980). *Physical education: Introductory analysis* (3rd ed.). Dubuque, IA: Brown.

———. (1981, August). Must competition be a zero-sum game? *The School Administrator,* 38, 11.

———. (1987). High school physical education: Still an endangered species. *Journal of Physical Education, Recreation, and Dance,* 58(2), 24–25.

———. (1989). The elementary specialist study. *Journal of Teaching in Physical Education,* 8(3), 187–270.

———. (1990). Commentary: The world according to Newell. *Quest,* 42(3), 315–322.

———. (1991). *Developing teaching skills in physical education* (3rd ed.). Mountain View, CA: Mayfield.

———. (1992). Thinking differently about secondary physical education. *Journal of Physical Education, Recreation, and Dance,* 63(7), 69–73.

———. (1994). *Sport education: Quality PE through positive sport experiences.* Champaign, IL: Human Kinetics.

———. (1996a). Physical education and education reform: The case for sport education. In S. Silverman & C. Ennis (Eds.), *Student learning in physical education: Applying research to enhance instruction* (pp. 247–268). Champaign, IL: Human Kinetics.

———. (1996b). Sport education: A curricular success story. *Teaching Secondary Physical Education,* 2(3), 8–9.

———. (1996c). Valuing the physically active life: Contemporary and future directions. *Quest,* 48(3), 266–274.

———. (1998). What is sport education and how does it work? *Journal of Physical Education, Recreation, and Dance,* 69(4), 18–20.

———. (2007). *The Ohio Project: Progress in preventing childhood/youth obesity: How do we measure up?* Columbus: The Ohio Collaborative: Research and Policy for Schools, Children, and Families, College of Education and Human Ecology, Ohio State University.

Siedentop, D., Hastie, P., & van der Mars, H. (2004). *The complete guide to sport education.* Champaign, IL: Human Kinetics.

Siedentop, D., Herkowitz, J., & Rink, J. (1984). *Elementary physical education methods.* Englewood Cliffs, NJ: Prentice-Hall.

Siedentop, D., & Locke, L. (1997). Making a difference for physical education: What professors and practitioners must build together. *Journal of Physical Education, Recreation, and Dance.* 68(4), 25–33.

Siedentop, D., Mand, C., & Taggart, A. (1986). *Physical education: Teaching and curriculum strategies for grades 5–12.* Palo Alto, CA: Mayfield.

Siedentop, D., & O'Sullivan, M. (1992). Preface. *Quest,* 44(3), 285–286.

Siedentop, D., & Siedentop, B. (1985). Daily fitness in Australia. *Journal of Physical Education, Recreation, and Dance,* 56(2), 41–43.

Siedentop, D., & Tannehill, D. (2000). *Developing teaching skills in physical education* (4th ed.). Mountain View, CA: Mayfield.

Simons-Morton, B. (1994). Implementing health-related physical education. In R. Pate & D. Hohn (Eds.). *Health and fitness through physical education* (pp. 137–146). Champaign, IL: Human Kinetics.

Simpson, K. (2000). Biomechanics of physical activity. In S. Hoffman & J. Harris (Eds.), *Introduction to kinesiology* (pp. 353–380). Champaign, IL: Human Kinetics.

Sinelnikov, O., Hastie, P., Cole, A., & Schneulle, D. (2005). Bicycle safety: Sport education style. *Journal of Physical Education, Recreation, and Dance,* 76(4), 24–29.

Singer, R. (Ed.). (1976). *Physical education: Foundations.* New York: Holt, Rinehart and Winston.

Sisley, B., & Capel, S. (1986). High school coaching: Filled with gender differences. *Journal of Physical Education, Recreation, and Dance,* 57(3), 39–44.

Sisley, B., & Weise, D. (1987). Current status: Requirements for interscholastic coaches. *Journal of Physical Education, Recreation, and Dance,* 58(7), 73–85.

Skidelsky, R. (1969). *English progressive schools.* Middlesex, England: Penguin Books.

Skinner, J. (1988). The fitness industry. *The Academy Papers,* 21, 67–72.

Slava, S., Laurie, D., & Corbin, C. (1984). The long-term effects of a conceptual physical education program. *Research Quarterly for Exercise and Sport,* 55(2), 161–165.

Smith, C. (1992a, August 16). Equality's hurdles. *New York Times,* Sports Pages, p. 27.

———. (1992b, August 16). Too few changes since Campanis. *New York Times,* Sports Pages, pp. 27–28.

Smith, L. (Ed.). (1970). *Psychology of motor learning.* Chicago: Athletic Institute.

Smith, R., Smoll, F., & Curtis, B. (1978). Coaching behaviors in Little League baseball. In F. Smoll & R. Smith (Eds.), *Psychological perspectives in youth sports* (pp. 173–201). Washington, DC: Hemisphere.

Smoll, F. (1986). Stress reduction strategies in youth sport. In M. Weiss & D. Gould (Eds.), *Sport for children and youths* (pp. 127–136). Champaign, IL: Human Kinetics.

Spain, C., & Franks, D. (2001). Healthy people 2010: Physical activity and fitness. *Research Digest,* 3(13), 1–12. President's Council on Physical Fitness and Sports.

Sparkes, A. (1991). Alternative visions of health-related fitness: An exploration of problem-setting and its consequences. In N. Armstrong & A. Sparkes (Eds.), *Issues in physical education* (pp. 204–227). London: Caswell Educational Limited.

Spears, B., & Swanson, R. (1978). *History of sport and physical activity in the United States.* Dubuque, IA: Brown.

Sporting Goods Manufacturing Association. (2006). *Youth sport participation trends.* www.sgma.com.

Stein, J. (2004). Adapted physical activity, the golden years. *Palaestra,* 20(1), 26–29, 56.

Steller, J. (1994). The physical education performance troupe: A skill and fitness approach. In R. Pate & D. Hohn (Eds.). *Health and fitness through physical education* (pp. 191–196). Champaign, IL: Human Kinetics.

Stevens, J. (1984). Special Olympics. *Journal of Physical Education, Recreation, and Dance,* 55(2), 42–43.

Stewart, C., & Sweet, L. (1992). Professional preparation of high school coaches: The problem continues. *Journal of Physical Education, Recreation, and Dance,* 63(6), 75–79.

Stourowsky, E. (1996). Blaming the victim: Resistance in the battle over gender equity in intercollegiate athletics. *Journal of Sport and Social Issues,* 20(2).

Strauss, R., & Pollock H. (2001). Epidemic increase in childhood overweight, 1986–1998. *JAMA,* 286(22), 2845–2848.

Strecker, L., & Young, J. (2007). Today's coaching. *Update Plus,* September–October, 26–27.

Strong, W., Malina, R., Cameron, J., Bumkie, R., Daniels, S., Dishman, R., Gutin, B., Hergenroeder, A., Must, A., Nixon, P., Parvinik, J., Rowland, T., Trost, S., & Trudeau, F. (2005). Evidence based physical activity for school-age youth. *Journal of Pediatrics,* 146(6), 732–737.

Stroot, S., Carpenter, M., & Eisnaugle, K. (1991). Focus of physical education: Academic and physical excellence at Westgate Alternative School. *Journal of Physical Education, Recreation, and Dance,* 62(7), 49–53.

Stroot, S., Collier, C., O'Sullivan, M., & England, K. (1994). Hoops and hurdles: Workplace conditions in secondary physical education. *Journal of Teaching in Physical Education,* 13, 342–360.

Stroot, S., Faucette, N., & Schwager, S. (1993). In the beginning: The induction of physical educators, *Journal of Teaching Physical Education,* 12(4), 375–385.

Struna, N. (1991). Further reactions to Newell: Chaos is wonderful! *Quest,* 43(2), 230–235.

Sui, X., LaMonte, M., & Blair, S. N. (2007). Cardiorespiratory fitness as a predictor of nonfatal cardiovascular events in asymptomatic women and men. *American Journal of Epidemiology,* 165(12), 1413–1423.

Sui, X., LaMonte, M., Laditka, J., Hardin, J., Chase, N., Hooker, J., & Blair, G. (2008). Cardiorespiratory fitness and a diposity as mortality predictors in older adults. *JAMA*, 298(21) 2507–2516.

Suits, B. (1976). What is a game? *Philosophy of Science*, 34, 148–156.

Sutton, A. (2000, May 19). Parents out of control *Chicago Tribune*, Internet Edition, www.chicagosports.com.

Sutton, W. (1984). Family involvement in youth sports: An examination of the YMCA Y-winners philosophy. *Journal of Physical Education, Recreation, and Dance*, 55(8), 59–60.

Sweeney, J., Tannehill, D., & Teeters, L. (1992). Team up for fitness. *Strategies*, 5(6), 20–23.

Swift, E. M. (1991). Why Johnny can't play. *Sports Illustrated*, 60–72.

Taggart, A., Taggart, J., & Siedentop, D. (1986). Effects of a home-based activity program. *Behavior Modification*, 10(4), 41–52.

Taylor, J., & Chiogioji, E. (1987). Implications of educational reform on high school programs. *Journal of Physical Education, Recreation, and Dance*, 58(2), 22–23.

Teague, M., & Mobily, K. (1983). Rustproofing people: Corporate recreation programs in perspective. *Journal of Physical Education, Recreation, and Dance*, 54(8), 42–44.

Templin, T., Sparkes, A., Grant, B., & Schemmp, P. (1994). Matching the self: The paradoxical case and life history of a late career teacher/coach, *Journal of Teaching in Physical Education*, 13, 274–294.

Thomas, J. (1977). *Youth sports guide*. Reston, VA: AAHPERD.

Thomas, J., & Thomas, K. (2000). Motor behavior. In S. Hoffman & J. Harris (Eds.), *Introduction to kinesiology* (pp. 243–281). Champaign, IL: Human Kinetics.

Thorpe, R., Bunker, D., & Almond, L. (Ed.). (1986). *Rethinking games teaching*. London: Esmonde.

Timmermans, H., & Martin, M. (1987). Top ten potentially dangerous exercises. *Journal of Physical Education, Recreation, and Dance*, 58(6), 29–31.

Tinning, R. (1985). Physical education and the cult of slenderness. *ACHPER National Journal*, 1(7), 10–13.

———. (1990). *Ideology and physical education*. Geelong, Australia: Deaking University.

Toufexis, A. (1986, July 21). Putting on the Ritz at the Y. *Time*, 65.

Treanor, L., Graber, K., Housner, L., & Wiegand, R. (1998). Middle school students' perceptions of coeducational and same-sex physical education classes. *Journal of Teaching in Physical Education*, 18, 43–56.

Treasure, D. (2007). Interscholastic athletics, coach certification and professional development: Current status and next steps. *The State Education Standard*, 8(1), 32–34.

Trembal, M., Barnes, J., Copeland, J., & Esliger, D. (2005). Conquering childhood inactivity: Is the answer in the past? *Medicine and Science in Sports and Exercise*, http://www.acsm-msse.org.

Trudeau, F., Laurencelle, L., Tremblay, J., Rajic, M., & Shephard, R. (1998). A long-term follow-up of participants in the Trois-Rivieres semi-longitudinal study of growth and development. *Pediatric Exercise Science*, 10, 366–377.

Trust for America's Health (2004, October). Issue Report: F As in Fat: How obesity policies are failing in America. www.healthyamericans.org.

Tucker Center for Research on Girls & Women in Sport. (2007). *Developing physically active girls: An evidence-based multidisciplinary approach*. University of Minnesota, Minneapolis, MN.

Turner, B. (1995). No more ifs, ands, or buts. *Teaching High School Physical Education*, 1(4), 11.

Turner, L. (2005, March 17). Obesity will cut U.S. life expectancy, researcher says. *Columbus Dispatch*, A5.

Ulrich, C. (1976). A ball of gold. In C. Ulrich (Ed.), *To seek and find* (pp. 150–160). Washington, DC: AAHPERD.

Update. (1995, July/September), AAHPERD, ACSM, AHA collaborate to launch national coalition for promoting physical activity. *American Alliance for Health, Physical Education, Recreation, and Dance*, 1.

USA Today. (1988, November 11). Anabolic steroids. *USA Today*, p. 1C.

U.S. Census Bureau. (2000). *Statistical abstract of the United States*. Washington, DC.

U.S. Congress. (2004). Child nutrition act (42 U.S.C 1751).

U.S. Congress Senate Report 108–345. (2006). Wellness initiative. Departments of Labor, Health and Human Services and Education, and Related Agencies, Appropriation Bill 2005.

U.S. Department of Health and Human Services. (1996). *Physical activity and health: A report of the surgeon general*. Atlanta: U.S. Department of Health and Human Services, Centers for Disease Control and Prevention, National Center for Chronic Disease Prevention and Health Promotion.

————. (2000). *Healthy People 2010: Physical Activity and Fitness.* Washington, DC: Government Printing Office.

————. (2000). *Promoting better health for young people through physical activity and sports,* Washington, DC: Government Printing Office.

————. (2002). *Physical activity fundamental to preventing disease.* Washington, DC: U.S. Department of Health and Human Services, Government Printing Office.

————. (2006). *Overweight and physical activity among children: A portrait of the states.* Health Resources and Services Administration.

U.S. Public Health Service. (1991). *Healthy people 2000: National health promotion and disease objectives* (DHHS Publication No. [PHS] 91–50212). Washington, DC: Government Printing Office.

U.S. Public Law 93-112. (1973). *Rehabilitation Act.*

Veal, M., Campbell, M., Johnson, D. & McKethan, R. (2002). The North Carolina PEPSE Project. *Journal of Physical Education, Recreation, and Dance,* 73(4), 19–23.

Vernon, J. (1980). Effects of vaulter and pole parameters on performance. In J. Cooper & B. Haven (Eds.), *Proceedings of the Biomechanics Symposium.* Indianapolis: Indiana State Board of Health.

Vertinsky, P. (1991). Science, social science, and the "hunger for wonders" in physical education: Moving toward a future healthy society. *The Academy Papers,* 24, 70–88.

————. (1992). Reclaiming space, revisioning the body: The quest for gender-sensitive physical education. *Quest,* 44(3), 373–397.

Vickers, J. (1992). While Rome burns: Meeting the challenge of the second wave of the reform movement in education. *Journal of Physical Education, Recreation, and Dance,* 63(7), 80–87.

Villeneuve, K., Weeks, D., & Schwied, M. (1983). Employee fitness: The bottom line. *Journal of Physical Education, Recreation, and Dance,* 54(8), 35–36.

Virgilio, S. (1996). A home, school, and community model for promoting healthy lifestyles. *Teaching Elementary Physical Education,* 7(1), 4–7.

Virgilio, S., & Berenson, G. (1988). SuperKids–SuperFit: A comprehensive fitness intervention model for elementary schools. *Journal of Physical Education, Recreation, and Dance,* 59(8), 19–25.

Walker, H. (1993). Youth sports: Parental concerns. *Physical Educator,* 50, 104–112.

Wallhead, T., & O'Sullivan, M. (2005). Sport Education: physical education for the new millennium? *Physical Education and Sport Pedagogy,* 10(2), 181–210.

Wang, Y., & Beydoun, M. (2007). The obesity epidemic in the Unites States—gender, age, socioeconomic, racial/ethnic, and geographic characteristics: A systematic review and meta-regression analysis. *Epidemiologic Reviews,* 1(29), 6–28.

Ward, D., Saunders, R., & Pate, R. (2007). *Physical activity interventions in children and adolescents.* Champaign, IL: Human Kinetics.

Weight-control Information Network. (2006). *Understanding adult obesity.* U.S. Department of Health and Human Services, National Institutes of Health.

Weight-control Information Network. (2007). *Statistics related to overweight and obesity.* U.S. Department of Health and Human Services, National Institutes of Health.

————. (2007). Do you know the health risks of being overweight? U.S. Department of Health and Human Services.

Weigle, S. (1994). A walking program in your school? Practice tips to make it work. In R. Pate & D. Hohn (Eds.). *Health and fitness through physical education* (pp. 201–204). Champaign, IL: Human Kinetics.

Weinberg, R., & Williams, J. (2001). Integrating and implementing a psychological skills training program. In J. Williams (Ed.), *Applied sport psychology* (4th ed., pp. 347–377). Mountain View, CA: Mayfield.

Weiss, M. (2000). Motivating kids in physical activity. *Research Digest,* 3(11), 1–8. President's Council on Physical Fitness and Sports.

Weiss, P. (1969). *Sport: A philosophic inquiry.* Carbondale: Southern Illinois Press.

Wells, C. (1996). Physical activity and women's health. *Physical Activity and Fitness Research Digest,* 2(5), 1–6.

Wessel, J., & Zittel, L. (1995). *Smart Start: A preschool movement curriculum for children of all abilities.* Austin, TX: PRO-ED.

Westcott, W. (1982). *Strength fitness.* Boston: Allyn & Bacon.

————. (1992). High school physical education: A fitness professional's perspective. *Quest,* 44(3), 342–351.

————. (1993). *Be strong: Strength training for muscular fitness for men and women.* Dubuque, IA: Brown & Benchmark.

Westcott, W., & Baechle, T. (1998). Strength training past 50. Champaign, IL: Human Kinetics.

Weston, A. (1962). *The making of American physical education*. New York: Appleton-Century-Crofts.

White, E., & Sheets, C. (2001). If you let them play, they will. *Journal of Physical Education, Recreation, and Dance*, 72(4), 27–28, 33.

Whitehead, J. (1994). Enhancing fitness and activity motivation in children. In R. Pate & D. Hohn (Eds.), *Health and fitness through physical education* (pp. 81–90). Champaign, IL: Human Kinetics.

Wier, T. (2004, December 16). New PE objective: Get kids in shape. *USA Today*, pp. 1, 4A.

Wilberg, R. (1975). The direction and definition of a field. In *Trabajos científicos* (Vol. 3). Madrid: Instituto Nacional de Education Fisica.

Wilkinson, C., Hillier, R., & Harrison, J. (1998). Improving the computer literacy of preservice teachers. *Journal of Physical Education, Recreation, and Dance*. 69(5), 10–13.

Wilkinson, R. (1994). The epidemiological transition: From material scarcity to social disadvantage? *Daedalus*, 123(4), 61–78.

Wilkinson, W., Eddy, N., MacFadden, G., & Burgess, B. (2002). *Increasing physical activity through community design: A guide for public health practitioners*. Washington, DC: National Center for Bicycling and Walking.

Williams, J., & Straub, W. (2001). Sport psychology: Past, present, future. In J. Williams (Ed.), *Applied sport psychology* (4th ed., pp. 1–12). Mountain View, CA: Mayfield.

Williams, J. F. (1930). Education through the physical. *Journal of Higher Education*, 1, 279–282.

Wilson, W. (1977). Social discontent and the growth of wilderness sport in America: 1965–1974. *Quest*, 27, 54–60.

Witt, P., & Baker, D. (1997). Developing after-school programs for youth in high risk environments. *Journal of Physical Education, Recreation, and Dance*, 68(9), 18–20.

Women's Sport Foundation. (2006). Report card on Olympic and Paralympic Winter Games. www.womenssportsfoundation.org.

———. (2007). Women in intercollegiate sport: A twenty-nine year update: 1977–2006. www.webpages.charter.net/womeninsport.

Wrisberg, C. (1996). Quality of life for male and female athletes. *Quest*, 48(3), 392–408.

Zeigler, E. (1962). A history of professional preparation for physical education (1861–1961). In *Professional preparation in health education, physical education, and recreation education* (pp. 116–133). Washington DC: AAHPERD.

———. (1979). *A history of physical education and sport*. Englewood Cliffs, NJ: Prentice-Hall.

Credits

PHOTO CREDITS

Chapter 1: p. 9 (left) © BananaStock/Alamy; p. 9 (right), © Royalty-Free/CORBIS; p. 10. © Design Pics/PunchStock; p. 11, © Sam Forencich; p. 13, © Ohio State University; P. 15, © Digital Vision/Getty Images; p. 16, © Ohio State University. *Chapter 2:* p. 27, © Ohio State University Archives; p. 31 (left), © Ohio State University Archives; p. 31 (right), © Ohio State University Archives; p. 34, Photograph by Katherine Elizabeth McClellan, Smith College Archives; p. 35, © Ohio State University Archives; p. 38, © Bettman/CORBIS; p. 41, © Ohio State University Archives; p. 47, © BananaStock/PunchStock; p. 50, © PhotoDisc; p. 51, © Ohio State University. *Chapter 3:* p. 62, © PhotoDisc; p. 64, © Digital Vision; p. 67, © Sam Forencich; p. 71, © Daryl Siedentop; p. 73, © PhotoDisc. *Chapter 4:* p. 79, © Royalty-Free/Corbis; p. 83, © Suburban News Publications; p. 88, © PhotoDisc; p. 93, © PhotoDisc; p. 94, © Royalty-Free/CORBIS; p. 95, © PhotoDisc. *Chapter 5:* p. 100 (left), © Ohio State University; p. 100 (right), © Lawrence M. Sawyer/Getty Images; p. 103, © PhotoDisc; p. 105, © Ohio State University; p. 106, © mylife photos/Alamy; p. 113, © U.S. Air Force photo by John Van Winkle; p. 115, © The McGraw-Hill Companies, Inc./Lars A. Niki, photographer; p. 121, © Palestra; p. 125, from Prentice, William E: Principles of Athletic Training, Thirteenth Edition, © 2009 McGraw-Hill. *Chapter 6:* p. 130, © Ohio State University; p. 133, © BananaStock/Alamy; p. 139, © PhotoDisc; p. 147, © Ohio State University; p. 149, © Royalty-Free/CORBIS. *Chapter 7:* p. 164 (left), © Ohio State University; p. 164 (right), © PhotoDisc; p. 175, © Daryl Siedentop; p. 177, © Daryl Siedentop; p. 179, © Daryl Siedentop. *Chapter 8:* p. 186, © Daryl Siedentop; p. 189, © Punchstock; p. 193, © Ohio State University; p. 194 (left), © Sam Forencich; p. 194 (right), © The McGraw-Hill Companies, Inc./Andrew Resek, photographer; pg 200–201, © 1999, The Cooper Institute for Aerobics Research, Dallas, Texas; p. 203, © Ohio State University; p. 204, © SwimEx, Inc. *Chapter 9:* p. 217, © liquidlibrary/PictureQuest; p. 218, © JupiterImages; p. 223, © Ohio State University; p. 224, © Corbis/Punchstock. *Chapter 10:* p. 232, © PhotoDisc; p. 237, © Ohio State University; p. 242, © PhotoDisc; p. 244, © Daryl Siedentop; p. 248 (left) © Palestra; p. 244 (right), © Lars Niki; p. 250, © Palestra. *Chapter 11:* p. 256, © Ohio State University; p. 261, © Ohio State University. *Chapter 12:* p. 283, © Ohio State University; p. 285, © Daryl Siedentop; p. 287, © image100 Ltd.; p. 293, © Wayne Glusker. *Chapter 13:* p. 308, © Ohio State University; p. 309, © PhotoLink/ Getty Images; p. 311, © Sam Forencich; p. 312, © PhotoDisc; p. 315, © The McGraw-Hill Companies, Inc./ Gerald Wolford, photographer. *Chapter 14:* p. 321, from Prentice, William E: *Principles of Athletic Training,* Thirteenth Edition, © 2009 McGraw-Hill; p. 323, © Ohio State University; p. 324, © Suburban News Publications; p. 326, © PhotoDisc; p. 328, © PhotoDisc. *Chapter 15:* p. 333, © Ohio State University; p. 337, © Ohio State University; p. 338, © Comstock/JupiterImages; p. 341, from Hamilton, N, Weimar, W, and Luttgens, K: *Kinesiology: Scientific Basis of Human Motion,* 11th Edition, © 2008, McGraw-Hill; p. 342, © Daryl Siedentop; p. 344, © Lars Niki; p. 345 © Image Source/Corbis. *Chapter 16:* *p. 353,* © Ohio State University; p. 354, © Stockbyte/PictureQuest; p. 355, © PhotoDisc; p. 360, © Sam Forencich; p. 363, © Brand X Pictures/PunchStock; p. 366, © Ohio State University; p. 370, © Daryl Siedentop; p. 372, © Royalty-Free/CORBIS; p. 375, Public Domain; p. 378 (left) © Ohio State University, p. 378 (right), © McGraw-Hill Companies, Inc./Gary He, photographer.

TEXT CREDITS

Figure 7.2, p. 171, Corbin, C., Welk, G., Corbin, W., & Welk, K., Concepts *of physical fitness: Active lifestyles for wellness,* 14th edition, 2008, Boston: McGraw-Hill; Figure 8.1, p. 191: U.S. Department of Health and Human Services, 2004, Healthy People 2010, 2nd ed. Washington, D.C.: DHHS; Focus on Box 8.2, p. 192: Adapted with permission from *Research Quarterly for Exercise Science and Sport* 62(2), 1991, 124–137, a publication of the American Alliance for Health, Physical Education, Recreation and Dance. 1900 Association Drive, Reston, VA 20191; Focus on Box 10.2, p. 233: Reprinted from *Moving into the Future: National Physical Education Standards: A Guide to Content and Assessment* with permission from the National Association for Sport and Physical Education (NASPE), 1900 Association Drive, Reston, VA 20191; Focus on Box 10.3, p. 234: Reprinted with permission from *Definition and Outcomes of the Physically Educated Person*, the National Association for Sport and Physical Education (NASPE), 1900 Association Drive, Reston, VA 20191; Focus On Box 11.2, p. 274: Reprinted from *Moving into the Future: National Physical Education Standards: A Guide to Content and Assessment* with permission from the National Association for Sport and Physical Education (NASPE), 1900 Association Drive, Reston, VA 20191.

Index